Lecture Notes in Computer Sc

Commenced Publication in 1973
Founding and Former Series Editors:
Gerhard Goos, Juris Hartmanis, and Jan van Leeuwen

Lecture Notes in Computer Science 3603

Commenced Publication in 1973
Founding and Former Series Editors:
Gerhard Goos, Juris Hartmanis, and Jan van Leeuwen

Editorial Board

David Hutchison
    Lancaster University, UK
Takeo Kanade
    Carnegie Mellon University, Pittsburgh, PA, USA
Josef Kittler
    University of Surrey, Guildford, UK
Jon M. Kleinberg
    Cornell University, Ithaca, NY, USA
Friedemann Mattern
    ETH Zurich, Switzerland
John C. Mitchell
    Stanford University, CA, USA
Moni Naor
    Weizmann Institute of Science, Rehovot, Israel
Oscar Nierstrasz
    University of Bern, Switzerland
C. Pandu Rangan
    Indian Institute of Technology, Madras, India
Bernhard Steffen
    University of Dortmund, Germany
Madhu Sudan
    Massachusetts Institute of Technology, MA, USA
Demetri Terzopoulos
    New York University, NY, USA
Doug Tygar
    University of California, Berkeley, CA, USA
Moshe Y. Vardi
    Rice University, Houston, TX, USA
Gerhard Weikum
    Max-Planck Institute of Computer Science, Saarbruecken, Germany

Victor Malyshkin (Ed.)

Parallel Computing Technologies

8th International Conference, PaCT 2005
Krasnoyarsk, Russia, September 5-9, 2005
Proceedings

 Springer

Volume Editor

Victor Malyshkin
Russian Academy of Sciences
Institute of Computational Mathematics and Mathematical Geophysics
Supercomputer Software Department
pr. Lavrentiev 6, ICM MG RAS, 630090 Novosibirsk, Russia
E-mail: malysh@ssd.sscc.ru

Library of Congress Control Number: 2005930458

CR Subject Classification (1998): D, F.1-2, C, I.6

ISSN   0302-9743
ISBN-10   3-540-28126-6 Springer Berlin Heidelberg New York
ISBN-13   978-3-540-28126-9 Springer Berlin Heidelberg New York

Springer is a part of Springer Science+Business Media

springeronline.com

© Springer-Verlag Berlin Heidelberg 2005
Printed in Germany

Typesetting: Camera-ready by author, data conversion by Scientific Publishing Services, Chennai, India
Printed on acid-free paper   SPIN: 11535294   06/3142   5 4 3 2 1 0

Preface

The PaCT 2005 (Parallel Computing Technologies) conference was a four-day conference held in Krasnoyarsk, September 5–9, 2005. This was the Eighth international conference in the PaCT series. The conferences are held in Russia every odd year. The first conference, PaCT '91, was held in Novosibirsk (Academgorodok), September 7 – 11, 1991. The next PaCT conferences were held in Obninsk (near Moscow), August 30 – September 4, 1993, in St. Petersburg, September 12–15, 1995, in Yaroslavl, September, 9–12 1997, in Pushkin (near St. Petersburg) September, 6–10 1999, in Academgorodok (Novosibirsk), September 3–7, 2001, and in Nizhni Novgorod, September 15–19, 2003. The PaCT proceedings are published by Springer in the LNCS series.

PaCT 2005 was jointly organized by the Institute of Computational Mathematics and Mathematical Geophysics of the Russian Academy of Sciences (RAS), the Institute of Computational Modeling also of the RAS and the State Technical University of Krasnoyarsk.

The purpose of the conference was to bring together scientists working on theory, architecture, software, hardware and the solution of large-scale problems in order to provide integrated discussions on Parallel Computing Technologies.

The conference attracted about 100 participants from around the world. Authors from 20 countries submitted 78 papers. Of those submitted, 38 papers were selected for the conference as regular ones; there was also 1 invited paper. In addition there were a number of posters presented. All the papers were internationally reviewed by at least three referees. The demo session was organized for the participants.

PaCT 2007 is planned to be held in Irlutsk, near lake Baikal, in September as usual.

Many thanks to our sponsors: the Russian Academy of Sciences, the Russian Fund for Basic Research, the Russian State Committee of Higher Education, and IBM, for their financial support. Organizers highly appreciated the help of the Association Antenne-Provence (France).

June 2005   Victor Malyshkin

Organization

PaCT 2005 was organized by the Supercomputer Software Department, Institute of Computational Mathematics and Mathematical Geophysics, Siberian Branch, Russian Academy of Sciences (SB RAS) in cooperation with the Institute of Computational Modelling, SB RAS (Krasnoyarsk) and the State Technical University of Krasnoyarsk.

Program Committee

V. Malyshkin	Chairman (Russian Academy of Sciences)
F. Arbab	(Centre for MCS, The Netherlands)
O. Bandman	(Russian Academy of Sciences)
F. Cappello	(INRIA, France)
T. Casavant	(University of Iowa, USA)
A. Chambarel	(University of Avignon, France)
P. Degano	(State University of Pisa, Italy)
D. Etiemble	(Université Paris Sud, Orsay, France)
B. Goossens	(University of Perpignan, France)
S. Gorlatch	(University of Muenster, Germany)
A. Hurson	(Pennsylvania State University, USA)
Yu. Karpov	(St.-Petersburg State Technical University, Russia)
B. Lecussan	(State University of Toulouse, France)
J. Li	(University of Tsukuba, Japan)
T. Ludwig	(Ruprecht-Karls-Universität Heidelberg, Germany)
G. Mauri	(University of Milan, Italy)
G. Papadopoulos	(University of Cyprus, Cyprus)
M. Raynal	(IRISA, Rennes, France)
B. Roux	(L3M, France)
V. Shaidurov	(Russian Academy of Sciences)
G. Silberman	(IBM, USA)
P. Sloot	(University of Amsterdam. The Netherlands)
C. Trinitis	(LRR, Munich, Germany)
M. Valero	(Universitat Politècnica de Catalunya, Spain)
V. Vshivkov	(Russian Academy of Sciences)

Organizing Committee

V. Malyshkin	Co-chairman (Novosibirsk)
V. Shaidurov	Co-chairman (Krasnoyarsk)
S. Achasova	Secretary (Novosibirsk)
O. Bandman	Publication Chair (Novosibirsk)
S. Isaev	Member (Krasnoyarsk)
F. Kazakov	Member (Krasnoyarsk)
N. Kuchin	Member (Novosibirsk)
A. Legalov	Member (Krasnoyarsk)
A. Malyshev	Member (Krasnoyarsk)
Yu. Medvedev	Member (Novosibirsk)
S. Nechaev	Member (Novosibirsk)
O. Nechaeva	Member (Novosibirsk)
G. Sadovskaya	Member (Krasnoyarsk)
E. Veysov	Member (Krasnoyarsk)

Referees

G. Acher	A. Glebovsky	G. Papodopoulos
M. Alt	B. Goossens	M. Raynal
F. Arbab	A. Gorlatch	L. Ricci
T. Bair	M. Gorodnichev	Y. Robert
S. Bandini	T. Hérault	L. Rosaz
O. Bandman	A. Hurson	B. Roux
H. Bischof	A. Iamnitchi	V. Shaidurov
C. Blanchet	E. Jeannot	G. Silberman
C. Bodei	Y. Karpov	V. Sokolov
N. Busi	T. Klostermann	A. Solopov
E. Caron	T. Klug	A. Starita
Y. Caniou	B. Lecussan	D. Stodden
T. Casavant	E. Kuzmin	E. Timofeev
D. Chaly	R. Leshchinskiy	P. Trifonov
A. Chambarel	J. Li	C. Trinitis
D. Clarke	O. Lodygensky	A. Tsigulin
D. Defour	T. Ludwig	M. Valero
P. Degano	A. Maggiolo-Schettini	V. Valkovskii
F. Desprez	N. Malyshkin	L. Vanneschi
J. Duennweber	V. Malyshkin	I. Virbitskaite
D. Etiemble	G. Mauri	V. Vshivkov
P. Faber	H. Mehammed	M. Walter
G. Fedak	J. Mueller	J. Weidendorfer
K. Fuerlinger	A. Nepomniaschaja	J. Zola
A. Giersch	L. Pagli	

Table of Contents

On Evaluating the Performance
of Security Protocols[*]

Chiara Bodei[1], Mikael Buchholtz[3], Michele Curti[1], Pierpaolo Degano[1],
Flemming Nielson[3], Hanne Riis Nielson[3], and Corrado Priami[2]

[1] Dipartimento di Informatica, Università di Pisa,
Largo B.Pontecorvo, 3, I-56127 Pisa, Italy
{chiara, curtim, degano}@di.unipi.it
[2] Dipartimento di Informatica e Telecomunicazioni,
Università di Trento, Via Sommarive, I-1438050 Povo (TN), Italy
priami@science.unitn.it
[3] Informatics and Mathematical Modelling, Technical University of Denmark,
Richard Petersens Plads bldg 321, DK-2800 Kongens Lyngby, Denmark
{mib, nielson, riis}@imm.dtu.dk

Abstract. We use an enhanced operational semantics to infer quantitative measures on systems describing cryptographic protocols. System transitions carry enhanced labels. We assign rates to transitions by only looking at these labels. The rates reflect the distributed architecture running applications and the use of possibly different crypto-systems. We then map transition systems to Markov chains and evaluate performance of systems, using standard tools.

1 Introduction

Cryptographic protocols are used in distributed systems for authentication and key exchange, and must therefore guarantee security. The mechanisms used are always the result of a judicious balance between their cost and benefits. Performance costs, in terms of time overhead and resource consumption, must be carefully evaluated when choosing security mechanisms.

Here, we extend a preliminary idea introduced in [6] for the development of a single, formal design methodology that supports designers in analysing the performance of protocols, with a semi-mechanizable procedure. We provide a general framework, where quantitative aspects, symbolically represented by parameters, can be formally estimated. By changing only these parameters on the architecture and the algorithm chosen, one can compare different implementations of the same protocol or different protocols. This allows the designer to choose among different alternatives, based on an evaluation of the trade-off between security guarantees and their price.

We are mainly interested in evaluating the cost of each cryptographic operation and of each message exchange. Here, "cost" means any measure of quantitative properties such as speed, availability, etc.

---

[*] Supported in part by the EU IST-2001-32072 project DEGAS.

V. Malyshkin (Ed.): PaCT 2005, LNCS 3606, pp. 1–15, 2005.

Usually protocols are described through informal narrations. These narrations include only a list of the messages to be exchanged, leaving it unspecified which are the actions to be performed in receiving these messages (inputs, decryptions and possible checks on them). This can lead, in general, to an inaccurate estimation of costs. The above motivates the choice of using the process algebra LySa [3,5], a close relative of the π- [24] and Spi-calculus [1], that details the protocol narration, in that outputs and the corresponding inputs are made explicit and similarly for encryptions and the corresponding decryptions. Also, LySa is explicit about which keys are fresh and about which checks are to be performed on the received values. More generally, LySa provides us with a unifying framework, in which security protocols can be specified and statically analysed [3,5] through Control Flow Analysis. This analysis, fully automatic and always terminating, is strong enough to report known flaws on a wide range of protocols, and even to find new ones [4].

Technically, we give LySa (Sect. 2) an enhanced semantics, following [14], and then we associate rates to each transition, in the style of [26]. It suffices to have information about the activities performed by the components of a system in isolation, and about some features of the network architecture. We then mechanically derive Markov chains using these rates (Sect. 3). The actual performance evaluation is carried out using standard techniques and tools [33,31,32]. Significantly, quantitative measures, typically on cryptography, here live together with the usual qualitative semantics, where instead these aspects are usually abstracted away. Specifically, there exists a very early prototype, based on π-calculus, on which it is possible to run LySa, that we used for the case study presented here (Sect. 4), along with a standard mathematical tool such as Mathematica. Relative approaches are EMPA[8] and PEPA[19], to cite only a few.

In comparing different versions of the same protocol or different protocols, specified in LySa, our technique can be suitably integrated with the Control Flow one, to check security at the same stage.

Our framework can be extended [7] to estimate the cost of security attacks. The typical capabilities of the Dolev-Yao attacker [16] go beyond the ones a legitimate principal has. The needed model includes a set of the possible extra actions in which the attacker exploits its computational power and its capability of guessing (see also [10] and [23]). It would be interesting to deal with timing attacks as well, even though this may considerably complicate our model.

2   LySa and Its Enhanced Semantics

The LySa calculus [3,5] is based on the π- [24] and Spi-calculus [1], but differs from these essentially in two aspects: (i) the absence of channels: there is only one global communication medium to which all processes have access; (ii) the tests associated with input and decryption are naturally expressed using pattern matching. Below, we assume that the reader is familiar with the basics of process calculi.

Syntax. The syntax consists of terms $E \in \mathcal{E}$ and processes $P \in \mathcal{P}$,

$$E ::= a \mid x \mid \{E_1, \cdots, E_k\}_{E_0}$$
$$P ::= 0 \mid out.P \mid in.P \mid P_1 \mid P_2 \mid (\nu\, a)P \mid dec \text{ in } P \mid A(y_1, \ldots, y_n)$$

where we introduced the following abbreviations: • $out \triangleq \langle E_1, \cdots, E_k \rangle$, • $in \triangleq$ $(E'_1, \cdots, E'_j; x_{j+1}, \cdots, x_k)$, • $dec \triangleq$ decrypt E as $\{E_1, \cdots, E_j; x_{j+1}, \cdots, x_k\}_{E_0}$. Intuitively, the process 0 or *nil* represents the null inactive process. The operator $|$ describes parallel composition of processes. The operator (νa) acts as a static declaration for the name a in the process P the restriction prefixes. Restriction is therefore used to create new names such as nonces or keys. The process $\langle E_1, \cdots, E_k \rangle. P$ sends $E_1, \cdots, E_k$ on the net and then continues like P. The process $(E_1, \cdots, E_j; x_{j+1}, \cdots, x_k). P$ receives the tuple $E'_1, \cdots, E'_k$ and continues as $P[E_{j+1}/x_{j+1}, \ldots, E_k/x_k]$, provided that $E_i = E'_i$ for all $i \in [1, j]$. The intuition is that the matching succeeds when the first j values E'_i pairwise correspond to the values E_i, and the effect is to bind the remaining $k - j$ values to the variables $x_{j+1}, \cdots, x_k$. Note that, syntactically, a semi-colon separates the components where matching is performed from those where only binding takes place. The same simple form of patterns is also used for decryption (see [9] for a more flexible choice). In fact, the process decrypt E as $\{E_1, \cdots, E_j; x_{j+1}, \cdots, x_k\}^{in}_{E_0}$ in P decrypts $E = \{E'_1, \cdots, E'_k\}_{E'_0}$ with the key E_0. Whenever $E_i = E'_i$ for all $i \in [0, j]$, the process behaves as $P[E_{j+1}/x_{j+1}, \ldots, E_k/x_k]$. Finally, an agent is a static definition of a parameterised process. Each agent identifier A has a unique defining equation of the form $A(\tilde{y}) = P$, where $\tilde{y}$ denotes a tuple $y_1, \ldots, y_n$ of distinct names occurring free in P.

Working Example. Consider the following basic Kerberos key agreement protocol [22] that is part of our case study. We assume that the AES algorithm [12] is the crypto-system used here.

$$(Kerberos)\quad\begin{array}{ll} 1. & A \rightarrow S : A, B \\ 2. & S \rightarrow A : \{B, T, L, K_{AB}\}_{K_A}, \{A, T, L, K_{AB}\}_{K_B} \\ 3. & A \rightarrow B : \{A, T, L, K_{AB}\}_{K_B}, \{A, T\}_{K_{AB}} \\ 4. & B \rightarrow A : \{T, T\}_{K_{AB}} \end{array}$$

Intuitively, principal A asks the Key Distribution Center S for a session key to share with B. S generates the key K_{AB}, a timestamp T and lifetime L and produces an encryption of these components for A and another one for B, including the identity of the other principal. Both encryptions are sent to A, that can decrypt the first and forward the second to B, along with another encryption that A obtains by encoding (A, T) with the new key. B can decrypt the first encryption so to obtain K_{AB} then B decrypts the second encryption, and uses K_{AB} to encrypt (T, T) as a replay to A. To simplify, we use $\{T, T\}_{K_{AB}}$ rather than the usual $\{T + 1\}_{K_{AB}}$.

The protocol specification in LySA is in Tab. 1, where the right column reports a concise explanation of the action on the left, in terms of the number of the message (called *msg*, while *enc* stands for an encrypted term) in the protocol narration. The whole system is given by the parallel composition ($|$) of the three processes A, B, S. Each part of the system performs a certain number of actions and then restarts.

Table 1. Specification of *Kerberos* Protocol

1 $Sys_1 = (\nu K_A)(\nu K_B)((A\|B)\|S)$	K_A, K_B long-term keys
2 $A = (\langle A, B \rangle. A')$	A sends msg (1)
4 $A' = (; v_{enc}^A, v_{enc}^B). A''$	A receives and checks msg (2)
5 $A'' = $ decrypt v_{enc}^A as $\{B; v_T, v_L, v_K\}_{K_A}$ in A'''	A decrypts the enc in msg (2)
6 $A''' = \langle v_{enc}^B, \{A, v_T\}_{v_K} \rangle. A''''$	A sends msg (3)
7 $A'''' = (; w_{enc}^A). A'''''$	A receives and checks msg (4)
8 $A''''' = $ decrypt w_{enc}^A as $\{v_T, v_T; \}_{v_K}$ in A	A decrypts the enc in msg (4)
9 $B = (; z_{enc}^1, z_{enc}^2). B'$	B receives and checks msg (3)
10 $B' = $ decrypt z_{enc}^1 as $\{; z_A, z_T, z_L, z_K\}_{K_B}$ in B''	B decrypts the 1st enc in msg (3)
11 $B'' = $ decrypt z_{enc}^2 as $\{z_A, z_T; \}_{z_K}$ in B'''	B decrypts the 2nd enc in msg (3)
12 $B''' = \langle \{z_T, z_T\}_{z_K} \rangle. B$	B sends msg (4)
13 $S = (; y^A, y^B). S'$	S receives and checks msg (1)
14 $S' = (\nu K_{AB})(\nu T)(\nu L)$	K_{AB} fresh session key
15 $(\langle \{y^B, T, L, K_{AB}\}_{K_A}, \{y^A, T, L, K_{AB}\}_{K_B} \rangle. S)$	S sends msg (2)

Enhanced Operational Semantics. Here, we give a concrete version of operational semantics, called *enhanced* in the style of [13,14]. Our enhanced semantics for LySa is a reduction semantics, built on top of the standard reduction semantics [3], where both processes and transitions are annotated with labels that will be helpful for computing costs.

Formally, each transition is enriched with an *enhanced label* θ which records both the action corresponding to the transition and its syntactic context. Actually, the label of a communication transition records the two actions (input and output) that lead to the transition. To facilitate the definition of our reduction semantics, for each given process, we annotate each of its sub-processes P with an encoding of the context in which P occurs. The encoding is a string of tags ϑ, that essentially record the syntactic position of P w.r.t. the parallel composition nesting. To do this, we exploit the abstract syntax tree of processes, built using the binary parallel composition as operator. We introduce a tag $\|_0$ ($\|_1$, resp.) for the left (for the right, resp.) branch of a parallel composition. Labels are defined as follows.

Definition 1. *Let* $\mathcal{L} = \{\|_0, \|_1\}$. *Then, the set of* context labels *is defined as* $\mathcal{L}^*$, *i.e. the set of all the string generated by* $\mathcal{L}$, *ranged over by* ϑ.

We choose to have tags concerned with the parallel structure of processes, i.e. linked to parallel composition "|". For our present purpose, this is the only necessary annotation (for other annotations, see [26,14]).

Technically, labelled processes are inductively obtained in a pre processing step, by using the function $\mathcal{T}$. This function (inductively) prefixes actions with context labels: $\mathcal{T}$ unwinds the syntactic structure of processes, until reaching a 0 or a constant. Given a process P, this transformation operates in linear time with the number of prefixes. Note that this pre-processing step can be completely mechanized. An auxiliary function $\triangleright$ is needed to distribute context labels on processes.

Definition 2. *Let* $\mathcal{LP}$ *be the set of* Labelled Processes, *ranged over by* T, T', T_0, T_1. *The functions* $\mathcal{T} : \mathcal{P} \to \mathcal{LP}$ *and* $\triangleright: \mathcal{L}^* \times \mathcal{LP} \to \mathcal{LP}$, *written as* $\vartheta \triangleright T$, *are defined by induction in the box below:*

$- \; \mathcal{T}(0) = 0$	$- \; \vartheta \triangleright 0 = 0$
$- \; \mathcal{T}(\mu.P) = \mu.\mathcal{T}(P), \quad \mu \in \{out, in\}$	$- \; \vartheta \triangleright (\vartheta'\mu.T) = \vartheta\vartheta'\mu.(\vartheta \triangleright T), \quad \mu \in \{out, in\}$
$- \; \mathcal{T}(P_0 \vert P_1) = \Vert_0 \triangleright \mathcal{T}(P_0) \mid \Vert_1 \triangleright \mathcal{T}(P_1)$	$- \; \vartheta \triangleright (T_0 \mid T_1) = (\vartheta \triangleright T_0) \mid (\vartheta \triangleright T_1)$
$- \; \mathcal{T}((\nu a)P) = (\nu a)\mathcal{T}(P)$	$- \; \vartheta \triangleright (\nu a)T = (\nu a)\; \vartheta \triangleright T$
$- \; \mathcal{T}(A(y_1, \ldots, y_n)) = A(y_1, \ldots, y_n)$	$- \; \vartheta \triangleright \vartheta' A(y_1, \ldots, y_n) = \vartheta\vartheta' A(y_1, \ldots, y_n)$
$- \; \mathcal{T}(dec \; in \; P) = dec \; in \; \mathcal{T}(P)$	$- \; \vartheta \triangleright \vartheta' \; dec \; in \; T = \vartheta\vartheta' \; dec \; in \; (\vartheta \triangleright T)$

The following example illustrates how $\mathcal{T}$ works on the process $Sys_1 = ((A \mid B) \mid S)$. The context labels preceding the prefixes of the three processes are: $\vartheta_A = \Vert_0\Vert_0$ for A, $\vartheta_B = \Vert_0\Vert_1$ for B, and $\vartheta_S = \Vert_1$ for S.

$$\mathcal{T}(((A \mid B) \mid S)) = \Vert_0 \triangleright (\mathcal{T}(A \mid B)) \mid \Vert_1 \triangleright \mathcal{T}(S) =$$

$$\Vert_0 \triangleright (\Vert_0 \triangleright (\mathcal{T}(A)) \mid \Vert_1 \triangleright (\mathcal{T}(B)) \mid \Vert_1 \triangleright \mathcal{T}(S) = (\Vert_0\Vert_0 \triangleright (\mathcal{T}(A) \mid \Vert_0\Vert_1 \triangleright (\mathcal{T}(B)) \mid \Vert_1 \triangleright \mathcal{T}(S)$$

For instance B is annotated with the label $\vartheta = \Vert_0\Vert_1$ as B is inside the right branch of the inner parallel composition $(A \mid B)$, and in turn on the left branch of the outermost parallel composition in $((A \mid B) \mid S)$.

The *enhanced label* of a transition records its *action*, i.e. decryption or input and output communications that lead to the transition. Also, actions come prefixed by their context labels.

Definition 3. *The set* $\Theta \ni \theta, \vartheta_O, \vartheta_I$ *of enhanced labels is defined by*

$$\theta ::= \langle \vartheta_O \; out, \vartheta_I \; in \rangle \mid \langle \vartheta \; dec \rangle$$

As usual, our semantics consists of the standard structural congruence $\equiv$ on processes and of a set of rules defining the transition relation.

Our *reduction relation* $\xrightarrow{\theta} \subseteq \mathcal{LP} \times \mathcal{LP}$ is the least relation on closed labelled processes that satisfies the rules in Tab. 2. In the rule (Com), the context labels ϑ_O (and ϑ_I, resp.) of both the partners are recorded in the pair $\langle \vartheta_O out, \vartheta_I in \rangle$ together with the corresponding output (and input, resp.) prefix. In the rule for decryption, the context label ϑ is recorded together with dec in the label of the transition. The other rules are quite standard. Our semantics differs from the standard one [3] because (i) processes are enriched with context labels ϑ and (ii) reductions carry enhanced labels θ. By eliminating labels from both transitions and processes, it is possible to recover the original reduction semantics $\longrightarrow \subseteq \mathcal{P} \times \mathcal{P}$.

For technical reasons, hereafter, we will restrict ourselves to *finite* state processes, i.e. whose corresponding transition systems have a finite set of states. Note that this does not mean that the behaviour of such processes is finite, because their transition systems may have loops.

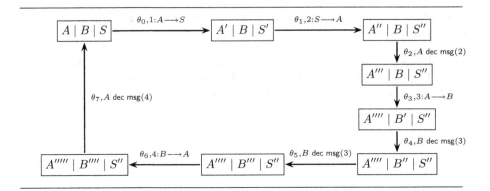

Fig. 1. Sys_1 Transition System

Table 2. Enhanced Reduction Semantics, $T \xrightarrow{\theta} T'$

(Com)
$$\frac{\wedge_{i=1}^{j} E_i = E'_i}{\vartheta_O \, out.T \;\; | \;\; \vartheta_I \, in.T' \xrightarrow{\langle \vartheta_O \, out, \vartheta_I \, in \rangle} T \;\; | \;\; T'[E_{j+1}/x_{j+1}, \cdots, E_k/x_k]}$$

(Decr)
$$\frac{\wedge_{i=0}^{j} E_i = E'_i}{\vartheta \, dec \, \text{in} \, T \xrightarrow{\langle \vartheta \, dec \rangle} T[E_{j+1}/x_{j+1}, \cdots, E_k/x_k]}$$

(Par)   (Res)   (Ide) :
$$\frac{T_0 \xrightarrow{\theta} T'_0}{T_0 \mid T_1 \xrightarrow{\theta} T'_0 \mid T_1} \qquad \frac{T \xrightarrow{\theta} T'}{(\nu a)T \xrightarrow{\theta} (\nu a)T'} \qquad \frac{\mathcal{T}(P)\{\tilde{K}/\tilde{y}\} \xrightarrow{\theta} T'}{\vartheta A(\tilde{K}) \xrightarrow{\vartheta\theta} \vartheta \triangleright T'}, \;\; A(\tilde{y}) = P$$

(Congr)
$$\frac{T \equiv T_0 \; \wedge \; T_0 \xrightarrow{\theta} T_1 \; \wedge \; T_1 \equiv T'}{T \xrightarrow{\theta} T'}$$

$out = \langle E_1, \cdots, E_k \rangle,$
$in = (E'_1, \cdots, E'_j; x_{j+1}, \cdots, x_k),$
$dec = \text{decrypt } E \text{ as } \{E_1, \cdots, E_j; x_{j+1}, \cdots, x_k\}_{E_0}$

Example (cont'd). In Fig. 1, we present the (finite) transition systems corresponding to Sys_1. To improve readability, we add a further component to the labels ϑ_i of transitions. A transition from state T to state T' has the form $T \xrightarrow{(\theta, caption)} T'$, where *caption* is a concise description of the step of the protocol narration. More precisely, it refers to message exchanges and decryptions (abbreviated as *dec*). Captions are of no other use.

The enhanced labels of Sys_1 are reported below. Since in our example, transitions have different labels each, we feel free to use hereafter the label θ_i for the i-th transition.

$$\theta_0 = \langle \vartheta_A \langle A, B \rangle, \vartheta_S(; z_{enc}^1, z_{enc}^2) \rangle$$
$$\theta_1 = \langle \vartheta_S \langle \{y^B, T, L, K_{AB}\}_{K_A}, \{y^A, T, L, K_{AB}\}_{K_B} \rangle, \vartheta_A(; v_{enc}^A, v_{enc}^B) \rangle$$
$$\theta_2 = \langle \vartheta_A \text{ decrypt } \{B, T, L, K_{AB}\}_{K_A} \text{ as } \{B; v_T, v_L, v_K\}_{K_A} \rangle$$
$$\theta_3 = \langle \vartheta_A \langle \{A, T, L, K_{AB}\}_{K_B}, \{A, T\}_{K_{AB}} \rangle, \vartheta_B(; z_{enc}^1, z_{enc}^2) \rangle$$
$$\theta_4 = \langle \vartheta_B \text{ decrypt } \{A, T, L, K_{AB}\}_{K_B} \text{ as } \{; z_A, z_T, z_L, z_K\}_{K_B} \rangle$$
$$\theta_5 = \langle \vartheta_B \text{ decrypt } \{A, T\}_{K_{AB}} \text{ as } \{A, T;\}_{K_{AB}} \rangle$$
$$\theta_6 = \langle \vartheta_B \langle \{T, T\}_{K_{AB}} \rangle, \vartheta_A(; w_{enc}^A) \rangle$$
$$\theta_7 = \langle \vartheta_A \text{ decrypt } \{T, T\}_{K_{AB}} \text{ as } \{T, T;\}_{K_B} \rangle$$

3 Stochastic Analysis

Costs of transitions are derived by inspecting enhanced labels, following [26]. This information is sufficient to extract the necessary quantitative information to obtain the Continuous Time Markov Chains (CTMC) (see [2,25] for more details on the theory of stochastic processes). In general, by "cost" we mean any measure that affects quantitative properties of transitions: here, we intend the time the system is likely to remain within a given transition. We specify the cost of a protocol in terms of the time overhead due to its primitives (along the same lines as [28]). The cost of (the component of) the transition depends on both the current action and on its context. Since the semantics of a language specifies its abstract machine, the context in which an action occurs represents the run-time support routines that the target machine performs to fire that action.

First, we intuitively present the main factors that influence the costs of actions and those due to their context. For simplicity, here we ignore the costs for other primitives, e.g. restriction or constant invocation (see [26] for a complete treatment).

- The cost of a *communication* depends on the costs of the input and output components. In particular, the cost of an (i) *output* depends on the size of the message and on the cost of each term of the message sent, in particular on its encryptions; (ii) *input* depends on the size of the message and on the cost of checks needed to accept the message. Actually, the two partners independently perform some low-level operations locally to their environment, each of which leads to a delay. Since communication is synchronous and handshaking, the overall cost corresponds to the cost paid by the slower partner.
- The cost of both *encryption* and *decryption* depends on the sizes of the cleartext and ciphertext, resp.; the complexity of the algorithm that implements it; the cipher mode adopted; the kind of the key (short/long, short-term/long-term). The length of the key is important: usually, the longer the key, the greater the computing time. In addition, the cost for *decryption* depends on the cost of the checks needed to accept the decryption.
- The cost of *parallel composition* is evaluated according to the number of available processors and to the speed of system clock.

To define a cost function, we start by considering the execution of each action on a dedicated architecture that only has to perform that action, and we estimate the corresponding duration with a fixed rate r. Then we model the performance degradation due to the run-time support. To do that, we introduce a scaling factor for r in correspondence with each routine called by the implementation of the transition θ under consideration. Here, we just propose a format for these functions, with parameters to be instantiated on need. Note that these parameters depend on the target machine, e.g. in a system where the cryptographic operations are performed at very high speed (e.g. by a cryptographic accelerator), but with a slow link (low bandwidth), the time will be low for encryptions and high for communication; vice versa, in a system offering a high bandwidth, but poor cryptography resources.

Technically, we interpret costs as parameters of exponential distributions $F(t) = 1 - e^{-rt}$, with rate r and t as time parameter (general distributions are also possible see [30]). The *rate* r associated with the transition is the parameter which identifies the exponential distribution of the duration times of the transition, as usual in stochastic process algebras (e.g. [19,18]). The shape of $F(t)$ is a curve which grows from 0 asymptotically approaching 1 for positive values of its argument t. The parameter r determines the slope of the curve: the greater r, the faster $F(t)$ approaches its asymptotic value. The probability of performing an action with parameter r within time x is $F(x) = 1 - e^{-rx}$, so r determines the time, Δt, needed to have a probability near to 1.

3.1   Cost Functions

We define in a few steps the function that associates rates with communication and decryption transitions, or, more precisely, with their enhanced labels. We first give the auxiliary function $f_E : \mathcal{E} \to \mathbb{R}^+$ that estimates the effort needed to manipulate terms $E \in \mathcal{E}$.

- $f_E(a) = size(a)$ • $f_E(\{E_1, \dots, E_k\}_{E_0}) = f_{enc}(f_E(E_1), \dots, f_E(E_1), kind(E_0))$

The size of a name a ($size(a)$) matters. For an encrypted term, we use the function f_{enc}, which in turn depends on the estimate of the terms to encrypt and on the kind of the key (represented by $kind(E_0)$), i.e. on its length and on the corresponding crypto-system.

Then we assign costs to actions in $\{in, out, dec\}$. Formally, the function $\$_\alpha : \{in, out, dec\} \to \mathbb{R}^+$ is defined as

- $\$_\alpha(\langle E_1, \dots, E_k \rangle) = f_{out}(f_E(E_1), \dots, f_E(E_1), bw)$
- $\$_\alpha((E_1, \dots, E_j; x_{j+1}, \dots, x_k)) = f_{in}(f_E(E_1), \dots, f_E(E_j), match(j), bw)$
- $\$_\alpha(\text{decrypt } E \text{ as } \{E_1, \cdots, E_j; x_{j+1}, \cdots, x_k\}_{E_0}) = f_{dec}(f_E(E), kind(E_0), match(j))$

The functions f_{out} and f_{in} define the costs of the routines which implement the send and receive primitives. Besides the implementation cost due to their own algorithms, the functions above depend on the bandwidth of the communication channel (represented by bw) and the cost of the exchanged terms, in turn computed by the auxiliary function f_E. Also, the cost of an input depends on the number of tests or matchings required (represented by $match(j)$). Finally, the function f_{dec} represents the cost of a decryption. It depends on the manipulated terms $(f_E(E))$, on the kind of key $(kind(E_0))$ and on the number of matchings $(match(j))$.

We now consider the context in which the actions occur. To determine the slowing factor due to parallel composition, we associate a cost to each context label ϑ, as expressed by the function $\$_l : \{\|_0, \|_1\}^* \to (0, 1]$. Parallel composition is evaluated according to the number np of processors available, and on the number of processes that run on them. Another factor is given by the speed of $clock$, the system clock.

- $\$_l(\vartheta) = f_{\|}(np, |\vartheta|, clock)$

Finally, the function $\$: \Theta \to \mathbb{R}^+$ associates rates with enhanced labels.

- $\$(\langle \vartheta_O out, \vartheta_I in \rangle) = \min\{\$_l(\vartheta_O) \cdot \$_\alpha(out), \$_l(\vartheta_I) \cdot \$_\alpha(in)\}$
- $\$\langle \vartheta dec \rangle = \$_l(\vartheta) \cdot \$_\alpha(dec)$

As mentioned above, the two partners independently perform some low-level operations locally to their environment, represented by the two context labels ϑ_O and ϑ_I. Each label leads to a delay ($\$_l(\vartheta_O)$ and $\$_l(\vartheta_I)$, resp.) in the rate of the corresponding action ($\$_\alpha(out)$ and $\$_\alpha(in)$, resp.). Thus, the cost paid by the slower partner corresponds to the minimum cost of the operations performed by the participants, in isolation. Indeed the lower the cost, i.e. the rate, the greater the time needed to complete an action and hence the slower the speed of the transition occurring. The smaller r, the slower $F(t) = 1 - e^{-rt}$ approaches its asymptotic value.

Note that we do not fix the actual cost function: we only propose for it a set of parameters to reflect some features of an idealized architecture and of a particular cryptosystem. Although very abstract, this suffices to make our point. A precise instantiation comes with the refinement steps from specification to implementations as soon as actual parameters become available.

We now associate a rate to each transition in the transition system Sys_1. For the sake of simplicity, we assume that each principal has enough processing power and then we can map each ϑ to 1. We could vary this value considering e.g. differences in the speed of clock for the two processes. We instantiate the cost functions given above, by using the following parameters each used to compute the rate corresponding to a particular action (sending, receiving and decryption) or a part of it, such as an encryption or a pattern matching: (i) e and d for encrypting and for decrypting, (ii) s and r for sending and for receiving, (iii) m for pattern matching. The functions are:

- $f_E(a) = 1$
- $f_E(\{E_1, \ldots, E_k\}_{E_0}) = \frac{e}{s} \cdot \sum_{i=1}^{k} f_E(E_i) + \sum_{i=1}^{k} f_E(E_i)$
- $\$_\alpha(\langle E_1, \ldots, E_k \rangle) = \frac{1}{s \cdot \sum_{i=1}^{i} f_E(E_i)}$
- $\$_\alpha(\langle E_1, \ldots, E_j; x_{j+1}, \ldots, x_k \rangle) = \frac{1}{r \cdot k + m \cdot j}$
- $\$_\alpha(\text{decrypt } E \text{ as } \{E_1, \cdots, E_j; x_{j+1}, \cdots, x_k\}_{E_0}) = \frac{1}{d \cdot k + m \cdot j}$

Intuitively, these parameters represent the time spent performing the corresponding action on a single term. They occur in the denominator, therefore keeping the rule that the faster the time, the slower the rate. Since transmission is usually more time-consuming than the corresponding reception, the rate of a communication, will always be that of output.

Example (cont'd) The rate c_0 of the first transition of Sys_1 is $\frac{1}{2s}$:

$$c_0 = \$(\theta_0) = min\{(\$_l(\vartheta_A) \cdot \$_\alpha(\langle A, B \rangle, \$_l(\vartheta_S) \cdot \$_\alpha((; z_{enc}^1, z_{enc}^2))\} = min\{\tfrac{1}{2s}, \tfrac{1}{2r}\}.$$

All the rates $c_i = \$(\theta_i)$ are: $c_0 = \frac{1}{2s}$, $c_1 = \frac{1}{8s+8e}$, $c_2 = \frac{1}{4d+m}$, $c_3 = \frac{1}{6s+6e}$, $c_4 = \frac{1}{4d+m}$, $c_5 = \frac{1}{2d+2m}$, $c_6 = \frac{1}{2s+2e}$ and $c_7 = \frac{1}{2d+2m}$.

3.2   Markov Chains and Performance Measures

Our first step is obtaining a Continuous Time Markov Chain (CTMC) from a transition system. Then, we shall calculate the actual performance measure, e.g. the throughput or utilization of a certain resource. We use the rates of transitions computed in Subsection 3.1, to transform a transition system T into its corresponding $CTMC(T)$: a state is associated with each node of the transition system, while the transitions between states are defined by the arcs.

Actually, the rate $q(T_i, T_j)$ at which a system changes from behaving like process T_i to behaving like T_j is the sum of the single rates of all the possible transitions from T_i to T_j. Note that $q(T_i, T_j)$ coincides with the off-diagonal element q_{ij} of the generator matrix of the CTMC, namely $\mathbf{Q}$. Recall that a CTMC can be seen as a directed graph and that its matrix $\mathbf{Q}$ (apart from its diagonal) represents its adjacency matrix. Hence, hereafter we will use indistinguishably CTMC and its corresponding $\mathbf{Q}$ to denote a Markov chain. More formally, the entries of the generator matrix $\mathbf{Q}$ are defined as $q_{ij} = $

$$q_{ij} = \begin{cases} q(T_i, T_j) = \displaystyle\sum_{T_i \xrightarrow{\theta_k} T_j} \$(\theta_k) & \text{if } i \neq j \\[2ex] -\displaystyle\sum_{j=0, j\neq i}^{n} q_{ij} & \text{if } i = j \end{cases}$$

Example (cont'd). Consider the transition system Sys_1. Since it is finite and has a cyclic initial state, then there exists its stationary distribution. The *stationary probability distribution* of a CTMC is $\Pi = (X_0, \ldots, X_{n-1})$ such that Π solves the matrix equation $\Pi^T \mathbf{Q} = \mathbf{0}$ and $\sum_{i=0}^{n} X_i = 1$. We derive the following generator matrix $\mathbf{Q}_1$ of $CTMC(Sys_1)$ and the corresponding stationary distributions is Π_1, where $C = 9s + 8e + 6d + 3m$.

$$\mathbf{Q}_1 = \begin{bmatrix} -c_0 & c_0 & 0 & 0 & 0 & 0 & 0 & 0 \\ 0 & -c_1 & c_1 & 0 & 0 & 0 & 0 & 0 \\ 0 & 0 & -c_2 & c_2 & 0 & 0 & 0 & 0 \\ 0 & 0 & 0 & -c_3 & c_3 & 0 & 0 & 0 \\ 0 & 0 & 0 & 0 & -c_4 & c_4 & 0 & 0 \\ 0 & 0 & 0 & 0 & 0 & -c_5 & c_5 & 0 \\ 0 & 0 & 0 & 0 & 0 & 0 & -c_6 & c_6 \\ c_7 & 0 & 0 & 0 & 0 & 0 & 0 & -c_7 \end{bmatrix}$$

$$\Pi_1 = \left[\frac{s}{C}, \frac{4(s+e)}{C}, \frac{4d+m}{C}, \frac{3(s+e)}{C}, \frac{4d+m}{C}, \frac{d+m}{C}, \frac{e+s}{C}, \frac{d+m}{C} \right]$$

Evaluating the Performance. In order to define performance measures for a process T, we define a *reward structure* associated with T, following [21,19,11]. Usually, a reward structure is simply a function that associates a reward with any state passed through in a computation of T. For instance, when calculating the utilisation of a resource, we assign value 1 to any state in which the use of the resource is enabled (typically the source of a transition that uses the resource). All the other states earn the value 0. Instead we use a slightly different notion, where rewards are computed from rates of transitions [26]. To measure instead the throughput of a system, i.e. the amount of useful work accomplished per unit time, a reasonable choice is to use as nonzero reward a value equal to the rate of the corresponding transition. The reward structure of a process T is a vector of rewards with as many elements as the number of states of T. By looking at the stationary distribution of and varying the reward structure, we can compute different performance measures. The total reward is obtained by multiplying the stationary distribution and the reward structure.

Definition 4. *Given a process T, let $\Pi = (X_0, \ldots, X_{n-1})$ be its stationary distribution and $\rho = \rho(0), \ldots, \rho(n-1)$ be its reward structure. The* total reward *of T is computed as $R(T) = \sum_i \rho(i) \cdot X_i$.*

Example (cont'd). The throughput for a given activity is found by first associating a transition reward equal to the activity rate with each transition. In our systems each transition is fired only once. Also, the graph of the corresponding CTMC is cyclic and all the labels represent different activities. This amounts to saying that the throughput of all the activities is the same, and we can freely choose one of them to compute the throughput of Sys_1. Thus we associate a transition reward equal to its rate with the last communication and a null transition reward with all the others communications. From them, we compute the reward structures as $\rho_1 = (0, 0, 0, 0, 0, 0, c_7)$, where $c_7 = \frac{1}{2d+2m}$. The total reward $R(Sys_1)$ of the system amounts then to $\frac{d+m}{(2d+2m)(9s14+d+3m)}$. To use this measure, it is necessary to instantiate our parameters under various hypotheses, depending on several factors, such as the network load, the packet size, the number of mobile stations and so on. We delay this kind of considerations to the next section, where this measure will be compared with the one obtained for a different protocol.

4 A Case Study

It is well known that asymmetric key cryptography is more expensive than symmetric key cryptography. This is why often the first technique is adopted for long-term keys, while the other is exploited for session keys. We want to apply our framework and compare public versus secret encryption techniques. Following [20], we compare the two key-agreement protocols Kerberos [22] (the one used as working example) and Diffie-Hellman, compared there for their energy consumption.

Before the comparison, we need to illustrate the second protocol and to apply it the introduced technique. The Diffie-Hellman protocol is based on the use of two functions, i.e. $g(x) = \alpha^x \bmod p$ and $f(x, y) = y^x \bmod p$, where p is a large prime (public) and α of Z_p^* (the set of all the numbers prime with p) is a generator. Here, we can safely abstract from the underlying number theory. We need to slightly extend the syntax with the following productions, where E and E' are terms and each of the two functions g and f are considered as term constructors. The semantics is modified accordingly, by adding a case for the function T and by adding an axiom to the reduction semantics.

$$E ::= g(E) \mid f(E, E')$$
$$P ::= \text{let } x \text{ be } f(E, E') \text{ in } P$$

$$T(\text{let } x \text{ be } f(E, E') \text{ in } P) = \text{let } x \text{ be } f(E, E') \text{ in } T(P)$$
$$\vartheta \triangleright \vartheta' \, (\text{let } x \text{ be } f(E, E') \text{ in } T) = \vartheta\vartheta' \, \text{let } x \text{ be } f(E, E') \text{ in } (\vartheta \triangleright T)$$
$$\vartheta \text{ let } x \text{ be } f(E, E') \text{ in } T \xrightarrow{\langle \vartheta f \rangle} T[f(E, E')/x]$$

The protocol is simply: $(Diffie\text{-}Hellman)$
$$\begin{array}{l} 1. \ A \rightarrow B : g(K_A) \\ 2. \ B \rightarrow A : g(K_B) \end{array}$$

At the end of the exchange A computes the key as $f(K_A, g(K_B))$, while B computes it as $f(g(K_A), K_B)$. These steps are made explicit in the LySa specification of the protocol, $Sys_2 = (A|B)$, given in Tab. 3. The two keys coincide, because of the following algebraic rule: $f(x, g(y)) = f(y, g(x))$. Here, K_A and K_B serve as private keys, while $g(K_A)$ and $g(K_B)$ serve as public keys. Note that here we do not need to extend our syntax with asymmetric encryption (we refer the reader to [3]).

The Diffie-Hellman protocol can be efficiently implemented using the Elliptic Curve Asymmetric-key (ECC) algorithm [17], that operates over a group of points on an elliptic curve. For each curve a base point G is fixed, a large random integer k acts as a private key, while kG (scalar point multiplication that results in another point on the curve) acts as the corresponding public key. Scalar point multiplication is obtained by a combination of point-additions and point-doublings. So, we can use (1) $g(x) = xG$ and (2) $f(x, y) = xy$.

Table 3. Specification of *Diffie-Hellman* Protocol

1 $Sys_2 = (A\|B)$	
2 $A = (\nu K_A)$	K_A private key
3 $(\langle g(K_A) \rangle . A')$	A sends msg (1)
4 $A' = (; v_g^A) . A''$	A receives msg (2)
5 $A'' = \text{let } v_g^A \text{ be } f(K_A, v_g^A) \text{ in } A$	A computes f
6 $B = (\nu K_B)$	K_B private key
7 $B' = (; v_g^B) . B''$	B receives msg (1)
8 $(\langle g(K_B) \rangle . B')$	B sends msg (2)
9 $B'' = \text{let } v_g^B \text{ be } f(K_B, v_g^A) \text{ in } B$	B computes f

For lack of space, we omit here the (finite) transition systems of Sys_2, that like the one of Sys_1 has a unique cyclic path. We directly give the rates corresponding to the transitions:

$$c_0' = \frac{1}{s+4pm}, \quad c_1' = \frac{1}{s+4pm}, \quad c_2' = \frac{1}{4pm}, \quad c_3' = \frac{1}{4pm}.$$

We use the same cost parameters as in Section 3. In particular, we assume that the sending parameter s is the same used for Sys_1 (again transmission is more expensive than reception). Since the functions g and f in Sys_2 are both implemented with four elliptic curve point multiplications, we assume that the cost for g and f depend on the parameter pm (parameter for point multiplication), more precisely $\$_\alpha(f(E, E')) = \frac{1}{4pm}$ and $\$_\alpha(\langle g(E)\rangle) = \frac{1}{s+4pm}$. Again, for the sake of simplicity, we assume that each principal has enough processing power, so $\$_{||}(\vartheta) = 1$ for each ϑ.

The stationary distribution Π_2, where $D = 2(8pm + s)$, corresponding to $\mathbf{Q}_2$ of $CTMC(Sys_2)$, here omitted, is:

$$\Pi_2 = \left[\frac{s + 4pm}{D}, \frac{s + 4pm}{D}, \frac{4pm}{D}, \frac{4pm}{D}\right]$$

We can now compare the performance of the two protocols by relating their throughputs. As done before, we associate a transition reward equal to its rate with the last communication and a null transition reward with all the others communications. We compute then the reward structure $\rho_2 = (0, 0, 0, c_3')$ for Sys_2 where $c_3' = \frac{1}{4pm}$. Furthermore, we assume the same cost for encryption and decryption, i.e. e = d. The total reward of Sys_2 is $R(Sys_2) = \frac{1}{2(s+8pm)}$ and is such that:

$$R(Sys_1) - R(Sys_2) = \frac{8pm - (8s + 14d + 3m)}{2((s + 8pm))((9s14 + d + 3m))} > 0 \text{ if } pm > \frac{(8s + 14d + 3m)}{8}$$

Experimentally, we know that point multiplication is significantly more time-consuming than decryption, therefore, we can assume that pm is significantly higher than d. Consequently, we conclude that $R(Sys_1) > R(Sys_2)$, i.e. the first system has a better performance. Clearly, energy consumption of a cryptographic algorithm is strongly related to its time complexity and thus our result agrees with the one obtained in [20].

Actually, our working example presents a simple setting, in which the involved transition systems have a unique cyclic path. In general, transition systems have more loops. Typically, this happens with a multi-session version of the protocols presented before, where more copies of each principal (A, B and S) running in parallel, lead to more transitions with the same source. Also, this happens with non-repudiation protocols.

References

1. M. Abadi and A. D. Gordon. A calculus for cryptographic protocols - The Spi calculus. *Information and Computation*, 148(1):1–70, Jan 1999.
2. A. A. Allen. *Probability, Statistics and Queueing Theory with Computer Science Applications*. Academic Press, 1978.

3. C. Bodei, M. Buchholtz, P. Degano, F. Nielson, and H. Riis Nielson. Automatic validation of protocol narration. *Proc. of CSFW'03*, pages 126–140. IEEE, 2003.
4. C. Bodei, M. Buchholtz, P. Degano, F. Nielson, and H. Riis Nielson. Control Flow Analysis can find new flaws too. *Proc. of Workshop on Issues in the Theory of Security (WITS'04)*, 2004.
5. C. Bodei, M. Buchholtz, P. Degano, F. Nielson, and H. Riis Nielson. Static validation of security protocos. To appear in *Journal of Computer Securuty.*
6. C. Bodei, M. Buchholtz, M. Curti, P. Degano, F. Nielson, and H. Riis Nielson and C. Priami. Performance Evaluation of Security Protocols specified in Lysa. *Proc. of (QAPL'04)*, ENTCS 112, 2005.
7. C. Bodei, M. Curti, P. Degano, C. Priami. A Quantitative Study of Two Attacks. *Proc. of (WISP'04)*, ENTCS 121, 2005.
8. M. Bravetti, M. Bernardo and R. Gorrieri. Towards Performance Evaluation with General Distributions in Process Algebras. *Proc. of CONCUR98*, LNCS 1466, 1998.
9. M. Buchholtz, F. Nielson, and H. Riis Nielson. A calculus for control flow analysis of security protocols. *International Journal of Information Security*, 2 (3-4), 2004.
10. I. Cervesato Fine-Grained MSR Specifications for Quantitative Security Analysis. *Proc. of WITS'04*, pp. 111-127, 2004.
11. G. Clark. Formalising the specifications of rewards with PEPA. *Proc. of PAPM'96*, pp. 136-160. CLUT, Torino, 1996.
12. J. Daemen and V. Rijndael. *The design of Rijndael.* Springer-Verlag, 2002.
13. P. Degano and C. Priami. Non Interleaving Semantics for Mobile Processes. *Theoretical Computer Science*, 216:237–270, 1999.
14. P. Degano and C. Priami. Enhanced Operational Semantics. *ACM Computing Surveys*, 33, 2 (June 2001), 135-176.
15. W. Diffie and M. E. Hellman. New directions in Cryptography. *IEEE Transactions on Information Theory*, IT-22(6):644-654, 1976.
16. D. Dolev and A. Yao. On the security of public key protocols. *IEEE TIT*, IT-29(12):198–208, 1983.
17. IEEE P1363 Standard Specification for Public-Key Cryptography, 1999
18. H. Hermanns and U. Herzog and V. Mertsiotakis. Stochastic process algebras – between LOTOS and Markov Chains. *Computer Networks and ISDN systems* 30(9-10):901-924, 1998.
19. J. Hillston. *A Compositional Approach to Performance Modelling.* Cambridge University Press, 1996.
20. A. Hodjat and I. Verbauwhede. *The Energy Cost of Secrets in Ad-hoc Networks.* IEEE Circuits and Systems Workshop on Wireless Communications and Networking, 2002.
21. R, Howard. *Dynamic Probabilistic Systems: Semi-Markov and Decision Systems.* Volume II, Wiley, 1971.
22. J.T. Kohl and B.C. Clifford. *The Kerberos network authentication service (V5).* The Internet Society, Sept. 1993.RCF 1510.
23. C. Meadows. A cost-based framework for analysis of denial of service in networks. *Journal of Computer Security*, 9(1/2), pp.143 - 164, 2001.
24. R. Milner, J. Parrow, and D. Walker. A calculus of mobile processes (I and II). *Info. & Co.*, 100(1):1–77, 1992.
25. R. Nelson. *Probability, Stochastic Processes and Queeing Theory.* Springer, 1995.
26. C. Nottegar, C. Priami and P. Degano. Performance Evaluation of Mobile Processes via Abstract Machines. *Transactions on Software Engineering*, 27(10), 2001.
27. D. Otway and O. Rees. Efficient and timely mutual authentication. *ACM Operating Systems Review*, 21(1):8–10, 1987.

28. A. Perrig and D.Song. A First Step towards the Automatic Generation of Security Protocols. *Proc. of Network and Distributed System Security Symposium*, 2000.

29. G. Plotkin. A Structural Approach to Operational Semantics. *Tech. Rep. Aarhus University, Denmark*, 1981, DAIMI FN-19

30. C. Priami. Language-based Performance Prediction of Distributed and Mobile Systems *Information and Computation* 175: 119-145, 2002.

31. A. Reibnam and R. Smith and K. Trivedi. Markov and Markov reward model transient analysis: an overview of numerical approaches. *European Journal of Operations Research*: 40:257-267, 1989.

32. W. J. Stewart. *Introduction to the numerical solutions of Markov chains*. Princeton University Press, 1994.

33. K. S. Trivedi. *Probability and Statistics with Reliability, Queeing and Computer Science Applications*. Edgewood Cliffs, NY, 1982.

Timed Equivalences
for Timed Event Structures

M.V. Andreeva and I.B. Virbitskaite

A.P. Ershov Institute of Informatics Systems,
Siberian Division of the Russian Academy of Sciences,
6, Acad. Lavrentiev avenue, 630090, Novosibirsk, Russia
Phone: +7 3833 30 40 47, Fax: +7 3833 32 34 94,
virb@iis.nsk.su

Abstract. The intention of the paper is to develop a framework for observational equivalences in the setting of a real-time partial order model. In particular, we introduce a family of equivalences of linear time – branching time spectrum based on interleaving, causal trees and partial order semantics, in the setting of event structures with dense time domain. We study the relationships between these approaches and show their discriminating power. Furthermore, when dealing with particular subclasses of the model under consideration there is no difference between a more concrete or a more abstract approach.

1 Introduction

For the purpose of specification and verification of the behaviour of systems, it is necessary to provide a number of suitable equivalence notions in order to be able to choose the simplest possible view of the system. When comparing behavioural equivalences for concurrency, it is common practice to distinguish between two aspects. The first one which is most dominant is the so-called *linear time – branching time* spectrum [11]. In the former, a process is determined by its possible executions, the behaviour of a system is represented by the set of its possible executions, whereas in the latter the branching structure of processes is taken in account as well. Branching time semantics is of fundamental importance in concurrency, exactly because it is independent of the precise nature of observability. The standard example of a linear time equivalence is (interleaving) *trace equivalence* as put forward in [15], the standard example of a branching time equivalence is (interleaving) *bisimulation equivalence* as proposed in [14]. Furthermore, there is (interleaving) *testing equivalence* [10] in between. The other aspect to consider is whether partial orders between action occurrences are taken into account. In the interleaving approach, these are neglected. Many attempts have been made to overcome the limits of the interleaving approach and to allow observer to discriminate systems via an equivalence accordingly to the degree of concurrency they exploit in their computations. As a result, various equivalences based on modelling causal relations explicitly by partial orders have appeared in the literature (see [1,12,13] among others). The culminating point here is history preserving bisimulation.

V. Malyshkin (Ed.): PaCT 2005, LNCS 3606, pp. 16–26, 2005.

Recently, a growing interest can be observed in modelling real-time systems which imply a need of a representation of the lapse of time. Several formal methods for specifying and reasoning about such systems have been proposed in the last ten years (see [3,4] as surveys). On the other hand, the incorporation of real time into equivalence notions is less advanced. There are a few papers (see, for example, [8,19,23]) where decidability questions of interleaving time-sensitive equivalences are investigated. However, to our best knowledge, the literature of real-time partial order models [7,16] has hitherto lacked such equivalences. In this regard, the paper [20] is a welcome exception, where step and partial order semantics of timed trace and bisimulation equivalences have been provided in the framework of timed event structures with urgent actions. Moreover, in the papers [5,18] time-sensitive testing has been treated for different real-time extensions of event structures. Finally, our origin has been the paper [21] where the open maps framework has been used to obtain abstract bisimilarities which are established to coincide with timed extensions of partial order based equivalences.

In this paper, we seek to develop a framework for observational equivalences in the setting of a real-time partial order model. In particular, we introduce a family of equivalences of linear time – branching time spectrum based on interleaving, causal trees and partial order semantics, in the setting of event structures with dense time domain. This allows us to take into account processes' timing behaviour in addition to their degrees of relative concurrency and nondeterminism. We study the relationships between these approaches to the semantics of real-time concurrent systems, and show their discriminating power. Furthermore, when dealing with particular subclasses of the model under consideration, such as sequential and deterministic timed event structures, there is no difference between a more concrete or a more abstract approach.

The rest of the paper is organized as follows. The basic notions concerning timed event structures are introduced in the next section. Three different families of behavioural equivalences based on interleaving, causal trees and partial orders semantics are given in the following three sections. In section 6, we establish the interrelationships between the equivalence notions in the setting of the model under consideration and its subclasses. Section 7 contains some conclusions and remarks on future work. For lack of the space, all the proofs have been omitted. They can be found in the full version of the paper [6].

2   Timed Event Structures

In this section, we introduce some basic notions and notations concerning timed event structures.

First, we recall a notion of event structures [22] which constitutes a major branch of partial order models. The main idea behind event structures is to view distributed computations as action occurrences, called events, together with a notion of causality dependency between events (which is reasonably characterized via a partial order). Moreover, in order to model nondeterminism, there is a notion of conflicting (mutually incompatible) events. A labelling function records which action an event corresponds to. Let Act be a finite set of actions and $\mathbf{E}$ a set of events. A *(labelled) event structure* is a tuple $S = (E, \leq, \#, l)$, where $E \subseteq \mathbf{E}$ is a set of events; $\leq\, \subseteq E \times E$ is a partial order (the *causality relation*), satisfying the *principle of finite causes*: $\forall e \in E \circ \downarrow e = \{e' \in E \mid e' \leq e\}$ is finite; $\# \subseteq E \times E$ is a symmetric and irreflexive relation (the *conflict relation*), satisfying the *principle of conflict heredity*: $\forall e, e', e'' \in E \circ e \# e' \leq e'' \Rightarrow e \# e''$; $l : E \longrightarrow Act$ is a labelling function. For an event structure $S = (E, \leq, \#, l)$, we define the following: $\smile = (E \times E) \setminus (\leq \cup \leq^{-1} \cup \#)$ (the *concurrency relation*), $e \#^1 d \iff e \# d \wedge \forall e', d' \in E \circ (e' \leq e \wedge d' \leq d \wedge e' \# d') \Rightarrow (e' = e\ \&\ d' = d)$ (the *minimal conflict relation*). For $C \subseteq E$, the *restriction* of S to C, denoted $S{\upharpoonright}C$, is defined as $(C, \leq \cap (C \times C), \# \cap (C \times C), l \mid_C)$. Let $C \subseteq E$. Then, C is *left-closed* iff $\forall e, e' \in E \circ e \in C \wedge e' \leq e \Rightarrow e' \in C$; C is *conflict-free* iff $\forall e, e' \in C \circ \neg(e \# e')$; C is a *configuration* of S iff C is left-closed and conflict-free. Let $\mathcal{C}(S)$ denote the set of all finite configurations of S.

We next present the model of *timed event structures* from [21]. Real time is incorporated into event structures by assuming that all events happen "instantaneously", while timing constraints w.r.t. a global real-valued clock restrict the times at which events may occur. Moreover, all events are non-urgent, i.e. they are allowed but not forced to occur once they are ready (their causal predecessors have occurred and their timing constraints are respected). Let $\mathbf{R}$ be the set of nonnegative real numbers.

Definition 1. *A* (labelled) timed event structure *is a triple* $TS = (S, Eot, Lot)$, *where* $S = (E, \leq, \#, l)$ *is a (labelled) event structure,* Eot, $Lot : E \to \mathbf{R}$ *are functions of the earliest and latest occurrence times of events, satisfying* $Eot(e) \leq Lot(e)$ *for all* $e \in E$.

For depicting timed event structures, we use the following conventions. The action labels and timing constraints associated with events are drawn near the events. If no confusion arises, we will often use action labels rather than event identities to denote events. The $<$-relation is depicted by arcs (omitting those derivable by transitivity), and conflicts are also drawn (omitting those derivable by conflict heredity).

Example 1. A trivial example of a labelled timed event structure is shown in Fig. 1.

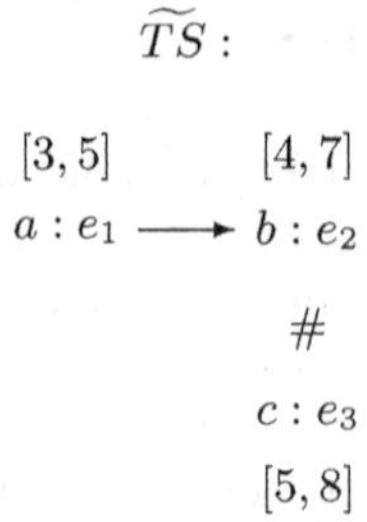

$$\widetilde{TS}:$$

$$[3,5] \qquad [4,7]$$
$$a : e_1 \longrightarrow b : e_2$$

$$\#$$

$$c : e_3$$
$$[5,8]$$

Fig. 1.

Timed event structures TS and TS' are *isomorphic* (denoted $TS \simeq TS'$), if there exists a bijection $\varphi : E_{TS} \longrightarrow E_{TS'}$ such that $e \leq_{TS} e'$ iff $\varphi(e) \leq_{TS'} \varphi(e')$, $e \#_{TS} e'$ iff $\varphi(e) \#_{TS'} \varphi(e')$, $l_{TS}(e) = l_{TS'}(\varphi(e))$, $Eot_{TS}(e) = Eot_{TS'}(\varphi(e))$, and $Lot_{TS}(e) = Lot_{TS'}(\varphi(e))$, for all $e, e' \in E_{TS}$.

An execution of a timed event structure is a *timed configuration* which consists of a configuration and a timing function recording global time moments at which events occur, and satisfies some additional requirements. Let $TS = (S, Eot, Lot)$ be a timed event structure, $C \in \mathcal{C}(S)$, and $T : C \longrightarrow \mathbf{R}$. Then $TC = (C, T)$ is a *timed configuration* of TS iff the following conditions hold: (i) $\forall e \in C \circ Eot(e) \leq T(e) \leq Lot(e)$, (ii) $\forall e, e' \in C \circ e \leq_{TS} e' \Rightarrow T(e) \leq T(e')$. Informally speaking, the condition (i) expresses that an event can occur at a time when its timing constraints are met; the condition (ii) says that for all two events e and e' occurred if e causally precedes e' then e should temporally precede e'. The *initial timed configuration* of TS is $(\emptyset, \emptyset)$. We use $\mathcal{TC}(TS)$ to denote the set of timed configurations of TS. To illustrate the concept, consider the timed event structure $\widetilde{TS}$ shown in Fig. 1. The set of possible timed configurations of $\widetilde{TS}$ is $\{(\emptyset, \emptyset), (\{e_1\}, T_1), (\{e_3\}, T_2), (\{e_1, e_3\}, T_3), (\{e_1, e_2\}, T_4) \mid T_1(e_1) \in [3, 5]; T_2(e_3) \in [5, 8]; T_3(e_1) \in [3, 5], T_3(e_3) \in [5, 8]; T_4(e_1) \in [3, 5], T_4(e_2) \in [4, 7], T_4(e_1) \leq T_4(e_2)\}$.

We need to introduce some auxiliary notions and notations. Let TS be a timed event structure and $TC = (C, T), TC' = (C', T') \in \mathcal{TC}(TS)$. We shall write $TC \longrightarrow TC'$ iff $C \subseteq C'$ and $T'|_C = T$. The *restriction* of TS to TC, denoted $TS \lceil TC$, is defined as $(S \lceil C, T)$.

3   Interleaving Semantics

In this section, we define timed trace, testing and bisimulation equivalences based on interleaving observations on timed event structures.

For this purpose we need the following notion. Let $(Act \times \mathbf{R})$ be the set of *timed actions*.

In the interleaving semantics, a timed event structure TS progresses through a sequence of timed configurations by occurrences of timed actions. In a timed configuration $TC_1 = (C_1, T_1)$, the *occurrence* of a timed action (a, d) *leads to* a timed configuration $TC_2 = (C_2, T_2)$ (denoted $TC_1 \xrightarrow{(a,d)} TC_2$), if $TC_1 \longrightarrow TC_2$, $C_2 \setminus C_1 = \{e\}$, $l_{TS}(e) = a$, and $T_2(e) = d$. The leading relation is extended to a sequence of timed actions from $(Act \times \mathbf{R})^*$ as follows: $TC \xrightarrow{(a_1,d_1)} \cdots \xrightarrow{(a_n,d_n)} TC' \Leftrightarrow TC \xrightarrow{(a_1,d_1)\ldots(a_n,d_n)} TC'$. The set $L_{ti}(TS) = \{w \in (Act \times \mathbf{R})^* \mid (\emptyset, \emptyset) \xrightarrow{w} TC$ for some $TC \in \mathcal{TC}(TS)\}$ is the *ti-language* of TS.

Say that timed event structures TS and TS' are *timed interleaving trace equivalent* (denoted $TS \equiv_{ti} TS'$) iff their *ti*-languages coincide.

Testing equivalences [10] are defined in terms of tests which processes may and must satisfy. A test is usually itself a process applied to a process by computing both together in parallel. A particular computation is considered to be successful if the test reaches a designated successful state, and the process guarantees the test if every computation is successful. However, following the papers [2,13], we use an alternative characterization of the testing concept. In timed interleaving semantics, a test consists of a timed word and a set of timed actions. A timed process passes this test if after every execution of the timed word the timed actions are inevitable next. Two timed event structures are *timed interleaving testing equivalent*, if there is no test which can distinguish them.

Definition 2. *Let TS and TS' be timed event structures. Then,*

- *for $w \in (Act \times \mathbf{R})^*$ and $L \subset (Act \times \mathbf{R})$, TS **after** w **MUST** L iff for all $TC \in TC(TS)$ such that $(\emptyset, \emptyset) \xrightarrow{w} TC$, there exists a timed action $(a, d) \in L$ such that $TC \xrightarrow{(a,d)} TC'$ for some $TC' \in TC(TS)$,*
- *TS and TS' are timed interleaving testing equivalent (denoted $TS \sim_{ti} TS'$) iff for all $w \in (Act \times \mathbf{R})^*$ and $L \subset (Act \times \mathbf{R})$ holds: TS **after** w **MUST** $L \Longleftrightarrow TS'$ **after** w **MUST** L.*

Further, consider the definition of *timed interleaving bisimulation* in the setting of timed event structures. We shall say that two timed event structures are *timed interleaving bisimilar*, if there exists a relation between their bisimilar timed configurations, among which the initial ones, such that the timed configurations obtained by occurring timed actions are also timed interleaving bisimilar.

Definition 3. *Timed event structures TS and TS' are* timed interleaving bisimilar *(denoted $TS \underline{\leftrightarrow}_{ti} TS'$) iff there exists a relation $\mathcal{B} \subseteq TC(TS) \times TC(TS')$ satisfying the following conditions: $((\emptyset, \emptyset), (\emptyset, \emptyset)) \in \mathcal{B}$ and for all $(TC, TC') \in \mathcal{B}$ it holds:*

(a) if $TC \xrightarrow{(a,d)} TC_1$ in TS, then $TC' \xrightarrow{(a,d)} TC'_1$ in TS' and $(TC_1, TC'_1) \in \mathcal{B}$ for some $TC'_1 \in TC(TS')$,

(b) symmetric to item (a).

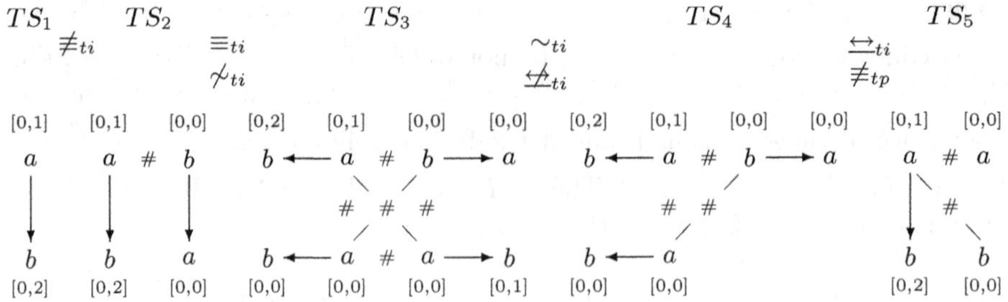

Fig. 2.

Example 2. Consider the timed event structures shown in Fig. 2. We have $TS_2 \equiv_{ti} TS_3$, while $TS_1 \not\equiv_{ti} TS_2$, since, for example, $(b,0)(a,0) \in L_{ti}(TS_2)$ but $(b,0)(a,0) \notin L_{ti}(TS_1)$. Next, we get $TS_3 \sim_{ti} TS_4$, while $TS_2 \not\sim_{ti} TS_3$, because, for instance, TS_2 **after** $(a,0)$ **MUST** $\{(b,1)\}$ but $\neg(TS_3$ **after** $(a,0)$ **MUST** $\{(b,1)\})$. Further, we have $TS_4 \underleftrightarrow{}_{ti} TS_5$ but $TS_3 \not\underleftrightarrow{}_{ti} TS_4$, since, for instance, the timed configuration TC of TS_3 containing the lower right timed action $(a,0)$ can not be related neither to the configuration TC' of TS_4 containing the lower left timed action $(a,0)$ nor to the configuration TC'' of TS_4 containing the upper left timed action $(a,0)$, because, on one hand, in TC the execution of timed action $(b,1)$ is possible, but it is not the case in TC', and on the other hand, in TC'' the execution of timed action $(b,2)$ is possible, but it is not the case in TC.

4   Causal Tree Semantics

The second semantics we use for the definition of timed equivalences are timed causal trees which are a timed extension of causal trees [9]. Causal trees are in turn synchronisation trees [17] which carry in their labels additional information about causes of actions, thus providing us with an interleaving description of timed concurrent processes which faithfully expresses causality.

We start with defining some needed notions and notations. A *timed causal tree* over $(Act \times \mathbf{R})$, TCT, is a tree (N, A, ϕ) where N is the set of nodes, $A \subseteq N \times N$ is the set of arcs, $\phi : A \longrightarrow (Act \times \mathbf{R} \times 2^{\mathbf{N}})$ is the labelling function. The labelling function is extended to paths in a timed causal tree in a standard way. From now on, we shall use the set $\mathcal{P}(TCT) = \{\phi(u) \in (Act \times \mathbf{R} \times 2^{\mathbf{N}})^* \mid u$ is a path in a timed causal tree TCT starting from its root$\}$.

We are ready to provide the definitions of equivalences on timed causal trees.

First, consider the definition of *trace equivalence on timed causal trees*. Timed causal trees TCT_1 and TCT_2 are *timed trace equivalent* (denoted $TCT_1 \equiv TCT_2$) iff $\mathcal{P}(TCT_1) = \mathcal{P}(TCT_2)$.

Second, the definition of *testing on timed causal trees* is developed. An untimed version of the notion was proposed in [13]. For our purpose, we adapt timed interleaving testing to timed causal trees, that is, the tests consist of words over and subsets of $(Act \times \mathbf{R} \times 2^{\mathbf{N}})$ instead of $(Act \times \mathbf{R})$.

Definition 4. *Let TCT_1 and TCT_2 be timed causal trees, $w \in (Act \times \mathbf{R} \times 2^{\mathbf{N}})^*$, and $L \subset (Act \times \mathbf{R} \times 2^{\mathbf{N}})$. Then,*

- *TCT_1 **after** w **MUST** L iff for all paths u in TCT_1 from its root to a node n such that $\phi_1(u) = w$, there exists a label $(a, d, K) \in L$ and an arc r starting from n such that $\phi_1(r) = (a, d, K)$,*
- *TCT_1 and TCT_2 are timed testing equivalent (denoted $TCT_1 \sim TCT_2$) iff for all $w \in (Act \times \mathbf{R} \times 2^{\mathbf{N}})^*$ and $L \subset (Act \times \mathbf{R} \times 2^{\mathbf{N}})$, TCT_1 **after** w **MUST** $L \Longleftrightarrow TCT_2$ **after** w **MUST** L.*

Third, the definition of *bisimulation on timed causal trees* is proposed.

Definition 5. *Timed causal trees TCT_1 and TCT_2 are* timed bisimilar *(denoted $TCT_1 \leftrightarrow TCT_2$) iff there exists a relation $\mathcal{B} \subseteq N_1 \times N_2$ satisfying the following conditions: the roots of the trees belong to $\mathcal{B}$ and for all $(n_1, n_2) \in \mathcal{B}$ it holds:*

(a) if there exists an arc, labelled by (a, d, K), from the node n_1 to a node n_1' in TCT_1, then there exists an arc, labelled by (a, d, K), from the node n_2 to a node n_2' in TCT_2 and $(n_1', n_2') \in \mathcal{B}$,
(b) symmetric to item (a).

Before introducing the notion of the timed causal tree of a timed event structure, we need some auxiliary notions and notations. A *timed trace* of a timed event structure TS is a word $\sigma = (e_1, d_1) \ldots (e_n, d_n)$ such that it holds: (i) $TC_\sigma = (C, T)$ (with $C = \{e_1, \ldots, e_n\}$ and $T(e_i) = d_i$), $1 \leq i \leq n$) is a timed configuration of TS, (ii) $e_i \neq e_j$ for all i, j ($i \neq j$), (iii) $e_i <_{TS} e_j$ implies $i < j$ for all i, j. Hence a timed trace is a causal linearization of a timed configuration. We use $\mathcal{TT}(TS)$ to denote the set of timed traces of TS. The length of a timed trace σ is denoted by $|\sigma|$.

In the timed causal tree of a timed event structure TS, the nodes are simply the timed traces of TS and an arc exists between two timed traces if the second one is an extension of the first one. The causes in the labels of the arc have to be computed from the causality relation of TS.

Definition 6. *Let $TS = (S, D)$ be a timed event structure. The* timed causal tree *of TS, $TCT(TS)$, is the tree $(\mathcal{TT}(TS), A, \phi)$ such that $A = \{(\sigma, \sigma(e, d)) \mid \sigma, \sigma(e, d) \in \mathcal{TT}(TS)\}$, $\phi((\sigma, \sigma(e, d))) = (l_{TS}(e), d, K)$ where $K = \{|\sigma_2| + 1 \mid \exists e' <_{TS} e, \text{ and } \sigma_1, \sigma_2 \text{ s.t. } \sigma = \sigma_1(e', d')\sigma_2 \text{ for some } d'\}$.*

Example 3. Consider the timed event structures, shown in Fig. 2 and 3. First, we have $TCT(TS_6) \equiv TCT(TS_7)$, while $TCT(TS_4) \not\equiv TCT(TS_5)$, since, for example, $(a, 0, \emptyset)(b, 0, \emptyset) \in \mathcal{P}(TCT(TS_5))$ but $(a, 0, \emptyset)(b, 0, \emptyset) \notin \mathcal{P}(TCT(TS_4))$. Second, we get $TCT(TS_7) \sim TCT(TS_8)$, but $TCT(TS_6) \not\sim_{tp} TCT(TS_7)$, because, for instance, $TCT(TS_6)$ **after** $(a, 1, \emptyset)$ **MUST** $\{(b, 1, \{1\})\}$ but $\neg(TCT(TS_7)$ **after** $(a, 1, \emptyset)$ **MUST** $\{(b, 1, \{1\})\})$. Third, we have $TCT(TS_8) \leftrightarrow TCT(TS_9)$, but $TCT(TS_7) \not\leftrightarrow TCT(TS_8)$, because, for instance, in $TCT(TS_8)$ there are arcs, labelled by $(b, 1, \{1\})$ and $(b, 1, \{2\})$, starting from a node reached by the path, labelled by $(a, 1, \emptyset)(a, 1, \emptyset)$, but it is not the case in $TCT(TS_7)$.

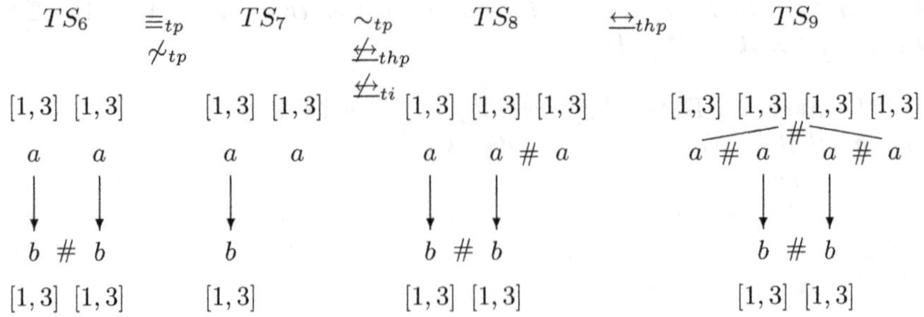

Fig. 3.

5   Partial Order Semantics

In this section, we consider several definitions of timed equivalence notions based on timed partial orders.

The partial order semantics of timed event structures is defined by means of timed pomsets. A *timed pomset* is a (labelled) timed event structure $TP = (E, \leq, \#, l, Eot, Lot)$ with $\# = \emptyset$ and $Eot(e) = Lot(e)$, for all $e \in E$. We use $\mathcal{TP}om$ to indicate the set of timed finite pomsets. The *empty timed pomset* is $(\emptyset, \emptyset, \emptyset, \emptyset, \emptyset)$. The set $L_{tp}(TS) = \{TP \in \mathcal{TP}om \mid TP \simeq TS \lceil TC$ for some $TC \in \mathcal{TC}(TS)\}$ is the *tp-language* of TS.

Using *tp*-languages we obtain timed pomset trace equivalence, i.e., two timed event structures TS and TS' are *timed pomset trace equivalent* (denoted $TS \equiv_{tp} TS'$) iff their *tp*-languages coincide.

Next, the definition of *timed pomset testing* which is a timed extension of causal testing defined in [13], is developed. For this purpose, we will use the following notion. For two timed pomsets TP and TP', TP is a *direct prefix* of TP' (denoted $TP \prec TP'$) if $E_{TP} \subseteq E_{TP'}$, $E_{TP'} \setminus E_{TP} = \{e'\}$, e' is a maximal element of $E_{TP'}$, $\leq_{TP'} |_{E_{TP} \times E_{TP}} = \leq_{TP}$, $l_{TP'}|_{E_{TP}} = l_{TP}$, and $Eot_{TP'}|_{E_{TP}} = Eot_{TP}$, $\forall e \in E_{TP'} \circ e \leq_{TP'} e' \Rightarrow Eot_{TP'}(e) \leq Eot_{TP'}(e')$.

Definition 7. *Let TS and TS' be timed event structures. Then,*

- *for $TP \in \mathcal{TP}om$ and a set of pomsets $\mathbf{TP}'$ such that $\forall TP' \in \mathbf{TP}' \circ TP \prec TP'$, TS **after** TP **MUST** $\mathbf{TP}'$ iff for all $TC \in \mathcal{TC}(TS)$ such that $TS \lceil TC \simeq TP$ and for all isomorphisms $f : TS \lceil TC \longrightarrow TP$ there exists $TP' \in \mathbf{TP}'$, $TC' \in \mathcal{TC}(TS)$, and $f' : TS \lceil TC' \longrightarrow TP'$ such that f' is an isomorphism and $f \subseteq f'$,*
- *TS and TS' are* timed pomset testing equivalent *(denoted $TS \sim_{tp} TS'$) iff for all TP and for all $\mathbf{TP}'$ it holds: TS **after** TP **MUST** $\mathbf{TP}' \iff TS'$ **after** TP **MUST** $\mathbf{TP}'$.*

Further, we define timed extensions of history preserving bisimulation [12]. It is well-known that the equivalence is the culminating point of the pomset bisimulation approach.

Definition 8. *Timed event structures TS and TS' are* timed history preserving bisimilar *(denoted $TS \underleftrightarrow{}_{thp} TS'$) if there exists a relation $\mathcal{B}$ consisting of triples (TC, f, TC'), where TC is a timed configuration of TS, TC' is a timed configuration of TS', and $f : TS \lceil TC \to TS' \lceil TC'$ is an isomorphism, such that $((\emptyset, \emptyset), \emptyset, (\emptyset, \emptyset)) \in \mathcal{B}$ and for all $(TC, f, TC') \in \mathcal{B}$ it holds:*

(a) if $TC \longrightarrow TC_1$ in TS, then $TC' \longrightarrow TC'_1$ in TS' and $(TC_1, f_1, TC'_1) \in \mathcal{B}$ with $f \subseteq f_1$, for some TC'_1 and f_1,
(b) symmetric to item (a).

Example 4. Consider the timed event structures, shown in Fig. 2 and 3. First, we have $TS_6 \equiv_{tp} TS_7$, while $TS_4 \not\equiv_{tp} TS_5$, since, for example, $\begin{smallmatrix}[0,0]\\a\\ \ \\ [0,0]\\b\end{smallmatrix} \in L_{tp}(TS_5)$

and $\begin{smallmatrix}[0,0]\\a\\{}_{[0,0]}\\b\end{smallmatrix} \notin L_{tp}(TS_4)$. Second, we get $TS_7 \sim_{tp} TS_8$, but $TS_6 \nsim_{tp} TS_7$, because,

for instance, TS_6 after $\overset{[1,1]}{a}$ MUST $\{\overset{[1,1]}{a} \to \overset{[1,1]}{b}\}$ and $\neg(TS_7$ after $\overset{[1,1]}{a}$ MUST $\{\overset{[1,1]}{a} \to \overset{[1,1]}{b}\})$. Third, we have $TS_8 \underleftrightarrow{}_{thp} TS_9$, but $TS_7 \nunderleftrightarrow{}_{thp} TS_8$, because, for instance, the timed configurations of TS_8, obtained first by the execution of the medium timed action $(a,3)$, and then by the execution of the left timed action $(a,1)$, can be related only to the timed configurations of TS_7 obtained first by the execution of the left timed action $(a,3)$ and then by the execution of the right timed action $(a,1)$, respectively, however the execution of the timed action $(b,1)$ is further possible in TC_8, but it is not the case in TC_7. Moreover, this means that $TS_7 \nunderleftrightarrow{}_{ti} TS_8$.

As was shown in [1,13], pomset testing and history preserving bisimulation coincide with testing and bisimulation on causal trees, respectively, in the setting of event structures. We extend the results to timed versions of the equivalences.

Theorem 1. *Let TS and TS' be timed event structures. Then,*

(i) $TS \equiv_{tp} TS' \iff TCT(TS) \equiv TCT(TS')$.
(ii) $TS \sim_{tp} TS' \iff TCT(TS) \sim TCT(TS')$.
(iii) $TS \underleftrightarrow{}_{thp} TS' \iff TCT(TS) \underleftrightarrow{} TCT(TS')$.

6   Comparison of Equivalences

The common framework used to define different observational equivalences allow us to study the relationships between the induced semantics. The theorems we state in the section are a step towards a better understanding of the interrelations between interleaving and partial order (also, causal tree) semantics. In particular, we will give the hierarchy for the equivalences and will establish that some of them coincide on special subclasses of timed event structures.

Theorem 2. *Let TS and TS' be timed event structures. Then,*

(i) $TS \equiv_{ti} TS' \Leftarrow TS \equiv_{tp} TS'$,
(ii) $TS \sim_{ti} TS' \Leftarrow TS \sim_{tp} TS'$,
(ii) $TS \underleftrightarrow{}_{ti} TS' \Leftarrow TS \underleftrightarrow{}_{thp} TS'$.

Theorem 3. *Let TS and TS' be timed event structures. Then,*

(i) $TS \equiv_{ti} TS' \Leftarrow TS \sim_{ti} TS' \Leftarrow TS \underleftrightarrow{}_{ti} TS'$,
(ii) $TS \equiv_{tp} TS' \Leftarrow TS \sim_{tp} TS' \Leftarrow TS \underleftrightarrow{}_{thp} TS'$.

The timed event structures in Fig. 2, 3 show that the converse implications of the above theorems do not hold and that the six equivalences are all different.

Now one can ask the obvious question what happens with all these equivalences if we restrict ourselves to some subclasses of the model under consideration. A timed event structure $TS = (S = (E, \leq, \#, l), Eot, Lot)$ is called *sequential*, if $\smile_S = \emptyset$; TS is *deterministic*, if $e \smile_S e'$ or $e \#_S^1 e' \Rightarrow l(e) \neq l(e')$ or $[Eot(e), Lot(e)] \cap [Eot(e'), Lot(e')] = \emptyset$.

The next theorem shows that if we only consider timed event structures which represent timed sequential processes then the interleaving and partial order semantics of the timed equivalences defined coincide.

Theorem 4. *Let TS and TS' be timed sequential event structures. Then,*

(i) $TS \equiv_{ti} TS' \Rightarrow TS \equiv_{tp} TS'$,
(ii) $TS \sim_{ti} TS' \Rightarrow TS \sim_{tp} TS'$,
(ii) $TS \underline{\leftrightarrow}_{ti} TS' \Rightarrow TS \underline{\leftrightarrow}_{thp} TS'$.

The theorem below establishes that if we only consider timed event structures which represent timed deterministic processes then there is no difference between the timed equivalences of linear time – branching time spectrum.

Theorem 5. *Let TS and TS' be timed deterministic event structures. Then,*

(i) $TS \equiv_{ti} TS' \Rightarrow TS \sim_{ti} TS' \Rightarrow TS \underline{\leftrightarrow}_{ti} TS'$,
(ii) $TS \equiv_{tp} TS' \Rightarrow TS \sim_{tp} TS' \Rightarrow TS \underline{\leftrightarrow}_{thp} TS'$.

7 Conclusion

In this paper, we have given a flexible abstract mechanism, based on observational equivalences which allows us to consider timed event structures as the basis of different approaches to the description of the semantics of concurrent and real-time systems. The results obtained show that the semantics proposed in general provide formal tools with an discriminative power. Furthermore, when dealing with particular subclasses of the model there is no difference between a more concrete or a more abstract approach.

In a future work, we plan to extend the obtained results to other observational equivalences (e.g., equivalences taking into account internal actions, etc.) and to other classes of timed event structures (e.g. timed stable event structures, timed local event structures, etc.). Some investigation on the development of timed event structure semantics of timed Petri nets are now under way, and we plan to report on this work elsewhere.

References

1. Aceto, L.: History Preserving, Causal and Mixed-ordering Equivalence over Stable Event Structures. Fundamenta Informaticae **17(4)** (1992) 319–331
2. Aceto, L., De Nicola, R., Fantechi, A.: Testing Equivalences for Event Structures. Lecture Notes in Computer Science, Vol. 280. Springer-Verlag, Berlin Heidelberg New York (1987) 1–20
3. Alur, R., Dill, D.: The Theory of Timed Automata. Theoretical Computer Science **126** (1994) 183–235

4. Alur, R., Henzinger, T.A.: Logics and Models of Real Time: a Survey. Lecture Notes in Computer Science, Vol. 600 Springer-Verlag, Berlin Heidelberg New York (1992) 74–106
5. Andreeva, M.V., Bozhenkova, E.N., Virbitskaite, I.B.: Analysis of Timed Concurrent Models Based on Testing Equivalence. Fundamenta Informaticae **43(1-4)** (2000) 1–20
6. Andreeva, M.A., Virbitskaite, I.B.: Timed Equivalences for Timed Event Structures. Available from http://www.iis.nsk.su/persons/virb/virb.zip
7. Baier, C., Katoen, J.-P., Latella, D.: Metric Semantics for True Concurrent Real Time. In Proc. 25th Int. Colloquium, ICALP'98, Aalborg, Denmark (1998) 568–579
8. Čerāns, K.: Decidability of Bisimulation Equivalences for Parallel Timer Processes. Lecture Notes in Computer Science, Vol. 663. Springer-Verlag, Berlin Heidelberg New York (1993) 302–315
9. Darondeau, Ph., Degano, P.: Causal Trees: Interleaving + Causality. Lecture Notes in Computer Science, Vol. 469. Springer-Verlag, Berlin Heidelberg New York (1990) 239–255
10. De Nicola, R., Hennessy, M.: Testing Equivalence for Processes. Theoretical Computer Science **34** (1984) 83–133
11. van Glabbeek, R.J.: The Linear Time – Branching Time Spectrum II: The Semantics of Sequential Systems with Silent Moves. Extended Abstract. Lecture Notes in Computer Science, Vol. 715. Springer-Verlag, Berlin Heidelberg New York (1993) 66–81
12. van Glabbeek, R.J., Goltz, U.: Equivalence Notions for Concurrent Systems and Refinement of Actions. Lecture Notes in Computer Science, Vol. 379. Springer-Verlag, Berlin Heidelberg New York (1989) 237–248
13. Goltz, U., Wehrheim, H.: Causal Testing. Lecture Notes in Computer Science, Vol. 1113. Springer-Verlag, Berlin Heidelberg New York (1996) 394–406
14. Hennessy, M., Milner, R.: Algebraic Laws for Nondeterminism and Concurrency. *Journal of ACM* **32** (1985) 137–162.
15. HOARE C.A.R. Communicating sequential processes. Prentice-Hall, London (1985)
16. Maggiolo-Schettini, A., Winkowski, J.: Towards an Algebra for Timed Behaviours. Theoretical Computer Science **103** (1992) 335–363
17. Milner, R.: Communication and Concurrency. Prentice-Hall, London (1989)
18. Murphy, D.: Time and Duration in Noninterleaving Concurrency. Fundamenta Informaticae **19** (1993) 403–416
19. Steffen, B., Weise, C.: Deciding Testing Equivalence for Real-Time Processes with Dense Time. Lecture Notes in Computer Science, Vol. 711. Springer-Verlag, Berlin Heidelberg New York (1993) 703–713
20. Virbitskaite, I.B.: An Observation Semantics for Timed Event Structures. Lecture Notes in Computer Science, Vol. 2244. Springer-Verlag, Berlin Heidelberg New York (2001) 215–225
21. Virbitskaite, I.B., Gribovskaya, N.S.: Open Maps and Observational Equivalences for Timed Partial Order Models. Fundamenta Informaticae **60(1-4)** (2004) 383–399
22. Winskel, G.: An introduction to event structures. Lecture Notes in Computer Science, Vol. 354. Springer-Verlag, Berlin Heidelberg New York (1988) 364–397
23. Weise, C., Lenzkes, D.: Efficient Scaling-Invariant Checking of Timed Bisimulation. Lecture Notes in Computer Science, Vol. 1200. Springer-Verlag, Berlin Heidelberg New York (1997) 176–188

Similarity of Generalized Resources in Petri Nets*

Vladimir A. Bashkin[1] and Irina A. Lomazova[2]

[1] Yaroslavl State University,
Yaroslavl, 150000, Russia
bas@uniyar.ac.ru
[2] Program Systems Institute of the Russian Academy of Science,
Pereslavl-Zalessky, 152020, Russia
irina@lomazova.pereslavl.ru

Abstract. *Generalized resources* are defined as multisets of Petri net vertices. Here places represent material resources (designated by tokens residing in these places). Transitions correspond to activity resources represented by transition firings. Two generalized resources are called *similar* if in any Petri net marking one resource can be replaced by another without changing the observable system's behaviour (modulo bisimulation). In this paper we study some basic properties of generalized resource similarity and prove that, being undecidable, generalized resource similarity is finitely based, and thus can be finitely described. We show also, that similarity of generalized resources allows to express some substantial properties of systems modelled by Petri nets.

1 Introduction

Petri nets is a well-known formalism of less than Turing power. It is suited for modelling parallel and distributed systems, such as protocol specifications, distributed algorithms and workflows. Petri nets offer a wide range of modelling primitives: sequential and parallel composition, choice, accumulation, expressed in a clear graphical notation.

The notion of bisimulation equivalence was introduced by Milner and Park. It captures the notion of observable system behaviour. Bisimulation equivalence is a binary relation on system states (Petri net markings). Two states are bisimilar, if an external observer (who sees only transition firings) cannot distinguish them.

For ordinary Petri nets the marking bisimulation is undecidable [6]. A more weak place bisimulation for ordinary Petri nets was studied in [1]. Place bisimulation is a binary relation on Petri net places. Two places in a Petri net are bisimilar, if replacing a token in one place by a token in another one in any

---

* This research was partly supported by the Russian Foundation for Basic Research (Grant 03-01-00804) and by the Presidium of the Russian Academy of Science, program "Intellectual computer systems", project 2.3.

V. Malyshkin (Ed.): PaCT 2005, LNCS 3606, pp. 27–41, 2005.

marking doesn't change the system behaviour. Place bisimulation is decidable. It can be used for reducing Petri nets by place fusion.

In [3] multisets of places were considered as system *resources* generating this or that net's behavior, and the relation of *resource similarity* was defined. Two resources are called similar if changing one resource by another in any marking can't be noticed by an external observer. The relation of resource similarity has a very natural interpretation and can be useful for analysis resource dependencies in modelled systems. It can be used also for net reduction. Resource similarities are undecidable, but they are closed under transitivity and addition of resources. Moreover, each resource similarity has a finite basis under transitivity and addition. Being undecidable, resource similarity can be in a certain sense "approximated" the by a stronger relation of *a resource bisimulation* [3]. In [4] *conditional resource similarity* was investigated. Two resources are called similar under a certain condition if one of them can be replaced by another without changing an observable behavior provided that a comprehending marking contains also some additional resources.

In many resource-dependent systems, such as e. g. workflow systems, stuff and devices, which deal with other resources, are changeable and can be considered as resources themselves. So, in this paper we introduce the notion of *generalized resource*. It includes not only statical but also dynamical components. Generalized resource is a pair of multisets: a multiset of places and a multiset of transitions. A multiset of places defines a *material resource,* a multiset of transition defines an *activity resource.*

Then we define the relation of *similarity* for generalized resources. Two generalized resources are similar, if in any state of the system we can replace tokens and firings of one of them by tokens and firings of another without changing the observable system behaviour. Here we suppose all transitions in the activity part of the resource to fire independently (in one parallel step).

This new kind of similarity allows to express some interesting properties of system components. The novelty is in the possibility to examine not only the static part of a Petri net (places and markings), but also it's active components (transitions and firings). Thus, for example, it allows to formalize the notions of "comparative effectiveness" and "equivalence under condition" for two multisets of events (transition firings). At the same time, generalized resource similarity is a natural extension of the resource similarity relation defined in [3]. Hence it allows to express all static resource properties such as "resource sufficiency" or "resource redundancy" as well.

In this paper we study basic properties of a generalized resource similarity. It is shown that a generalized resource similarity is an equivalence relation, and that it is closed under addition of pairs of generalized resources and under two specific operations — parallel step removal and parallel step addition. The set of all pairs of similar generalized resources is semilinear. We describe a special finite basis of a generalized resource similarity. It is also proven that a generalized resource similarity is a generalization of a resource similarity [3] and hence is undecidable.

2   Preliminaries

Let S be a finite set. A *multiset* m over a set S is a mapping $m : S \to Nat$, where Nat is the set of natural numbers (including zero), i. e. a multiset may contain several copies of the same element.

For two multisets m, m' we write $m \subseteq m'$ iff $\forall s \in S : m(s) \leq m'(s)$ (the inclusion relation). The sum and the union of two multisets m and m' are defined as usual: $\forall s \in S : m + m'(s) = m(s) + m'(s)$, $m \cup m'(s) = max(m(s), m'(s))$. By $\mathcal{M}(S)$ we denote the set of all finite multisets over S.

Non-negative integer vectors are often used to encode multisets. Actually, the set of all multisets over finite S is a homomorphic image of $Nat^{|S|}$. A binary relation $R \subseteq Nat^k \times Nat^k$ is a congruence if it is an equivalence relation and whenever $(v, w) \in R$, then $(v + u, w + u) \in R$ (here '+' denotes coordinate-wise addition). It was proved by L. Redei [7] that every congruence on Nat^k is generated by a finite set of pairs. Later P. Jančar [6] and J. Hirshfeld [5] presented a shorter proof and also showed that every congruence on Nat^k is a semilinear relation, i. e. it is a finite union of linear sets.

Let P and T be disjoint sets of *places* and *transitions* and let $F : (P \times T) \cup (T \times P) \to Nat$. Then $N = (P, T, F)$ is a *Petri net*. A *marking* in a Petri net is a function $M : P \to Nat$, mapping each place to some natural number (possibly zero). Thus a marking may be considered as a multiset over the set of places. Pictorially, P-elements are represented by circles, T-elements by boxes, and the flow relation F by directed arcs. Places may carry tokens represented by filled circles. A current marking M is designated by putting $M(p)$ tokens into each place $p \in P$. Tokens residing in a place are often interpreted as resources of some type consumed or produced by a transition firing. A simple example, where tokens represent molecules of hydrogen, oxygen and water respectively is shown in Fig. 1.

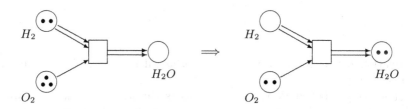

Fig. 1. A chemical reaction

For a transition $t \in T$ an arc (x, t) is called an *input arc*, and an arc (t, x) — an *output arc*; the *preset* $\bullet t$ and the *postset* $t \bullet$ are defined as the multisets over P such that $\bullet t(p) = F(p, t)$ and $t \bullet (p) = F(t, p)$ for each $p \in P$. A transition $t \in T$ is *enabled* in a marking M iff $\forall p \in P\ M(p) \geq F(p, t)$. An enabled transition t may *fire* yielding a new marking $M' =_{\text{def}} M - \bullet t + t \bullet$, i.e. $M'(p) = M(p) - F(p, t) + F(t, p)$ for each $p \in P$ (denoted $M \xrightarrow{t} M'$).

The transitions may *fire in parallel* (concurrently), if there are enough tokens for all of them. In particular, the transition may fire in parallel with itself. The concurrent firing of the multiset of transitions is called *a parallel step*. The precondition and postcondition for the multiset of transitions $\alpha \in \mathcal{M}(T)$ are:

$$^\bullet\alpha =_{def} \sum_{t \in \alpha} {}^\bullet t, \qquad \alpha^\bullet =_{def} \sum_{t \in \alpha} t^\bullet.$$

Note that if transition t occurs n times in α then its precondition $^\bullet t$ occurs n times in $^\bullet\alpha$. Obviously,

$$^\bullet(\alpha + \beta) = {}^\bullet\alpha + {}^\bullet\beta, \qquad (\alpha + \beta)^\bullet = \alpha^\bullet + \beta^\bullet.$$

To observe a net behavior transitions are marked by special labels representing observable actions or events. Let Act be a set of action names. A *labelled Petri net* is a tuple $N = (P, T, F, l)$, where (P, T, F) is a Petri net and $l : T \to Act$ is a labelling function. It can be generalized to multisets:

$$\text{for } \alpha \in \mathcal{M}(T) \qquad l(\alpha) =_{def} \sum_{t \in \alpha} l(t).$$

Again, we use not a union but a sum of multisets.

Let $N = (P, T, F, l)$ be a labelled Petri net. We say that a relation $R \subseteq \mathcal{M}(P) \times \mathcal{M}(P)$ conforms the *transfer property* iff for all $(M_1, M_2) \in R$ and for every step $t \in T$, s.t. $M_1 \xrightarrow{t} M_1'$, there exists an imitating step $u \in T$, s.t. $l(t) = l(u)$, $M_2 \xrightarrow{u} M_2'$ and $(M_1', M_2') \in R$. The transfer property can be represented by the following diagram:

$$
\begin{array}{ccc}
M_1 & \sim & M_2 \\[4pt]
\downarrow t & & \downarrow (\exists)u, \ l(u) = l(t) \\[4pt]
M_1' & \sim & M_2'
\end{array}
$$

A relation R is called a *marking bisimulation*, if both R and R^{-1} conform the transfer property.

For every labelled Petri net there exists the largest marking bisimulation (denoted by $\sim$) and this bisimulation is an equivalence. It was proved by P. Jančar [6], that the marking bisimulation is undecidable for Petri nets.

3   Similarity of Generalized Resources

Definition 1. *Let $N = (P, T, F, l)$ be a labelled Petri net. A pair (r, α) s. t. $r \in \mathcal{M}(P), \alpha \in \mathcal{M}(T)$ and $^\bullet\alpha \subseteq r$ is called a generalized resource of a Petri net N.*

The set of all generalized resources of N is denoted by $\Phi(N)$.

In other words, a generalized resource can be considered as a multiset over the set $P \cup T$ of vertices in Petri net graph. But we prefer to use the syntax (r, α) since for syntactical reasons it is more convenient to separate places and transitions explicitly.

So, the generalized resource (r, α) consists of two distinguished parts — a multiset of places r and a multiset of transitions α. We will call r a *material resource* and α an *activity resource*. The material part describes the availability of raw materials (tokens in Petri nets) and the activity part describes the possibility of tool usage (transition firings). Since we consider not sets but multisets, both tools and materials may have quantity.

The requirement of well-foundedness ${}^\bullet\alpha \subseteq r$ is very natural and guarantees that materials utilized by activity part are always included into material part.

Note that by definition ${}^\bullet\alpha$ contains enough tokens for *parallel* firing of *all* transitions in α. Hence α can be always considered as a parallel step. We consider only parallel firings of transitions constituting the activity part of a resource.

Generalized resources can be interchangeable:

Definition 2. *Generalized resources (r, α) and (s, β) are called* similar *(denoted by $(r, \alpha) \approx (s, \beta)$) if*

1. *$l(\alpha) = l(\beta)$;*
2. *for every marking $M \in \mathcal{M}(P)$ and parallel step $M + r \xrightarrow{\alpha} M'$ we have $M + s \xrightarrow{\beta} M''$ with $M' \sim M''$.*

Thus if two generalized resources are similar, then in every marking each of these resources can be replaced by another without changing the observable system behavior. The replacement of material parts means just replacement of corresponding tokens. The replacement of activity parts means determined firing of β instead of α.

The generalized resource similarity has natural interpretation. For example, it may express the possibility of replacement of one employee (making some work defined by a multiset of transitions) by another employee (another multiset of transitions), but only provided we replace also some tokens (raw materials at the store and salary on the employee's account) by another multiset of tokens. In this case the money and the raw materials are material resources, and the employees are activity resources. Different employees consume and produce different material resources.

Note that this replacement doesn't actually replace transitions in the net's graph. The structure of the net remains the same. We just replace the occurrences of transitions in the net's behaviour. The first employee is not fired, it is just substituted by the second for this certain work. Later he/she may carry out this kind of work himself/herself again.

Some examples of similar generalized resources are shown in Fig. 2.

Generalized resource similarity may capture a number of interesting facts about the system. Some of them are shown in Fig. 3.

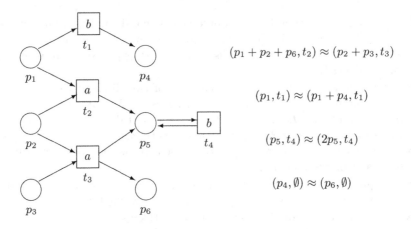

$$(p_1 + p_2 + p_6, t_2) \approx (p_2 + p_3, t_3)$$

$$(p_1, t_1) \approx (p_1 + p_4, t_1)$$

$$(p_5, t_4) \approx (2p_5, t_4)$$

$$(p_4, \emptyset) \approx (p_6, \emptyset)$$

Fig. 2. Examples of similar generalized resources

$(r, \alpha) \approx (s, \beta)$	Generalized resources (r, α) and (s, β) are **interchangeable** in any state of the system.
$(r, \alpha) \approx (r, \beta)$	Activities α and β are **equivalent** in any state of the system, containing context r.
$(r, \alpha) \approx (s, \alpha)$	Materials r and s are **equivalent** if the system necessarily executes α.
$(r, \alpha) \approx (r + s, \beta)$	Activity α is more **effective** than β.
$(r, \alpha) \approx (r + s, \alpha)$	Material s is **removable** if the system necessarily executes α.
$(r, \emptyset) \approx (r + s, \emptyset)$	A material s is **redundant**.

4   Properties of Generalized Resource Similarity

The generalized resource similarity has some nice properties. First of all, it is an equivalence:

Proposition 1. *Let* $(r, \alpha), (s, \beta), (u, \gamma) \in \Phi(N)$. *Then*

1. $(r, \alpha) \approx (r, \alpha)$;
2. $(r, \alpha) \approx (s, \beta) \Rightarrow (s, \beta) \approx (r, \alpha)$;
3. $(r, \alpha) \approx (s, \beta) \ \& \ (s, \beta) \approx (u, \gamma) \Rightarrow (r, \alpha) \approx (u, \gamma)$.

Proof. 1) From the definition.
2) Since the largest marking bisimulation $\sim$ is closed under the symmetry.
3) Since the largest marking bisimulation $\sim$ is closed under the transitivity.   □

The simplest nontrivial similar pairs can be generated by:

Proposition 2. *Let* $\alpha, \beta \in \mathcal{M}(T)$. *Then*

$$l(\alpha) = l(\beta) \quad \Rightarrow \quad (^{\bullet}\alpha + \beta^{\bullet}, \alpha) \approx (^{\bullet}\beta + \alpha^{\bullet}, \beta).$$

Proof. From the definition.   □

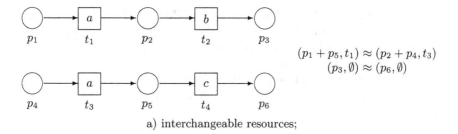

$$(p_1 + p_5, t_1) \approx (p_2 + p_4, t_3)$$
$$(p_3, \emptyset) \approx (p_6, \emptyset)$$

a) interchangeable resources;

$$(p_1, t_1) \not\approx (p_1, t_2)$$
$$(2p_1, t_1) \approx (2p_1, t_2)$$

b) equivalent activities;

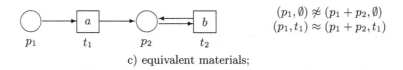

$$(p_1, \emptyset) \not\approx (p_1 + p_2, \emptyset)$$
$$(p_1, t_1) \approx (p_1 + p_2, t_1)$$

c) equivalent materials;

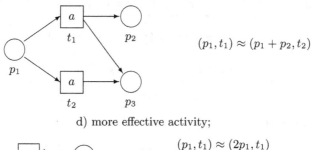

$$(p_1, t_1) \approx (p_1 + p_2, t_2)$$

d) more effective activity;

$$(p_1, t_1) \approx (2p_1, t_1)$$
$$(p_1, \emptyset) \approx (2p_1, \emptyset)$$
$$(\emptyset, \emptyset) \not\approx (p_1, \emptyset)$$

e) removable and redundant materials.

Fig. 3. Properties exposed by a generalized resource similarity

Generalized resource similarity is closed under the removal of a parallel step:

Proposition 3. *Let $(r, \alpha), (s, \beta) \in \Phi(N)$, $\gamma, \delta \in \mathcal{M}(T)$. Then*

$$(r, \alpha) \approx (s, \beta) \ \& \ l(\gamma) = l(\delta) \ \& \ \gamma \subseteq \alpha \ \& \ \delta \subseteq \beta \quad \Rightarrow$$
$$\Rightarrow \quad (r - {}^\bullet\gamma + \gamma^\bullet, \alpha - \gamma) \approx (s - {}^\bullet\delta + \delta^\bullet, \beta - \delta).$$

Proof. Assume the converse: $(r - {}^\bullet\gamma + \gamma^\bullet, \alpha - \gamma) \not\approx (s - {}^\bullet\delta + \delta^\bullet, \beta - \delta).$

First, note that $(r - {}^\bullet\gamma + \gamma^\bullet, \alpha - \gamma)$ and $(s - {}^\bullet\delta + \delta^\bullet, \beta - \delta)$ are well-formed generalized resources, since ${}^\bullet(\alpha - \gamma) \subseteq (r - {}^\bullet\gamma + \gamma^\bullet)$ and ${}^\bullet(\beta - \delta) \subseteq (s - {}^\bullet\delta + \delta^\bullet)$. From $(r, \alpha) \approx (s, \beta)$ and $l(\gamma) = l(\delta)$ we have $l(\alpha - \gamma) = l(\beta - \delta)$.

Hence, the multisets of transitions $\alpha - \gamma$ and $\beta - \delta$ may fire in parallel from the corresponding material resources and from any bigger markings.

So, our assumption implies that for some marking $M \in \mathcal{M}(P)$ and parallel steps

$$M + (r - {}^\bullet\gamma + \gamma^\bullet) \overset{\alpha - \gamma}{\to} M' \tag{1}$$

and

$$M + (s - {}^\bullet\delta + \delta^\bullet) \overset{\beta - \delta}{\to} M'' \tag{}$$

holds $M' \not\sim M''$.

Consider α and r. From the condition $\gamma \subseteq \alpha$ we have $\alpha = \gamma + \gamma'$. From the conditions ${}^\bullet\alpha \subseteq r$ and $\gamma \subseteq \alpha$ we have

$$r = {}^\bullet\gamma + {}^\bullet\gamma' + r'. \tag{2}$$

Applying (2) the step (1) can be rewritten as

$$M + (r - {}^\bullet\gamma + \gamma^\bullet) = M + \gamma^\bullet + {}^\bullet\gamma' + r' \overset{\gamma'}{\to} M + \gamma^\bullet + \gamma'^\bullet + r'.$$

Hence $M' = M + \gamma^\bullet + \gamma'^\bullet + r'$. Similarly we get $\beta = \delta + \delta'$, $s = {}^\bullet\delta + {}^\bullet\delta' + s'$ for some s' and $M'' = M + \delta^\bullet + \delta'^\bullet + s'$.

The generalized resource similarity $(r, \alpha) \approx (s, \beta)$ implies

$$M + r \overset{\alpha}{\to} G', \quad M + s \overset{\beta}{\to} G'',$$

$$G' \sim G''. \tag{3}$$

Applying (2) we can rewrite the firing $M + r \overset{\alpha}{\to} G'$ as

$$M + r = M + {}^\bullet\gamma + {}^\bullet\gamma' + r' \overset{\gamma + \gamma'}{\to} G' = M + \gamma^\bullet + \gamma'^\bullet + r'.$$

Hence $G' = M'$. Similarly $G'' = M''$. Therefore, we get contradiction between (3) and the assumption $M' \not\sim M''$. $\qquad\square$

Note that this is not a subtraction since we subtract only the activity component. The material component is not subtracted, it is transformed according to the step properties.

Generalized resource similarity is closed under the addition of a parallel step:

Proposition 4. Let $(r, \alpha), (s, \beta) \in \Phi(N)$, $\gamma, \delta \in \mathcal{M}(T)$. Then

$$(r, \alpha) \approx (s, \beta) \ \& \ l(\gamma) = l(\delta) \ \& \ \gamma^\bullet \subseteq (r - {}^\bullet\alpha) \ \& \ \delta^\bullet \subseteq (s - {}^\bullet\beta) \quad \Rightarrow$$
$$\Rightarrow \ (r - \gamma^\bullet + {}^\bullet\gamma, \alpha + \gamma) \approx (s - \delta^\bullet + {}^\bullet\delta, \beta + \delta).$$

Proof. Similarly to the proof of proposition 3. $\qquad\square$

This is also not a real addition. Again, we add only an activity component. Material component is not added or removed, it is transformed according to the step properties.

However, we can add both components at once. The generalized resource similarity is closed under the addition of pairs of resources:

Proposition 5. *Let* $(r, \alpha), (s, \beta), (u, \gamma), (v, \delta) \in \Phi(N)$. *Then*

$$(r, \alpha) \approx (s, \beta) \ \& \ (u, \gamma) \approx (v, \delta) \ \Rightarrow \ (r + u, \alpha + \gamma) \approx (s + v, \beta + \delta).$$

Proof. Assume the converse: $(r + u, \alpha + \gamma) \not\approx (s + v, \beta + \delta)$.

Reasoning as in the beginning of the proof of proposition 3, the assumption implies that for some marking $M \in \mathcal{M}(P)$ and parallel steps $M + r + u \overset{\alpha + \gamma}{\to} M'$ and $M + s + v \overset{\beta + \delta}{\to} M''$ holds $M' \not\sim M''$.

Consider (r, α). Since $\bullet \alpha \subseteq r$, we have

$$r \overset{\alpha}{\to} (r - \bullet\alpha + \alpha^\bullet).$$

Denote the multiset of places $r - \bullet\alpha + \alpha^\bullet$ by a primed letter r'. Similarly, denote the postsets of $(s, \beta), (u, \gamma)$ and (v, δ) by primed letters s', u' and v' :

$$r \overset{\alpha}{\to} r', \qquad s \overset{\beta}{\to} s', \qquad u \overset{\gamma}{\to} u', \qquad v \overset{\delta}{\to} v'.$$

Obviously, we have $M' = M + r' + u'$ and $M'' = M + s' + v'$ and hence the assumption can be rewritten as:

$$M + r' + u' \not\sim M + s' + v'. \tag{4}$$

Consider $G = M + r'$. From $(u, \gamma) \approx (v, \delta)$ we have

$$G + u \overset{\gamma}{\to} G + u', \qquad G + v \overset{\delta}{\to} G + v',$$

$$G + u' \sim G + v'. \tag{5}$$

Consider $H = M + v'$. From $(r, \alpha) \approx (s, \beta)$ we have

$$H + r \overset{\alpha}{\to} H + r', \qquad H + s \overset{\beta}{\to} H + s',$$

$$H + r' \sim H + s'. \tag{6}$$

Bisimilarities (5) and (6) can be rewritten:

$$(M + r') + u' \sim (M + r') + v', \qquad (M + v') + r' \sim (M + v') + s'.$$

Since the largest marking bisimulation $\sim$ is closed under the transitivity and the addition of multisets is commutative and associative we get

$$M + r' + u' \sim M + s' + v',$$

that contradicts to (4).   □

Note 1. The generalized resource similarity is not closed under the subtraction of pairs of resources. In particular, the subtraction may affect the well-foundedness of a resource.

From proposition 5 we get

Corollary 1. *The generalized resource similarity is a congruence.*

It was proved by L. Redei [7] that every congruence on the set of vectors Nat^k is generated by a finite set of pairs. Later P. Jančar [6] and J. Hirshfeld [5] presented a shorter proof and also showed that every congruence on Nat^k is a semilinear relation (modulo coordinate-wise addition), i. e. it is a finite union of linear sets.

Since the set of generalized resources $\Phi(N)$ can be considered as a subset of Nat^k with $k = |P| + |T|$, and the multiset addition coincides with the coordinate-wise vector addition, we immediately have

Corollary 2. *The generalized resource similarity is semilinear.*

Here we propose a description of a simple finite basis for $\approx$ (not semilinear).

Consider a finite set P and a congruence B over a set $\mathcal{M}(P) \times \mathcal{M}(P)$ of pairs of finite multisets over P. Since B is a congruence, there must be a finite representation of B ([7]).

It was proved [3], that a finite basis of B can be described as follows.

Define a partial order $\sqsubseteq$ on the set $B \subseteq \mathcal{M}(P) \times \mathcal{M}(P)$ of pairs of multisets: for "loop" pairs let

$$(r_1, r_1) \sqsubseteq (r_2, r_2) \overset{def}{\Leftrightarrow} r_1 \subseteq r_2;$$

for "non-loop" pairs "loop" and nonintersecting addend components are compared separately

$$(r_1 + o_1, r_1 + o_1') \sqsubseteq (r_2 + o_2, r_2 + o_2') \overset{def}{\Leftrightarrow}$$

$$\overset{def}{\Leftrightarrow} o_1 \cap o_1' = \emptyset \ \& \ o_2 \cap o_2' = \emptyset \ \& \ r_1 \subseteq r_2 \ \& \ o_1 \subseteq o_2 \ \& \ o_1' \subseteq o_2'.$$

Note that by this definition reflexive and non-reflexive pairs are incomparable.

Let B_s denote the set of all minimal (w.r.t. $\sqsubseteq$) elements of B. Since $\sqsubseteq$ is a well-quasi-ordering B_s is finite. We call B_s the *ground basis* of B.

Let B^{AT} denote the closure of the relation B under the transitivity and the addition of pairs of multisets.

Theorem 1. *[3] Let $B \subseteq \mathcal{M}(P) \times \mathcal{M}(P)$ be a symmetric and reflexive relation. Then $(B_s)^{AT} = B^{AT}$ and B_s is finite.*

It is easy to see that for any congruence B we have $B^{AT} = B$. So, it is sufficient to deal only with this ground basis.

But in the case of generalized resources the pair $(r, \alpha) \approx (s, \beta)$ is constituted of four distinguished multisets. Moreover, the material and the activity parts are bounded by the requirement ${}^\bullet\alpha \subseteq r$. However, the approach still works.

Define a partial order $\sqsubseteq$ on the set $R \subseteq \Phi(N) \times \Phi(N)$ of pairs of generalized resources as a "lifting" of the case $\mathcal{M}(P) \times \mathcal{M}(P)$:

$$\Big((r,\alpha),(s,\beta)\Big) \sqsubseteq \Big((u,\gamma),(v,\delta)\Big) \stackrel{def}{\Leftrightarrow} (r,s) \sqsubseteq (u,v) \ \& \ (\alpha,\beta) \sqsubseteq (\gamma,\delta).$$

Similarly, let R_s denote the set of all minimal (w.r.t. $\sqsubseteq$) elements of R and is called the *ground basis* of R.

So, we compare the material component and the activity components of resources separately. This can be argued by the fact that the operation of a generalized resource addition, introduced in the statement of proposition 5, also distinguishes them.

Theorem 2. *Let $R \subseteq \Phi(N) \times \Phi(N)$ be a symmetric and reflexive relation. Then $(R_s)^{AT} = R^{AT}$ and R_s is finite.*

The proof is long and technical and is omitted here.

Note 2. The complete relation R is constructed from it's finite ground basis not only with the addition, but also with the transitive closure. It is easy to give an example of a relation that can be generated only by infinitely many transitive closures of it's ground basis. Hence, this basis is not semilinear.

Corollary 3. *The generalized resource similarity is generated by a finite ground basis.*

5 Material and Activity Resources

There are two particularly interesting sorts of generalized resources.

Definition 3. *A generalized resource of the form $(r, \emptyset)$ is called a* material resource.
A generalized resource of the form $(^\bullet\alpha, \alpha)$ is called an activity resource.

Considering only pairs of similar material resources we obtain an important equivalence relation — a *material resource similarity*.

The material resource similarity coincides with the resource similarity, investigated in [3].

Definition 4. *[3] Let $N = (P, T, F, l)$ be a labelled Petri net. A resource $r \in \mathcal{M}(P)$ in a Petri net $N = (P, T, F, l)$ is a multiset over the set of places P.*
Resources $r, s \in \mathcal{M}(P)$ are called similar *(denoted by $r \approx s$) iff for every resource $m \in \mathcal{M}(P)$ we have $m + r \sim m + s$.*

The notion of a generalized resource similarity is a generalization of the notion of a resource similarity, that takes into account not only places (materials), but also transitions (activities).

It is easy to see that a resource similarity forms a distinguished subset of a generalized resource similarity:

Proposition 6. *Let $r, s \in \mathcal{M}(P)$. Then*

$$r \approx s \quad \Leftrightarrow \quad (r, \emptyset) \approx (s, \emptyset).$$

Proof. From the definitions. □

So, the set of all pairs of similar material resources coincides with the set of all pairs of similar resources (modulo notation). All properties of the resource similarity hold for the material resource similarity. In particular,

Corollary 4. *The material resource similarity is an equivalence relation, closed under the addition.*

It was proved in [3] that the resource similarity is undecidable for labelled Petri nets. Since the basis of the material resource similarity can be easily constructed from the ground basis of the complete generalized resource similarity, we get

Corollary 5. *The generalized resource similarity is undecidable for labelled Petri nets.*

Note 3. So, the generalized resource similarity is not computable in general. However, for a resource similarity there exist important subsets called *resource bisimulations* [3]. The problem whether the largest (w.r.t. inclusion) resource bisimulation is a proper subset of the resource similarity is still open. More likely they coincide.

On the other hand, the largest resource bisimulation can be constructively approximated. Hence it seems that it is very promising to look for some analogue in the case of generalized resources.

Considering only pairs of similar activity resources we obtain an activity resource similarity. It is not as rich as material one. More precisely, it is generated by a special subset of a material resource similarity:

Proposition 7. *Let $\alpha, \beta \in \mathcal{M}(T)$. Then*

$$(^{\bullet}\alpha, \alpha) \approx (^{\bullet}\beta, \beta) \quad \Leftrightarrow \quad (\alpha^{\bullet}, \emptyset) \approx (\beta^{\bullet}, \emptyset).$$

Proof.
($\Rightarrow$) From proposition 3.
($\Leftarrow$) From proposition 4. □

This is quite natural — we can exchange "tools" without additional requirements if and only if they are "completely" similar i. e. produce equivalent material resources.

6   Example

In this section we describe a toy example which demonstrates some possible applications of similarity relation.

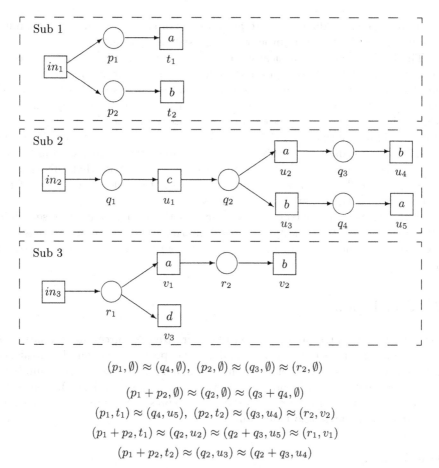

$$(p_1, \emptyset) \approx (q_4, \emptyset), \ (p_2, \emptyset) \approx (q_3, \emptyset) \approx (r_2, \emptyset)$$

$$(p_1 + p_2, \emptyset) \approx (q_2, \emptyset) \approx (q_3 + q_4, \emptyset)$$

$$(p_1, t_1) \approx (q_4, u_5), \ (p_2, t_2) \approx (q_3, u_4) \approx (r_2, v_2)$$

$$(p_1 + p_2, t_1) \approx (q_2, u_2) \approx (q_2 + q_3, u_5) \approx (r_1, v_1)$$

$$(p_1 + p_2, t_2) \approx (q_2, u_3) \approx (q_2 + q_3, u_4)$$

Fig. 4. Adaptive request processing

Consider a model of a request processing system shown in Fig. 4. It may be an organization, a web service or a computational device. The system consists of three separate modules (departments, servers or processors). Each of them can handle it's own type of request. The overall processing is different for different types of requests but, however, some of operations are identical. Specifically, there are "a" and "b" units in every module. So we want to know how this similarity may be used for *adaptive processing:* exchanging requests (resources) between subsystems for load balancing and exception handling. Of course, the replacement must not damage the overall system's behaviour.

The similarity of generalized resources offers a good opportunity for this. In the presented system we can find a number of similar resources.

The material resource similarity provides a nice set of rules for load balancing. For example, using the rule $(q_2, \emptyset) \approx (p_1 + p_2, \emptyset)$ one can decrease the load of subsystem 2 (at the cost of increasing the load of subsystem 1) by removing a token from q_2 and adding tokens to p_1 and p_2. (For simplicity we do not examine here in details the technical process of request transferring.)

The load balancing is basically imposed by some external events or reasons (load manager etc.). The exception handling is necessary for dealing with internal problems of the system. Consider a situation where subsystem 3 crushes during the execution of the task v_1 (or is executing it for an unacceptably long time while other – maybe more powerful – subsystems are standing idle). In this case the similarity rule $(r_1, v_1) \approx (p_1 + p_2, t_1) \approx (q_2, u_2)$ permits us to transfer all the incoming data from Sub 3 to another subsystem (Sub 1 or Sub 2) and then (transparently for the end user) restart the task. Note that this is not a "traditional" rollback, since we remember not only the state (marking) of the system but also the set of chosen activities.

Actually, one can exchange resources and activities not only because of failures. For example, the activity resource similarity $(p_1, t_1) \approx (q_4, u_5)$ displays the possibility to remove one of these activities from the system (permanently or during a hot-swap manipulations).

7   Conclusion

In this paper we presented a notion of generalized resource and a relation of generalized resource similarity, which allows to exposure behavioural equivalence between complex resources of a system. These aggregate resources contain both statical elements (tokens) and dynamical events (transition firings). Hence the relation of generalized resource similarity can express a wide range of properties of system components and behaviour.

References

1. Autant, C., Schnoebelen, Ph.:   Place bisimulations in Petri nets.   In Proc. of ICATPN'92. Lecture Notes in Computer Science, Vol. 616. Springer-Verlag, Berlin Heidelberg New York (1992) 45–61
2. Bashkin, V.A., Lomazova, I.A.: Reduction of Coloured Petri nets based on resource bisimulation. Joint Bulletin of NCC & IIS (Comp. Science), Vol. 13. Novosibirsk, Russia (2000) 12–17
3. Bashkin, V.A., Lomazova, I.A.: Petri Nets and resource bisimulation. Fundamenta Informaticae, Vol. 55, Nr. 2. (2003) 101–114
4. Bashkin, V.A., Lomazova, I.A.:   Resource similarities in Petri net models of distributed systems. In Proc. of PACT'2003. Lecture Notes in Computer Science, Vol. 2763. Springer-Verlag, Berlin Heidelberg New York (2003) 35–48
5. Hirshfeld, Y.:   Congruences in commutative semigroups.   Research report ECS-LFCS-94-291, Department of Computer Science, University of Edinburgh (1994)
6. Jančar, P.:   Decidability questions for bisimilarity of Petri nets and some related problems.   In Proc. of STACS'94. Lecture Notes in Computer Science, Vol. 775. Springer-Verlag, Berlin Heidelberg New York (1993) 581–592
7. Redei, L.: The theory of finitely generated commutative semigroups. Oxford University Press, New York (1965)

8. Milner, R.: A Calculus of Communicating Systems. Lecture Notes in Computer Science, Vol. 92. Springer-Verlag, Berlin Heidelberg New York (1980)
9. Shnoebelen, Ph., Sidorova, N.: Bisimulation and the reduction of Petri nets. In Proc. of ICATPN'2000. Lecture Notes in Computer Science, Vol. 1825. Springer-Verlag, Berlin Heidelberg New York (2000) 409–423

Real-Time Event Structures and Scott Domains

R.S. Dubtsov

A.P. Ershov Institute of Informatics Systems,
Siberian Division of the Russian Academy of Sciences,
6, Acad. Lavrentiev avenue, 630090, Novosibirsk, Russia
Phone: +7 3833 30 40 47, Fax: +7 3833 32 34 94
dubtsov@iis.nsk.su

Abstract. Event structures have come to play an important role in the formal study of the behaviour of distributed systems. The advantage of event structures is that they explicitly exhibit the interplay between concurrency and nondeterminism. In [14], it has been shown that event structures are closely related to Scott domains. The intention of the paper is to extend Winskel's approach to a real-time version of event structures, obtaining a coreflection between categories of the models.

1 Introduction

Category theory has been used to structure the seemingly confusing world of models for concurrency — see [15] for a survey. The general idea is to formalise that one model is more expressive than another in terms of an 'embedding', most often taking the form of a coreflection, i.e. an adjunction in which the unit is an isomorphism.

Event structures have come to play an important role in the formal study of the behaviour of distributed systems. The advantage of event structures is that they explicitly exhibit the interplay between concurrency and nondeterminism. Event structures essentially model processes as sets of events constrained by relations of causal dependency and conflict. On one hand, event structures consist of relations on events and bear a close relationship to Petri nets. On the other hand, configurations or states of an event structure naturally reflect information about which events have occurred and determine a Scott domain of information [2]. Thus, dual nature event structures stand as an intermediary between the theories of Petri nets and denotational semantics, sharing ideas with both. The facts have been shown by obtaining coreflections between categories of the models (see [5,11,14] among others).

Recently, the demand for correctness analysis of real-time systems, i.e. systems whose descriptions involve a quantitative notion of time, increases rapidly. Much of the theory of untimed systems have been lifted to real-time setting. Timed extensions of interleaving models have been investigated thoroughly in the last ten years (see, for instance, [1,6]). On the other hand, the incorporation of quantitative information into noninterleaving models has received scant

V. Malyshkin (Ed.): PaCT 2005, LNCS 3606, pp. 42–48, 2005.

attention: a few extensions are known of pomsets [4], configurations [12], asynchronous transition systems [3,9], net processes [8], and event structures [7,9]. More recently, the close relationships between probabilistic event structures and domains has been established in [13].

This paper follows the seminal work of Winskel [14], where prime event structures are categorically related to Scott domains via a coreflection (a particularly nice form of an adjunction). We extend Winskel's approach to real-time event structures and a specially developed class of Scott domains (marked domains), obtaining a coreflection between categories of the models.

The rest of the paper is organised as follows. The concepts of marked Scott domains and real-time event structures are developed in sections 2 and 3, respectively. In Section 4, categorical characterisation of the relationship between the models are treated.

2   Scott Domains

In this section we provide notions and notations related to Scott domains. First, recall some notions and notations concerning partial orders from [14].

Let $(D, \sqsubseteq)$ be a partial order, $d \in D$ and $X \subseteq D$. Then,

- $d{\uparrow} = \{d' \in \ | \ d \sqsubseteq d'\}$ is called the *upper cone of d*,
- $d{\downarrow} = \{d' \in \ | \ d' \sqsubseteq d\}$ is called the *lower cone of d*,
- X is said to be *compatible* (written $\mathrm{Cmp}(X)$) iff X has an upper bound. We shall denote the *least upper bound* (written lub) (*greatest lower bound* (written glb)), if it exists, as $\bigsqcup X$ ($\bigsqcap X$, respectively),
- X is said to be *finitely compatible* (written $\mathrm{Cmp}_{fin}(X)$), iff every finite subset $Y \subseteq_{fin} X$ has an upper bound,
- X is said to be *directed* iff all its finite subsets $X_0 \subseteq_{fin} X$ have upper bounds in X (so X is finitely compatible and cannot be empty). An element $e \in D$ is said to be *finite* iff for all directed sets $X \subseteq D$, if $e \sqsubseteq \bigsqcup X$ then $e \sqsubseteq x$ for some $x \in X$,
- D is *consistently complete* iff every finitely compatible subset $X \subseteq D$ has a least upper bound $\bigsqcup X$ (thus, D has the least element $\bot = \bigsqcup \varnothing$). A consistently complete partial order is *algebraic* iff for every element $d \in D$ holds: $d = \bigsqcup\{e \sqsubseteq d \ | \ e \text{ is finite}\}$.

We call a consistently complete algebraic partial order a *Scott domain* (or simply a domain). A *finitary* Scott domain is one in which every finite element e dominates only a finite number of elements, i.e. $\{d' \in D \ | \ d' \sqsubseteq e\}$ is finite.

Let $(D, \sqsubseteq)$ be a consistently complete partial order. A *(complete) prime* of D is an element $p \in D$ s.t. for any compatible set $X \subseteq D$ holds: $p \sqsubseteq \bigsqcup X \Rightarrow \exists x \in X \diamond p \sqsubseteq x$. Let P be the set of prime elements. D is a *prime algebraic domain* iff for every $d \in D$ holds: $d = \bigsqcup\{p \sqsubseteq d \ | \ p \in P\}$. Thus, a prime algebraic domain is a Scott domain with a special kind of sub-basis.

Let $(D, \sqsubseteq)$ be a prime algebraic Scott domain and $d, d' \in D$. Say d is *covered* by d' iff $d \prec d'$, where $\prec = \sqsubseteq \setminus \sqsubseteq^2$. A *prime interval* is a pair $[d, d']$ such that

$d \prec d'$. In the following, we shall use $I(D)$ to indicate the set of prime intervals of D. Given two prime intervals $[c, c'], [d, d'] \in I(D)$ define $[c, c'] \leqslant [d, d'] \iff c = c' \sqcap d \wedge d' = c' \sqcap d$. Define the equivalence relation $\sim$ as a symmetric, transitive closure of the relation $\leqslant$. A *covering chain* for an element $d \in D$, denoted $\sigma(d)$, is a (possibly infinite) sequence: $\bot = d_0 \prec d_1 \prec \ldots \prec d_n \prec \ldots$ s.t. $\bigsqcup\{d_j\} = d$.

Let $(D_0, \sqsubseteq_0)$ and $(D_1, \sqsubseteq_1)$ be partial orders and f be a mapping $f : D_0 \to D_1$. Say f is *additive* iff $\forall X \subseteq D_0 \circ \mathrm{Cmp}(X) \Rightarrow f(\bigsqcup X) = \bigsqcup fX$, *stable* iff $\forall X \subseteq D_0 \circ X \neq \varnothing \wedge \mathrm{Cmp}(X) \Rightarrow f(\bigsqcap X) = \bigsqcap fX$, $\prec$-*preserving* iff $\forall x, x' \in D_0 \circ x \prec x' \Rightarrow f(x) \prec f(x')$.

Prime algebraic finitary Scott domains with additive, stable and $\prec$-preserving mappings constitute the category **Dom**.

In the following, for a category **C** we shall use $|\mathbf{C}|$ to indicate the class of objects of **C** and for arbitrary objects $A, B \in |\mathbf{C}|$ we shall use $\mathbf{C}(A, B)$ to indicate the set of morphisms from A to B.

Next, the notion of *marked domains* is developed.

Definition 1. *Let $D \in |\mathbf{Dom}|$ be a prime-algebraic finitary Scott domain. A mapping $m : I(D) \to \{0, 1\}$ is called a* marking. *A pair (D, m) is called a* marked domain.

A marked domain (D, m) is called *correctly marked* iff m respects the $\sim$ relation, i.e $[c, c'] \sim [d, d'] \Rightarrow m([c, c']) = m([d, d'])$. In the following, we shall consider only correctly marked domains and call them simply marked domains.

Further, we need to define auxiliary notions and notations. Let $MD = (D, m)$ be a marked domain. For an element $d \in D$, define its *norm* $\|d\| = \sum_{d_j \in \sigma(d) \setminus \{d\}} m([d_{j-1}, d_j]) \in \widetilde{\mathbb{N}}$, where $\widetilde{\mathbb{N}} = \mathbb{N} \cup \{\omega\}$ ($\mathbb{N}$ is the set of natural numbers and $\omega > n$ for any $n \in \mathbb{N}$). Note that since m respects the $\sim$ relation, $\|d\|$ does not depend on the choice of a covering chain for d and thus is well defined. Calculate the *norm* of MD as follows: $\|MD\| = \max\{\|d\| \mid d \in D\}$.

Define the following relations: $d \prec^i d' \iff d \prec d' \wedge m([d, d']) = i$ for $i = 0, 1$. Form the relation $\sqsubseteq^i$ as a reflexive, transitive closure of $\prec^i$ $(i = 0, 1)$. For an element $d \in D$, define $d\uparrow^i = \{d' \in D \mid d \sqsubseteq^i d'\}$ (the i-marked upper cone of d).

Say that a marked domain $MD = (D, m)$ is

- *linear* iff for any $d \in D$ holds $d\uparrow^1 \cong \{n \in \widetilde{\mathbb{N}} \mid \|d\| \leqslant n \leqslant \|MD\|\}$ and for any $d, d' \in D$ holds $d\uparrow^1 \cap d'\uparrow^1 \neq \varnothing \iff (d \sqsubseteq^i d' \wedge d' \sqsubseteq^i d)$,
- *proper* iff the set P of prime elements is partitioned into two sets sets P^0 and P^1 such that: $P^0 = \{p \in P \mid m([d_p, p]) = 0\}$, where $d_p = \bigsqcup(p\downarrow, \setminus\{p\})$, and $P^1 = \bot\uparrow^1 \setminus \{\bot\}$.

Let (D_0, m_0) and (D_1, m_1) be marked domains and $f \in \mathbf{Dom}(D_0, D_1)$ be a morphism. Then f is called *marking-preserving* iff $m_0([d, d']) = m_1([f(d), f(d')])$ for any $[d, d'] \in I(D_0)$

Linear and proper marked domains with marking-preserving morphisms form the category **MDom**.

3   Real-Time Event Structures

In this section, we introduce a real-time extension of Winskel's model of prime event structures [14] by equipping events with time delays.

We first recall the terminology concerning event structures. An event structure is a partially ordered set of event occurrences together with a symmetric conflict relation. The ordering relation models causality, whereas the conflict relation expresses alternative choices between events. Two event occurrences that are neither comparable nor in conflict, may occur concurrently. In this sense, event structures provide explicit and separate representations of causality, choice and concurrency.

An *event structure* is a tuple $S = (E, \leqslant, \#)$, where E is a set of events; $\leqslant \subseteq E \times E$ is a partial order (the *causality relation*), satisfying the *principle of finite causes*: $\forall e \in E \, _\diamond \, e{\downarrow}$ is finite; $\# \subseteq E \times E$ is a symmetric and irreflexive relation (the *conflict relation*), satisfying the *principle of conflict heredity*: $\forall e, e', e'' \in E \, _\diamond \, e \, \# \, e' \leqslant e'' \Rightarrow e \,\#\, e''$. Let $C \subseteq E$. Then, C is *left-closed* iff $\forall e, e' \in E \, _\diamond \, e \in C \wedge e' \leqslant e \Rightarrow e' \in C$; C is *conflict-free* iff $\forall e, \, e' \in C \, _\diamond \, \neg(e \, \# \, e')$; C is a *configuration of* S iff C is left-closed and conflict-free. Let $\mathrm{Conf}(S)$ denote the set of all configurations of S. For $C \in \mathrm{Conf}(S)$ define $\mathrm{En}(C) = \{e \in E \backslash C \mid C \cup \{e\} \in \mathrm{Conf}(S)\}$ (the set of events *enabled* at C). For a set $E' \subseteq E$ define a *restriction* of S to E' as follows: $S{\lceil}E' = (E', \leqslant \cap (E' \times E'), \# \cap (E' \times E'))$.

For event structures $S_0 = (E_0, \leqslant_0, \#_0)$ and $S_1 = (E_1, \leqslant_1, \#_1)$, a total mapping $\theta : E_0 \to E_1$ is called a *morphism* from S_0 to S_1 if $\forall C \in \mathrm{Conf}(S_0) \, _\diamond \, f(C) \in \mathrm{Conf}(S_1) \wedge \forall e, e' \in C \, _\diamond \, \theta(e) = \theta(e') \Rightarrow e = e'$. Prime event structures with morphisms constitute the category **PES**.

We are now ready to introduce the concept of real-time event structures. In our model, we add time constraints to event structures by associating their events with time delays w.r.t. a global clock. Furthermore, all events are non-urgent, i.e. they are allowed but not forced to occur once they are ready (their causal predecessors have occurred and their time delays are respected). Moreover, the occurrence of an enabled event itself takes no time. A real-time event structure always proceeds in two ways — by occurring an event or by letting a certain amount of time pass. (See, for instance, [3,7,12] for more explanation of the concepts).

Definition 2. *A real-time event structure is a tuple* $(S = (E, \leqslant, \#), D)$*, where* S *is a prime event structure and* $D : E \to \mathbb{N}$ *is a timing function s.t.* $e \leqslant e' \Rightarrow D(e) \leqslant D(e')$.

In a graphic representation of a real-time event structure, delays are drawn near events. The $<$-relations are depicted by arcs (omitting those derivable by transitivity), and conflicts are also drawn (omitting those derivable by conflict heredity).

$$TS: \quad \begin{matrix} 0 & & 1 \\ e_0 & \longrightarrow & e_1 \\ & \# & \\ & e_2 & \\ & 1 & \end{matrix}$$

Example 1. Following the conventions, a trivial example of a real-time event structure is shown in Fig. 1.

A state of an execution of a real-time event structure $TS = (S = (E, \leqslant, \#), D)$ is called a *timed configuration* (C, t), which consists of a configuration $C \in \mathrm{Conf}(S)$ and $t \in \widetilde{\mathbb{N}}$, representing current value of a global clock. The initial timed configuration of TS is $(\varnothing, 0)$.

A real-time event structure progresses through a sequence of states in two ways: by occurring an event whose time delay is respected or by incrementing a global clock. Let $TC_0 = (C_0, t_0)$ and $TC_1 = (C_1, t_1)$ be timed configurations. An event $e \in \mathrm{En}(C_0)$ *may occur* at a timed configuration TC_0 iff $C_0 \cup \{e\} \in \mathrm{Conf}(S)$ and $D(e) \leqslant t_0$. In this case, an occurrence of an event e *leads* to the timed configuration TC_1 (denoted $TC_0 \longrightarrow_0 TC_1$) iff $C_1 \setminus C_0 = \{e\}$ and $t_0 = t_1$. The value of a global clock can be incremented at a timed configuration TC_0 iff $t < \sup\{D(e) \mid e \in E\}$. In this case the increment of a global clock *leads* to the timed configuration TC_1 (denoted $TC_0 \longrightarrow_1 TC_1$) iff $C_0 = C_1$ and $t_1 = t_0 + 1$. The timed configuration TC_0 is *reachable* if either $TC_0 = (\varnothing, 0)$ or there exists a reachable timed configuration TC_1 such that $TC_1 \longrightarrow_0 TC_0$ or $TC_1 \longrightarrow_1 TC_0$. We use $\mathrm{TConf}(TS)$ to denote the set of all reachable timed configurations of TS.

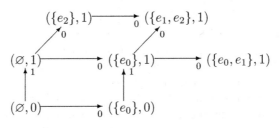

Fig. 2

Example 2. To illustrate the concept of timed configurations, the set of timed configurations of the real-time event structure TS shown in Fig. 1 is depicted in Fig. 2. Here, arcs marked with 0 and 1 denote the relations $\longrightarrow_0$ and $\longrightarrow_1$, respectively.

For real-time event structures $TS_0 = (S_0 = (E_0, \leqslant_0, \#_0), D_0)$ and $TS_1 = (S_1 = (E_1, \leqslant_1, \#_1), D_1)$, a total mapping $\theta : E_0 \to E_1$ is called a *morphism* from TS_0 to TS_1 iff θ is a morphism from S_0 to S_1 and θ respects event delays, i.e. for every $e \in E_0$ holds: $D_0(e) \leqslant D_1 \circ \theta(e)$.

Real-time event structures with morphisms form the category **TPES**.

4   Relating the Models

In this section we relate real-time event structures and marked Scott domains in a categorical setting. For this purpose, the definitions of two functors $\mathcal{TPr} : \underline{\mathbf{MDom}} \to \mathbf{TPES}$ and $\mathcal{TL} : \mathbf{TPES} \to \underline{\mathbf{MDom}}$ are developed. Note, we follow the paper [14], where the category **PES** of prime event structures and the category **Dom** of Scott domains are related by the functors $\mathcal{P}r : \underline{\mathbf{Dom}} \to \mathbf{PES}$ and $\mathcal{L} : \mathbf{PES} \to \underline{\mathbf{Dom}}$.

First, define the functor $\mathcal{TL} : \mathbf{TPES} \to \mathbf{MDom}$.

Definition 3. *For a real-time event structure $TS \in |\mathbf{TPES}|$, define $\mathcal{TL}(TS) = (\mathrm{TConf}(TS), m_{TS})$, where the marking m_{TS} is uniquely defined by the relations $\longrightarrow_0$ and $\longrightarrow_1$. For a morphism $\theta \in \mathbf{TPES}(TS_0, TS_1)$, define $\mathcal{TL}(\theta)$ as a mapping $(C, t) \mapsto (\theta(C), t)$ from $\mathrm{TConf}(TS_0)$ to $\mathrm{TConf}(TS_1)$.*

The following proposition establishes a property of the mapping $\mathcal{TL}$.

Proposition 1. *For a real-time event structure TS, $\mathcal{TL}(TS)$ is a linear and proper marked domain. Moreover, $\mathcal{TL} : \mathbf{TPES} \to \mathbf{TSDom}$ is a functor.*

Next, define the functor $\mathcal{TP}r : \mathbf{MDom} \to \mathbf{TPES}$, extending the functor $\mathcal{P}r$ from [14] in the following manner.

Definition 4. *For a marked domain $(D, m) \in |\mathbf{MDom}|$, define $\mathcal{TP}r(D, m) = (S\lceil P^0, \|\cdot\|)$ with $S = \mathcal{P}r(D)$. For a morphism $f \in \mathbf{MDom}(MD_0, MD_1)$, define $\mathcal{TP}r(f) = \mathcal{P}r(f)\lceil P_0^0$.*

Proposition 2. *$\mathcal{TP}r : \mathbf{TSDom} \to \mathbf{TPES}$ is a functor.*

Proof. The only non-trivial part of the proof is to show that $\mathcal{TP}r(f)$ respects time delays for any morphism $f \in \mathbf{TSDom}(TSD_0, TDS_1)$. It is straightforward due to the definition of $\mathcal{P}r(f)$ from [14] and the fact that f preserves markings and covering chains (hence, preserves the norms).

Theorem 1. *$\mathcal{TP}r$ and $\mathcal{TL}$ constitute a coreflection from $\mathbf{TSDom}$ to $\mathbf{TPES}$.*

Proof (sketch). Suppose $MD = (D, m) \in |\mathbf{MDom}|$ to be a marked domain. Consider a mapping $\eta_{MD} : D \to \mathrm{TConf}(\mathcal{TP}r(MD))$ defined as follows: $\eta_{MD} : d \mapsto (d{\downarrow} \cap P^0, \|d\|)$ for every $d \in D$. It is easy to show that η_{MD} is an isomorphism in $\mathbf{MDom}$.

Similarly, for any real-time event structure $TS \in |\mathbf{TSPES}|$ there exists an isomorphism $\mu_{TS} : TS \to \mathcal{TP}r \circ \mathcal{TL}(TS)$ defined as $\mu_{TS} : e \mapsto (e{\downarrow}, D(e))$. Moreover, it is easy to show that $\mathcal{TL}(\mu_{TS}) = \eta_{\mathcal{TL}(TS)}$.

Due to [10, Theorem 2, pg. 81], it is sufficient to show that for any $MD \in |\mathbf{MDom}|$ the isomorphism η_{MD} is universal, i.e. for any real-time event structure TS and any morphism $f \in \mathbf{MDom}(MD, \mathcal{TL}(TS))$ there exists a unique morphism $\theta \in \mathbf{TSPES}(\mathcal{TP}r(MD), TS)$ such that $f = \mathcal{TL}(\theta) \circ \eta_{MD}$. In [14] one can find the definition of the isomorphism $\varphi_D : D \to \mathcal{L} \circ \mathcal{P}r(D)$ for any domain $D \in \underline{\mathbf{Dom}}$, which is universal in the above-mentioned sense.

Using the fact that D is a prime algebraic finitary domain for every marked domain $MD = (D, m) \in |\mathbf{MDom}|$, there is an isomorphism $\varkappa_{MD} \in \underline{\mathbf{Dom}}(\mathrm{TConf}(\mathcal{TP}r(MD)), \mathcal{L} \circ \mathcal{P}r(D))$ defined as $\varkappa_{MD} = \varphi_D \circ \eta_{MD}^{-1}$.

Since φ_D is universal, there exists a unique morphism $\theta' \in \mathbf{PES}(\mathcal{P}r(D), \mathcal{P}r(\mathrm{TConf}(TS)))$ s.t. $\varphi_{\mathrm{TConf}(TS)} \circ f = \mathcal{L}(\theta') \circ \varphi_D$. Define $\theta = \mu_{TS}^{-1} \circ (\theta'\lceil P^0)$. Note that θ is unique because θ' is unique and μ_{TS}^{-1} is an isomorphism.

It is easy to show that $\theta \in \underline{\mathbf{TPES}}(\mathcal{TPr}(MD), TS)$ and $\mathcal{TL}(\theta) = \varphi_{\mathrm{TConf}(TS)}^{-1} \circ \mathcal{L}(\theta') \circ \varkappa_{MD}$. Thus, we have $f = \mathcal{TL}(\theta) \circ \eta_{MD}$.

5   Conclusions

In this paper, following Winskel's approach [14] we tried to relate a real-time prime event structures and Scott domains obtaining coreflections between categories of the models.

In a future work, we plan to extend the results to real-time generalisations of different classes of event structures. Some investigation on establishing the relationships between semantical representations (e.g., net processes, event structures, etc.) of the behaviour of timed Petri nets are now under way, and we plan to report on this work elsewhere.

References

1. Alur, R., Dill, D.: The theory of timed automata. *Theoretical Computer Science*, **126** (1994) 183–235.
2. Abramsky, S., Jung, A.: Domain theory. *Handbook of Logic in Computer Science*, vol. 3. Clarendon Press, 1994.
3. Aceto, L., Murphi, D.: Timing and causality in process algebra. *Acta Informatica* **33**(4) (1996) 317–350.
4. Casley, R.T., Crew, R.F., Meseguer J., Pratt V.R.: Temporal structures. *Mathematical Structures in Computer Science* **1**(2) (1991) 179–213.
5. Hoogers, P.W., Kleijn, H.C.M., Thiagarajan, P.S.: An event structure semantics for general Petri nets. *Theoretical Computer Science* **153** (1996) 129-170.
6. Henzinger, T.A., Manna, Z., Pnueli, A.: Timed transition systems. *Lecture Notes in Computer Science*, **600** (1991) 226–251.
7. Katoen, J.-P.: *Quantative and qualitative extensions of event structures*. PhD thesis, University of Twente, 1996.
8. Lilius, J.: Efficient state space search for time Petri nets. Proc. *MFCS'98 Workshop on Concurrency*, August 1998, Brno (Czech Republic), FIMU Report Series, FIMU RS-98-06 (1998) 123–130.
9. Murphy, D.: Time and duration in noninterleaving concurrency. *Fundamenta Informaticae* **19** (1993) 403–416.
10. MacLane, S.: Categories for the working mathematician. GTM, Springer-Verlag, 1971.
11. Mesguer, J., Montanari U., Sasonne V.: Process versus unfolding semantics for Place/Transition Petri nets. *Theoretical computer science* **153** (1996) 171-210.
12. Maggiolo-Schettini, A., Winkowski, J.: Towards an algebra for timed behaviours. *Theoretical Computer Science* **103** (1992) 335–363.
13. Varacca, D., Völzer, H., Winskel, G.: Probabilistic event structures and domains. *Lecture Notes in Computer Science*, **3170** (2004) 481–496.
14. Winskel, G.: Event Structures. *Lecture Notes in Computer Science*, **255** (1987) 325–392.
15. Winskel, G., Nielsen, N.: Models for concurrency. *Handbook of Logic in Computer Science*, 4, 1995.

Early-Stopping k-Set Agreement in Synchronous Systems Prone to Any Number of Process Crashes

Philippe Raipin Parvedy, Michel Raynal, and Corentin Travers

IRISA (INRIA-Université de Rennes 1-CNRS),
Campus de Beaulieu, 35042 Rennes, France
M. Raynal: Tel: 33 2 99 84 71 88, Fax: 33 2 99 84 71 71
{praipinp, raynal, travers}@irisa.fr

Abstract. The k-set agreement problem is a generalization of the consensus problem: each process proposes a value, and each non-faulty process has to decide a value such that a decided value is a proposed value, and no more than k different values are decided.

This paper presents a surprisingly simple protocol that solves the k-set agreement problem in synchronous systems prone to up to $t < n$ processes can crash (where n is the total number of processes). The proposed protocol is the first early stopping k-set agreement protocol that does not impose a constraint on t. It allows the processes to decide and stop by $\min(\lfloor f/k \rfloor + 2, \lfloor t/k \rfloor + 1)$ rounds where f is the number of actual crashes ($0 \leq f \leq t$). In addition to its conceptual simplicity, the protocol has an additional noteworthy feature, namely, it is particularly efficient in common case scenarios. This comes from the fact that it is based on a mechanism that allows the processes to take into account the actual pattern of failures and not only their number, thereby allowing the processes to decide in much less than $\lfloor f/k \rfloor + 2$ rounds in a lot of cases.

Keywords: Crash failure, Efficiency, k-set agreement, Message passing system, Round-based computation, Synchronous system, Uniform consensus.

1 Introduction

Context of the paper The k-set agreement problem generalizes the uniform consensus problem (that corresponds to the case $k = 1$). It has been introduced by S. Chaudhuri to investigate how the number of choices (k) allowed to the processes is related to the maximum number (t) of processes that can crash [5]. The problem can be defined as follows. Each of the n processes (processors) defining the system starts with a value (called a "proposed" value). Each process that does not crash has to decide a value (termination), in such a way that a decided value is a proposed value (validity) and no more than k different values are decided (agreement).

When we consider asynchronous systems, the problem can trivially be solved when $k > t$. Differently, it has been shown that there is no solution in these systems as soon as $k \leq t$ [3,13,19]. (The asynchronous consensus impossibility, case $k = 1$, was demonstrated before, using different techniques [9][1]). Several approaches have been proposed

---

[1] The impossibility to solve consensus in asynchronous systems is usually named "FLP result" according to the names of its authors [9].

V. Malyshkin (Ed.): PaCT 2005, LNCS 3606, pp. 49–58, 2005.

to circumvent the impossibility to solve the k-set agreement problem in asynchronous systems (e.g., probabilistic protocols [17], or unreliable failure detectors with limited scope accuracy [12,16]).

The situation is different in synchronous systems where the k-set agreement problem can always be solved, whatever the value of t (and k). It has also been shown that, in the worst case, the lower bound on the number of rounds (time complexity measured in communication steps) is $\lfloor t/k \rfloor + 1$ [6]. (This bound generalizes the $t+1$ lower bound associated with the consensus problem [1,2,8,15].)

Although failures do occur, they are rare in practice. For the uniform consensus problem ($k = 1$), this observation has motivated the design of early deciding synchronous protocols [4,7,14,18], i.e., protocols that can cope with up to t process crashes, but decide in less than $t+1$ rounds in favorable circumstances (when there are few failures). More precisely, these protocols allow the processes to decide in $\min(f+2, t+1)$ rounds, where f is the number of processes that crash during a run, $0 \le f \le t$, which has been shown to be optimal (the worst scenario being when there is exactly one crash per round).

In a very interesting way, it has very recently been shown that the early deciding lower bound for the k-set agreement problem is $\min(\lfloor f/k \rfloor + 2, \lfloor t/k \rfloor + 1)$ [10]. This lower bound, not only generalizes the corresponding uniform consensus lower bound, but also shows an "inescapable tradeoff" among the number t of faults tolerated, the number f of actual faults, the degree k of coordination we want to achieve, and the best running time achievable. It is also important to notice that, when compared to consensus, k-set agreement divides the running time by k (e.g., allowing two values to be decided halves the running time).

Related work. While there exist several not-early deciding k-set agreement protocols [2,6,15] (i.e., protocols that always terminate in $\lfloor t/k \rfloor + 1$ rounds), to our knowledge only one early deciding k-set agreement protocol has been proposed [11]. This protocol assumes $t < n - k$, which means that, contrarily to what we could "normally" hope, the maximum number t of processes that can crash decreases when the coordination degree k increases.

Content of the paper. We propose here a protocol that does not impose a constraint on t (it assumes only $t < n$, i.e., at least one process has to be correct for the problem to be meaningful). Moreover, differently from uniform consensus protocols where a correct process that decides in a round is required to halt only in the next round, the proposed protocol allows a process to decide and halt in the very same round. This means that, instead of the "early deciding" property, the protocol provides the stronger "early stopping" property in $\min(\lfloor f/k \rfloor + 2, \lfloor t/k \rfloor + 1)$.

The proposed protocol enjoys two noteworthy features. The first lies in its design simplicity (that is a first class property). Interestingly, when we take $k = 1$, we obtain a uniform consensus protocol simpler than some already proposed uniform consensus protocols (with a more general proof, based on a totally different approach). The second feature lies in its two dimensional efficiency. The first dimension concerns the size of the messages: they contain only one bit plus one proposed value. The second dimension is a "very quick decision" property, namely, except in extreme cases where the crashes are evenly distributed in the rounds, the processes decide and stop in much less than $\lfloor f/k \rfloor + 2$ rounds. The achievement of this first class efficiency property is provided by the introduction of a very simple mechanism that allows a process to count the number of processes that, from its point of view, have crashed during the last round, whatever the number of previous crashes. This differential approach allows a process to take into account the failure pattern and not only the number of failures that occur. If, during the very first rounds, there are either few crashes or a lot of crashes, the protocol terminates very quickly. As an example, the protocol stops after only three rounds when xk ($\forall\, x > 1$) processes have crashed before the protocol starts, and less than k processes crash thereafter. The $\lfloor f/k \rfloor + 2$ lower bound is attained only in the worst scenarios where there are k crashes per round. The proposed protocol is the first k-set agreement protocol enjoying this "very quick decision" property.

Roadmap. The paper consists 4 of parts. Section 2 presents the computation model and gives a definition of the k-set agreement problem. Section 3 presents the protocol and proves it is correct. Finally Section 4 discusses the local predicate used by bthe processes to early decide and stop.

2   Computation Model and k-Set Agreement

2.1   Round-Based Synchronous System

The system model consists of a finite set of processes, namely, $\Pi = \{p_1, \ldots, p_n\}$, that communicate and synchronize by sending and receiving messages through channels. Every pair of processes p_i and p_j is connected by a channel denoted (p_i, p_j).

The system is *synchronous*. This means that each of its executions consists of a sequence of *rounds*. Those are identified by the successive integers $1, 2$, etc. For the processes, the current round number appears as a global variable r that they can read, and whose progress is managed by the underlying system. A round is made up of three consecutive phases:

- A send phase in which each process sends messages.
- A receive phase in which each process receives messages.
  The fundamental property of the synchronous model lies in the fact that a message sent by a process p_i to a process p_j at round r, is received by p_j at the same round r.
- A computation phase during which each process processes the messages it received during that round and executes local computation.

The underlying communication system is assumed to be failure-free: there is no creation, alteration, loss or duplication of message.

2.2   Process Failure Model

A process is *faulty* during an execution if its behavior deviates from that prescribed by its protocol, otherwise it is *correct*. As already indicated, t is an upper bound on the number of faulty processes. A *failure model* defines how a faulty process can deviate from its protocol.

We consider here the **crash** failure model. A faulty process stops its execution prematurely. After it has crashed, a process does nothing. Let us observe that if a process crashes in the middle of a sending phase, only a subset of the messages it was supposed to send might actually be sent. As already indicated, t denotes the upper bound on the number of processes that can crash, while f denotes the number of actual crashes during a particular run. We have $0 \leq f \leq t < n$.

2.3   The k-Set Agreement Problem

The problem has been informally stated in the Introduction: every process p_i *proposes* a value v_i and each correct process has to *decide* on a value in relation to the set of proposed values. More precisely, the k-**set agreement** problem is defined by the following three properties:

- **Termination**: Every correct process eventually decides.
- **Validity**: If a process decides v, then v was proposed by some process.
- **Agreement**: No more than k different values are decided.

As we can see 1-set agreement is the uniform consensus problem. In the following, we implicitly assume $k \leq t$. This is because k-set agreement can trivially be solved in synchronous or asynchronous systems when $t < k$ [5]. A one communication step protocol is as follows: (1) k processes are arbitrarily selected prior the execution; (2) each of these k processes sends its value to all processes; (3) a process decides the first value it receives.

3   A k-Set Agreement Protocol

This section describes a k-set agreement protocol that allows the correct processes to decided by round $\min(\lfloor f/k \rfloor + 2, \lfloor t/k \rfloor + 1)$, for $t < n$. The protocol relies on a simple mechanism that allows a process to learn that it knows one of k smallest values currently present in the system.

3.1   Protocol Description

A process p_i invokes the k-set protocol by calling the function k-**set_agreement** (v_i) where v_i is the value it proposes (Figure 1). If it does not crash, p_i terminates when it executes **return** (est_i) at line 4 (early stopping) or line 11, where est_i is the value it decides.

The value decided by a process p_i is the smallest proposed value it has ever seen. That value is kept in the local variable est_i. The well-known "flooding strategy" (a basic technique encountered in nearly all agreement protocols [2,15,18]) is used to allow the processes to improve their knowledge on the smallest proposed values, namely, during each round, every active process sends the current value of est_i to all the processes. The achievement of the early stopping property is based on the following idea. Let $UP[r-1]$ be the set of processes not crashed by the end of round $r-1$, and $R_i[r]$ be the set of processes from which p_i has received messages during round r. Although p_i

---

Function k-set_agreement (v_i)

(1) $est_i \leftarrow v_i; nb_i[0] \leftarrow n; can\_dec_i \leftarrow false;$
(2)   **when** $r = 1, 2, \ldots, \lfloor t/k \rfloor + 1$ **do** % r: round number %
(3)   **begin_round**
(4)   send (est_i, can_decide_i) **to all**; % including p_i itself %
(5)   **if** can_decide_i **then** return (est_i) **end_if**;
(6)   **let** $nb_i[r]$ = number of messages received by p_i during r;
(7)   **let** $decide_i = \vee$ on the set of can_decide_j boolean values received during r;
(8) $est_i \leftarrow \min(\{est_j$ values received during the current round $r\})$;
(9)   **if** $\big((nb_i[r-1] - nb_i[r] < k) \vee decide_i\big)$ **then** $can\_decide_i \leftarrow true$ **end_if**
(10) **end_round**;
(11) return (est_i)

Fig. 1. Early stopping synchronous k-set agreement: code for p_i $(t < n)$

has no means to known the exact value of $UP[r-1]$ in the general case, as process crashes are stable we always have $R_i[r] \subseteq UP[r-1] \subseteq R_i[r-1]$. More, in the particular case where $R_i[r-1] = R_i[r]$, p_i has received a message from each process $p_j \in UP[r-1]$, i.e., from all the processes that were active at the beginning of r. It can then correctly conclude that it knows the smallest value among the values still present in the system at the beginning of r. Let us observe that, as the failure model is the crash model and a process p_i sends at most one message per round to each other process, we can use, instead of $R_i[r]$, a local variable $nb_i[r]$ counting the number of processes from which p_i has received a message during r. The predicate $R_i[r-1] = R_i[r]$ then becomes $nb_i[r-1] - nb_i[r] = 0$.

As we are interested in solving k-set agreement, it is not necessary for p_i to know the smallest value present in the system, it is sufficient for it to known one amongst the k smallest values present in the system. This knowledge can be obtained by weakening the locally evaluable predicate $nb_i[r-1] - nb_i[r] = 0$ into $nb_i[r-1] - nb_i[r] < k$. This weakening is due to the following observation. When $nb_i[r-1] - nb_i[r] < k$, p_i knows that it misses values from at most $k-1$ processes in the system. In the worst case these $k-1$ missing values are smaller than the value of est_i at the end of r, from which we conclude that, at the end of r, the value of its current estimate est_i is one of the k smallest values present in the system.

Unfortunately, the local predicate $nb_i[r-1] - nb_i[r] < k$ is not powerful enough to allow p_i to conclude that the other processes know it has one of the k smallest values. Consequently, p_i cannot decide and stop immediately. To be more explicit, let us consider the case where p_i has (not any of the k smallest values but) the smallest value v in the system, is the only process that knows v, decides it at the end of r and then crashes by the end of r. The other processes can then decide k other values as v is no longer is the system from round $r + 1$. An easy way to fix this problem consists in requiring p_i to proceed to $r + 1$ before deciding (this is similar to the way used to guarantee uniform agreement in consensus protocols). When $nb_i[r-1] - nb_i[r] < k$ becomes true, p_i sets a boolean (can_decide_i) to $true$ and proceeds to the next round $r + 1$. As, before deciding at line 4 of $r + 1$, p_i has first sent the pair (est_i, can_decide_i) to all processes, any process p_j active during $r + 1$ not only knows v but, as can_decide_i is true, knows also that v is one of k smallest values present in the system during $r + 1$.

3.2   Proof of the Protocol

Lemma 1. [Validity] *A decided value is a proposed value.*

Proof. The proof of the validity consists in showing that an est_i local variable always contains a proposed variable. This is initially true (round $r = 0$). Then, a simple induction reasoning proves the property: assuming the property is true at a round $r \geq 1$, it follows from the protocol code (lines 4 and 8), and the fact that a process receives at least the value it has sent, that the property remains true at round $r + 1$. $\square_{Lemma\ 1}$

Lemma 2. [Termination] *Every correct process decides.*

Proof. The proof is an immediate consequence of the fact that a process executes at most $\lfloor t/k \rfloor + 1$ rounds and the computation model is the synchronous round-based computation model. $\square_{Lemma\ 2}$

Lemma 3. [Agreement] *No more than k different values are decided.*

Proof. Let $EST[0]$ be the set of proposed values, and $EST[r]$ the set of est_i values of the processes that decide during r or proceed to $r + 1$ ($r \geq 1$). We first state and prove three claims.

Claim C1. $\forall r \geq 0$: $EST[r + 1] \subseteq EST[r]$.
Proof of the claim. The claim follows directly from the fact that, during a round, the new value of an est_i variable computed by a process is the smallest of the est_j values it has received. So values can only disappear, due to the minimum function used at line 8 or to process crashes. *End of the proof of the claim C1.*

Claim C2. Let p_i be a process such that can_decide_i is set to true at the end of r. Then est_i is one of the k smallest values in $EST[r]$.
Proof of the claim. Let v be the value of est_i at the end of r ($v \in EST[r]$). If can_decide_i is set to true at the end of r, $nb_i[r - 1] - nb_i[r] < k$ is satisfied or p_i has received a message carrying a pair $(v1, true)$, and $v1$ has been taken into account when computing the new value of est_i at line 8 during round r, i.e., $v \leq v1$. So, there is a chain of processes $j = j_a, j_{a-1}, \ldots, j_0 = i$ that has carried the boolean value $true$ to p_i. This chain is such that $a \geq 0$, $nb_j[r - a - 1] - nb_j[r - a] < k$ is satisfied, and any value v' sent by a process participating in this chain is such that $v \leq v'$ (as each process in the chain computes the minimum of the values it has received). In particular, we have $v \leq v''$ where v'' is the value sent by the first process in the chain. (The case $a = 0$ corresponds to the "one process" chain case where the local predicate is satisfied at p_i.) Due to claim C1, $EST[r] \subseteq EST[r - a]$. Consequently, if v'' is one of the k smallest values of $EST[r - a]$, $v \leq v''$ implies v is one of the k smallest values of $EST[r]$.

So, taking $r - a = r'$, we have to show that $nb_j[r' - 1] - nb_j[r'] < k$ implies that the value v'' of est_j at the end of r', is one of the k smallest values of $EST[r']$. As the crashes are stable, $nb_j[r' - 1] - nb_j[r'] < k$, allows concluding that p_j has received a message from all but at most $k - 1$ processes that where not crashed at the beginning of r'. As p_j computes the minimum of all the values it has received, and misses at most $k - 1$ values of $EST[r']$, this means that the value v'' computed by p_j at the end of r' is one of the k smallest values present in $EST[r']$. *End of the proof of the claim $C2$.*

Claim $C3$. Let p_i be process that decides (at line 5 or 11) during the round r. Its boolean flag can_decide_i is then equal to *true*.
Proof of the claim. The claim is trivially true if p_i decides at line 5. If p_i decides at line 11, it decides during the last round, namely $r = \lfloor t/k \rfloor + 1$. Let us consider two cases.

- At round r, p_i receives from a process p_j a message such as $can\_decide_j = true$. In that case, p_i sets can_decide_i to *true* at line 9, and the claim follows.
- In the other case, no process p_j has decided at a round $r' < r$ (otherwise, p_i would have received from p_j a message such that $can\_decide_j = true$). Let $t = k\,x + y$ with $y < k$ (hence, $x = \lfloor t/k \rfloor = r - 1$). As $nb_i[r' - 1] - nb_i[r'] < k$ was not satisfied at each round r' such that $1 \leq r' \leq x = r - 1$, we have $nb_i[x] \leq n - kx$. Moreover, as p_i has not received from any p_j a message such that can_decide_j is equal to *true*, if, during r, p_i does not receive a message from p_j it is because p_j has crashed. So, as at most t processes crash, we have $nb_i[x+1] \geq n - t = n - (k\,x + y)$. It follows that $nb_i[x] - nb_i[x + 1] \leq y < k$. the claim follows.

End of the proof of the claim $C3$.

To prove the lemma, we now consider two cases according to the line during which a process decides.

- No process decides at line 5. This means that a process p_i that decides, decides at line 11 during the last round. Due to the claim $C3$, such a p_i has then its flag can_decide_i equal to *true*. Due to the claim $C2$, it decides one of the k smallest values in $EST[\lfloor t/k \rfloor + 1]$.
- A process decides at line 5. Let r be the first round during which a process p_i decides at that line and v be the value it decides. Since p_i decides at r:
  - p_i has set its boolean flag can_decide_i to *true* at the end of $r - 1$, and its estimate $est_i = v$ is consequently one of the k smallest values in $EST[r - 1]$ (Claim $C2$). It follows that two processes that decide during r decide values that are among the the k smallest values in $EST[r - 1]$.
  - p_i has sent to all the processes (line 4) the pair $(v, true)$ before deciding at line 5 during r. This implies that a (non-crashed) process p_j that does not decide at r receives v at r and uses it to compute its new value of est_j. Due to the minimum function used at line 8, it follows that, from now on, we will always have $est_j \leq v$.
    Let us assume that p_j does not crash. If it decides, it decides at $r' > r$, and then it necessarily decides a value $v' \leq v$. As $EST[r'] \subseteq EST[r - 1]$ (claim $C1$), we have $v' \in EST[r - 1]$. Combining $v' \leq v$, $v' \in EST[r - 1]$, and the fact

that v is one of the k smallest values in $EST[r-1]$, it follows that the value v' decided by p_j is one of the k smallest values in $EST[r-1]$.

$$\square_{Lemma\ 3}$$

Theorem 1. [k-Set Agreement] *The protocol solves the k-set agreement problem.*

Proof. The proof follows from the Lemmas 1, 2, and 3. $\square_{Theorem\ 1}$

Theorem 2. [Early Stopping] *No process halts after the round* $\min(\lfloor f/k \rfloor + 2, \lfloor t/k \rfloor + 1)$.

Proof. Let us first observe that a process decides and halts at the same round; this occurs when it executes return (est_i) at line 4 or 11. As observed in Lemma 2, the fact that no process decides after $\lfloor t/k \rfloor + 1$ rounds is an immediate consequence of the code of the protocol and the round-based synchronous model. So, considering that $0 \leq f \leq t$ processes crash, we show that no process decides after the round $\lfloor f/k \rfloor + 2$. Let $f = xk + y$ (with $y < k$). This means that $x = \lfloor f/k \rfloor$.

The worst case scenario is when, for any process p_i that evaluates the local decision predicate $nb_i[r-1] - nb_i[r] < k$, this predicate is false as many times as possible. Due to the pigeonhole principle, this occurs when exactly k processes crash during each round. This means that we have $nb_i[1] = n - k, \cdots, nb_i[x] = n - kx$ and $nb_i[x+1] = n - f = n - (kx + y)$, from which we conclude that $r = x + 1$ is the first round such that $nb_i[r-1] - nb_i[r] = y < k$. It follows that the processes p_i that execute the round $x + 1$ set their can_decide_i boolean to $true$. Consequently, the processes that proceed to $x + 2$ decide at line 5 during that round. As $x = \lfloor f/k \rfloor$, they decide at round $\lfloor f/k \rfloor + 2$. $\square_{Theorem\ 2}$

4 Discussion

Instead of using the local predicate $nb_i[r-1] - nb_i[r] < k$, an early stopping protocol could be based on the local predicate $faulty_i[r] < k\,r$ where $faulty_i[r] = n - nb_i[r]$ (the number of processes perceived as faulty by $p_i)^2$. While both predicates can be used to ensure early stopping, we show here that $nb_i[r-1] - nb_i[r] < k$ is a more efficient predicate than $faulty_i[r] < k\,r$ (more efficient in the sense that it can allow for earlier termination). To prove it, we show the following:

- (*i*) Let r be the first round during which the local predicate $faulty_i[r] < k\,r$ is satisfied. The predicate $nb_i[r-1] - nb_i[r] < k$ is then also satisfied.
- (*ii*) Let r be the first round during which the local predicate $nb_i[r-1] - nb_i[r] < k$ is satisfied. It is possible that $faulty_i[r] < k\,r$ be not satisfied.

---

[2] This predicate is implicitly used in the proof of the (not-early deciding) k-set agreement protocol described in [15].

We first prove (i). As r is the first round during which $faulty_i[r] < k\,r$ is satisfied, we have $faulty_i[r-1] \geq k\,(r-1)$. So, we have $faulty_i[r] - faulty_i[r-1] < k\,r - k\,(r-1) = k$. Replacing the sets $faulty_i[r]$ and $faulty_i[r-1]$ by their definitions we obtain $(n - nb_i[r]) - (n - nb_i[r-1]) < k$, i.e., $(nb_i[r-1] - nb_i[r]) < k$.

A simple counter-example is sufficient to prove (ii). Let us consider a run where $f1 > ak$ $(a > 2)$ processes crash initially (i.e., before the protocol starts), and $f2 < k$ processes crash thereafter. We have $n - f1 \geq nb_i[1] \geq nb_i[2] \geq n - (f1 + f2)$, which implies that $(nb_i[r-1] - nb_i[r]) < k$ is satisfied at round $r = 2$. On an other side, $faulty_i[2] \geq f1 = ak > 2k$, from which we conclude that $faulty_i[r] < r\,k$ is not satisfied at $r = 2$.

This discussion shows that, while the early decision lower bound can be obtained with any of these predicates, the predicate $nb_i[r-1] - nb_i[r] < k$ is more efficient in the sense it takes into consideration the actual failure pattern (a process counts the number of failures it perceives during a round, and not only from the beginning of the run). Differently, the predicate $faulty_i[r] < r\,k$ considers only the actual number of failures and not their pattern (it basically always considers the worst case where there are k crashes per round, whatever their actual occurrence pattern).

References

1. Aguilera M.K. and Toueg S., A Simple Bivalency Proof that t-Resilient Consensus Requires $t+1$ Rounds. *Information Processing Letters*, 71:155-178, 1999.
2. Attiya H. and Welch J., *Distributed Computing: Fundamentals, Simulations and Advanced Topics*, McGraw-Hill, 451 pages, 1998.
3. Borowsky E. and Gafni E., Generalized FLP Impossibility Results for t-Resilient Asynchronous Computations. *Proc. 25th ACM Symposium on Theory of Computation*, California (USA), pp. 91-100, 1993.
4. Charron-Bost B. and Schiper A., Uniform Consensus is Harder than Consensus. *Journal of Algorithms*, 51(1):15-37, 2004.
5. Chaudhuri S., More *Choices* Allow More *Faults:* Set Consensus Problems in Totally Asynchronous Systems. *Information and Computation*, 105:132-158, 1993.
6. Chaudhuri S., Herlihy M., Lynch N. and Tuttle M., Tight Bounds for k-Set Agreement. *Journal of the ACM*, 47(5):912-943, 2000.
7. Dolev D., Reischuk R. and Strong R., Early Stopping in Byzantine Agreement. *Journal of the ACM*, 37(4):720-741, April 1990.
8. Fischer M.J., Lynch N.A., A Lower Bound on the Time to Assure Interactive Consistency. *Information Processing Letters*, 14(4):183-186, 1982.
9. Fischer M.J., Lynch N.A. and Paterson M.S., Impossibility of Distributed Consensus with One Faulty Process. *Journal of the ACM*, 32(2):374-382, 1985.
10. Gafni E., Guerraoui R. and Pochon B., From a Static Impossibility to an Adaptive Lower Bound: The Complexity of Early Deciding Set Agreement. *Proc. 37th ACM Symposium on Theory of Computing (STOC 2005)*, Baltimore (MD), May 2005.
11. Guerraoui R. and Pochon B., The Complexity of Early Deciding Set Agreement: how Topology Can Help? *Proc. 4th Workshop in Geometry and Topology in Concurrency and Distributed Computing (GETCO'04)*, BRICS Notes Series, NS-04-2, pp. 26-31, Amsterdam (NL), 2004.

12. Herlihy M.P. and Penso L. D., Tight Bounds for k-Set Agreement with Limited Scope Accuracy Failure Detectors. *Proc. 17th Int. Symposium on Distributed Computing (DISC'03)*, Springer Verlag LNCS #2848, pp. 279-291, Sorrento (Italy), 2003.
13. Herlihy M.P. and Shavit N., The Topological Structure of Asynchronous Computability. *Journal of the ACM*, 46(6):858-923, 1999.
14. Lamport L. and Fischer M., Byzantine Generals and Transaction Commit Protocols. *Unpublished manuscript*, 16 pages, April 1982.
15. Lynch N.A., Distributed Algorithms. *Morgan Kaufmann Pub.*, San Fransisco (CA), 872 pages, 1996.
16. Mostefaoui A. and Raynal M., k-Set Agreement with Limited Accuracy Failure Detectors. *Proc. 19th ACM Symposium on Principles of Distributed Computing*, ACM Press, pp. 143-152, Portland (OR), 2000.
17. Mostefaoui A. and Raynal M., Randomized Set Agreement. *Proc. 13th ACM Symposium on Parallel Algorithms and Architectures (SPAA'01)*, ACM Press, pp. 291-297, Hersonissos (Crete), 2001.
18. Raynal M., Consensus in Synchronous Systems: a Concise Guided Tour. *Proc. 9th IEEE Pacific Rim Int. Symposium on Dependable Computing (PRDC'02)*, Tsukuba (Japan), IEEE Computer Press, pp. 221-228, 2002.
19. Saks M. and Zaharoglou F., Wait-Free k-Set Agreement is Impossible: The Topology of Public Knowledge. *SIAM Journal on Computing*, 29(5):1449-1483, 2000.

Allowing Atomic Objects to Coexist with Sequentially Consistent Objects

Michel Raynal* and Matthieu Roy[†]

*IRISA, Campus de Beaulieu, 35042 Rennes Cedex, France
[†]LAAS CNRS, 7 Avenue du Colonel Roche, 31077, Toulouse cedex, France
raynal@irisa.fr, mroy@laas.fr

Abstract. A concurrent object is an object that can be concurrently accessed by several processes. Two well known consistency criteria for such objects are *atomic consistency* (also called *linearizability*) and *sequential consistency*. Both criteria require that all the operations on all the concurrent objects be totally ordered in such a way that each read operation obtains the last value written into the corresponding object. They differ in the meaning of the word "last" that refers to physical time for atomic consistency, and to logical time for sequential consistency. This paper investigates the merging of these consistency criteria. It presents a protocol that allows the upper layer multiprocess program to use simultaneously both types of consistency: purely atomic objects can coexist with purely sequentially consistent objects. The protocol is built on top of a message passing asynchronous distributed system. Interestingly, this protocol is generic in the sense that it can be tailored to provide only one of these consistency criteria.

Keywords: Asynchronous System, Atomic Consistency, Combination of consistency criteria, Linearizability, Message Passing, NP-Completeness, Shared Memory Abstraction, Sequential Consistency.

1 Introduction

Context of the study The definition of a consistency criterion is crucial for the correctness of a multiprocess program. Basically, a consistency criterion defines which value has to be returned when a read operation on a shared object is invoked by a process. The strongest (i.e., most constraining) consistency criterion is *atomic consistency* (also called *linearizability* [8]). It states that a read returns the value written by the last preceding write, "last" referring to real-time occurrence order (concurrent writes being ordered). *Causal consistency* [3,5] is a weaker criterion stating that a read does not get an overwritten value. Causal consistency allows concurrent writes; consequently, it is possible that concurrent read operations on the same object get different values (this occurs when those values have been produced by concurrent writes). Other consistency criteria (weaker than causal consistency) have been proposed [1,19].

Sequential consistency [10] is a criterion that lies between atomic consistency and causal consistency. Informally it states that a multiprocess program executes

V. Malyshkin (Ed.): PaCT 2005, LNCS 3606, pp. 59–73, 2005.

correctly if its results could have been produced by executing that program on a single processor system. This means that an execution is correct if we can totally order its operations in such a way that (1) the order of operations in each process is preserved, and (2) each read gets the last previously written value, "last" referring here to the total order. The difference between atomic consistency and sequential consistency lies in the meaning of the word "last". This word refers to real-time when we consider atomic consistency, while it refers to a logical time notion when we consider sequential consistency (namely the logical time defined by the total order). The main difference between sequential consistency and causal consistency lies in the fact that (as atomic consistency) sequential consistency orders all write operations, while causal consistency does not require to order concurrent writes.

Related work. It has been shown that determining whether a given execution is sequentially consistent is an NP-complete problem [21]. This has an important consequence as it rules out the possibility of designing efficient sequential consistency protocols (i.e., protocols that provide sequentially consistent executions and just these). This means that, in order to be able to design efficient sequential consistency protocols, additional constraints have to be imposed on executions. One of these constraints (that has been proposed in [13]) is the following. Let two operations *conflict* if both are on the same object and one of them is a write. Let us say that an execution satisfies the *OO-constraint* if any pair of conflicting operations are ordered. It is shown in [13] that an *OO*-constrained execution is sequentially consistent if its read operations are legal (i.e., do not provide over-written values). This approach shows that a sequential consistency protocol can be obtained by combining two mechanisms: one providing the *OO*-constraint and the other providing read legality.

On another side, It has been shown in [15] that sequential consistency can be seen as a form of lazy atomic consistency. The main difference between the two lies in the fact that sequential consistency allows a process to keep a cached value as long as it does not make inconsistent the other operations, while atomic consistency requires to update or invalidate the cached values of an object as soon as this object is modified.

Very recently, the combination of sequential consistency[10] and causal consistency [3] has been investigated in [22].

Content of the paper. This paper investigates a combination of sequential consistency with atomic consistency within the same parallel program. More precisely, it considers that the objects are divided into two classes, the objects that are atomically consistent and the objects that are sequentially consistent. A protocol is presented for this type of object semantics combination. This protocol generalizes the sequential consistency protocol we have introduced in [15]. (In addition to its own interest, the proposed protocol provides a better understanding of the link relating sequential consistency and atomic consistency.)

Roadmap. The paper consists of three sections. Section 2 presents the shared memory abstraction, atomic consistency, and sequential consistency. Section 3 presents the protocol. Finally, Section 4 provides a few concluding remarks.

2   The Consistent Shared Memory Abstraction

A parallel program defines a set of processes interacting through a set of concurrent objects. This set of shared objects defines a *shared memory abstraction*. Each object is defined by a sequential specification and provides processes with operations to manipulate it. When it is running, the parallel program produces a concurrent system [8]. As in such a system an object can be accessed concurrently by several processes, it is necessary to define consistency criteria for concurrent objects.

2.1   Shared Memory Abstraction, History and Legality

Shared Memory Abstraction A shared memory system is composed of a finite set of sequential processes $p_1, \ldots, p_n$ that interact via a finite set X of shared objects. Each object $x \in X$ can be accessed by read and write operations. A write into an object defines a new value for the object; a read allows to obtain a value of the object. A write of value v into object x by process p_i is denoted $w_i(x)v$; similarly a read of x by process p_j is denoted $r_j(x)v$ where v is the value returned by the read operation; *op* will denote either r (read) or w (write). For simplicity, as in [3,18], we assume all values written into an object x are distinct[1]. Moreover, the parameters of an operation are omitted when they are not important. Each object has an initial value (it is assumed that this value has been assigned by an initial fictitious write operation).

History concept. Histories are introduced to model the execution of shared memory parallel programs. The *local history* (or local computation) $\hat{h}_i$ of p_i is the sequence of operations issued by p_i. If *op1* and *op2* are issued by p_i and *op1* is issued first, then we say "*op1* precedes *op2* in p_i's process-order", which is noted $op1 \rightarrow_i op2$. Let h_i denote the set of operations executed by p_i; the local history $\hat{h}_i$ is the total order $(h_i, \rightarrow_i)$.

Definition 1. *An execution history (or simply history, or computation) $\hat{H}$ of a shared memory system is a partial order $\hat{H} = (H, \rightarrow_H)$ such that:*

- $H = \bigcup_i h_i$
- $op1 \rightarrow_H op2$ *if:*
    i) $\exists\, p_i : op1 \rightarrow_i op2$ *(in that case, $\rightarrow_H$ is called* process-order *relation),*

---

[1] Intuitively, this hypothesis can be seen as an implicit tagging of each value by a pair composed of the identity of the process that issued the write plus a sequence number.

or ii) $op1 = w_i(x)v$ *and* $op2 = r_j(x)v$ *(in that case* $\rightarrow_H$ *is called* read-from
   relation),

or iii) $\exists op3 : op1 \rightarrow_H op3$ *and* $op3 \rightarrow_H op2$.

Two operations $op1$ and $op2$ are *concurrent* in $\widehat{H}$ if we have neither $op1 \rightarrow_H op2$
nor $op2 \rightarrow_H op1$.

Legality notion. The legality concept is the key notion on which are based definitions of shared memory consistency criteria [3,5,7,12,19]. From an operational
point of view, it states that, in a legal history, no read operation can get an
overwritten value.

Definition 2. *A read operation* $r(x)v$ *is* legal *if: (i)* $\exists\, w(x)v : w(x)v \rightarrow_H r(x)v$
and (ii) $\not\exists\, op(x)u : (u \neq v) \wedge (w(x)v \rightarrow_H op(x)u \rightarrow_H r(x)v)$. *A history* $\widehat{H}$ *is*
legal *if all its read operations are legal.*

2.2   Sequential Consistency

Sequential consistency has been proposed by Lamport in 1979 to define a correctness criterion for multiprocessor shared memory systems [10]. A system is
sequentially consistent with respect to a multiprocess program, if "*the result
of any execution is the same as if (1) the operations of all the processors were
executed in some sequential order, and (2) the operations of each individual processor appear in this sequence in the order specified by its program*".

   This informal definition states that the execution of a program is sequentially
consistent if it could have been produced by executing this program on a single
processor system[2]. More formally, we define sequential consistency in the following way. Let us first recall the definition of *linear extension* of a partial order.
A linear extension $\widehat{S} = (S, \rightarrow_S)$ of a partial order $\widehat{H} = (H, \rightarrow_H)$ is a total order
that respects the partial order. This means we have the following: (i) $S = H$,
(ii) $op_1 \rightarrow_H op_2 \Rightarrow op_1 \rightarrow_S op_2$ ($\widehat{S}$ maintains the order of all ordered pairs of $\widehat{H}$)
and (iii) $\rightarrow_S$ defines a total order.

Definition 3. *A history* $\widehat{H} = (H, \rightarrow_H)$ *is* sequentially consistent *if it has a legal
linear extension.*

   As an example let us consider the history $\widehat{H}$ depicted in Figure 1 (only the
edges that are not due to transitivity are indicated, transitivity edges come from
process-order and *read-from* relations. Moreover, *process-order* edges are denoted
by continuous arrows and *read-from* edges by dotted arrows). Each process p_i
$(i{=}1,2)$ has issued three operations on the shared objects x and y. As we can

---

[2] In his definition, Lamport assumes that the *process-order* relation defined by the
   program (point 2) of the definition) is maintained in the equivalent sequential execution, but not necessarily in the execution itself. As we do not consider programs
   but only executions, we implicitly assume that the *process-order* relation displayed
   by the execution histories are the ones specified by the programs which gave rise to
   these execution histories.

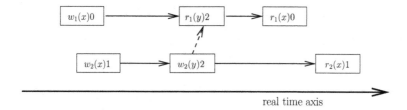

Fig. 1. A sequentially consistent execution

see, when looking at the real time axis, the write operations $w_1(x)0$ and $w_2(x)1$ are concurrent. The $r_1(y)2$ and $w_2(y)2$ are also concurrent. It is easy to see that $\widehat{H}$ is sequentially consistent by building a legal linear extension $\widehat{S}$ including first the operations issued by p_2 and then the ones issued by p_1, namely we have:

$$\widehat{S} = w_2(x)1 \; \; w_2(y)2 \; \; r_2(x)1 \; \; w_1(x)0 \; \; r_1(y)2 \; \; r_1(x)0.$$

This means that $\widehat{H}$ could have been produced by executing the multiprocess program on a machine with a single processor and a scheduler, which is the very essence of sequential consistency.

2.3   Atomic Consistency

Atomic consistency is the oldest consistency criterion in the sense that it has always been implicitly used. It has been extended to objects more sophisticated than read/write objects under the name *linearizability* [8].

   Atomic consistency considers that operations take time and consequently its definition is based on the real-time occurrence order of operations. Let $\prec_{rt}$ be a real-time precedence relation on operations defined as follows: $op_1 \prec_{rt} op_2$ if op_1 was terminated before op_2 started[3]. Let us notice that $\prec_{rt}$ is a partial order relation as two operations whose executions overlap in real-time are not ordered.

Definition 4. *A history* $\widehat{H} = (H, \rightarrow_H)$ *is* atomically consistent *if it has a legal linear extension that includes* $\prec_{rt}$.

This means that, to be atomically consistent, $\widehat{H}$ must have a legal linear extension $\widehat{S} = (H, \rightarrow_S)$ such that $\forall op_1, op_2 : (op_1 \prec_{rt} op_2) \Rightarrow (op_1 \rightarrow_S op_2)$. The linear extension $\widehat{S}$ has to keep real-time order. It is easy to see why invalidation-based atomic consistency protocols use an eager invalidation strategy: this ensures that the real-time occurrence order on operations cannot be ignored, a read always getting the last value (with respect to real-time).

   It is easy to see that the execution described in Figure 1 is not atomically consistent (the read operations on x issued by by p_1 and p_2 should return the same value, that value being determined by the ordering on $w_1(x)0$ and $w_2(x)1$ imposed by the execution). Differently, the execution described in Figure 2 is

---

[3] See [8] for a formal definition of "terminated before" and "started".

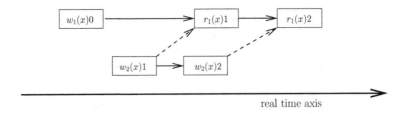

Fig. 2. An atomically consistent execution

atomically consistent. A base linear extension $\widehat{S_1}$ respecting real time order is the following:

$$\widehat{S_1} = w_1(x)0 \quad w_2(x)1 \quad r_1(x)1 \quad w_2(x)2 \quad r_1(x)2.$$

As we can see in $\widehat{S_1}$, the concurrent operations $r_1(x)1$ and $w_2(x)2$ have been ordered by the execution with the read operation first. Another execution could have ordered them differently, in that case we would have the base linear extension $S_2 = w_1(x)0 \quad w_2(x)1 \quad w_2(x)2 \quad r_1(x)2 \quad r_1(x)2$. It is important that to notice that, in all cases, the second read operation by p_1 obtains the value 2, as that value is the last value written into x (last with respect to real time).

Atomic consistency vs sequential consistency. Atomic consistency and sequential consistency are often confused, even in some textbooks! The fact that one has to respect real time order (atomic consistency) while the other has not (sequential consistency) has a fundamental consequence that has an important impact in practice. It is stated by the following property.

   A property P of a concurrent system is *local* if the system as a whole satisfies P whenever each individual object satisfies P. The following theorem is a main result of [8]. It states that atomic consistency is a local property. let $\widehat{H}|x$ ($\widehat{H}$ at x) be the projection of $\widehat{H}$ on x (i.e., $\widehat{H}|x$ includes only the operations that involve x).

Theorem 1. [8] $\widehat{H}$ *is atomically consistent iff, for each object x, $\widehat{H}|x$ is atomically consistent.*

This theorem is important as it states that a concurrent system can be designed in a modular way: atomically consistent objects can be implemented independently one from the other. Unfortunately, sequential consistency is not a local property [8]. As we will see in Section 3, the sequentially consistent objects have to cooperate to guarantee sequential consistency. From an operational point of view, this translates as follows. As atomic consistency considers real time while sequential consistency considers logical time, the way these consistency criteria use cached values are very different. Hence, there is a tradeoff between the *locality* of a consistency criterion and the *timeliness* (eager *vs* lazy) of the invalidation strategy used in the protocol that implements it.

2.4   The Constraint-Based Approach for Sequential Consistency

As indicated in the Introduction, determining whether a given execution is sequentially consistent is an NP-complete problem [21]. As we have noticed, this result rules out the possibility of designing efficient protocols providing sequentially consistent histories and just these.

The Constraint-Based Approach. Hence, the idea we have developed in [13] that consists in imposing additional constraints on histories in order to be able to design efficient sequential consistency protocols. This approach is similar to imposing constraints on view serializability for concurrency control protocols [9,14][4]. Let two operations *conflict* if both are on the same object x and one of them is a write. The two following additional constraints have introduced in [13].

Definition 5. *WW-constraint. A history $\widehat{H}$ satisfies the WW-constraint if any pair of write operations are ordered under $\widehat{H}$.*
OO-constraint. A history $\widehat{H}$ satisfies the OO-constraint if any pair of conflicting operations are ordered under $\widehat{H}$.

Hence, when $\widehat{H}$ satisfies the *WW*-constraint, all its write operations are totally ordered. Differently, when $\widehat{H}$ satisfies the *OO*-constraint, the operations on each object $x \in X$ follow the reader/writer synchronization discipline (for each x, the write operations are totally ordered, and the read operations are ordered with respect to the write operations). The following theorems are stated and proved in [13].

Theorem 2. [13] *Let $\widehat{H} = (H, \rightarrow_H)$ be a history that satisfies the WW-constraint. $\widehat{H}$ is sequentially consistent if and only if it is legal.*
Let $\widehat{H} = (H, \rightarrow_H)$ be a history that satisfies the OO-constraint. $\widehat{H}$ is sequentially consistent if and only if it is legal.

This theorem has important consequences. They mean that, to get sequential consistency, a protocol based on such a constraint only needs to ensure that the read operations are legal. In that way, efficient protocols ensuring sequential consistency can be obtained.

Constraint-Based Protocols for Sequential Consistency. Several protocols providing a sequentially consistent shared memory abstraction on top of an asynchronous message passing distributed system have been proposed. Among them, the protocols introduced in [2,6], although they do not explicitly identify the *WW*-constraint, are implicitly based on it. Differently, the protocols presented in [13,16] are explicitly based on the *WW*-constraint.

The protocol described in [2] implements a sequentially consistent shared memory abstraction on top of a physically shared memory and local caches. It

---

[4] Interestingly, *view equivalence* can be considered as a special case of sequential consistency, while *strict view equivalence* can be considered as a special case of atomic consistency.

uses an atomic n-queue update primitive and so implicitly relies on the the WW-constraint. The protocol described in [6] assumes each local memory contains a copy of the whole shared memory abstraction. It orders the write operations using an atomic broadcast facility: all the writes are sent to all processes and are delivered in the same order by each process. Read operations issued by a process are appropriately scheduled to ensure their legality.

The protocol described in [13] considers a server site that has a copy of the whole shared memory abstraction. The local memory of each process contains a copy of a shared memory abstraction, but the state of some of its objects can be "invalid". When a process wants to read an object, it reads its local copy if it is valid. When a process wants to read an object whose state is invalid, or wants to write an object, it sends a request to the server. In that way the server orders all write operations. An invalidation mechanism ensures that the reading by p_i of an object that is locally valid is legal. A variant of this protocol is described in [4]. The protocol described in [16] uses a token that orders all write operations and piggybacks updated values. As the protocol described in [6] it provides fast read operations[5].

A sequential consistency protocol fully based on the OO-constraint has been proposed in [15]. This protocol has no centralized control, it is based on a pure distributed control. A sequential consistency protocol for operations that can span several objects is described in [20].

3   Combining Atomic Consistency and Sequential Consistency

3.1   Two Types of Objects

We consider that each object accessed by a multiprocess program is either atomically consistent or sequentially consistent, i.e., the objects are partitionned in two subsets $sc\_objects$ and $ac\_objects$ such that if $x \in ac\_objects$ its read/write operations are atomically consistent, while if $x \in sc\_objects$ its read/write operations are sequentially consistent. Let $\widehat{H} = (H, \rightarrow_H)$ be an execution history. From a formal point of view, this means the following:

- If we suppress from $\widehat{H}$ all the operations accessing the objects in $sc\_objects$, we obtain an execution history $\widehat{H1} = (H1, \rightarrow_{H1})$ that is atomically consistent.
- If we suppress from $\widehat{H}$ all the operations accessing the objects in $ac\_objects$, we obtain an execution history $\widehat{H2} = (H2, \rightarrow_{H2})$ that is sequentially consistent.

This section presents a protocol providing such a combination of atomic consistency and sequential consistency.

---

[5] As shown in [6] atomic consistency does not allow protocols in which all read operations (or all write operations) are fast [8,12]. Differently, causal consistency allows protocols where all operations are fast [3,5,18].

3.2   Underlying System

The concurrent program is made up n processes $p_1, \ldots, p_n$ sharing m objects (denoted $x, y, \ldots$). The underlying system is made up of $n + m$ sites, divided into n process-sites and m object-sites (hence, without ambiguity, p_i denotes both a process and the associated site; M_x denotes the site hosting and managing x). As in the previous section, the sites communicate through reliable channels by sending and receiving messages. There are assumptions neither on the processing speed of the sites, nor on message transfer delays. Hence, the underlying distributed system is asynchronous.

To be as modular as possible, and in the spirit of clients/servers architectures, the proposed solution allows a process and an object to communicate, but no two processes -nor two objects- are allowed to send messages to each other. This constraint makes easier the addition of new processes or objects into the system.

3.3   Control Variables

The *OO*-constraint is used to get both atomic consistency on the objects in *ac_objects*, and sequential consistency on the objects in *sc_objects*. To that end, a manager M_x is associated with each object x. This makes the protocol distributed with respect to the set of objects as there is no centralized control. Basically, the manager M_x orders the write operations on the object x it is associated with. As in other protocols (e.g., the protocol ensuring atomic consistency described in [11]), and in order to get an efficient protocol, object values are cached and the last writer of an object x is considered as its *owner* until the value it wrote is overwritten or read by another process. The combination of value invalidation, value caching and object ownership allows processes to read cached values and to update the objects they own for free (i.e., without communicating with the corresponding managers). Depending on the read/write access pattern, this can be very efficient.

Local variables of a process. As just indicated, the protocol is based on cached copies and an invalidation strategy. A process p_i manages the following local variables:

- $present_i[x]$ is a boolean variable that is true when p_i has a legal copy of x (i.e., a read of the current cached value of x would be a legal read). This means that p_i can then locally read its cached copy of x.
- $C_i[x]$ is a cache containing a copy of x. Its value is meaningful only when $present_i[x]$ is true.
- $owner_i[x]$ is a boolean variable that is true if p_i is the last writer of x. Let us note that we have $owner_i[x] \Rightarrow present_i[x]$.

Local variables of an object manager. The site M_x associated with the object x manages the following local variables:

- C_x contains the last value of x (as known by M_x).
- $owner_x$ contains a process identity or $\bot$. Its meaning is the following: $owner_x = i$ means that no process but p_i has the last value of x (it is possible that M_x does not know this value). Differently, if $owner_x = \bot$, M_x has the last copy of x. The owner of an object x (if any) is the only process that can modify it.
- $hlw_x[1..n]$ is a boolean array, such that $hlw_x[i]$ is true iff p_i has the last value of x (hlw_x stands for "hold last write of x").

System initial state. Initially, only M_x knows the initial value of x which is kept in C_x. So, we have the following initial values: $\forall p_i: \forall x: owner_i[x] = false$, $present_i[x] = false$, $C_i[x] =$ undefined, $owner_x = \bot$, $hlw_x[i] = false$.

3.4 Behavior of a Manager for $x \in ac\_objects$

The behavior of the manager M_x of an object $x \in ac\_objects$ is described in Figure 3. It is made up of two statements that describe M_x's behaviour when it receives a message. The *write_req* and *read_req* messages are processed sequentially.

- M_x receives *write_req* (v) from p_i.
  In that case, p_i has issued a $w(x)v$ operation (and is not the current owner of x). The manager invalidates all the cached copies of x that currently exist.

---

upon reception of *write_req* (v) **from** p_i:
(1) **if** $(owner_x \neq \bot)$ **then** send *downgrade_req* (W, x) to p_{owner_x};
(2)   wait *downgrade_ack* $(-)$ from p_{owner_x}
(3)   **else** $\forall j \neq i:\ hlw_x[j]:$ **do** send *downgrade_req*(W, x) to p_j;
(4)   wait *downgrade_ack* $(-)$ from p_j
(5)   **enddo**
(6) **endif**;
(7) $C_x \leftarrow v;\ owner_x \leftarrow i$;
(8) $hlw_x[i] \leftarrow true;\ \forall j \neq i:\ hlw_x[j] \leftarrow false$;
(9) send *write_ack* () to p_i

upon reception of *read_req* () **from** p_i:
(10) **if** $(owner_x \neq \bot)$ **then** send *downgrade_req*(R, x) to p_{owner_x};
(11)   wait *downgrade_ack* (v) from p_{owner_x};
(12) $C_x \leftarrow v;\ owner_x \leftarrow \bot$
(13) **endif**;
(14) $hlw_x[i] \leftarrow true$;
(15) send *read_ack* (C_x) to p_i

Fig. 3. Behavior of an Object Manager M_x for $x \in ac\_objects$

In that way, no process will be able to read in the future a copy older than v, thereby ensuring atomic consistency

- M_x receives *read_req* (v) from p_i.

  In that case, p_i has issued a $r(x)$ operation, and does not have the last value of x. If x is currently owned by some process, M_x first gets the last value of x from this process and downgrades this previous owner (lines 10-11), that can only read its copy of x from now on. Then, it sends the current value of x to p_i (line 15) and updates $hlw_x[i]$ accordingly (line 14).

3.5   Behavior of a Manager for $x \in sc\_objects$

The behavior of the manager M_x of the object x is depicted in Figure 4. It consists of three statements that describe M_x's behaviour when it receives a message. The *write_req* and *read_req* messages are processed sequentially[6]. The *check_req* messages are processed as soon as they arrive (let us notice they do not modify M_x's context).

---

upon reception of *write_req* (v) **from** p_i:
(1)   **if** $(owner_x \neq \perp)$ **then send** *downgrade_req* (R, x) to p_{owner_x};
(2)   **wait** *downgrade_ack* $(-)$ **from** p_{owner_x}
(3)   **endif**;
(4) $C_x \leftarrow v$; $owner_x \leftarrow i$;
(5) $hlw_x[i] \leftarrow true$; $\forall j \neq i : hlw_x[j] \leftarrow false$;
(6)   **send** *write_ack* () **to** p_i

upon reception of *read_req* () **from** p_i:
(7)   **if** $(owner_x \neq \perp)$ **then send** *downgrade_req* (R, x) to p_{owner_x};
(8)   **wait** *downgrade_ack* (v) **from** p_{owner_x};
(9) $C_x \leftarrow v$; $owner_x \leftarrow \perp$
(10)   **endif**;
(11) $hlw_x[i] \leftarrow true$;
(12)   **send** *read_ack* (C_x) **to** p_i

upon reception of *check_req* () **from** p_i:
(13)   **let** $d = ($ $hlw_x[i] \wedge$ (no *write_req* is currently processed) $)$;
(14)   **send** *check_ack* (d) **to** p_i

Fig. 4. Behavior of an Object Manager M_x for $x \in sc\_objects$

- M_x receives *write_req* (v) from p_i.

  In that case, p_i has issued a $w(x)v$ operation. If x is currently owned by some process, M_x first downgrades this previous owner (lines 1-3). Then, M_x sets

---

[6] Assuming no message is indefinitely delayed, it is possible for M_x to reorder waiting messages if there is a need to favor some processes or some operations.

C_x and $owner_x$ to their new values (line 4), updates the boolean vector hlw_x accordingly (line 5), and sends back to p_i an ack message indicating it has taken its write operation into account (line 6).

- M_x receives $read\_req$ (v) from p_i.
  In that case, p_i has issued a $r(x)$ operation, and does not have a legal copy of x. If x is currently owned by some process, M_x first gets the last value of x from this process and downgrades this previous owner (lines 7-10). Then, it sends the current value of x to p_i (line 12) and updates $hlw_x[i]$ accordingly (line 11).
- M_x receives $check\_req$ $()$ from p_i.
  In that case, p_i has got a new value for some object and queries M_x to know if it still has the last value of x. As we will see, this inquiry is necessary for p_i to ensure its locally cached object values are legal. M_x answers $true$ if p_i has the last value of x, otherwise it returns $false$.

3.6   Behavior of a Process

The behavior of a process p_i is described in Figure 5. It is made of three statements that are executed atomically (the procedure $check\_legality(x)$ invoked at line 4 and at line 11 is considered as belonging to the invoking statement). The return statement terminates each write (line 7) and read operation (line 13).

- p_i invokes $w_i(x)v$.
  If p_i is the current owner of x, it was the last process that updated x. In that case, it simply updates its current cached copy of x (line 6). This value will be sent to M_x by p_i when it will leave its ownership of x (lines 19-20). If p_i is not the owner of x, it first becomes the current owner (line 3) by communicating with M_x (lines 1-2). As we have seen in Figure 3 if $x \in ac\_objects$, and in Figure 4 if $x \in sc\_objects$, this entails the downgrading of the previous owner if any. Then, p_i executes the $check\_legality(x)$ procedure. This procedure is explained in a next item. It is the core of the protocol as far as the OO-constraint and the legality of read operations are concerned.
- p_i invokes $r_i(x)$.
  If the local copy of x does not guarantee a legal read ($present_i[x]$ is false), p_i gets the last copy from M_x (lines 8-9), updates accordingly its context (line 10) and executes the $check\_legality(x)$ procedure (see next item).
- The $check\_legality(x)$ procedure.
  As we just claimed, this procedure is at the core of the protocol. It is invoked each time p_i questions M_x. This occurs when p_i's context is modified because (1) it becomes the new owner of x (lines 1-4), or (2) it reads the value of x from M_x (lines 8-11).
  The aim of the $check\_legality(x)$ procedure is to guarantee that all the values, associated with objects in the set $sc\_objects$, defined as present in p_i's local cache will provide legal read operations. To attain this goal, for each object y not currently owned by p_i but whose local readings by p_i were previously legal, p_i questions M_y to know if its current copy is still legal (line 15). M_y

operation $write_i(x)v$:

(1)   **if** $(\neg owner_i[x])$ **then** send $write\_req$ (v) to M_x;

(2)   wait $write\_ack$ () from M_x;

(3) $owner_i[x] \leftarrow true$; $present_i[x] \leftarrow true$;

(4) $check\_legality$ (x)

(5)   **endif**;

(6) $C_i[x] \leftarrow v$;

(7)   return ()

operation $read_i(x)$:

(8)   **if** $(\neg present_i[x])$ **then** send $read\_req$ () to M_x;

(9)   wait $read\_ack$ (v) from M_x;

(10) $present_i[x] \leftarrow true$; $C_i[x] \leftarrow v$;

(11) $check\_legality$ (x)

(12)   **endif**;

(13)   return $(C_i[x])$

procedure $check\_legality$ (x):

(14) $\forall y$ **such that** $(y \in sc\_objects \wedge present_i[y] \wedge \neg owner_i[y] \wedge y \neq x)$

(15)   **do** send $check\_req$ () to M_y;

(16)   wait $check\_ack$ (d) from M_y;

(17) $present_i[y] \leftarrow d$

(18)   **enddo**

upon reception of $downgrade\_req$ (TYPE, x):

(19) $owner_i[x] \leftarrow false$;

(20)   **if** (TYPE= W) **then** $present_i[y] \leftarrow false$ **endif**;
          % When TYPE=W, x is necessarily an atomically consistent object %

(21)   send $downgrade\_ack$ $(C_i[x])$ to M_x

Fig. 5. Behavior of a Process p_i

answers p_i if it has the last value of y (line 16), and accordingly p_i updates $present_i[y]$.

The *check_legality* procedure acts as a reset mechanism that invalidates object copies that cannot be guaranteed to provide legal read operations.

– p_i receives $downgrade\_req(x)$.

In that case, p_i is the current owner of x. It leaves it ownership on x (line 19) and sends the last value of x to M_x (line 20). Note that the current value of x is still present at p_i.

3.7   Considering a Single Criterion

Let us consider the particular case where all the objects belong to *sc_objects*. In this case there are only managers executing the behavior described in Figure 4

(Figure 3 disappears from the protocol). We then obtain the sequential consistency protocol based on the *OO*-constraint described in [15] (where the reader can find a correctness proof).

At the other extreme, if there is no sequentially consistent object (*sc_objects* is empty), the protocol simplifies as follows. Not only Figure 4 disappears, but the procedure *check_legality*() disappears also (as its aim is to check if values cached for sequential consistency are not too old). The protocol we obtain is then the atomic consistency protocol described in [11].

4   Concluding Remarks

This paper has explored a combination of sequential consistency with atomic consistency. As it is based on a consistent merging of the total orders defining each of these consistency criteria, the semantics of the proposed combination is well defined. Interestingly, the proposed protocol encompasses previous protocols designed for a single criterion. In that sense, this protocol provides a "global picture" on the way these consistency criteria can be implemented.

Another way to combine sequential consistency and atomic consistency has been investigated in [17]. For each object, this combination provides the processes with a single write operation and two read operations, namely, an atomic read operation and a sequentially consistent read operation. While the first read operation provides a process with the last "physical" value of an object, the second read operation provides its caller with the last value of the object (last referring here to a common logical time on which all the processes do agree).

References

1. Adve S.V. and Garachorloo K., Shared Memory Models: a Tutorial. *IEEE Computer*, 29(12):66-77, 1997.
2. Afek Y., Brown G. and Merritt M., Lazy Caching. *ACM Transactions on Programming Languages and Systems*, 15(1):182-205, 1993.
3. Ahamad M., Hutto P.W., Neiger G., Burns J.E. and Kohli P., Causal memory: Definitions, Implementations and Programming. *Distributed Comp.*, 9:37-49, 1995.
4. Ahamad M. and Kordale R., Scalable Consistency Protocols for Distributed Services. *IEEE Transactions on Parallel and Distributed Systems*, 10(9):888-903, 1999.
5. Ahamad M., Raynal M. and Thia-Kime G., An Adaptive Protocol for Implementing Causally Consistent Distributed Services. *Proc. 18th IEEE Int. Conf. on Distributed Computing Systems*, IEEE Computer Society Press, pp. 86-93, 1998.
6. Attiya H. and Welch J.L., Sequential Consistency versus Linearizability. *ACM Transactions on Computer Systems*, 12(2):91-122, 1994.
7. Garg V.K. and Raynal M., Normality: a Correctness Condition for Concurrent Objects. *Parallel Processing Letters*, 9(1):123-134, 1999.
8. Herlihy M.P. and Wing J.L., Linearizability: a Correctness Condition for Concurrent Objects. *ACM TOPLAS*, 12(3):463-492, 1990.
9. Ibaraki T., Kameda T. and Minoura T., Serializability with Constraints. *ACM Transactions on Database Systems*, 12(3):429-452, 1987.

10. Lamport L., How to Make a Multiprocessor Computer that Correctly Executes Multiprocess Programs. *IEEE Transactions on Computers*, C28(9):690-691, 1979.
11. Li K. and Hudak P., Memory Coherence in Shared Virtual Memory Systems. *ACM Transactions on Computer Systems*, 7(4):321-359, 1989.
12. Mizuno M., Nielsen M.L. and Raynal M., An Optimistic Protocol for a Linearizable Distributed Shared Memory System. *Parallel Proc. Letters*, 6(2):265-278, 1996.
13. Mizuno M., Raynal M. and Zhou J.Z., Sequential Consistency in Distributed Systems. *Proc. Int. Workshop on Theory and Practice of Distributed Systems*, Springer Verlag LNCS #938, pp. 224-241, 1994.
14. Papadimitriou C., The Theory of Concurrency Control. *Comp. Science Press*, 1986.
15. Raynal M., Sequential Consistency as Lazy Linearizability. *14th ACM Symposium on Parallel Algorithms and Architectures (SPAA'02)*, pp. 151-152, 2002.
16. Raynal M., Token-Based Sequential Consistency. *Journal of Computer Systems Science and Engineering*, 17(6):359-365, 2002.
17. Raynal M., Roy M. and Tutu C., A simple Protocol Offering Both Atomic Read Operations and Sequentially Consistent Read operations. *Proc. 19th Int. Conference on Advanced Information Networking and Applications (AINA'05)*, IEEE Computer Society Press, 2005.
18. Raynal M. and Schiper A., From Causal Consistency to Sequential Consistency in Shared Memory Systems. *Proc. 15th Int. Conf. on Foundations of Soft. Technology and Theor. Computer Science*, Springer-Verlag LNCS #1026, pp. 180-194, 1995.
19. Raynal M. and Schiper A., A Suite of Formal Definitions for Consistency Criteria in Distributed Shared Memories. *Proc. 9th Int. IEEE Conference on Parallel and Distributed Computing Systems (PDCS'96)*, pp. 125-131, 1996.
20. Raynal M. and Vidyasankar K., A Distributed Implementation of Sequential Consistency with Multi-Object Operations. *24th IEEE Int. Conf. on Distributed Computing Systems (ICDCS'04)*, IEEE Computer Society Press, pp. 544-551, 2004.
21. Taylor R.N., Complexity of Analyzing the Synchronization Structure of Concurrent Programs. *Acta Informatica*, 19:57-84, 1983.
22. Zhan Z., Ahamad M. and Raynal M., Mixed Consistency Model: Meeting Data Sharing Needs of Heterogeneous Users. *Proc. 25th IEEE Int. Conference on Distributed Computing Systems (ICDCS'05)*, IEEE Computer Society Press, 2005.

An Approach to the Implementation of the Dynamical Priorities Method

Valery A. Sokolov and Eugeny A. Timofeev

Yaroslavl State University,
150 000,Yaroslavl, Russia
{sokolov, tim}@uniyar.ac.ru

Abstract. In this work we consider a problem of optimizing the data transmission mechanism of Internet transport protocols. We use a priority discipline without time measurements by a receiver, which has the property of universality. The possibility of an application of this discipline for improving performances of the original Transmission Control Protocol (TCP) is discussed. We propose to apply the dynamical priority method to avoid time measurements by the receiver. Instead of this only mean queue lengths at the sending side have to be measured.

1 Introduction

We consider the problem of management optimization for a complex service system. Basic characteristic features of the considered system are:

- there is the possibility of the feed-back;
- the probability of the feed-back depends both on external (unknown) reasons and on the service discipline;
- the duration of customer service depends on time;
- there is a great number of customers with sharply various service durations.

The basic example of the considered problem is the management of the Transmission Control Protocol (TCP) [2].

It is easy to see that the listed properties hold for the TCP.

The main criteria of optimization are the minimization of losses of arriving customers and the minimization of the sojourn-time.

To optimize the management (see, for example, [4], [3]), adaptive service disciplines are usially used, which are adjusted to an input process. For improving the quality of service it is desirable to know as much as possible about characteristics of the system.

The duration of service is obviously one of the major characteristics. However, its measurements can happen to be impossible.

Thus, for example, in the TCP the duration of service contains an addend equal to the received time, but the standard TCP does not transfer this parameter.

In [5], [6] some updates of the TCP (TCP with an adaptive rate) are presented, which use the received time, and due to it the quality of the work is going upward. However, we have to bring into use an additional field to the TCP.

V. Malyshkin (Ed.): PaCT 2005, LNCS 3606, pp. 74–78, 2005.

In [1] we have described a service discipline which is also adaptive, but it uses only queue lengths and does not demand time measurements by a receiver.

In our work an algorithm of a choice of parameters for the presented service discipline is described. This discipline can be applied to the TCP without modifying it.

2 The Model

In this section a model of the considered service system will be described. We stress that the model is general, but the performance of the TCP keeps within this model.

2.1 General Characteristics of the System

1. The input process describes a sequence of customers to be served. Each customer consists of some number of segments. For simplicity, we suppose that the size of a segment is fixed and does not vary.
2. All segments arrive at the total queue.
3. Under available characteristics of customers and the current parameters of the service discipline some segments are chosen for service. The rules of the choice will be described below.
4. The service of the chosen segments consists in the following:
   - a segment is sent to the receiver;
   - if the confirmation does not come through the retranslation time, the segment is fed back to the total queue (the definition of the retranslation time will be described below);
   - if the confirmation comes, the segment is removed from the system.

We stress that here we do not consider rules of the creation of the confirmation because our main goal is the optimization of the data transfer.

Note, that the size of the window established by the receiver is much greater than a window for the data transfer, therefore it can be not taken into account (as it does occur in real systems).

2.2 Service of a Customer

Before every transmission of segments of the considered customer the following key parameters are thought to be known:

1. N is the number of segments in the total queue;
2. τ_i is the time of the previous transmission of the i-th segment;
3. ν_i is the number of the previous transmissions of the i-th segment.

The retransmission timer functions at the moment

$$t = \min_i \tau_i + R_0,$$

where R_0 is a constant which specifies the time required for passing a segment
from the sender to the receiver and for returning the confirmation (greater than
the Round Trip Time). By these parameters and by auxiliary parameters of
the choice algorithm described below we can find the value W, where W is
the number of segments (the width of a window). These W segments are to
be transmitted. After receiving confirmations for all transmitted segments, the
service of the customer is terminated.

2.3   The Algorithm of the Choice of Transmitted Segments

The basis of the algorithm of the choice of transmitted segments for a fixed
window width W is a probabilistic-divided discipline which is described in [1]
for service systems. Now we introduce parameters of the probabilistic-divided
service discipline.

To each segment we assign a type, i.e. one of the numbers $0, 1, 2, \ldots, 2n$ (n
is a given parameter) by the following rules:

- at the moment of arrival all segments receive the type 0;
- after obtaining the acknowledgement with the indication of a transmission
  mistake of a segment of type $i < n$, or if the retransmission timer fires on
  a segment of type i, the segment receives the type $2[(i + 1)/2] + 1$ with
  the probability $p_{[(i+1)/2]}$ and the type $2[(i + 1)/2] + 2$ with the probability
  $1 - p_{[(i+1)/2]}$;
- if $i = n$, the type does not vary.

Here, the probabilities $\mathbf{p} = (p_0, p_1, \ldots, p_{n-1})$ are auxiliary parameters of the
algorithm.

Another auxiliary parameter of the algorithm is the permutation

$$\pi = (\pi_0, \pi_1, \ldots, \pi_{2n})$$

of the numbers $0, 1 \ldots, 2n$.

The required W segments are defined by the permutation π: first, all segments
of type π_0, second, all segments of type π_1, etc. up to W segments.

Thus, to finish the description of the model, we have to specify the methods of changing auxiliary parameters of the algorithm: the permutation π, the
probabilities $\mathbf{p}$ and the window width W.

3   The Method of Finding the Auxiliary Parameters

At the initial moment the auxiliary parameters are set as follows:

$$W = 1, \quad \pi = (0, 1, \ldots, 2n), \quad \mathbf{p} = (1/2, \ldots, 1/2).$$

For recalculation of the auxiliary parameters the following characteristics will
be used:

$L_i(t)$ is a number of not transferred segments of type i at the moment t
$(0 \leq i \leq 2n)$;

$P(W)$ is the frequency of erratic transmission of a segment at the set width of the window W (it is clear that the values $P(W)$ will be known only for those values W which were set during the transmission, and for estimation of values $P(W)$ at other points we shall use the linear interpolation);

$RTT(t)$ is an estimation of the time required for passing a segment from a sender up to a receiver and for returning the confirmation (Round Trip Time).

These characteristics are recalculated before each moment of the transmission.

3.1   The Algorithm of Changing the Window Width W

If all segments have been transferred and $P(W) = 0$, the window width W is doubled.

If $P(W) > 0$, we do the following.

Considering the value $P(W)$ as a probability of the erratic transmission and the value $RTT(t)$ as the transfer time of a segment, we calculate an average time $\tau(W)$ of waiting for the segment till the complete sending.

Let $\tau_0(t)$ be an average retranslation time of a segment at the present moment, and T_0 be an auxiliary constant which defines an essential difference of average retranslation time.

If $\tau(W) < \tau_0(t) - T_0$, we increase the window so that $\tau(W) \approx \tau_0(t) - T_0$. For the calculation we extrapolate the value $P(W)$ linearly by the last two values, and we take the value $RTT(t)$ as a transfer time.

If $\tau(W) > \tau_0(t) + T_0$, we reduce the window so that $\tau(W) \approx \tau_0(t) - T_0$.

If $|\tau(W) - \tau_0(t)| \leq T_0$, the window is left without changing.

After the choice of a window width, we change the auxiliary parameters: the permutation π and probabilities $\mathbf{p}$.

3.2   The Algorithm of Changing π and p

When making the choice of these parameters, it is necessary to follow some heuristic rules, for example: the decreasing of the total queue of not transmitted segments, the decreasing of the time of residence in the system, etc. It is also possible to choose linear combinations of these rules and to optimize coefficients of this linear combination.

Under a chosen heuristic rule we obtain an optimization problem with continuous parameters $\mathbf{p}$ and with discrete parameters, namely, a permutation π. If the optimization problem is solved by the algorithm of the sequential improvement of the parameters $\mathbf{p}$ (for example, by the gradient method), then problems arise in the case when for some i the next value $p_i = 0$ or $p_i = 1$. In this case it is necessary to apply the algorithm of the choice of the following permutation from the work [1], which by a given permutation π and a given number i calculates probabilities $\tilde{\mathbf{p}}$ and a new permutation $\tilde{\pi}$, for which $\tilde{p}_i = 1$ (if $p_i = 0$) and $\tilde{p}_i = 0$ (if $p_i = 1$), and mean queue lengths are the same as for the parameters π and $\mathbf{p}$.

4   Conclusion

We have shown how it is possible to design a probabilistic-divided service discipline for managing the packet transfer in a network. The main advantage of such an approach consists in the fact that we eliminate time measurements of the receiver.

References

1. Sokolov V. A. , Timofeev E.A. : Dynamical Priorities without Time Measurement and Modification of the TCP, LNCS N.1649, (2001), p.240-245.
2. Stevens W.R. : TCP/IP Illustrated. Volume 1: The Protocols. Addison-Wesley, New York, 1994.
3. Balakrishnan H., Padmanabhan V., Katz R. : The Effects of Asymmetry on TCP Performance. ACM MobiCom, **9**, 1997.
4. Brakmo L., O'Malley S., Peterson L. : TCP Vegas: New Techniques for Congestion Detection and Avoidance. ACM SIGCOMM **8** (1994), p.24-35.
5. Alekseev I.V., Sokolov V.A. : The Adaptive Rate TCP. Model. and Anal. Inform. Syst. **6**, N.1 (1999), p.4–11.
6. Alekseev, I.V., Sokolov, V.A.: ARTCP: Efficient Algorithm for Transport Protocol for Packet Switched Networks. LNCS, N. 2127, Springer-Verlag (2001), p.159–174.
7. Alekseev, I.V., Sokolov, V.A.: Modelling and Traffic Analysis of the Adaptive Rate Transport Protocol. Future Generation Computer Systems, Number 6, Vol.18. NH Elsevier (2002), p.813–827.

Information Flow Analysis for VHDL

Terkel K. Tolstrup, Flemming Nielson, and Hanne Riis Nielson

Informatics and Mathematical Modelling, Technical University of Denmark
{tkt, nielson, hrn}@imm.dtu.dk

Abstract. We describe a fragment of the hardware description language VHDL that is suitable for implementing the *Advanced Encryption Standard* algorithm. We then define an Information Flow analysis as required by the international standard Common Criteria. The goal of the analysis is to identify the entire information flow through the VHDL program. The result of the analysis is presented as a non-transitive directed graph that connects those nodes (representing either variables or signals) where an information flow might occur. We compare our approach to that of Kemmerer and conclude that our approach yields more precise results.

1 Introduction

Modern technical equipment often depends on the reliable performance of embedded systems. The present work is part of an ongoing effort to validate the security properties of such systems. Here it is a key requirement that the programs maintain the confidentiality of information it handles. To document this, an evaluation against the criteria of the international standard *Common Criteria* [13] is a main objective.

In this paper we focus on the Covert Channel analysis described in Chapter 14 of [13]. The main technical ingredient of the analysis is to provide a description of the direct and indirect flows of information that might occur. This is then followed by a further step where the designer argues that all information flows are permissible — or where an independent code evaluator asks for further clarification. We present the result of the analysis as a directed graph: the nodes represent the resources, and there is a direct edge from one node to another whenever there might be a direct or indirect information flow from one to the other. In general, the graph will be non-transitive [4,14].

The programming language used is the *hardware description language* VHDL [7]. Systems consist of a number of processes running in parallel where each process has its own local data space and communication between processes is performed at synchronization points using *signals*. In Section 2 we give an overview of the fragment $VHDL_1$. We present a formal Semantics of $VHDL_1$ in Section 3.

The problem of analysing VHDL programs has already been addressed in previously published approaches. The paper by Hymans [6] uses abstract interpretation to give an over-approximation of the set of reachable configurations for a fragment of VHDL not unlike ours. This suffices for checking safety properties: if the safety property is true on all states in the over-approximation it

V. Malyshkin (Ed.): PaCT 2005, LNCS 3606, pp. 79–98, 2005.

will be true for all executions of the VHDL program. Hence when synthesizing the VHDL specification one does not need to generate circuits for enforcing the reference monitor (called an observer in [6]).

The paper by Hsieh and Levitan [5] considers a similar fragment of VHDL and is concerned with optimising the synthesis process by avoiding the generation of circuits needed to store values of signals. One component of the required analyses is a Reaching Definitions analysis with a similar scope to ours although specified in a rather different manner. Comparing the precision of their approach (to the extent actually explained in the paper) with ours, we believe that our analysis is more precise in that it allows also to kill signals being set in other processes than where they are used. Furthermore the presented analysis is only correct for processes with one synchronization point, because definition sets are only influenced by definitions in other processes at the end (or beginning) of a process. Therefore definitions is lost if they are present at a synchronization point within the process but overwritten before the end of the process.

Our approach is based around adapting a Reaching Definitions analysis (along the lines of [9]) to the setting of $VHDL_1$. A novel feature of our analysis is that it has two components for tracking the flow of values of active signals: one is the traditional over-approximation whereas the other is an under-approximation. Finally, a Reaching Definitions analysis tracks the flow of variables and present values of signals. The details are developed in Section 4.

The first step of the Information Flow analysis determines the local dependencies for each statement; this takes the form of an inference system that is local to each process. The second step constructs the directed graph by performing the necessary "transitive closure"; this takes the form of a constraint system and makes use of the Reaching Definitions analysis. The results obtained are therefore more precise than those obtained by more standard methods like that of Kemmerer [8] and only ignore issues like timing and power-consumption. The analysis is presented in Section 5 and has been implemented in the Succinct Solver Version 1.0 [10,11] and has been used to validate several programs for implementing the NSA *Advanced Encryption Standard* (AES) [17].

2   Background

$VHDL_1$ is a fragment of VHDL that concentrates on the behavioral specification of models. A program in $VHDL_1$ consists of *entities* and *architectures*, uniquely identified by indexes $i_e, i_a \in Id$. An entity describes how an architecture is connected to the environment. The architectures comprise the behavioral or structural specification of the entities.

An entity specifies a set of signals referred to as ports ($prt \in Prt$), each port is represented by a signal ($s \in Sig$) used for reference in the specification of the architecture; furthermore a notion of the intended usage of the signal is specified by the keywords in and out defining if the signals value can be altered or read by the environment, and the type of the signal's value (either logical values or vectors of logical values).

$pgm \in Pgm$ programs
pgm $::=$ **ent** $|$ $arch$ $|$ $pgm_1\ pgm_2$

$ent \in Ent$ entities
ent $::=$ **entity** i_e **is port**(prt)**; end** i_e**;**

$prt \in Prt$ ports
prt $::= s :$ **in** $type$ $|$ $s :$ **out** $type$ $|$ $prt_1; prt_2$

$type \in Type$ types
$type$ $::=$ **std_logic** $|$ **std_logic_vector**$(z_1$ **downto** $z_2)$
        $|$ **std_logic_vector**$(z_1$ **to** $z_2)$

$arch \in Arch$ architectures
$arch$ $::=$ **architecture** i_a **of** i_e **is begin** css**; end** i_a**;**

$css \in Css$ concurrent statements
css $::= s <= e$ $|$ $s(z_1$ **downto** $z_2) <= e$ $|$ $s(z_1$ **to** $z_2) <= e$
        $|$ $i_p :$ **process** $decl$**; begin** ss**; end process** i_p
        $|$ $i_b :$ **block** $decl$**; begin** css**; end block** i_b $|$ $css_1 | css_2$

$decl \in Decl$ declarations
$decl$ $::=$ **variable** $x : type := e$ $|$ **signal** $s : type := e$ $|$ $decl_1; decl_2$

$ss \in Stmt$ statements
ss $::=$ **null** $|$ $x := e$ $|$ $x(z_1$ **downto** $z_2) := e$ $|$ $x(z_1$ **to** $z_2) := e$ $|$ $s <= e$
        $|$ $s(z_1$ **downto** $z_2) <= e$ $|$ $s(z_1$ **to** $z_2) <= e$ $|$ **wait on** S **until** e
        $|$ $ss_1; ss_2$ $|$ **if** e **then** ss_1 **else** ss_2 $|$ **while** e **do** ss

$e \in Exp$ expressions
e $::= m$ $|$ a $|$ x $|$ $x(z_1$ **downto** $z_2)$ $|$ $x(z_1$ **to** $z_2)$ $|$ s $|$ $s(z_1$ **downto** $z_2)$
        $|$ $s(z_1$ **to** $z_2)$ $|$ $op^u_m\ e$ $|$ $e_1\ op^b_m\ e_2$ $|$ $e_1\ op_a\ e_2$

Fig. 1. The subset VHDL$_1$ of VHDL

An architecture model is specified by a family of concurrent statements ($css \in Css$) running in parallel; here the index $i_p \in Id$ is a unique identifier in a finite set of process identifiers ($I_p \subseteq_{fin} Id$). Each process has a statement ($ss \in Stmt$) as body and may use logical values ($m \in LVal$), vectors of logical values (we write $a \in VVal$, where a has the form "$m_1 \ldots m_k$" where $m_i \in LVal$), local variables ($x \in Var$) as well as signals ($s \in Sig$, $S \subseteq_{fin} Sig$). When accessing variables and signals we always refer to their present value and when we assign to variables it is always the present value that is modified. However, when assigning to a signal its present value is *not modified*, rather its so-called active value is modified; this representation of signal's values, as illustrated in Figure 2, is used to take care of the physical aspect of propagating an electrical current through a system, the time consumed by the propagation is usually called a *delta-cycle*. The wait statements are synchronization points, where the active values of signals are used to determine the new present values that will be common to all processes.

Concurrent statements could also be block statements that allow local signal declarations for the use of internal communication between processes declared

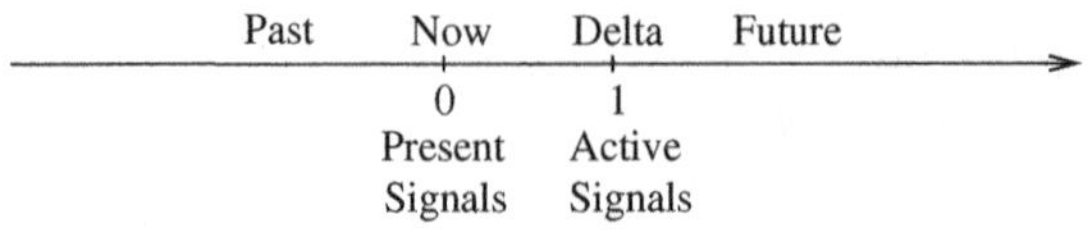

Fig. 2. The representation of abstract time in the signal store

within the block. The index $i_b \in Id$ is a unique identifier in a finite set of block identifiers ($I_b \subseteq_{fin} Id$). The scope of the local signals declared in the block definition is within the concurrent statements specified inside the block.

Signal assignment can also be performed as a concurrent statement, this corresponds to a process that is sensitive to the *free signals* in the right-hand side expression and that has the same assignment inside [2].

Since VHDL describe digital hardware we are concerned with the details of electrical signals, and it is therefore necessary to include types to represent digitally encoded values. We consider logical values ($LVal$) of the standard logic type *std_logic*, that includes traditional boolean values as well as values for electrical properties. $VHDL_1$ also allow the usage of vectors of logical values, values of this type is written using double quotes (e.g. "1" $\neq$ '1'). There are a number of arithmetic operators available on vectors of logical values.

The formal syntax is given in Figure 1. In VHDL it is allowed to omit components of wait statements. Writing $FS(e)$ for the free signals in e, the effect of 'on $FS(e)$' may be obtained by omitting the 'on S' component, and the effect of 'until true' may be obtained by omitting the 'until e' component. (In other words, the default values of S and e are $FS(e)$ and true, respectively.) Semantically, S is the set of signals waited on, i.e. at least one of the signals of S must have a new active value, and e is a condition on the new present values that must be fulfilled, in order to leave the wait statement.

In $VHDL_1$ the notion of signals is simplified with respect to full VHDL and thus does not allow references further into time than the following *delta-cycle*. This not only simplifies the analysis but also simplifies defining the semantics: Of the many accounts to be found in the literature [3,16] we have found the one of [16] to best correspond to our practical experiments, based on test programs simulated with the ModelSim SE 5.7d VHDL simulator. Even with this restriction $VHDL_1$ is sufficiently expressive to deal with the programs of the AES implementation.

3   Structural Operational Semantics

The main idea when defining the semantics for $VHDL_1$ programs is to execute each process by itself until a synchronization point is reached (i.e. a wait statement). When all processes of the program have reached a synchronization point synchronization is handled, while taking care of the resolution of signals in case a signal has been assigned different values by the processes. This synchronization will leave the processes in a state where they are ready either to continue execution by themselves or wait for the next synchronization.

Basic semantic domains. The syntax of programs in VHDL$_1$ is limited to statements operating on a state of logical values. These logical values are defined as $v \in LValue = \{$'U', 'X', '0', '1', 'Z', 'W', 'L', 'H', '-'$\}$ where the values indicate the properties

'U' Uninitialized	'X' Forcing Unknown	'0' Forcing zero
'1' Forcing one	'Z' High Impedance	'W' Weak Unknown
'L' Weak zero	'H' Weak one	'-' Don't care

these values are said to capture the behavior of an electrical system better than traditional boolean values [2].

Furthermore we have vectors of logical values $a \in AValue = LValue^*$. We have a function mapping logicals in the syntax to logical values in the semantics $\mathcal{L} : LVal \rightarrow LValue$, and vectors of logical values to their semantical equivalence $\mathcal{A} : VVal \rightarrow AValue$. The semantical values are collected in the set $Value = LValue \uplus AValue$.

Constructed semantic domains. VHDL$_1$ includes local variables and signals. The values of the local variables are stored in a local state. The local state is a mapping from variable names to logical values.

$$\sigma \in State = (Var \rightarrow Value)$$

The idea is that we have a local state for each process, keeping track of assignments to local variables encountered in the execution of the process so far.

For communication between the processes we have the signals, the values of signals are stored in local states. The processes can communicate by synchronizing the signals of their local signal state with other processes.

$$\varphi \in Signals = (Sig \rightarrow (\{0,1\} \hookrightarrow Value))$$

The value assigned to a signal is available after the following synchronization, therefore we keep the present value of a signal s in $\varphi\ s\ 0$. In $\varphi\ s\ 1$ we store the assigned value, meaning that it is available after a *delta-cycle*. Each signal state has a time line for each signal. Values in the past are not used and therefore forgotten by the semantics; in VHDL$_1$ it is not possible to assign values to signals further into the future than one delta-cycle.

All signals have a present value, so $\varphi\ s\ 0$ is defined for all s. Not all signals need to be active meaning they have a new value waiting in the following delta-cycle, thus $\varphi\ s\ 1$ need not be defined; hence we use $\{0,1\} \hookrightarrow Value$ in the definition of the signal state to indicate that it is a partial function.

The semantics handles expressions following the ideas of [12]. For expressions

$$\mathcal{E} : Expr \rightarrow (State \times Signals \hookrightarrow Value)$$

evaluates the expression. The function is defined in Table 1. Note that for signals we use the current value of the signal, i.e. $\varphi\ s\ 0$.

Table 1. Semantics of Expressions

$$
\begin{aligned}
\mathcal{E}[\![m]\!]\langle\sigma,\varphi\rangle &= \mathcal{L}[\![m]\!] \\
\mathcal{E}[\![a]\!]\langle\sigma,\varphi\rangle &= \mathcal{A}[\![a]\!] \\
\mathcal{E}[\![x]\!]\langle\sigma,\varphi\rangle &= \sigma\,x \\
\mathcal{E}[\![x(z_1 \; \texttt{downto} \; z_2)]\!]\langle\sigma,\varphi\rangle &= split(\sigma\,x, z_1, z_2) \\
\mathcal{E}[\![s]\!]\langle\sigma,\varphi\rangle &= \varphi\,s\,0 \\
\mathcal{E}[\![s(z_1 \; \texttt{downto} \; z_2)]\!]\langle\sigma,\varphi\rangle &= split(\varphi\,s\,0, z_1, z_2) \\
\mathcal{E}[\![op^u_m\,e]\!]\langle\sigma,\varphi\rangle &= \overline{op^u_m}\,v && \text{where } \mathcal{E}[\![e]\!]\varphi = v \\
& && \text{and } \overline{op^u_m}\,v \text{ defined} \\
\mathcal{E}[\![e_1\,op^b_m\,e_2]\!]\langle\sigma,\varphi\rangle &= v_1\,\overline{op^b_m}\,v_2 && \text{where } \mathcal{E}[\![e_1]\!]\varphi = v_1 \\
& && \text{and } \mathcal{E}[\![e_2]\!]\varphi = v_2 \\
& && \text{and } v_1\,\overline{op^b_m}\,v_2 \text{ defined} \\
\mathcal{E}[\![e_1\,op_a\,e_2]\!]\langle\sigma,\varphi\rangle &= v_1\,\overline{op_a}\,v_2 && \text{where } \mathcal{E}[\![e_1]\!]\varphi = v_1 \\
& && \text{and } \mathcal{E}[\![e_2]\!]\varphi = v_2 \\
& && \text{and } v_1\,\overline{op_a}\,v_2 \text{ defined}
\end{aligned}
$$

In the specification of the Semantics all vector values and definitions are normalized to the direction of ranging from a smaller index to a larger index. This simplification allows us to consider a significantly smaller number of rules. We define the function *split* which withdraws the elements of a vector in the range specified by the last two parameters ($split : a \times z \times z \to a$).

3.1 Statements

The semantics of statements and concurrent statements are specified by transition systems, more precisely by structural operational semantics. For statements we shall use configurations of the form:

$$\langle ss', \sigma, \varphi\rangle \in Stmt' \times State \times Signals$$

Here $Stmt'$ refers to the statements from the syntactical category $Stmt$ with an additional statement (`final`) indicating that a final configuration has been reached. Therefore the transition relation for statements has the form:

$$\langle ss, \sigma, \varphi\rangle \Rightarrow \langle ss', \sigma', \varphi'\rangle$$

which specifies one step of computation. The transition relation is specified in Table 2 and briefly commented upon below.

An assignment to a signal is defined as an update to the value at the delta-time, i.e. $\varphi\,s\,1$. We use the notation $\varphi^{[i]}[s \mapsto v]$ to mean $\varphi[s \mapsto \varphi(s)[i \mapsto v]]$. For updating the variable and signal store with vector values we use the notation $\sigma[x(z_i \ldots z_j) \mapsto v]$ to mean $\sigma[x \mapsto \sigma(x)[z_i \mapsto v_1]\ldots[z_j \mapsto v_{j-i}]]$, similarly for signals.

The wait statement is handled in Section 3.2, along with the handling of the concurrent processes. This is due to the fact that the wait statement is in fact a synchronization point of the processes.

Table 2. Statements

[Local Variable Assignment] :

$\langle x := e, \sigma, \varphi \rangle \Rightarrow \langle \mathbf{final}, \sigma[x \mapsto v], \varphi \rangle$ where $\mathcal{E}[\![e]\!]\langle \sigma, \varphi \rangle = v$

$\langle x(z_1 \ \mathbf{downto} \ z_2) := e, \sigma, \varphi \rangle \Rightarrow \langle \mathbf{final}, \sigma[x(z_1 \ldots z_2) \rightarrowtail v], \varphi \rangle$
where $\mathcal{E}[\![e]\!]\langle \sigma, \varphi \rangle = v$

[Signal Assignment] :

$\langle s <= e, \sigma, \varphi \rangle \Rightarrow \langle \mathbf{final}, \sigma, \varphi^{[1]}[s \mapsto v] \rangle$ where $\mathcal{E}[\![e]\!]\langle \sigma, \varphi \rangle = v$

$\langle s(z_1 \ \mathbf{downto} \ z_2) <= e, \sigma, \varphi \rangle \Rightarrow \langle \mathbf{final}, \sigma, \varphi^{[1]}[s(z_1 \ldots z_2) \rightarrowtail v] \rangle$
where $\mathcal{E}[\![e]\!]\langle \sigma, \varphi \rangle = v$

[Skip] :

$\langle \mathbf{null}, \sigma, \varphi \rangle \Rightarrow \langle \mathbf{final}, \sigma, \varphi \rangle$

[Composition] :

$$\frac{\langle ss_1, \sigma, \varphi \rangle \Rightarrow \langle ss_1', \sigma', \varphi' \rangle}{\langle ss_1; ss_2, \sigma, \varphi \rangle \Rightarrow \langle ss_1'; ss_2, \sigma', \varphi' \rangle} \quad \text{where } ss_1' \in Stmt$$

$$\frac{\langle ss_1, \sigma, \varphi \rangle \Rightarrow \langle \mathbf{final}, \sigma', \varphi' \rangle}{\langle ss_1; ss_2, \sigma, \varphi \rangle \Rightarrow \langle ss_2, \sigma', \varphi' \rangle}$$

[Conditional] :

$\langle \mathbf{if} \ e \ \mathbf{then} \ ss_1 \ \mathbf{else} \ ss_2, \varphi \rangle \Rightarrow \langle ss_1, \sigma, \varphi \rangle$ if $\mathcal{E}[\![e]\!]\langle \sigma, \varphi \rangle = \text{'1'}$
$\langle \mathbf{if} \ e \ \mathbf{then} \ ss_1 \ \mathbf{else} \ ss_2, \varphi \rangle \Rightarrow \langle ss_2, \sigma, \varphi \rangle$ if $\mathcal{E}[\![e]\!]\langle \sigma, \varphi \rangle = \text{'0'}$

[Loop] :

$\langle \mathbf{while} \ e \ \mathbf{do} \ ss, \sigma, \varphi \rangle \Rightarrow \langle \mathbf{if} \ e \ \mathbf{then} \ (ss; \mathbf{while} \ e \ \mathbf{do} \ ss) \ \mathbf{else} \ \mathbf{null}, \sigma, \varphi \rangle$

3.2 Concurrent Statements

The semantics for concurrent statements handles the concurrent processes and their synchronizations of a VHDL$_1$ program. We rewrite process declarations into statements so the process declaration $i\colon \mathbf{process} \ \ decl_i; \ \mathbf{begin} \ ss_i; \ \mathbf{end} \ \mathbf{process} \ \ i$ is rewritten to $\mathbf{null}; \mathbf{while} \ \text{'1'} \ \mathbf{do} \ \ ss_i$ as the intention is that the statement ss is repeated indefinitely.

The transition system for concurrent statements has configurations of the form:

$$\|_{i \in I} \langle ss_i', \sigma_i, \varphi_i \rangle$$

for $I \subseteq_{fin} Id$ and $ss_i' \in Stmt'$, $\sigma_i \in State$, $\varphi_i \in Signals$ for all $i \in Id$. Thus each process has a local variable and signal state.

The initial configuration of a VHDL$_1$ program is:

$$\|_{i \in I} \langle \mathbf{null}; \mathbf{while} \ \mathbf{true} \ \mathbf{do} \ ss_i, \sigma_i^0, \varphi_i^0 \rangle$$

The ith process uses an initial state for signals defined by the Semantics for declarations of signals. If no initial value is specified the following are used: $\sigma_i^0 \ x = \text{'U'}$ and $\varphi_i^0 \ s \ 0 = \text{'U'}$ for all non-vector signals used in the process ss_i. All vectors has a string of 'U''s corresponding to the length of the vector (i.e. "U...U"). $\varphi_i^0 \ s \ 1$ is *undef* for all signals used in the process ss_i.

Table 3. Concurrent statements

[Handle non-waiting processes (H)] :

$$\frac{\langle ss_j, \sigma_j, \varphi_j \rangle \Rightarrow \langle ss'_j, \sigma'_j, \varphi'_j \rangle}{\|_{i \in I \cup \{j\}} \langle ss_i, \sigma_i, \varphi_i \rangle \Longrightarrow \|_{i \in I \cup \{j\}} \langle ss'_i, \sigma'_i, \varphi'_i \rangle}$$

where $ss'_i = ss_i \wedge \sigma'_i = \sigma_i \wedge \varphi'_i = \varphi_i$ for all $i \neq j$.

[Active signals (A)] :

$$\|_{i \in I} \langle \texttt{wait on } S_i \texttt{ until } e_i; ss_i, \sigma_i, \varphi_i \rangle \Longrightarrow \|_{i \in I} \langle ss'_i, \sigma_i, \varphi'_i \rangle$$

if $\exists i \in I.\ active(\varphi_i)$

where

$$\varphi'_i\ s\ 0 = \begin{cases} f_s\{\{v_j | \varphi_j\ s\ 1 = v_j\}\} & \text{if } \exists j \in I.\ \varphi_j\ s\ 1 \text{ is defined} \\ \varphi_i\ s\ 0 & \text{otherwise} \end{cases}$$

$$\varphi'_i\ s\ 1 = undef$$

$$ss'_i = \begin{cases} ss_i & \text{if } ((\exists s \in S_i.\ \varphi_i\ s\ 0 \neq \varphi'_i\ s\ 0) \wedge \\ & \mathcal{E}[\![e_i]\!]\langle \sigma'_i, \varphi'_i \rangle =' 1') \\ \texttt{wait on } S_i \texttt{ until } b_i; ss_i & \text{otherwise} \end{cases}$$

The transition relation for concurrent statements has the form:

$$\|_{i \in I} \langle ss'_i, \sigma, \varphi_i \rangle \Longrightarrow \|_{i \in I} \langle ss''_i, \sigma'_i, \varphi'_i \rangle$$

which specifies one step of computation.

The transition relation is specified in Table 3 and explained below.

As mentioned the idea when defining the semantics of programs in VHDL$_1$ is that we execute processes locally until they have all arrived at a wait statement, this is reflected in the rule [**Handle non-waiting processes (H)**].

When all processes are ready to execute a wait statement we perform a synchronization covered by the rule [**Active signals (A)**]. If one signal waited for is active, those processes waiting for that signal may proceed; this is expressed using the predicate $active(\varphi)$ defined by

$$active(\varphi) \equiv \exists s \exists v : \varphi\ s\ 1 = v$$

The delta-time values of signals will be synchronized for all processes and in order to do this we use a resolution function $f_s : multiset(Value) \rightarrow Value$. Thus f_s combines the *multi-set* of values assigned to a signal into one value that then will be the new (unique) value of the signal.

Notice that even though a signal that a wait statement is waiting for becomes active, it is not enough to guarantee that it proceeds with its execution. This is because we have the side condition 'until e'. This is reflected in the definition of the statement ss'_i of the next configuration. Notice that the state of local variables is unchanged.

3.3 Architectures

The Semantics for architectures basically initializes the local variable and signal stores for each process and rewrites the other constructions to processes. Concurrent assignments are rewritten to processes and blocks are handled by adding the signals the block declares to the scope of the processes declared inside the block. Vector variables or signals declared using the *to* specifier, where the value is reversed to match the expected ordering in the Semantics of expressions and statements.

4   Reaching Definitions Analysis

The main purpose of the Reaching Definitions analysis is to gather information about which assignments **may** have been made and not overwritten, when the execution reaches each point in the program.

The semantics divides signal states into two parts, namely the present value of a signal and the active value of a signal. Following this the analysis is divided into two parts as well, one for the active value of a signal and one for local variables and the present value of a signal. The two parts are connected since the active values of a signal influence the present value of the signal after the following synchronization. Therefore we will first define the analysis of active signals in Section 4.1, and then, that of the local variables and present values of signals in Section 4.2.

The analysis for active signals is concerned only with a single process, and thus has no information about the other processes. It collects information about which signals **might** be active in order to gather all the influences on the present value; this information is gathered for the process i by an over-approximation analysis of the active signals $RD_\varphi^\cup {}^i$. It also collects information about which signals **must** be active so that the overwritten signals can be removed from the analysis result; this information is gathered for the process i by an under-approximation analysis of the active signals $RD_\varphi^\cap {}^i$.

The analysis of the local variables and present values of signals will be an over-approximation. It is concerned with the entire program and thus collects information for all processes at the same time.

Common analysis domains. The analyses use a labeling scheme, a block definition and a flow relation, similar to the ones described in [9], the only difference being the wait statements which are given labels and treated as blocks. For each process i in a program $\|_{i \in I}\ i :$ **process** $decl_i;$ **begin** $ss_i;$ **end process** i the set of blocks is denoted $blocks(ss_i)$ and the flow relation is denoted $flow(ss_i)$. Similarly we use $init(ss_i)$ to denote the label of the initial block when executing the process i.

We define the cross flow relation cf for a program as the set of all possible synchronizations, i.e. cf is the Cartesian product of the set of labels of wait statements in each process.

The labeling scheme is defined so that each block has a label which is initially unique for the program. During execution the labels might not be unique within the processes, but the same label is not found in two different processes. Hence, we shall sometimes implicitly use that to each label ($l \in Lab$) there is a unique process identifier ($i \in Id$) in which it occurs.

The analyses are presented in a simplified way, following the tradition of the literature (see [9]), where all programs considered are assumed to have so-called isolated entries (meaning that the entry nodes cannot be reentered once left). This is reasonable as each process in $VHDL_1$ can be considered as a skip statement followed by a loop with an always true condition around the statement defining the process. We shall write $FV(ss)$ for the set of free variables of the statement ss and similarly $FS(ss)$ for the set of free signals.

4.1   Analysis of Active Signals

The Reaching Definitions analysis takes the form of a Monotone Framework as given in [9]. It is a *forward* Data Flow analysis, with both an over- $(RD_\varphi^{\cup\ i})$ and an under- $(RD_\varphi^{\cap\ i})$ approximation part; it operates over a complete lattice $\mathcal{P}(Sig_\star \times Lab_\star)$ where $Sig_\star$ is the set of signals and $Lab_\star$ is the set of labels present in the program.

In both cases we shall introduce functions recording the required information at the *entry* and at the *exit* of the program points. So for the over-approximation we have

$$RD_{\varphi entry}^{\cup\ i}, RD_{\varphi exit}^{\cup\ i} : Lab_\star \rightarrow \mathcal{P}(Sig_\star \times Lab_\star)$$

and similarly for the under-approximation

$$RD_{\varphi entry}^{\cap\ i}, RD_{\varphi exit}^{\cap\ i} : Lab_\star \rightarrow \mathcal{P}(Sig_\star \times Lab_\star)$$

To define the analysis we define in Table 4 a function

$$kill_{RD\varphi}^i : Blocks_\star \rightarrow \mathcal{P}(Sig_\star \times Lab_\star)$$

which produces a set of pairs of signals and labels corresponding to the assignments that are killed by the block. A signal assignment can be killed for two reasons: Another block in the same process assigns a new value to the already active signal, or a wait statement in the same process will synchronize all active signals, and therefore kill all signal assignments.

In Table 4 we also define the function

$$gen_{RD\varphi}^i : Blocks_\star \rightarrow \mathcal{P}(Sig_\star \times Lab_\star)$$

that produces a set of pairs of signals and labels corresponding to the assignments generated by the block.

The over-approximation part of the analysis is defined in terms of the information that *may* be available at the entry of the statement. Therefore the over-approximation part considers a union of the information available at the exit of all statements that have a flow directly to the statement considered.

The under-approximation part of the analysis is defined in terms of the information that *must* be available at the entry of the statement. Therefore the under-approximation part considers an intersection of the information available at the exit of all statements that have a flow directly to the statement considered.

The full details are presented in Table 4.

Table 4. Reaching Definitions Analysis for active signals; labels l are implicitly assumed to occur in process i : **process** $decl_i$; **begin** ss_i; **end process** i

---

kill and gen functions for the process i : **process** $decl_i$; **begin** ss_i; **end process** i

$$kill^i_{RD\varphi}([s <= e]^l) = \{(s, l')|B^{l'} \text{ assigns to } s \text{ in process } i\}$$
$$kill^i_{RD\varphi}([\textbf{wait on } S \textbf{ until } e]^l) = \{(s, l')|B^{l'} \text{ assigns to } s \text{ in process } i\}$$
$$kill^i_{RD\varphi}([\dots]^l) = \emptyset \text{ otherwise}$$

$$gen^i_{RD\varphi}([s <= e]^l) = \{(s, l)\}$$
$$gen^i_{RD\varphi}([s(z_1 \textbf{ downto } z_2) <= e]^l) = \{(s, l)\}$$
$$gen^i_{RD\varphi}([s(z_1 \textbf{ to } z_2) <= e]^l) = \{(s, l)\}$$
$$gen^i_{RD\varphi}([\dots]^l) = \emptyset \text{ otherwise}$$

---

data flow equations: RD_φ for the process i : **process** $decl_i$; **begin** ss_i; **end process** i

$$RD^{\cup\ i}_{\varphi entry}(l) = \begin{cases} \emptyset & \text{if } l = init(ss_i) \\ \bigcup\{RD^{\cup\ i}_{\varphi exit}(l')|(l', l) \in flow(ss_i)\} & \text{otherwise} \end{cases}$$

$$RD^{\cup\ i}_{\varphi exit}(l) = (RD^{\cup\ i}_{\varphi entry}(l)\backslash kill^i_{RD\varphi}(B^l)) \cup gen^i_{RD\varphi}(B^l)$$

$$RD^{\cap\ i}_{\varphi entry}(l) = \begin{cases} \emptyset & \text{if } l = init(ss_i) \\ \dot{\bigcap}\{RD^{\cap\ i}_{\varphi exit}(l')|(l', l) \in flow(ss_i)\} & \text{otherwise} \end{cases}$$

$$RD^{\cap\ i}_{\varphi exit}(l) = (RD^{\cap\ i}_{\varphi entry}(l)\backslash kill^i_{RD\varphi}(B^l)) \cup gen^i_{RD\varphi}(B^l)$$

For the under-approximation analysis we define a special intersection operator; $\dot{\bigcap}\emptyset = \emptyset$, and $\dot{\bigcap}X = \bigcap X$ for $X \neq \emptyset$, to guarantee that $RD^{\cap\ i}_{\varphi entry} \subseteq RD^{\cup\ i}_{\varphi entry}$, will hold for the smallest solution to the equation systems.

4.2   Analysis of Local Variables and Present Values of Signals

The Reaching Definitions analysis for the local variables corresponds to the Reaching Definitions analysis given in [9]. For the present value of signals it will use the result of the Reaching Definitions analysis for active signals. The idea is that if a signal has an active value when execution of the program arrives at a synchronization point, then the active value of the signal will become the present value of the signal after the synchronization.

The result of the Reaching Definitions analysis for active signals can be computed *before* we perform the Reaching Definitions analysis for local variables and signals. Hence the result can be considered a static set, and therefore the Reaching Definitions analysis for local variables and signals remains an instance of a Monotone Framework.

The Reaching Definitions analysis for present values of signals operates over the complete lattice $\mathcal{P}(Sig_\star \times Lab_\star)$ and is a *forward* data flow analysis. It yields an over-approximation of the assignments that **might** have influenced the present value of the signal. Its goal is to define two functions holding the information at the *entry* and *exit* of a given label in the program:

Table 5. Reaching Definitions Analysis for the local variables and present value of signals, for all labels l in the program $\|_{i \in I} i : \texttt{process } decl_i; \texttt{ begin } ss_i; \texttt{ end process } i$

$$kill \text{ and } gen \text{ functions}$$

$$kill_{RD}^{cf}([x := e]^l) = \{(x, ?)\} \cup$$
$$\{(x, l') | B^{l'} \text{ assigns to } x \text{ in process } i\}$$
$$kill_{RD}^{cf}([\texttt{wait on } S \texttt{ until } e]^l) = \hat{\bigcap}_{(l_1,\ldots,l_n) \in cf, s.t.\ l_i = l}$$
$$\bigcup_{j=1}^{n} fst(RD_{\varphi entry}^{\cap\ i}(l_j)) \times wS(ss_i)$$
$$kill_{RD}^{cf}([\ldots]^l) = \emptyset \text{ otherwise}$$

$$gen_{RD}^{cf}([x := e]^l) = \{(x, l)\}$$
$$gen_{RD}^{cf}([x(z_1 \texttt{ downto } z_2) := e]^l) = \{(x, l)\}$$
$$gen_{RD}^{cf}([x(z_1 \texttt{ to } z_2) := e]^l) = \{(x, l)\}$$
$$gen_{RD}^{cf}([\texttt{wait on } S \texttt{ until } e]^l) = \bigcup_{(l_1,\ldots,l_n) \in cf, s.t.\ l_i = l}$$
$$\bigcup_{j=1}^{n} fst(RD_{\varphi entry}^{\cup\ i}(l_j)) \times \{l\}$$
$$gen_{RD}^{cf}([\ldots]^l) = \emptyset \text{ otherwise}$$

$$\text{data flow equations: } RD$$

$$RD_{entry}^{cf}(l) = \begin{cases} \{(x, ?) \mid x \in FV(ss_i)\} \cup \{(s, ?) \mid s \in FS(ss_i)\} & \text{if } l = init(ss_i) \\ \bigcup\{RD_{exit}^{cf}(l') | (l', l) \in flow(ss_i)\} & \text{otherwise} \end{cases}$$
$$\text{where } B \text{ and } i \text{ is uniquely given by } B^l \in blocks(ss_i)$$

$$RD_{exit}^{cf}(l) = RD_{entry}^{cf}(l) \backslash kill_{RD}^{cf}(B^l) \cup gen_{RD}^{cf}(B^l)$$

$$RD_{entry}^{cf}, RD_{exit}^{cf} : Lab_\star \to \mathcal{P}((Var_\star \cup Sig_\star) \times Lab_\star)$$

The Reaching Definitions analysis for local variables and signals is given in Table 5 and makes use of two auxiliary functions. One is

$$kill_{RD}^{cf} : Blocks_\star \to \mathcal{P}((Var_\star \cup Sig_\star) \times Lab_\star)$$

that produces a set of pairs of variables or signals and labels corresponding to assignments that are overwritten by the block. An assignment to a local variable will overwrite all previous assignments on the execution path. A signal value can only be overwritten by a wait statement where at least one of the synchronizing processes has an active value for the signal. To guarantee that an active value for a signal is available, the under-approximation analysis ($RD_\varphi^{\cap\ i}$) described above in Section 4.1 is used.

Since the active signal has to be present in all possible processes the considered wait statement could synchronize with, an intersection over the set cf of cross flow information is needed.

The other auxiliary function is

$$gen_{RD}^{cf} : Blocks_\star \to \mathcal{P}((Var_\star \cup Sig_\star) \times Lab_\star)$$

that produces a set of pairs of variables or signals, and labels corresponding to the assignments generated by the block. Only assignments to local variables generate definitions of a variable. Only wait statements are capable of changing a signal's value at present time. This means that in our analysis signals will get their present value at wait statements in the processes. The result of the over-approximation analysis $(RD_\varphi^{\cup\ i})$ contains all the signals that might be active and thus defines the present value after the synchronization. Therefore we perform a union over all the signals that might be active in any process, that might be synchronized with.

Finally, all signals are considered to have an initial value in VHDL$_1$ hence a special label (?) is introduced to indicate that the initial value might be the one defining a signal at present time. The operator *fst* is defined by $fst(D) = \{s \mid (s, l) \in D\}$ and extracts the first components of pairs.

5   Information Flow Analysis

The Information Flow analysis is performed in two steps. First we identify the flow of information to a variable or signal locally at each assignment; this is specified in Section 5.1. Then we perform a transitive closure of this information guided by our Reaching Definitions analysis; this is described in Section 5.2 where we also compare the result of our method with that of Kemmerer [8].

The result of the Information Flow analysis is given in the form of a directed graph. The graph has a node for each variable or signal used in the program, and an edge from the node n_1 to the node n_2 if information **might** flow from n_1 to n_2 in the program. This graph will in general be non-transitive. To illustrate this point consider the following programs:

$$(a):\ [c := b]^1; [b := a]^2 \qquad\qquad (b):\ [b := a]^1; [c := b]^2$$

In program (a) there is a flow from b to c and a flow from a to b and therefore the resulting graph shown in Figure 3(a) has an edge from node b to node c and an edge from node a to node b. There is no flow from a to c and indeed there is no edge from a to c. In program (b) on the other hand there is a flow from a to c and the resulting graph shown in Figure 3(b) indeed has an edge from a to c.

5.1   Local Dependencies

It is clear that an assignment of a variable to another variable will cause a flow of information. As an example, a := b causes a flow of information from b to a. We also need to consider implicit flows due to conditional statements. As an example, if c then a := b else null has an implicit flow from c to a because an observer could use the resulting value of a to gain information about the value of c.

In this fashion we must consider all the statements of VHDL$_1$ and determine how information might flow. For a VHDL$_1$ program we define a set of structural rules that define the set of dependencies between local variables and signals. The analysis is defined using judgments of the form

$$B \vdash ss : RM$$

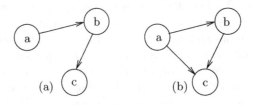

Fig. 3. Result of the Information Flow Analysis for programs (a) and (b)

where $B \subseteq (\mathbf{Var} \cup \mathbf{Sig})$, $ss \in \mathbf{Stmt}$ and $RM \subseteq ((\mathbf{Var} \cup \mathbf{Sig}) \times \mathbf{Lab} \times \{M_0, M_1, R_0, R_1\})$. Here ss is the statement analyzed under the assumption that it is only reachable when values of variables and signals in B have certain values. The result is the set RM containing entries (n, l, M_j) if the variable or signal n might be modified at label l in ss; we use M_0 for variables and present values of signals and M_1 for active values of signals. Similarly, RM contains entries (n, l, R_j) if the variable or signal n might be read at label l in ss; we use R_0 for variables and present values of signals and R_1 for the synchronization of active values of signals.

The local dependency analysis of the flow between variables and signals is specified in Table 6 and is explained below. Assignments to variables result in local dependencies, there are no other statements that causes information to flow into variables.

For the active signals in a program it holds that information can only flow to the signal through signal assignment. Hence only the signal assignment contributes dependencies to the resulting set. Notice that the information flowing to active signals (M_1) might come from both local variables and the present value of signals, but never from the active value of signals.

The variables and signals used in the evaluation of conditions within **if** and **while** statements are collected in the *block-set B* as they might implicitly flow into assigned variables or signals in the branches. This is taken care of in rules [**Conditional**] and [**Loop**]. Notice that these rules do not handle termination or timing channels that might occur.

The synchronization statements (i.e. **wait**) cause information about the active signals to flow to the present value of the same signals. Hence we will update (writing R_1) all signals present in the process considered.

5.2   Global Dependencies

Using the local dependencies defined above we can construct a Resource Matrix specifying for each point in the program which resources (i.e. a variable or signal) was modified and which resources were read meanwhile [8]. First we apply the local dependency analysis on each process in the considered program the result is collected in $RM_{lo} = \bigcup_i RM_i$ where $\emptyset \vdash ss_i : RM_i$. Then we need to compute the global dependencies; one way to do this is to take the transitive closure of

Table 6. Structural rules for constructing a Resource Matrix for the process i : process $decl_i$ begin ss_i; end process i

---

[Local Variable Assignment] :
$$B \vdash [x := e]^l : \{(x, l, M_0)\} \cup \{(n, l, R_0) \mid n \in FV(e) \cup FS(e) \cup B\}$$

$$B \vdash [x(z_1 \text{ downto } z_2) := e]^l :$$
$$\{(x, l, M_0)\} \cup \{(n, l, R_0) \mid n \in FV(e) \cup FS(e) \cup B\}$$

$$B \vdash [x(z_1 \text{ to } z_2) := e]^l :$$
$$\{(x, l, M_0)\} \cup \{(n, l, R_0) \mid n \in FV(e) \cup FS(e) \cup B\}$$

[Signal Assignment] :
$$B \vdash [s <= e]^l : \{(s, l, M_1)\} \cup \{(n, l, R_0) \mid n \in FV(e) \cup FS(e) \cup B\}$$

$$B \vdash [s(z_1 \text{ downto } z_2) <= e]^l :$$
$$\{(s, l, M_1)\} \cup \{(n, l, R_0) \mid n \in FV(e) \cup FS(e) \cup B\}$$

$$B \vdash [s(z_1 \text{ to } z_2) <= e]^l :$$
$$\{(s, l, M_1)\} \cup \{(n, l, R_0) \mid n \in FV(e) \cup FS(e) \cup B\}$$

[Skip] :
$$B \vdash [\text{null}]^l : \emptyset$$

[Composition] :
$$\frac{B \vdash ss_1 : RM_1 \qquad B \vdash ss_2 : RM_2}{B \vdash ss_1; ss_2 : RM_1 \cup RM_2}$$

[Conditional] :
$$\frac{B' \vdash ss_1 : RM_1 \qquad B' \vdash ss_2 : RM_2}{B \vdash \text{if } [e]^l \text{ then } ss_1 \text{ else } ss_2 : RM_1 \cup RM_2}$$
where $B' = B \cup FV(e) \cup FS(e)$

[Loop] :
$$\frac{B' \vdash ss : RM}{B \vdash \text{while } [e]^l \text{ do } ss : RM}$$
where $B' = B \cup FV(e) \cup FS(e)$

[Synchronization] :
$$B \vdash [\text{wait on } S \text{ until } e]^l : \{(s, l, R_1) \mid s \in FS(ss_i)\} \cup$$
$$\{(n, l, R_0) \mid n \in B \cup S \cup FV(e) \cup FS(e)\}$$
where ss_i is the body of process i in which l resides

---

the local dependencies; this method is attributed to Kemmerer and is described in [8] in case of traditional programming languages.

Let us evaluate the traditional method for constructing the Resource Matrix. For this we consider the program (a) defined above. The result of the transitive closure will correspond to the graph presented in Figure 3(b), but not to the true behavior of the program as depicted in the graph in Figure 3(a). This is due to the flow-insensitivity of the transitive closure method: The imprecision is a result of the method failing to consider information about the flow between labels in the programs.

Table 7. Specialization of $RD^{\cup\ i}_{\varphi entry}$ and RD^{cf}_{entry}

[RD for active signals]

$$\frac{(s, l_i, R_1) \in RM_{lo} \quad (s, l) \in RD^{\cup\ i}_{\varphi entry}(l_i)}{(s, l) \in RD^{\dagger}_{\varphi}(l_i)} \quad \text{if } \exists\,\overrightarrow{l} \in cf : l_i \text{ occurs in } \overrightarrow{l}$$

[RD for present signals and local variables]

$$\frac{(n, l', R_0) \in RM_{lo} \quad (n, l) \in RD^{cf}_{entry}(l')}{(n, l) \in RD^{\dagger}(l')}$$

Table 8. Transitive closure of Resource Matrix, based on $RD^{\dagger}$ and $RD^{\dagger}_{\varphi}$

[Initialization]

$$\frac{(n, l, A) \in RM_{lo}}{(n, l, A) \in RM_{gl}} \quad \text{where } A \in \{R_0, R_1, M_0, M_1\}$$

[Present values and local variables]

$$\frac{(n', l') \in RD^{\dagger}(l) \quad (n, l', R_0) \in RM_{gl}}{(n, l, R_0) \in RM_{gl}}$$

[Synchronized values]

$$\frac{(s', l_i) \in RD^{\dagger}(l) \quad (s', l'') \in RD^{\dagger}_{\varphi}(l_j) \quad (s, l'', R_0) \in RM_{gl}}{(s, l, R_0) \in RM_{gl}}$$
$$\text{if } \exists\,\overrightarrow{l} \in cf : l_i \text{ and } l_j \text{ occur in } \overrightarrow{l}$$

Closure based on Reaching Definitions. This motivates modifying the closure condition to make use of Reaching Definitions information. Indeed the Reaching Definitions analysis specified in Section 4 supplies us with the needed information to exclude some of the "spurious flows" when performing the transitive closure.

Before doing so we specialize in Table 7 the result of the Reaching Definitions analysis to allow a better precision in the closure of the Resource Matrix. The specialization ensures that definitions are only considered to reach a labeled construct if they are actually used in the labeled construct. This is done by considering the result of the local dependency analysis; notice the usage of the cross flow relation in rule **[RD for active signals]** which determines if the signal might in fact be synchronized.

We can now update the specification of the transitive closure using the result of the Reaching Definitions analysis, as is done in Table 8. We specify a rule for initializing the Global Resource Matrix **[Initialization]**.

The closure is done by rule **[Present values and local variables]** considering the result of the Reaching Definitions analyses for the program. For the present value of a signal and for local variables we consider each entry in the Resource Matrix, if the present value of a variable or signal is read (R_0) we can use the information of the Reaching Definitions analysis to find the label where the variable or signal was defined. Therefore we copy all the entries about variables and signals read at this label in the Resource Matrix. This rule also handles the

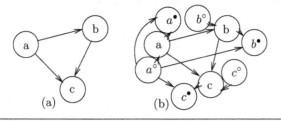

Fig. 4. Result of the Information Flow Analysis for program (b)

case where information flows from the variables and signals in a condition on a synchronization point.

The rule [**Synchronized values**] uses the result of the Reaching Definitions analysis to determine which signals were read in the Resource Matrix and follow them to their definition. When synchronizing signals the matter is complicated as the signal is defined at a synchronization point, therefore the rule needs to consider all the information about signals flowing into the synchronization points that might be synchronized with. Which synchronization points the definition point synchronizes with is gathered in the *cf* predicate, hence we apply the Reaching Definitions analysis for active signals on all the synchronization points and copy all the entries indicating variables and signals being read from the point the signal could be defined.

5.3   Improvement of the Information Flow Analysis

For the example program (b) (i.e. $[b := a]^1; [c := b]^2$) we previously described how the Information Flow Analysis would yield the result presented in Figure 4(a). In fact the resulting graph indicates that the resulting value of the variable b can be read from the resulting value of the variable c, which is entirely correct. However, the initial value of the variable b cannot be read from the variable c; to see this consider a scenario where b initially contained a value, this value would never flow to c, as the first assignment would overwrite the variable.

The Information Flow Analysis based on the Reaching Definitions Analysis can be improved to handle the initial and outgoing values of signals with greater accuracy. The idea is to add a node to the graph for each incoming signal, annotating the incoming node of a variable with a ∘, and for each outgoing signal, annotating the outgoing node with a •. Using this scheme a more precise result for program (b) can be constructed as shown in Figure 4(b), where we consider the last statement to be outcoming and therefore update the Resource Matrix in the same fashion as for wait statements.

The extension of the analysis is based on adding special variables and signals for incoming and outgoing values. The rules for improving the information flow analysis are presented in Table 9 and explained below.

In a traditional sequential programming language the improvement could be handled by adding assignments of the form $x := x^{\circ}$ for each variable read in front of the program, and similarly adding assignments $x^{\bullet} := x$ in the end for

Table 9. Rules for the improved Information Flow Analysis

[Initial values]	[Incoming values]		
$\dfrac{(n,?) \in RD^\dagger(l)}{(n^\circ, l, R_0) \in RM_{gl}}$	$\dfrac{(n, l') \in RD^\dagger(l) \qquad l' \in WS}{(n^\circ, l, R_0) \in RM_{gl}}$		
[Outgoing values]	[Outcoming values]		
$\dfrac{n \in Sig^{out}}{(n^\bullet, l_{n^\bullet}, M_1) \in RM_{gl}}$	$\dfrac{l \in WS \qquad (n, l') \in RD_\varphi^\dagger(l) \qquad (n', l', R_0) \in RM_{gl}}{(n', l_{n^\bullet}, R_0) \in RM_{gl}}$		

handling the outgoing values. Having this in mind we introduce the rule [**Initial values**] that uses the special symbol (?) from the Reaching Definitions analysis to propagate the initial value of a variable or locally defined signal.

$VHDL_1$ consists of processes running as infinite loops in parallel with other processes and under the influence of the environment. Therefore signals might carry incoming values at any synchronization point, similarly a process might communicate values out of the system at any synchronization point. We introduce a new process π to illustrate how the incoming and outgoing signals are handled. The process has the form

$$\pi : \texttt{process begin } [s_1^{in} <= s_1^\circ]; \ldots [\texttt{wait on } S^\pi]; [s_1^\bullet <= s_1^{out}]^{l_{s_1^\bullet}}; \ldots$$
$$\texttt{end process } \pi$$

where $s_1^{in}, s_2^{in}, \ldots$ are the incoming signals, $s_1^{out}, s_2^{out}, \ldots$ are the outgoing signals and S^π is the set of all incoming and outgoing signals, as specified in the entity declaration of the program.

The assignments prior to the synchronization point in process π can be synchronized into the system at each wait statement and this is handled by rule [**Incoming values**] where $WS = \bigcup_i WS(ss_i)$ are all the wait statements in the program.

We add two rules for the outgoing values to the closure method. The first rule [**Outgoing values**] specifies a special label for each signal (i.e. the label of the assignment to $n^\bullet$ in process π) used on the left-hand side in an assignment, at which the signal is set to be modified in the Resource Matrix. The second rule [**Outcoming values**] handles the right-hand side of the outgoing assignments in process π by considering all active signals coming into a wait statement, the values read when these active signals where modified are the signals that influence the outgoing value. Sig^{out} is the set of signals that are declared as outgoing (i.e. with the keyword out in the entity declaration).

6   Results

In order to compare our work to Kemmerer's method we shall consider part of the NSA *Advanced Encryption Standard* test implementation of the 128 bit version of the encryption algorithm [17]. Both the presented analyses and Kemmerer's method have been implemented using the Succinct Solver.

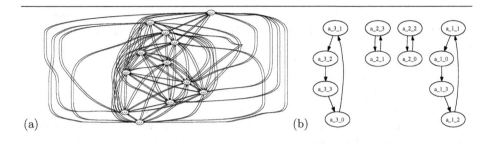

Fig. 5. Resulting graphs of Kemmerer's method (a) and our analysis (b) on a shift function

The analysed programs use several temporary variables. These variables are overwritten and reused for each input state. The graphs computed by Kemmerer's method indicate the problem of the method not taking control flow information into account; many edges are false positives resulting from the over approximation. Our analysis correctly eliminates the edges introduced by the overwritten variables.

To illustrate the difference between the two approaches, we consider the function shifting rows in a block. The first row is not altered by the function, while the last three rows are shifted 1, 2 and 3 positions respectively. The values flow through temporary variables, which are used for all three rows. The function is preprocessed by unrolling the loops and replacing constants with their values.

The resulting graphs are simplified so that only the nodes for the three shifted rows are presented. Furthermore we have merged incoming and outgoing nodes in the graph of our analysis. Therefore both of the resulting graphs for the three shifted rows have 12 nodes, and are now comparable. Kemmerer's method is unable to separate the shifts on each row as shown in Figure 5(a). Our analysis computes the precise result as shown in Figure 5(b).

7   Conclusion

One main achievement of the paper is the adaptation of the classical notion of Reaching Definitions analysis from traditional programming languages to real-time languages in the context of hardware description languages. We performed a development for a useful fragment of VHDL and correctly deal with the complications due to active and present values of signals. One unusual ingredient is the under-approximation analysis for active signals in order to be able to specify non-trivial kill-components for present values.

The other main achievement is the demonstration of the usefulness of the Reaching Definitions analysis for developing an Information Flow analysis that is more precise than the traditional method of Kemmerer. The local dependencies were specified by a straightforward inference system in the manner of information flow analyses. The global dependencies made good use of all aspects of the Reaching Definitions analysis.

Furthermore the improved information flow analysis correctly analyses programs that would incorrectly be rejected by typical security-type systems; as it is described in the *Open Challenge F* of [15]. This is due to the fact that the Reaching Definitions analysis allows us to kill overwritten variables and signals.

The current implementation directly follows the structure of the specifications given in the previous sections and one can argue that its worst case complexity is $O(n^5)$. So far this has posed no problems, however we conjecture that the implementation can be improved to have a cubic worst case complexity. The reason is that the analysis basically is a combination of three bit-vector frameworks (each being linear time in practice) [9] and a cubic time reachability analysis [1].

References

1. A. Aho, J. Hopcroft, and J. Ullman. *Data Structures and Algorithms*. Addison-Wesley, 1983.
2. P. J. Ashenden. *The Designer's Guide To VHDL*. Morgan Kaufmann, 2nd edition, 2002.
3. K. G. W. Goossens. Reasoning About VHDL Using Operational and Observational Semantics. In *CHDM*, volume 987 of *LNCS*, pages 311–327. Springer, 1995.
4. J. T. Haigh and W. D. Young. Extending the Non-Interference Version of MLS for SAT. In *IEEE Symposium on Security and Privacy*, pages 232–239, 1986.
5. Y-W. Hsieh and S. P. Levitan. Control/Data-Flow Analysis for VHDL Semantic Extraction. *Journal of Information Science and Engineering*, 14(3):547–565, 1998.
6. C. Hymans. Checking Safety Properties of Behavioral VHDL Descriptions by Abstract Interpretation. In *SAS*, volume 2477 of *LNCS*, pages 444–460. Springer, 2002.
7. IEEE inc. *IEEE Standard VHDL Language Reference Manual*. IEEE, 1988.
8. J. McHugh. Covert Channel Analysis. *Handbook for the Computer Security Certification of Trusted Systems*, 1995.
9. F. Nielson, H. R. Nielson, and C. Hankin. *Principles of Program Analysis*. Springer, 1999.
10. F. Nielson, H. R. Nielson, and H. Seidl. A Succinct Solver for ALFP. *Nordic Journal of Computing*, 9(4):335–372, 2002.
11. F. Nielson, H. R. Nielson, H. Sun, M. Buchholtz, R. R. Hansen, H. Pilegaard, and H. Seidl. The Succinct Solver Suite. In *TACAS*, volume 2988 of *LNCS*, pages 251–265. Springer, 2004.
12. H. R. Nielson and F. Nielson. *Semantics with Applications - A Formal Introduction*. John Wiley & Sons, 1992.
13. International Standards Organisation. Common Criteria for information technology security (CC). *ISO/IS 15408 Final Committee Draft, version 2.0.*, 1998.
14. J. Rushby. Noninterference, Transitivity, and Channel-Control Security Policies. Technical Report CSL-92-02, SRI International, December 1992.
15. A. Sabelfeld and A. C. Myers. Language-Based Information-Flow Security. *IEEE Journal on Selected Areas in Communications*, 21(1):5–19, 2003.
16. K. Thirunarayan and R. L. Ewing. Structural Operational Semantics for a Portable Subset of Behavioral VHDL-93. *FMSD*, 18(1):69–88, 2001.
17. B. Weeks, M. Bean, T. Rozylowicz, and C. Ficke. Hardware performance simulations of round 2 advanced encryption standard algorithms. Technical report, National Security Agency, 2000.

Composing Fine-Grained Parallel Algorithms for Spatial Dynamics Simulation*

Olga Bandman

Supercomputer Software Department,
ICMMG, Siberian Branch Russian Academy of Sciences,
Pr. Lavrentieva, 6, Novosibirsk, 630090, Russia
bandman@ssd.sscc.ru

Abstract. A class of fine-grained (FG) parallel models and algorithms is defined as a generalization of Cellular Automata (CA). It comprises all CA-modifications, in which two main CA-properties (locality and parallelism of intercell interaction) are preserved, no constraint being imposed on state alphabets and transition functions. A set of methods for composing a complex FG-algorithm out of a number of simple ones is proposed. To make compatible FG-algorithms with different alphabets, a number of algebraic operations on cellular arrays are introduced. The set of proposed composition methods has a two-level structure: the lower level comprises composition of cell transition functions, while the higher level deals with global operators on cellular arrays. For each type of proposed methods an example is given and the domain of application is determined.

1 Introduction

The problem of finding a proper mathematical model for simulation spatial dynamics of a complex phenomenon, which is given by some kind of qualitative or quantitative description, is sometimes extremely hard. The simulation is usually associated with a natural process investigation and requires large space-time dimensions, as well as the necessity of observing the process evolution in detail. The above requirements determine the main features of the models to be used. First, due to their complexity it should be easy to allocate the program on a number of processors to run it in parallel. Second, the computation should allow to construct a visual pattern at any time of the program run. To afford the above properties the simulation models have to rely upon two main principles: 1) inherent spatial parallelism, and 2) locality of state transition functions. Nowadays these principles characterize a number of spatial dynamics models. All of them take origin from the classical Cellular Automaton by von-Neumann, being its modification or generalization, having extended state alphabet (integer, real, symbolic), and/or arbitrary state transition functions (logical, arithmetic, deterministic, probabilistic). Moreover, different modes of operation (synchronous,

---

* Supported by Presidium of Russian Academy of Sciences, Basic Research Program N 17-6 (2004).

V. Malyshkin (Ed.): PaCT 2005, LNCS 3606, pp. 99–113, 2005.

n-step synchronous, asynchronous) are also studied. Being allocated according to the degree of discreteness, the set of FG parallel models represents a sequence with Boolean CA on one border, and the so called "continuous CA" – on the other border. The latter comprises the explicit form of PDE discretization, and may be considered as a representative of differential mathematics in a FG-models community.

By that time a large amount of FG–models of simple natural processes are proposed and well studied. The most known and practically used are CA models of diffusion [1], Gas-Lattice [2], phase-separation, pattern formation [3], chemical reactions [4], etc. Unfortunately, there is no formal procedure to construct a new fine-grained model according to a given qualitative or quantitative specification of the phenomenon to be simulated. It may be done either by experimental trial-and-error method or by combining simple models to represent the more complicated ones. The first way is rather heuristic and requires both good experience in CA modeling and sophisticated understanding of the phenomenon itself. The second way may be formalized but needs to accumulate case studies of simple models and develop a set of algebraic operations on them. The latter is a hard problem born of used alphabets (data types) differentiation, which do not allow to obey usual arithmetical rules. So, new operations on FG-algorithms are needed to express the results of several interacting processes, whose known models are of different type. For example, in reaction-diffusion and prey-predatory processes, diffusion may be given as a CA, and reaction – as a real function. Snow-flakes formation may be modeled by a Boolean CA, while if it happens in active medium, a chemical component should be added. So, to develop composition methods in FG domain the models belonging to it should be made compatible to allow mathematical operations on them. Some particular cases of composing Boolean CA with real spatial functions have been introduced in [5,6] for combining diffusion and reaction components. Moreover, some attempts to create a theoretical foundation for composition is presented in [7]. The main purpose of this article is to fill the gap and to present composition methods of FG-algorithms in a generalized and systematic form. To capture all features of the great diversity of FG-models the more general formalism for FG-algorithms representation, namely, Parallel Substitution Algorithm [8], is chosen as a mathematical tool.

Apart from the Introduction and the Conclusion the paper contains four sections. The second section contains definitions of the used concepts. In the third section algebraic operations on cellular arrays are proposed and analyzed. The fourth and the fifth sections are dedicated to composition methods on local and global FG-operators, respectively. All methods are illustrated by examples.

2   Formal Statement of the Problem

2.1   Main Concepts and Definitions

Fine-grained algorithms are intended for processing spatially distributed functions, represented by *cellular arrays* $\Omega = \{(u, m) : u \in A, m \in M\}$, which are finite sets of pairs (u, m) called *cells*, u being a *cell state variable* from the domain A, referred to as *alphabet*, m - a *cell name* from a discrete *naming set* M. No constraint is imposed on A, which is allowed to be Boolean vectors $A_B = \{(v_1 \ldots, v_n) : v_k \in \{0, 1\}\}$, real numbers from the closed interval $A_R = [0, 1]$, and a set of symbols $A_S = A, B, C, ..., K$. When any of above alphabets is implied the symbol u is used as a state variable. When the precise indication of the state variable domain is essential, v is used for the Boolean and z for the real ones. To indicate the state variable of a cell named m both notations $u(m)$ and u_m are used.

In the general case the naming set M may be of any kind, but further integer vector set, representing coordinates of a Cartesian space of finite size is used. For example, in the 2D case $M = \{(i, j) : i, j = 0, 1, \ldots, N\}$. A notion m instead of (i, j) is used for simplify general expressions and to indicate, that they are valid for any other kind of a naming set. A set of all cellular arrays having identical naming sets form a *cellular array class* denoted as Ω_M.

A mapping $\phi : M \rightarrow M$, called a *naming function* is defined on M. It determines for any m a neighbor $\phi(m)$ with whom a cell is allowed to interact. For the set $M = \{(i, j)\}$ naming functions are usually given in the form of shifts $\phi_k = (i + a, j + b)$, a, b being integers not exceeding a fixed r, called a *radius of neighborhood*. By condition, $\phi_0(m) = m$. The neighborhood of a cell is determined by a *template* as a set of naming functions

$$T(m) = \{m, \phi_1(m), \ldots, \phi_n(m)\}, \tag{1}$$

which associates to each name $m \in M$ a number of cell names, thereby determining the cell neighborhood, which is a subset of cells

$$S(m) = \{(u_0, m), (u_1, \phi_1(m)), \ldots, (u_n, \phi_n(m))\}, \tag{2}$$

which is called a *local configuration*, and $T(m)$ being its *underlying template*. The set $U(m) = \{u_0, u_1, \ldots, u_n\}$ forms a set of local confugaration state variables.

A cell $(u_m(t), m)$ changes its state to the next one $u_m(t + 1), m$ when a *local operator* is applied to it, which is expressed in the form of a *substitution* [8] as follows

$$\Phi(m) : S(m) \rightarrow S'(m), \tag{3}$$

where $S(m)$ is called a *base*, and $S'(m)$ – a *next state* of the substitution. The underlying templates of $S(m)$ and $S'(m)$ are in the following relation. $T'(m) \subseteq T(m)$, which means that some cells may remain unchanged by the substitution application. These cells form *a context* of the substitution $\Phi(m)$ with the underlying template $T''(m) = T(m) \setminus T'(m)$.

The cell states in $S'(m)$ are the results of a *cell transition function*,

$$u_m(t + 1) = f(u_0, u_1, \ldots, u_n), \quad u_j \in U(m). \tag{4}$$

where $U(m)$ is a state variables set of $S(m)$.

A *global operator* $\Phi(\Omega)$, which performs a transition from $\Omega(t)$ to $\Omega(t+1)$ is referred to as a *parallel substitution* [8]. An execution of a parallel substitution is the application of (3) to all $m \in M$. There are two main modes of parallel substitution application to a cellular array. The *synchronous* mode when all cells compute their next states in parallel and transit to the next state at once on time steps $t = 0, 1, \dots, \dots$, changing the global cellular array state, and the *asynchronous* mode when the cells execute the transitions at random or in a certain order. In all cases a computation of $\Phi(\Omega(t)) = \Omega(t+1)$ is considered as *an iteration*. The sequence $\Omega(0), \Omega(1), \dots, \Omega(t), \dots, \Omega(T)$ obtained by iterative application of a global operator to the initial array $\Omega(0)$, is called the *evolution*. The time T undicates the terminal step.

With the above notions an *FG-algorithm* Θ is defined as a global operator $\Phi(\Omega)$ which may be applied to any cellular array from a class Ω_M, i.e.

$$\Theta = (\Omega_M, \Phi(\Omega))$$

together with the indication of the operation mode. When $\Phi(\Omega)$ is a single parallel substitution of the form (3) Θ is considered to be an elementary FG-algorithm.

2.2   Operations on Cellular Arrays

In any class of cellular arrays Ω_M some algebraic operations are defined bellow to be used as tools in FG-composition methods. Like in any algebraic system unary and binary operations are recognized.

Unary operations are represented by parallel substitutions, which are considered to be *universal operators* due to their great expressive power. In fact, any mapping $\Omega_M \to \Omega_M$ may be represented in terms of parallel substitutions [8]. Nevertheless, two particular unary operators: averaging and Boolean discretization, are to be distinguished, because they serve as transformers of Boolean arrays into the equivalent real ones and vice versa.

Averaging of the Boolean cellular array $Av(\Omega_B)$ is a substitution of the form

$$\Phi_{Av}(m) : Av(m) \to \{(z, m)\}, \tag{5}$$

applied to all cells $m \in M$.

$$Av(m) = \{(v_0, \psi_0(m)), (v_1, \psi_1(m)), \dots, (v_q, \psi_q(m))\}, \tag{6}$$

is a base of $\Phi_{Av}(m)$, the next state local configuration is a single cell, whose state is computed according to the following local transition function

$$z = \frac{1}{q} \sum_{k=0}^{q} v_k, \quad v_k \in \{0, 1\}, \ z \in [0, 1]. \tag{7}$$

Boolean discretization of a real cellular array $Disc(\Omega_R)$ is a single-cell substitution of the form

$$\Phi_{Disc}(m) : \ \{(z, m)\} \to \{(v, m)\}, \text{ where } v = \begin{cases} 1, & \text{if } u < rand, \\ 0 & \text{otherwise} \end{cases} \tag{8}$$

applied to all $m \in M$. In (8) and further *rand* is a real random number in the interval [0,1].

The above two transformations are in the following relationship.

$$
\begin{aligned}
Disc(\Omega_B) &= \Omega_B, \\
Av(\Omega_R) &= \Omega_R, \\
Disc(Av(\Omega_B)) &= \Omega_B, \\
Av(Disc(\Omega_R)) &= \Omega_R.
\end{aligned}
\tag{9}
$$

Binary operators on a class of cellular arrays are defined on the basis of the requirement that ordinary arithmetical rules be valid for their averaged forms, i.e.

$$
\begin{aligned}
\Omega_1 \diamond \Omega_2 &\Leftrightarrow Av(\Omega_1) \diamond Av(\Omega_2), \\
u_1(m) \diamond u_2(m) &\Leftrightarrow \langle u_1(m) \rangle \diamond \langle u_1(m) \rangle \quad \forall m \in M,
\end{aligned}
\tag{10}
$$

where $\diamond$ stands for the cellular array operations: addition $\oplus$, subtraction $\ominus$ or multiplication $\otimes$, and $\diamond$ stands for arithmetical $+, -, \times$, respectively. Angle brackets denote averaged state values.

The reason of taking averaged state values as a generalized alphabet is twofold: 1) to allow ordinary arithmetic to be used for modeling spatial functions interactions, and 2) to make the results more comprehensive from physical point of view. The underlying template of the averaging area is chosen at the stage of simulation problem discretization according to accuracy requirement [9].

From (10) it follows that when all operands have real alphabets, the cellular array arithmetic coincides with the corresponding real cell-by-cell *arithmetical* rules. But when one or both operands have Boolean alphabet, cell-by-cell operations are not valid. So, if Ω_1 has Boolean alphabet, Ω_2 has a real one, and a Boolean arrays $\Omega_3 = \Omega_1 \oplus \Omega_2$ is wanted, the single cell local operator with the following transition function should be used [10].

$$
v_3(m) = \begin{cases} 1 & \text{if } v_1(m) = 0 \ \& \ rand < \frac{z_2(m)}{(1 - \langle v_1(m) \rangle)}, \\ v_1(m) & \text{otherwise.} \end{cases}
\tag{11}
$$

When $\Omega_3 = \Omega_1 \ominus \Omega_2$ is to be obtained a transition function should be as follows [10]

$$
v_3(m) = \begin{cases} 0 & \text{if } v_1(m) = 1 \ \& \ rand < \frac{z_2(m)}{\langle v_1(m) \rangle}. \\ v_1(m) & \text{otherwise.} \end{cases}
\tag{12}
$$

Since addition and subtraction are defined on cellular arrays with the alphabet restricted by the interval [0,1], the condition $0 \le u \le 1$ should be satisfied for all cells (u, m) in the resulting cellular array. If it is not so, the alphabet is to be renormalized. When both operands are Boolean and Boolean result is wanted, the values z_2 in (11) and (12) should be replaced by $\langle v_2 \rangle$. The above operations on cellular arrays form a set of tools for constructing complex FG-algorithms of a number of simple ones.

The set of FG-algorithms composition methods has two levels of hierarchy. The lower level (*local composition*) contains methods which aim to construct a composed local operator from a number of elementary substitutions. The higher level methods (*global composition*) aim to obtain a composed global operator from a number of parallel substitutions.

3   Local Composition Methods

A local composition operator $\lambda(\Phi_1(m), \ldots, \Phi_l(m))$ represents the common functioning of several simple local operators. Being applied to a cell (u, m) it results in its next state $u(t + 1)$. There are two forms of local composition: sequential and parallel.

3.1   Sequential Local Composition

The local composition $\lambda_s(\Phi_1(m), \ldots, \Phi_l(m))$ is said to be *sequential*, when l sequential substeps are needed to obtain the next state $u_m(t + 1)$.

The operation used for local sequential composition is a *local superposition*, i.e. application of a substitution $\Phi_k(m)$ to the result of $\Phi_{(k-1)}(m)$, so that the result is a single local operator of the following form.

$$\Phi(m) = \Phi_l(\Phi_{l-1}(\ldots(\Phi_1(m)))), \tag{13}$$

When the transition functions $f_k(U_k)$ and $f_g(U_g)$ of the form (4) in the component substitutions Φ_k and Φ_g, $k, g = 1, \ldots, l$, have different complexities, the sequential substep times $\tau_k(m)$ and $\tau_g(m)$, may be different, i.e. $\tau_k(m) \neq \tau_g(m)$. So, the time step needed for a cell to transit to the next iteration is as follows.

$$\tau(m) = \sum_{k=1}^{l} \tau_k(m), \tag{14}$$

In case when all $\tau_k(m)$ are identical, $\tau(m) = l\tau(m)$. Obviously, the time step for the global transition should be taken not less than the maximal $\tau(m)$ over all $m \in M$.

In the general case local superposition is neither commutative nor associative, i.e. if $\Phi_1 \neq \Phi_2 \neq \Phi_3$, then

$$\begin{aligned} \Phi_1(\Phi_2(m)) &\neq \Phi_2(\Phi_1(m)), \\ \Phi_3(\Phi_2(\Phi_1(m))) &\neq (\Phi_3(\Phi_2))(\Phi_1(m)). \end{aligned} \tag{15}$$

The above two properties are very important, because the results of the simulation may differ essentially if the order of superpositions is changed. Although in case of long evolution, the repetitive sequence of superpositions, for example, such as $\Phi_1(\Phi_2(\Phi_1(\Phi_2(m)\ldots)))$, makes the composition insensitive of the substitution being the first. If it is not the case, the only way to make the result independent of the order of substitutions in the composition is their random choice at any step of application (the Monte-Carlo method).

Example 1. A chemical reaction of CO oxidation over platinum metals, studied by means of a number of kinetic and continuous models [4,11], is represented by a local superposition of elementary substitutions as follows. The cellular array $\Omega(A, M)$ corresponds to a metallic plate, each site on it being named by $(i, j) \in M, |M| = N \times N$. The alphabet contains three symbols $A = \{a, b, 0\}$, so that $(a, (i, j)), (b, (i, j))$, and $(0, (i, j))$ are cells corresponding to the sites occupied by the molecules of CO, O or being empty, respectively. In the initial array all cells are empty. The reaction mechanism consists of the following elementary molecular actions in any cell named (i, j).

1) Adsorption of CO from the gas: if the cell (i, j) is empty, it becomes occupied by a CO molecule with probability p_a.

2) Adsorption of O_2 from the gas: if the cell (i, j) is empty and has an empty neighbor, both become occupied by a molecule of oxygen with probability p_b. One of the four neighbors of the cell (i, j) is chosen with probability $p_n = 0.25$.

3) Reaction of oxidation of CO (CO+0 $\rightarrow$ CO$_2$): if the cell (i, j) occurs to be in a CO state and its neighbor in O state, then the molecule CO$_2$, formed by the reaction, transits to the gas and both cells become empty. The neighbor to be tested for the cell (i, j) is chosen with probability $p_n = 0.25$.

4) Reaction of oxidation of CO (O+CO $\rightarrow$ CO$_2$), which is the same than in 3) but the cell (i, j) is in a state O and its neighbor is in the state CO.

The above chemical process is expressed in terms of a local superposition $\Phi(i, j) = \Phi_4(\Phi_3(\Phi_2(\Phi_1(i, j))))$ of the following substitutions:

$$\begin{aligned}
\Phi_1(i, j): & \ \{(0, (i, j))\} \rightarrow \{(a, (i, j))\}, \quad \text{if} \quad p_a > rand, \\
\Phi_2(i, j): & \ \{(0, (i, j))(0, \phi_k(i, j))\} \rightarrow \{(b, (i, j)), (b, (\phi_k(i, j))\}, \\
& \ \text{if} \ ((k-1)p_n < rand < kp_n) \ \& \ p_b > rand) \\
\Phi_3(i, j): & \ \{(a, (i, j))(b, \phi_k(i, j))\} \rightarrow \{(0, (i, j)), (0, (\phi_k(i, j))\}, \quad (16) \\
& \ \text{if} \ ((k-1)p_n < rand < kp_n)) \\
\Phi_4(i, j): & \ \{(b, (i, j))(a, \phi_k(i, j))\} \rightarrow \{(0, (i, j)), (0, (\phi_k(i, j))\}, \\
& \ \text{if} \ ((k-1)p_n < rand < kp_n))
\end{aligned}$$

In (16), each substitution $\Phi_l(i, j)$ (l=1,2,3,4) represents a molecular action mentioned in lth point in the above description of of the process. In Φ_2, Φ_3, and Φ_4, the naming function $\phi_k(i, j), k \in \{1, 2, 3, 4\}$, indicates to one of the four neighbors of the cell (i, j), namely $\phi_1(i, j) = (i, j + 1), \phi_2(i, j) = (i + 1, j), \phi_3(i, j) = (i, j - 1), \phi_4(i, j) = (i - 1, j)$.

Following [4], where Monte-Carlo simulation method is applied, i,e, asynchronous mode of simulation is chosen, the composed local operator $\Phi(i, j)$ should be applied $N \times N$ times to randomly chosen cells of Ω to obtain $\Omega(t+1)$.

In fig.1 three snapshots of the simulation process are shown, the initial cellular array $\Omega(0) = \{(0, (i, j)) : \forall (i, j) \in M\}, |M| = 200 \times 200$ with periodic boudary conditions.

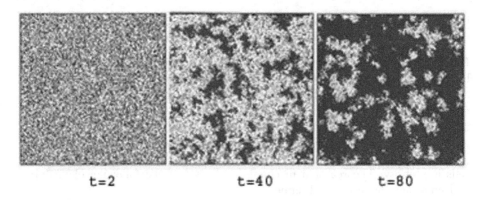

t=2   t=40   t=80

Fig. 1. Three snapshots of the simulation process given as a sequential local composition of the substitutions (16) with $|M| = 200 \times 200$. Black pixels stand for CO, gray pixels – for 0, and white pixels – for empty sites

3.2   Parallel Local Composition

A local composition $\lambda_p(\Phi_1(m), \ldots, \Phi_l(m))$ is called *parallel*, when all l component substitutions are executed in parallel, i.e. simultaneously or independently.

When the substitutions to be composed are completely independent, that is

$$T_k(m) \cap T_g(m) = \emptyset \quad \forall g, k, \in \{1, \ldots, l\},$$

parallel local composition is referred to as *trivial*.

When it is not the case, the set of substitutions should meet the condition of noncontradictoriness [8]. Necessary and sufficient conditions for two substitutions Φ_k and Φ_g to be *noncontradictory* are as follows. If there exists $m \in T'_k(m) \cap T'_g(m)$, with $T'_k(m)$ and $T'_g(m)$ being the underlying templates for $S'_k(m)$ and $S'_g(m)$, respectively, then

$$(u_k, m) \in S'_k(m) \& (u_g, m) \in S'_g(m) \Rightarrow u_k = u_g.$$

In other words, no cell with the same name may occur in different states at the same time-step. Some methods for providing a parallel substitution set to be noncontradictory are given in [8]. All of them require a great amount of computation. So, it seems reasonable to use the most simple sufficient noncontradictoriness condition. In terms of the next state local configurations it is as follows.

$$T'_k(m) \cap T'_g(m) = \emptyset,$$
$$S'_k(m) \cap S'_g(m) = \emptyset, \quad \forall k, g \in \{1, \ldots, l\}. \tag{17}$$

On the other hand, to operate in common, component substitution transition function should use common variables, i.e. each cell next state is the function of the state values of cells in local configurations of all substitutions under the composition.

$$u_k(t+1) = f_k(U_1(m) \cup U_2(m) \cup \ldots \cup U_l(m)) \quad \forall k = 1, \ldots, l,$$

where $U_k(m), k \in \{1, \ldots, l\}$ is a set of local configuration state variables from $S_k(m)$. Hence, the bases of the component substitutions as well as their underlying templates, should have nonempty intersections.

$$S_k(m) \cap S_g(m) \neq \emptyset,$$
$$T_k(m) \cap T_g(m) \neq \emptyset \quad \forall k, g \in \{1, \ldots, l\}, \tag{18}$$

Combining (17) and (18) the condition for nontrivial local parallel substitution is formulated as follows. The component substitutions may have nonempty intersections only by their context parts.

$$T'_k(m) \cap T'_g(m) = \emptyset$$
$$T''_k(m) \cap T''_g(m) \neq \emptyset \quad \forall k, g \in \{1, \ldots, l\}, \tag{19}$$

From the above it follows, that, as distinct from a sequential case, a parallel local composition is represented by a set of substitutions, i.e.

$$\lambda(\Phi_1(m), \ldots, \Phi_l(m)) = \{\Phi_1(m), \ldots, \Phi_l(m)\},$$

such that for any $\Phi_k : S_k(m) \to S'_k(m), \ k = 1, \ldots, l$, the following holds.

$$S'_k(m) \in \Omega_k, \quad S_k(m) \in \Omega, \quad \Omega = \bigcup_{k=1}^{l} \Omega_k \tag{20}$$

Example 2. A one-dimensional prey-predatory process in [12] is represented in the form of the following PDE system.

$$u_t = d_u u_{xx} + f_u(u, w)$$
$$w_t = d_w w_{xx} + f_w(w, u),$$

where d_u, d_w are diffusion coefficients for the two species, respectively.

$$f_u(u, w) = \left(\frac{35 + 16u - u^2}{9} - w\right)u, \quad f_w(u, w) = \left(u - \frac{5 + 2w}{5}\right)w. \tag{21}$$

In (21) u stands for predatory (fish) density, w stands for prey (plankton) density in an area of the ocean. When explicit scheme of time and space discretization is used the above process is expressed in terms of a fine-grained algorithm with real alphabet. Since two species are involved in the process, the composed parallel local operator requires the naming set to be the union of two isomorphic parts: $M_u = \{i_u\}$ and $M_w = \{i_w\}$, $i_u, i_w = 0, 1, \ldots, N$. Space and time steps for both parts being identical, $h_u = h_w = h$, $\tau_u = \tau_w = \tau$. The alphabet is a set of reals, state variables being denoted as u, w. The local configurations bases have three cells according to diffusion term discrete representation. Hence, the parallel composition consists of two following substitutions.

$$\Phi_u(i_u) : \{(u_{i-1}, i_u - 1), (u, i_u), (u_{i+1}, i_u + 1), (w, i_w)\} \to \{(u(t+1), i_u)\},$$
$$\Phi_w(i_w) : \{(w_{i-1}, i_w - 1), (w, i_w), (w_{i+1}, i_w + 1), (u, i_u)\} \to \{(w(t+1), i_w)\}, \tag{22}$$

the next states being as follows.

$$u(t + 1) = u + D_u(u_{i-1} - 2u + u_{i+1} + \tau f_u(u, w)),$$
$$w(t + 1) = w + D_w(w_{i-1} - 2w + w_{i+1} + \tau f_w(u, w)),$$
$$(23)$$

where $D_u = \tau d_u / h^2$ and $D_w = \tau d_w / h^2$

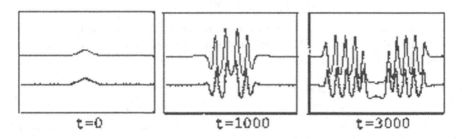

t=0   t=1000   t=3000

Fig. 2. Three snapshots of of the simulation of the prey-predatory process given by a parallel local composition (22) with $|N| = 251$. Black line stand for $u(i_u)$, gray line stands for for $w(i_w)$

From (21) it is seen that with $u(i_u) = 5, w(i_w) = 10, i_u, i_w = 0, 1, \ldots, N$, the system is stable and nothing is going on. But, when at any place the equilibrium is violated (Fig.2, t=0), then redistribution over the space starts on, resulting in propagating oscillations. In Fig.2 three snapshots $u(i), w(i)$ with $t = 0, t = 1000$, and $t = 3000$ of the process evolution are shown. The simulation is performed with the following parameters: the time-step τ=0.03 sec, the space-step h=120 cm, diffusion coefficients $d_u = 0.0125 \mathrm{cm}^2/\mathrm{sec}, d_w = 0.1 d_u$, which yields in $D_u = (\tau d_u / h^2) = 0.05, D_w = 0.005$.

4   Global Composition Methods

The *global composition* $\gamma(\Phi_1(\Omega), \ldots, \Phi_l(\Omega))$ is a representation of common functioning of a number of global operators, expressed in terms of parallel substitutions. Like in the case of local composition, sequential and parallel global compositions are distinguished.

4.1   Sequential Global Composition

The global composition $\Phi(\Omega) = \gamma_s(\Phi_1(\Omega), \ldots, \Phi_l(\Omega))$ is said to be *sequential*, when a set of parallel substitutions are applied sequentially on cellular arrays with identical naming sets, each next operator Φ_{k+1} being applied to the result of the previous one, $\Omega(k + 1) = \Phi_k(\Omega_k), k = 1, \ldots, l$. So, each iteration consists of l sequentially applied parallel substitutions, the result being a single global operator. The substep times $\tau_1, \ldots, \tau_l$, as well as the modes of operation may differ in different components. So, (13) is valid for sequential global composition, having regard to the fact that each τ_k is the timestep for $\Phi_k(\Omega)$. Hence, the timestep of the composed global operator τ depends also on the mode of operation of the components at any time being not less than the sum of time steps of all of them.

The operation used for the sequential global composition is a *global superposition*.

$$\Phi(\Omega) = \Phi_l(\Phi_{l-1}(\ldots(\Phi_1(\Omega)))), \tag{24}$$

Like in the local case, superposition of global operators is neither commutative nor associative. So, it is important to keep strictly the order of superposition prescribed by the process under simulation.

Example 3. A 2D phase separation process in an active medium is represented as a global superposition of three FG-algorithms: phase separation Boolean CA [13], Boolean diffusion by Margolus [1], and a nonlionear reaction function.

Phase separation CA is as follows.

$$\Phi_1(\Omega_1) : \{(v_k, \phi_k(i,j)) : \phi_k(i,j) = (i+g, j+h), g, h \in \{-2, 0, 2\} \rightarrow \atop \{(v', (i,j))\} \qquad \forall (i,j) \in M, \tag{25}$$

where

$$v' = \begin{cases} 1, & \text{if} \quad s < 24 \text{ or } v = 25, \\ 0, & \text{if} \quad s > 25 \text{ or } v = 24. \end{cases} \quad \text{where} \quad s = \sum_{g=-2}^{2} \sum_{h=-2}^{2} v_{i+g, j+h}.$$

Diffusion CA is represented as follows.

$$\Phi_2(\Omega_2) : \{(v_0, (i,j)), (v_1, (i+1, j)), (v_2, (i+1, j+1)), (v_3(i, j+1))\} \rightarrow \atop \{(v_0', (i,j)), (v_1', (i+1, j)), (v_2', (i+1, j+1)), (v_3', (i, j+1))\}, \tag{26} \atop \forall (i,j) \in M.$$

where

$$v_k' = \begin{cases} v_{(k+1)mod4}, & \text{if} \quad (rand > 0.5 \;\&\; t_{mod2} = i_{mod2} = j_{mod2} = 0), \\ v_{(k-1)mod4}, & \text{if} \quad (rand < 0.5 \;\&\; t_{mod2} = i_{mod2} = j_{mod2} = 1), \end{cases}$$

$k = 0, 1, 2, 3$, $rand$ is a random number in the interval [0,1]. From (26) it follows that diffusion component iteration has two substeps:an even substep when the even local configurations cell states are changed, and an odd substep when the odd local configurations cell states are updated. Changing states in local configarations is shifting them in the configuration blocks clockwise or counterclockwise with probability $p = 0.5$.

The activeness of the medium is modeled by a reaction function, which is given as a real function $F(z) = 0.5z(1 - z)$, which should be applied to each cell state of the array. Since the real function application to a Boolean array Ω_2 requires the latter to be averaged, the resulting cell states should be computed as $F(\langle v_{ij} \rangle)$, which is expressed in terms of substitution as follows.

$$\Phi_3(\Omega_2) : \{(\langle v_{ij} \rangle, (i,j))\} \rightarrow \{(v_{ij}', (i,j))\}, \quad \forall (i,j) \in M, \tag{27}$$

where

$$v'_{ij} = 0.5\langle v_{ij}\rangle(1 - \langle v_{ij}\rangle,) \quad \langle v_{ij}\rangle \in [0,1].$$

If a Boolean array is wanted as a final result, then $\Omega_3 = \Phi_3(\Omega_2)$ should be discretized according to (8).

So, the composed global operator is $\Phi(\Omega) = \Phi_3(\Phi_2(\Phi_1(\Omega_1)))$. The composition has been applied to an initial Boolean cellular array $\Omega(0)$ with randomly distributed $v = 1$ with the density $Av(i,j)) \approx 0.5$ for all $(v,(i,j)) \in \Omega(0)$, border conditions being periodic. In Fig.3 three snapshots of the process are shown, cellular arrays being averaged for making the observation more comprehensive. It is seen that on the first iterations the total amount of the substance decreases, but if some concentrated spots remain large enough, the chemical activeness enhances their growth up to the saturation.

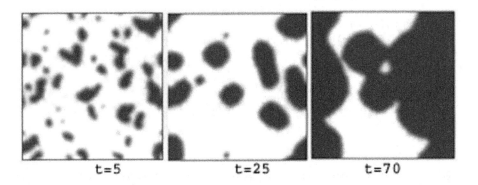

Fig. 3. Three snapshots of averaged cellular arrays of the phase separation process simulation according to the superposition of parallel substitutions given as (25),(26) and (27)

4.2   Parallel Global Composition

The global composition $\gamma_p(\Phi_1(\Omega),\ldots,\Phi_l(\Omega))$, is called *parallel*, if all its global components are to be executed in parallel. If therewith they do not interact, each functioning on its own cellular array and using its own variables, i.e. the condition (17) is met, then composition is referred to as a *trivial parallel composition*.

If the substitutions to be composed are functioning in common interacting at every iteration, then noncontradictoriness conditions are to be satisfied. In case of global parallel composition they are as follows.

$$\begin{matrix} T'_k \subset M'_k & T'_g \subset M'_g \\ M_k \cap M_g = \emptyset & \Omega_k \cap \Omega_g = \emptyset, & \forall k,g = 1,\ldots,l. \end{matrix} \tag{28}$$

It is clear, that from (28) the condition (17) for local parallel composition is straightforward, from what it appears, that any global parallel composition is locally parallel. The contrary is not always true.

In order to provide common functioning, the component substitutions should use common state variables from any cellular array involved in the composition. Thus, the underlying templates of the substitutions bases have nonempty intersections, i.e. (18) is satisfied. Hence, they belong to the common naming set $M = \bigcup_{k=1}^{l}(M_k)$.

From the above it follows, that a parallel global composition is a set of substitutions

$$\gamma_p(\Phi_1(\Omega_1), \ldots, \Phi_l(\Omega_l)) = \{\Phi_1(\Omega), \ldots, \Phi_l(\Omega)\},$$

each being a branch of a parallel computation, where

$$\Phi_k(\Omega) : S_k(m) \rightarrow S_k'(m_k) \quad S_k(m) \in \Omega, \quad S_k'(m_k) \in \Omega_k, \tag{29}$$

and

$$\Omega = \bigcup_{k=1}^{l} \Omega_k \tag{30}$$

all M_k, $k = 1, \ldots, l$ being identical, and, hence, all Ω_k, belong to one and the same class Ω_M.

Example 4. Phase separation process given by a CA $\Phi_1(\Omega_1))$ as a substitution (25) in Example 3, may also be simulated by the following PDE [6].

$$u_t = 0, 2(u_{xx} + u_{yy}) - 0.2(u - 0.1)(u - 0.5)(u - 0.9), \tag{31}$$

After applying exlicit scheme of discretization which corresponds to a tempate

$$T(i,j) = (u_0, (i,j), (u_1, (i-1, j)), (u_2, i, j+1)), (u_3, (i+1, j)), (u_4, (i, j-1)),$$

the equation (31) takes a form of the following parallel substitution.

$$\Phi_2(\Omega_2) : \{(u, (i,j)), (u_1, (i-1, j)), (u_2, (i, j+1)), (u_3, (i+1, j)), (u_4, (i, j-1))\}$$
$$\rightarrow \{(u(t+1), (i,j)\}. \tag{32}$$

In order to compare the evolutions generated by the above two phase separation algorithms, a parallel composition $\gamma_p(\Phi_1, \Phi_2, \Phi_3)$ is constructed, where $\Phi_1(\Omega_1)$ given by (25) and $\Phi_2(\Omega_2)$ given by (32) are functioning independently and the third algorithm computes at every iteration the absolute value of the their difference, $\Omega_3(t) = |\Omega_2(t) \ominus \Omega_1(t)|$, $\Omega_3(t) = \{(z, (i,j))\}$ being a real cellular array.

$$\Phi_3(\Omega) : \{(\langle v(i,j) \rangle, (i,j)\} - \{(u, (i,j)\} \rightarrow \{(z(t+1), (i,j)\},$$
$$\forall(i,j) \in M_3, \tag{33}$$

where according to (7) and (10)

$$z(t+1) = \frac{1}{q} \left| \sum_{k=0}^{q} v_k - z \right|, \quad q = |Av(i,j)|.$$

In Fig.4 three snapshots of $\Phi_3(\Omega)$ are shown.

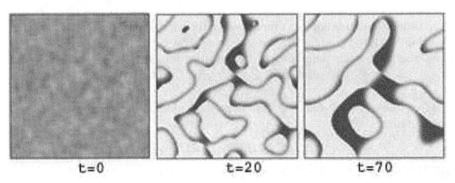

Fig. 4. Three snapshots of global parallel composition simulating the difference (33) between PDE (31) and CA phase-separation model (25)

Of course, the composition of composed algorithms is also allowed provided that all components are on the one and the same level. It means, that in local compositions only locally composed components may be used. Similarly, in global compositions only global ones may serve as components, which is on no account a constraint due to the fact that any global operator is a local one applied to all cells of the cellular array.

5   Conclusion

The proposed methodology of fine-grained algorithm composition allows to extend the domain of their application. Due to the introduced operations on cellular arrays with Boolean and real data types, it diminishes the gap between two main types of spatial dynamics models: cellular automata and partial differential equations. Explicit numerical methods of PDE solutions may be considered as a bridge across the gap which makes possible the use of both types of models in a single complex simulation task. It seems to be very important in view of modern computational technologies oriented to be implemented on multiprocessor systems, because of the simplicity and efficiency of fine-grained algorithms parallel realization.

References

1. Toffolli T., Margolus N.: Cellular Automata Machines. MIT Press, USA (1987)
2. Rothman D.H., Zaleski S.: Lattice-Gas Cellular Automata. Simple Models of Complex Hydrodynamics. Cambridge University Press, London (1997)
3. Wolfram S.: A New Kind of Science. Wolfram Media Inc., Champaign, Ill., USA (2002)
4. Latkin E.I.,Elokhin V.I.,Gorodetskii V.V.: Spiral concentration waves in the Monte-Carlo model of CO oxidation over Pd(110) caused by synchronization via $CO_a ds$ diffusion between separate parts of catalytic surface. Chemical Engineering Journal 91 (2003) 123-131.
5. O.Bandman. Simulation Spatial Dynamics by Probabilistic Cellular Automata. Lecture Notes in Computer Science 2493 (Eds S.Bandini, B,Chopard,M.Tomassini) Springer, Berlin (2002) 10-19.

6. Weimar J.R. Cellular Automata for reaction-diffusion systems. Parallel Computing 23 (11) (1997) 1699-1715.

7. Bandman O. Algebraic Properties of Cellular Automata: the Basis for Composition Technique. Lecture Notes in Computer Science 3305 (Eds. Sloot P.M.A., Chopard B., Hoekstra A.G.) (2004) 688-698.

8. Achasova S., Bandman O., Markova V., Piskunov S. Parallel Substitution Algorithm. Theory and Application. World Scientific, Singapoore (1994).

9. Bandman O. Accuracy and Stability of Spatial dynamics Simulation by Cellular Automata Evolution. Lecture Notes in Computer Science 2763 (Ed. V.Malyshkin) (2003) 20-34.

10. O.Bandman Spatial Functions Approximation by Boolean Arrays. Bulletin of Novosibirsk Computer Center, series Computer Science, N 19, Novosibirsk, ICMMG (2003) 10-19.

11. Chopard B., Droz M. Cellular Automata Approach to nonequilibrium phase transition in a surface reaction model: static and dynamics properties. Journal of Phisics A. Mathematical and General 21 (1988) 205-211.

12. Svirezhev Yu. Nonlinear waves, dissipsative structures and catastrophes in ecology. Nauka, Moscow (1987)

13. Vichniac G. Simulating Physics by Cellular Automata. Physica D, 10 (1984) 86-112.

Situated Agents Interaction: Coordinated Change of State for Adjacent Agents

Stefania Bandini, Sara Manzoni, and Giuseppe Vizzari

Dipartimento di Informatica, Sistemistica e Comunicazione,
Università degli Studi di Milano–Bicocca,
Via Bicocca degli Arcimboldi 8, 20126 Milano, Italy
{bandini, manzoni, vizzari}@disco.unimib.it

Abstract. Situated Multi Agent System models are characterized by the fact that the environment in which these autonomous entities are placed has an explicit spatial structure influencing their behaviours and interactions. Coordination mechanisms for agents exploiting the contextual spatial information can be defined. In particular this paper focuses on issues and proposed solutions related to the coordinated change of state for agents positioned in adjacent places.

1 Introduction

Agent coordination represents a very active and challenging area of the research in Multi-Agent Systems (MAS). The term coordination refers to the interaction mechanisms that allow autonomous agents to select and carry out their actions within a concerted framework. The separation of the agent computation model, specifying the behaviour of a single agent, from the coordination model is a proposal that goes back to the early nineties [6]. In particular, the concept of Linda tuple space [5] and the related coordination language is the most diffused metaphor adopted by current coordination languages and approaches. The basic model has been enhanced in order to allow a distributed implementation of the conceptually centered tuple space [14]. Moreover tuple spaces have been also extended to allow the specification of tuple-based coordination media presenting reactive and programmable behaviours (see, e.g., [12,13,4]), and also the specification and enforcement of organizational abstractions and constraints (e.g. roles, access control rules) to agent coordination [15].

Situated MASs (see, e.g., [1,8,17]) are particular agent based models which provide the representation and exploitation of spatial information related to agents and their position into the environment they inhabit. While the previously defined approaches to agent coordination provide general-purpose coordination languages and mechanisms, situated MASs present issues that could benefit from specific mechanisms for agent interaction. For instance, the concept of *field* (i.e. a signal that agents may spread in their environment, which can influence the behaviour of other entities) has been widely adopted for the generation of coordinated movements (see, e.g., [2,8]). This kind of mechanism is devoted to the interaction of agents which may be positioned on distant points of their space,

V. Malyshkin (Ed.): PaCT 2005, LNCS 3606, pp. 114–128, 2005.

but there can be situations in which agents which are in direct contact (considering a discrete representation of agents' environment) may wish to perform a coordinated change in the respective state (for instance in order to model the exchange of information) without causing modifications in the environment. In fact, field based interaction and other approaches focused on modelling agent environment, are intrinsically multicast interaction mechanisms that may be useful to represent actions and interactions that should be *observable* by other entities in the system. However this observability property should not automatically characterize all possible actions and interactions of a Multi Agent model. To this purpose, Multilayered Multi Agent Situated System (MMASS) [1] defines the *reaction* action which allows the coordinated change of the states of agents which are positioned in sites forming a clique (i.e. a complete subgraph) in the spatial structure of their environment. This operation, which also allows a direct exchange of information among the involved entities, is not observable by other agents. The aim of this paper is to describe issues related to coordinated changes in the state of situated agents, and propose approaches for the management of these issues, with specific reference to the reaction MMASS action.

The following section will better describe the problem, showing how existing situated MAS approaches tackle the issue of coordinated agent change of state. Section 3 will focus on the design and implementation of mechanisms supporting coordinated change of state of situated agents, discussing synchronous and asynchronous cases. Conclusions and future developments will end the paper.

2 Coordinated Change of State in Situated MASs

Despite most agent definitions emphasize the role of the environment, currently most model do not include it as a first class abstraction. The number of situated MAS models (that are models providing a representation of spatial features of agent environment) is thus relatively small, and the topic of coordinating the change of state of situated agents is still not widely analyzed.

One of the first approaches providing the possibility to define the spatial structure of agents' environment is represented by Swarm [10]. Swarm and platforms derived by it (e.g. Repast[1], Mason [7]) generally provide an explicit representation of the environment in which agents are placed, and often provide mechanisms for the diffusion of signals. Nonetheless they generally represent useful libraries and tools for the implementation of simulations, but do not provide a comprehensive, formally defined *interaction model*. In other words they do not provide support to the coordinated change of state among agents, but just define and implement a spatial structure in which agents, and sometimes signals, may be placed. Moreover, they generally provide a sequential execution of agents' behaviours (that are triggered by the environment, which is related to the only thread of execution in the whole system). This approach prevents concurrency issues and allows to obtain compact and efficient simulations even with a very high number of entities. The price of these characteristics is essentially

---

[1] http://repast.sourceforge.net

that agents are not provided with a thread of execution of their own (i.e. they have a very limited autonomy and proactiveness), and the execution of their behaviours is sequential (although not necessarily deterministic).

The Co-Fields [8] approach and the Tuples On The Air (TOTA) middleware [9] provide the definition and implementation of a field based interaction model, which specifically supports this kind of interaction that implies a local modification of agents' environment. However the defined interaction mechanism does not provide the possibility to have a coordinated change of agent state without such a modification. A different approach to the modelling and implementation of situated MAS [17] instead focuses on the definition of a model for simultaneous agent actions, including centralized and (local) regional synchronization mechanisms for agent coordination. In particular, actions can be independent or interfering among each other; in the latter case, they can be mutually exclusive (*concurrent* actions), requiring a contemporary execution in order to have a successful outcome (*joint* actions), or having a more complex influence among each other (both positive or negative).

The previously introduced MMASS model provides two mechanisms for agent interaction. The first is based on the concept of *field*, that is a signal that may be emitted by agents, and will spread in the environment according to its topology and to specific rules specifying field diffusion functions. These signals may be perceived by agents which will react according to their specific behavioural specification. The model also defines the possibility for having a coordinated change of agent state through the *reaction* operation. The outcome of this joint action depends on three factors:

- agents' *positions*: reacting agents must be placed in sites forming a complete subgraph in the spatial structure of the environment;
- agents' *behavioural specifications*: agents must include compatible reaction actions in their behavioural specification;
- agents' *willingness* to perform the joint action: one of the preconditions for the reaction is the agreement among the involved agents.

The following section will discuss issues related to the design and implementation of this operation, but several considerations are of general interest in the development of mechanisms supporting the coordinated change of state for situated agents.

3   Reaction

Reaction is an activity that involves two or more agents that are placed in sites forming a clique (i.e. a complete subgraph) and allows them to change their state in a coordinated way, after they have performed an agreement. The MMASS model does not formally specify what this agreement process consists of, and how the activities related to this process influence agent behaviour. This choice is due

```
begin
turn:=0;
do
    begin
    localContext:=environment.sense(turn);
    nextAction:=actionSelect(localContext);
    outcome:=environment.act(nextAction,turn);
    if outcome<>fail then
        turn:=turn+1;
    end
while(true);
end
```

Fig. 1. Agent behaviour thread in a synchronous situation.

to the fact that such an agreement process could be very different in different application domains (e.g. user authentication, transactions). For instance, in some of these situations an agent should block its activities while waiting for the outcome of the agreement process, while in others this would be unnecessary. Especially in a distributed environment this agreement process could bring to possible deadlocks, and in order to better focus this subject, more details on internal mechanisms related to agent, to the environment and its composing parts must be given.

3.1 Synchronous Environments

In synchronous situations a global time step regulates the execution of agents actions; in particular, every agent should be allowed to carry out one action per turn. In order to enforce synchronicity, the management of system time step and agent actions can be delegated to agents' *environment*, that they invoke not only for functional reasons (i.e. perform an action which modifies the environment) but also to maintain system synchronicity (i.e. agent threads are put into a wait condition until the environment signals them that the global system time step has advanced). This proposal assumes that agents are provided with one thread of execution, and also provides that the environment has at least one thread of execution of its own. In fact the environment is responsible for the management of field diffusion (more details on this subject can be found in [3]), other modifications of the environment (as consequences of agents' actions), and to enforce system synchronicity.

In the following, more details on agent and environment activities and threads of execution will be given; the situation that will be considered provides one thread for every agent, and a synchronous system. The described approach is valid both for centralized and for distributed situations; in the latter case one of the sites must be elected as a representative of the whole environment, and interactions with the environment can be implemented through a remote invocation protocol (e.g. RMI or others, according to the chosen implementation platform).

Agent Behaviour Management Thread. The sequence of actions performed in the agent behaviour thread is the following:

```
begin
turn:=0;
do
    begin
    until(forall i in 1..n, agent_i.actionperformed=true)
        begin
        collect(agent_i,action,agentTurn)
        if agentTurn=turn then
            begin
            manage(agent_i,action, turn);
            agent_i.actionperformed:=true;
            end
        else
            agent_i.wait();
        end
    turn:=turn+1;
    forall i in 1..n
        agent_i.actionperformed:=false;
    notifyAllAgents();
    end
while(true);
end
```

Fig. 2. Environment behaviour thread in a synchronous situation

- *sense its local context*: in order to understand what are the actions whose preconditions are verified, the agent has to collect information required for action selection, and more precisely: *active fields* in the site it is positioned on and adjacent ones; *agents* placed in adjacent sites, and their types;
- *select which action to perform*: according to the action selection strategy specified for the system (or for the specific agent type), the agent must select one action to be performed at that turn (if no action's preconditions are satisfied, the agent will simply skip the turn);
- *perform the selected action*: in order to perform the previously selected action, the agent must notify the environment, because the action provides a modification of agent's local context or even simply to maintain system synchronicity.

The last step in agent behavioural management cycle may cause a suspension of the related thread by the environment. In fact an agent may be trying to perform an action for turn t while other ones still did not perform their actions for turn $t - 1$. A pseudo-code specification of agent behavioural thread sequence of activities is shown in Figure 1. Agents must thus keep track of current turn and of the previously performed action. In fact, as will be introduced in the following subsection, system dynamics might require an agent to reconsider its action when it is involved in a reaction process.

Environment Management Thread. The environment, more than just managing information on agents' spatial context, also acts as a monitor in order to handle concurrency issues (e.g. synchronization, agreements among agents). Agents must notify the environment of their actions, and the latter will manage these actions performing modifications to the involved structures (e.g. sites and active fields) related to the following turn. The state of the current one must be preserved, in order to allow its sensing and inspection by agents which still did

```
procedure reactionManagement(agent, action, turn)
    begin
    involvedAgents:=action.getReactionPartners();
    reactingAgents:=new list();
    reactingAgents.add(agent);
    agreed:=true;
    forall agent_i in involvedAgents
        begin
        if agent_i.agreeReaction(involvedAgents) = false then
            begin
            agreed:=false;
            break;
            end
        reactingAgents.add(agent_i);
        end
    if agreed=true then
        forall agent_i in reactingAgents
            agent_i.performReact(turn);
    else
        forall agent_i in reactingAgents
            agent_i.notifyFailure(turn);
    end
```

Fig. 3. Reaction management procedure in a synchronous situation

not act in that turn. The environment may also put an agent into a *wait* condition, whenever performing its action would break system synchronicity. This wait ends when all agents have performed their action for the current turn, and thus all entities are free to perform actions for the next one. The environment must thus keep track of the actions performed by agents in the current turn, and then notify waiting agents whenever system time advances. More schematically, a pseudo-code description of the environment thread of execution is shown in Figure 2. In particular the **manage** function inspects the specified action (which includes the required preconditions and parameters), checks if it is valid and then calls the appropriate subroutines which effectively perform actions. The previously introduced sequences require a slight integration to specify how reaction actions are managed. In this case the beginning of an agreement process stops other agent actions until this process is over, either positively (when all other involved agents agreed) or negatively (when the agreement failed). In this way, also system time advancement is stopped until the reaction process is over, preserving system synchronicity.

The reaction is triggered by the agent which first requires the execution of this action to the environment. The latter becomes the leader of the group of involved agents, queries them asking if they agree to take part in the reaction, if an agreement is reached it signals them to change their state, then starts again the normal system behaviour, allowing the advancement of global system time step and thus agent execution. More schematically the environment procedure devoted to the management of reaction is shown in Figure 3. An agent receiving a **notifyFailure** will have a **fail** outcome, and thus will not advance its time step and will start over again its behavioural cycle for the current turn. The **reactionManagement** procedure is one of the specific subroutines invoked by the the environment thread of execution previously shown in Figure 2 through the **manage** function.

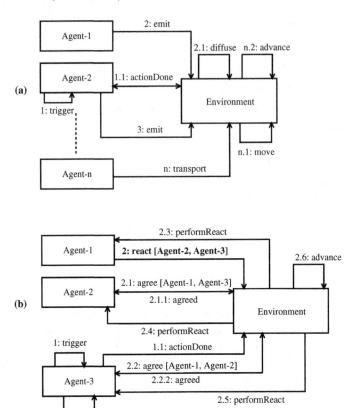

Fig. 4. A sample scenario illustrating the evolution of a centralized synchronous MMASS system

Examples. A sample scenario illustrating the evolution of a centralized synchronous MMASS system is shown is Figure 4. Scenario (a) provides the presence of a set of agents (Agent-1, ..., Agent-n), which do not require the execution of reaction actions. The system dynamics is the following:

• Agent-2 performs a trigger (action 1);
• Agent-1 emits a field (action 2) and as a consequence the environment performs its diffusion (action 2.1);
• Agent-2 also tries to perform an emission (action 3), but the environment puts it into a wait condition, as other agents did not perform their actions in that turn;
• agents that are not shown in the Figure perform their actions, which are managed by the environment;
• eventually Agent-n performs a transport action (action n), and as a consequence the environment performs its movement (action n.1), advances system time (action n.2) and eventually notifies agents. Agent-2 emit action (action 3) will now be managed.

```
begin
do
    begin
    localContext:=mysite.sense();
    nextAction:=actionSelect(localContext);
    outcome:=site.act(nextAction);
while(true);
end
```

Fig. 5. Agent behaviour thread in an asynchronous situation

A different case is shown in scenario (b), which exemplifies the sequence generated by a reaction request. Agent-1, Agent-2 and Agent-3 are positioned in sites forming a clique. In this case system dynamics is the following:

• Agent-3 performs a trigger (action 1);
• Agent-1 requires the environment to perform a reaction with Agent-2 and Agent-3 (action 2);
• as a consequence to this request, the environment asks Agent-2 if it intends to agree in preforming the reaction (action 2.1) and it receives a positive reply (action 2.1.1); the environment then asks Agent-3 if it wishes to reconsider its action for the current turn (action 2.2); the agent performs anew an action selection (action 2.2.1) and decides to agree(action 2.2.1);
• the environment indicates all involved agents that they must perform the reaction (actions 2.3 – 2.5) and then advances system time.

Discussion. The previously described approach to the management of agents, their cycle of execution, their environment and reaction mechanisms provides a key role of the environment, which represents a sort of medium ensuring specific properties, and especially system synchronicity. This is a global feature of the system, and the simplest way to ensure it is to have a conceptually centralized unit to which all entities must refer in order to perform their actions. This medium and coordination models providing a centralized medium (e.g. a tuple space) seem thus similar, in fact, both provide an indirect interaction among agents and must tackle issues related to the concurrent access to shared resources. The main difference is the fact that, for instance, a Linda tuple space does not provide abstractions for the definition of spatial information (e.g. a topology, an adjacency relation), that should be modelled, represented and implemented. An interesting feature of advanced artifact based interaction models, and more precisely reactive and programmable tuple spaces, is the possibility to specify a behaviour for the artifact, which could be a way to implement interaction mechanisms defined by the MMASS model.

The described approach provides computational costs that could be avoided, in a centralized situation, by providing a single thread of execution, preventing synchronization issues by activating agents in a sequential (although non necessarily deterministic) way (i.e. adopting the approach exploited by Swarm–like simulation platforms). Whenever autonomy and proactiveness are not central elements in agent modelling, this could be a feasible and cost effective choice. It could be the case of simulations characterized by a large number of enti-

```
begin
do
    begin
    reactionRequest:=mysite.getReactionRequest();
    newReactManager:=new ReactManagerThread(reactionRequest);
    newReactManager.start();
while(true);
end
```

Fig. 6. Agent reaction detection thread in an asynchronous situation

ties endowed with very simple behavioural specification. However, the described approach can useful when integrating into a single environment entities characterized by a higher degree of autonomy, proactiveness and heterogeneity (for instance, reactive and deliberative agents developed with deeply different approaches).

3.2   Asynchronous Environments

In an asynchronous situation, the mechanisms for the management of agents and their interactions with the environment, are on one hand simpler than in a synchronous case (i.e. there is no need to ensure that every agent acts once per turn), but can also be more complex as there are less constraints on action timings. In a centralized situation, it is still possible to delegate the management of shared resources to an environment entity, whose task is actually simpler than in a synchronous situation as it does not have to maintain global system synchronicity, although it must guarantee the consistent access to shared resources. In a distributed and asynchronous situation, even if it would be possible to elect a single representative of agents' environment (like in the synchronous and distributed case, described in the previous Section), this possibility would represent a bottleneck and is not even necessary. In fact, the main reason for the presence of a single representative of agent environment was to assure system synchronicity. This Section will then focus on a distributed and asynchronous scenario, and will describe a distributed approach providing the collaboration of *sites*, instead of a single centralized environment, for the management of coordinated change of agents' states.

Agent Related Threads. As previously introduced, agents will now collaborate directly with the sites they are placed on, and their behavioural threads must thus be changed. A pseudo-code formalization of agent behaviour thread in an asynchronous situation is shown in Figure 5.

Another change that can be introduced in the agent is the presence of a distinct thread for the management of reaction requests. In fact the agreement process required by the reaction process can require a certain number of interaction among agents which are placed in computational units spread over a network. This means that a relevant delay may occur from the beginning of an agreement process and its outcome (either positive or negative). Being in an asynchronous situation there is no need to stop agent behavior in order to wait for this process to end. An agent may be provided with three kinds of threads:

```
begin
myReactAction:=this.getAction(reactionRequest);
if myReactAction<>null then
    begin
    if reactionRequest.author <> this then
        begin
        agreed:=checkAgreement(reactionRequest);
        site.replyReactReq(reactionRequest, agreed);
        end
    if agreed=true then
        begin
        agreemReached:=site.getReactAgreement(reactionRequest);
        if agreemReached=true then
            this.changeState(myReaction.nextState);
        end
    end
else
    site.replyReactReq(reactionRequest, false);
end
```

Fig. 7. Agent reaction management thread in an asynchronous situation

- its behavioural thread, which is very similar to the one related to the synchronous situation, and whose structure is shown in Figure 5;
- a thread which is devoted to the detection of reaction requests; this thread is responsible to query the site for pending reaction requests (which may occur concurrently) and start the third kind of thread which will manage the agreement process; a pseudo-code formalization of this thread is shown in Figure 6;
- threads that are devoted to the effective management of the reaction process; a pseudo-code formalization of this thread is shown in Figure 7. This kind of thread must check if the agent effectively agrees to perform the reaction, through the **checkAgreement** invocation (only if it is not the one which actually started the reaction process). This means that first of all the agent must have a react action matching the one specified by the request (this is checked through the **getAction** invocation). Then it must wait the notification of the success or failure of the agreement (the **getReactAgreement** invocation may in fact suspend this thread) and, in the former case, change the agent state.

Site Related Threads. Similar considerations on the internal structure of agents may be also done for sites. The latter act as a interfaces between agents and the rest of the environment, and must manage events generated both internally and externally. In particular, *internal events* are generated by an agent that is positioned on the site, and more precisely they are the following ones:

- *sense the local context*: the site must provide an agent with the information it needs to select which action it may perform (active fields in the site and adjacent ones, agents in adjacent positions and related types);
- *transport request*: when an agent attempts a transport action, the site it is positioned on must communicate with the destination one in order to verify if it is empty, and eventually allow the agent movement, which frees the current site;

- *reaction request*: upon reception of a reaction request by the overlaying agent, the site must propagate it to involved agents' sites, which in turn will notify them. The site must wait for their replies and then notify all involved entities of the agreement operation outcome; in other words, the site where the reaction is generated is the *leader* of the group of involved sites; a pseudo-code formalization of the reaction management procedure for the leader site is shown in Figure 8;
- *field emission*: when a field is generated in a site it must be added to the set of active fields present in the site, and it must be propagated to other adjacent sites according to the chosen diffusion algorithm.

With reference to reaction, and especially on the selection of a leader site, there are some additional elements that must be integrated with the previous description of site behaviour. In an asynchronous environment, there is the possibility that two agents concurrently start two related reactions. For instance, given three agents A, B and C, placed in sites forming a clique, agent A and Agent B require their respective sites to react among themselves and with agent C. There is not a single site which started the reaction, so a leader must be chosen. Whenever this kind of situation occurs an election protocol must be invoked. The first and probably simplest solution, is to associate a unique identifier related to every site (a very simple way of obtaining it could be the adoption of a combination of the IP address and TCP port related to the site) and assume that the one with the lowest identifier becomes the leader of the reaction group, and others will behave as the reaction request was generated by the leader.

Externally generated events are consequences of internal events generated by agents in other sites; more precisely they are the following ones:

- *inspect the site*: upon request, the site must provide to adjacent sites information related to active fields and to the presence (or absence) of an agent in it;
- *diffusion propagation*: when a field generated in a different site is propagated to the current one the latter must evaluate its value through the related diffusion function and, if the value is not null, it must propagate the field to other adjacent sites according to the adopted diffusion algorithm;
- *reaction request*: upon reception of a reaction request by the leader of a reaction group, the site must forward it to the overlaying agent, wait for its response and transmit it back to the leader; then it must wait for the outcome of the reaction and notify the overlaying agent; a more schematic description of non-leader sites behavior for management of reaction is shown in Figure 9;
- *transport*: when a remote agent attempts a transport action, the destination site must verify if its state has changed from the previous inspection performed by the agent, and if it is still empty will allow the transport action, blocking subsequent incoming transports.

Site is thus responsible for many concurrent activities; the proposed approach provides thus to endow a site with two threads, respectively detecting internal

```
procedure reactionManagement(agent, action)
    begin
    involvedAgents:=action.getReactionPartners();
    reactingAgents:=new list();
    reactingAgents.add(agent);
    agreed:=true;
    forall agent_i in involvedAgents
        begin
        adjSite:=agent_i.getSite();
        adjSite.reqAgreement(action);
        end
    until(forall a in involvedAgents, a.gotResponse)
        begin
        if receiveAgreeResp(agent_i,action) = false then
            begin
            agreed:=false;
            break;
            end
        reactingAgents.add(agent_i)
        end
    if agreed=true then
        forall agent_i in reactingAgents
            begin
            adjSite:=agent_i.getSite();
            adjSite.performReact(action);
            end
    else
        forall agent_i in reactingAgents
            begin
            adjSite:=agent_i.getSite();
            adjSite.performReact(adjSite);
            end
    end
```

Fig. 8. Reaction management procedure for the leader site in an asynchronous situation

and external events. These threads are also able to generate additional ones which effectively manage these events.

Inter-thread Communication. Both agents and sites are provided with a set of threads which must be able to communicate among themselves in a safe and consistent way. For instance, agent reaction management thread in an asynchronous situation communicates to the underlying site by means of a `replyReactRequest` invocation (see Figure 7). The latter performs a write operation on a thread-safe queue, that is a structure with synchronized accessors (observers and modifiers) that may be accessed by site threads but also by the ones related to the agent that is placed on it. The `replyReactRequest` invocation inserts an event in this queue, and notifies threads that were waiting for the generation of events. In this case the thread interested in the agent reply to the reaction request is the one related to the underlying site which effectively manages the agreement process with other involved entities. It could be either the leader, which is put into a wait condition by the and the `receiveAgreeResp` invocation (see Figure 8), or any other involved site, which is put into a wait condition by a `getReactReply` invocation (see Figure 9).

Precautions on Network Communication. So far the possibility to have failures in network transmission was not considered, as the design of a robust distributed protocol for reaction management is not the focus of this work. Moreover

```
procedure reactionManagement(site, action)
    begin
    if this.agent <> null then
        begin
        this.agent.notifyReaction(action);
        agreed:=getReactReply(agent,action);
        site.replyReact(agreed);
        if agreed=true then
            if site.reqAgreement()=true then
                this.agent.setReactAgreement(action,true);
        end
    else
        site.replyReact(false);
    end
```

Fig. 9. Reaction management procedure for non-leader sites in an asynchronous situation

the chosen technologies supporting network communication could implement mechanisms assuring a reliable form of communication. However, considering the simple loss of messages related to the orchestration of reaction, a simple protocol providing the transmission acknowledgements and the definition of timeouts in order to avoid deadlock situations could be easily implemented. Whenever this kind of issue is detected, the agents' threads related to the management of reaction could simply try to repeat the whole process from the beginning. Moreover, the fact that every agent is related to multiple threads of control, greatly reduces the dangers and issues related to possible deadlocks: the agent behaviour thread is separated from the management of reactions, and the same can be said for what concerns site specific functions (e.g. threads related to field diffusion are separated from those managing reactions). Thus, a failure in a reaction process does not hinder the possibility of the agent to continue its behaviour, leaving aside the specific reaction that caused the problem. The price of these advantages is that agents and sites are more complex from a computational perspective, and require more resources both in terms of memory and processor time. There are also functional requirements that must be considered: the execution of an action during an agreement process might change the preconditions that brought an agent to accept the reaction proposal. This could represent a serious issue, and in this case the possibility of the reaction management thread to temporarily block the agent behavioural one should be introduced, suitably exploiting the inter thread interaction mechanism.

Discussion. Some of the concurrency issues that were described in this Section are common also in direct agent interaction models. In fact, they are generally designed to work in an asynchronous situation in which messages may be sent and received at any time. In order not to miss any message, the communication partners require some kind of indirection mechanism and structure (e.g. *mailboxes* in Zeus [11], and *queues* in Jade [16]).

Unlike the synchronous approach, in this case no single entity managing the coordinated change of state among agents is provided. While managing this kind of operation in a distributed way provides a more complex implementation of sites, to which this activity is delegated, this approach seems more suitable in distributed situations, unless synchronization is absolutely necessary. In fact, a single entity managing this operation may represent a bottleneck and a single point of failure, hindering system robustness.

4 Conclusions and Future Developments

The paper has discussed issues related to the coordinated change of state for situated MASs, proposing specific solutions for synchronous and asynchronous situations. In particular, the MMASS reaction action was considered as a specific case of coordinated change of state in situated agents, but most considerations are of general interest in the design and implementation of mechanisms supporting this form of coordinated action in situated MASs. In particular the approach described in [17] provides a similar approach to situated agents coordination: in fact it provides a centralized synchronization, similar to the one provided by the environment described in Section 3.1. A distributed mechanism for agent coordination is also described, but it provides a personal synchronizer for every agent while in the approach described in Section 3.2 every site is responsible for providing this kind of service to the hosted agent.

References

1. Stefania Bandini, Sara Manzoni, and Carla Simone, "Heterogeneous Agents Situated in Heterogeneous Spaces.," *Applied Artificial Intelligence*, vol. 16, no. 9-10, pp. 831–852, 2002.
2. Stefania Bandini, Sara Manzoni, and Giuseppe Vizzari, "Situated Cellular Agents: a Model to Simulate Crowding Dynamics," *IEICE Transactions on Information and Systems: Special Issues on Cellular Automata*, vol. E87-D, no. 3, pp. 669–676, 2004.
3. Stefania Bandini, Sara Manzoni, and Giuseppe Vizzari, "Towards a Specification and Execution Environment for Simulations Based on MMASS: Managing At-a-distance Interaction," in *Proceedings of the 17th European Meeting on Cybernetics and Systems Research*, 2004, pp. 636–641, Austrian Society for Cybernetic Studies.
4. Giacomo Cabri, Letizia Leonardi, and Franco Zambonelli, "MARS: a Programmable Coordination Architecture for Mobile Agents," *IEEE Internet Computing*, vol. 4, no. 4, pp. 26–35, 2000.
5. David Gelernter, "Generative Communication in Linda," *ACM Trans. Program. Lang. Syst.*, vol. 7, no. 1, pp. 80–112, 1985.
6. David Gelernter and Nicholas Carriero, "Coordination Languages and Their Significance," *Communications of the ACM*, vol. 35, no. 2, pp. 97–107, 1992.
7. Sean Luke, G. C. Balan, Liviu A. Panait, C. Cioffi-Revilla, and S. Paus, "Mason: a Java Multi-Agent Simulation Library," in *Proceedings of Agent 2003 Conference on Challenges in Social Simulation*, 2003.
8. Marco Mamei, Franco Zambonelli, and Letizia Leonardi, "Co-fields: Towards a Unifying Approach to the Engineering of Swarm Intelligent Systems," in *Engineering Societies in the Agents World III: Third International Workshop (ESAW2002)*. 2002, vol. 2577 of *LNAI*, pp. 68–81, Springer–Verlag.

9. Marco Mamei and Franco Zambonelli, "Programming Pervasive and Mobile Computing Applications with the Tota Middleware," in *2nd IEEE International Conference on Pervasive Computing and Communication (Percom2004)*. 2004, pp. 263–273, IEEE Computer Society.

10. Nelson Minar, Roger Burkhart, Chris Langton, and Manor Askenazi, "The Swarm Simulation System: A Toolkit for Building Multi-Agent Simulations," Working Paper 96-06-042, Santa Fe Institute, 1996.

11. Hyacinth S. Nwana, Divine T. Ndumu, Lyndon C. Lee, and Jaron C. Collis, "Zeus: A toolkit for Building Distributed Multiagent Systems," *Applied Artificial Intelligence*, vol. 13, no. 1-2, pp. 129–185, 1999.

12. Andrea Omicini and Enrico Denti, "From Tuple Spaces to Tuple Centres," *Science of Computer Programming*, vol. 41, no. 3, pp. 277–294, 2001.

13. Andrea Omicini and Franco Zambonelli, "Coordination for Internet Application Development," *Autonomous Agents and Multi-Agent Systems*, vol. 2, no. 3, pp. 251–269, Sept. 1999, Special Issue: Coordination Mechanisms for Web Agents.

14. Gian Pietro Picco, Amy L. Murphy, and Gruia-Catalin Roman, "Lime: Linda Meets Mobility," in *Proceedings of the 21st International Conference on Software Engineering (ICSE99)*. 1999, pp. 368–377, ACM press.

15. Alessandro Ricci, Mirko Viroli, and Andrea Omicini, "Agent Coordination Context: from Theory to Practice," in *Proceedings of the 17th European Meeting on Cybernetics and Systems Research*, 2004, pp. 618–623, Austrian Society for Cybernetic Studies.

16. Giovanni Rimassa, *Runtime Support for Distributed Multi-Agent Systems*, Ph.D. thesis, University of Parma, January 2003.

17. Danny Weyns and Tom Holvoet, "Model for Simultaneous Actions in Situated Multi-Agent Systems," in *First International German Conference on Multi-Agent System Technologies, MATES.* 2003, vol. 2831 of *LNCS*, pp. 105–119, Springer–Verlag.

Optimal Behavior of a Moving Creature in the Cellular Automata Model

Mathias Halbach and Rolf Hoffmann

TU Darmstadt, FB Informatik, FG Rechnerarchitektur,
Hochschulstraße 10, D-64289 Darmstadt,
Phone: +49 6151 16 {3713, 3606}, Fax: +49 6151 16 5410
{halbach, hoffmann}@ra.informatik.tu-darmstadt.de

Abstract. The goal of our investigation is to find automatically the best rule for a cell in the cellular automata model. The cells are either of type OBSTACLE, EMPTY or CREATURE. Only CREATURE can move around in the cell space and can perform one of the four actions: if the path to the next cell is blocked: turn left or right, if the path is free: move ahead and simultaneously turn left or right. The task of the creature is to cross all empty cells with a minimum number of steps. The behavior was modeled using a variable state machine represented by a state table. Input to the state table is the neighbor's state in front of its moving direction. The goal is to find the absolutely best rule in the set of all possible rules. The search space grows exponentially with the number of states. As simulation, testing and evaluating the quality are very time consuming in software, the migration of the problem to a parallel hardware platform is a promising solution. In order to reduce the computation time, the search procedure was (1) implemented in hardware and (2) solutions which are equivalent under state permutations were not generated and (3) solutions which show or expect bad or trivial behavior were excluded as soon as possible in a preselection phase. Exactly six different five-state algorithms could be detected, which allow to cross all empty cells for all the given initial configurations. We described this model in Verilog HDL and in AHDL. A hardware synthesizing tool transforms the description into a configuration file which was loaded into a field programmable gate array (FPGA). Hardware implementation offers a significant speed up of many thousands compared to software.

1 Introduction

We are presenting results of the project "Behavior of Artificial Creatures and their Simulation under Massively Parallel Hardware". The general goal of the project is the design of a massively parallel model which allows describing many moving and learning creatures in artificial worlds. The simulation of such models is very time consuming and therefore the model should be massively parallel in such a way that it can efficiently be supported by special hardware or multiprocessor systems. There are many fields of applications for such artificial worlds:

V. Malyshkin (Ed.): PaCT 2005, LNCS 3606, pp. 129–140, 2005.

- Synthetic worlds: Games, genetic art, optimization of the behavior of the creatures to reach global goals, social behavior, self organization.
- Computational worlds: Creatures are considered as active moving objects. Passive objects contain data. Creatures are programmed or are able to learn to solve a complex algorithmic problem.

2   Previous Work

Cellular Automata (CA). The popular CA model dates back to J. von Neumann. Well known are the self replication rules of Von Neumann and Conway (LIFE). In our group the language CDL [7] was defined to describe such rules in an easy and concise way. CDL was enhanced to CDL++ [8] in order to describe moving objects and features to resolve conflict situations. A number of FPGA-based configurable special processors were developed to support the CA model in hardware (CEPRA family) [9]. We have shown that CA can efficiently be implemented in FPGA logic reaching speed-ups up to thousands compared to software implementations on a PC [6][5].

Global Cellular Automata (GCA). [10, etc.] For the simulation of artificial worlds direct communication between arbitrary cells should be available. The CA model offers only local communication. Global communication between remote cells has to be emulated step by step through local communication. A new massively parallel model called GCA was defined, which allows direct access to any remote cell. The model is more complex than the CA, but it can still be computed in a synchronous parallel way like the CA because there are no write conflicts. As the model allows long distance communication it is better suited for complex Artificial Life problems. This model will not be used for the presented problem but is well suited for problems where creatures can move and communicate over long distances in one time step. Other related models are the PSA [1] model and the pointer machines [15].

Other Work. This work is related to the general research field Artificial Life. Steven Levy gives in his book [12] an overview over this field. Thomas Ray [14], an American environmentalist and bio-scientist has developed a simulation program allowing the simulation of artificial individuals. The individuals are able to mutate and they survive only if they have certain fitness. He developed the language TIERRA to describe the behavior of the individuals by simple programs based on 32 different instructions. Individuals are able to learn and to use program parts from other individuals. There is a lot of other relevant work which will not be discussed here in detail, like Genetic Algorithms, Neural Networks, Classifier Systems, and Rule Based Learning Models. The task to find a path to all cells is also related to space filling curves like the Hilbert curve and to the snake tiling problem [11]. In [13] an agent learns smart behavior which is stored in a FSM table using a reinforcement learning procedure.

3   The Task: Cross All Empty Cells in Shortest Time

We have studied a simplified problem in order to perceive the open questions and to find some first solutions in the context of learning creatures. The problem is defined as follows.

Consider a two-dimensional grid of cells. There are three types of objects: OBSTACLE, EMPTY, or CREATURE. Border cells and obstacles are both modeled as OBSTACLE and they are located at fixed positions. CREATURE is a more complex type with a simple brain and it is able to move around. All these objects act according to a given set of rules which are as follows: CREATURE is variable in nature, it can move within the space from one place to other but it cannot go to a cell where a border cell or an obstacle is placed. At any time the creature can look in a certain direction one cell ahead and it will move in that direction if possible.

The actions. The creature may perform four different actions.

- R (turn Right)
- L (turn Left)
- Rm (turn Right and move) move forward and simultaneously turn right
- Lm (turn Left and move) move forward and simultaneously turn left

If the path (one cell ahead) is not free because of obstacle or border, either action R or L will be performed. If the path is free, either action Rm or Lm is performed (fig. 1

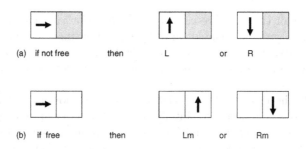

Fig. 1. The actions of the creature

Initial configuration. At the beginning the number and the placement of the obstacles are given. Also the creature is placed in a certain start position with a defined direction.

Goal. The goal is to find an optimal and simple local algorithm for the creature to cross a maximum number of empty cells with a minimum number of time steps for a given set of initial configurations.

3.1   CA-Model of the Moving Creature

To keep the problem simple, the moving of the creature is emulated in the CA model according to the following rules (in simplified pseudo code). The center cell is called **My**.

Rule for My.Type = EMPTY
(a1) {CASE Free}
    if (Neighbor.Type = CREATURE) and
    (Neighbor.Direction points to My) then
      My.Type := CREATURE   //create (move by copy)
      My.Direction := TurnRight/Left (Neighbor.Direction)   //new direction
Rule for My.Type = CREATURE
(a2) {CASE Free}
    if (ahead Neighbor.Type = EMPTY) then My.Type := EMPTY   //delete
(b) {CASE not free}
    My.Direction:= TurnRight/Left (My.Direction)   //only turn R, L

In case a1 and a2 where a creature can move ahead in its direction, it changes its own type to EMPTY (case a2) and at the same time a new creature will be created by the empty cell ahead of the creature (case a1). In case b where the cell cannot move, it will only turn right or left.

3.2   Behavior of the Creature

The behavior of the creature can be either fixed or variable. We have experimented with a variable behavior in order to find optimal solutions for our problem. In our first approach we use a variable state machine for that purpose. The state machine can also be seen as control logic, intelligence or brain of the creature.

To study the basic problems with variable behavior (fig. 2) we reduced the intelligence to a minimum. The intelligence is stored in a state machine with two state tables called *TableFree* and *TableNotFree*. Input to the tables is the state S which is either 0 or 1 (if the brain is modeled only with two states). *TableFree* is selected if the creature is able to move, *TableNotFree* is selected if the creature cannot move because an obstacle or border is in front.

The principle of operation will be explained for the case of two states. There are totally 256 different two-state algorithms, because each table consists of four bit. The tables can be concatenated to one table with 8 bit information. These 8 bits can be represented as a number. E. g. the algorithm 0x39 shown in fig. 2 is abbreviated 0R1L-1R0L. The number 0x39 is the hexadecimal equivalent to 0011-1001, where R is coded with 0 and L is coded with 1. The first part 0R1L is the line by line contents of *TableNotFree*, the second part is the line by line contents of *TableFree*. The second part can also be written as 1Rm0Lm, where Lm means: turn left and move, Rm means: turn right and move. This algorithm can be represented clearer as a state graph (fig. 2(c)).

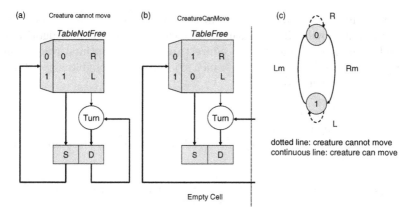

Fig. 2. Table driven state machine (a, b). Two-state algorithm 0x39 as state graph (c)

In the general case where the different values of the states, inputs and outputs are not restricted to powers of two, the number of different algorithms will be

$$N = (s\,y)^{(s\,x)}$$

where s is the number of used states, x is the number of different input states and y is the number of different output actions. The set of N algorithms can be divided into classes of equivalent algorithms with respect to state encoding permutations. Note that N increases dramatically which makes it impossible to check sequentially the quality of all algorithms in a reasonable time.

We liked to characterize the number of possible algorithms with a smaller number. We have defined the "capacity of intelligence" (COI) to be the minimum number of bits which are necessary to code all possible algorithms including permutations.

$$\text{COI} = \text{ld}\,N, \text{ or } N = 2\,\text{COI}$$

For example $x = y = 2$, $s = 5$: $N = (2s)^{2s} = 10^{10}$. $\text{COI}(10^{10}) = 33.2$. In our implementation using a binary state table the states, inputs and outputs are coded in different bit strings. For the above example the state table has a size of 64 bits.

4 Experimental Result of Optimal Rules

We have evaluated all two-state, all four-state and all five-state rules. Whereas we were able to check all four state-algorithms in optimized software, we needed hardware support to check all five-state-algorithms (see section 5).

The two-state table contains 8 bit of information. Each code corresponds to a certain algorithm.

Input to the state-machine algorithm is the old control state S and the signal $X = CreatureCanMove$. Output is $Y = L/R$. In case of $X = true$ the creature turns left or right and moves forward, in case $X = false$ the creature turns left or right without moving. The creature can learn and optimize the algorithm by itself. Before implementing the procedure to detect the optimal rule in hardware we used a software simulation which tried out all possible algorithms by enumeration and evaluation.

> *for all algorithms do*
>   *for all configurations do*
>   *count the cells which are crossed and how many steps are needed*
>   *evaluate the quality*

All algorithms were tested for the following five configurations (fig. 3).

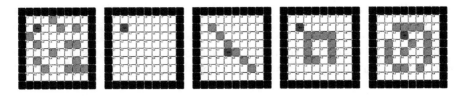

Fig. 3. The initial configurations 1 to 5 from left to right

In order to reduce simulation time, algorithms (tables) were deleted in advance if not all possible states are used. Also the further simulation was aborted when a path turned out to be a loop or the number of crossed cells did not increase after a certain time.

Two-State Algorithms. The best average algorithms found are algorithm 0x39 with 61 % crossed cells and algorithm 0x6C with 60 % crossed cells (table 1). The number of time steps (generations) was big enough that no improvement over time was possible. It can be realized, that no two-state algorithm exists, which is able to cross all cells for all these configurations.

Table 1. The best two states algorithms 0x39 = 0R1L 1R0L and 0x6C = 0L1R 1L0R

Crossed Cells	config. 1	config. 2	config. 3	config. 4	config. 5	crossed % av.
Empty cells	50	64	58	53	48	
Algorithm 0x39	50	22	28	34	34	61 %
Algorithm 0x6C	50	28	10	36	41	60 %

Another result of the analysis is that only 144 of the 256 algorithms are real two-state algorithms, where both states are reached or used. Before simulation an algorithm can formally check the bit pattern if it is a real two-state algorithm or if it is trivial. By this technique the simulation time was significantly reduced. Only 19 of the 144 algorithms allow the creature to cross 42 to 61 % of the empty cells. Many of the algorithms yield bad or unacceptable results mainly because they cyclically cross the same cells in a loop without any improvement after having visited a certain number of cells.

Four-State Algorithms. As expected the four-state algorithms lead to better results compared to two-state algorithms. The algorithms with four states, one input and one output can be represented by a 24 bit table, meaning that 2^{24} different algorithm have to be checked. The COI is 24.

The five best algorithms found are:

- A4: Algorithm 0x0E67D5 = 0R1L2R3R 1L3L1R2L
- B4: Algorithm 0x7E0A72 = 1L3L2R0R 2L0L3R1R
- C4: Algorithm 0x1EACCC = 0R3L2L1R 3R1L0L2R
- D4: Algorithm 0x1EA8F1 = 0R3L2L1R 2R1L3R0L
- E4: Algorithm 0x95EDD4 = 2R2L1L3R 3R3L1R2R

For each algorithm a number of equivalent algorithms were found, which only differ by the state encoding. However, the initial state is always state 0. The state graphs for the algorithms A4 and B4 are shown in fig. 4.

Algorithm A4 is not able to reach all cells of the configuration 2 and 3. Algorithm B4 is not able to reach all cells of the configuration 4, even if the number of generations (computation steps in the CA model) is very high (tested for 40 000). Algorithms C4 and D4 are not able to reach all cells of the configuration 2 and 4. Algorithm E4 is not able to reach all cells of the configuration 1, 2, 3, and 4. Only the algorithm B is able to reach all cells of the empty configuration 2 of size 8 × 8.

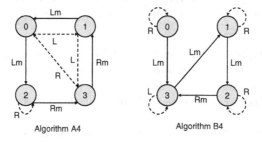

Algorithm A4   Algorithm B4

Fig. 4. The best four-state algorithms. Dotted line: creature cannot move. Continuous line: creature can move

Note that the performance of the algorithm depends on the starting position and starting direction of the creature, the size of the field and on the number and arrangement of the obstacles.

Another criterion for the performance of the algorithms is the speed, meaning how fast the cells are crossed. Figure 5a shows for the first configuration with many scattered obstacles that the five algorithms differ in their speed. Algorithm E4 is the fastest, but it is not able to cross all cells. Algorithm B4 is slower than E4, but it can cross all cells. The other algorithms are even slower and cannot cross all cells.

Table 2. Four-state Algorithms

crossed cells	config. 1	config. 2	config. 3	config. 4	config. 5	crossed % av.
max	50	64	58	53	48	
algorithm A4	50	60	56	53	48	97 %
algorithm B4	50	64	58	50	48	97 %
algorithm C4	50	60	58	48	48	96 %
algorithm D4	50	60	58	47	48	95 %
algorithm E4	48	60	47	48	48	91 %

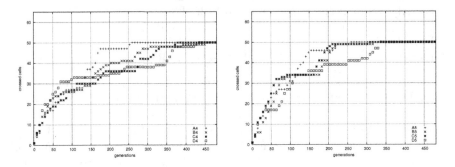

Fig. 5. The speed of the algorithms for the first configuration of (a) 4 states and (b) 5 states

The optimizations needed minutes to days on a regular PC, depending on the field size, number of initial configurations, and the capacity of intelligence. In order to speed up the optimizations significantly, the problem was mapped into programmable FPGA logic.

Five-State Algorithms. There are 10^{10} different algorithms with five states, one input and one output. It would take a very long time to test all algorithms by software. For example

$n = 64$ cells, 5 configurations, 200 simulation steps, on simulation step = 100ns

$t = 64 \times 5 \times 200 \times 10^{-7} \,\text{s} \times 10^{10} = 64 \times 10^6 \,\text{s} = 741 \,\text{days}.$

Therefore we implemented the procedure in hardware using FPGA technology. The best six algorithms are

- A5: Algorithm 0x4368021759 = 2R1L3R4R0R 1R0L3L2L4L
- B5: Algorithm 0x1852634790 = 0L4R2L1R3R 1L2R3L4L0R
- C5: Algorithm 0x1827435690 = 0L4R1R3L2R 1L2L3R4L0R
- D5: Algorithm 0x5126834790 = 2L0L1R3R4R 1L2R3L4L0R
- E5: Algorithm 0x4368021597 = 2R1L3R4R0R 1R0L2L4L3L
- F5: Algorithm 0x4379021685 = 2R1L3L4L0R 1R0L3R4R2L

All and only these six algorithms are able to cross all empty cells (100 %) for all configurations. The speed of the first four algorithms is shown in fig. 5b. Algorithm A5 is the fastest for all configurations on average. It needs 1164 steps to reach all 273 empty cells for all configurations. (Mean step value $1164/273 =$ 4.26). Compared to the 4-state algorithms the 5-state algorithms are faster in general.

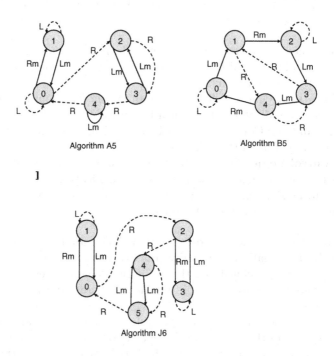

Algorithm A5

Algorithm B5

]

Algorithm J6

Fig. 7. One of the best six-state algorithms

The state-diagram (fig. 6) of algorithm A5 and B5 show a more complex behavior compared to the 4-state algorithms which results in the better performance.

In order to analyse the behavior of the creature, one could detect the cycles or watch the behavior if the paths are always blocked or always free. So a graph can be split into two graphs, one with dotted arcs and one with continues arcs. For example algorithm A5 dotted represents the sequence $(RRRRL^*)^* + L^*$, where * means repetition. But by the moment we are not able to detect clear relations between the graph's structure and the behavior.

We are just investigating the 6-state algorithms. The best 6-state algorithm (fig. 7) we detected needs only 959 generations to cross all cells of the five configurations. This means a mean step value of $959/273 = 3.51$ which is 21 % faster compared to the best 5-state algorithm.

5   Some Details of the Hardware Implementations

The hardware for the cell field is described in the hardware description languages Verilog and AHDL and synthesized into basic logic, which can be loaded into a FPGA. We used the Altera chip Cyclone EP1C20F324C7 and the Quartus II tools for the synthesis. The major part is the "CA-world" which calculates the movement of the creature on the surface. In order to reduce the amount of logic, the CA-world is divided into the two parts (surface and creature). The hardware consists of the following parts.

1. **Surface:** An array of simple cells which are either of type BOARDER or EMPTY. Because of hardware limitations the environment is limited to the size of 16×16 in a first step.
2. **Creature:** One complex cell containing the position, the actual state, the direction and the ability to turn left or right.
3. **Evaluation:** Counters and test logic which are used to control the simulation and evaluation of the behavior.
4. **Control Logic:** The control logic starts, stops, and synchronizes the different parallel emulations and allows communicating with the host computer.
5. **Glue Logic:** This part connects the other parts, for instance the connection of 1. and 2. yields the CA model.

Two phases are needed for operation: The initialization and the calculation phase. In the initialization phase obstacles are placed on the surface, the position of the creature is defined and the evaluation logic is reset. In calculation mode the creature moves around until the amount of crossed fields doesn't increase for a certain time.

Our example consists of five possible surfaces, so we can calculate them in parallel. Each of the five "worlds" operates on the same algorithm. Whensoever the behavior an one surface is too bad, the calculations on the other surfaces don't need to be continued. By this method the time of finding the best algorithm can be reduced.

Algorithms where a state can only be reached but never left can be excluded because they are not powerful enough. In the same way some algorithm representations can be excluded without loosing results, e. g. one kind of permutation: a state transition is only allowed if the difference between the destination and start state numbers is less than 2.

The best results are preselected and transferred via USB to a computer (host). For verification it is possible to simulate and observe a selected "world" step by step using a direct connection to the hardware. For all these hardware parts 8,423 logic cells were needed on the FPGA, which is around 41 % of the chip capacity. The maximum clock frequency which can be achieved is 62.05 MHz for this chip. Compared to a software solution on a PC the total speed-up is in the range of many thousands which has been shown in another investigation [4].

6   Conclusion and Future Work

We implemented a learning moving creature both in software and in hardware. The creature has the task to cross as many as possible empty cells using a local algorithm. This algorithm can be seen as the brain of the creature which implements a certain behavior. A variable state machine was used for the hardware and software implementation of the algorithm. The synthesized hardware allows working massively parallel yielding to speed-ups of many thousands compared to software simulation on a PC.

All 256 two-state algorithms, all 2^{14} four-state algorithms and all 10^{10} five-state algorithms have been investigated systematically. Only one four-state algorithm was found, which is able to cross all cells of the 8×8 empty configuration 2. Six five-state algorithms were found which are able to cross all empty cells of all configurations. Also the speed of the five-state algorithms is higher than for the four-state algorithms.

The goal is to discover better algorithms using a higher capacity of intelligence. The capacity intelligence can be enhanced by increasing the number of states, the number of inputs from the environment or the number and type of outputs (actions).

There is a lot of interesting future work to do, like:

- Find efficient and robust behaviors for a higher capacity of intelligence.
- Analyze and evaluate the performance of the algorithms in relation to the state graph.
- Speeding up the optimizing procedures.
- Use more complex worlds and tasks.
- Improve the hardware architectures.

References

1. S. Achasova, O. Bandman, V. Markova, and S. Piskunov. *Parallel Substitution Algorithm*. World Scientific, P.O.BOX 128, Farrer Road, Singapore 9128, 1994.
2. M. Dascalu, E. Franti, and G. Stefan. Modeling production with artificial societies: the emergence of social structure. In *Cellular Automata Research Towards Industry*, 1998.
3. J. M. Epstein and R. Axtell. *Growing artificial societies – social science from the bottom up*. Brooking Institution Press, Washington D. C., 1996.
4. M. Halbach, W. Heenes, R. Hoffmann, and J. Tisje. Optimizing the Behavior of a Moving Creature in Software and in Hardware. In *ACRI 2004*, Amsterdam, 2004. Springer.
5. M. Halbach and R. Hoffmann. Implementing Cellular Automata in FPGA Logic. In *International Parallel & Distributed Processing Symposium (IPDPS), Workshop on Massively Parallel Processing (WMPP)*, Santa Fe, NM, 2004. IEEE Computer Society.
6. M. Halbach, R. Hoffmann, and P. Röder. FPGA Implementation of Cellular Automata Compared to Software Implementation. In *PASA Workshop*, ARCS, Augsburg, 2004.
7. C. Hochberger. *CDL - Eine Sprache für die Zellularverarbeitung auf verschiedenen Zielplattformen*. PhD thesis, Darmstädter Dissertation D17, 1998.
8. C. Hochberger, R. Hoffmann, and S. Waldschmidt. CDL++ for the Description of Moving Objects in Cellular Automata. In *PaCT99, Par. Comp. Technologies*, LNCS 1662. Springer, 1999.

9. R. Hoffmann, B. Ulmann, K.-P. Völkmann, and S. Waldschmidt. A Stream Processor Architecture Based on the Configurable CEPRA-S. In *FPL 2000*, LNCS 1896. Springer, 2000.

10. R. Hoffmann, K.-P. Völkmann, S. Waldschmidt, and W. Heenes. Global Cellular Automata, A Flexible Parallel Model. In *6th International Conference on Parallel Computing Technologies PaCT2001*, Lecture Notes in Computer Science (LNCS 2127). Springer, 2001.

11. J. Kari. Infinite snake tiling problems. In *DLT'2002, Developments in Language Theory*, Lecture Notes in Computer Science. Springer, 2002.

12. S. Levy. *KL - Künstliches Leben aus dem Computer*. Droemer Knaur, 1993. translation from the English, 'Artificial Life' (1992).

13. B. Mesot, E. Sanchez, C. A. Pena, and A. Perez-Uribe. SOS++: Finding Smart Behaviors Using Learning and Evolution. In Standish, Abbass, and Bedau, editors, *Artificial Life VIII*, page 264ff., 2002.

14. T. Ray. An Approach to the Synthesis of Life. In *Artificial Life II*, 1991.

15. A. Schönhage. Real-time simulation of multidimensional turing machines by storage modification machines. In *SIAM Journal on Computing*, volume 9, Issue 3, pages 490 – 508. August 1980.

Systolic Routing in an Optical Butterfly

Risto T. Honkanen

Department of Computer Science, University of Kuopio, P.O.Box 1627,
FIN-70211 Kuopio, Finland
rthonkan@cs.uku.fi

Abstract. In this paper we present an all-optical network architecture and a systolic routing protocol for it. The r-dimensional optical butterfly ($\mathcal{OBF}$) network consists of $r2^r$ nodes and $r2^{r+1}$ edges. Processors are deployed at the level 0 (identical to level r) nodes of the network. Routing is based on the use of cyclical control bit sequence and scheduling. The systolic routing protocol ensures that no electro-optical conversion is needed in the intermediate routing nodes and all the packets injected into the routing machinery will reach their target without collisions. A work-optimal routing of an h-relation is achieved with a reasonable size of h.

1 Introduction

Optics offers a possibility to increase the bandwidth of intercommunication networks. Optical communication offers several advantages in comparison with its electronic counterpart, for example, a possibility to use broader bandwidth and insensitivity to external interferences. These advantages have been covered, e.g., by Saleh and Teich in their book [12].

Our work is motivated by another kind of communication problem, namely the emulation of shared memory with distributed memory modules [6]. If a parallel computation has enough parallel *slackness*, the implementation of shared memory can be reduced to efficient routing of h-relation [14]. An h-relation is a routing problem where each processor has at most h packets to send and it is the target of at most h packets [1]. An implementation of an h-relation is said to be *work-optimal* at *cost* c, if all the packets arrive at their targets in time ch. A precondition for work-optimality is that h is greater than the diameter ϕ of the network and the network can move $\Omega(n\phi)$ packets in each step, where n is the number of processors. Otherwise slackness cannot be used to "hide" diameter influenced latency [6]. For an r-dimensional optical butterfly ($\mathcal{OBF}$) having $n = 2^r$ processors the diameter $\phi = r$ fulfills this condition.

Butterfly networks are widely used in intercommunication machineries. There are several reasons to the popularity of butterfly networks. Firstly, they have a simple recursive structure. Secondly, in a r-dimensional butterfly any input p is linked to any output p' by a unique path of length r [7]. Most of implementations of butterfly based networks use packet switching as the routing strategy [7,9,13].

V. Malyshkin (Ed.): PaCT 2005, LNCS 3606, pp. 141–150, 2005.

A drawback of packet switching is that routing decisions must be done in electronic form. Liu and Gu have presented an all-optical implementation based on wavelength-division multiplexing (WDM) in their paper [8]. An advantage of their implementation is that electro-optic conversions are avoided. A disadvantage is that a number of wavelengths and wavelength converters are needed to realize connections [8].

In this work we present an all-optical network architecture and a systolic routing protocol for it. The r-dimensional optical butterfly network consists of $r2^r$ nodes and $r2^{r+1}$ edges. Processors are deployed at the level 0 nodes of the network. Routing nodes are connected to each other by optical links. In this paper we present a novel packet routing protocol, called the *systolic routing protocol*. Additionally, when a packet is injected into the routing machinery, neither electro-optic conversions are needed during its path from source to target processor nor any collisions may happen between two distinct packets. An r-dimensional $\mathcal{OBF}$ can route an h-relation in $\Theta(h)$ time, if $h \in \Theta(n \log n)$. Section 2 presents the internal structure of routing nodes and the structure of $\mathcal{OBF}$ network. In Section 3 we introduce the systolic routing protocol. Section 4 presents the analysis of our construction. Section 5 sketches conclusions and future work.

2   Optical Butterfly with Systolic Routers

We study on the r-dimensional structure of $\mathcal{OBF}$ of diameter $\phi = r$ and having $n = 2^r$ processing nodes. We represent the structure of routing nodes in Section 2.1. Section 2.2 introduces the construction of $\mathcal{OBF}$. Section 2.3 sketches the feasibility of our construction.

2.1   Systolic Routers for $\mathcal{OBF}$

Each routing node of $\mathcal{OBF}$ has two incoming and two outgoing links. A routing node can be in two states. When a routing node routes incoming packets from input links in_{up} and in_{down} to output links out_{down} and out_{up} respectively, it is said to be in *invert* state and when it routes incoming signals from input links in_{up} and in_{down} to output links out_{up} and out_{down} respectively, it is said to be in *push* state. The two possible states of routing nodes are presented in Figure 1.

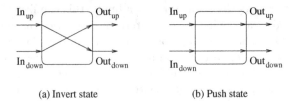

(a) Invert state   (b) Push state

Fig. 1. Two possible states of routing nodes

The basic component of routing nodes is the electrically controlled all-optical 2×2 switch. Switches can be implemented by LiNbO$_3$ technology [12]. The construction of routing nodes ensures that signals never collide and routing of the packets works correctly if we can arrange a situation that both incoming packets never prefer the same output link. We will show that this kind of situation is arrangeable.

2.2   Construction of Optical Butterfly

The r-dimensional butterfly consists of $r2^r$ nodes and $r2^{r+1}$ edges. The nodes correspond to pairs $\langle w, i \rangle$, where i is the level of the node ($0 \le i \le r$) and w is an r-bit binary string denoting the row number of the node. Two nodes $\langle w, i \rangle$ and $\langle w', i' \rangle$ are connected by an edge (optical link) if and only if $i' = i + 1$, and either [7]

   i. w and w' are identical (straight edges), or
  ii. w and w' differ in precisely the i'th bit (cross edges).

The construction of 3-dimensional $\mathcal{OBF}$ out of two 2-dimensional $\mathcal{OBF}$'s is presented in Figure 2. In Figure 2, a circle indicates a processing node, a rounded square indicates a routing node, and an arrow between two nodes indicates a link between the nodes. Two attachable subnetworks are called blocks of the network. Straight edges are always connecting the output out_{up} from the i'th level router to the input in_{up} of the $i + 1$'th level input (in the same block), and cross edges are always connected from the output out_{down} of the i'th level router to the input in_{down} of the $i + 1$'th level input (adjacent block).

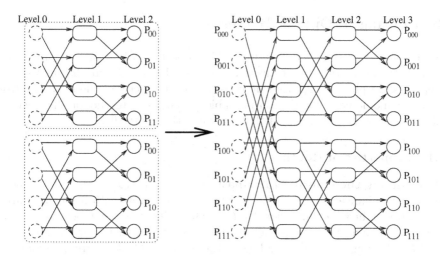

Fig. 2. Construction of 3-dimensional $\mathcal{OBF}$ out of two 2-dimensional $\mathcal{OBF}$'s with relabeling of processing nodes and levels

Our construction has two characteristics. Firstly, straight edges are always leading to the same block and cross edges are always leading to the adjacent block of the (sub)butterfly. Secondly, treatment of packets can be arranged uniformly at each router at the network because of uniform connections between routers.

Nodes $\langle w, 0 \rangle$ and $\langle w, r \rangle$ are considered identical processing nodes. A useful property of the r-dimensional butterfly is that for any source/destination processing node pairs $\langle w_s, 0 \rangle$ and $\langle w_d, r \rangle$ the packets can be routed by a unique path of length r.

2.3   Feasibility of $\mathcal{OBF}$ for Using as a Systolic Router

The switching time of LiNbO$_3$ switches lies in the range of 10–15 ps [12]. The length of packet (l_p) can be evaluated by equation $l_p = \frac{N_p \times v_c}{B \times r}$, where N_p is the size of the packet in bits, $v_c = 0.3$ m/ns is the speed of light in vacuum, $r = 1.5$ is the refraction index of fiber [12], and B is the link bandwidth. Assuming the bandwidth to be B=100 Gb/s, the length of a bit in a fiber is $\frac{v_c}{B \times r} = 2$ mm.

In order to estimate the feasibility of a 6-dimensional $\mathcal{OBF}$ (having 64 processing nodes) let us assume the link bandwidth to be $B = 100$ Gb/s, and the size of packets to be $N_p = 128$ b. The corresponding length of a packet in a fiber is $l_p \simeq 256$ mm, and the length of time slot is $t_p \simeq 1.3$ ns. Assuming the length of clock cycle of processing nodes to be $t_{cc} = 1$ ns (corresponding the frequency of 1 GHz), it will take 1.3 clock cycles for a packet to travel between two adjacent routing nodes. The overall amount of fibers is $L_f \simeq 200$ m, and the routing time of packet is $t_r \simeq 8$ clock cycles for each packet. We consider the requested parameters to be reasonable and the architecture to be feasible to construct in the near future.

3   Routing in Optical Butterfly

We develope a routing algorithm for $\mathcal{OBF}$. In Section 3.1 we present properties of routing information and transitions between blocks. Section 3.2 introduces preprocessing phase. Preprocessing phase consists of determining of the control sequence and determining the routing table that will control the routing. Section 3.3 introduces the routing algorithm for the optical butterfly.

3.1   Properties of Routing

Determining the Routing Information. Let $a_0 a_1 \ldots a_{r-1}$ ($a_i \in \{0, 1\}$) be a bit sequence indicating the edges used by a packet on its path from the source to the target in an r-dimensional $\mathcal{OBF}$. The value 1 in a bit position a_k indicates that at level k the packet should be routed from router on level k to level $k + 1$ using cross edge leading to the adjacent block. Correspondingly, if $a_k = 0$ the packet should be routed from router on level k to level $k + 1$ using the straight edge leading to the same block. Clearly, we can construct an r-ary routing bit sequence for any source/destination pair so that it leads correctly the

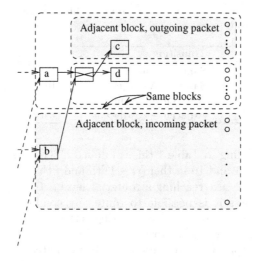

Fig. 3. Example of transitions between blocks

packet through the $\mathcal{OBF}$. To notice this, let us assume that in a bit sequence $a_0a_1 \ldots a_k \ldots a_{r-1}$, the k'th bit stands for the edge leading to the wrong subnetwork. We just substitute the initial bit sequence by $a_0a_1 \ldots \bar{a}_k \ldots a_{r-1}$, where $\bar{a}_k$ is the complement of a_k.

The routing information for packets can be evaluated by the bitwise XOR-operation $\oplus$. For example, if processor P_{011} has a packet destined to processor P_{111}, the routing information can be expressed as $011 \oplus 111 = 100$. The meaning of the information is that the packet from P_{011} to P_{111} must be routed from the sender to the 1'st level router using cross edge, from 1'st level router to 2'nd level router using straight edge, and from 2'nd level router to destination using straight edge.

Determining Transitions Between Blocks. An r-dimensional $\mathcal{OBF}$ has $r - 1$ levels of routers. According to the recursive contruction of $\mathcal{OBF}$ and our definition every routing node at level r' is connected to two subnetworks of dimension $r - r' - 1$ by two outgoing links. We call these subnetworks as blocks. Additionally it is a target of two incoming links from two subnetworks (blocks) whose dimension is $r - r' + 1$, except routing nodes at level 1 that are targets of processors. Figure 3 clarifies the idea of blocks.

Routers can be considered to be an interface between blocks. Let us assume that a packet has bits $\ldots 10 \ldots$ in its $(i - 1)$'th and i'th bit positions of routing information. Router responsible to route this packet (at the i'th level) receives the packet from adjacent block into its in_{down} input and it should route the packet to the same block of the $\mathcal{OBF}$. According to our construction the router should be in invert state. Correspondence between two-bit routing information, transitions between blocks, and required state of router is presented in Table 1.

Because all the routers have two incoming and two outgoing links, each router can route two packets at the same time, if the packets do not prefer the same

Table 1. Correspondence between two-bit routing information, transitions between blocks, and required state of router

Routing information	Transition	Required state
00	Same → Same	Push
01	Same → Adjacent	Invert
10	Adjacent → Same	Invert
11	Adjacent → Adjacent	Push

outgoing link. According to Table 1 this is fulfilled if the incoming packets have either 00 and 11 or 01 and 10 in their $(i-1)$'th and i'th bit position of routing information when they are reaching a router at level i. Clearly we can see that using these two states it is possible to route any combination of transitions between blocks. Precondition of correct routing is that arrival of packets and the state of router are synchronized correctly.

The transition information for packets can be evaluated by the bitwise XOR-operation $\oplus$. Let $w = s \oplus d$ denote the routing information of a packet from processor P_s to P_d and w_j denote the value at the bit position j of the routing information. We are able to determine a unique transition bit sequence τ by $\tau_j = w_j \oplus w_{j+1}, j = 0 \ldots r-1$.

3.2 Initialization Phase

In our contruction injected packets have no routing information. When a packet arrives a routing node it is routed into an adjacent or the same block according to the state of the router. Anyway we are able to arrange a control system so that every packet injected into the $\mathcal{OBF}$ reaches its target. We will use a syclical control bit sequence and timing of injections of packets.

Determining the Control Sequence. An r-dimensional $\mathcal{OBF}$ has r levels of routing nodes. Packet routing in an r-dimensional $\mathcal{OBF}$ can be implemented by constructing a long control bit sequence $s_0 s_1 s_2 \ldots$, applying at time step t the state corresponding to the value of bit position s_t to all the routing nodes of the $\mathcal{OBF}$, and synchronizing injections of packets so that they reach every routing node in the correct state. Precondition of all-to-all routing is that the bit sequence includes (cyclically) all bit sequences of $l = r-1$ bits. A naive solution would be to construct the control bit sequence of all l-ary bit combinations. The length of control cycle would be $l2^l$. The control sequence can be reduced to $T = 2^l$ by using *de Bruijn sequences* [3].

A de Bruijn sequence (in alphabet $\mathcal{A} = \{/, \infty\}$) of length 2^l is a sequence of 2^l bits in which every subsequence of $l = r-1$ bits appears once, including wraparound [7]. For $l = 4$, for example, $\boldsymbol{\xi} = 0000111101100101$ is a de Bruijn sequence applicable for our purpose. All sixteen 4-bit sequences occur exactly once as subsequence of $\boldsymbol{\xi}$.

Fredricksen has presented an algorithm to construct a de Bruijn sequence [2]. The algorithm is *Prefer one* and it can be presented as follows [2]:

Algorithm Prefer one
   1: Write $l = r$ zeros;
   2: **for** the kth bit of the sequence, $k > l$, write a one;
      if the newly formed l-tuple has not previously appeared in
          the sequence then $k := k + 1$
     else
   3: **for** the kth bit of the sequence, write a zero;
      if the newly formed l-tuple has not previously appeared in
          the sequence then $k := k + 1$ and go to step 2
     else stop;

Bit positions of $\boldsymbol{\xi}$ present states of routers of $\mathcal{OBF}$. Let $\boldsymbol{\xi}_m$ denote the value of de Bruijn sequence at m'th bit position. At each time step t all the routers are set in push state if $\boldsymbol{\xi}_{t \bmod \|\boldsymbol{\xi}\|} = 0$, where $\|\boldsymbol{\xi}\|$ is the length of de Bruijn sequence, and in invert states otherwise. Determining of the control sequence is necessary to do only once at the initialization phase of the $\mathcal{OBF}$.

Determining the Routing Table. The optical butterfly has a number of properties. Firstly, structure of routers and connections between them are uniform. Secondly, it is possible to determine a unique routing bit sequence for any packet from a source P_s to the destination P_d for any pair (s, d). Thirdly, determination of unique transitions between blocks is possible as well because of uniformness of the construction of the $\mathcal{OBF}$ and uniqueness of the routing bit sequences. Fourthly, the $\mathcal{OBF}$ is controlled by the static control bit sequence $\boldsymbol{\xi}$. For these reasons we are able to determine a routing table for every connections at the initialization phase.

Let us consider an r-ary $\mathcal{OBF}$ having $p = 2^r$ processors. For this construction the length of routing bit sequence is $\|w\| = r$, the length of transition bit sequence is $\|\boldsymbol{\tau}\| = \|w\| - 1 = r - 1$, and the length of control sequence is $\|\boldsymbol{\xi}\| = 2^{r-1}$. A packet having $w_0 = 0$ is routed correctly if it is injected into output link out_{up} leading to the same block and during the next $r - 1$ time steps stands $\tau_t = \boldsymbol{\xi}_{t \bmod \|\boldsymbol{\xi}\|}, t = 0 \ldots r - 2$. At the same time the sending processor can inject another packet into the output link out_{down} for which $w_0 = 1$ and $\tau_t = \boldsymbol{\xi}_{t \bmod \|\boldsymbol{\xi}\|}, t = 0 \ldots r - 2$ during the next $r - 1$ time steps. For these two packets destined to processors d and d' stand $d_i = \bar{d'_i}, j = 0 \ldots r - 1$, i.e., d' is the complement of d.

At the initialization phase every processor P_i determines a routing table R having $\|\boldsymbol{\xi}\| = 2^{r-1}$ rows. Let R_i denote the value of i'th row of the routing table. The algorithm determining routing table is *Routing table* and it can be presented as follows:

Algorithm Routing table
   1: $i = 0$;
   2: **repeat**
     In the i'th position of routing table R write the index
     value of destination processor for which $w_0 = 0$ and
     $\tau_t = \boldsymbol{\xi}_{i+t+1 \bmod \|\boldsymbol{\xi}\|}, t = 0 \ldots r - 2$; $i := i + 1$;
   3: **until** $i = 2^{r-1} - 1$;

Algorithm Routing table is necessary to do only once at the initialization phase of the $\mathcal{OBF}$.

3.3   Routing Algorithm for the Optical Butterfly

At the initialization phase each processor determines the control sequence and the routing table. This must be done when the system is set up. At the beginning of routing each processor of the $\mathcal{OBF}$ has a number of packets to send. In the preprocessing phase each processor P_s inserts packets destined to processor P_d into sending buffer $B_{(s,d)}$.

At each time step t each processor s picks up a packet from sending buffer $B_{(s,d')}$, where $d' = R_{t \bmod \|\xi\|}$ is the value of $(t \bmod \|\xi\|)$'th position in the routing table. The packet is injected into the outgoing link out_{up} leading to the same block. A packet from sending buffer $\bar{d}'$ is picked up as well and injected into the outgoing link out_{down}.

4   Analysis of Systolic Routing

In preprocessing phase, each of the h packets of a processor P_i are inserted into sending buffers according to their target. Clearly, all of the packets have been routed after time $O(Tn)$, where T is the maximum size of all buffers. According to Mitzenmacher et al. [10], supposing that we throw n balls into n bins with each ball choosing a bin independently and uniformly at random, then the *maximum load* is approximately $\log n / \log \log n$ with high probability[1]. Maximum load means the largest number of balls in any bin. Correspondingly, if we have n packets to send and n sending buffers during a simulation step, then the maximum load of sending buffers is approximately $\log n / \log \log n$ *whp*. The overall routing time of those packets is $n \log n / \log \log n + \Theta(1)$ that is not work-optimal according to the definition of work-optimality.

If the size of h-relation is enlarged to $h \geq n \log n$, the maximum load is $\Theta(h/n)$ [11]. Assuming that $h = n \log n$ the maximum load is $\Theta(\log n)$ and the corresponding routing time is $\Theta(n \log n)$. A work-optimal result is achieved according to the definition of work-optimality.

Routing h packets in time $\Theta(h)$ implies work-optimality. We ran some experiments to get an idea about the cost. We ran 5 simulation rounds for each occurrence using a visualizator programmed with Java programming language [4]. Packets were randomly put into output buffers and the average value of the routing time over all the 5 simulation rounds were evaluated. The average cost was evaluated using equation $c_{ave} = \frac{t_r}{h}$, where t_r is the average routing time. Figure 4 gives support to the idea that h does not need to be extremely high to get a reasonable routing cost.

---

[1] We use *whp*, *with high probability* to mean with probability at least $1 - O(1/n^\alpha)$ for some constant α.

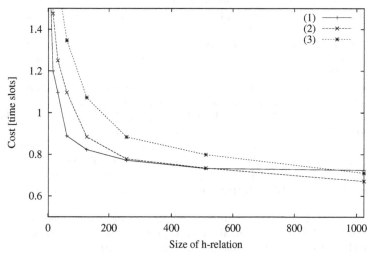

Fig. 4. Routing costs, when the size of h-relation varies. (1) $n = 4$, (2) $n = 8$, and (3) $n = 16$

5   Conclusions and Future Work

We have presented the systolic routing protocol for optical butterfly. No electro-optical conversion is needed during the transfer and all the packets injected into the routing machinery are guaranteed to reach their destination. We believe that the simple structure presented and the systolic routing protocol are useful and realistic and offer work-optimal routing of h-relation if $h \in \Theta(n \log n)$.

An advantage of our construction is that the overall number of links is $\Theta(n \log n)$. Honkanen presented the systolic routing protocol for Sparse Optical Torus ($\mathcal{SOT}$) is his paper [5]. For $\mathcal{SOT}$, the number of links is $\Theta(n^2)$.

However, a drawbacks arise, when the systems are scaled up. Putting M elements in the physical space requires at least a volume of size $\Theta(\sqrt[3]{M})$ [15,16]. The length of wires between routing nodes increase with respect to the physical space required.

References

1. Adler, M., Byers, J.W., Karp, R.M.: Scheduling Parallel Communication: The h-relation Problem. Proceedings of Mathematical Foundation of Computer Science (MFCS). Prague Czech Republic (1995) 1–20
2. Fredricksen, H.: A Survey of Full Length Nonlinear Shift Register Cycle Algorithms. SIAM Review **24**,2 (1982) 195–221
3. Golomb, S.W.: Shift Register Sequences. Aegean Park Press, Laguna Hills California (1982)
4. Haikarainen, T.: Visualisator for $\mathcal{OBF}$ network. Special project, University of Kuopio, Kuopio. URL: http://www.cs.uku.fi/~rthonkan/OBF/ (March 30, 2005)

5. Honkanen, R.T.: Systolic Routing in Sparse Optical Torus. Proceedings of the 8th Symposium on Programming Languages and Programming Tools (SPLST'03). Kuopio Finland (2003) 14–20

6. Honkanen, R., Leppänen, V., Penttonen M.: Hot-Potato routing Algorithms for Sparse Optical Torus. Proceedings of the 2001 ICPP Workshops. Valencia Spain (2001) 302–307

7. Leighton, F.T.: Introduction to parallel algorithms and architecture: arrays, trees, hypercubes. Morgan Kaufmann Publishers Inc., California (1992)

8. Liu, X., Gu, Q.-P.: Multicasts on WDM All-Optical Butterfly Networks. Journal of Information Science and Engineering **18** (2002) 1049–1058

9. Maggs, B.M., Sitaraman, R.K.: Simple Algorithms for Routing on Butterfly Networks with Bounded Queues. Siam J. Comput. **28**,3 (1999) 984–1003

10. Mitzenmacher, M., Richa, A.W., Sitaraman, R.: To appear in: Handbook of Randomized Algorithm. URL: http://www.eecs.harvard.edu/~michaelm/ (June 24, 2002)

11. Raab, M., Steger, A.: "Balls into Bins"—A Simple and Tight Analysis. Proceedings of 2nd Workshop on Randomize and Approximation Techniques on Computer Science (RANDOM'98). Barcelona Spain (1998) 159–170

12. Saleh, B.E.A., Teich, M.C.: Fundamentals of Photonics. John Wiley & Sons Inc., New York (1991)

13. Upfal, E., Felperin, S., Snir, M.: Randomized Routing with Shorter Paths. IEEE Transactions on Parallel and Distributed Systems **7**,4 (1996) 356–362

14. Valiant L.G.: General Purpose Parallel Architectures. In Algorithms and Complexity. Handbook of Theoretical Computer Science vol. A (1990) 943–971

15. Vitányi P.B.M., 1988: Locality, Communication, and Interconnect Length in Multicomputers. SIAM Journal of Computing **17**,4 (1988) 659–672

16. Vitányi P.B.M., 1994: Multiprocessor Architectures and Physical Law. Proceedings of 2nd Workshop on Physics and Computation (PhysComp'94). Dallas Texas (1994) 24–29

Feasibility of the Circularly Connected Analog CNN Cell Array-Based Viterbi Decoder

Hongrak Son[1], Hyunjung Kim[2], Hyongsuk Kim[2], and Kil To Chong[2]

[1] Communicatin and Network Lab. Samsung Advance Institute of Technology,
Yongin, Repulbic of Korea
[2] Division of Electronics and Information Engineering, Chonbuk National University,
561-756, Chonju, Republic of Korea
hskim@chobuk.ac.kr

Abstract. The feasibility of the high speed Viterbi decoder with a circularly connected 2-dimensional analog CNN cell array has been investigated. In the previous study, the CNN-based analog Viterbi decoder was reported, in which a part of the trellis diagram of the convolutional coder is designed with analog circuit-based cells and connections. The circuits of the trellis diagram are connected circularly, forming a cylindrical shape so that the cells of the last stage are connected to those of the first stage. In this study, the performance of the CNN-based analog Viterbi decoder circuits have been measured through circuit simulations and its hardware feasibility has been investigated with two different kinds of tests such as the worst-case simulation and the Monte Carlo analysis. Results of such simulations are included.

1 Introduction

The Viterbi decoder [1][2] is the convolutional code decoder which is widely used for error correction in numerous high-speed data communication areas. The decoder is a simple model of dynamic programming [3], performing efficient data correction by utilizing the most likely path-finding on the trellis diagram. One weakness is the requirement of a heavy computation load.

There were approaches to fulfill such computational requirement utilizes digital technology [4] where a one-dimensional array of computational units for one stage is implemented into circuits. The trace-back requirement for finding the path with the minimum error forces the circuits to employ the large size of path memory and additional circuitry. Also, the high speed A/D converter which consumes a lot of power is required in such a digital Viterbi decoder. Different approach alleviating the problems in the digital Viterbi decoder is the analog Viterbi decoder [3] in which the digital processor for each node is replaced with an analog processing unit. However, it is not freed from the requirement of the path memory and trace-back procedure.

The Cellular Neural/Nonlinear Networks by Chua et [4][5] is the technology of full parallelism employing massive processing array. Since the speed of the CNN processing is potentially very high, its application to the Viterbi decoder is expected to be a good technical combination. The decoding structure of the fully parallel

V. Malyshkin (Ed.): PaCT 2005, LNCS 3606, pp. 151–158, 2005.
© Springer-Verlag Berlin Heidelberg 2005

Viterbi decoder in which the infinitively expanding trellis diagram is implemented with the circularly connected cell array was reported [8]. The nodes of the trellis diagram are devised with the cells of the Cellular Neural Network (CNN). To test the feasibility of the structure, diverse simulations have been done such as the worst case simulations and the Monte Carlo analysis. The results of such study is reported in this paper.

2 Operational Principle of the Proposed Viterbi Decoder

The principle of the Viterbi decoder is explained with the operation of trellis diagram as in Figure 1 where vertical and horizontal locations are called states and stages, respectively. Each branch between the states contains symbol error for a data bit. Each node of the trellis diagram performs (1) to accumulate minimum error as in the operation of dynamic programming [3].

$$E_{i,j} = min \ \{ \ E_{k,l} + e_{ij,kl}, \ (k,l) \in S \} \tag{1}$$

where $E_{k,l}$ is the minimum total error from the start node to the node (k, l) and $e_{ij,kl}$ is a symbol error for a data bit assigned on the branch between the two nodes (i, j) and (k, l). Also, S is a set of the cells in the neighbor of the cell (i,j), and min is the function of minimum. Since a greater number of states allows for better error correcting performance, the conventional Viterbi decoder has a heavy computational burden due to the loads of the nonlinear processes at many nodes on one hand and the optimal path finding operation on the trellis diagram on the other hand.

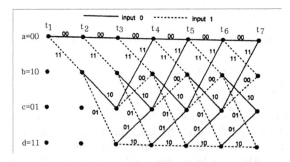

Fig. 1. An example of trellis diagram

The CNN is inherently the parallel processing structure with massive parallelism. Since the CNN is potentially high in processing speed due to its massive parallelism, its application to Viterbi decoding process can be expected to produce a great performance: a cell in CNN acts as a node on the trellis diagram. One problem that has arisen is the difficulty of hardware implementation since the trellis diagram expands infinitively as the data are received continuously. The idea proposed in this study is that the finite length of the circularly connected CNN as shown in Figure 2 performs for the infinitively expanding trellis diagram. Since such 2D networks are

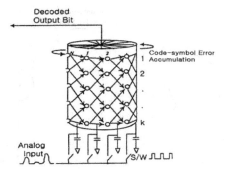

Fig. 2. Proposed CNN-based Viterbi decoder with cylindrical connection to perform the operation of trellis diagram

configured to have a cylindrical shape, the decoding is performed continuously through the reference value propagation around the networks. The identification whether a branch passes the optimal path or not is performed by adding a negative triggering pulse to the branch and checking the alteration level of the output stage. The values appear at the output stage are influenced only when the branch on the optimal path is triggered. In this processing structure, each CNN cell is implemented with analog circuits. Therefore, the A/D converter is not required and quantization error does not occur. Also, the parallel analog structure of the proposed Viterbi decoder allows the decoding speed to be very high, and the trigger-based decoding mechanism does not require the path memory and circuits for the trace. The details of the operation and its structure are included in [8].

3   CNN Cell Circuits

In the cylindrical shape of the proposed Viterbi decoder, each node has partial connections since the error flows and accumulates only in the rotational direction. The cell structure of the proposed CNN is unsymmetrical as in Figure 3(b) in contrast to symmetrical in the ordinary cell as in Figure 3(a). In networks with such connections, information flows in one direction, while flowing out to other directions. Since the computation (1) includes min operation, its implementation with electronic circuits is complicated. Introducing a big reference value I_{ref} and with some arrangement, (1) could be expressed with max circuits which are simpler circuits than min as in (2).

$$y_{i,j} = \max\{y_{k,l} - E_{i,j}; \ (k,l) \in S(i,j)\} \tag{2}$$

where $y_{k,l}$ is defined as

$$y_{k,l} = I_{ref} - E_{k,l}. \tag{3}$$

The circuits to compute (2) or the nonlinear cell function in Figure 3(b) can be implemented with the current mode circuits as in Figure 4. Let $u(i,j)$ be the input of

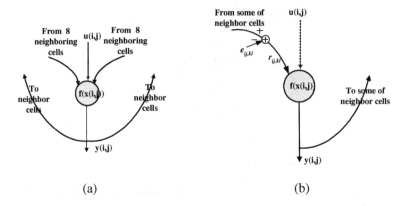

Fig. 3. Comparison of CNN cell structures (a) ordinary CNN cell (b) proposed CNN cell

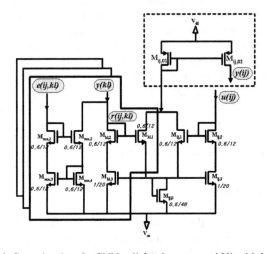

Fig. 4. Core circuits of a CNN cell for the proposed Viterbi decoder

the cell at the i th state of the j th stage on the trellis diagram. Transistors at the center of the circuits compose the max function, where transistors $M_{ij,1}$, $M_{ij,2}$, $M_{ij,3}$ make an input terminal of the current mode max circuit at the cell (i,j). The transistor $M_{ij,c}$ is a common transistor for the max operation at the cell (i, j). For example, the transistors $M_{ij,1}$, $M_{ij,2}$, $M_{ij,3}$ are for the input $u(ij)$ and the transistors $M_{kl,1}$, $M_{kl,2}$, $M_{kl,3}$ are for the input r(ij,kl). The circuits choose the bigger one between u(ij) and r(ij,kl) where r(ij,kl) is the difference between y(kl) and e(ij,kl). Such subtraction is performed simply by parallel connection of a current mirror which drains the current corresponding to e(ij,kl) out of y(kl) as shown at the left side of the Figure 4. The output of the circuits is obtained at a terminal y_{ij} of the current mirror $M_{ij,01}$ and $M_{ij,02}$. Such input and output terminals correspond to those in the cell structure of Figure 3(b).

Figure 5 shows the complete circuits of a cell including the subsidiary blocks. The voltage signals of the input code symbol and the branch code symbol are converted into the corresponding currents with V-to-I converting circuits. Such circuits are at the left most block divided by the dotted line, where V_{cap} and V_{br} are the input symbol and the reference branch code symbol voltages, respectively. Also, the V_{bias} is the bias voltage. Note that the input code symbols are expressed as a quadrature signal with multi-levels. The current mode signals of the V-to-I output are fed into the difference and absolute computing circuits at the center block. The output of the center block is provided as the branch metric error to the core circuits at the lower part of the right most blocks. The upper part of the right most blocks is the V-to-I circuits for the reference input signal I_{ref}. The sizes and types of the transistors are listed in the Table 1.

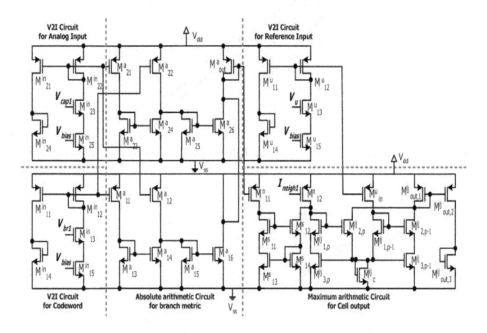

Fig. 5. Complete circuits of a cell including the subsidiary blocks

4   Circuit Simulations

The circuits of the proposed Viterbi decoder in Figure 2 have been designed and its performance has been tested with HSPICE simulation. The constraint length and code rate of the proposed decoder are K=7(64 states) and R=1/2, respectively. The simulation of the proposed Viterbi decoder has been done under the AGWN environment. The technology and simulation model used is Hyundai 0.35um and BSIM3v3 MOS model level 49.

Figure 6 shows the comparison of error correction performance between the conventional and the proposed Viterbi decoder at various decoding speed. With the same performance, the speed in the proposed decoding scheme is much superior to the digital Viterbi decoder. Though the speed of a specially designed digital Viterbi decoder can reach 91 Mbps, it requires about ten times more transistors than the proposed decoder. Note that the speed of the ordinary sized digital Viterbi decoder is less than 30 Mbps.

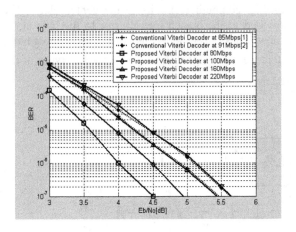

Fig. 6. Performance comparison between the digital Viterbi decoder and the proposed Viterbi decoder

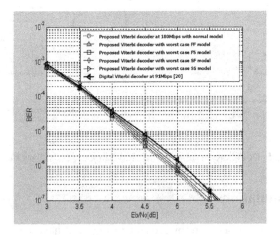

Fig. 7. Simulation results of the worst case models. F and S denote fast and slow options. The first and the second characters in FF, FS, SF and SS are for the NMOS and the PMOS, respectively. Performances of all the worst case models of the proposed circuits are better than that of digital counter part with the half of decoding speed

The results of Figure 6 are the ones without considering the fabrication inaccuracy. To estimate the decoding speed of the real chip, two different kinds of tests have been done: the worst-case simulation and the Monte Carlo analysis.

In the worst-case simulation, the performance of the circuits has been tested assuming the size (W/L) is normal, bigger or smaller than that of the nominal one for NMOS and PMOS, respectively. The different kinds of size (W/L) deviation of the transistors of NMOS and PM OS are chosen by the speed options of the chip in HSPICE simulator. For example, a slow-fast (SF) option assumes that NMOS is larger and the PMOS is smaller than that of the nominal ones, respectively. Therefore, the option SS is the worst case where all the NMOS and PMOS are assumed to be slow. Observing the error correction performance of the proposed Viterbi decoder for 4 different worst-case models at 180Mb/s in Figure 7, we see that the speed of the proposed circuits to achieve the same performance of the digital counter part [20] is two times faster than that of the digital one.

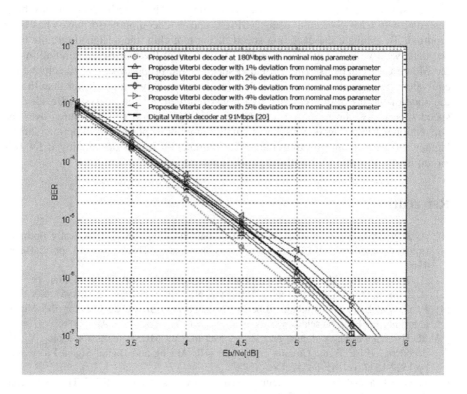

Fig. 8. Performance of the proposed Viterbi decoder when mismatching among transistors is considered. The mismatching is allowed by deviating the MOS parameters of each transistor by randomly generated amount

The circuit simulation to show the mismatching effect has also been done based on the Monte Carlo analysis. For this end, V_t and T_{ox} values of all transistors are varied randomly within the ranges of m% of their nominal values while the value of m varies from 1 to 5. For example, if m is 2, the deviation of the parameters is the randomly selected number within the range of [-2%, 2%] of its nominal value. Therefore, V_t and T_{ox} values are assigned differently for every transistors and the mismatching condition of the circuits is established. Figure 8 shows the performance of the proposed Viterbi decoder at 180 Mbps, which is about two times higher speed than that of the conventional digital counter part. As shown in the figure, the performance of the Viterbi decoder degrades gracefully as the deviation increases. However, it is still better than that of the digital counter part with one half speed until 3% of deviation.

5 Conclusion

A very high speed and low power Viterbi decoder employing a circularly connected 2-dimensional analog CNN cell array is proposed. The Viterbi decoder has been designed with CMOS circuits using HSPICE and its decoding performance has been reported. To estimate the decoding speed of the real chip, the designed circuits have been analyzed with two different kinds of tests such as the worst-case simulation and the Monte Carlo analysis. The estimated speed of the proposed circuit to achieve the equivalent performance to the digital Viterbi decoders is two times faster than that of the state-of-the art digital counter part consistently in all the analyses. Besides the speed superiority, the proposed Viterbi decoder has several better features over the conventional Viterbi decoders such as smaller amount of power consumption, shorter latency, no path memory requirement. The number of transistors employed for this circuit is also less than that of the digital counter part.

References

[1] A. J. Viterbi, "Error bounds for convolutional codes and an asymptotically optimum decoding algorithm," IEEE Transactions on Information Theory, vol. 13, pp. 260-269, 1967.
[2] G. D. Forney, JR. "The Viterbi algorithm," Proc. of the IEEE, vol. 61, No. 3, Mar. 1973.
[3] R. Bellman, Dynamic Programming, Princeton, NJ: Princeton Univ. Press, 1957.
[4] P. G. Gulak and T. Kailath, "Locally connected VLSI architecture for the Viterbi algorithm," IEEE J. on selected areas in comm., vol. 6, pp. 527-537, Apr. 1988.
[5] M. H. Shakiba, D. A. Johns, and K. W. Martin, "BiCMOS circuits for analog Viterbi decoders," IEEE Trans. Circuits and Systems-II: Analog and Digital Signal Processing, pp.1527-1537, vol. 45, no. 12, Dec. 1998
[6] L. O. Chua and L. Yang, "Cellular neural networks: theory," IEEE Tr. on Circuits Systems, vol.35, pp. 1257-1272, 1988.
[7] T. Roska and L. O. Chua, "The CNN universal machine: an analogic array computer", IEEE Tr. on Circuits Systems II, CAS-40, pp. 163-173, 1993.
[8] H. Kim, H. Son, T. Roska, L. O. Chua, "Very high speed Viterbi decoder with circularly connected analog CNN cell array," IEEE International Symposium on Circuits and Systems Vol.3, pp.III-97-100 Vol.3, 2004.

Associative Parallel Algorithm for Dynamic Reconstruction of a Minimum Spanning Tree After Deletion of a Vertex*

Anna Nepomniaschaya

Institute of Computational Mathematics and Mathematical Geophysics,
Siberian Division of Russian Academy of Sciences,
pr. Lavrentieva, 6, Novosibirsk, 630090, Russia
anep@ssd.sscc.ru

Abstract. In this paper, we propose an associative parallel algorithm for updating a minimum spanning tree when a vertex and all its incident edges are deleted from the underlying graph. This algorithm is represented as the corresponding procedure implemented on a model of associative parallel systems of the SIMD type with vertical data processing (the STAR–machine). We justify the correctness of this procedure and evaluate its time complexity.

1 Introduction

Updating a minimum spanning tree (MST) after changes in the network topology is a fundamental problem. Let G be an undirected graph with n vertices and m edges and T be its MST. Let one of the following changes be performed in G: deletion or insertion of an edge, or deletion or insertion of a vertex along with its incident edges. We want to compute a new MST for the altered graph by performing changes in the given T. In particular, such a problem arises in computer networks that use broadcast or multicast routing protocols [2]. The dynamic graph algorithms are designed to handle graph changes. They maintain some property of a changing graph more efficiently than recomputation of the entire graph from scratch with a static algorithm after every change.

We study the vertex deletion problem. Let us enumerate the main results obtained for this task. Chin and Houck [1] proposed an $O(n^2)$ sequential algorithm for reconstructing an MST after deletion of any vertex. Tsin [13] presented a parallel algorithm that updates an MST after a single vertex deletion. Tsin's algorithm uses $n^2/\log n$ CREW PRAM processors and runs in $O(\log n + \log^2 \delta_T(v))$ time, where $\delta_T(v)$ is the tree degree of a deleted vertex v. Pawagi and Kaser [12] have generalized Tsin's algorithm to handle the k-vertex deletion problem. Das and Loui [2] proposed two algorithms for reconstructing an MST after deletion of any vertex. Their sequential algorithm takes $O(m \log n)$ time in general and their parallel algorithm takes $O(\log^2 n)$ time using m CREW PRAM processors.

---

* This work was supported in part by the Russian Foundation for Basic Research under Grant 03-01-00399.

In this paper, we first propose a simple and elegant associative parallel algorithm for dynamic reconstructing an MST after deletion of a vertex and all its incident edges from the underlying graph. Our model of computation (the STAR–machine) simulates the run of associative (content addressable) parallel systems of the SIMD type with bit–serial (vertical) processing and simple single–bit processing elements (PEs). Such an architecture is best suited to solving graph problems. By analogy with [9], our associative algorithm for the vertex deletion problem uses a graph represented on the STAR–machine as a list of triples (edge vertices and the weight) and a matrix of tree paths consisting of m rows and n columns. Its every i-th column saves the tree path from the root v_1 to vertex v_i. In view of [10], initially the source MST and the corresponding matrix of tree paths are known. Such a matrix is used both to select the connected components obtained after deleting a vertex from the graph and to construct a new MST. To achieve the dynamic reconstruction of an MST, we perform the corresponding changes in the matrix of tree paths each time after finding a new MST.

The associative parallel algorithm for updating the MST after a single vertex deletion is represented on the STAR–machine as procedure DeleteVert whose correctness is proved. We obtain that this procedure takes $O(h \log n)$ time, where h is the number of vertices whose tree paths change after deletion of a vertex. Following Foster [3], it is assumed that each elementary operation of the STAR–machine (its microstep) takes one unit of time.

2   An Associative Parallel Machine Model

We define the model as an abstract STAR–machine of the SIMD type with vertical processing and simple single–bit PEs. It consists of the following components:

- a sequential control unit (CU), where programs and scalar constants are stored;
- an associative processing unit consisting of p single–bit PEs;
- a matrix memory for the associative processing unit.

The CU broadcasts an instruction to all PEs per unit time. All active PEs execute it simultaneously while inactive PEs do not perform it. Activation of a PE depends on data.

Input binary data are loaded in the matrix memory in the form of two–dimensional tables, where each data item occupies an individual row and it is updated by a dedicated PE. The rows are numbered from top to bottom and the columns – from left to right.

The associative processing unit is represented as h vertical registers, each consisting of p bits. A vertical register can be regarded as a one–column array that maintains an entire column of a table. Bit columns of tabular data are stored in the registers which perform the necessary bitwise operations.

The STAR–machine run is described by means of the language STAR [7] being an extension of Pascal. To simulate data processing in the matrix memory, we use the data types **slice** and **word** for the bit column access and the bit row access, respectively, and the type **table** for defining the tabular data. Assume that any variable of the type **slice** consists of p components. For simplicity, let us call "slice" any variable of the type **slice**.

Let X, Y be variables of the type **slice** and i be a variable of the type **integer**. We use the following elementary operations:

SET(Y) sets all components of the slice Y to $'1'$; CLR(Y) sets all components of Y to $'0'$; $Y(i)$ selects the i-th component of Y; FND(Y) returns the ordinal number i of the first (the uppermost) component $'1'$ of Y; STEP(Y) returns the same result as FND(Y) and then resets the first $'1'$ found to $'0'$; NUMB(Y) returns the number of components $'1'$ in the slice Y.

In the usual way we introduce predicates ZERO(Y) and SOME(Y) and the bitwise Boolean operations X *and* Y, X *or* Y, *not* Y, X *xor* Y.

The above–mentioned operations are also used for variables of the type **word**.

Let T be a variable of the type **table**. We use the following two operations:

ROW(i,T) returns the i-th row of the matrix T; COL(i,T) returns its i-th column.

Remark 1. Note that the STAR statements are defined in the same manner as for Pascal. They will be used for presenting our procedures.

We will employ the following three basic procedures implemented on the STAR–machine [8]. They use a global slice X to mark with ones the positions of rows which will be processed. As shown in [8], these procedures run in $O(k)$ time each, where k is the number of columns in T.

The procedure MATCH(T, X, v, Z) defines in parallel positions of the given matrix T rows which coincide with the given pattern v written in binary code. It returns the slice Z, where $Z(i) =' 1'$ if and only if ROW(i,T) $= v$ and $X(i) =' 1'$.

The procedure MIN(T, X, Z) defines in parallel positions of the given matrix T rows, where minimum elements are located. It returns the slice Z, where $Z(i) =' 1'$ if and only if ROW(i,T) is the minimum element in T and $X(i) =' 1'$.

The procedure TCOPY(T, h, F) writes the given matrix T, consisting of h columns, into the resulting matrix F.

3   Preliminaries

Let $G = (V, E)$ denote an *undirected graph*, where V is a set of vertices and E is a set of edges. Let $wt(e)$ denote the weight of the edge e. We assume that $V = \{1, 2, \ldots, n\}$, $|V| = n$, and $|E| = m$.

A *path* from v_1 to v_k in G is a sequence of the vertices $v_1, v_2, \ldots, v_k$, where $(v_i, v_{i+1}) \in E$ for $1 \leq i < k$.

A *minimum spanning tree* $T = (V, E')$ is a connected acyclic subgraph of G, where $E' \subseteq E$ and the sum of weights of the corresponding edges is minimum.

Each edge $e \in E - E'$ is called a *chord* of G.

Let $\delta_T(v)$ denote the number of edges of T incident on v.

A *connected component* is a maximal connected subgraph of G.

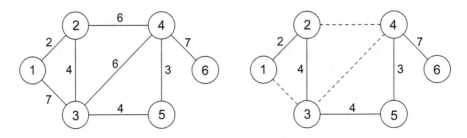

Fig. 1. Graph G and its MST T

Let every edge (u, v) be matched with the triple $(u, v, wt(u, v))$. Note that vertices and weights are written in binary code. In the STAR–machine memory, a graph is represented as association of matrices *left*, *right*, and *weight*, where every triple $(u, v, wt(u, v))$ occupies an individual row, and $u \in left$, $v \in right$, and $wt(u, v) \in weight$. A minimum spanning tree is represented as a slice, where *positions* of edges belonging to it are marked with $'1'$.

We also use a matrix of tree paths M consisting of m rows and n columns. Its every i-th column saves the tree path from the root v_1 to vertex v_i. Initially, it is obtained along with the MST [10].

Let an edge from the i-th row of the graph representation be deleted from the MST. Then the vertices marked with $'1'$ in the i-th row of M form a separate connected component.

We will illustrate the use of the matrix M by means of a graph given in Figure 1. In the right part of this figure, solid edges form the MST T.

Let the edge $(3, 5)$ be deleted from the MST. In Table 1, this edge is written in the seventh row of the graph representation. Therefore vertices $\{4, 5, 6\}$ marked with $'1'$ in the seventh row of the matrix M form a separate connected component.

In [9], we proposed two associative parallel algorithms for the dynamic edge update of an MST. They employ the matrix of tree paths M. After finding a new MST, this matrix changes by means of the auxiliary procedure TreePaths.

Table 1. Representations of a graph, its MST, and the matrix of tree paths on the STAR–machine

	left	right	weight	S	T
		Table		Slice	
1	001	010	010	1	1
2	001	011	111	1	0
3	010	011	100	1	1
4	010	100	110	1	0
5	011	100	110	1	0
6	100	101	011	1	1
7	011	101	100	1	1
8	100	110	111	1	1

	1	2	3	4	5	6
1	0	1	1	1	1	1
2	0	0	0	0	0	0
3	0	0	1	1	1	1
4	0	0	0	0	0	0
5	0	0	0	0	0	0
6	0	0	0	1	0	1
7	0	0	0	1	1	1
8	0	0	0	0	0	1

4 Associative Parallel Algorithm for Updating an MST After Deletion of a Vertex

Let $G - v$ be a graph after deleting the vertex v and all its incident edges. We assume that this graph is connected and has an MST.

The algorithm consists of the following three stages.

At the *first stage*, we determine connected components obtained after deleting vertex v and all its incident edges. Then we save vertices adjacent to vertex v.

At the *second stage*, we first determine positions of chords. Then positions of edges incident on v are deleted from the current MST. Finally, we determine the positions of chords being included in the new MST and save their endpoints.

At the *third stage*, we recompute the matrix of tree paths M.

4.1 Finding Connected Components

Let a vertex v and all its incident edges be deleted from the MST T. By definition of a tree, there is such a unique edge, say γ, incident on v that vertex v is not reachable from v_1 after deleting this edge from the MST. Therefore the MST is divided into two subtrees T_1 and T_2 such that T_1 includes vertex v_1 and T_2 includes vertex v along with vertices reachable from v. Let γ be written in the i-th row of the graph representation. Since the subtree T_2 also includes edges incident on v that will be deleted from the MST, one can determine the subtree that includes vertex v_1. It is precisely those vertices that are not marked with $'1'$ in the i-th row of the matrix M.

Now, we propose an associative parallel algorithm for finding connected components obtained after deleting vertex v from the MST. Knowing the given MST, vertex v, and the matrix of tree paths M, it builds a matrix of connected components *comp*, consisting of n bit columns and $\delta_T(v)$ rows. Its every row saves a separate connected component. The algorithm performs the following steps.

Step 1. Save *positions* of edges from the MST incident on vertex v.
Update the selected edges using Steps 2–5.
Step 2. Select position i of the current edge from the MST incident on v.
Step 3. Save the i-th row of the matrix M using a variable, say w_1.
Step 4. Verify whether vertex v belongs to the row w_1.
The following two cases are possible.
Case 1. The vertex v is marked with $'1'$ in w_1. Then *not* w_1 is written in the current row of the matrix *comp*.
Case 2. The vertex v is marked with $'0'$ in w_1. Then w_1 is written in the current row of the matrix *comp*.
Step 5. Determine the vertex adjacent to vertex v and save its number in the variable *vdel*.

Let in Figure 1 vertex 5 and its incident edges be deleted from the MST. Then in view of the rule from Step 4, we determine connected components $\{4, 6\}$ and $\{1, 2, 3\}$ using the sixth and the seventh rows of the matrix M, respectively. Hence, the matrix *comp* will consist of the following two rows: $0\,0\,0\,1\,0\,1$ and $1\,1\,1\,0\,0\,0$. One can check that $vdel = 0\,0\,1\,1\,0\,0$.

On the STAR–machine, the algorithm is realized by means of the procedure Subtrees. It returns the following parameters: a matrix *comp*; a variable *vdel* to save vertices adjacent to vertex *v*; a slice *S* to save positions of edges that remain after deleting vertex *v* and all its incident edges; a slice *Y* to save positions of edges from the MST incident on *v*.

Now, we propose the following procedure.

```
procedure Subtrees(left,right: table; code: table; M: table;
    T: slice(left); v: integer; var S,Y: slice(left);
    var vdel: word; var comp: table);
/* Here, S is the slice that saves positions of all graph edges,
    T is the MST and v is the deleted vertex. */
var X: slice(left);
    Z,Z1: slice(code);
    i,j,k: integer;
    node1,node2,w1,w2: word;
1. Begin SET(Z); j:=0; CLR(vdel);
2.    node1:=ROW(v,code);
3.    MATCH(left,S,node1,X);
4.    MATCH(right,S,node1,Y);
5.    X:=X or Y;
/* The slice X saves positions of all graph edges incident on v. */
6.    S:=S and (not X);
/* Positions of edges incident on v are deleted from the slice S. */
7.    Y:=X and T;
/* The slice Y saves positions of edges from T incident on v. */
8.    X:=Y;
9.    while SOME(X) do
10.       begin i:=STEP(X);
/* We select the position of the current deleted edge. */
11.           w1:=ROW(i,M); j:=j+1;
12.           if w1(v)='1' then
/* The connected component includes vertex v. */
13.               begin w2:=not w1;
14.                   ROW(j,comp):=w2;
15.               end
16.               else ROW(j,comp):=w1;
17.           node2:=ROW(i,left);
18.           if node1=node2 then node2:=ROW(i,right);
19.           MATCH(code,Z,node2,Z1);
20.           k:=FND(Z1);
/* The endpoint k of the deleted edge belongs to the connected
    component located in the j-th row of the matrix comp. */
21.           vdel(k):='1';
22.       end;
23. End;
```

Theorem 1. *Let a graph G be given as association of the matrices left and right, and the matrix code save binary representations of vertices. Let an MST be given as a slice T and vertex v be deleted from it. Then the procedure Subtrees returns the matrix comp and the above described variables vdel, S, and Y.*

Proof. (Sketch) We prove this by induction on the number of edges k being incident on vertex v in the MST.

Basis is checked for $k = 1$. After performing lines 1–6, the variable $node1$ saves the binary code of vertex v and positions of *all* its incident edges are deleted from the global slice S. After performing lines 7–8, each of slices X and Y saves position of a single edge, say γ, incident on v in the MST.

After performing lines 10–11, we first extract position i of γ and then we save the i-th row of the matrix M using the variable $w1$. Since there is a single edge incident on v in the MST, after deleting γ only vertex v is not reachable from vertex v_1. Therefore $w1(v) =' 1'$. Hence, after performing lines 12–15, we obtain a single connected component consisting of all vertices except v and write it in the first row of the matrix $comp$. One can immediately verify that after performing lines 17–21, the variable $vdel$ saves the vertex of γ adjacent to v. Since the slice X consists of zeros, the procedure terminates.

Step of induction. Let the assertion be true for MSTs that include no more than $k - 1$ edges incident on v. We prove this for MSTs having k such edges.

Again, after performing lines 1–8, positions of *all* edges incident on v are deleted from the slice S, and each of slices X and Y saves positions of k edges from the MST incident on v.

By inductive assumption, after updating the first $k-1$ edges incident on v in the MST, the first $k-1$ connected components are written in the corresponding rows of the matrix $comp$, the variable $vdel$ saves $k-1$ vertices adjacent to vertex v and the slice X saves position of a single edge incident on v. Since X is a non–empty slice, we start with line 10. By analogy with the basis, after performing lines 10–22, we first select the last connected component and write it in the k-th row of the matrix $comp$. Then we include the endpoint of this edge adjacent to v in $vdel$. Since the slice X consists of zeros, the procedure terminates.   □

Now, we enumerate two properties of the matrix $comp$ and three rules being used for constructing a new MST.

Property 1. $\forall i \neq j$, $\text{ROW}(i, comp) \neq \text{ROW}(j, comp)$.

Property 2. There is a unique bit $'1'$ in every column of the matrix $comp$.

Rule 1. To determine the connected component that includes the vertex having number i, we need to select the i-th column of the matrix $comp$ and to find the position of $'1'$.

Rule 2. To determine whether endpoints of a chord (i, j) belong to the same connected component of the matrix $comp$, we need to find the row of $comp$ that includes vertex i (using Rule 1) and then check whether the j-th bit of this row is equal to $'1'$.

Rule 3. Let endpoints of a chord (i, j) belong to different connected components from the matrix *comp*. Then a new connected component is obtained by including the connected component containing its right endpoint (vertex j) into the connected component containing its left endpoint (vertex i). Then we write zeros in the matrix *comp* row, where the connected component including the vertex j was written.

4.2   Finding a New MST

Here, we propose an associative parallel algorithm that constructs a new MST from the current one after deletion of vertex v and all its incident edges. Knowing connected components obtained after deleting vertex v from the MST and positions of edges incident on v, the algorithm determines a new MST, positions of chords joining different connected components and their endpoints.

To obtain a new MST, we will simulate the run of Kruskal's algorithm [6] on the STAR–machine. Initially, this algorithm acts on $\delta_T(v)$ connected components each being an MST on the corresponding graph induced by its vertices [1].

At every iteration when the current selected chord of the minimum weight connects two *different* connected components, we unite them together with this chord forming a single connected component which is also an MST on the corresponding graph induced by its vertices.

The process continues until all connected components are united in a single connected component.

Let $\delta_T(v) = q$. Let us agree to denote by $C(u)$ a connected component that includes vertex u.

The associative parallel algorithm is performed as follows.

Step 1. Make a copy of the matrix *comp*, namely, *comp*1.
While $q > 1$, perform Steps 2–5.
Step 2. Find position i of the minimum weight chord. Then delete this chord from further consideration.
Step 3. Determine both vertices of this chord. Let the chord (l, r) be written in the i-th row of the graph representation.
Step 4. Determine the matrix *comp*1 row that contains vertex l.
Step 5. Check whether vertex r belongs to the same connected component.

The following two cases are possible.

Case 1. Both vertices belong to the same connected component. Then go to Step 2.

Case 2. Both vertices belong to different connected components. Then include the chord from the i-th row in the MST and in the slice *Rep*. Further, save its endpoints l and r in the i-th row of the matrix *endpoints* and perform the statement $q := q - 1$. Moreover, by means of Rule 3, determine a new connected component that unites $C(l)$ and $C(r)$ and change the corresponding rows of the matrix *comp*1.

On the STAR–machine, this algorithm is realized by means of the procedure NewMST. It returns the following parameters: a slice T to save the new MST; a slice *Rep* to save positions of chords joining different connected components; a matrix *endpoints* whose every i-th row saves both vertices of the chord from the i-th row of the graph representation being included in the slice *Rep*.

Initially, the slice T saves the current MST and the slice *Rep* consists of zeros. Let us present the following procedure.

```
procedure NewMST(left,right:table; weight:table; code:table;
   comp:table; Y,S:slice(left); n:integer; var T,Rep:
   slice(left); var endpoints:table);
var comp1:table;
   X,NT:slice(left);
   Z,Z1:slice(code);
   F:slice(comp);
   i,j,k,l,r,q:integer;
   w1,w2,w3:word;
1. Begin SET(Z); CLR(Rep);
2.    TCOPY(comp,n,comp1);
3.    NT:=S and (not T);
/* The slice NT saves positions of chords. */
4.    T:=T and (not Y);
/* We delete positions of edges incident on v from the slice T. */
5.    q:=NUMB(Y);
6.    while q>1 do
7.       begin MIN(weight,NT,X);
8.          i:=FND(X); NT(i):='0';
/* The position of the minimum weight chord is located
   in the i-th row of the graph representation. */
9.          w1:=ROW(i,left);
10.         MATCH(code,Z,w1,Z1); l:=FND(Z1);
11.         w1:=ROW(i,right);
12.         MATCH(code,Z,w1,Z1); r:=FND(Z1);
/* Here, (l,r) is the edge (say γ) from the i-th row. */
13.         F:=COL(l,comp1); j:=FND(F);
14.         w2:=ROW(j,comp1);
/* The endpoint l of the edge γ belongs to the connected
   component written in the j-th row of comp1. */
15.         if w2(r)='0' then
/* The case when the endpoint r of γ doesn't belong
   to the same connected component. */
16.            begin Rep(i):='1';
17.               T(i):='1'; CLR(w3);
18.               w3(l):='1'; w3(r):='1';
/* The variable w3 saves the edge (l,r). */
19.               ROW(i,endpoints):=w3;
```

```
20.              F:=COL(r,comp1); k:=FND(F);
21.              w3:=ROW(k,comp1);
/* The endpoint r of γ belongs to the connected component
   written in the k-th row of the matrix comp1. */
22.              w2:=w2 or w3;
/* Here, w2 saves the join of two connected components. */
23.              ROW(j,comp1):=w2;
24.              CLR(w3); ROW(k,comp1):=w3;
25.              q:=q-1;
26.          end;
27.      end;
28. End;
```

Theorem 2. *Let a graph G be given as a list of triples and the matrix code save binary representations of vertices. Let a matrix comp save the selected connected components, a slice Y save positions of edges incident on the deleted vertex, and n be the number of graph vertices. Then the procedure NewMST returns the slices T and Rep and the matrix endpoints described above.*

Proof. (Sketch) We prove this by induction on the number of connected components k obtained after performing the procedure Subtrees.

Basis is checked for $k = 2$. If there is a single connected component, the new MST is obtained from the current MST by deleting a single edge incident on v.

After performing lines 1–3, the slice Rep consists of zeros, the matrix $comp1$ is a copy of the matrix $comp$, and the slice NT saves positions of chords. After performing lines 4–5, positions of edges incident on v are deleted from the slice T and q saves the number of edges incident on v in the MST. Since $q = 2$, we fulfil the cycle from line 6.

Here, after performing lines 7–8, we determine *position i* of the minimum weight chord, say γ, and exclude it from the slice NT. After performing lines 9–12, we find out that $\gamma = (l, r)$.

After performing lines 13–15, using Rule 1, we first determine the connected component $C(l)$ that includes vertex l . Then by means of Rule 2, we verify whether r belongs to $C(l)$. We consider the following two cases:

Case 1. Let $r \notin C(l)$. Then after performing lines 16–19, we save position i of γ both in the slice Rep and in the slice T. Moreover, we save this chord in the i-th row of the matrix *endpoints*. On performing lines 20–25, we first determine the connected component $C(r)$. Then by means of Rule 3, we merge together $C(l)$ and $C(r)$ and change the corresponding rows of the matrix $comp1$. Finally, we perform the statement $q := q - 1$. Since $q = 1$, the procedure terminates.

Case 2. Let $r \in C(l)$. Then we go to line 7 and select another chord of the minimum weight because the previous chord was deleted from the slice NT.

It remains to show that the slice T saves positions of edges from the *new* MST. Really, we have deleted from T the positions of two edges incident on v (line 4) and have included the position of the minimum weight chord that links two connected components (line 17).

Step of induction. Let the assertion be true for MSTs having no more than $k - 1$ connected components. We prove this for MSTs that include k connected components. After performing lines 1–5, we obtain the matrix $comp1$ and update slices Rep, NT, and T by analogy with the basis. Since $q > 1$, we perform the cycle from line 6.

By inductive assumption, after selecting the first $k - 1$ chords of the minimum weight that link two different connected components, there is such a row in the matrix $comp1$ that the union of $k - 1$ connected components is written. In view of Rule 3, $k - 2$ rows of $comp1$ consist of zeros. Positions of these chords are included both in the slice T and in the slice Rep, their endpoints are written in the corresponding rows of the matrix $endpoints$ and $q = 2$. Therefore we perform line 6. Further we reason by analogy with the basis. □

4.3   Recomputing Tree Paths

Let us explain the main idea of the associative parallel algorithm for recomputing the matrix of tree paths M.

We first select the connected component w_1 that includes root v_1. Tree paths for vertices from w_1 do not change. Then we select the connected component w_2 which is linked with w_1 by means of a chord. After that, we determine *new* tree paths for all vertices from w_2 using the auxiliary procedure TreePaths. Further, we unite w_1 and w_2 and obtain a new connected component w_1.

The process is carried out until all connected components are included in w_1.

The associative parallel algorithm for recomputing tree paths is realized as procedure ChangePaths. It uses the following input parameters: matrices $comp$ and $endpoints$, and a slice Y described before. The procedure returns a slice Rep, a variable $vdel$, and the recomputed matrix M.

Initially, the slice Rep saves the positions of chords being included in the new MST, the variable $vdel$ saves vertices adjacent to vertex v, and the matrix M saves tree paths to all vertices of the source graph.

Really, the procedure NewMST does not change the matrix $comp$ and variables $vdel$ and Y obtained in the procedure Subtrees. Moreover, the matrix $endpoints$ and the slice Rep are obtained in the procedure NewMST. Note that the procedures Subtrees and NewMST do not change the matrix M.

The associative parallel algorithm is performed as follows.

Step 1. Make a copy of the matrix M, namely $M1$, to save tree paths from root v_1 to all vertices of the source graph.

Step 2. In the matrix $comp$, select a connected component w_1 that includes root v_1. Tree paths for vertices from w_1 do not change.

While $q > 1$ [1], perform Steps 3–8.

Step 3. In the matrix $endpoints$, select position i of a chord whose endpoint k belongs to w_1. Delete this chord from the slice Rep.

Step 4. Define another endpoint ins of this chord. Hence, we assume that the chord (k, ins) is written in the i-th row of the matrix $endpoints$.

---

[1] Here, $q = \delta_T(v)$.

Step 5. Select the connected component w_2 that includes vertex *ins*. In w_2, determine vertex *del* being adjacent to the deleted vertex v. Delete vertex *del* from the row *vdel*.

Step 6. By means of the matrix $M1$, determine both a *new* tree path W to vertex *ins* and a slice P to save *positions* of tree edges that link the vertices *ins* and *del*.

Step 7. By means of the procedure TreePaths, compute new tree paths for all vertices from the connected component w_2. Write down them in the corresponding columns of the matrix M.

Step 8. Join the connected component w_2 to the connected component w_1. Then perform the statement $q := q - 1$.

Now we propose the following procedure.

```
procedure ChangePaths(comp: table; endpoints: table;
    Y: slice(left); n: integer; var Rep: slice(left);
    var vdel: word; var M: table);
var M1: table;
    i,j,j1,k,l,q,del,ins: integer;
    X1,X2,P,W,Rep1: slice(left);
    F: slice(comp);
    w1,w2,w3: word;
 1. Begin TCOPY(M,n,M1);
 2.   q:=NUMB(Y); Rep1:=Rep;
/* Here, q saves the number of connected components. */
 3.   F:=COL(1,comp); j:=FND(F);
 4.   w1:=ROW(j,comp);
/* Here, w1 saves the connected component that includes root v1. */
 5.   while q>1 do
 6.     begin i:=STEP(Rep1);
 7.        w2:=ROW(i,endpoints);
 8.        w3:=w1 and w2;
 9.        while ZERO(w3) do
10.           begin i:=STEP(Rep1);
11.              w2:=ROW(i,endpoints);
12.              w3:=w1 and w2;
13.           end;
/* We select the position of the edge that joins the connected
   component having root v1 and another one. */
14.        Rep(i):='0'; Rep1:=Rep;
15.        k:=FND(w3);
16.        w2(k):='0'; ins:=FND(w2);
/* The edge (k,ins) is located in the i-th row
   of the matrix endpoints. */
17.        F:=COL(ins,comp); j1:=FND(F);
/* Vertex ins belongs to the connected component written
   in the j1-th row of the matrix comp. */
```

```
18.        w2:=ROW(j1,comp);
/* Here, w2 saves a connected component whose tree paths
   are recomputed. */
19.        w3:=w2 and vdel;
20.        del:=FND(w3); vdel(del):='0';
/* We determine endpoint of the deleted edge belonging
   to the same connected component as vertex ins. */
21.        W:=COL(k,M1); W(i):='1';
/* The slice W saves the new tree path to vertex ins. */
22.        X1:=COL(ins,M1);
23.        X2:=COL(del,M1);
24.        P:=X1 xor X2;
25.        TreePaths(left,right,code,M1,ins,del,M,P,W,w2);
/* We have determined new tree paths for every vertex from w2. */
26.        w1:=w1 or w2;
27.        q:=q-1;
28.   end;
29. End;
```

Theorem 3. *Let matrices comp and endpoints be obtained after deleting the vertex v and all its incident edges from the given graph. Let Y save positions of edges from the MST incident on v and n be the number of graph vertices. Then the procedure ChangePaths returns the slice Rep, the variable vdel, and the recomputed matrix of tree paths M.*

Proof. (Sketch) We prove this theorem by induction on the number of connected components obtained after performing the procedure Subtrees.

Basis is checked for $k = 2$. After performing lines 1–4, the slice $Rep1$ is a copy of Rep, the matrix $M1$ saves paths to all vertices of the source graph, and $w1$ is a connected component that includes vertex v_1. Since $q = 2$, we perform the cycle from line 5. Here, after performing lines 6–13, we select position i of the chord included in the new MST whose endpoint belongs to $w1$. This can be done because the matrix *endpoints* saves all chords included in the new MST. After performing line 14, we first delete position of the selected chord from the slice Rep and then perform $Rep1 := Rep$. After fulfilling lines 15–18, we first determine endpoint k of the selected chord that belongs to $w1$. Then we define its endpoint ins and the connected component $w2$ that includes it. Tree paths for $w2$ will be recomputed. After performing lines 19–24, we determine other parameters for the auxiliary procedure TreePaths.

Finally, after computing new tree paths for all vertices from $w2$, we join $w2$ to $w1$ and obtain a new connected component $w1$. Since $q = 1$ (line 27), the procedure terminates.

Step of induction is proved as in Theorem 2. It should be noted that the current connected component being joined to $w1$ is easily determined because at any iteration we update slices Rep and $Rep1$ and the variable $vdel$.   □

Now, we present the procedure DeleteVert that implements the associative paralel algorithm for updating an MST after deletion of a vertex.

```
procedure DeleteVert(left,right: table; weight: table;
   code: table; n,v: integer; var endpoints: table;
   var S,T,Rep: slice(left); var M: table);
var comp: table;
   Y: slice(left);
   vdel: word;
Begin
   Subtrees(left,right,code,M,T,v,S,Y,vdel,comp);
   NewMST(left,right,weight,code,comp,Y,S,n,T,Rep,endpoints);
   ChangePaths(comp,endpoints,Y,n,Rep,vdel,M);
End;
```

Let us evaluate time complexity of the procedure DeleteVert. One can check that the procedures Subtrees and NewMST take $O(\delta_T(v) \log n)$ time each. The procedure ChangePaths requires $O(s \log n)$ time, where s is the number of vertices whose tree paths are recomputed. Let $h = max\{\delta_T(v), s\}$. Then the procedure DeleteVert takes $O(h \log n)$ time on the STAR–machine having no less than m PEs. Note that the factor $\log n$ appears due to the use of the basic procedures inside the cycle.

Now, we briefly compare our algorithm and the sequential algorithm Find Node Replacements (FNR) by Das and Loui [2]. Let $T - v$ be the graph after deleting vertex v and its incident edges from T. Let $R(v)$ be a set of edges such that $T - v + R(v)$ is the MST of $G - v$. Let $F(v)$ be a component graph of v whose vertices correspond to the connected components of $T - v$ and its edges correspond to nontree edges that are not incident to v and connect different components of $T - v$. To determine $R(v)$ for all v, the FNR algorithm simulates Kruskal's algorithm on each $F(v)$. Note that adjacency lists of each $F(v)$ are determined by means of the parallel algorithm from [4] and the MSTs of each $F(v)$ are found using the parallel algorithm from [5]. Our algorithm determines the connected components of $T - v$ using the corresponding rows of the given matrix of tree paths. Moreover, MSTs of these components are obtained automatically due to the tabular data structures and the vertical data processing. The FNR algorithm simulates Kruskal's algorithm on a graph modified via star transformation. Our algorithm offers an original approach to obtaining a simple simulation of Kruskal's algorithm on the STAR–machine.

5   Conclusions

We have proposed a simple and natural associative parallel algorithm for the dynamic updating an MST after deletion of a vertex. It uses a matrix of tree paths to easily determine both a tree path between any pair of vertices and the connected components obtained after deleting a vertex along with its incident edges. We have also proposed a simple and natural method to easily determine a new MST from the current MST by means of Kruskal's algorithm. We have obtained that the corresponding procedure DeleteVert takes $O(h \log n)$ time on the STAR–machine having m PEs, where $h = max\{\delta_T(v), s\}$ and s is the number of vertices whose tree paths are recomputed. Moreover, we have compared our algorithm and the FNR algorithm by Das and Loui [2].

We are planning to implement our algorithm on the associative graph machine [11] that carries out both the bit–serial and the bit–parallel processing.

References

1. Chin, F., Houck, D.: Algorithms for Updating Minimum Spanning Trees. In: J. of Computer and System Sciences, Vol. 16 (1978) 333–344
2. Das, B., Loui, M. C.: Reconstructing a Minimum Spanning Tree after Deletion of Any Node. In: Algorithmica, Vol. 31 (2001) 530–547
3. Foster, C. C.: Content Addressable Parallel Processors. Van Nostrand Reinhold Company, New York (1976)
4. Johnson, D. B., Metaxas, P.: Connected components in $O(\lg^{3/2} \mid V \mid)$ parallel time for the CREW PRAM. In: J. Systems Sci., Vol. 54, No. 2 (1997) 227–242
5. Johnson, D. B., Metaxas, P.: A parallel algorithm for computing minimum spanning trees. In: J. Algorithms, Vol. 19 (1995) 383–401
6. Kruskal, J. B.: On the Shortest Spanning Subtree of a Graph and the Traveling Salesman Problem. In: Proc. Amer. Math. Soc., Vol. 7 (1956) 48–50
7. Nepomniaschaya, A. S.: Language STAR for Associative and Parallel Computation with Vertical Data Processing. In: Mirenkov, N. N. (ed.): Proc. of the Intern. Conf. "Parallel Computing Technologies". World Scientific, Singapure (1991) 258–265
8. Nepomniaschaya, A. S., Dvoskina, M. A.: A Simple Implementation of Dijkstra's Shortest Path Algorithm on Associative Parallel Processors. In: Fundamenta Informaticae, Vol. 43. IOS Press, Amsterdam (2000) 227-243
9. Nepomniaschaya, A. S.: Associative parallel algorithms for dynamic edge update of minimum spanning trees. In: Malyshkin, V. (ed.): Parallel Computing Technologies. 7th Intern. Conference, PaCT 2003, Proceedings. Lecture Notes in Computer Science, Vol. 2763. Springer–Verlag, Berlin Heidelberg New York (2003) 141–150
10. Nepomniaschaya, A. S.: A New Technique for Updating Tree Paths on Associative Parallel Processors. In: Bulletin of the Novosibirsk Computing Center, Series: Computer Science, Issue: 21 (2004) 85-97
11. Nepomniaschaya, A. S., Kokosinski, Z.: Associative Graph Processor and its Properties. In: Proc. of the International Conference on Parallel Computing in Electrical Engineering (PARELEC 2004), Dresden, Germany. IEEE Computer Society Press (2004) 297-302
12. Pawagi, S., Kaser, O.: Optimal Parallel Algorithms for Multiple Updates of Minimum Spanning Trees. In: Algorithmica, Vol. 9 (1993) 357–381
13. Tsin, Y. H.: On Handling Vertex Deletion in Updating Minimum Spanning Trees. In: Information Processing Letters, Vol. 27, No. 4 (1988) 167–168

The Use of Vertical Processing Principle in Parallel Image Processing on Conventional MIMD Computers*

Evgeny V. Rusin

Institute of Computational Mathematics and Mathematical Geophysics,
Siberian Branch, Russian Academy of Sciences,
6 Acad. Lavrentiev Ave, Novosibirsk, 630090 Russia
rev@ooi.sscc.ru

Abstract. PLVIP, experimental library for parallel image processing, designed and implemented in the Image Processing Laboratory of the Institute of Computational Mathematics and Mathematical Geophysics SB RAS, is described. The library is built on the principle of vertical processing and is installed on two multiprocessor computers of the Siberian Supercomputer Center, the 32-processor Linux cluster MVS–1000/M and the 8-processor SMP server RM600–E30. Basic characteristics of the library (supported data formats, organization of computational process, and implemented subprograms) and an example of its application are considered.

1   Introduction

Enormous size of remote sensing data (information flows up to 128 Mbps, single image size of about 1 GB, daily content of receive data up to 60 GB) and the need for its real-time interpretation (for example in problems of monitoring forest fires and floods) require the high performance of the computers involved in processing. Today it is obvious that the necessary performance cannot be reached by the means of increasing the computer clock cycle alone, and parallel processing is the only way to obtain the results within the required time frame.

Existing image processing systems belong, as a rule, to one of the following three classes: multipurpose and highly optimized libraries for personal computers and workstations, such as Intel IPP [1] or open source library OpenCV [2]; programs for a single problem solution on multiprocessor computers; or yet more specialized systems based on custom hardware. Unlike some other fields of informatics that require a large amount of computations (solution of linear algebra problems, building of high-performance data bases, etc.), basic image processing systems for conventional multiprocessor computers do not exist today.

The present work describes an experimental library for parallel image processing PLVIP designed and implemented in the Image Processing Laboratory

* Supported by Russian Academy of Sciences (integration project No. 13.14) and Russian Foundation for Basic Research (project No. 05-07-90057).

V. Malyshkin (Ed.): PaCT 2005, LNCS 3606, pp. 174–185, 2005.

of the Institute of Computational Mathematics and Mathematical Geophysics SB RAS. The principle of vertical processing was chosen as the algorithmic base of the library, which provides effective processing of the arrays of short data, for example halftone images with small color depth. The library is installed on two multiprocessor computers of the Siberian Supercomputer Center, the 32-processor Linux cluster MVS–1000/M and the 8-processor SMP server RM600–E30.

In the paper, after a brief description of the vertical processing method, the basic principles of the building of the library PLVIP are considered: supported data formats, organization of computational process, and implemented subprograms. Next, the way of optimization of the calculations based on vertical processing is considered. The application of the created software is illustrated by the example of the solution of the classic digital cartography problem, the recovery of an elevation map from a given contours set. In the conclusion, the author's considerations about the further work direction are stated.

2   Vertical Processing

In 1970s, for the support of the solution of the problems permitting the mass information processing, including the image processing problems, specialized fine-grained SIMD computers were created. This computers consisted of a very large number (up to a hundred of thousands) of synchronously operating one-bit processor elements with own memories and an interconnection network connecting them [3]. The characteristic feature of SIMD computers was a *vertical*, or word-parallel bit-serial, approach to data processing (vertical processing, VP) [4].

The VP principle is schematically shown in Fig. 1, which represents the example of the processing of a data array by the traditional and the "vertical" way. Unlike the traditional processing, when the elements of the array are loaded into

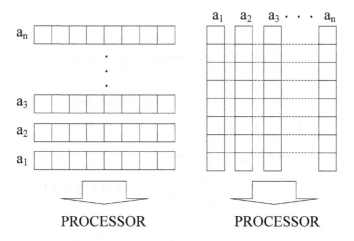

Fig. 1. Traditional (at left) and vertical (at right) approaches to data processing

processor by turns, and a single element is processed as a whole, during VP the same-named (i.e., of the same significance) bits of multiple elements are loaded into processor together.

The set of the values of the same-named bits of all pixels of an image is called a *bit plane* of the image. It is bit planes that are the handling units of the vertical image processing (VIP); the value of a pixel is composed of the values of the corresponding bits of image planes (Fig. 2).

The algorithmic basis of VIP is formed by the operations on bit planes:

- bitwise Boolean operations;
- shifts to the horizontal (X-shifts) and the vertical (Y-shifts) direction;
- calculation of a "mass" of a bit plane, i.e., of the number of the one bits in it;
- checks on the presence of at least one 1 (or 0) bit in a bit plane and on the equality of two bit planes.

The data model used in VP didn't find an application out of specially designed processors; in particular, the questions of the implementation of VIP in conventional computers are still unexplored today. Meanwhile, there are the following reasons to study these questions.

1. The performance of bit-serial computations grows with the decrease of the size of an individual datum being processed; this allows making the processing of arrays of short data more efficient, for example the processing of halftone images with small color depth.
2. For VP, there are no limitations on the size of a single datum being processed; this makes calculations with an arbitrary accuracy easy to perform.
3. The algorithmic basis of VIP can be effectively implemented on conventional computers by the operations on machine words (bitwise Boolean operations and shifts); present-day 64-bit microprocessors allow processing 64 pixels of an image in parallel.

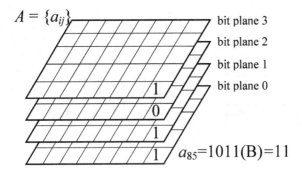

Fig. 2. A 16-color image A consists of four bit planes. The value of the pixel $(8, 5)$ of A is composed of the values of the corresponding bits of A planes

4. The intrinsic parallelism of VP allows using multiprocessor computers of the traditional architecture for VIP implementation.

Given considerations became the reasons for creating an experimental image processing library for traditional MIMD-computers. The library was designed on the base of VP principle and called PLVIP (Parallel Library for Vertical Image Processing).

3   The PLVIP Library

The library PLVIP is implemented as a set of C-subprograms [5]. The programming language C and the parallel programming interface MPI were chosen as implementation tools; that provides both possibility of low-level manipulations with bit planes and portability of the source code of the library to most present-day multiprocessor architectures.

3.1   Data Formats

The key problem in carrying the idea of VP to conventional computers was the design of the format of a bit plane. The impossibility of the implementation of the full two-dimensional topology on the linear address space of a conventional computer resulted in a compromise settlement that is similar to the way the VGA video adapter maps video memory onto main memory in some graphics modes. A bit plane of an $M \times N$ image is represented by the set of M-bit strings formed by sequentially kept machine words. The number of words in a string is equal to M/DC, where DC is the machine word width (suppose that M is divisible by DC). To support the neighborhood relation by shifts of machine words, the correspondence between bits of a plane and pixels of the image is defined as follows: the i-th (from leftmost) bit of the j-th (from lower address) word of the k-th string of the bit plane corresponds to the pixel with the coordinates $(jDC + i, k)$ (Fig. 3).

On this basis, the formats of halftone images, as sets of bit planes, are built: integer and fixed-point. The color depth of fixed-point images is an even number, and the binary point divides the bit representation of a pixel value in half.

3.2   Organization of Computational Process

The domain decomposition was chosen as the basis principle of computations parallelization: bit planes (and therefore halftone images) are cut into contiguous horizontal strips whose number is equal to the number of the executing processors; the strips are then distributed among the processors (Fig. 4).

This principle provides the effective parallelization of Boolean operations and X-shifts, but Y-shifts, calculation of mass, and comparisons, in their general form, require data transfer between processors. While comparisons of bit planes and calculation of mass, intensity of interprocessor communications can be essentially weakened in practical cases by using on a single processor P the result

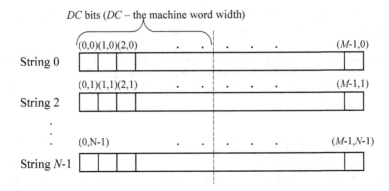

Fig. 3. The representation of a bit plane

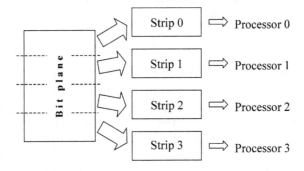

Fig. 4. The basic parallelization principle of the PLVIP library: bit planes are cut into strips

of these operations in the strip corresponding to P. However the intensive use of Y-shifts by an algorithm makes it unsuitable for such parallelization. Therefore, to provide alternative ways of parallelization, most operations are implemented in the PLVIP library both for images cut into strips and for whole images on one processor.

A "star" was chosen as the topology of computations: all input/output operations and conversions of image formats are carried out by the one, "root", processor; the other processors receive data from the root, process it, and, if necessary, return results to the root. The choice of such topology is stipulated by features of the file system of the MVS–1000/M computer.

3.3 Subprograms of the Library

The set of the library subprograms includes ones for:

- library initialization/termination;
- image input/output in BMP and PCX format;

- image distribution among processors and assembling on the root processor from strips;
- binary images (bit planes) handling: copying, bitwise Boolean operations, shifts, comparisons, and calculation of the mass;
- halftone images handling: copying, converting between the vertical and the traditional image formats, setting/getting the value of a pixel, etc.;
- halftone images arithmetic: pixel-wise summation, subtraction, multiplication, and division; calculation of the sum of image pixels and of the inner product of two images;
- halftone images processing: building a histogram, profiles, a level set of pixels values; thinning by Zhang and Suen's method [6]; and calculating the Euclidean Distance Transform (EDT).

Table 1 shows the speed-up values of the execution of some subprograms of the library on 2, 4, 8, 16, and 24 processors relative to the one-processor execution (the size of the test images is 640×640 pixels, the calculations were carried out on MVS–1000/M).

The exceeding, in some cases, the number of executing processors N by speed-up values can be explained by the following two factors.

1. The size of data a single processor manipulates with decreases with the growth of N, and beginning from some $N = N^*$, the processor places all data to be processed in the CPU cache memory, which is much faster then the main memory.
2. An optimization was applied in a number of the subprograms, which allows reducing the volume of computations on a single processor. The optimization is based on global properties of the strips processed by the processor (absence of one (or zero) bits in a strip, coincidence of corresponding strips of two planes, etc.) (see Sect. 4). With the growth of N and, respectively, with the decrease of the size of the strips to be processed by a single processor, the effectiveness of such optimization increases.

Table 1. Speed-up values of the execution of some PLVIP subprograms relative to one-processor execution

Subprogram	Number of processors				
	2	4	4	16	24
Pixel-wise multiplication	1.6	4.4	10.5	18.0	24.4
Inner product	2.0	3.8	7.4	14.4	19.9
Building a histogram	2.2	3.7	10.0	18.5	21.7
Thinning by Zhang and Suen	1.7	3.6	6.1	8.8	10.3
Building a level set of pixels values	1.7	3.3	7.6	10.0	20.0
Calculation of the EDT	2.0	4.7	7.5	15.5	20.0

4   Optimization of Algorithms of Vertical Image Processing

Bit-serial character of vertical processing results in direct relation of algorithm execution time to the color depth of processed image. However, the optimization of calculations by the branching of kind "if the i-th bit plane of an image is filled exclusively with one bits (or zero bits), perform A; otherwise, B" allows, in a number of cases, making the execution time of the "vertical" calculations dependent not on a formal size of a pixel, but on the number of different values that pixels of the image being processed take. This can be illustrated by the example of the optimization of the histogram building and vertical profile building algorithms. Table 2 shows the time results (in seconds) of application of the non-optimized and optimized algorithms of histogram building and of vertical profile building to two similar grayscale images I_1 and I_2 of size 1600×1400 pixels, pixels of which take 231 different values in the range from 0 up to 255. For I_1 pixel representation, 8 bit planes are used (256 gray gradations); and for I_2, 16 (65536 gray gradations).

Table 2. The results of optimization of vertical image processing algorithms

Algorithm	Image	
	I_1 (8 bits per pixel)	I_2 (16 bits per pixel)
Building histogram (not optimized)	.3700	93.0000
Building histogram (optimized)	.3000	.3200
Building vertical profile (not optimized)	.0072	.0178
Building vertical profile (optimized)	.0072	.0103

The time complexity of the non-optimized algorithm of histogram building, i.e. its execution time as a function of image color depth L, is $O(2^L)$ [7]. As the table shows, the time of execution of the optimized algorithm turns out to be almost independent on L. The optimization of the algorithm of vertical profile building, whose time complexity is $O(L)$, turns out to be less effective because of comparability of computational costs of optimization with costs of calculations themselves. Nevertheless, the growth of the execution time of the optimized algorithm with the increase of the color depth is slower than linear.

5   Application of the Library PLVIP: Solution of the Problem of Recovery of an Elevation Map from a Set of Contours

5.1   Statement of the Problem

The library PLVIP was used for solving a problem of the recovery of an elevation map from a set of contours. The problem is considered in the following statement [8].

1. Let a rectangular region B of raster plane with square elements (pixels) be given; B will represent the result of discretization of some region of the Earth surface.
2. The set of B pixels in which the value of the height of the Earth surface is equal to H is called a *contour of the level* H.
3. Let the set $C_1, C_2, \ldots, C_S$ of the contours of the level $L_1, L_2, \ldots, L_S$ respectively be given on B, and $L_i < L_j$ when $i < j$.
4. The set of contours reflects the Earth surface continuity, that is, there are no contours C_i and $C_j, j > i + 1$, that are not separated from one another by the contours $C_{i+1}, C_{i+2}, \ldots, C_{j-1}$.

On the basis of (1-4), it is required to approximate the value of Earth elevation in the pixels of the set $U = B \backslash \bigcup_{i=1}^{S} C_i$.

It was shown in [9] that the condition (4) can be weakened and one can allow even an intersection of contours of different levels. However, the respective changes in the algorithm do not influence its parallelization so all the reasonings below will be referred to the simpler statement (1-4).

5.2   Algorithm of Solution

The considered algorithm of the problem solution is described in details in [9]. Without going in details, note that the algorithm consists of the following steps.

1. Each contour C_i is divided into non-intersecting subsets of pixels $C_{ij}, j = 1, \ldots, J(i)$ (segments) such that two different segments of one contour C_i are separated from one another by the set $D_i = \bigcup_{k \neq i} C_k$.
2. For each segment C_{ij}, a *region of dependency* $dep(C_{ij})$ is built, which consists of pixels not separated from C_{ij} by D_i (Fig. 5); in $dep(C_{ij})$, a field $Dist_{ij}$ of Euclidean distances to C_{ij} and a field of the segment level $Height_{ij}$, which value is equal to L_i in every pixel, is built.
3. Four global fields are assembled from the built local ones: $\mathbf{Dist_0}$ and $\mathbf{Dist_1}$, which are the compositions of the fields of distances to the segments of even- and odd-numbered contours respectively, and $\mathbf{Height_0}$ and $\mathbf{Height_1}$, which

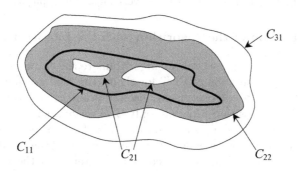

Fig. 5. The segments of the contours C_1, C_2, and C_3; the gray region is $dep(C_{11})$

are the the similar compositions of the fields of segments levels (the operation of the composition is correct because the regions of dependency of either two segments of non-neighbor contours or two different segments of one contour do not intersect).

4. The field of height approximating values $\mathbf{H}$ is obtained as the result of an array arithmetic operation applied to the global fields built:

$$\mathbf{H} = \frac{\mathbf{Dist_0Height_1 + Dist_1Height_0}}{\mathbf{Dist_1 + Dist_0}}.$$

This formula is a two-dimensional generalization of one-dimensional linear interpolation; in the case of the "continuous" plane, it provides the continuous 3D surface recovery.

The example of the algorithm application is shown on Fig. 6: the left picture is the set of 15 contours on the raster map of the size 500×500 pixels (black pixels on white background), the right picture is the result elevation map.

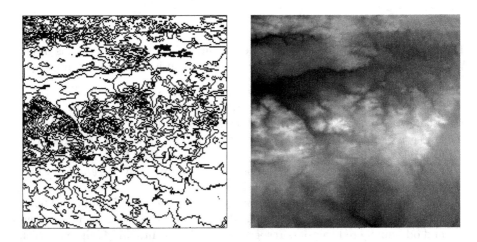

Fig. 6. The example of the recovery algorithm application

5.3   Parallelization of the Algorithm with the Library PLVIP

The most time-consuming parts of the algorithm are the extraction of segments from contours and calculation of EDT for them (the final arithmetic operation takes the small part of the algorithm execution time and can be easily parallelized by the domain decomposition). At that, only EDT calculation is well parallelized by the domain decomposition (as is seen from Table 1). The operation of segment extraction and its region of dependency building consists of the iterative sequence of the shifts of a contour image; moreover the criterion of the termination of segment extraction is a predicate concerning some image as a whole, and this image is changed from iteration to iteration.

Consider three approaches to the parallelization of the algorithm, implemented with the PLVIP library.

Algorithm A_1, the base parallelization way of the PLVIP library. Each image involved in calculations is cut into horizontal strips, which are then distributed among processors. Here an image Y-shift results in the data transfer across the boundary between neighbor strips, and the check of the condition of the termination of segment extraction requires the synchronization of the work of all executing processors. Next, for the parallel calculation of the distances field of a segment, each processor needs the whole image of the segment obtained, so it is necessary to assemble it on every processor. The obvious disadvantage of this approach is the intensive interprocessor interaction.

Algorithm A_2, parallelization by contours. Each processor processes (i.e., extracts segments, builds regions of their dependency, and calculates distances and levels fields) its own subset of contours, and a contour is processed as a whole by one processor. After that, the local fields of distances and of levels are gathered on the root processor, where then the global fields $\mathbf{Dist}_{0(1)}$ and $\mathbf{Height}_{0(1)}$ are composed. Next, the global fields, which are fixed-point images, are cut into strips and distributed among the processors for the final arithmetic operation carrying out. The advantage of this approach is the small dependency of parallel processes, as synchronization and interprocessor interaction is required only when the data obtained are assembled. The disadvantage is limiting the number of processors by the number of contours and the possibility of non-uniform load of the processors, since the workload of a single processor depends on the number and complexity of the contours it processes.

Algorithm A_3, parallelization by contours with the equalization of workload. The extraction of segments from each contour is carried out by one processor. Processors that have no contours or that have already processed their contours get extracted segments by request and calculate EDT for them. If there are no requests for the segment, it is processed by the processor that have extracted it. The processing of requests is carried out by the root processor, which does not take part in the calculations themselves. This approach seems to be the most flexible of three listed ones; there is no strong processes dependency as in A_1, and more uniform processors load is reached than in A_2.

The computational experiments were carried out on MVS–1000/M for the set of 15 contours on the raster map of the size 1600×1400 pixels (total segments number is 29951). The results of the experiments are shown in Table 3.

In the table, for each algorithm A_i, its execution time T_{A_i} (in seconds) and its speed-up Ac_{A_i} relative to the one-processor execution (2574 sec) are given for different numbers of the executing processors. As it is seen, the algorithm A_3 loses to other approaches in the execution speed for small (2-3) numbers of the processors only.

The detailed analysis of the critical sections of all three algorithms is done in [10]. Here we just note that the results of the experiments give illustration in support of the chosen strategy of the library PLVIP building, providing the alternative ways for the parallelization of computations.

Table 3. The execution time of the parallel versions of the elevation map recovery algorithm

Number of processors	Algorithm					
	A_1		A_2		A_3	
	T_{A_1}	Ac_{A_1}	T_{A_2}	Ac_{A_2}	T_{A_3}	Ac_{A_3}
2	1136	2.27	1270	2.03	1943	1.33
3	911	2.83	965	2.67	1004	2.57
5	909	2.83	690	3.73	584	4.41
7	785	3.28	507	5.08	436	5.91
11	780	3.30	429	6.00	311	8.28
13	866	2.97	323	7.98	262	9.83
15	833	3.09	246	10.47	236	10.92
20	935	2.76	-	-	220	11.71
24	-	-	-	-	211	12.21

6   Conclusion

Despite the serious limitations posed by the vertical image representation (uniformity of computational algorithms, growth of computational costs with increase of color depth, etc.), the creation of the library PLVIP is an important step toward the understanding of the principles of building image processing systems on conventional multiprocessor MIMD-computers. Based on the received experience, the work on creation of the universal high-performance image processing library on the multiprocessor computers of the Siberian Supercomputer Center starts in the Image Processing Laboratory of ICMMG SB RAS. Support of both vertical and traditional image formats and a variety of parallelization methods ("image on single processor", "cutting image into strips", "cutting image into strips with overlapping", etc.) have been chosen as the important principles of building the library. In addition to the basis algorithms of image processing, the original ones elaborated in the laboratory and oriented to the aerospace images will be also included in the library.

References

1. Intel IPP. http://intel.com/software/products/ipp/
2. OpenCV. http://sourceforge.net/projects/opencvlibrary/
3. Potter J.L., Meilander W.C.: Array Processor Supercomputers. Proc. IEEE. **77** (1989) 1896–1914.
4. Shooman W.: Parallel computing with vertical data. AFIPS Conf. Proc. **18** (1960) 111–115.
5. PLVIP: the programmer's manual.
   http://loi.sscc.ru/web/lab/RFFI03/rusin/PLVIPman_eng.htm
6. Zhang T. Y., Suen S.Y.: A Fast Parallel Algorithm for Thinning Digital Patterns. Comm. ACM **3** (1984) 236–239.

7. Reeves A.P.: On Efficient Information Extraction Method For Parallel Processing. Computer Graphics and Image Processing **14** (1980) 159–169.

8. Rusin E.V.: The Parallel Algorithm of Approximation of Earth Elevation Matrix by Given Contours. Proc. Int. Conf. "Mathematical Methods in Geophysics", Vol. 2. ICMMG SB RAS, Novosibirsk (2003) 612–617 (in Russian).

9. Kim P.A., Pyatkin V.P., Rusin E.V.: Three Massively Parallel Algorithms for Solving Computational Geometry Problems by Using Euclidean Distance Transform. Pattern Recognition and Image Analysis **14** (2004) 267–275.

10. Rusin E.V.: About Parallelization of an Algorithm of Earth Elevation Map Recovery from Given Contours. Proc. Int. Conf. Comp. Math. ICCM–2004, Vol. 2. ICMMG SB RAS, Novosibirsk (2004) 197–202 (in Russian).

Parallel Implementation of Back-Propagation Neural Network Software on SMP Computers[*]

Victor G. Tsaregorodtsev

Institute of Computational Modeling SB RAS, Krasnoyarsk, Russian Federation
tsar@neuropro.ru

Abstract. Experiments of neural network training procedure parallelization are conducted. Several styles of parallelization are described and
compared, estimations of neural network size and training set size that
allow speedup on two-processors SMP machine are obtained.

1 Introduction

Artificial neural networks are a flexible instrument for solving a lot of problems
including non-linear regression, supervised learning and pattern recognition, unsupervised learning, associative memory, optimization tasks etc. Here we study
only a back-propagation neural networks introduced in 1986 and named so because of the main part of its training algorithm doing "back propagation of
errors" to compute gradient vector along adjustable (trainable) variables.

Experiments of running neural networks on parallel computers start at the
end of 1980-ies [1,2,3], but mostly focus on the specific architectures – transputers, connection machines, massively parallel computers. This epoch of investigations ends in the middle of 1990-ies with a remarkable works of [4,5,6,7,8]
(see also references therein). Moreover, results of [8] were confirmed recently
[9,10,11]: so-called online training is theoretically faster than batch-training, but
unparallelizable (batch training that accumulates penalties and updates over the
patterns of the training set can be parallelized, but in general converges slowly).

Here we study parallelization for SMP (symmetric multiprocessors) computers. This research becomes necessary due to wide usage of multiprocessor servers,
HyperThreading technology that was introduced by Intel Corp. recently, and
plans of Intel Corp. to step to multicore processors, each core of which will
support HyperThreading (i.e. can run two threads simultaneously under some
restrictions). So in a nearest future we will be able to run up to 4 parallel threads
on a single dual-core processor, and SMP computations will be of usual use.

Such a perspectives of hardware evolution makes SMP-programming more
valuable than clustering techniques because of widely usage of a common computers (with multikernel processors therein) in a nearest future. Also, results
obtained for SMP-software give some landmarks for a cluster platforms too.

In the paper we briefly describe neural network structure and training algorithm and possible parallelization schemes, then describe data bases used in

---

[*] This work was supported by the Krasnoyarsk regional scientific fund, grant 15G277.

V. Malyshkin (Ed.): PaCT 2005, LNCS 3606, pp. 186–192, 2005.

experiments and provide experimental results. Then we discuss some additional questions and perspectives.

2 Artificial Neural Networks

2.1 Neural Network Structure

Here we use only a most convenient network structure – feedforward network with a single hidden layer of neurons. For a input vector $\mathbf{x}$ of n components and vector of desired outputs $\mathbf{y}$ of m components we can describe neural network as follows. Firstly, we compute the outputs of a hidden layer of N neurons as

$$z_i = f(\sum_{k=1}^{n} x_k w_{ki} + w_{0i})$$ for each that neuron i using nonlinear function f, usually

of sigmoidal form a-la $f(\theta) = \dfrac{\theta}{c + |\theta|}, c > 0$. Then we compute each j-th output

signal $\hat{y}_j = \sum_{l=1}^{N} z_l u_{lj} + u_{0j}$. Variables w_{ab}, u_{cd} are trainable network coefficients

that should be adjusted during training. Training should minimize differences between desired and obtained signals (y_j and $\hat{y}_j$ respectively) using some error measure, e.g. of a mean square error form.

Different optimization methods can be used during training – random search, genetic algorithms, gradient optimization techniques. Here we use the last one because "back propagation of errors" (precisely, back propagation of partial derivatives of the error measure) algorithm allows fast computation of gradient vector of error measure function along values of trainable network variables. When we obtain gradient vector, we can use gradient descent equation to improve quality of network's response by making step along the antigradient direction.

2.2 Training Scheme and Possibilities of Parallelization

Here we use batch training – accumulation of gradients for all the patterns collected in training set to compute overall gradient: for error measure $H_i(\mathbf{x}_i, \mathbf{y}_i) = \|\mathbf{y}_i - \hat{\mathbf{y}}_i(\mathbf{x}_i)\|$ for a training pattern $\{\mathbf{x}_i, \mathbf{y}_i\}$ and overall error $H = \sum H_i$ we can compute ∇H as $\nabla H = \nabla \sum H_i = \sum \nabla H_i$, therefore computation of different H_i's and their gradients can be done in parallel over a different parts of the training set. I.e. for two parallel threads and K training patterns we can divide training set onto sets with pattern indexes $\{1, ..., K/2\}$ and $\{K/2 + 1, ..., K\}$, simultaneously compute H^1 and ∇H^1 by the first and H^2 and ∇H^2 by the second thread and then obtain final values of $H = H^1 + H^2$ and $\nabla H = \nabla H^1 + \nabla H^2$.

Oppositely, online-training corrects network after each pattern processing (along ∇H_i, not ∇H) – this is unparallelizable due to frequent modifications of the network and loss of suitability for any other parallelly computed gradient (which becomes obsolete after model correction along the concurrent one).

Each batch-training epoch consists of overall gradient computation, unnecessary phase of step size and/or descent direction selection (e.g. using conjugate gradient method) and network modification. Iterations last until the desired value of H is obtained or some stopping criteria is met, e.g. local minima found.

For SMP-parallelization, i.e. fast memory access without any slow network links, we propose the following three data separation schemes:

1. Thread requests for a next unprocessed pattern, i.e. there is no hard or formal separation of the training set. But we should additionally synchronize access and modification of a pointer to a next pattern.
2. Hard separation – training set is divided onto a parts which number is equal to a number of processors without any redivisioning lately. Each processor (thread) here will work with a constant subset of patterns that can be cached.
3. Hard separation, but if the thread finishes his prescribed data processing, it handles some of currently unprocessed data assigned to the other thread.

The third scheme is required because we can stop i-th pattern training when the desired H_i is obtained. So we can skip ∇H_i computation, and when the numbers of already-trained patterns in a sets corresponded to different threads differs greatly, some threads may finish their work earlier and should wait others.

3   Data Bases Used in Experiments

We use 20 real-world data bases available from http://kdd.ics.uci.edu/. All of them are classification tasks. Table 1 summarize data base properties (number of classes, number of training examples and the number of bytes to store prepro-cessed data base and some additional information needed) and neural networks properties (number of neurons, input signals, number of adaptive variables in network). For three data bases we use neural networks of two different size in order to propagate results further along the network size scale.

4   Results of Experiments

Parallelization properties was implemented into author's own neural network software package running under MS Windows. We did not use any high-level parallelization package but create and synchronize threads using Window API. Neural network kernel previously was programmed careful enough – without object orientation that can hurt performance, with manual reprogramming of some routines using Assembler.

Experiments was conducted on a SMP workstation with two 1Ghz Pentium III processors. For the last two parallelization schemes (as numbered in Section 2.2) we also study implementations with hard assignment of every thread to a definite processor in order to maximize cache hitting for non-changing partitions of training set. Curiously, this versions help to increase speedup further (about $3 \div 5\%$) not for the small data bases but also for the great ones too, where only a little amount of data can be cached, but this results are not shown here.

Results of experiments are presented on Figures 1-3 where vertical axes count speedup obtained over the initial single-threaded version.

Table 1. Data base sizes and corresponded neural network sizes

Database name	Num. of patterns	Num. of input signals	Num. of classes	Num. of neurons	Num. of adaptive variables	Data size, in bytes
AnnThyroid	3772	21	3	10	253	437552
Car	1728	6	4	15	169	110592
HypoThyroid	3162	19	2	10	222	316200
Letter	20000	16	26	25	1101	5600000
Mushrooms	8124	111	2	10	1142	3802032
Musk	6598	166	2	10 / 15	1692 / 2537	4539424
Nursery	12960	8	5	20	285	1036800
OptDigits	3823	62	10	10	740	1284528
PageBlocks	5473	10	5	10	165	481624
PenDigits	7494	16	10	10	280	1139088
Satellite	4435	36	6	20	866	887000
Shuttle	43500	9	7	15	262	4350000
Spambase	4601	57	2	25	1502	1159452
Vowel	990	11	11	15	356	138600
Yeast	1484	8	10	40	770	178080
MF-Fac	2000	216	10	10 / 15	2280 / 3415	1904000
MF-Fou	2000	76	10	15	1315	784000
MF-Kar	2000	64	10	10	760	688000
MF-Pix	2000	240	10	10 /15	2520 / 3775	2096000
MF-Zer	2000	47	10	15	880	552000

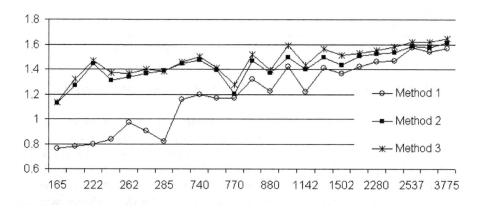

Fig. 1. Speedup obtained using two threads over single thread. Marks on a horizontal axis are from the simple ordering of the neural networks along their size

Fig.1 show speedup values when neural networks are simply ordered by their size. Effectivenesses correspond to parallelization schemes numbering, which is clear enough: for the scheme where threads simultaneously ask for the next unprocessed pattern great enough fraction of time is thrown away because of synchronization waits. When data set is divided between threads the third scheme with adaptive capturing of some examples unprocessed by the other thread runs faster than scheme with no-helping-to-each-other threads.

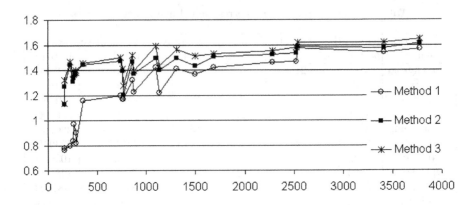

Fig. 2. The same results as in Fig.1, but horizontal axis counts real network size

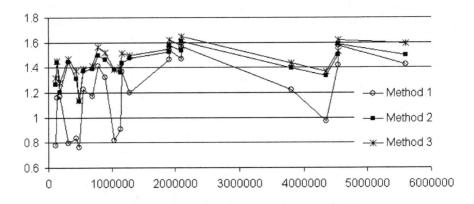

Fig. 3. Dependencies between data size, in bytes, and achieved speedup

Fig.2 shows the same results as Fig.1 but horizontal axis correspond to a real number of adaptive parameters in the network, so we can see more clearly that concurrent (first one) scheme gives no speedup for nets with less than 300 coefficients. Both Fig.1 and Fig.2 indicate speedup improvement with the network size growth, so it's possible to conclude that parallelization can be efficient (gives, at least, speedup of 1.5 for two-processors computer) only for the back-propagation networks with 1000 synapses at least. Network of that size is suitable for the great number of real world problems, and it's difficult to find a problem where a network with 10000 or more weights is required – but only for such a big networks we can achieve speedup near the theoretical limit of 2.

We should note that computations during neural network training are mainly of multiplication/accumulation instructions (see Section 2) that can be efficiently encoded by the compiler using SSE instructions (or programmer by itself can use vector-matrix computation package with SSE optimization therein) – this is the reason for the great influence of threads synchronization routines because each training epoch for small and medium-sized nets last only fraction of a second.

There may exist some dependence between speedup ratio and data base size (e.g., cache size influence), but less certain. Data base size affect on effectiveness less than network size, all the speedup drops on Fig.3 correspond to small nets.

5 Conclusion

We study the effectiveness of neural network software parallelization on two-processors SMP computer, explore three methods of data separation and some additional tricks. Obtained results are promising: for the most efficient scheme we obtain average speedup about 1.5 over a single-threaded program, and speedup varies from 1.2 to more than 1.6 over a wide pairs of network and data sizes.

We plan to step to heterogeneous parallel scemes which is necessary for HyperThreading feature of Intel Pentium IV Prescott processor where two threads can run simultaneously only while using different blocks of CPU, e.g. floating point and general purpose blocks. Also we'll study techniques and influental things more carefully, for other network structures and methods too [12].

References

1. Beyon T. A parallel implementation of the back-propagation algorithm on a network of transputers / Proc. First IEEE Int. Neural Network Conf. 1987.
2. Murali, P., Wechsler, H., Manohar, M. Fault-tolerance and learning performance of the back-propagation algorithm using massively parallel implementation / Proc. of Frontiers'90, The Third Symposium on the Frontiers of Massively Parallel Processing. College Park, MD, USA. 1990. – pp.364-367.
3. Paugam-Moisy H. On parallel algorithm for backpropagation by partitioning the training set / Proc. Fifth Int. Conf. Neural Networks and Their Applications. Nimes, France. 1992. – pp.53-65.
4. Kumar V., Shekhar S, Amin M.B. A scalable parallel formulation of backpropagation algorithm for hypercubes and related architectures / IEEE Trans. on Parallel and Distributed Systems, 1994. Vol.5. Issue 10. – pp.1073-1090.
5. Prechelt L. Data locality and load balancing for parallel neural network learning / Proc. Workshop on Compilers for Parallel Computers. Spain, 1995. – pp.111-127.
6. Misra M. Parallel environments for implementing neural networks / Neural Computing Surveys, 1997. Vol.1. – pp.48-60.
7. Strey A. EpsiloNN – A tool for the abstract specification and parallel simulation of neural networks / System analysis - Modeling - Simulation, special issue on Simulation of Artificial Neural Networks, 1999. Vol.34. No.4.
8. Torresen J., Tomita S., Landsverk O. The relation of weight update frequency to convergence of BP / Proc. World Conf. Neural Networks (WCNN'1995). Washington, USA. 1995. – pp.679-682.
9. Wilson D.R., Martinez T.R. The general inefficiency of batch training for gradient descent learning / Neural Networks. 2003, Vol.16. Issue 10. – pp.1429-1451.
10. Bottou L., LeCun Y. Large scale online learning / Advances in Neural Information Processing Systems 16 (2003). MIT Press, 2004. – pp.217-224.

11. Tsaregorodtsev V.G. General inefficiency of batch gradient usage for neural network training / Proc. XII Conf. "Neuroinformatics and their applications". Krasnoyarsk, Russia. 2004. – pp.145-151. (in Russian).
12. Tsaregorodtsev V.G. Perspectives for parallelization of neural-network data processing and analysis software/ Proc. III Conf. "Mathematics, Informatics, Control". Irkutsk, Russia. 2004. – 6p. (in Russian).

Development of Predictive TFRC with Neural Network

Sung-goo Yoo[1], Kil To Chong[2], and Hyong-suk Kim[2]

[1] Chonbuk National Univ., Control and Instrumentation, 664-14 1Ga Duckjin-Dong,
Duckjin-Gu Jeonju Jeonbuk 561-756, South Korea
ding5@chonbuk.ac.kr
[2] Chonbuk National Univ., Electronics and Information, 664-14 1Ga Duckjin-Dong,
Duckjin-Gu Jeonju Jeonbuk 561-756, South Korea
{kitchong, hskim}@chonbuk.ac.kr

Abstract. As Internet real-time multimedia applications increase, the
bandwidth available to TCP connections is stifled by UDP traffic, which
results in the performance of overall system to be extremely deterio-
rated. Therefore, developing a new transmission protocol is necessary.
The TCP-friendly algorithm is an example satisfying this necessity. The
TCP-Friendly Rate Control (TFRC) is an UDP-based protocol that controls the transmission rate based on the variables such as RTT and PLR.
In the conventional data transmission processing, the transmission rate is
determined by the RTT and PLR of the previous transmission period. If
the one-step ahead predicted values of RTT and PLR are used to determine the transmission rate, the performance of network will be improved
significantly. This paper proposes a predictive TFRC protocol with one-
step ahead RTT and PLR. A multi-layer perceptron neural network is
used as the prediction model, and the Levenberg-Marquardt algorithm is
used as a training algorithm. The values of RTT and PLR were collected
using UDP protocol in the real system used for NN modeling. The performance of the predictive TFRC was evaluated by the share of Internet
bandwidth with various protocols in terms of the packet transmission
rate. The extensive experiment of the suggested system in real system
was performed and proves its advantages.

1 Introduction

Most Internet traffics are caused by TCP based protocols, such as HTTP (Hy-
pertext Transfer Protocol), SMTP (Simple Mail Transfer Protocol), FTP (File
Transfer Protocol). In addition, there is a new issue stemming from an increase
Internet traffic, which is due to the real-time audio/video streaming applications,
in using an UDP, such as an IP telephony, Internet audio player, and VOD. A
real-time application generally doesn't use a TCP [1], and uses a UDP [1] algorithm, which doesn't consider congestion control. If congestion control applied
in the network where a TCP and UDP share the same link, the TCP will reduce
the transmission rate to solve the congestion problem; however, the UDP will
maintain its transmission rate and increase the congestion due to it occupies a

V. Malyshkin (Ed.): PaCT 2005, LNCS 3606, pp. 193–205, 2005.

large part of the effective bandwidth. This property will facilitate an imbalance in the use of a network.

In order to solve these problems, a modified rule of transmission rate control can be applied to non-TCP traffics for sharing the bandwidth fairly with the mechanism of TCP transmission. This transmission rule should have the property that non-TCP applications include the TCP-friendly property, in which the system should support a fair distribution. There have been various TCP-friendly algorithms reported to solve unequal distributions [2][3][4]. The most prominent algorithms among them are the Rate Adaptation Protocol (RAP)[5], and TCP Friendly Rate Control (TFRC)[6].

An important property of a TCP-friendly algorithm is control the transmission rate adaptively by measuring the network condition. However, this property doesn't consider a QoS (Quality of Service), which affects the quality of a transmitted image, due to focus on the fairness aspect for TCP flows. In addition, the existing TCP-friendly algorithm determines the control transmission rates based on RTT and PLR of the previous states. Therefore, when the packets are transmitted through network based on the transmission rate is not appropriate for the present network condition anymore. The transmission rate is optimal for the past packet transmission condition. This suggested algorithm estimates the Internet bandwidth during data transmission, which is called the RTT, and PLR and predict the one-step-ahead value of them using a neural network. The predicted RTT and PLR were used as important factors for a prediction of transmission rate. Moreover, the prediction model included a transmission protocol that developed through this study are evaluated its performance through real network system tests.

A decision tree, rule based, and neural network were generally used to build the prediction model. This study used a neural network, which can model the nonlinear system [7]. A multi-layer perceptron (MLP) structure [8] was used as a model structure. The Levenberg-Marquardt Back-propagation (LMBP)[9] solving the problem converges to a local minimum, which is a demerit of the back-propagation algorithm [10], was used to train the neural network(NN).

In order to improve the accuracy of the prediction model, the NN was trained by using a moving average value, which has been applied to the transmission rate control mechanism of the TCP [11][12]. In addition, a hybrid method, which operates the prediction model when the network is under a congestion situation, and the general TFRC was operates when the network is in a normal operating condition. The main contributions of this paper are

1. Development of a neural network model for the RTT and PLR of the network.
2. Propose a predictive TFRC protocol.
3. Improvethe valid transmission packet rate compare to the TFRC protocol.
4. The suggested predictive TFRC does not deteriorate the TCP transmission compare to the UDP protocol.

After brief reviewing the basic concept of TFRC and NN in section 2 and 3, the real experimental system has been set up in order to verify the suggested system in section 4. The measurement of the RTT and PLR has also been discussed in section 5.1 and 5.2. Section 5.3 shows the neural network modeling and the packet transmission rate control tests in the real system and the brief concluding remarks are offered in section 6.

2   TCP-Friendly Transmission Rate Control

Multimedia transmission can be classified into two main methods, which involve either replaying the entire multimedia file previously downloaded from a web server or streaming. In the latter case, a part of the entire file is downloaded and the multimedia content is displayed while the rest of the file is being downloaded. The method of streaming is well suited to the real-time broadcasting of audio and video data.

In the case of multimedia transmission using the Internet, packet loss occurs mainly as a result of transmission errors and congestion. In response to this, the TCP protocol reduces the transmission rate using its own method of congestion control. Therefore, if a number of TCP connections that have a similar RTT delay share the same channel, they will share the available bandwidth equally. The problem of bandwidth distribution was not studied in detail in the past, because almost all traffic utilized a TCP based protocol, but it is becoming one of the most important issues, due to the increasing use of real-time applications, such as IP telephony, video conferencing, etc., and Non-TCP traffic such as audio/video streaming services and various other services. Unfortunately, whereas TCP reduces the transmission rate when the network is under congestion condition, but Non-TCP protocols increase the overall amount of traffic by continuing to transmit at their original transmission rate, because Non-TCP traffic does not incorporate any method of rate control that is compatible with TCP. Therefore, a mechanism is needed which allows the transmission rate of Non-TCP traffic to be controlled and which is compatible with that of TCP. In addition, it is necessary to distribute the available bandwidth, by making the Non-TCP traffic adhere to the TCP-Friendly protocol, in order to solve the problem referred to as TCP-Friendly congestion.

Any method based on TCP-Friendly congestion control should calculate the transmission rate based on a TCP model [11], in which the average transmission rate over time can modeled by considering the operation of TCP in the steady state. This depends on the operation of the TCP protocol, but can basically be expressed as Eq. (1).

$$R = f\,(PLR, RTT) \tag{1}$$

where R is the transmission rate, PLR is the packet loss rate, and RTT is the round trip time.

The transmission rate used in this paper is in Eq. (2). The derivation of the Eq. (2) is shown in [2].

$$R = \frac{s}{RTT\sqrt{\frac{2p}{3}} + t_{RTO}\left(3\sqrt{\frac{3p}{8}}\right)p\left(1 + 32p^2\right)} \tag{2}$$

where, t_{RTO} is the retransmission time out, p is the packet loss rate.

3   Neural Netowork

The structure of the predictive model used in this study is the multi-layer perceptron NN and consists of an input layer, hidden layer and output layer. The output of the multi-layer perceptron is presented in Eq. (3) [13].

$$\hat{y}_i(t) = g_i[\varphi,\theta] \ F_i\left[\sum_{j=1}^{n_h} w_{i,j} f_j\left(\sum_{l=1}^{n_\varphi} w_{j,l}\varphi_l + w_{j,0}\right) + W_{i,0}\right] \tag{3}$$

where θ is a parameter vector that includes all of the adjustable parameters in the neural network structure, and $\{w_{j,l}, W_{i,j}\}$ are weights and biases, respectively.

The error function, E, that represents the error between the output of the training data and the output of the neural network can be defined as in Eq. (4)

$$E = \frac{1}{2}\sum_{n=1}^{k}(y_n - o_n)^2 \tag{4}$$

where y_n is the target value of the training data and o_n is the output of the neural network.

The LM algorithm was used in training. This algorithm can solve dynamically the problems presented in the Steepest Descent and Newton methods. The weight w can be obtained by using Eq. (5).

$$w_{i+1} = w_i - (H + \lambda I)^{-1}\nabla F(w_i) \tag{5}$$

where $\nabla F(w_i) = \frac{\partial F}{\partial w_i}$:gradient $F = \sum_{k=0}^{N} e_k^2$ is SSE(square-sum error) k is the kth sample,$H = \nabla^2 F(w)$ is the Hessian matrix, and λ is a parameter varying dynamically.

However, the LMBP algorithm adopts the Gauss-Newton method that approximates the value of H since the second derivative produces computational problems. That is, the value of H used in the Newton method can be obtained by means of Eq. (6).

$$H = \left[\nabla^2 F(w)\right]_{ij} = \frac{\partial^2 F(x)}{\partial w_i \partial w_j} = 2\sum_{k=0}^{N}\left[\frac{\partial e_k(w)}{\partial w_i}\frac{\partial e_k(w)}{\partial w_j} + e_k(w)\frac{\partial^2 e_k(w)}{\partial w_i \partial w_j}\right] \tag{6}$$

where the second term of Eq. (6) can be neglected, hence

$$\left[\nabla^2 F(w)\right]_{ij} \cong 2\sum_{k=0}^{N}\frac{\partial e_k(w)}{\partial w_i}\frac{\partial e_k(w)}{\partial w_j} = 2J^T(w)J(w) \tag{7}$$

where $J_{ki} = \frac{\partial e_k}{\partial w_i}$ is a Jacobian matrix. By using this approximation, the necessity to use the second derivative can be eliminated. $\nabla F(w_i)$ presented in Eq. (8) is defined by

$$\nabla F(w_i) = J^T(w_i)e(w_i) \qquad (8)$$

Therefore, the modified LMBP algorithm can be expressed as Eq. (9).

$$w_{m+1} = w_m - \left[J^T(w_m)J(w_m) + \lambda_m I\right]^{-1} J^T(w_m)e(w_m) \qquad (9)$$

4   Experimental Set Up

4.1   End-to-End- System

A VBR(Variable Bit Rate) video transmission system through the Internet is a type of end-to-end(ENDE) system based on a server-client configuration. Fig. 1 presents a typical server-client model[13]. The server-client system used in this study was configured by a server, which was located in Cheonbuk National University and had an IP address of 210.117.183.41, and a client, which was located at Seoul National University and had an IP address of 147.46.156.91. The operation system of the server is Wow Linux 7.3(kernel 2.4.18-4) and the CPU is PIV 1.7 MHz, and memory size is 512 Mbyte. The client computer using Redhat Linux 8.0(kernel 2.4.20), AMD Athlon 1200, and the memory size is same as the server.

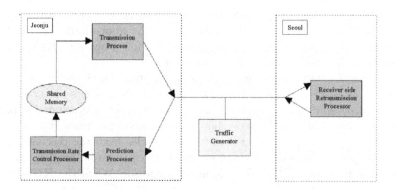

Fig. 1. Structure of Server-Client system

The server has two processes, one is the data transmission processor and the other one is transmission prediction processor, and the client also has tow processors such as data receiving and retransmission processor. Each processor was independently operated. The transmission prediction processor in the server stores the predicted transmission rate to the shared memory in real-time, and the data transmission processor transmitted data according to the transmission rate, which was stored in the shared memory. The receiving and retransmission processor located in the client side retransmits the probe header of the packet to the transmission rate prediction processor. Once the client processor receives the packet, it divides the packet into a probe header and a data file, it then retransmits the probe header, which has a new time data required to figure out the RTT and PLR, to the transmission rate prediction processor.

The suggested system uses a shared memory for real time data transmission. The main reason using a shared memory in the system is that fast access to data can be achieved. Communication between different processors required four different duplications of data; however, the shared memory method presented two different duplications of data. Since rapid communication between the processors can be achieved using a shared memory method, it is possible for the data transmission processor and transmission rate prediction processor to operate their own processing without any interrupts.

4.2   Data Transmission Rate Control Algorithm

The transmission processor can transmit packets using the TCP-Friendly method, as mentioned in Chapter 2. The packet transmission test was conducted using Eq. (2). The initial transmission speed is 100kb/s, and the whole packet size is 625 bytes, of which 64 bytes are reserved for the probe header. The probe header is attached to the header of the transmission packet, in order to measure the RTT and PLR. The probe header constitutes 7 segments; Sequence Number(tp), Sequence Number(rp), Sequence Number(RTT-PLR ep), Time Stamp(tp), Time Stamp(rp), Time Stamp(RTT-PLR ep), and the User Data. The transmission processor (tp), receiving-retransmission processor (rp), and RTT-PLR estimation processor (RTT-PLR ep) were implemented using a socket program written in the ANSI C language. The 'ep' appeared in the above indicates the transmission processor, 'rp' is for receiving-retransmission processor, 'RTT-PLR ep' represents the RTT-PLR estimation processor.

In addition, it has a storage area used to store numbers of transmitted packets, so as to keep track of the order in which the packets are transmitted from each processor and their transmission time. When the transmission processor transmits a packet to the receiving-retransmission processor, the receiving-retransmission processor separates the probe header from the received packet, inserts the packet number and current time into the probe header, and then retransmits it to the RTT-PLR estimation processor. When the RTT-PLR ep processor receives the probe header, it estimates the RTT and PLR using Eqs. (10) and (11), respectively.

$$\text{RTT} = \text{packet arrival time of RTT-PLR ep - Transmission time of tp} \quad (10)$$

$$\text{PLR(\%)} = 1 - \frac{\text{total sum of the received packets at the round } i}{\text{total sum of the transmitted packets at the round } i} \times 100$$

$$= 1 - \frac{R_i - R_{i-1}}{S_i - S_{i-1}} \times 100 \quad (11)$$

R_i : the sequence number of the latest received data at i
S_i : the sequence number of the latest transmitted data at i

R_{i-1} : the sequence number of the latest received data at $(i-1)$
S_{i-1} : the sequence number of the latest transmitted data at $(i-1)$

The RTT and PLR are measured in every 2 seconds called 'round' in this paper. where the round refers to a time interval of 2 seconds. When the Internet is under the congested situation, the values of RTT and PLR are likely to fluctuate rapidly. Even though controlling the transmission rate can help reducing the amount of traffic problems by rapidly applying these suddenly changed values of RTT and PLR directly to the TFRC mechanism, the quality of service of real-time applications will rapidly deteriorate. In order to prevent this problem, the RTT and PLR of the TFRC algorithm should adhere to the calculation method used by the RTT and PLR of the TCP algorithm. The TCP protocol can change the estimated values of RTT and PLR naturally by using a low-pass filter. The estimated values of RTT and PLR can be obtained by using the moving average as described in Eq. (12).

$$\text{RTT}^* = \alpha \text{RTT}^* + (1-\alpha)\,\text{newRTT} \ , \ \text{PLR}^* = \alpha \text{PLR}^* + (1-\alpha)\,\text{newPLR} \quad (12)$$

where α is a parameter that has a recommended value of 0.9, and newRTT and newPLR are recently estimated values of RTT and PLR, respectively. The moving average can be used to control the transmission rate, by reducing any sudden changes in the values of the RTT and PLR when the network is congested. In the transmission test, the RTT and PLR are estimated at every round, and the moving average RTT and moving average PLR are determined using Eq. (12). Although a prediction model presented an excellent performance, in the case of the prediction of RTT and PLR using a prediction model after passing one round, some errors could possibly be occur. In this study, a TCP-friendly algorithm was used to send data for the stable state having no loads in the network. A predictive TFRC method, which controls the transmission rate using the proposed prediction model, was used to decide the transmission rate when the PLR was over 5%. This hybrid method can be effectively used to control the transmission rate by removing an error of the prediction model, which can occur in the network that has less loads. If PLR is less than 5%, use Eq. (13), otherwise use Eq. (14).

$$R = \frac{s}{RTT\sqrt{\frac{2p}{3}} + t_{RTO}\left(3\sqrt{\frac{3p}{8}}\right)p\left(1 + 32p^2\right)} \quad (13)$$

$$R = \frac{s}{RTT_2\sqrt{\frac{2p_2}{3}} + t_{RTO}\left(3\sqrt{\frac{3p_2}{8}}\right)p_2\left(1 + 32p_2^2\right)} \quad (14)$$

where, t_{RTO} is the retransmission time out, RTT_2 and p_2 are RTT and PLR obtained using prediction NN.

5   Experimental Results

5.1   Neural Network Modeling

This section evaluates NN predictive modeling performance for the RTT and PLR. The training data of the RTT and PLR was collected using the real system mentioned in section 4 using UDP. A traffic generator IPERF [14] was used to produce the various situations involving network control in this experiment.

Table 1 shows the amount of traffic generated by IPERF, and the measured values of the RTT and PLR from the experimental test, the first row shows the amount of traffic generated. The average RTT is about 10.3ms when there is no traffic, and the average PLR is about 0.5%. The RTT and PLR increased rapidly when the traffic load is increased.

A multi-layer NN structure and LMBP training algorithm were used to obtain one-step-ahead values of RTT and PLR. The NN model consists of 20 nodes in the input layer, 8 nodes in the hidden layer, and the output layer has a single node. The packet transmission test was performed by the communicating between Cheonju and Seoul, 30 minutes long in every hour. The experiment performed 15 times a day for more than one week. Approximately 70% of the collected data was used to train the NN, and the rest was used to validate the obtained NN model.

Fig. 2 depicts a part of the RTT data collected from the UDP transmission while a load was applied as shown in table 1.

The NN was trained until the error reaches smaller than 1.4%. Also the PLR data was collected with similar method as in the RTT case in order to obtain

Table 1. Experiment Results of RTT and PLR

	0 Mbyte	1 Mbyte	2 Mbyte	5 Mbyte	7 Mbyte
Max.RTT(ms)	10.8	17.3	23.9	45.2	79.3
Min.RTT(ms)	10.1	115.	19.4	29.7	34.9
Max.PLR(%)	1.2	2.4	8.1	12.7	14.4
Min.PLR(%)	0	0.5	3.8	11.3	12.5

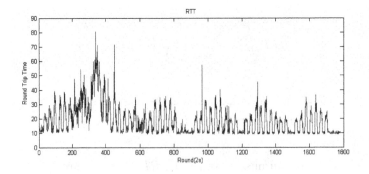

Fig. 2. Response of RTT obtained using UDP

the training and the validation data for PLR as shown in Table 1. The training procedures performed until the error reduces to as low as 1.52%.

NN Modeling of RTT and PLR using the moving average method also has been performed. It demonstrated that the moving average produces better results when the data set characterized with high variation. By reducing the rapid change, it was easier to train the NN, which improved the training where the error can be low as 1.1% for RTT and 0.87% for PLR case.

5.2   Validation of a Prediction NN Model

Validation of a RTT and PLR. Fig. 3 and 4 present the validation results of the RTT and PLR prediction model using data that was not applied to the training process. The dotted line is the output of the neural network. It reveals that an error occurred in the normal state, however, the error was reduced when a large load was applied, where the error rate for RTT was 5% and the PLR was

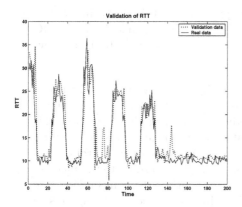

Fig. 3. Validation for RTT

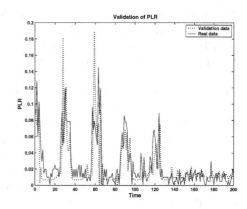

Fig. 4. Validation for PLR

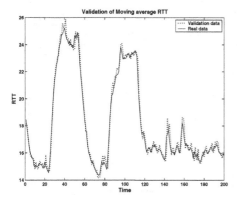

Fig. 5. Results of the validation with moving average RTT

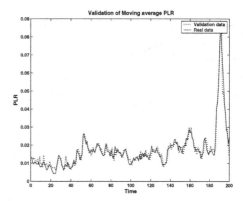

Fig. 6. Results of the validation with moving average PLR

3.82%. This paper improved the performance of a prediction model by reducing the variation range of the PLR using the moving average value in the next section.

Validation of RTT and PLR with moving average method. Fig. 5 presents the validation results of the RTT neural network model that estimates using a moving average values. An error occurred at the maximum value was negligible. In addition, the error rate was about 1.125% and significantly improved compare to the case that didn't apply the moving average, where the error rate was 5%.

Fig. 6 presents the validation results of the NN model that estimates the PLR using the moving average values. The graph showed improved results compared to the case without moving average method, where the error rate was about 0.9%.

5.3   Measuring a Bandwidth Sharing Rate

This section conducted a test from the viewpoint of bandwidth sharing for the TFRC (pTFRC1) that was simply applied by a prediction model, and TFRC (pTFRC2) that was applied by the prediction transmission using both the moving average and hybrid method.

Simultaneous Transmission of TCP and UDP. Fig. 7 presents the transmission rate for the simultaneous transmission of TCP and UDP by applying the load from 0 to 7Mbps, which were produced using a traffic generator. This process revealed that the UDP transmits data with a constant transmission rate, regardless of the network condition, because it has no congestion control mechanism. However, the TCP reduced its transmission rate according to the increase in loads using a congestion control algorithm. In addition, the transmission rate of TCP significantly decreased when loads is increased due to the aggressive transmission of the UDP.

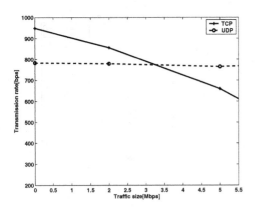

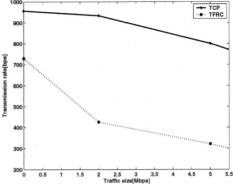

Fig. 7. Simultaneous Transmission rate for TCP and UDP

Fig. 8. Simultaneous Transmission rate for TCP and TFRC

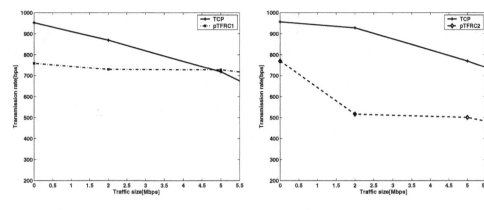

Fig. 9. Simultaneous Transmission rate for TCP and pTFRC1

Fig. 10. Simultaneous Transmission rate for TCP and pTFRC2

Fig. 8 presents the transmission rate for the simultaneous transmission of TCP and TFRC by applying the same load as in the previous case. It revealed that the TFRC significantly decreased the transmission rate according to the increase in loads using a congestion control algorithm. The TCP also decreased the transmission rate in proportion to the size of loads. However, the TCP presented a higher transmission rate than that of the simultaneous transmission with the UDP. This result was achieved due to the fact that the TFRC has mechanism sharing the bandwidth with other protocols.

Simultaneous Transmission of TCP/pTFRC1 and TCP/pTFRC2. Fig. 9 presents the simultaneous transmission of the TFRC (pTFRC1) and TCP algorithms, which decide the transmission rate by predicting the RTT and PLR, which did not using either a moving average or hybrid method. The pTFRC1 reduced the transmission rate according to the size of the loads. However, this demonstrates that the change in the transmission rate was minute. This means that the prediction error still existed, and the aggressive transmission of the UDP continued, even though the traffic was predicted.

Fig. 10 presents the simultaneous transmission of the TFRC (pTFRC2) and TCP that were applied using the moving average and hybrid method. The pTFRC2 reduces its transmission rate compared to the existing pTFRC1, according to the increase in loads, and presented higher transmission rate than that of the TFRC. This means that the transmission rate was controlled by adapting the traffic situation, while the sharing rate of TCP was maintained.

Simultaneous Transmission of every protocol. Fig. 11 presents the transmission rate using the four different TCP protocols studied so far. It revealed that the transmission rate of the TCP significantly decreased compared to other protocols, because the UDP and pTFRC1 presented an aggressive transmission. However, the TFRC and pTFRC2 provide a smooth reduction in TCP. The pTFRC2 guaranteed the transmission rate of the TCP, while it maintained a

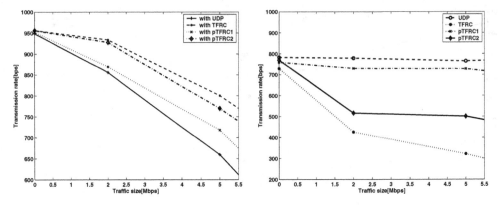

Fig. 11. Transmission rate of all protocol

Fig. 12. Transmission rate with respect to the packet size

higher transmission rate than that of the TFRC, even though the TFRC presented smoother changes than those of the pTFRC2.

Fig. 12 presents the transmission rate for each protocol according to the size of loads. It reveals that the UDP transmits data using a constant speed because it has no congestion control algorithm. The pTFRC1 still aggressively transmits data due to a lack of prediction performance, even though it reduces the transmission rate according to the load. The TFRC significantly reduced the transmission rate in order to guarantee the sharing rate of the TCP. However, the pTFRC2 maintained a higher transmission rate than that of the pTFRC1, while it guarantees the sharing rate of the TCP.

6   Conclusion

This paper developed and evaluated a protocol, which controls the transmission rate by predicting an Internet bandwidth in the data transmission through the Internet. A neural network that is able to produce a nonlinear system was used as a predictive modeling method. In addition, a LMBP algorithm, which showed a fast convergence, was applied to train the model.

The RTT and PLR were collected using the UDP transmission method, and the collected data was used to train the prediction model. In order to improve the performance of the prediction model, the moving average values of the RTT and PLR were used. Moreover, a hybrid method was used to improve the performance when the network is not congested.

In order to evaluate the performance of the prediction model proposed in this paper, a system was set up that transmits a packet between the systems located in Cheonju and Seoul. The possible various situations of the Internet were produced using a traffic generator. The sharing rate of the bandwidth in the congestion situation was measured using the simultaneous transmission of each protocol conjunction with the TCP, one of the typical transmission methods for the Internet. The test revealed that the prediction model trained by using the moving average value presented a good transmission rate, while it maintained the transmission rate of the TCP.

References

1. A.S Tanenbaum: Computer Networks(third edition). Prentice Hall International, Inc. (1996)
2. Joerg Widmer, Robert Denda, Martin Mauve: A Survey on TCP-Friendly Congestion Control. IEEE Network, vol 3 (2001) 28-37
3. L. Rizzo: Pgmcc: A TCP-Friendly single-rate multicast Congestion control scheme. Proc. ACM SIGCOMM, Stocholm, Sweden (2000) 17-28
4. S. Sisalem, A. Wolisz: MLDA: A TCP-Friendly Congestion Control Framework for Heterogeneous Multicast Environments. 8th Intĺ. Wksp. QoS (2000)
5. D. Rajate, M. Handley, D. Estrin: RAP : An end-to-end rate-based congestion control mechanism or realtime streams in the Internet. INFOCOM'99, vol 3 (1999) 1337-1345
6. J. Mahadavi and S. Floyd: TCP-Friendly unicast rate-based flow control. Tech. Rep., Technical note sent to end2end interest ailing list (1997)
7. K. S. Narendra and K. Parthasarathy: Identification and control of dynamical systems using neural network. IEEE Trans. Neural Networks, vol 1 (1990) 4-27
8. M. Norgaard, O. Ravn, N.K. Poulsen, L. K. Hansen: Neural Networks for Modeling and Control of Dynamic System. A practitioner's Handbook, Springer
9. Finschi: An implementation of the Levenberg-Marquardt algorithm. clausiusstrasses 45, CH-8092, Zuerich (1996)
10. S. Haykin: Neural Networks. MacMillan (1994)
11. V. Jacobson: Congesion Avoidance and contro. SIGCOMM Symposium on Communications Architectures and Protocols (1988) 214-329
12. Michael J. Donahoo, Kenneth L. Calvert: The Pocket Guide to TCP/IP Socket : C Version. Morgan Kaufmann Publishers, Inc. (2001)
13. Ikjun Yeom: ENDE An End-To-End Network Delay Emulator. Texas A & M University (1998)
14. The IPERF: http://dast.nlanr.net/Projects/Iperf/

Planning of Parallel Abstract Programs as Boolean Satisfiability

Gennady A. Oparin and Alexei P. Novopashin

Institute of Systems Dynamics and Control Theory,
Siberian Branch of Russian Academy of Sciences,
134, Lermontov st., 664033, Irkutsk, Russia
{oparin, apn}@icc.ru

Abstract. In this paper [1], a new formulation is proposed for the problem of constructing parallel abstract programs of a required length in parallel computing systems. The conditions of a planning problem are represented as a system of Boolean equations (constraints), whose solutions determine the possible plans for activating the program modules. Specifications of modules are stored in the knowledgebase of the planner. Constraint on number of processors and time delays at execution of modules are taken into account.

1 Introduction

The declarative languages and systems of parallel modular programming [1], [2] allow to accumulate knowledge of computing modules of a subject domain in a computer memory and to use this knowledge for the automatic decision of problems of given class. However the efficient use of this technology demands the decision of a difficult problem of planning of the parallel abstract program (constructing the plan for the problem solving).

Descriptions of modules (related by data) are located in the knowledgebase of the planner. It is necessary to define what modules, in what sequence and on what processors (from accessible) of the parallel computing system are to be executed to calculate the required set B_0 of target parameters from the given set A_0 of parameters (input data). The objective is to obtain a parallel plan for solving the problem $T = (A_0, B_0)$, which is:

(1) admissible (the modules must be ordered so that each be provided with necessary input data at its starting moment or, in other words, for any input parameter of the plan module, there must be at least one previously encountered module with the same output parameter),

(2) repetition-free (each module cannot enter into the plan more than once),

(3) irredundant (elimination of any module from the plan leads to an inadmissible plan),

(4) efficient (the plan length must be less than or equal to a given value k).

---

[1] Supported by the Russian Foundation for Basic Research (project 04-07-90358).

We assume, that during constructing the parallel plan with the aforementioned properties the number of accessible processors of the parallel computing system is limited by some size, there are time delays at execution of modules, time of data transmission between modules is ignored. In this formulation, the planning problem is NP-hard, its conditions can be represented as a system of Boolean equations (constraints), and the proper plan of module execution is a solution to this system. The advantage of Boolean modeling over the traditional deductive approach is that the first makes it possible to (1) obtain parallel plans of required lengths, (2) take into account various constraints on the plan, and, finally, (3) make use of existing efficient solvers for Boolean equations (or, SAT-solvers), which, in some cases, are faster than special-purpose planning algorithms. On the whole as noted in [3] such approach not only provides a more flexible framework for stating different kinds of constraints on plans, but also more accurately reflects the theory behind modern constraint-based planning systems.

2   The Planner Knowledgebase

As a planner knowledgebase, we use a computational model $KB = (F, Z, In, Out)$, where $F = \{F_1, ..., F_n\}$ is the set of available modules acting on the field of common transit data $Z = \{Z_1, ..., Z_m\}$, which are input or output parameters for these modules; $In \subset F \times Z$ and $Out \subset F \times Z$ are relations reflecting the interaction of modules with input or output data, respectively. Thus, each module F_i is connected with two parametric sets $A_i, B_i \subset Z$ called the input and output, correspondingly. The input A_i identifies the data that are needed to obtain the results represented by the output B_i. Hereafter, this will be denoted by $F_i(A_i; B_i)$. Without loss of generality, we assume that F_1 and F_2 modules of the set F model the conditions of the statement of the planning problem $T = (A_0, B_0)$: the knowledgebase KB includes the modules $F_1(; A_0)$ and $F_2(B_0;)$, where $A_0, B_0 \subset Z$. The absence of any attribute before or after the semicolon means that the corresponding set is empty. F_1 is called the module of input data and F_2 the target module.

The knowledgebase KB is assumed to be redundant in the sense that only a part of modules of F are used to solve the problem, and/or the problem T has several alternative solution plans.

The relations In and Out are conveniently given as two $n \times m$ Boolean matrices A and B with the following elements: $a_{ij} = 1$ ($b_{ij} = 1$), if Z_j is an input (output) parameter for the module F_i. Furthermore, A_i and B_i $(i = 1, ..., n)$ denote the rows of these matrices, A'_i and B'_i $(i = 1, ..., m)$ - their columns. The rows and columns of A and B are the binary representations of subsets of parameters and modules, respectively. The notation $q \in S$ (where S is a binary row of A_i, B_i, A'_i or B'_i) means that q takes the numbers of unit entries in the binary row S.

3   Boolean Modeling Without Resource Constraints

First of all we shall consider a case when constraint on number of processors is absent, and time delays at execution of modules are ignored (constructing the synchronous plan). Let us define the plan as a $(k \times n)$-matrix X of Boolean variables x_{ij}, where $x_{ij} = 1$ means that the module F_j is at the i-th place in the plan X. The total length of the plan is k, its row gives a set of parallel-executable modules, and its columns correspond to the set of available F modules. Then, Boolean constraints on entries of the matrix X have the following form.

Condition 1. The condition of the statement of the planning problem $T = (A_0, B_0)$ (the input-data module $F_1 = (; A_0)$ and the target module $F_2 = (B_0;)$ are located at the first and last rows of the plan, respectively, and there are no other modules in these rows):

$$\overline{x}_{11} = 0, \quad \bigvee_{j=2}^{n} x_{1j} = 0, \quad \overline{x}_{k2} = 0, \quad x_{k1} = 0, \quad \bigvee_{j=3}^{n} x_{kj} = 0.$$

Condition 2. The plan should be continuous (each row of the plan contains at least one module):

$$\bigvee_{i=2}^{k-1} \bigwedge_{j=1}^{n} \overline{x}_{ij} = 0.$$

Condition 3. The plan should be repetition-free:

$$\bigvee_{j=1}^{n} \bigvee_{i=1}^{k-1} \bigvee_{p=i+1}^{k} (x_{ij} \wedge x_{pj}) = 0.$$

Condition 4. The plan should be admissible:

$$\bigvee_{t=2}^{k} \bigvee_{p=1}^{n} (x_{tp} \wedge y) = 0,$$

where

$$y = \begin{cases} \bigvee_{q \in A_p} \bigwedge_{i=1}^{t-1} \bigwedge_{j \in B'_q} \overline{x}_{ij} \ , \ \text{if } (A_p \neq 0 \ ) \wedge ((\forall q \in A_p)(B'_q \neq 0)); \\ 1, \ \text{if } (A_p \neq 0) \wedge ((\exists \ q \in A_p)(B'_q = 0)); \\ 0, \ \text{if } A_p = 0. \end{cases}$$

Condition 5. The plan should be ordered (if the data preparation for a module is completed at the $(t-1)$-*th* row of the plan, then this module is necessarily included in its t-*th* row):

$$\bigvee_{t=2}^{k} \bigvee_{p=1}^{n} (x_{tp} \wedge v) = 0,$$

where

$$v = \begin{cases} \bigwedge_{q \in A_p} \bigwedge_{j \in B'_q} \overline{x}_{t-1,j}, \ \text{if } (A_p \neq 0) \wedge ((\forall q \in A_p)(B'_q \neq 0)); \\ 1, \ \text{if } (A_p \neq 0) \wedge ((\exists \ q \in A_p)(B'_q = 0)); \\ 0, \ \text{if } (A_p = 0) \wedge (\ t = 2); \\ 1, \ \text{if } (A_p = 0) \wedge (\ t > 2). \end{cases}$$

Condition 6. The plan should be irredundant:

$$\overset{k-1}{\underset{s=2}{\vee}} \overset{n}{\underset{r=1}{\vee}} (x_{sr} \wedge \overline{u}) = 0,$$

where

$$u = \overset{k}{\underset{t=2}{\vee}} \overset{n}{\underset{p=1}{\vee}} (x_{tp} \wedge y),$$

t and p subscripts satisfy the condition $\overline{(t = s) \wedge (p = r)}$, and y is determined from the expression in condition 4.

Additional conditions are given by the originator of the planning problem:

$$g(x_{11}, ..., x_{1n}, ..., x_{k1}, ..., x_{kn}) = 0.$$

As examples we can consider the following:

a) The condition that the module F_j is necessarily included in the plan:

$$h_j = \overset{k-1}{\underset{i=2}{\wedge}} \overline{x}_{ij} = 0;$$

b) The condition that the module F_j is not included in the plan:

$$z_j = \overset{k-1}{\underset{i=2}{\vee}} x_{ij} = 0;$$

c) The condition that the modules F_j and F_p are alternatively included in the plan:

$$z_j \wedge z_p \vee h_j \wedge h_p = 0.$$

The requirement that the plan is ordered allows one to reduce the search space essentially during solving the system of Boolean equations given by conditions 1-6, although denying this requirement extends the list of additional conditions set by the originator of the planning problem. By eliminating the condition of continuity, one can synthesize plans of length $\leq k$. The number of unknown Boolean variables (the problem dimension) is n^2 in a worst case. If the module set F is very redundant, the problem dimension can be reduced through a preliminary processing of the solver knowledgebase by forward and backward search algorithms conventionally used in planning.

As an example, we shall consider the following solver knowledgebase:

$KB = \{F_1(; z_1), F_2(z_6, z_7;), F_3(z_1; z_2), F_4(z_1; z_3), F_5(z_1; z_4), F_6(z_2; z_6),$
$F_7(z_2, z_3; z_7), F_8(z_3, z_4; z_5), F_9(z_4; z_7), F_{10}(z_5; z_6)\}.$

The dependence graph for KB is shown on a Fig. 1. The modules are represented as circles, parameters – as points. The modules F_1 and F_2 determine the statement of the planning problem: parameter z_1 is given; it is required to calculate parameters z_6 and z_7.

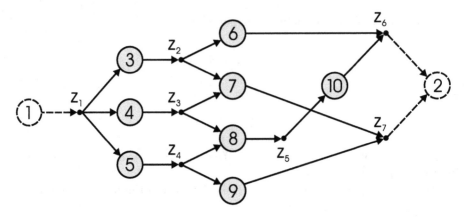

Fig. 1. The dependence graph for KB

In this case, the binary matrices A and B have the form

$$
A = \begin{bmatrix} 0000000 \\ 0000011 \\ 1000000 \\ 1000000 \\ 1000000 \\ 0100000 \\ 0110000 \\ 0011000 \\ 0001000 \\ 0000100 \end{bmatrix}, \quad
B = \begin{bmatrix} 1000000 \\ 0000000 \\ 0100000 \\ 0010000 \\ 0001000 \\ 0000010 \\ 0000001 \\ 0000100 \\ 0000001 \\ 0000010 \end{bmatrix}.
$$

The additional conditions given by the originator of the planning problem are missing. To solve the system of equations from conditions 1-6, we used the REBUS Boolean equation solver [4]. The solution method relies on the representation of Boolean functions in the left-hand side of equations in the general form (condition 6 is of this type, and conditions 1-5 are given in the disjunctive normal form), realizing the technique of chronological backtracking with the use of Kleene's three-valued logic.

We found two plans of length 4 (nr.1 and nr.2) and two plans of length 5 (nr.3 and nr.4): nr.1: F_1, $F_3 - F_5$, $F_6 - F_9$, F_2;

nr.2: F_1, $F_3 - F_4$, $F_6 - F_7$, F_2;
nr.3: F_1, $F_3 - F_4 - F_5$, $F_7 - F_8$, F_{10}, F_2;
nr.4: F_1, $F_4 - F_5$, $F_8 - F_9$, F_{10}, F_2.

There are no plans of different length. The "$-$" symbol denotes parallel-executable modules.

The comparison with different solvers of Boolean equations (or, SAT-solvers; see, for example, [5]) is complicated by the fact that the initial Boolean constraints on them must be in the normal form (in our case, condition 6 is of a general form and its reduction to the disjunctive normal form in the general case is a hard problem).

4   Boolean Constraints in DNF-Form

If we impose more strict conditions of admissibility and non-redundancy of the plan, Boolean constraints can be obtained in the disjunctive normal form.

Condition 4.1. The condition that the plan is admissible: for any input parameter of the plan module, there must be just a single previously encountered module with the same output parameter. In such a formulation, this condition ensures that the plan is non-alternative inside and Boolean equation

$$\bigvee_{t=2}^{k} \bigvee_{p=1}^{n} (x_{tp} \wedge y) = 0$$

corresponds to it, where

$$
y = \begin{cases}
\bigvee_{q \in A_p} \left(\bigvee_{r=1}^{l-1} \bigvee_{s=r+1}^{l} (z_r \wedge z_s) \vee \bigwedge_{r=1}^{l} \overline{z}_r \right), & \text{if } (A_p \neq 0) \wedge ((\forall q \in A_p)(B'_q \neq 0)); \\
1, & \text{if } (A_p \neq 0) \wedge ((\exists \, q \in A_p)(B'_q = 0)); \\
0, & \text{if } A_p = 0.
\end{cases}
$$

The symbol z denotes an array of length l of the matrix X, which is formed for each $q \in A_p$ in the following way:

$$z = \left\{ x_{ij} : \; i = \overline{1, \, t-1}, \; j \in B'_q \right\}.$$

Condition 6.1. Then, in view of 4.1., the non-redundancy condition can be formulated in the following way: each module of the plan includes (at least one) output parameter being input for at least a single module, encountered later in the plan. In this case, Boolean constraint has the form:

$$\bigvee_{t=1}^{k-1} \bigvee_{p=1}^{n} (x_{tp} \wedge w) = 0,$$

where

$$
w = \begin{cases}
\bigwedge_{q \in B_p} \bigwedge_{i=t+1}^{k} \bigwedge_{j \in A'_q} \overline{x}_{ij}, & \text{if } B_p \neq 0 ; \\
1, & \text{if } B_p = 0.
\end{cases}
$$

As an example, we shall consider the following solver knowledgebase:
$KB1 = \{F_1(; z_1), F_2(z_6;), F_3(z_1; z_2, z_3), F_4(z_1; z_3, z_4), F_5(z_3; z_5),$
$F_6(z_2, z_4, z_5; z_6)\}$.

In this case, the binary matrices A and B have the form:

$$
A = \begin{bmatrix} 000000 \\ 000001 \\ 100000 \\ 100000 \\ 001000 \\ 010110 \end{bmatrix}, \quad
B = \begin{bmatrix} 100000 \\ 000000 \\ 011000 \\ 001100 \\ 000010 \\ 000001 \end{bmatrix}.
$$

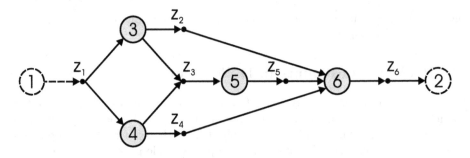

Fig. 2. The dependence graph for $KB1$

The dependence graph for $KB1$ is shown on a Fig. 2.

There is a single plan for the problem solving $(F_1, F_3 - F_4, F_5, F_6, F_2)$, which satisfies conditions 1-6. However, no plans will be found if more strict constraints 4.1 and 6.1 (instead of 4 and 6) are used. These conditions eliminate the possibility to calculate the parameter z_3 by two alternative ways (either F_3 or F_4).

5   Boolean Modeling with Resource Constraints

In this section we shall consider a case, when all processors are identical and number of processors is limited by pr. Each module can be executed on any processor. Time of execution τ_j of the module $F_j \in F$ is discrete value: $\tau_j \in N = \{1, 2, ...\}$. Time of data transmission from one processor to another is ignored. The processor can execute only one module at each moment of time. The general directory period of the problem solving $k \in N$ is set. It is required to construct the asynchronous plan which length is equal to the given value k or does not exceed it.

To allow for time delays at execution of modules (τ_j) it is necessary to modify two conditions (continuity (2) and admissibility (4)) and to exclude the condition 5 (orderliness of the plan) from system of Boolean constraints.

Condition 2.1. The plan should be continuous (with time delays at execution of modules):

$$\bigvee_{t=2}^{k-1} \bigwedge_{j=1}^{n} \bigwedge_{i=t-\tau_j+1}^{t} \bar{x}_{ij} = 0.$$

Here τ_j $(j = \overline{1, n})$ - the execution time of module F_j. When $\tau_j = 1$ for all j we have equivalence $i = t$, i.e. condition 2.

Condition 4.2. The condition that the plan is admissible (with time delays at execution of modules):

$$\bigvee_{t=2}^{k} \bigvee_{p=1}^{n} (x_{tp} \wedge y) = 0,$$

where

$$y = \begin{cases} \bigvee_{q \in A_p} \bigwedge_{j \in B'_q} \bigwedge_{i=1}^{t-\tau_j} \bar{x}_{ij} \,, \text{ if } (A_p \neq 0) \wedge ((\forall q \in A_p)(B'_q \neq 0)); \\ 1, \text{ if } (A_p \neq 0) \wedge ((\exists \, q \in A_p)(B'_q = 0)); \\ 0, \text{ if } A_p = 0. \end{cases}$$

To allow for number of accessible processors (pr) it is necessary to incorporate additional constraints.

Condition 7. The constraint on number of processors, assigned for solving the problem T. This condition allows us to find plans for pr processors without taking into account delays.

$$\bigvee_{t=2}^{k-1} \Big(\bigvee_{1 \leq j_1 \leq j_2 \leq \ldots \leq j_{pr+1} \leq n} (x_{t,j_1} \wedge x_{t,j_2} \wedge \ldots \wedge x_{t,j_{pr+1}}) \Big) \vee$$
$$\bigvee_{t=2}^{k-1} \bigwedge \Big(\bigvee_{1 \leq j_1 \leq j_2 \leq \ldots \leq j_{n-pr+1} \leq n} (\bar{x}_{t,j_1} \wedge \bar{x}_{t,j_2} \wedge \ldots \wedge \bar{x}_{t,j_{n-pr+1}}) \Big) = 0.$$

Condition 7.1. The constraint on number of processors with time delays at execution of modules:

$$\bigvee_{t=2}^{k-1} \Big(\bigvee_{1 \leq j_1 \leq j_2 \leq \ldots \leq j_{pr+1} \leq n} \Big(\bigvee_{i=t-\tau_{j_1}+1}^{t} x_{i,j_1} \wedge$$
$$\wedge \bigvee_{i=t-\tau_{j_2}+1}^{t} x_{i,j_2} \wedge \ldots \wedge \bigvee_{i=t-\tau_{j_{pr+1}}+1}^{t} x_{i,j_{pr+1}} \Big) \Big) \vee$$
$$\vee \bigvee_{t=2}^{k-1} \bigwedge \Big(\bigvee_{1 \leq j_1 \leq j_2 \leq \ldots \leq j_{n-pr+1} \leq n} \Big(\bigwedge_{i=t-\tau_{j_1}+1}^{t} \bar{x}_{i,j_1} \wedge$$
$$\wedge \bigwedge_{i=t-\tau_{j_2}+1}^{t} \bar{x}_{i,j_2} \wedge \ldots \wedge \bigwedge_{i=t-\tau_{j_{n-pr+1}}+1}^{t} \bar{x}_{i,j_{n-pr+1}} \Big) \Big) = 0.$$

For example, we shall consider the following solver knowledgebase:
$KB2 = \{F_1(; z_1), F_2(z_4, z_5;), F_3(z_1; z_2), F_4(z_1; z_3), F_5(z_1; z_5), F_6(z_2, z_3; z_4)\}$.
In this case, the binary matrices A and B have the form:

$$A = \begin{bmatrix} 000000 \\ 000110 \\ 100000 \\ 100000 \\ 100000 \\ 011000 \end{bmatrix}, \quad B = \begin{bmatrix} 100000 \\ 000000 \\ 010000 \\ 001000 \\ 000010 \\ 000100 \end{bmatrix}.$$

The dependence graph for $KB2$ is shown on a Fig. 3 .

The single problem solving plan is found when the resource constraints are absent (with constraints 1-6):

$F_1, F_3 - F_4 - F_5, F_6, F_2$.

Let us define number of accessible processors $pr = 2$ and time delays at execution of modules $\tau_j = 1 \ (j = \overline{1, n})$. Boolean equations system which consists of constraints 1, 2, 3, 4, 6 and 7 is solved by REBUS. As a result 10 synchronous plans are found: 1 plan of length 4 (nr.1) and 9 plans of length 5 (nr.3 − nr.10):

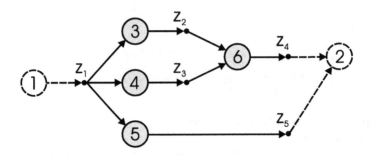

Fig. 3. The dependence graph for $KB2$

nr.1: F_1, $F_3 - F_4$, $F_5 - F_6$, F_2;
nr.2: F_1, $F_3 - F_4$, F_5, F_6, F_2;
nr.3: F_1, $F_3 - F_4$, F_6, F_5, F_2;
nr.4: F_1, $F_3 - F_5$, F_4, F_6, F_2;
nr.5: F_1, F_3, $F_4 - F_5$, F_6, F_2;
nr.6: F_1, F_3, F_4, $F_5 - F_6$, F_2;
nr.7: F_1, $F_4 - F_5$, F_3, F_6, F_2;
nr.8: F_1, F_4, $F_3 - F_5$, F_6, F_2;
nr.9: F_1, F_4, F_3, $F_5 - F_6$, F_2;
nr.10: F_1, F_5, $F_3 - F_4$, F_6, F_2.

To allow for time delays we shall replace condition 2 (continuity of the plan), condition 4 (admissibility of the plan) and condition 7 (on number of accessible processors) by constraints 2.1, 4.2 and 7.1 respectively.

Let us define time delays at execution of modules $\tau_3 = 3$ (for F_3), $\tau_5 = 4$ (for F_5) and $\tau_j = 1$ (for others). Boolean equations system which consists of constraints 1, 2.1, 3, 4.2, 6 and 7 is solved. As a result 6/21/35/29 asynchronous plans of length 7/8/9/10 are found. In the set of the solutions we shall consider three plans:

A. F_1, $F_3 - F_4$, F_3^+, F_3^+, $F_5 - F_6$, F_5^+, F_5^+, F_5^+, F_2;
B. F_1, $F_3 - F_4$, $F_3^+ - F_5$, $F_3^+ - F_5^+$, $F_6 - F_5^+$, F_5^+, F_2;
C. F_1, $F_3 - F_4$, $F_3^+ - F_5$, $F_3^+ - F_5^+$, F_5^+, $F_6 - F_5^+$, F_2.

The symbol "+" denotes continuation of the module execution.

Analysis of the result shows: the plan A corresponds to the plan nr.1 (when $\tau_3 = \tau_5 = 1$) from above-stated list of 10 plans. Similarly, the plan B and the plan C correspond to the plan nr.2. The length of the plan nr.1 is equal 4, length of the plan nr.2 – 5. The situation changes when we take into account time delays: the plan A is realized at 9 steps, B and C – at 7 steps. Clearly, B and C are preferable as they have smaller length and more effectively load processors of the parallel computing system.

6   Conclusion

A new formulation was given for the problem of constructing asynchronous action plans in parallel computing systems. In addition we took into account time delays at execution of modules, constraint on number of accessible processors, constraint on a length of the plan. Time of data transmission between modules was ignored. Boolean model for constructing successive plans of a given length in mediator systems, realizing structural data requests on the Internet is considered in [6]. In the related work [7] Boolean model for constructing parallel synchronous plans of action for organization the distributed computing in Internet is offered by authors. A comparative analysis shows, that the requirements to the plan parallelism and asynchronism and other constraints make the model significantly difficult, which gives no way of using well-known SAT-solvers oriented to the fact that Boolean constraints are in the normal form. Boolean equation solver REBUS is efficient enough to be applied in declarative languages and systems of the parallel modular programming.

References

1. Valkovskii, V., Malyshkin, V.: Parallel Programs and Systems Synthesis on the basis of Computational Models. Nauka, Novosibirsk (1988) 129
2. Oparin, G.A., Feoktistov, A.G.: Instrumental'naya raspredelennaya vychislitel'naya SATURN-sreda. Program. Prod. Sist., No. 2 (2002) 27–30 [in Russian]
3. Kautz, H., Selman, B.: Planning as Satisfiability. In: Proceedings of the 10th European Conference on Artificial Intelligence (ECAI) (1992) 359–363
4. Oparin, G.A., Bogdanova, V.G.: Algoritmy resheniya bol'shikh razrezhennykh sistem bulevykh uravnenii. Metody optimizatsii i ikh prilozheniya: Tr. 12-i Baikal'skoi mezhdunar. konf. Sektsiya 5. Diskretnaya matematika. IGU, Irkutsk (2001) 114–118 [in Russian]
5. Simon, L.: The experimentation web site around the satisfiability problem. [http://www.lri.fr/ simon/satex/satex.php3]
6. Prestwich, S., Bressan, S.: A SAT Approach to Query Optimization in Mediator Systems. In: Proceedings of the Fifth International Symposium on the Theory and Applications of Satisfiability Testing, University of Cincinnati (2002) 252–259
7. Oparin, G.A., Novopashin, A.P.: Boolevo modelirovanie planirovaniya deystvii v raspedelennykh vychislitel'nykh systemakh. Izvestia RAN, Teoria i systemy upravleniya, No. 5 (2004) 105–108 [in Russian]

Efficient Communication Scheduling Methods for Irregular Data Redistribution in Parallelizing Compilers[1]

Shih-Chang Chen[1], Ching-Hsien Hsu[1,*], Chao-Yang Lan[1],
Chao-Tung Yang[2], and Kuan-Ching Li[3]

[1] Department of Computer Science and Information Engineering,
Chung Hua University, Hsinchu 300 Taiwan
chh@chu.edu.tw
[2] Department of Computer Science and Information Engineering,
Tunghai University, Taichung 40704 Taiwan
ctyang@mail.thu.edu.tw
[3] Department of Computer Science and Information Management,
Providence University, Taichung 43301 Taiwan
kuancli@pu.edu.tw

Abstract. Irregular array redistribution has been paid attention recently since it can distribute different size of data segment to processors according to their own computation ability. It's also the reason why it has been kept an eye on load balance. In this work, we present a *two-phase degree-reduction* (*TPDR*) method for scheduling HPF2 irregular data redistribution. An extended algorithm based on *TPDR* is also presented. Effectiveness of the proposed methods not only avoids node contention but also shortens the overall communication length. To evaluate the performance of our methods, we have implemented both algorithms along with the divide-and-conquer algorithm. The simulation results show improvement of communication costs.

1 Introduction

In order to achieve a good performance of load balancing, using an appropriate data distribution scheme when processing different phase of application is necessary. In general, data distribution can be classified into regular and irregular. The regular distribution usually employs BLOCK, CYCLIC, or BLOCK-CYCLIC(c) to specify array decomposition. The irregular distribution uses user-defined functions to specify unevenly array distribution.

To map unequal sized continuous segments of array onto processors, High Performance Fortran version 2 (HPF2) provides GEN_BLOCK distribution format which facilitates generalized block distributions. GEN_BLOCK allows unequal sized data segments of an array to be mapped onto processors. This makes it possible to let different processors dealing with appropriate data quantity according to their computation ability.

---

[1] This research is supported partially by National Science Council, Taiwan, under grant number NSC-93-2213-E-216-029.
[*] The correspondence address.

V. Malyshkin (Ed.): PaCT 2005, LNCS 3606, pp. 216–225, 2005.

In some algorithms, an array distribution that is well-suited for one phase may not be good for a subsequent phase in terms of performance. Array redistribution is needed when applications running from one sub-algorithm to another during run-time. Therefore, many data parallel programming languages support run-time primitives for changing a program's array decomposition. Efficient methods for performing array redistribution are of great importance for the development of distributed memory compilers for those languages.

In this paper, we present a two-phase degree reduction (*TPDR*) algorithm to efficiently perform GEN_BLOCK array redistribution. Communication scheduling is one of the most important issues on developing runtime array redistribution techniques. The main idea of the two-phase degree reduction method is to schedules communications of processors that with degree (number of communication messages) greater than two in the first phase (named degree reduction phase). A communication step will be scheduled after performing one of the serial degree-reduction iterations. The second phase (named coloring phase) schedules all messages of processors that with degree-2 and degree-1 using an adjustable coloring mechanism. Based on the *TPDR* method, we also present an extended *TPDR* algorithm (*E-TPDR*).

The rest of this paper is organized as follows. In Section 2, a brief survey of related work will be presented. In section 3, we will introduce an example of GEN_BLOCK array redistribution as preliminary. Section 4 presents two communication scheduling algorithms for irregular redistribution problem. The performance analysis and simulation results will be presented in section 5. Finally, the conclusions will be given in section 6.

2 Related Work

Techniques for regular array redistribution, in general, can be classified into two approaches: the communication sets identification techniques and communication optimizations. The former includes the *PITFALLS* [14] and the *ScaLAPACK* [13] methods for index sets generation; Park *et al.* [11] devised algorithms for BLOCK-CYCLIC Data redistribution between processor sets; Dongarra *et al.* [12] proposed algorithmic redistribution methods for BLOCK-CYCLIC decompositions; Zapata *et al.* [1] proposed parallel sparse redistribution code for BLOCK-CYCLIC data redistribution based on *CRS* structure. The *Generalized Basic-Cycle Calculation* method was presented in [3].

Techniques for communication optimizations category, in general, provide different approaches to reduce the communication overheads in a redistribution operation. Examples are the processor mapping techniques [7, 9, 4] for minimizing data transmission overheads, the multiphase redistribution strategy [8] for reducing message startup cost, the communication scheduling approaches [2, 5, 10, 18] for avoiding node contention and the strip mining approach [15] for overlapping communication and computational overheads.

On irregular array redistribution, Guo *et al.* [6] presented a symbolic analysis method for communication set generation and to reduce communication cost of irregular array redistribution. On communication efficiency, Lee *et al.* [9] presented a logical processor reordering algorithm on irregular array redistribution. Four algorithms were discussed in this work for reducing communication cost. Guo *et al.* [16, 17] proposed a divide-and-conquer algorithm for performing irregular array redistribution. In this method, communication messages are first divided into groups using Neighbor Message Set (NMS), messages have the same sender or receiver; the communication steps will be scheduled after those NMSs are merged according to the relationship of contention. In [18], a relocation algorithm was proposed by Yook and Park. The relocation algorithm consists of two scheduling phases, the list scheduling phase and the relocation phase. The list scheduling phase sorts global messages and allocates them into communication steps in decreasing order. Because of conventional sorting operation, list scheduling indeed performs well in term of algorithmic complexity. If a contention happened, the relocation phase will perform a serial of re-schedule operations. While algorithm flow goes to the relocation phase, it has to allocate an appropriate location for the messages that can't be scheduled at that moment. This leads to high scheduling overheads and degrades the performance of a redistribution algorithm.

3 Preliminaries

A bipartite graph $G = (V, E)$ is used to represent the communications of an irregular array redistribution on $A[1:N]$ over P processors. Vertices in G are used to represent the source and destination processors. Edge e_{ij} in G denotes the message sent from source processor SP_i to destination processor DP_j, where $e_{ij} \in E$. $|E|$ is the total number of communication messages through the redistribution.

Unlike regular problem, there is no repetition communication pattern in irregular GEN_BLOCK array redistribution. It is also noticed that if SP_i sends messages to DP_{j-1} and DP_{j+1}, the communication between SP_i and DP_j must exist, where $0 \le i, j \le P-1$. This result was mentioned as the consecutive communication property [9]. Figure 1(a) shows an example of redistributing two GEN_BLOCK distributions on a n array $A[1:100]$. Distributions I and II are mapped to source processors and destination processors, respectively. The communications between source and destination processor sets are depicted in Figure 1(b). There are totally eleven communication messages ($|E|=11$), m_1, m_2, m_3..., m_{11} among processors involved in the redistribution. In general, to avoid conflict communication or node contention, a processor can only send one message to destination processors at a communication step. Similarly, one can only receive a message from source processors at any communication step. Figure 1(c) shows a simple schedule for this example.

4 Scheduling Algorithms of GEN_BLOCK Redistribution

The communication time depends on total number of communication steps and the length of these steps. In general, the message startup cost is proportional to the number of communication steps. The length of these steps determines the data transmission overheads. A minimal steps scheduling can be obtained using the coloring mechanism. However, there are two drawbacks in this method; first, it can not minimize total size of communication steps; second, the graph coloring algorithmic complexity is often high. In the following subsections, we will present two low complexity and high availability scheduling methods.

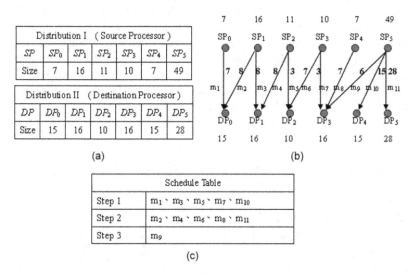

Distribution I	(Source Processor)				
SP	SP_0	SP_1	SP_2	SP_3	SP_4	SP_5
Size	7	16	11	10	7	49

Distribution II	(Destination Processor)				
DP	DP_0	DP_1	DP_2	DP_3	DP_4	DP_5
Size	15	16	10	16	15	28

(a)

(b)

Schedule Table	
Step 1	$m_1 \cdot m_3 \cdot m_5 \cdot m_7 \cdot m_{10}$
Step 2	$m_2 \cdot m_4 \cdot m_6 \cdot m_8 \cdot m_{11}$
Step 3	m_9

(c)

Fig. 1. An example of irregular array redistribution. (a) The source and destination distributions. (b) Bipartite communications. (c) Simple schedule

4.1 The Two-Phase Degree Reduction Method

The Two-Phase Degree Reduction (*TPDR*) method consists of two parts. The first part schedules communications of processors with degree greater than two. In a bipartite graph representation, the *TPDR* reduces the degree of vertices with maximum degree by one every reduction iteration. The second part schedules all messages of processors that with degree-2 and degree-1 using an adjustable coloring mechanism. The degree reduction is performed as follows.

Step1: Sort the vertices that with maximum degree d by total size of messages in decreasing order. Assume there are k nodes with degree d. The sorted vertices would be $<V_{i1}, V_{i2}, ..., V_{ik}>$.

Step2: Schedule the minimum message $m_j = \min\{m_1, m_2, ..., m_d\}$ into step d for vertices $V_{i1}, V_{i2}, ..., V_{ik}$, where $1 \leq j \leq d$.

Step3: Maximum degree $d = d-1$. Repeat Steps 1 and 2.

Figure 2(a) shows an example of initial communication patterns. The redistribution is carried out over seven processors with maximum degree 3. Therefore, the communications can be scheduled in three steps. According to the above description in step 1, there are two nodes with degree 3, SP_6 and DP_1. The total message size of SP_6 (36) is greater than DP_1 (14). Thus, SP_6 is the first candidate to select a minimum message (m_{11}) of it into step 3. A similar selection is then performed on DP_1. Since m_5 is the minimum message of DP_1 at present, therefore, m_5 is scheduled into step 3 as well. As messages m_{11} and m_5 are removed from the bipartite graph, adjacent nodes of edges m_{11} and m_5, i.e., SP_6, DP_4, DP_1 and SP_3 should update their total message size. After the degree reduction iteration, the maximum degree of the bipartite graph will become 2. Figure 2(b) shows this scenario. Figures 2(c) and 2(d) show the similar process of above on degree = 2 bipartite graph. In Figure 2(c), vertices SP_6, SP_5, SP_4, SP_1, DP_3, DP_2, DP_1 and DP_0 have the maximum degree 2 and are candidates to schedule their messages into step 2. According to the degree reduction method, m_{12}, m_{10} and m_7 are scheduled in order. The next message to be selected is m_8. However, both messages of DP_3 will result node contention (one with SP_4 and one with SP_5) if we are going to schedule one of DP_3's messages. This means that the degree reduction method might not reduce degree-2 edges completely when the degree is 2.

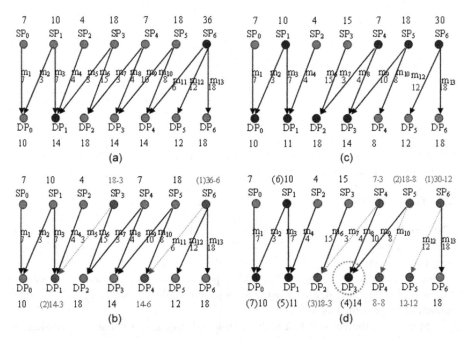

Fig. 2. The process of degree reduction (a) initial bipartition communications. (b) SP_6 and DP_1 have the maximum degree 3, m_{11} and m_5 are scheduled. Total message size of adjacent nodes of edges m_{11} and m_5 (SP_6, DP_4, DP_1 and SP_3) should be updated. (c) m_{11} and m_5 are removed from the bipartite graph. The maximum degree is 2 after degree reduction. SP_6, SP_5, SP_4, SP_1, DP_3, DP_2, DP_1 and DP_0 have the maximum degree 2, they are marked blue. (d) m_{12}, m_{10}, m_7, m_2 and m_4 are scheduled. Adjacent nodes of edges m_{12}, m_{10}, m_7, m_2 and m_4 (SP_6, DP_5, SP_5, DP_4, DP_2, SP_4,...) should be updated. After remove messages m_7 and m_{10}, the degree of DP_3 can't be reduced

To avoid the above situation, an adjustable coloring mechanism to schedule degree-2 and degree-1 communications in bipartite graph can be applied. Since the consecutive edges must be scheduled into two steps, there is no need to care about the size of messages. That means we don't have to schedule the large messages together on purpose.

Let's consider again the example in Figure 2(c). Figure 3 demonstrates scheduling of the coloring phase for communication steps 1 and 2. To facilitate our illustration, we denote each connected component in G' as a *Consecutive Section (CS)*. In Figure 3, there are three *Consecutive Sections*, the CS_1 is consisted of four messages m_1, m_2, m_3 and m_4; the CS_2 is consisted of five messages m_6, m_7, m_8, m_9 and m_{10}; the CS_3 is consisted of two messages m_{12} and m_{13}. A simple coloring scheme is to use two colors on adjacency edges alternatively. For example, we first color m_1, m_6 and m_{12} red; then, color m_2, m_7 and m_{13} blue; and so on. The scheduling results for CS_1 and CS_2 are shown in row 1 and row 2 beside the bipartite graph. Row 3 shows the merging result of CS_1 with CS_2 and the schedule of CS_3. In row 3, messages m_6 (15) and m_{13} (18) dominate the communication time at steps 1 and 2, respectively. This results total communication cost = 33. If we change the order of steps 1 and 2 in CS_3, it becomes m_{13} dominates the communication time in step 1 and m_{12} dominates the communication time in step 2. This will result total communication cost = 30. Therefore, the colors of two steps in CS_3 are exchanged in Row 3 for less communication cost. Row 4 shows communication scheduling of the adjustable coloring phase for degree-2 and degree-1 communications.

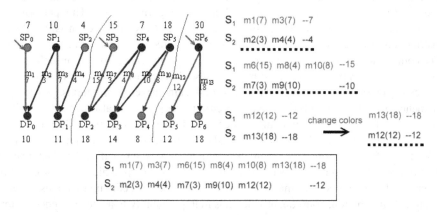

Fig. 3. Adjustable coloring mechanism for scheduling degree-2 and degree 1 communications

4.2 Extended TPDR

Based on *TPDR*, we present an extended two-phase degree reduction (*E-TPDR*) algorithm in this subsection. An edge-complement operation is added in the degree-reduction phase. As the *TPDR* algorithm stated, the original degree-reduction operation only schedules degree-k nodes' messages into communication step k. This might not fully utilize the available space in step k and remains heavy communications in the previous steps (less than k). Therefore, a principle for adding extra messages into these steps is to select the maximum message that is smaller than the length of current step and with un-marked adjacent vertices.

The key concept of this modification is to schedule messages into communication steps during reduction phase as many as possible into the existing communication steps. Because the additional scheduled messages are with smaller message size than the current step length, the edge-complement operation will not influence the cost of original scheduling from *TPDR*. Figure 4 shows the communication schedule of the example given in Figure 2 using *E-TPDR*. Although this example does not reflect lower total cost of *E-TPDR*, section 5 will demonstrate the improvement of *E-TPDR* method from the simulation results.

S_1: $m_1(7)$, $m_3(7)$, $m_6(15)$, $m_9(10)$, $m_{13}(18)$

S_2: $m_4(4)$, $m_7(3)$, $m_{10}(8)$, $m_{12}(12)$

S_3: $m_{11}(6)$, $m_5(3)$, $m_8(4)$, $m_2(3)$

Fig. 4. The *E-TPDR* scheduling of communications for the example in Figure 2

5   Performance Evaluation

To evaluate the performance of the proposed methods, we have implemented the *TPDR* and *E-TPDR* along with the divide-and-conquer algorithm [16]. The performance simulation is discussed in two classes, even GEN_BLOCK and uneven GEN_BLOCK distributions. In even GEN_BLOCK distribution, each processor owns similar size of data. The communication cost will not be dominated by specific processor, because the size of messages between processors could be very close. In contrast to even distributions, few processors might be allocated grand volume of data in uneven distributions. Since array elements could be centralized to some specific processors, it is also possible for those processors to have the maximum degree of communications. Therefore, the communication cost will be dominated by these processors. To accomplish an optimal scheduling, it is obvious that even distribution case is more difficult than uneven distribution. This observation was comprehended by that communication cost could be determined by one processor that with maximum degree or maximum total message size in uneven distribution; consequently, it leads high probability to achieve a schedule that has the same cost as the processor's total message size.

To determine the redistribution is on even GEN_BLOCK or uneven GEN_BLOCK, we define upper and lower bounds of data size in GEN_BLOCK distribution. Given an irregular array redistribution on $A[1:N]$ over P processors, the average block size will be N/P. In even distribution, the range of upper and lower bounds is set to ±30%. Thus, size of data blocks could be 130% N/P ~ 70% N/P. In uneven distribution, the range of upper and lower bounds is set to ±100%. Thus, size of data blocks could be 200% N/P ~ 1.

5.1   Simulation A – Uneven Distribution

Simulation A is carried out to examine the performance of *TPDR* and *E-TPDR* algorithms on uneven cases. We use a random generator to generate 10,000 test data sets. Figure 5(a) shows the comparisons of *TPDR* algorithm and the *divide-and-conquer* (*DC*) algorithm. We run tests by different processor numbers from 4 to 24. In 10,000 samples, the number of cases of *TPDR* better than *DC*, *DC* better than *TPDR* and the same are counted. When the number of processors is 4, there are lots of cases both algorithms have the same result. This is because that the size of messages could be larger when number of processors is less. It's easier to derive schedules that have minimum size of total communication steps. When the number of processors becomes numerous, the *TPDR* provides significant improvements generally. This phenomenon can be explained by size of data blocks in these processors are relative small. Therefore, processors have lower possibility to have high degree of communication links. In other words, the number of degree-2 nodes increases largely. Since the *TPDR* uses an optimal adjustable coloring mechanism for scheduling degree-2 and degree-1 communications, therefore, we expect that *TPDR* performs better when the number of degree-2 nodes is large.

Figure 5(b) gives the comparisons of the *E-TPDR* algorithm and the divide-and-conquer algorithm. When the number of processors is 4, there are about 60% cases has the same result by both algorithms. Similar to the previous observations, the *E-TPDR* performs well when number of processors is numerous.

	4	6	8	10	12	14	16	18	20	22	24
TPDR better than DC	3134	6724	8253	8926	9288	9481	9662	9766	9811	9843	9908
DC better than TPDR	511	901	884	698	555	420	293	204	168	139	76
the same	6355	2375	863	376	157	99	45	30	21	18	16

(a)   TPDR vs DC with uneven data distribution scheme

	4	6	8	10	12	14	16	18	20	22	24
E-TPDR better than DC	3159	7020	8600	9284	9595	9788	9861	9888	9951	9956	9964
DC better than E-TPDR	291	442	363	281	214	119	81	73	30	29	32
the same	6550	2538	1037	435	191	93	58	39	19	15	4

(b)   E-TPDR vs DC with uneven data distribution scheme

	4	6	8	10	12	14	16	18	20	22	24
TPDR better than DC	2672	5724	5946	7658	8107	8477	8672	8951	9157	9351	9390
DC better than TPDR	68	130	149	149	139	119	160	132	116	108	83
the same	7260	4146	2905	2193	1754	1404	1168	917	727	641	527

(c)   TPDR vs DC with even data distribution scheme

	4	6	8	10	12	14	16	18	20	22	24
E-TPDR better than DC	2599	5819	6916	7599	8137	8592	8810	9040	9239	9392	9463
DC better than E-TPDR	0	43	64	72	86	80	84	80	58	63	64
the same	7401	4138	3020	2329	1777	1328	1106	880	703	545	473

(d)   E-TPDR vs DC with even data distribution scheme

Fig. 5. Performance achievement of different algorithms in 10,000 GEN_BLOCK test samples

5.2 Simulation B – Even Distribution

Simulation B is carried out to examine the performance of *TPDR* and *E-TPDR* algorithms on even cases. We also use the random generator to produce 10,000 data sets for this test.

Figures 5(c) and 5(d) show the performance comparisons of *TPDR* and *DC*, *E-TPDR* and *DC*, respectively. Overall speaking, we have similar observations as those described in Figures 5(a) and 5(b). The *E-TPDR* performs better than *TPDR*. When number of processors is large, the *TPDR* and *E-TPDR* both provide significant improvements. Compare to the results in uneven cases (simulation A), the ratio of our algorithms outperform the *DC* algorithm become lower. In even distribution, we observed that there is no vertices with degree higher than 4. In other words, the maximum degree of nodes of these 10,000 test samples is 3. On this aspect, the *DC* algorithm and the *TPDR* methods have more cases that are the same. This is also why the *TPDR* and *E-TPDR* have better ratio from 99% to 93%.

6   Conclusions

In this paper, we have presented a *two-phase degree-reduction* (*TPDR*) scheduling technique to efficiently perform HPF2 irregular array redistribution on distributed memory multi-computer. The *TPDR* is a simple method with low algorithmic complexity to perform GEN_BLOCK array redistribution. An extended algorithm based on *TPDR* is also presented. Effectiveness of the proposed methods not only avoids node contention but also shortens the overall communication length. The simulation results show improvement of communication costs and high practicability on different processor hierarchy.

In HPF, it supports array redistribution with arbitrary source and destination processor sets. The technique developed in this paper assumes that the source and the destination processor sets are the same. In the future, we will study efficient methods for array redistribution with arbitrary source and destination processor sets. Besides, the issues of scheduling irregular problems on grid system and considering network communication latency in heterogeneous environments are also interesting and will be investigated. Also, we will also study realistic applications and analyze their performance.

References

[1] G. Bandera and E.L. Zapata, "Sparse Matrix Block-Cyclic Redistribution," *Proceeding of IEEE Int'l. Parallel Processing Symposium* (IPPS'99), San Juan, Puerto Rico, April 1999.

[2] Frederic Desprez, Jack Dongarra and Antoine Petitet, "Scheduling Block-Cyclic Data redistribution," *IEEE Trans. on PDS*, vol. 9, no. 2, pp. 192-205, Feb. 1998.

[3] C.-H Hsu, S.-W Bai, Y.-C Chung and C.-S Yang, "A Generalized Basic-Cycle Calculation Method for Efficient Array Redistribution," *IEEE TPDS*, vol. 11, no. 12, pp. 1201-1216, Dec. 2000.

[4] C.-H Hsu, Dong-Lin Yang, Yeh-Ching Chung and Chyi-Ren Dow, "A Generalized Processor Mapping Technique for Array Redistribution," *IEEE TPDS*, vol. 12, vol. 7, pp. 743-757, July 2001.

[5] Minyi Guo, I. Nakata and Y. Yamashita, "Contention-Free Communication Scheduling for Array Redistribution," *Parallel Computing*, vol. 26, no.8, pp. 1325-1343, 2000.

[6] Minyi Guo, Yi Pan and Zhen Liu, "Symbolic Communication Set Generation for Irregular Parallel Applications," *The Journal of Supercomputing*, vol. 25, pp. 199-214, 2003.

[7] Edgar T. Kalns, and Lionel M. Ni, "Processor Mapping Technique Toward Efficient Data Redistribution," *IEEE Trans. on PDS*, vol. 6, no. 12, December 1995.

[8] S. D. Kaushik, C. H. Huang, J. Ramanujam and P. Sadayappan, "Multiphase data redistribution: Modeling and evaluation," *Proceeding of IPPS'95*, pp. 441-445, 1995.

[9] S. Lee, H. Yook, M. Koo and M. Park, "Processor reordering algorithms toward efficient GEN_BLOCK redistribution," *Proceedings of the ACM symposium on Applied computing*, 2001.

[10] Y. W. Lim, Prashanth B. Bhat and Viktor and K. Prasanna, "Efficient Algorithms for Block-Cyclic Redistribution of Arrays," *Algorithmica*, vol. 24, no. 3-4, pp. 298-330, 1999.

[11] Neungsoo Park, Viktor K. Prasanna and Cauligi S. Raghavendra, "Efficient Algorithms for Block-Cyclic Data redistribution Between Processor Sets," *IEEE TPDS*, vol. 10, No. 12, pp.1217-1240, Dec. 1999.

[12] Antoine P. Petitet and Jack J. Dongarra, "Algorithmic Redistribution Methods for Block-Cyclic Decompositions," *IEEE Trans. on PDS*, vol. 10, no. 12, pp. 1201-1216, Dec. 1999.

[13] L. Prylli and B. Touranchean, "Fast runtime block cyclic data redistribution on multiprocessors," *Journal of Parallel and Distributed Computing,* vol. 45, pp. 63-72, Aug. 1997.

[14] S. Ramaswamy, B. Simons, and P. Banerjee, "Optimization for Efficient Data redistribution on Distributed Memory Multicomputers," *Journal of Parallel and Distributed Computing,* vol. 38, pp. 217-228, 1996.

[15] Akiyoshi Wakatani and Michael Wolfe, "Optimization of Data redistribution for Distributed Memory Multicomputers," short communication, *Parallel Computing*, vol. 21, no. 9, pp. 1485-1490, September 1995.

[16] Hui Wang, Minyi Guo and Daming Wei, "Divide-and-conquer Algorithm for Irregular Redistributions in Parallelizing Compilers", *The Journal of Supercomputing*, vol. 29, no. 2, 2004.

[17] Hui Wang, Minyi Guo and Wenxi Chen, "An Efficient Algorithm for Irregular Redistribution in Parallelizing Compilers," *Proceedings of 2003 International Symposium on Parallel and Distributed Processing with Applications*, LNCS 2745, 2003.

[18] H.-G. Yook and Myung-Soon Park, "Scheduling GEN_BLOCK Array Redistribution," *Proceedings of the IASTED International Conference Parallel and Distributed Computing and Systems*, November, 1999.

Online Virtual Disk Migration with Performance Guarantees in a Shared Storage Environment

Yong Feng, Yan-yuan Zhang, Rui-yong Jia, and Xiao Zhang

Computer Science & Engineering School, Northwestern Polytechnical University,
Xi'an, Shaanxi 710072, P. R. China
{fengyong, zhangyy, jiary, zhangxiao}@co-think.com

Abstract. In this paper, we present a novel approach of online virtual disk migration with performance guarantees, which is important for storage maintenance tasks. Our approach can be applied to moving virtual disk and exchanging virtual disks. It identifies the surplus I/O resource of storage pools after satisfying performance requirement of virtual disks with EPYFQ scheduling algorithm, and gives high priority of using these I/O resource to migration tasks. Thus, the performance of virtual disks is guaranteed during migration, and the migration is completed in the shortest possible time. Moreover, our approach divides migration task into multiple storage transactions, which can protect the consistency of the data in the migrated virtual disks when application I/O and migration I/O execute concurrently. We implement our approach into E-DM, a kernel module of Linux, and evaluate it. The result shows that the IOPS of virtual disks is decreased not more than 3% during migration.

1 Introduction

The consolidation of the storage systems that are connected by a dedicated storage network, called SAN (Storage Area Network), makes it possible to manage more and more data with fewer people. Moreover, to use storage resource efficiently, a new abstraction layer between host view and storage system implementation, called storage virtualization, is introduced. This software makes a transformation between a logical address space that is presented to the servers and the access to the physical storage devices.

With these trends in storage technologies, a shared storage model is now widely accepted in storage management [1]. In a shared storage environment, it is possible to use the available storage resource (Without loss of generality we refer to processor, physical disk, cache, bandwidth etc. as storage resource) of the storage systems as one or more storage pools. Virtual disks are built from these storage pools without worrying about the limitations of the underlying hardware, such as physical disks. From the standpoint of virtual disk consumer, virtual disk is highly desired to be as concrete as physical disks, implying that it demands to have a guaranteed storage service, especially I/O performance, at all times. To meet the requirement, some storage virtualization systems are designed to provide performance guarantees for virtual disks [2,3,4,5].

V. Malyshkin (Ed.): PaCT 2005, LNCS 3606, pp. 226–238, 2005.
© Springer-Verlag Berlin Heidelberg 2005

Keeping such systems operating in the face of changing access patterns, new applications, equipment failures, new resource, the needs to balance loads to achieve acceptable performance requires migrating virtual disks between storage pools. Existing approaches to migrating virtual disks are seldom designed with performance guarantees in mind. The I/O resource consumption engendered by the migration process will interfere with foreground application accesses and show them down. It will destroy the performance guarantees of virtual disk provided by storage virtualization systems.

This paper explores our approach to the problem of how to maintain performance guarantees for virtual disks during virtual disks migration, and aims at the following objectives.

Online: Today's applications can not tolerant the downtime of storage system. Thus, the migrated virtual disk should be accessed by applications in parallel with the migration.

Performance guarantees: The virtual disk with performance guarantees has similar performance characteristics as physical disk, such as Bandwidth and IOPS. These performance characteristics should be met while migration takes place.

Short migration time: After satisfying the above two objectives, the migration is desired to complete in the shortest possible time.

We implement our approach into the E-DM (Enhanced Device Mapper) [5], a kernel module of Linux that provides logic volume management service with performance guarantees, and evaluate it using synthesized I/O load generated by Iometer [6]. The remainder of this paper is organized as follows: Section 2 describes some related works. Section 3 explains how our approach guarantees the I/O resource necessary to meet the performance requirements of virtual disks. Section 4 explains how our approach protects the consistency of the data in the migrated virtual disks when the application I/O and the migration I/O execute concurrently. Section 5 gives some comments about the current implementation of our approach. After present the results of our experimental evaluation in section 6, the conclusion will be drawn in the seventh section.

2 Related Works

Currently, some logical volume managers, such as LVM [7], VxVM [8], are able to provide continuing access to volume while it is being moved. This is achieved by creating a mirror of the volume to be moved, with the new replica in the place where the volume is to end up. The mirror is made consistent by bringing the new copy up to date. After the mirror is completed, the original copy can be disconnected and discarded. This trick is also used by other migration tools, such as Aqueduct [9]. However, they cannot achieve continuing access during exchanging two virtual disks with one virtual disk in the place where the other virtual disk originally resides. Our approach can provide continuing access not only when moving virtual disk, but also when exchanging virtual disks.

In order to avoid the impact of migration on the performance of virtual disks, it is best choice to migrate virtual disks when storage system is nearly idle. Therefore, former storage administrators usually chose to perform migration tasks at night for the workload is low at that time. However, as for current worldwide applications, such as WWW and e-business, the workloads are not bound by time zone any more. Then storage administrators want the ability to control the workload of migration. VxVM provides limited support through a parameter vol_default_iodelay, which can be used to throttle the I/O operation of migration. Some high-end disk arrays (e.g. NEC S4300 [10]) provide the similar function. Unfortunately, they leave the problem, how to adjust the control parameter according to current workload of applications, to storage administrators.

Aqueduct uses a feedback method to realize an automatic throttling system, which takes the place of storage administrators to adjust the workload of migration through forecasting the change of application workload. The effect of Aqueduct is influenced by many factors, such as parameters of feedback control algorithm, sample interval, and so on. Storage administrators still need to adjust these parameters according to different applications and storage devices, which is also a hard work. Furthermore, Aqueduct only puts the performance requirement of the virtual disks in the source storage pool into consideration, and ignores the performance requirement of the virtual disks in the target storage pool. However, they are both important.

The scheduler of storage system has the knowledge of current workload of applications and need not to forecast them. Eno Thereska et al. present a free-block scheduling algorithm for disk maintenance applications [11], which predicts rotational latency delays and tries to fill them with media transfers for disk maintenance applications. Unfortunately, storage pool is different from disks. We have no priori knowledge of the internal structure of storage pool, thus cannot predict rotational latency delays. In COMFORT file system [12], only when disk is idle, the hot data block can be transferred to cool disk for load balance purpose. However a storage pool is shared by many virtual disks, it is impossible that all these virtual disks are idle simultaneously. Therefore we need a method to know whether there is a virtual disk whose workload is below its performance requirement and what is the difference between them.

3 I/O Resource Allocation

The performance provided by virtual disk depends on consumed I/O resource. Based on the following three points, our approach can guarantee the I/O resource virtual disks required to meet their performance requirement and leave as much I/O resource as possible to virtual disk migration.

Firstly, to guarantee the performance of virtual disks in the storage pools involved in migration, our approach uses EPYFQ scheduling algorithm [5], which is designed to provide performance virtualization in a shared storage environment, to correctly identify the amount of I/O resource, which should be allocated to virtual disks currently to meet their performance requirement, and assign the surplus to virtual disks migration.

Secondly, to guarantee the performance of the migrated virtual disks, our approach spreads the workload of migrated virtual disks to both source storage pool and target storage pool, and then dynamically allocates I/O resource to the migrated virtual disks from the two storage pools with migration going on.

Thirdly, to reduce the I/O resource used by migration, our approach enables some I/O operations of foreground applications to execute virtual disk migration.

The following three subsections will explain these points respectively in details.

3.1 Stealing Free I/O Resource

EPYFQ is the core technology of our storage management system with performance guarantees. Assuming that to meet the performance requirement, virtual disk i is assigned a share of I/O resource s_i and the total I/O resource of the storage pool is s, EPYFQ can allocate at least s_i/s of the I/O resource of the storage pool to virtual disk i. Moreover if the load of a virtual disk is below its share, EPYFQ will reallocate the spare storage resource from it to other overloaded virtual disks. Now, we will give the brief description of EPYFQ.

In our storage management system, every virtual disk has an input queue, and the storage pool has an execute queue. EPYFQ associates a start tag S_i and a finish tag F_i with the input queue q_i of the virtual disk VD_i, and also associates a tag E with the execute queue q_e. S_i, F_i and E are all initially zero. The virtual work function, $v(t)$, of EPYFQ is defined as:

$$v(t) = \begin{cases} 0 & \text{if} & t = 0 \\ E & \text{if} & storage \quad pool \quad is \quad active \\ max(F_i) & \text{if} & storage \quad pool \quad is \quad inactive \end{cases} \quad (1)$$

Here, the storage pool is active if there are requests being serviced in execute queue; otherwise, it is inactive.

When a new request r_i^n towards VD_i arrives: Firstly, if q_i was previously empty, EPYFQ calculates S_i and F_i with formula (2).

$$S_i = max(v(t), F_i)$$
$$F_i = S_i + e_i(r_i^n) \quad (2)$$

Here, $e_i(r_i^n)$ is the virtual service time of request r_i^n in VD_i. Secondly, EPYFQ appends r_i^n to q_i.

If the number of requests in the execute queue is less than p, which is the max number of outstanding requests we prescribed in the execute queue, and there are requests waiting in the input queues of virtual disks, EPYFQ selects the request r_i^n at the head of the non-empty q_i of VD_i, which meets the conditions list in formula (3) until the number of requests in the execute queue equals to p, or there is no request meets the conditions.

$$\begin{cases} F_i = \left\{min\left(F_j \mid VD_j \in S\right)\right\} \\ \forall VD_j \in U, e(r_i^n) \le \begin{pmatrix} e_j(\overline{r}_j) - e(\overline{r}_j) + max\left(v(t), F_j\right) - \\ v(t) - \sum_{r' \in q_e} e(r') + \varepsilon \end{pmatrix} \end{cases} \quad (3)$$

Here, S is the set of all virtual disks; U is the set of the virtual disk whose input queue is empty; $e_j(\overline{r}_j)$ and $e(\overline{r}_j)$ are average values of virtual service times of a request in VD_j and in storage pool respectively, which can be measured with run-time performance monitor; ε is a positive value, which can be used as a tradeoff between tight resource control and storage pool resource utilization. The bigger ε allows more requests to execute concurrently, however the smaller ε makes scheduler reserve more resource for underloaded virtual disks.

When r_i^n is selected, EPYFQ removes r_i^n from q_i and attaches the current value of F_i to r_i^n as F_i^n. If q_i is still non-empty, EPYFQ recalculates S_i and F_i with formula (2). When r_i^n is completed, EPYFQ recalculates E with formula (4).

$$E = \left\{ min\left(F_i^n\right) \mid r_i^n \in q_e \right\} \qquad (4)$$

Since EPYFQ can reallocates the spare storage resource from the underloaded virtual disks to overloaded virtual disks, if we give high priority of using spare I/O resource to virtual disk migration, the migration will do no harm to the performance of virtual disks.

In EPYFQ, v(t) can identify the spare I/O resource. For virtual disk VD_i, the difference between v(t) and its finish tag F_i is the amount of I/O resource it left. Thus formula (5) gives the condition when the I/O operation of migration executes.

$$\begin{cases} \qquad\qquad true & if \quad K = S \\ e\left(r_{migrate}\right) \le \sum_{VD_i \in K}\left(v(t) - F_i\right) & if \quad K \subset S \end{cases} \qquad (5)$$

Here, K is the set of virtual disks whose finish tag is smaller than v(t); S is the set of all virtual disks; $e(r_{migrate})$ is the virtual service time of a migration request in the storage pool.

To avoid that the spare I/O resource is used repeatedly, after a migration request is dispatched, the finish tags of virtual disks in S should be added by $e(r_{migrate})$, but the added finish tag is limited under the current value of v(t).

3.2 Allocating I/O Resource for Migrated Virtual Disk

Usually, the cause of migration is that the source storage pool cannot afford the performance requirement of its virtual disks. Moving a virtual disk to other underloaded storage pool will address the problem. However if there is no storage pool can afford a whole virtual disk, we can only exchange a virtual disk with heavy load in the overloaded storage pool for a virtual disk with light load in the underloaded storage pool, and there is a precondition that the two virtual disks must have the same capacity. Unfortunately the former migration approaches through creating a mirror of virtual disk cannot use the spare I/O resource of the target storage pool until the migration is completed, and cannot be applied to exchanging virtual disks either.

Our approach can eliminate these drawbacks. In our approach, a bitmap, named MST (the abbreviation for Migration State Table), is used to mark the current migration state of chunks (a group of data blocks) of the migrated virtual disk. Every chunk has a bit in MST: 0 means the chunk has not been migrated, whereas 1 means the chunk has been migrated. When a request towards the migrated virtual disk comes, if the migration state of the target chunk is 0, the request will be sent to the source storage pool, but if the migration state of the target chunk is 1, the request will be sent to the target storage pool. Thus the workload of migrated blocks will be transferred to the target storage pool, which is underloaded.

Similarly, when exchanging virtual disks, the MST can be used to mark the migration state of chunks of both virtual disks simultaneously. In that case, the chunk with the same offset in the exchanged virtual disks has the same migration state. Thus, through MST, we can know where a requested block is stored during exchanging virtual disks, and then provide continuing access to virtual disks while they are being exchanged.

For moving virtual disk, the target storage pool can afford the performance requirement of the migrated virtual disk. Therefore we allocate the same amount of I/O resource to migrated virtual disk from the target storage pool as what we allocate from the source storage pool. Thus, during migration, the performance of application I/O towards the migrated part of virtual disk will be guaranteed.

However, for exchanging virtual disks, neither of the two storage pools can afford another virtual disk. Therefore we cannot allocate the double I/O resource that the exchanged virtual disks required to those virtual disks in advance. The dynamic allocation of I/O resource is a good choice. We suppose that the workload spreads around the virtual disk evenly. Thus, when a virtual disk spreads around two storage pools and is divided into two parts, the I/O resource required by any part of virtual disk is in proportion with the number of blocks it owns. Then, the amount of I/O resource that should be allocated to VD_i from the target storage pool currently can be calculated with formula (6).

$$S_i^t = V_i^t / V_i \times S_i \qquad (6)$$

Here, S_i is the total I/O resource that should be allocated to VD_i from the target storage pool after migration; S_i^t is the amount of I/O resource currently allocated to VD_i from the target storage pool; V_i is the total number of blocks of VD_i; V_i^t is the current number of migrated blocks of VD_i.

3.3 Combining Application I/O and Migration I/O

When a write request towards the migrated virtual disk comes, if the migration state of target chunk is 0, the block in the source storage pool will be updated. After a while, this block will be migrated to the target storage pool. In this case, if the write request is not sent to the source storage pool but redirected to the target storage pool, the I/O operation of migration will be saved.

Therefore, when moving a virtual disk, if a write request comes and the migration state of the target chunk is 0, the write request will be sent to the target storage pool, and after the request is completed, the migration state of the target chunk is set as 1. However, the method will not work when exchanging two virtual disks, for exchanging a pair of data chunks involves two write operations. We need a more complicated method to deal with this situation. The following section will explain the methods used in moving a virtual disk and exchanged two virtual disks in details.

4 Storage Transaction

Moving a virtual disk and exchanging two virtual disks both translate into multiple I/O operations towards the storage pools and update operation towards MST. Thus concurrent application I/O operation may corrupt MST and cause application to lose updated data or read inconsistent data.

In this section, we propose an approach, which allows the migration I/O operations to be a transaction, called storage transaction, to coordinate the migration I/O operation and the application I/O operation, such that the application I/O and the migration I/O can execute concurrently.

4.1 Moving a Virtual Disk

Moving a virtual disk involves reading from the source storage pool, writing to the target storage pool and updating MST. The storage transaction of moving a virtual disk is divided into three phrases, reading, waiting and writing. Fig. 1 gives the state transition of the storage transaction of moving a virtual disk.

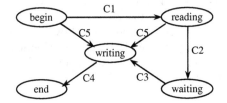

C1: Formula (5) is true in the source storage pool ;
C2: reading request is completed;
C3: Formula (5) is true in the target storage pool;
C4: writing request is completed;
C5: writing request from application comes

Fig. 1. State transition of the storage transaction of moving a virtual disk

When formula (5) is true in the source storage pool, a reading request will be sent to the source storage pool, and then a storage transaction in the reading state is created. After the reading request is completed, the storage transaction is in waiting state. When formula (5) is true in the target storage pool, if there is a storage transaction in the waiting state, a writing request will be sent to target storage pool, and then the storage transaction turns into the writing state. Before sending the writing request, the migration state of the writing chunk should be set as 1. After the writing request is completed, the storage transaction is completed. Furthermore, when a writing request from application towards the migrated virtual disk comes, if the migrated state of the written chunk is 0, the writing request will be send to the target storage pool and the migrated state will be set as 1, which will create a storage transaction in the writing state. Especially, if the written chunk belongs to a storage transaction, which is in the reading state or waiting state, the original storage transaction will be cancelled.

The approach of moving a virtual disk explained above only uses the spare I/O resource to execute the migration task and protects the consistency of the data of the moved virtual disk during migration with storage transaction. When the conflict between the migration I/O and the application I/O occurs, the approach will combine the application I/O and the migration I/O. Thus, the application I/O and the migration I/O will execute concurrently.

4.2 Exchanging Virtual Disks

Different from moving a virtual disk, exchanging two virtual disks involves two pairs of I/O operations, and either of the involved storage pools is not only source storage pool but also target storage pool. The state of either of the storage pools is not enough to identify the state of storage transaction during exchanging two virtual disks. Therefore, we use a pair of states, the state of the source storage pool and the state of the target storage pool instead. For convenience, we call the overloaded storage pool as source storage pool and the underloaded storage pool as target storage pool. Fig. 2 shows the state transition of the storage transaction of exchanging two virtual disks.

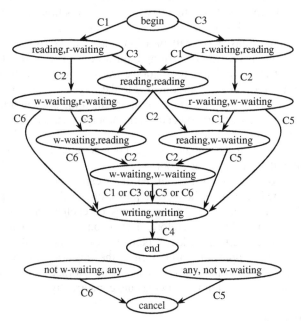

C1: Formula (5) is true in the source storage pool;
C2: reading request is completed;
C3: Formula (5) is true in the target storage pool;
C4: writing request is completed;
C5: writing request from application towards the source storage pool comes;
C6: writing request from application towards the target storage pool comes.

Fig. 2. State transition of the storage transaction of exchanging two virtual disks

In Fig. 2, the state of storage transaction is represented by (s-state, t-state). Here, s-state is the state of source storage pool; t-state is the state of target storage pool. There are four kinds of state, including r-waiting, reading, w-waiting and writing. r-waiting means a reading request needs to be dispatched; reading means a reading request has been dispatched; w-waiting means a reading request has been finished and the corresponding writing request needs to be dispatched to the other storage pool; writing means a writing request has been dispatched. In addition, the word "any" means any kind of states; the word "not w-waiting" means any kind of states except w-waiting.

When formula (5) is true in the source storage pool, if there is a storage transaction in the state of (w-waiting, w-waiting), a pair of writing requests will be sent to the source storage pool and the target storage pool, and then the storage transaction turns into the state of (writing, writing). Before sending the writing requests, the migration state of the writing chunks should be set as 1. When the pair of writing requests is completed, the corresponding storage transaction is completed. Otherwise, if there is a storage transaction in the state of (w-reading, any), a reading request will be sent to source storage pool, and the storage transaction turns into the state of (reading, any). If there is no storage transaction in the state of (writing, writing) or (w-reading, any), a reading request towards a trunk, which has not been exchanged, will be sent to the source storage pool, which will create a new storage transaction in the state (reading, w-reading). When a reading request is completed in the source storage pool, the corresponding storage transaction will turn into the state of (w-writing, any) from (reading, any). Furthermore, when a writing request towards the source storage pool comes, if the target chunk belongs to a storage transaction, which is in the state of (any, w-writing), the request will be redirected to the target storage pool and a writing request will be sent to the source storage pool, and then the storage transaction turns into the state of (writing, writing). Otherwise, the storage transaction, which the target chunk belongs to, will be cancelled.

The process method in the target storage pool is same as the process method explained above in the source storage pool.

In the approach of exchanging two virtual disks explained above, although when writing the exchanged chunks to the storage pools, one of the storage pools may not have spare I/O resource, most of I/O operations of exchanging two virtual disks execute with spare I/O resource. Therefore, there is only a little impact of migration on the performance of virtual disks. Moreover, when the conflict between the migration I/O and the application I/O occurs, the approach either combines the application I/O and the migration I/O, or cancels the storage transaction. Thus, the application I/O and the migration I/O will execute concurrently.

4.3 Disaster Recovery

In order to preserve the consistency of the migrated virtual disks in the event of a disaster, such as power failure, during migration, we need store some metadata in disks permanently. After the disaster, a user space tool can recover the migration task through scanning the metadata in disks. It is not necessary to explicitly store all the information in disks. Instead, enough information can be maintained to allow migration task to be reconstructed after disaster.

The MST keeps the rate of progress of migration and is important for address resolving. Moreover all other information, such as storage transaction state, can be reconstructed from it. Therefore the MST is the only metadata need to be stored in disks. For moving a virtual disk, the MST in disks is updated only after the writing request of migration is completed in the target storage pool. For exchanging two virtual disks, before the pair of writing requests of migration is sent to storage pools, the migrated chunks must be stored in the migration log in disks. After the writing requests are both completed, the MST can be updated and the migration log can be deleted.

5 Prototype

The approach of online virtual disk migration presented in this paper is designed for storage maintenance tasks, especially for load balance, in a shared storage environment with performance guarantees. To evaluate the approach, we implement it into E-DM, which is based on DM (Device Mapper) [13]. Like DM, E-DM groups some physical volumes (PV) into a volume group (VG), and allocates logic volume (LV) from VG. The PV, VG and LV are equivalents of physical disk, storage pool and virtual disk referred in this paper respectively. However, different from DM, which can only provide capacity virtualization, E-DM can provide both capacity and performance virtualization. In addition, we also implement some facilities to enable E-DM to support continuous availability [14].

In E-DM, the approach of online virtual disk migration is added into I/O scheduling thread, a kernel thread that schedules requests from all virtual disks in the storage system with EPYFQ scheduling algorithm to guarantee the performance requirement of virtual disks. When executing migration task, firstly a migration plan, including source storage pool, target storage pool and migrated virtual disks, is submitted to E-DM through dmsetup, a user space configure tool of E-DM. After that, E-DM establishes a MST for the migrated virtual disks, and expands the address-resolving table of migrated virtual disks, in which a block is mapped into both source storage pool and target storage pool. When a request comes, E-DM firstly decides which storage pool the request is sent to according to the migration state in MST, and then resolves the physical address according to the address-resolving table of the selected storage pool. During migration, E-DM migrates virtual disks with the approach presented in this paper. When the migration task is completed, E-DM will delete the MST and the address-resolving table of migrated virtual disks in the target storage pool. If a disaster occurs during migration, the administrator can use dmscan, another user space configure tool of E-DM, to scan the permanent metadata of E-DM in disks to reconstruct the metadata of E-DM and recover the migration tasks. In addition, the migration of virtual disks is transparent to the upper applications of E-DM, such as database, file system and raw device. There is not any restriction for these applications during migration.

6 Experimental Evaluation

The experiments are run on a dual Pentium 700 MHz computer with 256 MB of RAM. The versions of Linux kernel and E-DM module are 2.4.20 and 1.00.05 respectively. A NEC S2100 disk array is connected directly to an Emulex Lightplus 750 HBA card in the PC. NEC S2100 is a midrange disk array with 15 HITACHI DK32DJ-36FC disks (10025RPM, 36.9GB each). We set up two RAID0 Logic Units (LU) using four disks, each with two disks, on the disk array, and configure them as two VGs, VG1 and VG2, in E-DM. After that, we allocate two logic disks, VD1 and VD2, from VG1 and allocate one logic disk VD3 from VG2. These VDs are configured as following: They both have a capacity of 1GB; VD_1 has an 80% share of the I/O resource of the VG1; VD_2 has a 20% share of the I/O resource of the VG1; VD3 has a 40% share of the I/O resource of the VG2. The synthetic workloads used in the experiments are generated by Iometer. The workloads of VD1, VD2 and VD3 all issue purely random 64 KB read/write mix (67% read, 33% write). The maximum number of outstanding I/O of the workloads is set as 5. We use the delay time to regulate the intensity of the workload. In Iometer, the delay time specifies the time between two adjacent requests. Furthermore, to avoid the influence of Linux buffer cache, "raw" devices associated with the VDs are used.

Table 1. The test results during moving VD2

No.	disk	delay time (ms)	IOPS	ART (ms)	move time (s)	difference of IOPS
1	VD1	5	104.01	33.40	N/A	N/A
	VD2	5	26.34	85.82		
2	VD1	40	20.36	17.93	N/A	N/A
	VD2	20	34.02	19.10		
	VD1	40	20.02	19.67	409	-1.7%
	VD2	20	29.22	40.46		+10.9%
3	VD1	30	25.32	18.51	N/A	N/A
	VD2	20	33.87	20.56		
	VD1	30	24.67	20.44	488	-2.6%
	VD2	20	28.43	44.32		+7.9%
4	VD1	20	36.02	19.60	N/A	N/A
	VD2	20	32.52	22.02		
	VD1	20	35.23	21.74	841	-2.2%
	VD2	20	28.88	51.68		+9.6%
5	VD1	15	51.56	21.15	N/A	N/A
	VD2	20	30.34	29.39		
	VD1	15	50.03	24.72	1169	-3.0%
	VD2	20	28.74	59.27		+8.7%

VD2 is the migrated virtual disk, and after migration, VD2 will have a 40% share of the I/O resource of the VG2. Table 1 gives five groups of test results. The first is IOPS and ART (Average Response Time) of VD1 and VD2 when VD1 and VD2 are both overloaded, which indicates the performance requirements of VD1 and VD2. The following four groups are IOPS and ART of VD1 and VD2 with different delay times. In each group, the first two lines are tested before migration, and the last two lines are tested during moving VD2 from VG1 to VG2. In the last column of table 1, "Difference of IOPS", we give the difference ratio of IOPS. For VD1, the value is difference ration of IOPS in the same line to the difference between IOPS in the same line and IOPS in the first line of the same group, which indicates the impact of migration on the performance of underloaded virtual disks. For VD2, the value is difference ration of IOPS in the same line to the difference between IOPS in the same line and IOPS in the second line of the first group, which indicate the impact of migration on the performance of overloaded virtual disks.

From the second group of test results to the fifth group of test results, the delay time of workload of VD2 is set as 20ms, which exceeds the performance that VD2 is requested to provide, that is to say, VD2 is overloaded. At the same time, the delay time of workload of VD1 is changed from 40ms in the second group to 15 ms in the fifth group, however is still under the performance that VD1 is requested to provide, that is to say, VD1 is underloaded. From the last column "difference of IOPS", we can see that the decrease of IOPS of VD1 is not more than 3%, which means that there is only a little impact of migration on the performance of underloaded virtual disk. Meanwhile, the IOPS of VD2 during migration is still more than the IOPS that VD2 is requested to provide (26.34, list in the second line). However the difference is less than 11%, which indicates that most of the spare I/O resource left by VD1 is used by migration I/O operations, and only a little is used by application I/O operations towards VD2.

As described above, we can draw a conclusion that the approach presented in this paper only uses the spare I/O resource to execute migration I/O operation. Therefore the performance of virtual disks is guaranteed during migration. Moreover it gives high priority of using spare I/O resource to migration tasks, which make migration is completed as soon as possible. Undoubtedly, the approach is a kind of online virtual disks migration and can provide continuous access to virtual disks during migration.

7 Conclusion

In order to guarantee the performance of virtual disks during executing storage maintenance tasks, especially load balance, in a shared storage environment. We present an approach of on-line virtual disks migration and implement it into E-DM. We also evaluate it using synthesized I/O load generated by Iometer.

Our approach guarantees the I/O resource of virtual disks during migration from the following three aspects. Firstly, based on EPYFQ scheduling algorithm, it only uses the spare I/O resource to execute migration I/O operations. Secondly, it allocates enough I/O resource to the migrated virtual disks from the source storage pool and the target storage pool during migration. Thirdly, it enables some I/O operations of foreground applications to replace the migration I/O operations, thus reduces the I/O resource used by migration. Moreover, it uses storage transactions to protect the consistency of the data in the migrated virtual disks during migration, so that it can provide continuous access to migrated virtual disks. In addition, our approach can be applied to moving a virtual disk and exchanging virtual disks, which is not provided by former approaches. The test results also show that our approach can provide performance guarantees and continuous access to virtual disks during migration.

References

1. Wilkes, J., Rickard, W., Gibson, G. et al.: Shared Storage Model A Framework for Describing Storage Architectures. SNIA Technical Council Proposal Document (2003)
2. Wilkes, J.: Traveling to Rome: QoS Specifications for Automated Storage System Management. In Wolf, L. C., Hutchison, D., Steinmetz, R. (eds.): Quality of Service. Lecture Notes in Computer Science, Vol.2092. Springer-Verlag, Berlin Heidelberg New York (2001) 75-91

3. Anderson, E., Hobbs, M., Keeton, K. et al.: Hippodrome: Running Circles Around Storage Administration. In Proc. of the 1st Conference on File system and Storage Technology. USENIX, Berkeley CA. (2002) 175-188

4. Huang, L.:Stonehenge: A High Performance Virtualized Storage Cluster with QoS Guarantee. Technical Report TR-138. ECSL, Computer Science Department, SUNY Stony Brook (2003)

5. Feng, Y., Zhang, Y. Y., Jia, R. Y.: EPYFQ: A Novel Scheduling Algorithm for Performance Virtualization in Shared Storage Environment, In Proc. of the 5th International Workshop on Software and Performance. ACM, New York (2005)

6. Iometer project. Available from http://www.iometer.org/

7. LVM project. Available from http://www.sistina.com/

8. Veritas Software Corp.: Veritas Volume Manager. Available from http://www.veritas.com/

9. Lu, C., Alvarez, G. A., Wilkes, J.: Aqueduct: Online Data Migration with Performance Guarantees. In Proc. of the 1st Conference on File and Storage Technologies. USENIX, Berkeley CA. (2002) 219-230.

10. NEC Corp Ltd.: DataSheet of Diskarray S4300. Available from http://www.sw.nec.co.jp/necstorage/global/product/san/s4300/index.shtml

11. Thereska, E., Schindler, J., Bucy, J. et al.: A Framework for Building Unobtrusive Disk Maintenance Applications. In Proc. of the 3rd Conference on File and Storage Technologies. USENIX, Berkeley CA. (2004) 213-226

12. Scheuermann, P., Weikum, G., Zabback, P.: Data Partitioning and Load Balancing in Parallel Disk Systems. Int. J. VLDB 1 (1998) 48-66

13. Device-mapper project. Available from http://sources.redhat.com/dm/

14. Feng, Y., Zhang, Y. Y., Jia, R. Y.: Research and Implementation of a Snapshot Facility Suitable for Soft-Failure Recovery. In: Jin, H., Gao, G. R., Xu, Z. W., Chen, H. (eds.): Network and Parallel Computing. Lecture Notes in Computer Science, Vol.3222. Springer-Verlag, Berlin Heidelberg New York (2004) 256-260

ParC#: Parallel Computing with C# in .Net

João Fernando Ferreira and João Luís Sobral

Departamento de Informática - Universidade do Minho,
4710 - 057 BRAGA – Portugal
{joaoferreira, jls}@di.uminho.pt

Abstract. This paper describes experiments with the development of a parallel computing platform on top of a compatible C# implementation: the Mono project. This implementation has the advantage of running on both Windows and UNIX platforms and has reached a stable state. This paper presents performance results obtained and compares these results with implementations in Java/RMI. The results show that the Mono network performance, critical for parallel applications, has greatly improved in recent releases, that it is superior to the Java RMI and is close to the performance of the new Java nio package. The Mono virtual machine is not yet so highly tuned as the Sun JVM and Thread scheduling needs to be improved. Overall, this platform is a new alternative to explore in the future for parallel computing.

1 Introduction

Traditional parallel computing is based on languages such as C/C++ and Fortran, since these languages provide a very good performance. Message passing libraries such as MPI and PVM are also very popular, since there are bindings for several languages and implementations for high performance networks, like Myrinet and Infiniband. These message passing libraries support the CSP model, where parallel applications are decomposed into a set of processes that communicate through message passing. It has been recognised that this programming model is not the most appropriated for object-oriented applications [1], since the natural mechanism for communication on these applications is the method invocation. Several extensions to C++ have been proposed [2] that use the object as the base unit of parallelism (instead of process) and objects communicate through remote method invocations (instead of message passing).

The Java programming language has gained an increasing acceptation in the last decade. It is a much cleaner object oriented language than C++, since it removes the burden of pointer management and memory allocation. It also has an increased portability, since it is based on a virtual machine and an application can run anywhere that has a virtual machine implementation. This approach also resolves the communication problem among heterogeneous machines, since the communication is always between virtual machines. These are also important advantages for the increasing popular GRID computing field. The Java language also includes support for threads, remote method invocation (RMI) and object serialisation. Object serialisation allows object copies to move between virtual machines, even when objects are not allocated on a continuous memory range or when they are composed

V. Malyshkin (Ed.): PaCT 2005, LNCS 3606, pp. 239–248, 2005.

by several objects. The serialisation mechanism can automatically copy the object to a continuous stream that can be sent to another virtual machine, which can reconstruct a copy of the original object structure on the remote machine.

Several works are based on the Java platform for parallel computing: performance improvements to the original RMI implementation [3], thread distribution among virtual machines [4][5], MPI bindings [6] and implementation of higher level programming paradigms [7], just to name a few.

Microsoft has proposed the .Net platform to compete against the Java success. In particular, the C# language closely resembles to Java: it is also based on a virtual machine; it relieves the programmer from memory allocation and pointer management issues; it includes thread support in the language specification and supports RMI. However, the C# language includes some improvements; namely, it provides support for asynchronous method invocation and several ways to publish remote objects, which will be discussed in more detail in the next section. The main Microsoft .Net platform drawback is the lack of support in other platforms besides Microsoft Windows. This may explain the limited number of research projects related to .Net platform on clusters, since clusters mainly run Linux operating systems or other UNIX variants.

The Mono project is a free .Net platform implementation that runs on several operating systems, including Linux machines. This paper describes the experience acquired when porting a parallel object oriented system to this platform. The rest of this paper is organised as follows. Section 2 presents a more detailed comparison of the supported concurrency and distribution mechanisms of MPI, Java and C#. Section 3 presents the proposed platform, including the programming model and its implementation on the Mono platform. Section 4 presents performance results. Section 5 closes the paper with suggestions for future work.

2   C# Remoting Versus MPI and JAVA RMI

The Message Passing Interface (MPI) is a collection of routines for inter process communication. The mechanisms for communication are based on explicit message send and receive, where each process is identified by its rank in the communication group. MPI has a large set of primitives to send and receive messages, namely, blocking and unblocking sends and receives; broadcasts and reductions. MPI requires explicit packing and unpacking of messages (i.e., a data structure residing in a non-continuous memory must be packed into a continuous memory area before being sent and must be unpacked in the receiver). A thread library such as Pthreads can be used to create multithreaded applications. However, most MPI implementations are not thread safe, increasing the application complexity, when several threads in the same process need to access to the MPI library.

The Java language specification includes support for multithreaded applications through the Thread class and the Runnable interface. The thread method start initiates the execution of a new thread that executes the run method of an object implementing the Runnable interface. Synchronised methods prevent two threads from simultaneously executing code in the same object, avoiding data races. The Java RMI provides remote method invocations among Java virtual machines. Using RMI involves several steps, which considerably increase the burden to use it:

1. Server classes must implement an interface, which must extend the *Remote* interface, and its methods must throw a *RemoteException.*
2. Each server object must be manually instantiated (by introducing a *main* method on the server class), exported to be remotely available and registered in a name server to provide remote references to it;
3. Client classes must contact a name server to obtain a local reference to a remote object;
4. Each remote call must include a *try { ... } catch* statement to deal with *RemoteExcetions*;
5. For each server class it is required to run the *rmic* utility to generate proxies and ties that are, respectively, used by the client and server class in a transparent way.

Fig. 1 illustrates these required transforms for a simple remote class that performs a division of two numbers.

```
public class DServer {
  public double divide(double d1, double d2) {
    return d1 / d2;
  }
}

public class DivideClient {
  public static void main(String args[]) {
    DServer ds = new DServer();
    double d1 = Double.valueOf(args[0]).doubleValue();
    double d2 = Double.valueOf(args[1]).doubleValue();
    double result = ds.divide(d1, d2);
  }
}
```

```
public interface IDServer extends Remote {
  double divide(double d1, double d2) throws RemoteException;
}                                                                ⎫
                                                                 ⎬ ❶
public class DServer extends UnicastRemoteObject implements IDServer {
  public double divide(double d1, double d2) throws RemoteException {
    return d1 / d2;                                               ⎭
  }
  public static void main(String args[]) {                        ⎫
    try {                                                         ⎬ ❷
      DServer dsi = new DServer();
      Naming.rebind("rmi://host:1050/DivideServer",dsi);
    } catch(Exception e) { e.printStackTrace(); }                 ⎭
  }
}

public class DivideClient {
  public static void main(String args[]) {
    try {
      IDServer ds; // Obtains a reference to the remote object
      ds = (IDServer) Naming.lookup("rmi://host:1050/DivideServer");   ⎫
      double d1 = Double.valueOf(args[0]).doubleValue();               ⎬ ❸
      double d2 = Double.valueOf(args[1]).doubleValue();
      double result = ds.divide(d1, d2);                               ⎭
    } catch(RemoteException ex) { ex.printStackTrace(); }        } ❹
  }
}
```

Fig. 1. Conversion of a Java class to a remote class

With RMI the only binding between the client and the server is the registered name of the server object (*host:1050/DivideServer* in the figure), which truly provides location transparency. All objects passed among remote classes should implement the interface *serializable*, providing a way to automatically send object copies among virtual machines.

The .Net platform implements threads in a way similar to Java, but the use of remote method invocations has become simpler and several improvements have been added. One important difference is the various alternatives to publish remote objects (step 2 from the previous list). In addition to publish objects explicitly instantiated, it is possible to register an object factory that instantiates objects at request. This object factory has two alternatives to instantiate objects:

1. singleton - all remote calls are executed by the same object instance;
2. singlecall – each remote call may be executed by a different instance (i.e., object state is not maintained between remote calls).

Fig. 2 presents the code in Fig. 1 converted to C#.

```
public interface IDServer {
  double divide(double d1, double d2);
}

public class DServer : MarshalByRefObject, IDServer {
  public double divide(double d1, double d2) {
    return d1 / d2;
  }
  public static int Main (string [] args) {
    TcpChannel cn = new TcpChannel (1050);
    ChannelServices.RegisterChannel(cn);
    RemotingConfiguration.RegisterWellKnownServiceType( typeof(DServer),
      "DivideServer", WellKnownObjectMode.Singleton);
  }
}

public class DivideClient {
  public static int Main (string [] args) {
    TcpChannel cn = new TcpChannel();
    ChannelServices.RegisterChannel(cn);
    IDServer ds = (IDServer) Activator.GetObject( typeof(DivideServer),
      "tcp://localhost:1050/DivideServer");
    double d1 = Convert.ToDouble(args[0]);
    double d2 = Convert.ToDouble(args[1]);
    double result = ds.divide(d1, d2);
  }
}
```

Fig. 2. Remote class in C#

There are two important differences: no *RemoteException* needs to be thrown/caught and the server code only publishes the object factory (*RemotingConfiguration* line), not an object instance. Conversely to the Java version it is not required to generate proxy and ties, since they are automatically generated.

C# Remoting also includes support for asynchronous method invocation through *delegates*. A delegate can perform a method call in background and provides a mechanism to get the remote method return value, if required. In Java, a similar functionality must be explicitly programmed using threads.

3 The Platform

The ParC# is a SCOOPP (Scalable Object Oriented Parallel Programming) implementation [8], which has been previously implemented in C++/MPI (implementation called ParC++). The C# implementation is much simpler, since the C++ version must contain code to explicitly pack/unpack method tags and parameters into MPI messages, required to implement synchronous or asynchronous remote method invocations. This section shortly reviews the programming model and details the main differences between these two implementations.

3.1 Programming Paradigm

SCOOPP is based on an object oriented programming paradigm supporting active and passive objects. Active objects are called parallel objects and they specify explicit parallelism, having its own thread of control. These objects model parallel tasks and are automatically distributed among processing nodes. They communicate through either asynchronous (when no value is returned) or synchronous method calls (when a value is returned).

References to parallel objects may be copied or sent as a method argument, which may lead to cycles in a dependence graph. The application's dependence graph becomes a DAG when this feature is not used.

Passive objects are supported to make easier the reuse of existing code. These objects are placed in the context of the parallel object that created them, and only copies of them are allowed to move between parallel objects.

SCOOPP removes parallelism overheads at run-time by transforming (packing) parallel objects in passive ones and by aggregating method calls [9]. These run-time optimisations are implemented through:

- method call aggregation: (delay and) combine a series of asynchronous method calls into a single aggregate call message; this reduces message overheads and per-message latency;
- object agglomeration: when a new object is created, create it locally so that its subsequent (asynchronous parallel) method invocations are actually executed synchronously and serially.

3.2 Implementation

The ParC++ implementation supports some extensions to C++. It includes a pre-processor, several C++ support classes and a run-time system. The pre-processor analyses the application - retrieving information about the declared parallel objects - and generates code for remote object creation and remote method invocation.

The ParC++ run-time system (RTS) is based on three object classes: proxy objects (PO), implementation objects (IO) and server objects (SO).

A PO represents a local or a remote parallel object and has the same interface as the object it represents. It transparently replaces remote parallel objects and forwards all method invocations to the remote parallel object implementation (IO/SO in Fig. 3). A PO maintains the remote identification of its IO and SO. On inter-grains method calls the PO forwards the call to a remote SO, which activates the corresponding method on the IO (calls a in Fig.3). On intra-grain calls, the PO directly calls the corresponding method on the local IO (call b in Fig.3).

Converting the ParC++ prototype to C# removed a large amount of code from PO objects, since most of its functionality is already implemented by C# remoting.

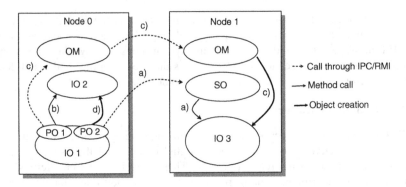

Fig. 3. Inter-grains a) and intra-grain b) method calls; RTS c) and d) direct object creation

However, PO objects are still required, since they perform much of the grain-size adaptation. The main simplification of PO objects arises from the elimination of code required to pack a method tag and method arguments into a MPI message. This code is directly replaced by a direct call to the corresponding method in the IO, using C# remoting. This change also allowed PO objects to transparently use remote objects or local objects (i.e., those objects created directly, when performing object agglomeration). Implementing asynchronous method invocation was simpler, since it only required the use of delegates. During the preprocessing phase, the original parallel object classes are replaced by generated PO classes.

Fig. 4 presents a simple source code and the PO code generated by the preprocessor. This code calls the *process* method asynchronously, using a delegate.

```
public class PrimeServer : PrimeFilter {
  public void process(int[] num) {
  ...
  }
}
```

```
public class PrimeServer : PrimeFilter {   // PO object
  public delegate void RemoteAsyncDelegate (int[] num );    // delegate decl.
  PrimeServerImpl obj;                              // reference to IO object

  public void process(int[] num) {    // asynchronous call using delegates
    RemoteAsyncDelegate RemoteDel= new RemoteAsyncDelegate(obj.process);
    IAsyncResult RemAr=RemoteDel.BeginInvoke(num,null,null);
  }
}
```

Fig. 4. PO object using delegates

The ParC++ RTS provides run-time grain-size adaptation and load balancing through cooperation among object managers (OM) and POs. The application entry code creates one instance of the OM on each processing node. The OM controls the grain-size adaptation by instructing PO objects to perform method call aggregation and/or object agglomeration.

When a parallel object is created in the original code, the generated code creates a PO object instead. The first task of the newly created PO is to request the creation of the IO. When parallelism is not being removed, the OM selects a processing node to create a new IO (according to the current load distribution policy), selects or creates the associated SO and returns their identifier to the PO (calls c̲ in Fig.3). When the RTS is removing excess of parallelism, the PO directly creates the parallel object, by locally creating the IO (call d̲ in Fig.3) and notifying the RTS. In ParC# this generated code is very similar to the ParC++ code and it is placed on the PO object constructor. shows the PO generated constructor from the example in Fig. 4.

```
public class PrimeServer : PrimeFilter {  // PO object
  ...
  PrimeServerImpl obj;                             // reference to IO object
  ...
  public PrimeServer() {
    if (aglomerateObj) {                           // perform agglomeration?
      obj = new PrimeServerImpl();                 // intra-grain object creation
      ... // notify local OM
    }
    else {
      ... // contact OM to get a (host) and tcp (port) for the new object
      string uri="tcp://"+host+":"+port+"/factory.soap";
      // gets a reference to the remote factory (rf)
      rf =(RemoteFactory)Activator.GetObject(typeof(RemoteFactory),uri);
      obj=(PrimeServerImpl)rf.PrimeServer(); // request remote object creation
    }
  }
}
```

Fig. 5. PO generated code for IO object creation

```
public class PrimeServerImpl : MarshalByRefObject {
  ...
  public void process(int[] num) {
    ... // copy of the original method implementation
  }
}
// object factory
public class RemoteFactory : MarshalByRefObject  {
  ...
  public PrimeServerImpl PrimeServer() {
    return new PrimeServerImpl();
  }
}
// main code the register the factory
public static void Main (string [] args) {
  ...
  RemotingConfiguration.RegisterWellKnownServiceType(typeof(RemoteFactory),
      "factory.soap",WellKnownObjectMode.Singleton);
}
```

Fig. 6. IO code and the corresponding factory

In ParC++ SO objects are active entities (i.e., threads) that continuously receive messages from PO objects, calling the requested method on local IO and, if needed, returning the result value to the caller. The ParC# implementation no longer requires SO objects and the corresponding message loop to receive external messages, since this loop is implemented by the C# remoting.

The object manager in the ParC++ implementation had the responsibility to perform load management and explicit object creation. A factory was generated for each class and instantiated on each node to implement this functionality. On the C#

prototype this functionality was separated form the OM code since object factories can be automatically registered in the boot code of each node. Fig. 6 shows the code of the generated IO from the previous example and also shows the generated object factory and the code to register this factory.

Aggregating several method calls in a single message required the introduction of a new method in the implementation object to process a pack of several method calls. The parameters of the several invocations are placed in an array structure that is constructed on the PO side and fetched from the array on the IO side. Fig. 7. presents the generated code for method call aggregation.

```
public class PrimeServer : PrimeFilter {     // PO with method call aggregation
  [Serializable]
  struct paramsprocess {
     public int[] num;
  }                                   // array structure for multiple invocations
  public ArrayList processList = new ArrayList();
  paramsprocess processStruct = new paramsprocess();

  public void process (int[] num) {
     if (currentCall++<maxCalls) {              // maxCalls = calls per message
     processStruct.num=num;
     processList.Add(processStruct);
     currentCall++;
     } else {
     obj.processN(processList, maxCalls);
     }
}
public class PrimeServerImpl : MarshalByRefObject {                 // IO code
  ...
  public void processN (ArrayList a, int nInv) {
     paramsprocess b;
     for (int i=0;i<maxCalls;i++) {
     b=(paramsprocess)(a[i]);
     process(b.num);
  }
}
```

Fig. 7. Method call aggregation code

4 Performance Results

Performance evaluation was performed through low and high level tests. The low level evaluation measures the base communication latency and bandwidth. The high level evaluation measures the application performance with a simple application. These tests were run in a Linux cluster, connected through a 100 Mbit Ethernet. Each node is a dual Athlon MP 1800+ and has 512 MB of RAM.

Low-level performance was evaluated by a ping-pong test, where messages with several sizes are exchanged between two nodes. These tests compare the Mono Remoting (version 1.1.7) performance against an equivalent Java RMI (SDK 1.4.2) application and an MPI version (MPICH 1.2.6 and GNU g++ 3.2.2). Both Java and the Mono implementations use a remote object, where an array of integers is sent and received as the method parameter and return type. In these results the performance penalty introduced by the ParC# platform is not noticeable (results not shown). The MPI version uses the MPI_Send and MPI_Recv primitives.

Inter-node bandwidth (Fig. 8b) shows that the MPI bandwidth performance is superior to Java and Mono. This is explained by the high level nature of the remote method invocation and the well-optimised version of MPI. Also, for large messages, the Mono performance lags behind the Java implementation. This may be explained by the fact that the Mono platform is relatively new, when compared to the other alternatives and it is not yet so well tuned.

Inter node latency in Mono (not shown) is between the Java RMI and the MPI latency (respectively, 520, 273 and 100us). This low latency is promising for parallel applications since it is in the same order as highly optimised Java RMI

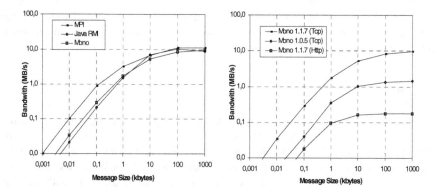

Fig. 8. Inter-node bandwidth a) Mono versus other; b) Mono implementations

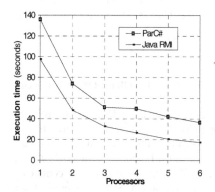

Fig. 9. Parallel Ray Tracer execution time

implementations [3]. This latency is very close to the performance of the Java nio package (introduced in Java 4). However, this Java package is more low level, based on message passing. Fig. 8b compares the performance of various Mono implementations; it shows that Mono performance has radically increased from release 1.0.5 and the low performance of an Http channel.

The high level evaluation was performed using a parallel Ray Tracer from the Java Grande Forum, converted to C#. This application was parallelised using a farming approach, where each worker renders several lines from the generated image.

Fig. 9 compares the execution times of Java and ParC# to render a scene with 500x500 pixels. The C# sequential execution time in this particular application is 40% superior to the Java version (using the Microsoft virtual machine, on a Windows machine, it is only 10% superior). This indicates that the Mono virtual machine is not as highly tuned as the JVM. However, running another application, a prime number sieve, the Mono execution time is about the same as the JVM.

The parallel Ray Tracer execution time in several processors is higher in ParC# mainly due to the higher sequential time and due to thread management. The Mono implementation uses a thread pool to reduce the thread creation cost; however limiting the number of running threads in parallel applications reduces the overlap among computation and communication and also produces starvation in some application threads.

5   Conclusion

This paper presented the implementation of a parallel programming paradigm on top of a C# and .Net platform. The experience with this implementation revealed that the platform greatly simplifies the implementation of the ParC++ and that it is possible to use C# and the .Net platform for parallel applications, both on Windows and UNIX machines. Code can be moved between these two platforms without any recompilation and it is even possible to use it simultaneously on both platforms (something that Java does since its appearance). However, performance gains would be achieved by a more performance tuned Mono implementation; specifically, the virtual machine JIT and the Thread scheduling policy should be improved.

References

[1] Yonezawa, A., Tokoro, M. (eds): Object-Oriented Concurrent Programming, MIT Press (1987)
[2] Wilson G. (ed): Parallel Programming Using C++, MIT Press (1996).
[3] Nester, C. ,Philippsen M., Haumacher, B. : A More Efficient RMI for Java, Proceedings of the ACM 1999 Java Grande Conference, San Francisco, June (1999)
[4] MacBeth, M., McGuigan, K., Hatcher: Executing Java threads in parallel in a distributed-memory environment, Proceedings of the 1998 conference of the Centre for Advanced Studies on Collaborative research, Cascon'98, Ontario, Canada, November (1998)
[5] Aridor, Y., Factor, M., Teperman, A.: cJVM: A Single System Image of a JVM on a Cluster, Int. Conference on Parallel Processing, Wakamatsu, Japan, September (1999)
[6] Baker, M., Carpenter, B., Fox, G., Ko, S., Lim, S.: MPIJAVA:An Object-Oriented JAVA Interface to MPI, International Workshop on Java for Parallel and Distributed Computing, Proceedings of the 11 IPPS/SPDP'99 Workshops, San Juan, Puerto Rico , April (1999)
[7] Philippsen, M., Zenger, M.: JavaParty – transparent remote objects in Java. Concurrency: Practice and Experience. v. n. 11, November (1997)
[8] Sobral, J., Proença, A.: Designing Scalable Object Oriented Parallel Applications, Proceedings of the 8th Int. European Conference on Parallel Processing (Euro-Par'02), Parderborn, Germany, August (2002)
[9] Sobral, J., Proença. A.: A Run-time System for Dynamic Grain Packing, Proceedings of the 5th Int. EuroPar Conference (Euro-Par'99), Toulouse, France, September (1999)

Minimizing Hotspot Delay by Fully Utilizing the Link Bandwidth on 2D Mesh with Virtual Cut-Through Switching

MinHwan Ok and Myong-soon Park

Department of Computer Science and Engineering, Korea University,
Anam-dong, Seongbuk-gu, Seoul 136-701, South Korea
Phone: +82-31-460-5287, Fax: +82-31-460-5279
panflute@korea.ac.kr, myongsp@ilab.korea.ac.kr

Abstract. The hotspot seriously degrades the performance of a parallel algorithm but there have not been many methods proposed for this problem. Without modification of mesh topology a reasonable method is fully utilizing all the links of the hotspot node. A new routing method that incorporates both minimal routes and non-minimal routes was proposed and approved with the hotspot traffic patterns. In particular the routing method decide on misrouting without the congestion detection. The routing method requires only little addition of hardware and it is relatively simple.

1 Introduction

Collective communications such as global synchronization operation essentially incur non-uniform traffic situation. Where the non-uniform traffic situation arise, the center of the situation, might become a 'hotspot.' The other cause of hotspot is not-even data-access. In this case, many other nodes transmit packets to a hotspot node to get information from the node. Contention caused by accesses to the hotspot is notorious for degrading performance of a parallel algorithm[1]. The phenomenon by hotspot is not only the problem in multistage networks. Although mesh networks have multiple physical links, the number of nodes that participate in collective communication or the group size sharing information of a node grows multiple times when compared to those of multistage networks. The objective of this work is to seek the method that reduces the delay by the hotspot on the mesh topology.

Enlarging the physical consumption channel could be a straight solution to the hotspot. Basak and Panda have used multiple consumption channels than single one for each processor on wormhole-routed k-ary n-cube[10]. Their approach is to analyze various factors of interconnection network with message consumption, and derive the minimum number of required consumption channels for alleviating consumption bottleneck. In the approach, additional channel per processor is necessary thus additional hardware cost is imposed. Sun and Cheung have developed a tree-based routing scheme for supporting barrier synchronization[2]. However since each router should have knowledge of barrier group to maintain a collective synchronization tree, special

V. Malyshkin (Ed.): PaCT 2005, LNCS 3606, pp. 249–262, 2005.

hardware is added into the routers. The cost/performance trade-off of the synchronization hardware is analyzed[3], and it is the cost for only the synchronization, not for all the cases of hotspots. Without enlarging the channel bandwidth or the knowledge of collective communication which is at application-level, one solution would be using all available network resources efficiently to alleviate the hotspot effect. Routing algorithms govern the use of network resources, and the underlying switching method concerns the routing.

To provide good network performance, a key point is to develop a traffic-balanced network with minimum diameter and average path length[6]. Traffic-balancing means even usage of network resources and efficient usage is achieved by minimum average path length. Virtual channels employed in wormhole switching prevent the deadlock. However a few algorithms results in uneven load distribution in using the virtual channels[7]. Even usage of network resources is gained by load balancing between virtual channels in mesh. Chuang et al. have proposed buffer utilization scheme for mesh with virtual channels[8]. They defined a particular area of high traffic load, where hotspot might emerge, and restricted passage to or through the area by remained area. However the schemes don't aim at hotspot problem directly, but to distribute the traffic load evenly over the network. Once hotspot situation arose it is desirable to complete the communication that caused the hotspot as soon as possible, either it is collective communication or not, since the situation affects much of the overall system performance[2].

Among network resources two major resources are the link bandwidth and buffer capacity. Adaptive routing is a primary way to gain more link bandwidth from given interconnection topology. Misrouting is necessary if there is an idle link available around the hotspot but it is important not to extend the path much since the longer path charges the more network resources. By this reason there were not much works with misrouting so far. Most of them were for fault-tolerance and a little were for reducing packet latency. Moreover it is rare what dealt with the hotspot case. In [14] misrouting or Non-minimal algorithm was slightly worse than the best algorithm since it charged more network resources, although the hotspot was not dealt with.

Virtual cut-through switching has some merit such that wire length is independent of buffer size and preventing deadlock is more flexible when adaptive routes are considered[4][5]. Adaptive routing methods that select only minimal paths including one presented by Pifarre et al.[9] don't utilize all available paths to the destination. The main problem with minimal adaptive routers is that, in general, the number of paths available decreases as the distance to the destination decreases. Because of this, packets near their destinations lose their ability to maneuver around the congestion, and a worse, hotspot[13].

Non-minimal adaptive routings that selects misroutes have been proposed[11][12], and the effect of various misroute limits is presented in [12]. The motivation in misrouting is it would be better go misroute than being blocked in each router buffer and that was proved for high network load in many works. For 2D mesh fully utilizing the 4 links of a hotspot node by misrouting could alleviate the hotspot problem. In this paper we propose a new routing algorithm with virtual cut-through switching to reduce hotspot delay, which is blocking time in each router or switch buffer. A new method to distribute packets evenly on 2D mesh is introduced in Section 2, and a misrouting based on the method is described in the Section 3. Section 4 presents performance evaluation for the proposed routing method including one recent famous routing, and Section 5 finalizes the contribution.

2 Link Selection to Distribute Packets Evenly

This section introduces a new method to utilize links evenly on 2D mesh. Utilizing links evenly would induce even usage of buffers in the network. On 2D mesh a node has 4 pairs of input and output links, each pair for each direction, east, west, north and south, respectively, except for boundary nodes. Each node has the buffer to capture income packets from each direction. To avoid blocking in the buffer of each intermediate switch, we utilize all available links of each switch by devising a new link selection method as follows. The objective of the method is that a switch receives the incoming packets along two links then sends the outgoing packets along the other two links with the same numbers of packets. The packet length is fixed and all the same in virtual cut-through switching.

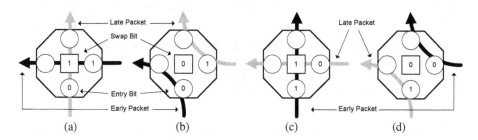

Fig. 1. The node (switch) internal operation

To memorize which dimension a packet came in and which dimension it came out, we introduce a one-bit named 'swap bit.' To memorize the previous series of packets has passed whether in even number or in odd number of packets, four one-bits named 'entry bits' for each direction are located in the switch. The central routing logic of a switch contains the swap bit. A pair of unidirectional links connects neighboring switches for each direction and there are 4 FIFO queues for incoming packets from 4 neighboring switches except for boundary switches.

The usage of the swap bit and entry bits in <Swap selection> is as follows;

  0. Each entry bit is preset to 0.
  1. If a packet comes through any link, the entry bit of that income direction is negated.
      A. Negate the swap bit.
      B. If the dimension determining the swap bit has changed, copy its entry bit to the swap bit.
      C. According to the swap bit;

i.   1 : the packet go straight to the opposite link of the same dimension; if it has come in through X-dimension it will go out through X-dimension and vice-versa. We call this 'crossing' the switch.

ii.   0 : the packet go left or right direction for its destination, thus to the link of the other dimension; if it has come in through X-dimension it will go out through Y-dimension and vice-versa. We call this 'detouring' the switch.

2. For next incoming packet, go to 1.

<Swap Selection>

The role of the swap bit is to alternate the dimensions of output links on packet by packet. Each entry bit remembers whether the previous packet of the input links has crossed or detoured the switch. Through this scenario the packets should be distributed evenly.

The swap selection extends to the case two series come from both dimensions at about the same time. The swap bit is determined by a little early-arrived packet than the other so the little-late packet takes the remained dimension. This technique is inherent from *deflection routing*[16]. Modification to the above scenario has two aspects.

– The little-late packet does not execute 1-A and 1-B from <Swap Selection> and the little-late packets' entry bit is copied from the swap bit.
– The swap bit should not be changed until the transmission of the little-late packet has finished, thus the swap bit is not always negated when a next little-early arrived packet determines it.

Fig. 2 depicts the behavior of the swap selection with this modification by an example. In Fig. 2(a) 4 packets are approaching to Z, an intermediate node to reach for D, the destination node. Assume the packet 'a' has entered Z first and the packet b has second. The entry bit of Z's west link is negated to 1. Let the swap bit was 0(What value the swap bit was is not important). The packet 'a' negates the swap bit to '1'. Then the packet 'a' crosses the node Z. If the packet 'b' has entered Z while the packet 'a' is still crossing Z then 'b' should also cross the node Z according the swap bit, 1. In this case the entry bit of Z's north link is copied to 1 from the swap bit. If the packet 'b' has entered Z after the packet 'a' has already left Z then 'b' copies its entry bit of Z' north link (which is now 1) to the swap bit and it should cross the node Z.

Now the packet 'c' or 'd' would enter Z. If the packet 'c' has entered early, it would detour the node Z. The packet 'd' should detour the node Z whether it has entered while the packet 'c' is still crossing the node Z or not. Fig. 2(b) shows this case. If the packet 'd' has entered early and the packet 'b' has already left Z, 'd' would detour the node Z. The packet 'c' should detour the node Z whether it has entered while the packet 'd' is still detouring the node Z or not. Fig. 2(c) shows this case. If the packet 'b' is still crossing when 'd' has entered the node Z, 'd' should also cross the node Z. If the packet 'c' has entered while 'd' is still crossing the node Z, 'c' should also cross the node Z. However if the packet 'c' has entered after 'd' has already crossed Z, 'c' would detour the node Z. This is the case the packets are not distributed evenly. Note that, the packet 'c' should not change the swap bit when 'b' was still in transmitting. This should be better than 'c' would wait until it can change the swap bit. More importantly all the neighbor nodes before and after the node Z use the swap selection. The packets are eventually distributed evenly fully utilizing the links.

In summary, by using the swap selection every intermediate node distributes income packets evenly, toward the destination, violating the evenness only not to introduce unnecessary waiting time in the buffer. The packet generated at each node may select any idle link or be interposed between packets with some adequate priority level.

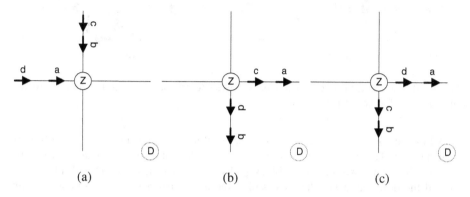

Fig. 2. The packets passing through an intermediate node Z according to the swap bit

3   Non-minimal Swap Routing

This section presents a new routing method to fully utilize the links' bandwidth in the paths toward the hotspot. The routing is founded on the swap routing introduced in Section 2. On 2D mesh any node except boundary nodes has its 4 input links, and the bandwidth sum of the 4 links is the physical maximum in receiving packets headed to the node. We exclude any physical link addition to gain more bandwidth, which may change the topology of mesh and increase the cost of its implementation. As each node is attached to the mesh by its switch we use the terms a node and a switch interchangeably from now on. We say that a node in 2D mesh has the *consumption capability* of 4, the number of input links for nodes that means maximum capacity of receiving each flit of packets passing through the 4 links at any given instant.

We suppose an occasion the hotspot would emerge which some of other nodes (equals to a switch) has one packet each to send to a node, called *hotspot node*. Fig. 3(a) shows the movements of packets heading to the hotspot node in a profitable routing method. The profitable routing method that selects only the shortest paths in this occasion utilizes only a half of the hotspot node's consumption capability. The hotspot node, D, has another half of its consumption capability unused thus misrouting method is required, in the manner that some of the shortest paths are extended by the least additional hop. Without misrouting, packets generated at the black nodes would suffer evitable blocking delay to eventually enter the node D. The goal of this paper is to minimize the blocking time in the buffer of each intermediate switch by utilizing the consumption capability fully as possible.

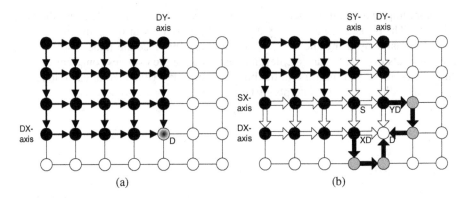

Fig. 3. (a) Black nodes may generate hotspot packets for the node D, and (b) profitable routes and misroutes for the hotspot node are provided

All the hotspot packets traverse the mesh heading to the destination D as written in their headers. The proposed routing method is applied at each intermediate switch in the Fig. 3(b), and two additional black paths emerged from two XD and YD nodes toward the destination D. The idea behind the additional paths is each node, XD or YD, sends the same number of packets along both dimensions after receiving any even number of packets.

Suppose there are 2p nodes that generate one hotspot packet each among black nodes in the Fig. 3(b). Assume that the number of packets entered the node YD along SX-axis and that entered XD along DX-axis is the same, h. Assume also that the number of packets entered the node XD along SY-axis and that entered YD along DY-axis is the same, v. In this case packets sent by the node S are h along SX-axis, and v along SY-axis. Then XD sends (h+v)/2 packets along DX-axis and (h+v)/2 along SY-axis, to D and an additional path toward D, respectively. YD shows the same behavior. For this routing each packet header contains two control bits in addition to its destination address. It is inherent from [18]. The packet header format is depicted in Fig. 6, and the meanings of the control bits are as follows;

```
11 - The packet is heading to (X_Dest - 0, Y_Dest - 0), that
is, the destination.

01 - The packet is heading to (X_Dest - 0, Y_Dest - 1), that
is, the node YD. In this case it is on either SX- or
DY-axis and the swap bit of each switch is ignored.

10 - The packet is heading to (X_Dest - 1, Y_Dest - 0), that
is, the node XD. In this case it is on either SY- or
DX-axis and the swap bit of each switch is ignored.

00 - The packet is heading to (X_Dest - 0, Y_Dest - 0), the
destination, from XD or YD and it could make a curve,
following the black arrows in the Fig. 3(b), or not.
The swap bits are ignored.
```

And the routing is divided into three phases.

- Phase 1 – Destination: (X_{Dest}, Y_{Dest})

Packets leave their source node with the control bits '11.' When they enter any node over SX- or SY-axis, they are forwarded to either XD or YD.

- Phase 2 - Destination: $(X_{Dest} - 1, Y_{Dest})$ or $(X_{Dest}, Y_{Dest} -1)$

Packets advance to either XD with the control bits '10' or YD with the control bits '01.' When they enter either XD or YD, they are forwarded to the destination, D.

- Phase 3 - Destination: (X_{Dest}, Y_{Dest})

Packets enter the destination directly or make a curve to the destination. In both cases the control bit is '00', and any node receiving a packet with '00' should make the link selection as 'detouring.'

In the phase 2, if the packets has entered a node over SX-axis, the half of the packets are destined for YD and the other half are destined for XD to advance toward the destination, D(Fig. 4(a)). If the packets has entered a node over SY-axis, the half of the packets are destined for XD and the other half are destined for YD to advance toward the destination, D(Fig. 4(b)). In the phase 3, misrouting occurs with a probability 1/2 at the node XD or YD and only these two nodes use $(X_{Dest}, Y_{Dest}+1)$ or $(X_{Dest}+1, Y_{Dest})$ for next false direction instantly. If the packet enters D directly the control bits '00' is of no use since it has arrived at the destination.

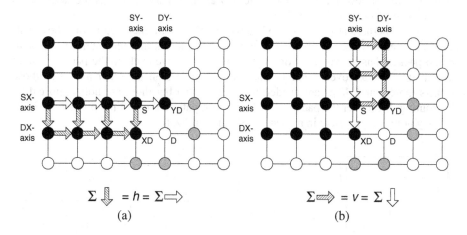

$$\Sigma \Downarrow = h = \Sigma \Rightarrow \qquad \Sigma \Rightarrow = v = \Sigma \Downarrow$$

(a)   (b)

Fig. 4. The node XD and YD receive the same number of packets

'11' is the initial value of control bits. Once a packet enters a node over SX- or SY-axis, the control bits are changed into '10' or '01'. Packets that starts at a source node over DX- or DY- axis begins with '10' or '01.' If the packet enters XD or YD, the bits are changed into '00' at the node and then it enters the destination or makes a curve to the destination. The proposed routing algorithm is in the Fig. 8. Note that, after the control bits are changed into '10' or '01', the packet advances along either X-dimension only or Y-dimension only, until it enters XD or YD. Let a_i be the packet arrival rate at each node over SX-axis then the packet arrival rate at YD along SX-axis is equal with that at XD along DX-axis.

$$ARsx(YD) = \frac{1}{2}\sum_{i=1}^{4} a_i \qquad (1) \qquad ARDx(XD) = \frac{1}{2}\sum_{i=1}^{4} a_i \qquad (2)$$

Let b_j be the packet arrival rate at each node over SY-axis then the packet arrival rate at XD along SY-axis is equal with that at YD along DY-axis.

$$ARsy(XD) = \frac{1}{2}\sum_{j=1}^{3} b_j \qquad (3) \qquad ARDy(YD) = \frac{1}{2}\sum_{j=1}^{3} b_j \qquad (4)$$

In general;

$$ARDx(XD) + ARsy(XD) = \frac{1}{2}\sum_{i=1}^{I} a_i + \frac{1}{2}\sum_{j=1}^{J} b_j , \qquad (5)$$

and

$$ARsx(YD) + ARDy(YD) = \frac{1}{2}\sum_{i=1}^{I} a_i + \frac{1}{2}\sum_{j=1}^{J} b_j , \qquad (6)$$

where I is the largest hop from the node YD along SX-axis and J is the largest hop from the node XD along SY-axis.

Packets generated at nodes over SX-axis or SY-axis are included in the above calculation. Therefore the destination D receives p/2 packets through each link, thus all the 2p packets has arrived the common destination, if we exclude the packets "more generated" at nodes over either DX-axis or DY-axis than the other axis. For those packets more than 2 hops are needed to be misrouted but those are not supported by this routing. Moreover the packets have a straight path to the destination thus misrouting may not be appropriate in respect of resource utilization.

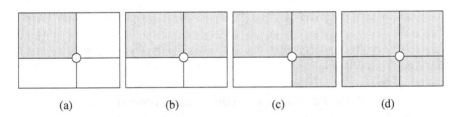

(a)   (b)   (c)   (d)

Fig. 5. Distributions of the source nodes

Each entry bit of the switches memorizes whether even number of packets has entered or not through each input link, except the packets of the control bits '00.' Therefore the flow of misrouted packets does not affect that of other packets in the distribution of source nodes (b), (c), or (d) of the Fig. 5. $(X_{Dest}-1, Y_{Dest})$ or $(X_{Dest}, Y_{Dest}-1)$, the coordinates of XD or YD, of the routing algorithm, should be changed into either $(X_{Dest}+1, Y_{Dest})$ or $(X_{Dest}, Y_{Dest}+1)$ according to the location of the source node.

The packet arrival is depicted in the Fig. 7, (a) shows the case from source locations of the Fig. 5(b). White arrows are direct entrances and black arrows are curved entrances. There are no interferences between the flows of misrouted packets since their control bits '00' means just 'detouring' each intermediate switch and packets with the control bits '00' do not change each entry bit. Superimposing the Fig. 7(b) on 5(a) makes the case for the Fig. 5(c).

- Deadlock freedom

    There is no cycle of packets since the path of misrouted packets starts at a node only one hop apart from the destination, and the path finishes at the destination.

- Livelock freedom

    The path of a misrouted packet is fixed by the control bit '00' thus the packet eventually arrives at the destination.

X_{Dest}	Y_{Dest}	SX	SY

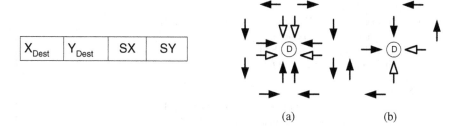

(a)   (b)

Fig. 6. Packet header format   **Fig. 7.** Packets approaching to the destination

Theorem 1. For the traffic that is centralized to one node on 2D mesh, if all the 4 input links of the node receive packets in their full bandwidth in parallel, the traffic should be consumed in the minimal time.

Proof. This is the topological and physical limit.

Theorem 2. Under the N-Swap routing the destination node's 4 input links receive the packets in their full bandwidths in parallel. The average path length of all the packets arrived the destination is 1 hop plus the average of each packet's the shortest path length.

Proof. Using the swap selection packets reach SX- or SY-axis through the shortest path in the phase 1. In the phase 2, packets advance to XD or YD through the shortest path. The node XD has two input links for two input links of the node D and the node YD has two input links for the other two input links of the node D. The destination node D's 4 input links are capable to consume both every two packets from XD and every two packets from YD. Thus the N-Swap routing utilizes the full bandwidths of the destination's 4 input links. Since a half of packets arrives at the destination took 2 hops more than its shortest path in the phase 3, a packet takes the length of its shortest path plus 1 hop, on average, to arrive at the destination.

IF the packet's current coordinates (X, Y) are equal to (X_{Dest}, Y_{Dest})
    EXIT the algorithm.
ENDIF
CASE of SX and SY;
   00: /* *The packet is making a curve to the destination* */
     Insert the packet to the queue of link toward the node D.
   01: /* *The packet is heading to YD* */
     IF the packet's current coordinates (X, Y) are equal to $(X_{Dest}, Y_{Dest}-1)$
       THEN change the control bit to 00, and CALL SelectLink.
       ELSE Insert the packet to the queue of link toward the node YD.
     ENDIF
   10: /* *The packet is heading to XD* */
     IF the packet's current coordinates (X,Y) are equal to $(X_{Dest}-1, Y_{Dest})$
       THEN change the control bit to 00, and CALL SelectLink.
       ELSE Insert the packet to the queue of link toward the node XD.
     ENDIF
   11: /* *The packet has not reached SX- or SY-axis* */
     CALL SelectLink.
     IF the packet's current Y coordinate is equal to $Y_{Dest}-1$;
       IF the packets next Y coordinate is equal to Y_{Dest}
         THEN change to control bit to 10.
         ELSE change the control bit to 01.
       ENDIF
     ENDIF
     IF the packet's current X coordinate is equal to $X_{Dest}-1$;
       IF the packets next X coordinate is equal to X_{Dest}
         THEN change the control bit to 01.
         ELSE change the control bit to 10.
       ENDIF
     ENDIF
ENDCASE
SUB SelectLink
    CASE of the swap bit;
        0: Insert the packet to the queue, of X-dimension link where it entered along Y-dimension, or of Y-dimension link where it entered along X-dimension.
        1: Insert the packet to the queue, of X-dimension link where it entered along X-dimension, or of Y-dimension link where it entered along Y-dimension.
    ENDCASE
ENDSUB

Fig. 8. N-Swap Routing Algorithm

Previous works employed multiqueue or bypass buffer to store blocked packets not to block other flow of packets[7][8]. To prevent starvation packets in the bypass buffer gets higher priority than those in the input buffer. Bypass buffer is installed as one central multiqueue as in [7] or as distributed single buffers for each direction as in [8]. One linear central queue was adopted and its capacity is four packets, in this paper, the same multiqueue capacity in [7]. If a switch designer determine input buffers with its capacity of multiple packets, the packet at the top of FIFO queue(buffer) should change its entry bit and the swap bit.

4   Performance Evaluation

4.1   Simulation Model

The simulations are conducted in a 16x16 2D mesh. A pair of unidirectional links connects each pair of neighboring switches, and each switch connects to its local processor through four pairs of unidirectional links. Input buffering is assumed, i.e., buffers are partitioned into flits and are associated with input links from neighboring switches. A flit may contain a predetermined number of bits. The processor generates packets (assumed to have 20 flits per packet) at time intervals chosen from an exponential distribution. Packets that are generated from the source processor enter the attached switch are immediately enqueued, and those enter a destination switch are immediately dequeued and arrive at the processor. Every simulation has iterated 100 times and the average values are obtained. A packet generated at the source node is injected at the bottom of an input buffer. Ejection of a packet arrived at its destination is also done at the bottom of an input buffer.

Three cases of hotspot occasion are simulated to evaluate the effect of non-minimal paths. Node (8,8), (5,5), and (2,2) are selected as the hotspot nodes, respectively, and packets from other nodes will be headed to the hotspot node. Communication latency and throughput[15] are the performance metrics of interest in the simulations. Communication latency is measured from the time a packet is generated at the source node until the tail flit reaches the destination. Throughput is the average number of packets that complete transmission per unit time. The issue rate is defined to be the ratio of the number of packets generated during a simulation to the number of nodes in the network.

Three routing methods were evaluated, M-Swap, N-Swap and Chaos[17]. M-Swap is a swap routing that takes only minimal path thus misrouting doesn't occur (Fig. 3(a)). N-Swap, Non-minimal Swap routing of the Fig. 8, is a swap routing that takes minimal or non-minimal paths at the probability of 1/2. Chaos is the most relevant router and the recent one. Latencies and throughputs are measured in unit times.

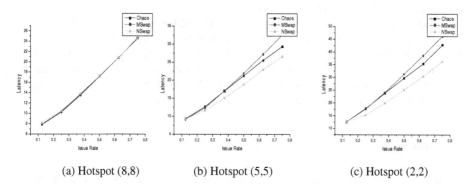

(a) Hotspot (8,8)   (b) Hotspot (5,5)   (c) Hotspot (2,2)

Fig. 9. Average latencies in 3 locations of the hotspot node

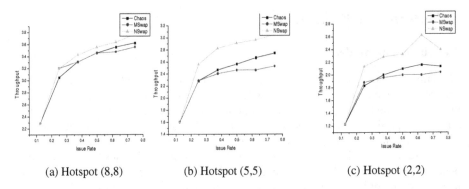

(a) Hotspot (8,8)   (b) Hotspot (5,5)   (c) Hotspot (2,2)

Fig. 10. Average throughputs in 3 locations of the hotspot node

4.2 Hotspot Traffic

Traffic patterns may vary by the locations of the hotspot node. Hotspot simulation was conducted in three cases. In 16x16 mesh a number of nodes would send their packets to one hotspot node. The central node (8,8) is the first hotspot case. In the Fig. 9(a) the destination hotspot node is surrounded by evenly distributed source nodes and the expectations that hotspot packets would come through one of four input links would be all the same for each input link. Thus misrouting achieves hardly any throughput improvement. For the case the hotspot node locates apart from the center, the Fig. 9(b), idle input links should work by misrouting for non-minimal paths and non-minimal swap routing performs much better than the minimal one. Chaos performs over M-Swap but under N-Swap. The reasons are two; firstly, the Chaos switches the income packet to the first available output link on a profitable path[17]. This chaotic link selection achieves high link utilization, however, does not guarantee even distribution of income packets for output links. This tendency of unsymmetrical link selection makes imbalanced usage between input buffers toward the hotspot node. Although misrouting of Chaos relieves the imbalance, however, its misrouting is originally not for balanced buffer usage.

Secondly, misrouting of N-Swap routing is devised for full utilization of all the input links of the destination hotspot node. This implies balanced usage among the 4 input link's bandwidth thus N-Swap shows lower latency in the Fig. 10(b). As the hotspot node is more apart from the center, throughput improvement is more apparent. Fig. 10(c) means link utilization with non-minimal paths is more effective on the performance than that with only the minimal paths.

5 Conclusion

Hotspot is an inevitable situation for many parallel applications. Various approaches were proposed but the routing method to alleviate hotspot problem without extra physical links is rare. Without modification of mesh topology a reasonable method is fully utilizing all the links of the hotspot node. Non-minimal paths are the way for utilizing the idle links. A new routing method that incorporates both profitable routes and misroutes was proposed and approved in the hotspot traffics. In particular this routing method does not consider congestion to decide on misrouting. Although not presented in this paper, the proposed routing method showed effectiveness also for other traffic patterns.

Every node owns its swap bit. This swap bit enables two output links be in transmitting state continuously, simultaneously enabling two input links be in receiving state. A packet come into the switch might go out through either dimensional link with the probability of 1/2, which corresponds to one link every hop to the destination. This property makes the bandwidth of links fully utilized together with minimizing the buffer occupations until one of the two output links is not available due to the topological limitation, i.e., the edge nodes. Fully utilizing the link bandwidth and minimizing the buffer occupation should conduce to the maximal utilization of network resources.

The routing method requires only little addition of hardware and it is relatively simple. This merit is very important since most of proposed routing methods was not implemented due to their high complexities[11]. In this respect the proposed routing method is rather practical.

As virtual cut-through switching defines fixed packet length, i.e., a fixed number of flits, the proposed routing method assumes only a fixed packet length. However the proposed routing is able to work with variant packet lengths after appropriate modification. Memorizing whether even or odd of flits than that of packets and some adaptation in the flow control may result in such a routing method.

References

1. G. F. Pfister and V. A. Norton, Hot Spot Contention and Combining in Multistage Interconnection Networks, IEEE Trans. Computers, vol. 34, (1985) 943-948.
2. Y. Sun, P. Cheng and X. Lin, Barrier Synchronization on Wormhole-routed Networks, IEEE Trans. Parallel and Distributed Systems, vol. 12, (2001) 583-597.
3. R. S. Hyder and D. A. Wood, Synchronization Hardware for Networks of Workstations: Performance v.s. cost, in: ACM ICS'96, (1996) 245-252.
4. J. Duato, A. Robles and F. Silla, A Comparison of Router Architectures for Virtual Cut-Through and Wormhole Switching in a NOW Environment, in: 13th International Parallel Processing Symposium and 10th Symposium on Parallel and Distributed Processing, (1999) 240-248.
5. H. S. Lee, H. W. Kim, J. Kim and S. Lee, Adaptive Virtual Cut-through as an Alternative to Wormhole Routing, in: Proceedings of the 24th International Conference on Parallel Processing, vol. I, (1995) 68-75.
6. Lionel M. Ni, Wenjian Qiao and Mingyao Yang, Switches and Switch Interconnects, in: 4th International Conference on Massively Parallel Processing Using Optical Interconnections, (1997) 122-130.
7. J. H. Upadhyay, V. Varavithya and P. Mohapatra, Efficient and Balanced Adaptive Routing in Two-Dimensional Meshes, in: 1st IEEE Symposium on High-Performance Computer Architecture, (1995) 112-121.
8. P.-Jen Chuang, J.-Tang Chen and Y.-T. Jiang, Balancing Buffer Utilization in Meshes Using a "Restricted Area" Concept, IEEE Trans. Parallel and Distributed Systems, vol. 13, (2002) 814-827.

9. G. D. Pifarre, L. Gravano, S. A. Felperin, and J. L.C. Sanz, Fully Adaptive Minimal Dead-lock-Free Packet Routing in Hypercubes, Meshes, and Other Networks: Algorithms and Simulations, IEEE Trans. Parallel and Distributed Systems, vol. 5, (1994) 247-263.
10. D. Basak, D. K. Panda, Alleviating Consumption Channel Bottleneck in Wormhole-routed k-ary n-cube Systems, IEEE Trans. Parallel and Distributed Systems, vol. 9, (1998) 481-496.
11. K. Bolding, M. Fulgham and L. Snyder, The Case for Chaotic Adaptive Routing, IEEE Trans. Computers, vol. 46, (1997) 1281-1997.
12. M. S. Thottethodi, A. R. Lebeck, and S. Mukherjee, BLAM : A High-Performance Rout-ing Algorithm for Virtual Cut-Through Networks, in: Proceedings of the International Par-allel and Distributed Processing Symposium, (2003).
13. T. Nguyen and L. Snyder, Performance of Minimal Adaptive Routers, in: Proc. Parallel Computer Routing and Comm. Workshop, (1994) 60-71.
14. G. D. Pifarre, L. Gravano, G. Denicolay and J. L.C. Sanz, Adaptive Deadlock- and Live-lock-Free Routing in the Hypercube Network, IEEE Trans. Parallel and Distributed Sys-tems, vol. 5, (1994) 1121-1139.
15. W.J. Dally, Performance Analysis of k-ary n-cube Interconnection Networks, IEEE Trans. Computers, vol. 39, no. 6, (1990) 775-785.
16. A. G. Greenberg and B. Hajek, Deflection Routing in Hypercube Networks, IEEE Trans. Communications, vol. COM-40, (1992) 1070-1081.
17. S. Konstantinidou and L. Snyder, The Chaos Router, IEEE Trans. Computers, vol. 43, (1994) 1386-1397.
18. M. –H. Ok and M.-S. Park, A Novel Collective Communication Scheme on Packet-switched 2-D Mesh Interconnection, in: Proc. Int'l Conf. VECPAR '2000, (2000) 147-158.

A Shape Optimizing Load Distribution Heuristic for Parallel Adaptive FEM Computations*

Stefan Schamberger

Universität Paderborn,
Fakultät für Elektrotechnik, Informatik und Mathematik,
Fürstenallee 11, D-33102 Paderborn
schaum@uni-paderborn.de

Abstract. Load balancing plays an important role in parallel numerical simulations. To address this problem, some general purpose libraries as well as a number of more specific approaches have been developed. Many of them base on vertex exchange operations like the Kerninghan-Lin heuristic which, due to their sequential nature, are hard to parallelize. Furthermore, libraries like Metis and Jostle primarily minimize the edge-cut and cannot obey constraints like connectivity and straight partition boundaries, which are important for some numerical solvers.

In this paper we present a new approach to address the load balancing problem. In contrast to existing heuristics, we are able to guarantee connectivity and the resulting partitions are usually well shaped. Furthermore, our experiments indicate that we can outperform the two parallel state-of-the-art libraries Metis and Jostle also according to the classic metrics like edge-cut and boundary length. The proposed algorithm thereby contains a high degree of natural parallelism, while its drawback is the long run-time, especially if the parallelism is not exploited.

Keywords: Parallel FEM computations, load balancing, graph partitioning, diffusion schemes.

1 Introduction

Finite Element Methods (FEM) are used extensively by engineers to analyze a variety of physical processes which can be expressed via Partial Differential Equations (PDE). The domain on which the PDEs have to be solved is discretized into a mesh, and the PDEs are transformed into a set of equations defined on the mesh's elements (see e. g. [4]). These can then be solved by iterative methods such as onjugate Gradient (CG) and Multigrid. Due to the very large amount of elements needed to obtain an accurate approximation of the original problem, this method has become a classical application for parallel computers. The parallelization of numerical simulation algorithms usually follows the Single-Program Multiple-Data (SPMD) paradigm: Each processor executes the same code on

---

* This work is supported by the German Science Foundation (DFG) project SFB-376.

V. Malyshkin (Ed.): PaCT 2005, LNCS 3606, pp. 263–277, 2005.

a different part of the data. This means that the mesh has to be split into P sub-domains and each sub-domain is then assigned to one of the P processors. To minimize the overall computation time, all processors should thereby roughly contain the same amount of elements. Since iterative solution algorithms perform mainly local operations, i. e. data dependencies are defined by the mesh, the parallel algorithm mainly requires communication at the partition boundaries. Hence, these should be as small as possible. The described problem can be expressed as a graph partitioning problem. The mesh is transformed into a graph where the vertices represent the computational work on the elements and the edges their interdependencies. Libraries working on graphs are referred to as *general purpose libraries*, since they are not provided with any additional problem related information.

Depending on the application, some areas of the simulation space require a higher resolution and therefore more elements. Since the location of these areas is not known beforehand or can even vary over time, the mesh is refined and coarsened during the computation. However, this can cause an imbalance between the processors' load and therefore delay the simulation. To avoid this, the distribution of elements needs to be rebalanced. The application is interrupted and the at this program state static repartitioning problem is solved. To keep the interruption as short as possible, it is necessary to find a new balanced partitioning with small boundaries quickly, with the additional objective not to cause too many elements to change their processor. Migrating elements can be an extremely costly operation since a lot of data has to be sent over communication links and reinserted into complex data structures. Note, that the re-balancing problem is similar to the initial balancing problem. Modeling it as a graph, the difference is that the vertices are already assigned to partitions beforehand and additional migration costs should be considered.

Due to the complexity of the problem, the large input sizes and the given time constraints, existing libraries that address the graph (re-)partitioning problem are based on heuristics. Even if approximation algorithms are applied for some calculations, the overall computation is still a heuristic, because the influence between the different components has not been theoretically investigated yet. State-of-the-art graph partitioning libraries like Metis [8], Jostle [19] or Party [15] follow the multilevel scheme [6]. Vertices of the graph are contracted according to a matching and a new level consisting of a smaller graph with a similar structure is generated. This is repeated, until in the lowest level only a small graph remains. The partitioning problem is then solved for this small graph and vertices in higher levels are assigned to partitions according to their representatives in lower levels. Additionally, a local refinement phase (also called uncoarsening phase) is applied in every level to further enhance the solution. This process finally leads to a partitioning of the original graph. Hence, a multilevel algorithm consists of three important tasks: A matching algorithm, deciding which vertices are combined in the next level, a global partitioning algorithm applied in the lowest level (which can be omitted if the number of vertices meets the number of desired partitions), and a local refinement algorithm improving the quality of a given partitioning by exchanging vertices. Implementations of the latter are usually based on the Kerninghan-Lin (KL) heuristic [9], while the local refinement algorithm in Party is derived from theoretical analysis with Helpful-Sets (HS) [7,15].

To address the load balancing problem during parallel computations, distributed versions of the libraries Metis and Jostle have been developed. Both of them apply about the same multilevel techniques as their single processor version, but some phases of the computation need special attention due to their sequential nature. As an example, a coloring of the graph's vertices is used by the parallel library ParMetis [18] to assure that during the KL refinement no two neighboring vertices change their partition simultaneously and therefore destroy the consistency of the data structures. In contrast to Metis where vertices stay on their partition until a new distribution has been computed, the parallel version of Jostle [20] maps each sub-domain to a single processor and vertices which migrate do so already during the computation of the repartitioning. Furthermore, Jostle, apart from the edge-cut minimization, seems to incorporate a shape optimization presented in [21]. However, since the sources are not available, we can only make assumptions here. Usually, Metis is very fast while Jostle takes longer but often computes better solutions.

Another, widely applied geometric approach to partition a mesh is based on Space-Filling curves (see e.g. [12,22]). The vertices of the graph are sorted by a certain recursive scheme covering the whole domain. Then, the now linear array of vertices is split into equal sized parts, each representing a partition. In contrast to partitioning heuristics, this method only works if vertex coordinates are present. It has been shown that this method is extremely fast, but problems arise if the simulation area contains holes [17] since only the provided (sometimes misleading) geometric information is used and the structural data is ignored.

While the global edge-cut is the classical metric that most graph partitioners optimize, it is not necessarily the best metric to follow because it does not model the real communication and runtime costs of FEM computations as described in [5]. Hence, different metrics have been implemented inside the local refinement process modeling the real objectives more closely. In [11], the costs emerging from vertex transfers is taken into consideration while Metis is capable of minimizing the sub-domain connectivity as well as the number of boundary vertices.

A completely different approach is undertaken in [2]. Since the convergence rate of the CGBI domain decomposition solver in the PadFEM environment depends on the geometric shape of a partition, the integrated load balancer focuses on iteratively optimizing the aspect ratios by applying a bubble like algorithm. Although different to the multilevel-schemes, this approach still contains a strictly sequential part and suffers from some other difficulties that are described in more detail in [16]. However, the latter paper introduces an implementation that eliminates most of these problems by replacing the sequential growing mechanism of the bubble framework by a few iterations of the first order diffusion scheme (FOS) [3]. This leads to a graph partitioning algorithm that contains a high degree of parallelism and produces well shaped partitions. However, it is not clear how many FOS iterations must be performed and since this number depends on the graph, a wrong choice leads to bad or even no results.

In this paper we refine the technique from [16] and extend the FOS by adding absolute draining. The modified version converges and the properties of the converged state are similar to the state that is reached after a few FOS iterations. Hence, the termination criterion question mentioned above is solved. Furthermore, we demonstrate that the new resulting heuristic can be successfully applied to repartition meshes in parallel adaptive FEM simulations and surpasses state-of-the-art load balancing libraries concerning the solution-quality.

The remaining part of this paper is organized as follows. The next Section briefly recaptures the bubble frame work and the diffusive operations from [16]. In Sec. 3, we describe the modified FOS scheme which we implemented in the Party/DB library and illustrate some of its properties. Selected results of a comparison between the new heuristic and state-of-the-art load balancing libraries are presented in Sec. 4.

2   DB - A Diffusive Bubble Algorithm

As already mentioned, the DB algorithm [16] is based on the bubble framework [2]. Algorithms within this framework start with an initial, often randomly chosen vertex (seed) per partition, and all sub-domains are then grown simultaneously in a breadth-first manner. Colliding parts form a common border and keep on growing along this border – "just like soap bubbles". After the whole mesh has been covered and all vertices of the graph have been assigned this way, each component computes its new center that acts as the seed in the next iteration. This is usually repeated until a stable state, where the movement of all seeds is small enough, is reached. This procedure is based on the observation that within "perfect" bubbles, the center and the seed vertex coincide.

In the DB algorithm, the growth process is implemented via a small number of FOS iterations. Note, that diffusion in graphs has been studied very well because it can be applied to solve load balancing problems in various scenarios (e. g. [1,3]). The main idea behind applying it in a graph partitioning heuristic is the fact that load primarily diffuses into densely connected regions of the graph rather than into sparsely connected ones. Following this observation one can expect to identify sets of vertices that possess a high number of internal and a small number of external edges.

Independently for each partition, we place load on some (so called source vertices) of the graph and run a few FOS iterations. Then, we assign the vertices to that partition they have obtained most load from. Hence, a partition can crowd others out of parts of the graph if it itself already contains a higher load nearby. These dynamical movements are addressed by the bubble framework. During its iterations, the seeds from which the diffusion process is initiated are rearranged such that they are finally well distributed over the graph and are preferably placed within a densely connected region. Two different operations cause this movement. The first one, called contraction, chooses a single vertex in the center of each partition containing the maximal load of the according color. This vertex becomes the new seed (or single source) for the next iteration. However, since only a few FOS iterations are performed, this will be very likely the same vertex that initiated the diffusion process in the previous iteration. Hence, no movement would occur. Therefore, a second operation called consolidation is introduced. In contrast to the contraction, not a single vertex is assigned as new seed but the whole partition is used as source. Since more vertices are within the dense regions of the graph, this operation will direct the partition toward its desired position and also insures that in the following loops a different vertex contains the maximum load, as long as the final state has not been reached. The resulting algorithm is sketched in Fig. 1. As with all other bubble implementations, some difficulties arise establishing the balance of the partitioning. However, adjusting the total load of each color (either placed on a single vertex or equally distributed on the partition) provides a handy method to address this problem [16].

The drawback of the described implementation is the difficulty in determining the number of FOS iterations to be performed. If too many iterations are executed, the load diffuses to far into the graph and the load differences between the different kinds of load on the vertices vanish. Hence, it becomes difficult to assign the vertices to the partitions. On the other hand, too little iterations inhibit partition interaction. Therefore, very little or even no movement will occur. As a solution, the right number of FOS iterations must be determined, but because this number depends on the graph properties as well as the current partitioning, and experiments show that the range of "good selections" is rather small, this number is difficult to obtain.

```
00  Algorithm DB(G, t, s)
01     in each iteration t
02        if t = 1
03           determine-seeds(G)
04        else
05           parallel for each partition p
06              place-load-on-seeds(G, p)
07              load-diffusion(G, p)
08              contraction(G)
09        in each loop s
10           parallel for each partition p
11              place-load-on-parts(G, p)
12              load-diffusion(G, p)
13           π = consolidation(G)
14     return π
```

Fig. 1. Sketch of the DB algorithm

The solution presented here applies an alternative diffusion scheme. This scheme must provide similar information than the state after some iterations of the FOS. First, load must diffuse faster into densely connected regions of the graph, which is important for the movement. Second, in order to guarantee connectivity, vertices must obtain more load the closer they are to the load originating vertices. Hence, we want to construct a scheme that converges toward such solutions.

3   A New Diffusion Scheme with Absolute Draining

In this Section, we introduce an new diffusion scheme. This scheme also converges, but in contrast to the original FOS, not toward the completely balanced

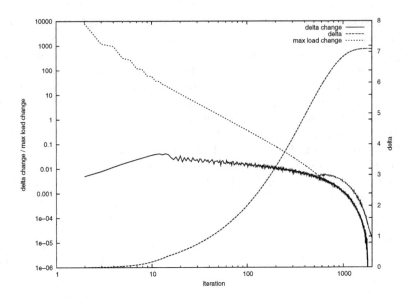

Fig. 2. FOS/A on the 100×100 Grid. $L = |V|$ load is initially placed on vertex (50,50) and $\delta_A = 0.001$. The plot shows Δ, its difference $|\Delta^i - \Delta^{i-1}|$ between two iterations and the maximal change of the load on a vertex $\max_v(|l_v^i - l_v^{i-1}|)$

load situation. It is disturbed such that the converged solution has similar properties as the state after some FOS iterations which is described in the last Section. The disturbance is realized by decreasing the load on each vertex by an absolute value δ_A. Note, that if a vertex contains less load than δ_A, only the existing load will be subtracted, and therefore load values are still non-negative. To keep the total load amount in the system constant, all subtracted load will be added equally to the set of source vertices $S \subseteq V$. Recall, that for each partition this set contains either the single seed vertex or all its vertices. Formally, the proposed scheme can be described as follows.

Definition 1 (FOS/A). *Let $G = (V, E)$ be a connected graph and $S \subseteq V$ be the chosen set of source vertices. The entries of the vector s are either set to $s_v = 1/|S|$, if $v \in S$, or 0 otherwise. Let $\delta_A \geq 0$ be the absolute drain constant and $L > 0$ the total load in the system. Furthermore, set $\alpha_{(u,v)} = 1 + \max\{deg(u), deg(v)\}$ for each edge $e = (u, v)$ in G. In iteration i, let l_v^i denote the load on vertex v and f_e^i the flow over edge e. Initially, set $l^0 = 0$ and $\Delta^0 = L$. Then, the iteration scheme **FOS/A** performs in each iteration i the following computations:*

$$f_{e=(u,v)}^i = \frac{1}{\alpha_e} \cdot \left(l_u^i - l_v^i \right) \tag{1}$$

$$t_v^{i+1} = l_v^i - \sum_{e=(v,*)} f_e^i + s_v \Delta^i \tag{2}$$

$$d_v^{i+1} = \min \left(t_v^{i+1}, \delta_A \right) \tag{3}$$

$$l_v^{i+1} = t_v^{i+1} - d_v^{i+1} \tag{4}$$

$$\Delta^{i+1} = \sum_{v \in V} d_v^{i+1} \tag{5}$$

Initially, all load is placed on the source vertices. During the first iterations, this load diffuses into the graph, similar to the original FOS scheme, because the subtracted load compared to the load amount on a vertex is relatively small. Since the load spreads into the graph, more and more vertices acquire load and therefore Δ increases. At some point however, all load of the furthest vertices is subtracted and sent back to the source, such that no load on these vertices remains. Hence, the spreading slows down and eventually stops. Fig. 2 shows some important variables of a sample experiment. We can see that during the first iterations, Δ increases quickly, but the increase slows down such that $|\Delta^i - \Delta^{i-1}|$ becomes finally zero. Consequently, the flow over the edges has reached a stable state and therefore also the load on each vertex does not change anymore.

4   Experiments

This Section describes our experiments with the Party/DB library. In this library we have implemented the DB algorithm from [16] and replaced the original growing mechanism by the proposed FOS/A diffusion scheme.

Unfortunately, in contrast to the graph partitioning problem, there are no load balancing benchmarks available to the public. This might be due to the number of involved components that are needed to run numerical simulations and that are often very problem specific. In order to run comprehensible tests, We have created a set of benchmark instances as described in [10] which are available via [13]. While a graph partitioning benchmark only consists out of a single graph, the evaluation of load balancing heuristics requires a sequence of them. This sequence reflects the changes of the mesh caused by the refinement and coarsening procedure and each graph, also called frame, reflects the static mesh at that point when the load balancing algorithm is started. All benchmarks contain 101 frames, each consisting of around 15000 triangles. Though the instances are quite small, important observations can already be made while we are still able to include some examples in this paper. However, due to the space limitations, we have to restrict our presentation to three instances. Furthermore, we decided to only include the results of 12 partitionings since we have seen that other partition numbers lead to very similar results. The same holds for tests with 3-dimensional meshes created with the modified version of the $padfem^2$ environment. Although we know that different vertex orderings can influence the results [14], we only perform one computation per benchmark due to time restrictions.

In the experiments, we compare our implementation to the parallel libraries of Metis (version 3.1) and Jostle (version 3.0). Both offer a large number of options. For the presented evaluation, we chose the recommended values from their manual, respectively, and left the remaining parameters at their default. This means that Metis operates with an *itr* value of 1000.0 and Jostle uses

Mesh	Metis	Jostle	Party/DB

Fig. 3. Frames 0, 49, 50, 51 and 100 of the 'heat' benchmark

the options *threshold = 20, matching = local, imbalance = 3*. Note, that Jostle seems to ignore the imbalance setting and computes totally balanced partitions, except for the initial solution where the sequential versions of the libraries are applied. The Party/DB library is invoked with $\delta_A = |V|^{1/2}$ and $L = |V|$, which is automatically doubled in case of an empty vertex stay after the diffusion process.

To measure the quality of a partitioning, a number of metrics are possible. The traditional one is the edge-cut, that is the number of edges between different partitions, but it is known that this usually does not model the real costs [5].

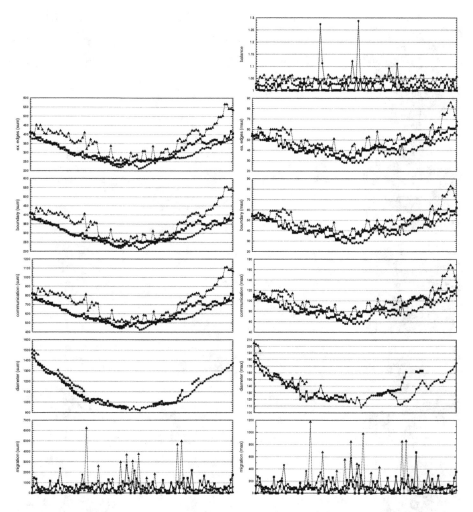

Fig. 4. Results of all 101 frames of the 'heat' benchmark for Metis (blue triangles), Jostle (red squares) and Party/DB (green pentagons)

Depending on the application, some of the metrics might be more important than others, and more information is provided if we list them separately. The metrics included in out tests can be described as follows: *External edges:* Number of edges that are incident to exactly one vertex of partition p. *Boundary vertices:* Number of vertices of partition p that are adjacent to at least one vertex from a different partition. *Send volume:* The amount of outgoing information is the sum of the adjacent partitions different to p that each vertex residing inside partition p has. *Receive volume:* The amount of incoming information is the number of vertices of partitions different to p adjacent to at least one vertex of partition p. *Diameter:* The longest shortest path between two vertices of the same partition. Infinity, if the partition is not connected. *Outgoing migration:* Number of vertices

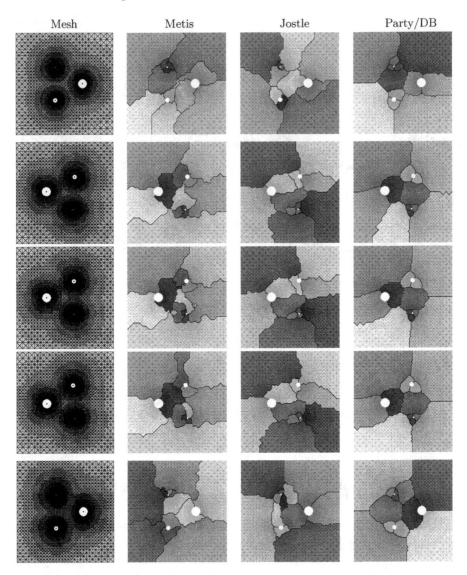

Fig. 5. Frames 0, 49, 50, 51 and 100 of the 'slowtric' benchmark

that have to be migrated to a different partition. *Incoming migration:* Number of vertices that have to be migrated from a different partition. Furthermore, the quality of a partitioning depends on its balance. A less balanced solution does not necessarily cause problems during the computation, but of course allows other metrics to improve further and makes comparisons less meaningful. Please note that we have omitted the run-times since the Party/DB library is some magnitudes slower then its competitors.

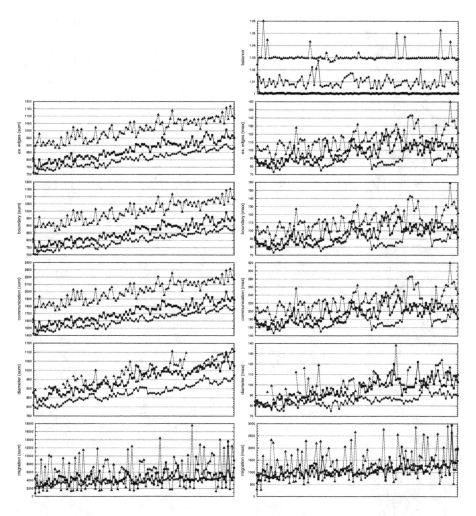

Fig. 6. Results of all 101 frames of the 'slowtric' benchmark for Metis (blue triangles), Jostle (red squares) and Party/DB (green pentagons)

In addition, for the listed metrics we consider three different norms. Given the values $x_1, \ldots, x_P$, the norms are defined as follows: $l_1(X) := x_1 + \ldots + x_P$, $l_2(X) := (x_1^2 + \cdots + x_P^2)^{1/2}$ and $l_\infty(X) := \max_{i=1..P} x_i$. The l_1-norm (summation norm) is a global norm. The global edge cut belongs into this category (it equals half the external edges in this norm). In contrast to the l_1-norm, the l_∞-norm (maximum norm) is a local norm only considering the worst value. This norm is favorable if synchronized processes are involved. The l_2-norm (Euclidean norm) lays in between the l_1 and the l_∞-norm and reflects the global situation as well as local peaks. However, due to space limitations, we omit the l_2-norm here and also combine some of the metrics.

Mesh	Metis	Jostle	Party/DB

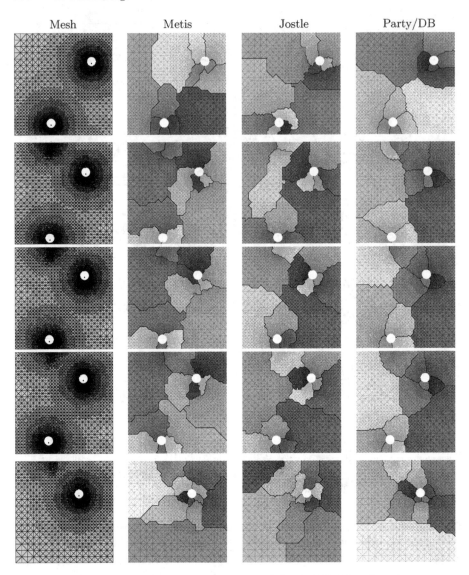

Fig. 7. Frames 0, 49, 50, 51 and 100 of the 'bubbles' benchmark

The first example is derived from a heat simulation on a square cooker with four plates. Fig.3 shows some frames of the mesh and the computed partitions, respectively. At the beginning, the area around the upper left plate is refined more deeply. This changes over the simulation time toward the lower right plate as indicated in the left column. The solutions of Metis are shown in the middle left column. While the initial solution looks acceptable, there seem to be some problems in later balancing steps. A closer look to e. g. frame 50 reveals that one partition is degenerated into three parts, one of them only consisting out of

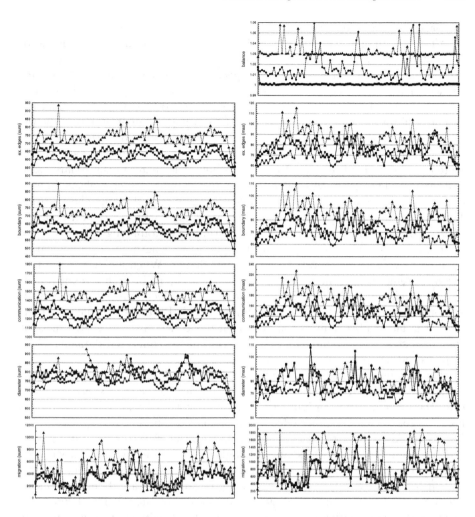

Fig. 8. Results of all 101 frames of the 'bubbles' benchmark for Metis (blue triangles), Jostle (red squares) and Party/DB (green pentagons)

two vertices. Metis applies a local exchange heuristic that usually takes care of a few isolated vertices and assigns them to adjacent partitions. However, we guess that this problem is related to the parallelization of the exchange procedure. The distributions calculated with Jostle (middle right) are usually of a better shape, though partitions are sometimes disconnected. Party/DB guarantees connectivity, but shows a few balancing problems in this benchmark, which becomes clearer in Fig. 4 which shows the recorded metrics. The left column contains the data according to the l_1-norm while on the right side the l_∞-norm has been applied. The first row contains the balance, displayed as the maximal size of a partition. The next four rows contain the edge-cut, the number of boundary vertices, the communication volume (send and receive volumes are added) and the partition diameter. One can see that the values of the solutions computed by Metis are higher than those for the partitionings obtained with Jostle or Party/DB. This is a general observation and holds for all of our benchmark sets. Looking at the diameter, Jostle and especially Metis compute sometimes disconnected domains. The last row displays the migration (outgoing and incoming elements are added). Here, Metis seems to follow a different strategy than the two other libraries, moving either very little or a huge amount of data while the migration volume of Jostle and Party/DB is more constant over the frames.

Fig. 5 shows some frames of the 'slowtric' benchmark. Here, the mesh is generated according to three circles rotating around the center of the squared simulation area. The circle sizes differ and due to a similar attractor placed in each of the circles, the area around the smaller circles is refined more. The resulting 12 partitionings are better shaped if using Jostle or Party/DB than if applying Metis. Applying Metis, partitions are often thin or contain long extensions into their neighbors, which both increases the boundary length and communication volumes as well as deteriorates the partition shapes. When looking at the partition movement, it is interesting too see that domains in deeply refined areas (e. g. around the smallest circle) try to follow these locations. This property is even more distinct in the solutions obtained with Party/DB (right). Furthermore, the latter library finds the best solutions concerning the classic metrics, computes straighter boundaries and also guarantees connected domains. Fig.6 displays the numerical data.

The last benchmark presented in Fig. 7 is as well created by moving some circles over the squared simulation area. In contrast to the last experiment however, the movement in the 'bubbles' instance is not continuous, but the refined areas disappear on the upper edge of the simulation space and reappear on the lower one. Also, the attractors are not placed in the circle centers but closer to the lower side. The idea is to simulate a higher computational complexity caused by some turbulences. Although the discontinuous movements will very unlikely appear in real world applications, it is a good example for a fast changing mesh. The numerical results shown in figure 8 are similar to the previous two experiments and the evaluation of this as well as of the remaining examples that can be found in [13] is left to the reader.

5   Conclusion and Future Work

In this paper, we have introduced a new heuristic to balance load in parallel adaptive FEM computations. Replacing a former implementation, the proposed diffusion scheme FOS/A increases the reliability of the growing algorithm in the bubble framework. Integrated into the prototypic library Party/DB, the latter computes solutions that outperform those obtained with Jostle and especially Metis concerning all considered metrics. However, since the run-time of the current version is indiscussable high it is not applicable in practice. Nevertheless, due to the obtained solution qualities, we think that further investigations are justified. Besides the parallelization, the run-time could be further reduced, e. g. by adopting the multilevel paradigm or applying a faster diffusion scheme.

References

[1] G. Cybenko. Load balancing for distributed memory multiprocessors. *Parallel and Distributed Computing*, 7:279–301, 1989.

[2] R. Diekmann, R. Preis, F. Schlimbach, and C. Walshaw. Shape-optimized mesh partitioning and load balancing for parallel adaptive FEM. *Parallel Computing*, 26:1555–1581, 2000.

[3] R. Elsässer, B. Monien, and R. Preis. Diffusion schemes for load balancing on heterogeneous networks. *Theory of Computing Systems*, 35:305–320, 2002.

[4] G. Fox, R. Williams, and P. Messina. *Parallel Computing Works!* Morgan Kaufmann, 1994.

[5] B. Hendrickson. Graph partitioning and parallel solvers: Has the emperor no clothes? In *Irregular'98*, number 1457 in LNCS, pages 218–225, 1998.

[6] B. Hendrickson and R. Leland. A multi-level algorithm for partitioning graphs. In *Proc. of Supercomputing'95*, 1995.

[7] J. Hromkovic and B. Monien. The bisection problem for graphs of degree 4. In *Proc. of Mathematical Foundations of Computer Science (MFCS '91)*, volume 520 of *LNCS*, pages 211–220, 1991.

[8] G. Karypis and V. Kumar. *MeTis: A Software Package for Partitioning Unstrctured Graphs, Partitioning Meshes, and Computing Fill Reducing Orderings of Sparse Matrices, Version 4.0*, 1998.

[9] B. W. Kernighan and S. Lin. An efficient heuristic for partitioning graphs. *Bell Systems Technical Journal*, 49:291–308, 1970.

[10] O. Marquardt and S. Schamberger. Open benchmarks for load balancing heuristics in parallel adaptive finite element computations. Submitted to PDPTA'05.

[11] L. Oliker and R. Biswas. PLUM: Parallel load balancing for adaptive unstructured meshes. *Journal of Parallel and Distributed Computing*, 52(2):150–177, 1998.

[12] H. Sagan. *Space Filling Curves*. Springer, 1994.

[13] S. Schamberger. http://www.upb.de/cs/schaum/benchmark.html.

[14] S. Schamberger. Improvements to the helpful-set heuristic and a new evaluation scheme for graphs-partitioners. In *Intern. Conf. on Computational Science and its Applications, ICCSA'03*, number 2667 in LNCS, pages 49–59, 2003.

[15] S. Schamberger. Graph partitioning with the Party library: Helpful-sets in practice. In *Computer Architecture and High Performance Computing, SBAC-PAD'04*, pages 198–205, 2004.

[16] S. Schamberger. On partitioning FEM graphs using diffusion. In *HPGC, Intern. Parallel and Distributed Processing Symposium, IPDPS'04*, page 277 (CD), 2004.

[17] S. Schamberger and J. M. Wierum. Graph partitioning in scientific simulations: Multilevel schemes vs. space-filling curves. In *Parallel Computing Technologies, PACT'03*, number 2763 in LNCS, pages 165–179, 2003.

[18] Kirk Schloegel, George Karypis, and Vipin Kumar. Multilevel diffusion schemes for repartitioning of adaptive meshes. *J. Parallel Distributed Computing*, 47(2):109–124, 1997.

[19] C. Walshaw. *The parallel JOSTLE library user guide: Version 3.0*, 2002.

[20] C. Walshaw and M. Cross. Parallel optimisation algorithms for multilevel mesh partitioning. *Parallel Computing*, 26(12):1635–1660, 2000.

[21] C. Walshaw, M. Cross, R. Diekmann, and F. Schlimbach. Multilevel mesh partitioning for optimising domain shape. *Intl. J. High Performance Comput. Appl.*, 13(4):334–353, 1999.

[22] G. Zumbusch. *Parallel Multilevel Methods: Adaptive Mesh Refinement and Load-balancing*. Teubner, 2003.

Performance Analysis of Applying Replica Selection Technology for Data Grid Environments*

Chao-Tung Yang[1,†], Chun-Hsiang Chen[1], Kuan-Ching Li[2], and Ching-Hsien Hsu[3]

[1] High-Performance Computing Laboratory,
Department of Computer Science and Information Engineering,
Tunghai University, Taichung 40704, Taiwan
ctyang@mail.thu.edu.tw
[2] Parallel and Distributed Processing Center,
Department of Computer Science and Information Management,
Providence University, Taichung 43301, Taiwan
kuancli@pu.edu.tw
[3] Department of Computer Science and Information Engineering,
Chung Hua University, Hsinchu 300, Taiwan
chh@chu.edu.tw

Abstract. The Data Grid enables the sharing, selection, and connection of a wide variety of geographically distributed computational and storage resources for solving large-scale data intensive scientific applications. Such technology efficiently manage and transfer terabytes or even petabytes of data for data-intensive, high-performance computing applications in wide-area, distributed computing environments. Replica selection process allows an application to choose a replica from replica catalog, based on its performance and data access features. In this paper, we build a Grid environment based on three existing PC Cluster environments and perform performance analysis of data transfers using GridFTP protocol over these systems. In addition, based on experimental results, it is proposed a cost model to pick the best replica, in real and dynamic network situations.

Keywords: Grid computing, Data Grid, Replica selection, Globus, GridFTP.

1 Introduction

Grid computing is utilization of many computers' resources in a network to a single problem at the same time - usually to a scientific or technical problem that requires a great number of computer processing cycles or access to large amounts of data. A Grid computing environment provides a platform for scientific applications and physical experiments. A Grid is a large-scale virtual organization which resources are shared in order to solve problems [4, 7, 9, 10, 11 12]. Grid computing is distributed computing taken to the next evolutionary level. The goal is to create the vision of

---

* This paper is supported in part by NSC Taiwan (National Science Council), under grants no. NSC92-2213-E-029-025, NSC92-2119-M-002-024, NSC 93-2119-M-002-004 and NSC93-2213-E-029-026.
† The corresponding author.

V. Malyshkin (Ed.): PaCT 2005, LNCS 3606, pp. 278–287, 2005.
© Springer-Verlag Berlin Heidelberg 2005

large and powerful self-managing virtual computer, which is a huge collection of connected heterogeneous systems. The emerging mechanism is resources sharing through the availability of high bandwidth network. The "computational Grid" is a term used to provider the users a better performance, especially in terms of speed and throughput. The term "Data Grid" aggregate distributed resources to produce results for large size problems. Most of these Data Grid applications are executed simultaneously and access a large number of shared data files in Grid.

In certain data intensive scientific applications, such as high-energy physics, bioinformatics applications and astrophysical virtual observatory, we confront with huge amount of data. A Data Grid provides two essential basic services, which are a secure, reliable, efficient data transport protocol and replica management [2]. The high-speed transport protocol, GridFTP, extends the popular FTP protocol with some new features required for Data Grid applications, such as partial file transfer and third-party transfer [5]. The replica management service take advantage of replica catalog with GridFTP transfer to provide for the creation, registration, location and management of data replicas [1].

In this paper, we build a Grid environment based on three existing PC Cluster environments and perform performance analysis of data transfers using GridFTP protocol over these systems. In addition, based on experimental results, it is proposed a cost model to pick the best replica, in real and dynamic network situations. In this paper, we propose a cost model according to the three significant parameters: network bandwidth, CPU load and I/O state. Although the network situation is constantly changing and the storage equipments are busy or idle, we can use our cost model to determine the best replica immediately. The replica selection can be conducted accurately because our cost model is based on the system monitoring information that update continuously.

2 Background Review

2.1 Globus Toolkit

The Globus Project [10, 11, 12] provides software tools that make it easier to build computational Grids and Grid-based applications. These tools are collectively called The Globus Toolkit. The Globus Toolkit is used by many organizations to build computational Grids that can support their applications. The composition of the Globus Toolkit can be pictured as three pillars: Resource Management, Information Services, and Data Management. Each pillar represents a primary component of the Globus Toolkit and makes use of a common foundation of security. GRAM implements a resource management protocol, MDS implements an information services protocol, and GridFTP implements a data transfer protocol. They all use the GSI security protocol at the connection layer [8, 11, 12, 13].

2.2 NWS

The Network Weather Service (NWS) [16] is a generalized and distributed monitoring system for producing short-term performance forecasts based on historical performance measurements. The goal of the system is to dynamically characterize and forecast the performance deliverable at the application level from a set of network and computational resources. It is composed of three component processes:

- *nws_nameserver*: implements a naming and discovery service used to manage a system of nws_sensor and nws_memory,
- *nws_memory*: provides persistent storage for the measurement data collected by the NWS deployment,
- *nws_sensor*: gathers performance measurements from a specified resource and communicates it to a set of *nws_memory* specified on the command line.

A typical installation would involve one *nws_nameserver*, one or more *nws_memory* (which may reside on different machines), and a *nws_sensor* running on each machine for which resources are to be monitored. The system includes sensors for end-to-end TCP/IP performance (bandwidth and latency), available CPU percentage, and available non-paged memory.

2.3 Sysstat Utilities

The Sysstat [15] utilities are a collection of performance monitoring tools for Linux OS, which sysstat package contains the *sar*, *mpstat*, and *iostat* commands. The *sar* command collects and reports system activity information. This information can also be saved in a system activity file for future inspection. The *iostat* command reports CPU statistics and I/O statistics for *tty* devices and disks. The statistics reported by *sar* concern I/O transfer rates, paging activity, process-related activities, interrupts, network activity, memory and swap space utilization, CPU utilization, kernel activities, and *tty* statistics, among others. Both uniprocessor (UP) and Symmetric multiprocessor (SMP) machines are fully supported.

3 Replica Selection

3.1 Replica Selection Scenario

The system established in this research used the following architecture. Figure 1 shows our proposed replica selection model, to show how a client identifies the best location for a desired replica transfer.

At first, the client login at the site *local site* and execute parallel applications in the Data Grid platform. This application checks the files are located in local site or not. If they are present at the local site, the application accesses them immediately. Otherwise, the application passes the logical file names to replica catalog server, which returns a list of physical locations for all registered copies. The application passes this list of replica locations to a replica selection server, which identifies the destination locations of storage system for all candidate data transfer operations.

The replica selection server sends the possible destination locations to information server, which provides the performance of measurements and predictions of three system factors, as described in next section. According to these estimates, the replica selection server chooses the best replica location and returns location information to the parallel application, which receives the replica through GridFTP. Once finished the application's computation, the application returns the results to user.

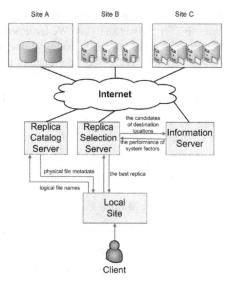

Fig. 1. Replica selection scenario

3.2 System Factors

We propose a replication selection model for Data Grid environments. In this environment, we can treat a biological database as a replica of Data Grid. When we execute large-scale data intensive applications in these environments, a site has both data stores and computational capabilities. To determine the best database from many of same replications is a significant problem. In our model, we consider three system factors that affect the replica selection:

- Network bandwidth: Network bandwidth is one of the most significant factors in Data Grid, since the size of a data file in Data Grid environment is usually very large. In other words, the data file transfer time is tightly dependent on network bandwidth situations. Because network bandwidth is unstable and dynamic factor, we should often measure and predict it as most accurate as possible. NWS (Network Weather Service) is a powerful toolkit for such purpose,
- CPU load: a Grid platform consists of a number of heterogeneous systems, built with different system architectures, e.g., cluster platforms, supercomputers, PCs. CPU load is a dynamic system factor, and if the CPU load of a system is heavy, it will certainly affect the data file download process from this site. The measurement of CPU status is done through the Globus Toolkit / MDS,
- I/O state: Data Grid nodes consist of different heterogeneous storage systems. The size of data in Data Grid is huge. If I/O state of the site that we would like to download file from is very busy, it will directly affect the data transfer performance. We measure the I/O state using *sysstat* utilities.

3.3 Replica Selection Cost Model

The target function of a cost model for distributed and replicated data storage is the score of information from information service. We listed different influencing factors for our cost model in the previous section. However, we have to express these factors within a mathematical notation for further analysis. We assume node I is the local site which the user or application is logged in, while node j possesses the replica which the user or application wanted. The seven system parameters in our replica selection cost model are:

- $Score_{i-j}$: The score high or low represents the user or application acquiring the replica effectively or not is from node I to node j,
- P_{i-j}^{BW} : The percentage of bandwidth from node I to node j. In other words, the current bandwidth divided the highest theoretical bandwidth,
- W^{BW} : The weight of the network bandwidth defined by the administrator of the Data Grid,
- P_{j}^{CPU} : The percentage of CPU idles of node j,
- W^{CPU} : The weight of the CPU load defined by the administrator of the Data Grid,
- $P_{j}^{I/O}$: The percentage of I/O idles of node j,
- $W^{I/O}$: The weight of the I/O state defined by the administrator of the Data Grid,

According to the given three system factors, we define the following general formula as:

$$Score_{i-j} = P_{i-j}^{BW} \cdot W^{BW} + P_{j}^{CPU} \cdot W^{CPU} + P_{j}^{I/O} \cdot W^{I/O} \qquad (1)$$

In this formula, three influencing factors: W^{BW}, W^{CPU}, and $W^{I/O}$, described as the weights of network bandwidth, CPU, and I/O. These weights can be determined by the administrator of the Data Grid organization. According to different attributes of storage systems in Data Grid nodes, administrator can decide for different weights, because some storage equipment does not affect CPU load. After several experimental measurements, we consider that network bandwidth is the most significant factor, influencing directly the data transfer time. When we perform data transfer using GridFTP protocol, we discover that the CPU and I/O statuses slightly affect the performance of data transfer. In our Data Grid environment, we define the values as 80%, 10%, and 10%, respectively.

4 Experimental Environments and Results

In this section, there are experimental results using GridFTP protocol. First, we measure and compare the FTP with GridFTP, as their file transfer time. Secondly, we focused in the parallel data transfer in this paper, measuring and comparing the GridFTP with 1, 2, 4, 8 and 16 TCP streams of file transfer time.

The Data Grid testbed consisting of three Linux PC clusters is built as:

- THU site: four PCs with dual AMD AthlonMP 2.0GHz processors, 1GB DDR memory, 60GB HD, 1Gbps network bandwidth,
- Li-Zen site: four PCs with Intel Celeron 900MHz processor, 256MB DDR memory, 10GB HD, 30 Mbps network bandwidth,
- HIT site: four PCs with Intel P4 2.8GHz processors, 512MB DDR memory, 80GB HD, 1Gbps network bandwidth.

Figure 2 shows the hardware and network configuration of our Data Grid testbed. The THU site is located in Tunghai University, Taichung City; Li-Zen site is located at Li-Zen High School, Taichung County, while HIT site is located in Hsiuping Institute of Technology, Taichung County, all in Taiwan.

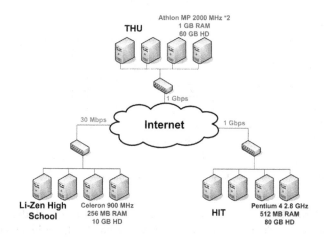

Fig. 2. Our Data Grid testbed

4.1   FTP Versus GridFTP

The Globus Project surveyed available protocols and technologies, implemented some prototypes, and settled on using FTP and its existing extensions as a base, and then extending it again to add missing required functionality. The Globus alliance propose a common data transfer and access protocol named GridFTP that provides secure, efficient data movement in Grid environments. This protocol, which extends the standard FTP protocol, provides a superset of the features offered by the various Grid storage systems currently in use.

In Grid environments, access to distributed data is typically as important as access to distributed computational resources. Distributed scientific and engineering applications require transfers of large amounts of data between storage systems, and access to large amounts of data by many geographically distributed applications and users for analyzing and visualization. We note that GridFTP protocol is extended from FTP protocol, and suitable for Grid environments. Figure 3 shows the performance of FTP and GridFTP by transferring four different file sizes. We transferred these files (256, 512, 1024 and 2048 megabytes) from THU site alpha01 to HIT site gridhit3 in our first experiment.

4.2   GridFTP with Parallel Data Transfer

Using multiple TCP streams can improve aggregate bandwidth over using a single TCP stream in WAN environments. We apply this feature of GridFTP protocol to transfer different sizes files in Data Grid environments. GridFTP (as well as normal FTP) defines multiple wire protocols, or MODES, for the data channel. Most normal

FTP servers only implement stream mode, i.e., the bytes flow in order over a single TCP connection. GridFTP defaults to this mode so that it is compatible with normal FTP servers.

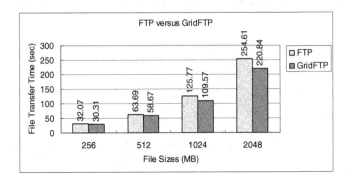

Fig. 3. FTP versus GridFTP

However, GridFTP has another mode, called Extended Block Mode, or MODE E. This mode sends the data over the data channel in blocks. Each block consists of 8 bits of flags, a 64 bit integer indicating the offset from the start of the transfer, and a 64 bit integer indicating the length of the block in bytes, followed by a payload of length bytes. Because the offset and length are provided, out of order arrival is acceptable, i.e., the 10th block could arrive before the 9th because you know explicitly where it belongs. This allows us to use multiple TCP channels. If you use the parallelism option, *globus-url-copy* automatically puts the servers into MODE E. Note that parallel data transfer with one TCP stream is not the same as no parallel data transfer at all. Both will use a single stream, but the default will use stream mode and the parallel data transfer with one TCP stream will use mode E [12].

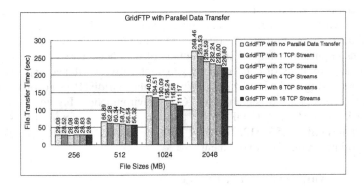

Fig. 4. GridFTP with parallel data transfer

The parallelism option is used by the source data note to control how many parallel data connections may be established to each destination data node. Figure 4 shows the performance of GridFTP transferring 256, 512, 1024 and 2048 megabytes files with 1, 2, 4, 8 and 16 TCP streams from THU site alpha02 to Li-Zen site lz04. According to the experiment result, we observed that parallel data transfer technique showed better performance for larger file sizes. Parallel data transfer really improves aggregate bandwidth, with the establishment of multiple data channels.

4.3 Replica Selection Cost Model

According to the replica selection scenario in 3.1, a user logins the local site THU site alpha1, and specifies the characteristics of the desired data and passes this attribute description to replica catalog server. The replica catalog server queries its database and produces a list of logical files that contain data with the specified characteristics. The replica catalog server returns the information of physical locations for all registered replicas of the desired logical files. In this experiment, there is only one logical file, file-a, conform to user's request, and the size of file-a is 1024 megabytes.

Table 1. The value of replica selection cost model and file transfer time

alpha1	Alpha4	hit0	lz02
P_{i-j}^{BW}	88.25	29.09	20.91
P_j^{CPU}	98.67	99.56	98.33
$P_j^{I/O}$	2.88	100.00	3.78
Replica Selection Cost model	80.76	43.228	26.939
Practical Data transfer time	101.9	128.09	164.99

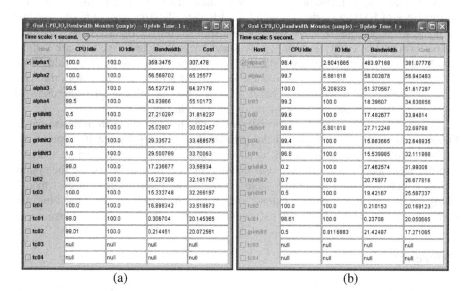

(a)   (b)

Fig. 5. GUI of replica selection cost model program

Next, the user passes this list of replica locations to the replica selection server, which identifies the destination storage system locations for all candidate data transfer operations. There are three replicas mapping to the logical file file-a. These three replicas are individually located at different sites, alpha4, hit0, and lz02. The replica selection server sends the candidate destination locations to the information server [17], which provide the three system factors mentioned in 3.2. Based on the replica cost model referred in 3.3, the replica selection server chooses the best replica and transfers it to the local site alpha1 by GridFTP. Table 1 shows the values of system factors and the scores of the replica selection cost model, and the physical file transfer time. According to discussions given in 3.3, we implemented a replica selection cost model computer program. We also executed the program in our Data Grid testbed. Because the program is developed using Java programming language, we can execute it in any computing platform with JVM. Fig. 5(a) shows costs that are calculated based on the three system factors (the percentage of CPU idle, I/O idle and bandwidth from other sites) to alpha1. Figure 5(b) displays the average value based on the selected time scale, which is adjustable on the top scroll bar. We also can get the sort list of the costs by clicking the "Cost" button.

5   Conclusions and Future Work

In this paper, we have presented the design and implementation of two fundamental services. The GridFTP protocol was extended from FTP protocol, and it provides beneficial features. In this research paper, we focused in parallel data transfer issues. After measuring the performance of GridFTP with parallel data transfer feature, we confirm that such technology improves data transfer. After measuring the performance of FTP and GridFTP with four different file sizes, we could observe that even file size is 2 gigabytes; the data transfer time is similar. However, we measured the performance of GridFTP with 1, 2, 4, 8 and 16 TCP streams. We are sure that the parallel data transfer technology efficiently saves data transfer time. After calculating the score of replica selection cost model, we can sort a list of replicas from the most efficient replica to worst one. Therefore, our cost model can provide users or applications the best choice mechanism for replica selection.

As future work, there are three investigations will be carried out from this research. First, although we have employed the parallel data transfer feature to improve the performance of data transfer, there is another striped data transfer feature that can improve aggregate bandwidth. Second, we will consider how to determine the system factors weight and refer to more system factors in the replica selection cost model. Third and last one, we will extend our Data Grid testbed for analyzing the performance of replica selection in a dynamic and larger number of sites environment.

References

1. B. Allcock, J. Bester, J. Bresnahan, A. Chervenak, I. Foster, C. Kesselman, S. Meder, V. Nefedova, D. Quesnal, S. Tuecke, "Data Management and Transfer in High Performance Computational Grid Environments," *Parallel Computing*, Vol. 28 (5), pp. 749-771, May 2002.

2. B. Allcock, J. Bester, J. Bresnahan, A. Chervenak, I. Foster, C. Kesselman, S. Meder, V. Nefedova, D. Quesnel, S. Tuecke, "Secure, Efficient Data Transport and Replica Management for High-Performance Data-Intensive Computing," *IEEE Mass Storage Conference, 2001.*

3. B. Allcock, S. Tuecke, I. Foster, A. Chervenak, and C. Kesselman, "Protocols and Services for Distributed Data-Intensive Science," *ACAT2000 Proceedings*, pp. 161-163, 2000.

4. K. Czajkowski, S. Fitzgerald, I. Foster and C. Kesselman, "Grid Information Services for Distributed Resource Sharing," *Proceedings of the Tenth IEEE International Symposium on High-Performance Distributed Computing (HPDC-10)*, IEEE CS Press, August 2001.

5. K. Czajkowski, I. Foster, N. Karonis, C. Kesselman, S. Martin, W. Smith and S. Tuecke, "A Resource Management Architecture for Metacomputing Systems," *Proc. IPPS/SPDP '98 Workshop on Job Scheduling Strategies for Parallel Processing*, pp. 62-82, 1998.

6. R. L. De, C. Costa and S. Lifschitz, "Database Allocation Strategies for Parallel BLAST Evaluation on Clusters", *Proceedings of the Distributed and Parallel Databases*, Vol. 13, Issue1, pp. 99-127, Hingham, MA, USA, January 2003.

7. I. Foster, "The Grid: A New Infrastructure for 21st Century Science," *Physics Today*, 55(2):42-47, 2002.

8. I. Foster, C. Kesselman, "Globus: A Metacomputing Infrastructure Toolkit," *Intl J. Supercomputer Applications*, 11(2):115-128, 1997.

9. I. Foster and C. Kesselman, *The Grid: Blueprint for a New Computing Infrastructure*, Morgan-Kaufmann, 1999.

10. I. Foster, C. Kesselman and S. Tuecke, "The Anatomy of the Grid: Enabling Scalable Virtual Organizations," *Intl J. Supercomputer Applications*, 15(3), 2001.

11. Global Grid Forum, http://www.ggf.org/

12. The Globus Project, http://www.globus.org/

13. Introduction to Grid Computing with Globus, http://www.ibm.com/redbooks/

14. SETI@home: Search for Extraterrestrial Intelligence at home, http://setiathome.ssl. berkeley. edu/

15. SYSSTAT utilities home page, http://perso.wanadoo.fr/sebastien.godard/

16. R. Wolski, N. Spring and J. Hayes, "The Network Weather Service: A Distributed Resource Performance Forecasting Service for Metacomputing," *Journal of Future Generation Computing Systems*, Vol. 15, No. 5-6, pp. 757-768, October 1999.

17. X. Zhang, J. Freschl, and J. Schopf, "A Performance Study of Monitoring and Information Services for Distributed Systems," *Proceedings of HPDC*, August 2003.

RAxML-OMP: An Efficient Program for Phylogenetic Inference on SMPs[*]

Alexandros Stamatakis[1], Michael Ott[2], and Thomas Ludwig[3]

[1] Institute of Computer Science, Foundation for Research and Technology-Hellas,
P.O. Box 1385, GR-71110 Heraklion, Crete, Greece
[2] Technical University of Munich, Department of Computer Science,
Boltzmannstr. 3, D-85748 Garching b. München, Germany
[3] Ruprecht-Karls University, Department of Computer Science,
Im Neuenheimer Feld 348, D-69120 Heidelberg, Germany

Abstract. Inference of phylogenetic trees comprising hundreds or even thousands of organisms based on the Maximum Likelihood (ML) method is computationally extremely intensive. In order to accelerate computations we implemented RAxML-OMP, an efficient OpenMP-parallelization for Symmetric Multi-Processing machines (SMPs) based on the sequential program RAxML-V (Randomized Axelerated Maximum Likelihood). RAxML-V is a program for inference of evolutionary trees based upon the ML method and incorporates several advanced search algorithms like fast hill-climbing and simulated annealing. We assess performance of RAxML-OMP on the widely used Intel Xeon, Intel Itanium, and AMD Opteron architectures. RAxML-OMP scales particularly well on the AMD Opteron architecture and achieves even super-linear speedups for large datasets (with a length $\geq$ 5.000 base pairs) due to improved cache-efficiency and data locality. RAxML-OMP is freely available as open source code.

1 Introduction

Phylogenetic (evolutionary) trees are used to represent the evolutionary history of a set of n organisms which are often also called taxa within this context. A multiple alignment of a—in a biological context—suitable small region of their DNA or protein sequences can be used as input for the computation of phylogenetic trees. Note, that a high-quality multiple alignment of the organisms is a necessary prerequisite to conduct a phylogenetic analysis: *The quality of the evolutionary tree can only be as good as the quality of the multiple alignment!* Other computational approaches to phylogenetics also use gene order data [24].

In a computational context phylogenetic trees are usually strictly bifurcating (binary) unrooted trees. The organisms of the alignment are located at the tips (leaves) of such a tree whereas the inner nodes represent extinct common

---

[*] This work is funded by a Postdoc-fellowship granted by the German Academic Exchange Service (DAAD) and by the "Competence Network for Technical, Scientific High Performance Computing in Bavaria (KONWIHR)".

V. Malyshkin (Ed.): PaCT 2005, LNCS 3606, pp. 288–302, 2005.
© Springer-Verlag Berlin Heidelberg 2005

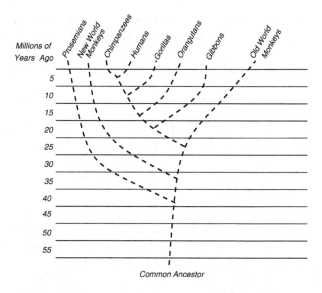

Fig. 1. Phylogenetic tree representing the evolutionary relationship between monkeys and the homo sapiens

ancestors. The branches of the tree represent the time which was required for the mutation of one species into another—new—one. An example for the evolutionary tree of the monkeys and the homo sapiens is provided in Figure 1. Note, that the tree need not be *the* model of evolution. Therefore, approaches using phylogenetic networks are becoming more popular recently [8].

The inference of phylogenies with computational methods has many important applications in medical and biological research, such as e.g. drug discovery and conservation biology. A paper by D. Bader *et al* [1] addresses potential industrial applications of evolutionary tree inference and contains numerous useful references to important biological results obtained via phylogenetic analysis.

Due to the rapid growth of available sequence data over the last years and the constant improvement of multiple alignment methods it has now become feasible to compute very large trees which comprise more than 1.000 organisms. The computation of the tree-of-life containing representatives of all living beings on earth is considered to be one of the *grand challenges* in Bioinformatics.

The most fundamental algorithmic problem computational phylogeny faces consists in the immense amount of potential alternative tree topologies. This number grows exponentially with the number of sequences n, e.g. for $n = 50$ organisms there already exist $2.84 * 10^{76}$ alternative topologies; a number almost as large as the number of atoms in the universe ($\approx 10^{80}$). Thus, given some—biologically meaningful—optimality criterion for evaluating all alternative configurations (topologies) in order to search for the best tree, one can quickly assume that the problem might be NP-hard. In fact, this has already been demonstrated for the general version of the *perfect phylogeny* problem [3] and *maximum parsimony* (MP) [4]. The *maximum likelihood* (ML) criterion [5] is also believed to be NP-hard, though this could not be demonstrated so far because of the significantly superior mathematical complexity of the model. Due to the large amount of alternative trees, intelligent search space heuristics have to be deployed for ML-based phylogenetic inference. Another important aspect for the design of such heuristics consists in the very high degree of accuracy (difference to the score of the optimal or best-known solution) which is required to obtain reasonable biological as well as topologically closely related results. While an accuracy of 90% is considered to be a "good" value for heuristics designed to solve other NP-hard optimization problems, e.g. the traveling salesman problem, recent results [29] suggest that phylogenetic analyses require an accuracy $\geq 99.99\%$, in particular for large trees. This observation yields the whole field more difficult and challenging.

When comparing the various optimality criteria which have been devised for phylogenetic trees one can observe a *trade-off* between speed and quality. This means that a phylogenetic analysis conducted with an elaborate model such as maximum likelihood requires significantly more computation time but yields trees with superior accuracy than e.g. *neighbor joining* [6] (NJ) or MP [7] [28]. However, due to the higher accuracy it is desirable to infer large and complex trees with maximum likelihood or closely related Bayesian methods.

Within this context it is important to note that the design of maximum likelihood programs is primarily an *algorithmic discipline,* due to the gigantesque number of alternative tree topologies and the high computational cost of the likelihood function. Thus, progress in the field has mainly been attained via algorithmic improvements rather than by brute force allocation of all available computational resources. As an example consider the performance of parallel fastD-NAml [21] (state-of-the-art parallel ML program in 2001) and RAxML-V [19] (Randomized Axelerated Maximum Likelihood, one of the fastest sequential ML programs in 2004) on a 1.000-organism alignment: For this large alignment parallel fastDNAml consumed approximately 9.000 accumulated CPU hours on a Linux PC cluster in contrast to less than 20 hours required by RAxML-V on a single Intel Xeon processor. In addition, the likelihood of the tree computed by RAxML-V was *significantly better* than the likelihood score obtained by parallel fastDNAml.

However, as algorithmic research in phylogenetics comes of age and novel powerful algorithms allow for computation of trees which comprise more than 500 sequences, a new category of problems arises. Those problems mainly concern memory shortage, cache efficiency, and a still very large demand for computation time. Thus, the main focus of this paper is on the deployment of the shared memory programming paradigm for the computation of large trees (containing ≥ 500 sequences) based on statistic models of sequence evolution.

The remainder of this paper is organized as follows: Section 2 describes related work in the area of ML phylogeny programs. The following Section 3 briefly describes the main components of the sequential version of RAxML-V. In Section 4 the computation of the likelihood score for a tree is explained and the OpenMP [14] parallelization of RAxML-V is outlined. In Section 5 we report

RAxML-OMP speedups on Xeon, Itanium, and Opteron SMPs. Finally, Section 6 provides a conclusion and briefly addresses current and future issues of work.

2   Related Work

The survey of related work is restrained to statistical phylogeny methods since they have shown to be the most accurate methods currently available. On the one hand there exist "traditional" maximum likelihood methods and a large variety of programs implementing maximum likelihood searches. The recently updated site maintained by J. Felsenstein [17] lists most available programs. On the other hand there exist Bayesian methods which are relatively new compared to maximum likelihood and have experienced great impact, especially through the release of a program called MrBayes [9].

A thorough comparison of popular phylogeny programs using statistical approaches such as fastDNAml [13], MrBayes, PAUP [15], and TREE-PUZZLE [22] on *small* simulated datasets (up to 60 sequences) has been conducted by T.L. Williams *et al* [28]. The most important result of this paper is that MrBayes outperforms all other phylogeny programs in terms of speed and tree quality. However, the results of this survey do not necessarily apply to large real data sets since simulated alignment data has different properties and a significantly stronger phylogenetic signal than real world data (see [20] for a discussion), i.e. typically much more computational effort is required to find a "good" phylogenetic tree for real-world data. Due to these significant differences between real and simulated datasets comparative surveys should include collections of simulated *and* real datasets in order to yield a more complete image of program performance. In fact, there exist some real datasets for which MrBayes fails to converge to acceptable likelihood values within reasonable time [19]. Huelsenbeck *et al* [10] provide an in-depth discussion of potential pitfalls of Bayesian inference.

More recently, Guidon and Gascuel published an interesting paper about their new program PHYML [7], which is very fast and seems to be able to compete with MrBayes. PHYML is a "traditional" maximum likelihood hillclimbing program which seeks to find the optimal tree in respect to the likelihood value. Moreover, the respective performance analysis includes larger simulated datasets of 100 sequences and two well-studied real data sets containing 218 and 500 sequences. Their experiments show that PHYML is extremely fast on real and simulated data. However, the accuracy on real data needs improvement [19]. Moreover, the results show that well-established sequential programs like PAUP* [15], TREE-PUZZLE [22], and fastDNAml [13] are prohibitively slow on datasets containing more than 200 sequences, at least in sequential execution mode.

Vinh *et al* [27] recently published a program called IQPNNI which yields better trees than PHYML on real world data but is significantly slower.

Finally, the current hill-climbing and simulated annealing algorithms implemented in RAxML-V clearly outperform PHYML and IQPNNI on real world data, both in terms of execution time and final tree quality [20].

The main problem which parallel implementations of ML analyses face is that technical development drags behind algorithmic development. This means that programs are parallelized that do not represent the state-of-the-art algorithms any more. Thus, it can be observed that parallel or distributed codes like parallel fastDNAml [21], DPRml [12] (both based on a search algorithm from 1994) or parallel TREE-PUZZLE [18] are just as good as the currently best sequential codes in terms of tree quality. However, they require *significantly* more CPU hours to attain the same results. The above programs have all been parallelized with MPI.

To the best of our knowledge, apart from RAxML-OMP, there exists only one distributed shared-memory implementation of an ML program for NUMA architectures: veryfastDNAml [26] which is based on the TreadMarks library [25]. The veryfastDNAml implementation is also based on the old and slow fastDNAml algorithm from 1994. The technical details of the veryfastDNAml implementation have not been published anywhere such that it is not known if the parallelization is based on loop-level parallelism or a coarse-grained master-worker scheme.

3   RAxML-V

In this Section we provide a brief outline of the basic components and algorithms of RAxML-V, which are required to understand the structure of the parallelization. The program initially computes a starting tree which contains all sequences of the alignment using a fast greedy MP search. The MP search is performed by an appropriately modified version of Joe Felsenstein's dnapars program [17]. One important property of dnapars is that it yields distinct starting trees depending on the input order permutation of the sequences. By randomizing the sequence input order, the program can start the optimization from different points of search space each time it is executed. Therefore, by executing several RAxML-V runs it is more likely to find good trees and avoid local maxima since each run will yield a distinct final tree. Thus, the confidence into the final results obtained by RAxML-V is higher than for strictly *deterministic* programs.

The procedure by which the parsimony score is computed in dnapars is very similar to ML. Thus, the loop-level parallelization of the parsimony component is analogous to that for ML which we describe in more detail in the following Section 4.

After the computation of the parsimony starting tree, the likelihood of the candidate topology is improved by subsequent application of topological alterations. To evaluate and select candidate alternative topologies RAxML-V uses a mechanism called *lazy subtree rearrangements* [19]. This mechanism initially performs a rapid pre-scoring of a comparatively large number of alternative topologies. After the pre-scoring step a few of the best pre-scored topologies are analyzed more thoroughly. The fact, that RAxML-V is currently the fastest *and*

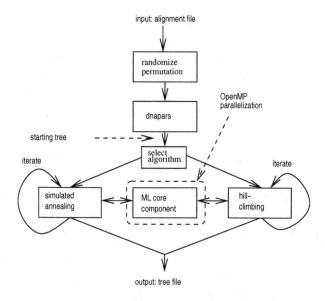

Fig. 2. Basic components of RAxML-V

most accurate program on real alignment data is due to this ability to quickly evaluate (pre-score) a large number of alternative tree topologies. Furthermore, RAxML-V currently implements two basic search procedures which exploit the lazy subtree rearrangement mechanism:

1. A strict hill-climbing procedure which applies lazy subtree rearrangements until the candidate tree can not be improved upon any more [19].
2. A simulated annealing algorithm which is slightly slower than hill-climbing on the one hand but able to escape local maxima on the other hand [20].

Finally, it is important to know that both search algorithms use the same core component to calculate maximum likelihood values, such that the parallelization applies to both search strategies. Figure 2 provides an overview of RAxML-V as described in this Section.

4   Parallelization

The current Section does not intend to provide a detailed introduction to ML for phylogenetic trees. The goal is to give a notion of the complexity and amount of arithmetic operations required to compute the maximum likelihood score for one *single* tree topology. Furthermore, it aims to explain where the intrinsic loop-level parallelism occurs and how it can be exploited.

The seminal paper by Felsenstein [5] which actually introduces the application of ML to phylogenetic trees and the comprehensive and readable chapter by Swofford et al. [23] provide detailed descriptions of the mathematical background and models of nucleotide substitution (see below).

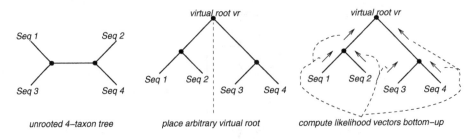

Fig. 3. Computation of the likelihood vectors of a 4-taxon tree

To calculate the likelihood of a tree topology with given branch lengths one requires a probabilistic model of nucleotide substitution $P_{ij}(t)$ which allows for computing the probability P that a nucleotide i (e.g. A) mutates to another nucleotide j (e.g. G) within time t (branch length).

Given the model of nucleotide substitution and an *unrooted* tree topology with fixed branch lengths where the data (the individual sequences of the multiple alignment) is located at the tips, one can proceed with the computation of the likelihood score for that tree. In order to compute the likelihood a *virtual root* (*vr*) has to be placed into an *arbitrary* branch of the unrooted tree in order to calculate/update the individual entries of each *likelihood vector* with length n (alignment length) in the tree bottom-up, i.e. starting at the tips and moving towards *vr*. It is important to note, that the likelihood of the tree is identic irrespectively of where *vr* is placed. After having updated all likelihood vectors the vectors to the right and left of *vr* can be used to compute the overall likelihood value of the tree. The process of rooting and updating the likelihood vectors for a 4-taxon tree is outlined in Figure 3.

To understand how the individual likelihood vectors are updated consider a subtree rooted at node p with immediate descendants r and q and likelihood vectors l_p, l_q, and l_r respectively. When the likelihood vectors l_q and l_r have been computed the entries of l_p can be calculated—in an extremely simplified manner—as outlined by the pseudo-code below and in Figure 4:

```
for(i = 0; i < n; i++)
    l_p[i] = f(g(l_q[i], b_pq), g(l_r[i], b_pr));
```

where f() is a simple function, i.e. requires just a few FLOPs, to combine the values of g(l_q[i], b_pq) and g(l_r[i], b_pr). The g() function however is more complex and computationally intensive since it contains the evaluation of $P_{ij}(t)$. The parameter t corresponds to the branch lengths b_pq and b_pr respectively. Since entries l_p[i] and l_p[i + 1] can be computed *independently* this for-loop can be parallelized by insertion of an appropriate OpenMP directive to exploit the inherent loop-level parallelism:

```
#pragma omp parallel for private(...)
for(i = 0; i < n; i++)
    l_p[i] = f(g(l_q[i], b_pq), g(l_r[i], b_pr));
```

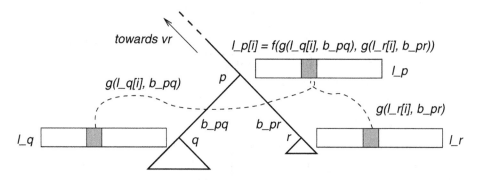

Fig. 4. Updating the likelihood vector of node p at position i

Up to this point it has been described how to compute the likelihood of a tree given some arbitrary branch lengths. However, in order to obtain the *maximum* likelihood value for a given tree topology the length of *all* branches in the tree has to be optimized. Since the likelihood of the tree is not altered by distinct rootings of the tree the virtual root can be subsequently placed into all branches of the tree. Each branch can then be optimized individually to improve the likelihood value of the entire tree. In general—depending on the implementation—this process is continued until no further branch length alteration yields an improved likelihood score. Branch length optimization can be regarded as maximization of a one-parameter function $lh(t)$ where lh is the phylogenetic likelihood function and t the current branch length at vr.

Typically, the three basic operations: computation of the likelihood vectors, optimization of the branch lengths, and computation of the overall likelihood value require $\approx 90\%$ of the complete execution time of every ML implementation. For example 92.72% of total execution time for a typical dataset with 150 sequences in PHYML and 92.89% for the same dataset in RAxML-V. Thus, an acceleration of these functions on a technical level by optimization of the C code, the memory access behavior and consumption, as well as the exploitation of loop-level parallelism can lead to substantial performance improvements. The structure of the loops in the three basic functions is very similar to the abstract pseudocode representation provided above. The main **for**-loops of RAxML have been parallelized in an analogous way.

Memory consumption is becoming a problem for inference of large phylogenetic trees containing more than 1.000 sequences. Table 1 provides some figures for memory requirements of RAxML, PHYML, and MrBayes for large datasets. Note that MrBayes could not handle the 10.000-taxon dataset, even when compiled on a 64-bit architecture. In fact only the sequential RAxML-version could still be executed on a 32-bit processor with this large dataset. The memory requirements of RAxML-V are directly proportional to the alignment size, i.e. $\Theta(n * m)$ where n is the number of sequences and m the number of base pairs (length of the alignment). Figure 5 depicts how the memory allocated by RAxML-OMP is accessed by 2 individual threads, each running on a separate CPU. The situation is particularly favorable because memory accesses are inde-

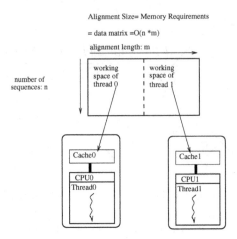

Fig. 5. Memory access scheme of RAxML-OMP

Table 1. Memory consumption of RAxML-III, MrBayes, and PHYML for large data sets

Program	1.000 taxa	10.000 taxa
RAxML-III	200 MB	750 MB
PHYML	900 MB	8.8 GB
MrBayes	1.2 GB	not available

pendent and equally distributed among threads, i.e. *thread 0* in the figure works exclusively on the left half of the data matrix and *thread 1* on the right half.

Thus, we believe that RAxML-OMP provides a viable approach to resolve both memory shortage problems and allow for higher cache efficiency at the same time. It is important to emphasize that memory efficiency is becoming an important issue because evolutionary biology has already entered the whole-genome era. This means that alignments used for phylogenetic analyses will particularly grow in length m which will have typical values of around 10.000 or 20.000 base pairs and do not fit into cache any more. Moreover, inferences of large trees containing more than 1.000 sequences which are now becoming algorithmically feasible also require *long* alignments in terms of m to produce a reliable phylogenetic signal [2]. Finally, RAxML-OMP can serve as a basis for hybrid MPI/OpenMP implementations on constellations of PC-clusters which are widely available nowadays.

5   Results

Initially, we provide a brief description of the test platforms and datasets used in this study. Thereafter, we provide measured speedup values for various platform/dataset combinations and compare the performance on the different SMP architectures.

Test data, platforms and experimental setup: For measuring the efficiency of RAxML-OMP we executed the program on three common SMP architectures: a dual-processor Intel Xeon 2.4GHz with 4 Gbyte of main memory, a quad-processor Intel Itanium2 1.3GHz with 8 Gbyte of main memory, and a quad-processor AMD Opteron 850 2.4 GHz with 8 Gbyte of memory. We used several real world alignment data sets containing 150, 218, 500, and 1.000 taxa (150_SC, 218_RDPII, 500_ARB, 1000_ARB). In addition we generated 3 simulated alignment data sets with 300 sequences (sim300_1000, sim300_5000, sim300_10000) to evaluate the effect of increasing alignment length on program performance. For the sake of completeness we indicate the alignment lengths (# of base pairs) of all datasets we used in Table 2.

Table 2. Alignment lengths

Dataset	# bp	Dataset	# bp
150_SC	1.130	sim300_1000	1.000
218_RDPII	1.847	sim300_5000	5.000
500_ARB	2.751	sim300_10000	10.000
1000_ARB	3.364		

We compiled RAxML-OMP with the native Intel compiler `icc -O3` and the respective OpenMP flags for the Itanium and Xeon architectures. For the Opteron we used the PGI [16] compiler `pgcc -O3`. In order to measure execution times and calculate speedup values we executed RAxML-OMP with 1 and 2 threads on the Xeon, and 1,2, and 4 threads on the Itanium and Opteron processors respectively. We executed 3 runs for each dataset/architecture/number-of-threads combination and report average values. To be able to reproduce comparable results we used a fixed parsimony starting tree. This was achieved by using a standard input sequence permutation order instead of a randomized one. Moreover, we also measured the execution times of the parsimony and maximum likelihood components separately to analyze the efficiency for each part. A separate analysis is of particular interest since the parsimony component exclusively performs integer operations while maximum likelihood performs mainly a large number of floating point operations. Moreover, ML requires approximately 5 times higher per-loop execution times than MP, e.g. for the 150_SC dataset 18.3 μs for one complete iteration of a parsimony `for`-loop and 97.2 μs for an ML `for`-loop[1]

Experimental results: A complete analytical table containing the execution times of *all* experiments conducted within the framework of this study is available

---

[1] These times have been measured on an Intel Centrino.

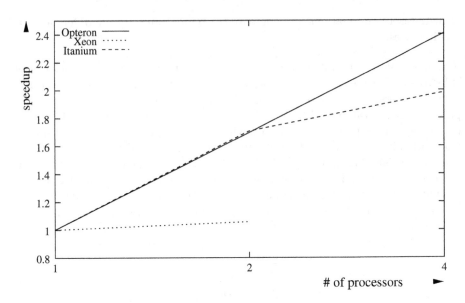

Fig. 6. Speedup on Xeon, Opteron, and Itanium for 218_RDPII

at: wwwbode.in.tum.de/~ottmi/results_jan_05.html. Therefore, we present some representative examples of RAxML-OMP performance.

Figure 6 indicates the speedup values for the relatively small—in terms of alignment length m (see Table 2 and Figure 5)—dataset 218_RDPII on Xeon,

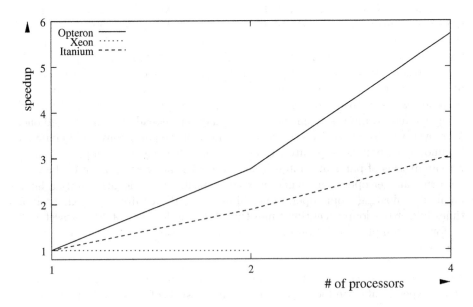

Fig. 7. Speedup on Xeon, Opteron, and Itanium for sim300_10000

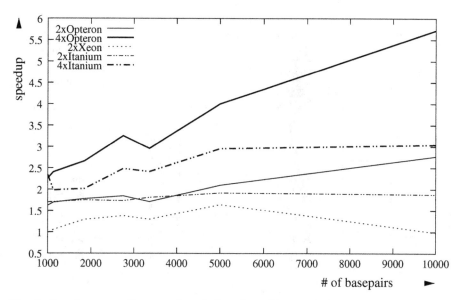

Fig. 8. Speedup over alignment length (number of base pairs) per processor type and number of CPUs

Opteron, and Itanium architectures. The generally better scalability of the Opteron processor is most probably due to the HTT (Hyper Transport Technology [11]) memory access architecture which suits the program structure of RAxML-OMP. However, this issue requires further investigation. On the other hand, due to an unfavorable memory access design the Xeon processor yields only marginal speedups.

Figure 7 provides the speedup values for the sim300_10000 dataset. Though, comparable in size in respect to the number of taxa with 218_RDPII, the length of this alignment and consequently the length of the parallelized for-loops is significantly longer: 10.000 nucleotides = 10.000 iterations (also called base pairs). Note, that the speedup on the AMD Opteron on 2 *and* 4 CPUs is clearly *superlinear* (≈ 2.8 and ≈ 5.6 respectively). This is due to the improved cache efficiency and data locality inherent to RAxML-OMP in conjunction with AMD's HTT and a "long" alignment. In order to demonstrate the impact of alignment length on speedup values in Figure 8 we plot the speedup over the number of base pairs—for all datasets used in this study—per processor type and number of CPUs. The general tendency is that the parallel efficiency increases with alignment length due to the aforementioned reasons on the Opteron. Note, that for an AMD Opteron equipped with significantly less main memory (512MB) and a smaller cache the speedups became already super-linear at significantly lower alignment lengths (≥ 2.000 base pairs). Another point worth mentioning is that a "large" number of taxa n (see Figure 5) in the alignment has a negative effect on speedup-values since the amount of allocated memory increases significantly. This explains the buckling which can be observed at ≈ 3.500 base pairs. This value corresponds to the large—in terms of taxa—1000_ARB dataset. In Fig-

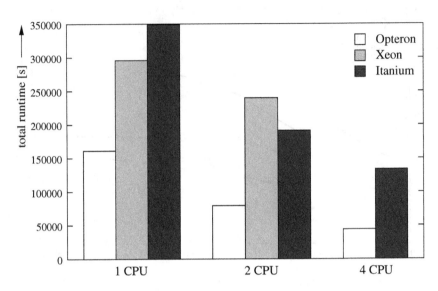

Fig. 9. Accumulated average execution times over all datasets per processor type and number of CPUs

ure 9 we present the accumulated average runtime over all datasets per number of CPUs for the Itanium, Opteron, and Xeon architectures. In all cases RAxML-OMP is at least $\approx 50\%$ faster on Opteron than on the Xeon and Itanium.

Finally, as expected the parallel efficiency of the ML component was significantly better than for MP due to the aforementioned reasons (please refer to the results web-site for exact figures).

6   Conclusion, Availability and Future Work

We have presented an efficient OpenMP parallelization of RAxML-V which scales particularly well on the AMD Opteron SMP architecture. Due to improved cache efficiency and data locality RAxML-OMP yields clearly superlinear speedups for long (in terms of base pairs) datasets on 2-way and 4-way Opteron nodes. Moreover, the current implementation allows for inference of large 1.000-taxon trees on a single Opteron node in less than 6 hours. The program is freely available for download as open source code at www.ics.forth.gr/~stamatak. Currently, we are working on an OpenMP-version of PHYML which faces more serious memory problems than RAxML.

Since scalability of parallel programs which exploit fine-grained loop-level parallelism is limited, future work will mainly cover the implementation of a mixed MPI/OpenMP parallelization of RAxML for hybrid supercomputer architectures. Moreover, the architectural causes for the relatively bad performance of RAxML-OMP on both Intel architectures in comparison to the efficiency on the Opteron need to be further investigated.

References

1. Bader, D.A., Moret, B.M.E., Vawter, L.: Industrial Applications of High-Performance Computing for Phylogeny Reconstruction. Proceedings of SPIE IT-Com: Commercial Applications for High-Performance Computing **4528** (2001) 159–168

2. Bininda-Emonds, O.R.P., Brady, S.G., Sanderson, M.J., Kim, J.: Scaling of accuracy in extremely large phylogenetic trees. Proceedings of Pacific Symposium on Biocomputing (2000) 547–558

3. Bodlaender, H.L., Fellows, M.R., Hallett, M.T., Wareham, T., Warnow, T.: The hardness of perfect phylogeny, feasible register assignment and other problems on thin colored graphs. Theor. Comp. Sci. **244** (2000) 167–188

4. Day, W.E., Johnson, D.S., Sankoff, D.: The computational Complexity of inferring rooted phylogenies by parsimony. Math. Bios. **81** (1986) 33–42

5. Felsenstein, J.: Evolutionary Trees from DNA Sequences: A Maximum Likelihood Approach. J. Mol. Evol. **17** (1981) 368–376

6. Gascuel, O.: BIONJ: An improved version of the NJ algorithm based on a simple model of sequence data. Mol. Biol. Evol. **14** (1997) 685–695

7. Guindon, S., Gascuel, O.: A Simple, Fast, and Accurate Algorithm to Estimate Large Phylogenies by Maximum Likelihood. Syst. Biol. **52(5)** (2003) 696–704

8. Gusfield, D., Eddhu, S., Langley, C.: Efficient Reconstruction of Phylogenetic Networks with Constrained Recombination. Proceedings of 2nd IEEE Computer Society Bioinformatics Conference (2003) 363–371

9. Huelsenbeck, J.P., Ronquist, F., Nielsen, R., Bollback, J.P.: Bayesian Inference and its Impact on Evolutionary Biology. Science **294** (2001) 2310–2314

10. Huelsenbeck, J.P., Larget, B., Miller, R.E., Ronquist, F.: Potential Applications and Pitfalls of Bayesian Inference of Phylogeny. Syst. Biol. **51(5)** (2002) 673–688

11. Hyper Transport Technology: WWW.HYPERTRANSPORT.ORG.

12. Keane, T.M., Naughton, T.J., Travers, S.A.A., McInerney, J.O., McCormack, G.P.: DPRml: Distributed Phylogeny Reconstruction by Maximum Likelihood. Bioinformatics **21(7)** (2005) 969–974

13. Olsen, G., Matsuda, H., Hagstrom, R., Overbeek, R.: fastdnaml: A Tool for Construction of Phylogenetic Trees of DNA Sequences using Maximum Likelihood. Comput. Appl. Biosci.**10** (1994) 41–48

14. OpenMP: WWW.OPENMP.ORG/DRUPAL.

15. PAUP project site: PAUP.CSIT.FSU.EDU.

16. Portland Group High-Performance Compilers and Tools: WWW.PGROUP.COM.

17. PHYLIP downlaod site and list of phylogeny software: EVOLUTION.GENETICS.WASHINGTON.EDU.

18. Schmidt, H.A., Strimmer, K., Vingron, M., Haeseler, A.v.: TREE-PUZZLE: maximum likelihood phylogenetic analysis using quartets and parallel computing. Bioinformatics **18** (2002) 502–504

19. Stamatakis, A., Ludwig, T., Meier, H.: RAxML-III: A Fast Program for Maximum Likelihood-based Inference of Large Phylogenetic Trees. Bioinformatics **21(4)** (2005) 456–463

20. Stamatakis, A.: An Efficient Program for phylogenetic Inference Using Simulated Annealing. Proceedings of 19th International Parallel and Distributed Processing Symposium (2005) to be published

21. Stewart, C., Hart, D., Berry, D., Olsen, G., Wernert, E., Fischer, W.: Parallel Implementation and Performance of fastdnaml - a Program for Maximum Likelihood Phylogenetic Inference. Proceedings of SC2001 (2001)

22. Strimmer, K., Haeseler, A.v.: Quartet Puzzling: A Maximum-Likelihood Method for Reconstructing Tree Topologies. Mol. Biol. Evol. **13** (1996) 964–969
23. Swofford, D.L., Olsen, G.J., Wadell, P.J., Hillis, D.M.: Phylogenetic Inference. Hillis, D.M., Moritz, C., Mabel, B.K., (editors) Molecular Systematics, **Chapter 11** (1996) Sinauer Associates, Sunderland, MA
24. Tang, J., Moret, B.M.E., Cui, L., dePamphilis, C.W.: Phylogenetic reconstruction from arbitrary gene-order data. Proc. 4th IEEE Conf. on Bioinformatics and Bioengineering BIBE'04 (2004) 592–599
25. The TreadMarks Distributed Shared Memory (DSM) System: WWW.CS.RICE.EDU/~WILLY/TREADMARKS/OVERVIEW.HTML
26. VeryFastDNAml: WWW-BIOWEB.PASTEUR.FR/SEQANAL/SOFT-PASTEUR.HTML#VERYFASTDNAML
27. Vinh L.S., Haeseler, A.v.: IQPNNI: Moving fast through tree space and stopping in time. Mol. Biol. Evol. **21(8)** (2004) 1565–1571
28. Williams, T.L., Moret, B.M.E.: An Investigation of Phylogenetic Likelihood Methods. Proceedings of 3rd IEEE Symposium on Bioinformatics and Bioengineering (2003)
29. Williams, T.L., Berger-Wolf, B.M., Roshan, U., Warnow, T.: The relationship between maximum parsimony scores and phylogenetic tree topologies. Tech. Report, **TR-CS-2004-04** (2004) Department of Computer Science, The University of New Mexico

OpenTS: An Outline of
Dynamic Parallelization Approach

Sergey Abramov[1], Alexei Adamovich[1], Alexander Inyukhin[2], Alexander Moskovsky[1],
Vladimir Roganov[1], Elena Shevchuk[1], Yuri Shevchuk[1], and Alexander Vodomerov[2]

[1] Program System Institute, Russian Academy of Sciences, Pereslavl-Zalessky, 152020,
Russia, Yaroslavl Region.
+7 08535 98 064 (phone&fax)
abram@botik.ru
[2] Moscow, 119192, Michurinsky prosp., 1, Institute of Mechanics of MSU, Russia

Abstract. The paper is dedicated to an open T-system (OpenTS) — a
programming system that supports automatic parallelization of computations
for high-performance and distributed applications. In this paper, we describe the
system architecture and input programming language as well as system's
distinctive features. The paper focuses on the achievements of the last two years
of development, including support of distributed, meta-cluster computations.

1 Open T-System Outline

Open T-System (Open TS) is a recent dynamic program parallelization technology for
high-performance and distributed applications. It originates from functional and meta-
programming technologies [1, 2] and tries to achieve maximum performance of
single/multi-processors, supercomputers, clusters and meta-clusters. Another goal was
the development of easy-to-use tools for parallel programming, with high learning
curve and easy legacy code support. With initial implementations of T-system dated
back to nineties and end of eighties of the last century, Open TS is a third generation
of the T-system [3]. The Open TS approach allows addressing in a uniform way
parallel computing problem for mutli-core processors, SMP systems, computational
clusters and distributed systems. As well, Open TS facilitates parallel applications
with non-uniform parallelism grains or parallelism grains defined at runtime.

1.1 Related Work

The Open TS design utilizes many concepts of parallel computing. First of all, it
devises high-level parallelizing approach, while many of them currently exist [4].
Secondly it utilizes an extension of C++ language to express parallelism, while many
other extensions of C and C++ for parallel computing were developed [5]. Thirdly,
the concept of T-system is based upon functional programming approach [1], that
make it very similar to parallel implementations of functional languages [6]. At last,
Open TS runtime implementation utilizes Distributed Shared Memory (DSM) [7],
mutli-tier architecture [8] and C++ template- based design [9]. Here we note
separately only small fraction of all works in this field, not comprehensive but
representative, as we hope:

V. Malyshkin (Ed.): PaCT 2005, LNCS 3606, pp. 303–312, 2005.

1. Charm++ [10] is a C++ extension for parallel computing, which is used to create high-performance codes for supercomputers [11]. Open TS is different in many aspects – from runtime implementation to language semantics. The most important is that Open TS uses functional approach for parallelization, while Charm++ uses asynchronous communication with object-oriented model.
2. mpC++ is another example of successful implementation of "parallel C" for computational clusters and heterogeneous clusters [12]. While mpC uses explicit language constructions to express parallelism, Open TS has implicit parallelization constructs.
3. Cilk is a language for multithreaded parallel programming based on ANSI C [13]. Cilk is designed for shared memory computers only, in contrary Open TS can be run on computational clusters and meta-clusters.
4. Glasgow Parallel Haskell is a well-known extension of Haskell programming language [14]. Open TS is similar with GPH by utilizing some implicit approach to parallelizing computation, while enabling low-level optimization on C++ level, unavailable in Haskell.
5. OMPC++[15] is very similar to Open TS in many aspects, especially in the way of using C++ templates in runtime. However, language extensions are of primary importance for Open TS concept.

While many parallel programming techniques, like Unified Parallel C [16] and CxC [17] are not covered in our comparison, Open TS distinctions will be virtually the same.

1.2 Programming Model

Unlike many tools for parallel programming, T-System does not try to change the usual programming model too much. Native input language is a transparent attribute-based extension of C++; however, other T-dialects of programming languages are in the development stage: T-FORTRAN, T-REFAL. Only two new notions are really important for programming: T-function and T-value. T-values are extensions of basic C values with non-ready value, read access to a non-ready value stops execution of a T-function, unless C-value is provided during computation. T-functions are pure C-functions forming functional model at the top level of program structure. However, imperative C exists inside T-functions enabling potential for low-level optimization. Support for object oriented-model is forthcoming.

An important feature of Open TS is a separation of the computation code from the scheduling code. In Open TS, the programmer is enabled to develop complex strategies for dynamic parallelization without affecting the computational code itself.

1.3 Execution Model

Parallel execution is based on a completely conflict-free data-flow model, and the "macro-scheduling" algorithm distributes computational tasks (active T-functions) over all available computing resources on the fly. Thus, latency hiding should enable very high computational power utilization. Moreover, heterogeneous (e.g. different CPU speeds) computational clusters can be efficiently loaded with that approach.

Special hardware such as application-specific accelerators and processors can be also considered as specific computational resources, it is dynamically loaded in the same way.

Millions of threads[1] can work in a cooperative and conflict-free way enabling latency hiding: any time non-ready T-value is reached, T-System switches rapidly to another ready-to-compute task. In this way, T-System avoids blocking computation in many cases when communication infrastructure permits. In brief, T-System may be a good candidate to fill up the gap between fast recent CPUs and latency-restricted communications.

1.4 T-Applications

T-application is a self-contained, dynamically linked executable. In a nutshell, it recognizes the execution environment and automatically loads a corresponding communication driver on the fly. The execution environment may be one of the following.

- Unicomputer – runs as a single process
- SMP — runs on a machine with symmetric multi processing capabilities
- MPI (6 flavors are supported now, including PACX MPI and MPICH-G2 for the meta-cluster environment)
- PVM.

Thus, T-applications don't need to be recompiled or re-linked for all possible communication flavors. This is important in many cases, especially in meta-clusters with heterogeneous MPI implementations.

2 Open T-System Design Notes

Open T-System runtime has a microkernel-based design. Microkernel, or T-Superstructure, is a central part of the runtime. It contains all essential entities that a typical program needs to be run on. T-Superstructure has a "snowman" architecture of three tiers: `S' ("super-memory" and "super-threads"), `M' (mobile objects and references) and `T' (T-values, variables, references, functions). Being compact in size (less than 5 000 lines in about 100 C++ classes), it suits for various extensions: enhanced task schedulers, memory allocation schemes, custom thread systems, and so on. A special class 'Feature' is used to register extension plug-ins, which are typically dynamically linked at the startup stage. The microkernel can be easily ported to `almost pure' hardware, because it is almost self-contained. C++ [cross] compiler only is required for such porting. However, since C++ templates are used extensively, a modern C++ compiler is required.

Fast context switch is a special feature of Open TS, which is very important for efficient T-applications. Since T-applications are known to create millions of simultaneous threads, fast switching is key important. Today, the T-context switch is 10 times faster than the fastest standard thread library switch.

---

[1] Opens supports the usage of more than one million of threads even in one usual processor — this was shown practically, this was used in real applications.

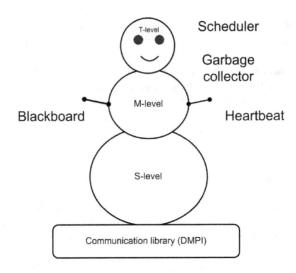

A "Supermemory", or special kind of distributed shared memory, is located outside of program data and used to manage T-values. Novel communication technologies such as hyper-transport can be directly incorporated into the "Supermemory" layer to avoid an unnecessary MPI overhead. Super memory is utilized in six different ways:

1. T-Values
2. Task exchange
3. Resource information exchange
4. Memorization table
5. "Heartbeat" (see below)
6. Shutdown signal

The fault-tolerance support has been implemented with the help of LAM MPI BLCR checkpoint system [18]. It is integrated with the T-System runtime, thus making fault-tolerant computing easier.

Since the T-system originates from the functional programming model, it is possible to implement the fault-tolerance on the base of re-computing of T-functions. This work is forthcoming.

3 Compilation of T-Programs

Two approaches are followed to develop compilers for T++ programs.

The first, "converter", approach utilizes OpenC++ [19] parser to translate a T++ program to a C++ program using Open TS runtime library calls. Advantage of that approach is that the best-of-breed C++ compiler can be used, with the best processor-specific optimization available. The drawback is some C++ syntax features that are not supported seamlessly due to Open C++ limitations.

An alternate, "compiler", approach is based on an open-source GNU C++ compiler. An extra front-end language for T++ has been implemented, it has a smooth and comprehensive support of all C++ language features. However, if the GNU C compiler optimization is not on a par with the other compilers of the target platform, a performance loss might happen.

4 T-Application Development Stages

First of all, T++ is a transparent attribute-based dialect of C++. The T++ code can be trivially mapped to the sequential C++ program by masking T-attributes on the preprocessor stage. To start, the T++ code may be developed and debugged without T-System.

Then, the `t++' compiler may be used to obtain T-executables which should be able to normally run on the unicomputer. Thus, the second stage of the development process is to check whether everything works correctly on the unicomputer — this involves usual testing and debugging for the traditional (one-processor) case.

Furthermore, the same executable may be run on the `cluster emulation'. The simplest way to do this is to use LAM on various Linux systems: the command

```
mpirun n0,0,0,0 <t-executable>
```

will emulate the 4-node cluster. Some tuning can be done at this stage.

Finally, run T-executable on the desired target platform.

5 T-Application Debugging and Tuning

T-System has a number of built-in profiling, tracing and debugging facilities.

First of all, debugging is facilitated by several modes of compilation: "optimized", "normal" and "debug". The "optimized" mode uses the runtime version with heavy optimization. The runtime of the "normal" mode is simplified as compared to the "optimized" version. If an application is compiled in the "normal" mode and a problem persists, it should be attributed to the application itself — not the runtime — with high degree of confidence. Moreover, the "debug" mode generates a large amount of debug output, which helps programmers to understand the current situation in T-runtime and applications. This output can be filtered with the help of regular expressions.

A full-fledged Trace facility has also been implemented for T-applications.

When the program is finished, some statistical data is printed (see figures below). It includes minimal/medium/maximal (depending on computational nodes) values of the following parameters: used CPU time, communication time, idle time. This hot profiling information may be very useful for the tuning of applications.

Communication message logs can be called in order to understand which communication traffic occurred during the program execution. A T-function call graph can also be obtained.

If the program crashes, some information (including program call stack with source line numbers) is printed. Optionally, the debugger is started at the same time, which may be very convenient for a rapid problem discovery.

Finally, a special heartbeat logic is used to discover broken program/communication state. If heartbeat timeout is reached without any data exchange, then all T-processes will exit automatically.

6 Sample Program Run

The example program is the calculation the Fibonacci number. Since it is not very hard computationally, it is a good test for the runtime system, and it illustrates well the simplicity of T++ programming.

```
tfun int fib(int n)
{
        if (n<2) return 1;
        return (fib(n-1)+fib(n-2));
}
tfun int main (int argc, char *argv[])
{
        int n = atoi(argv[1]);
        printf("Fibonacci %d is %d\n",n,(int)fib(n));
        return 0;

}
```

The only T-function is the "fib" function which recursively calls itself. Since the result of "fib" is a non-ready value, explicit casting to **int** is necessary for the program to run correctly. The casting results in the "main" thread wait until the result of "fib" is ready. "fib" recursively calls itself creating a tree, while the tree branches can be computed in parallel.

Compiling the program is possible with either t++ or tg++.

```
t+ -o fib0 fib0.tcc
```

The process of the program execution is illustrated in Fig. 1 (running on single processor) and Fig. 2 (running on four-cluster nodes). You may see some speedup demonstrated by "fib". The example has been a mere illustration that doesn't reflect the real quality of T-system, benchmarking results will be published elsewhere.

```
[alexanderm@skif demos]$ ./fib 29
Open T-System Runtime v3.0, 2003-2004, PSI RAS, Russia.
Running under unicomputer MPI on 1-rank cluster:
  [3.3Gf,3322BM,0.86GiB]
Starting tfun main, good luck!

fib(29) = 514229
Tasks activated:      1664080
Tasks exported:       0
Msgs sent:            0
Async Msgs:           0
Msgs size:            0
Taskboard visits:     1664080
Scheduler time:       2.724
MPI time:             0.000
Idle time:            0.000
Tasks time:           30.260
Total time:           36.897
```

Fig. 1. Sample program run result in console

```
[alexanderm@skif demos]$ mpirun n1,2,3,4 ./fib 29
Open T-System Runtime v3.0, 2003-2004, PSI RAS, Russia.
Running under LAM MPI on 4-rank cluster:
  ([3.1Gf,3060BM,0.86GiB]+[3.1Gf,3060BM,0.49GiB]+[3.1Gf,3060BM,0.86GiB]*2) ~= [1
2.2Gf,12240BM,3.08GiB]
Starting tfun main, good luck!

fib(29) = 514229
Tasks activated:     [407582/416020/420993]
Tasks exported:      [33/35/40]
Msgs sent:           [1534/1577/1639]
Async Msgs:          [0/0/0]
Msgs size:           [114472/118405/124576]
Taskboard visits:    [408080/416657/421748]
Scheduler time:      [1.188/1.219/1.234]
MPI time:            [0.031/0.033/0.035]
Idle time:           [0.011/0.013/0.015]
Tasks time:          [8.942/9.059/9.190]
Total time:          [16.368/16.375/16.380]
```

Fig. 2. Sample program run on multiple cluster nodes

7 T++ Language in a Nutshell

The T++ language is a semantically and syntactically "seamless" extension of C++. The language constructions are enumerated below with short descriptions following them:

tfun — a function attribute which should be placed just before the function declaration. Now, the function cannot represent a class method but must be an ordinary C function. A function with the "tfun" attribute is named "T-function".

tval — a variable type attribute which enables variables to contain a non-ready value. The variable can be cast to the "original" C++-type variable, which makes the thread of execution suspend until the value becomes ready.

tptr — a T++ analogue of C++ pointers which can hold references to a non-ready value.

tout — a function parameter attribute used to specify parameters whose values are produced by the function. This is a T++ analog of the "by-reference" parameter passing in C++.

tct — an explicit T-context specification. This keyword is used for specification of additional attributes of T-entities.

tdrop — a T++ -specific macro which makes a variable value ready. It may be very helpful in optimization when it's necessary to make non-ready values ready before the producer function finishes.

8 Runtime Performance

The detailed performance study of Open TS runtime is out of the current paper scope and will be published elsewhere. However, overall runtime performance and quality is good enough to stimulate many groups outside of Program Systems Institute to develop their own applications with Open TS (see below). Best speedup achieved with image-processing application is approximately 60% of linear speedup on 32-processor computational cluster with Scalable Coherent Interface (SCI) interconnect.

9 Applications

Approximately a dozen of applications have been developed with the help of T-system. Some of them are the following:

- Plasma physics modeling tool
- Aerodynamics simulation package
- Tools for computational modeling in chemistry
- Automatic text categorization package
- Radar image modeling application
- Remote sensing images processing

10 Support

Open T-System is being developed in the Program System Institute of the Russian Academy of Sciences (PSI RAS) as a key technology in the SKIF Super-Computing project.   The system support can be obtained via e-mail: opents@botik.ru (developers' conference).

11 Work in Progress

We are also working on various application-oriented T-libraries. Such libraries are represented as the T++ code (working also in pure C++) and may be used without any knowledge of T++ or even parallel programming at all. Using the C++ inheritance mechanism, an application programmer just needs to define several application-specific methods — virtual functions — to obtain a complete highly-parallel computational component for a custom high-performance application. Other development areas if macro-scheduling schemas for meta-clusters and other distributed systems.

Acknowledgements

This work is supported by joint "SKIF" supercomputing project of Russia and Belarus and basic research grant from Russian Academy of Science program "High-performance computing systems on new principles of computational process organization" and basic research program of Presidium of Russian Academy of Science "Development of basics for implementation of distributed scientific informational-computational environment on GRID technologies".

References

1. Field A.J, Harrison P.: Functional Programming (International Computer Science Series), Addison-Wesley (1988)
2. (a) Turchin V.F.: The concept of a supercompiler Transactions on Programming Languages and Systems.—v .8, N 3 (1986) .292 –325. (b) Ershov A.P., D.,Futamura Yo.,Furukawa K.,Haraldsson A.,Scherlis W.L.:Selected Papers from the Workshop on Partial Evaluation and Mixed Computation. New Generation Computing. v.6 , N 2 –3.
3. (a) Abramov S. M., Adamovich A. I., Kovalenko M. R.: T-system as a programming environment with automatic dynamic support parallelization support. An example with implementation of ray-tracing algorithm Programmirovanie, № 25 (2), 100–107.(in Russian) (b) Abramov S. M., Vasenin V. A. , Mamchits E. E., Roganov V. A.: Slepukhin A.F. Dynamic parallelization of programs based on parallel graph reduction. A software architecture of new T-system version. Proceedings book of MIPHI scientific session, 22-26 January 2001, v. 2, Moscow, 2001. (in Russian)
4. High-level Parallel Programming and Applications Workshop 2003 Proceedings in Parallel Processing Letters , .v. 13, issue 3.
5. Gregory V.: Wilson (Editor), Paul Lu (Ed.) Parallel Programming Using C++ MIT Press, 1996
6. H-W. Loidl , F. Rubio , N. Scaife, K. Hammond , S. Horiguchi , U.Klusik , R. Loogen , G.J. Michaelson , R. Pena , S. Priebe ,A.J. Rebon and P.W. Trinder: Comparing parallel functional languages,: programming and performance. J. of Higher-order and Symbolic Computation, 2003
7. J.B. Carter, D. Khandekar, L. Kamb: Distributed shared memory: where we are and where we should be headed. Fifth Workshop on Hot Topics in Operating Systems (HotOS-V) May 04 - 05, 1995 Orcas Island, Washington
8. M. J. Vianna. E. Silva, S. Carvalho, J. Kapson,: In Proceedings of the 2nd European Conference on Pattern Languages of Programming (EuroPLoP '97). Siemens Technical Report 120/SW1/FB. Munich, Germany: 1997
9. Andrei Alexandrescu.: "Modern C++ Design: Generic Programming and Design Patterns Applied" , Addison Wesley Professional., ISBN: 0201704315;2001
10. L. V. Kaleev, Sanjeev, Krishnan :Charm++: Parallel Programming with Message-Driven Objects. In [5] 175-213
11. James C. Phillips Gengbin Zhengy Sameer Kumary Laxmikant V. Kaley :NAMD: Biomolecular Simulation on Thousands of Processors. In: Supercomputing 2002 conference proceedings http://sc-2002.org/paperpdfs/pap.pap277.pdf
12. Alexey Lastovetsky: mpC - a Multi-Paradigm Programming Language for Massively Parallel Computers, ACM SIGPLAN Notices, 31(2):13-20, February 1996
13. Cilk: Efficient Multithreaded Computing by Keith H. Randall. Ph. D. Thesis, MIT Department of Electrical Engineering and Computer Science. June 1998. http://supertech.lcs.mit.edu/cilk/
14. Pointon R.F. Trinder P.W. Loidl H-W.: The Design and Implementation of Glasgow distributed Haskell: IFL'00 - 12th International Workshop on the Implementation of Functional Languages, Aachen, Germany (September 2000) Springer Verlag LNCS 2011, pp 53-70
15. Yukihiko Sohda, Hirotaka Ogawa, Satoshi Matsuoka OMPC++ - A Portable High-Performance Implementation of DSM using OpenC++ Reflection. Lecture Notes In Computer Science; Vol. 1616 pp 215-234   Proceedings of the Second International Conference on Meta-Level Architectures and Reflection , 1999,

16. F. Cantonnet, T. El-Ghazawi: UPC Performance and Potential: A NPB Experimental Study, in Supercomputing 2002 conference proceedings   http://sc-2002.org/paperpdfs/pap. pap316.pdf
17. CxC Programmer's Manual. Engineering Intelligence Corporation, 2004, available at http://www.engineeredintelligence.com/
18. Sankaran S. , Squyres J.M. , Barrett D., Lumsdaine A. , Duell J. , Hargrove P. Roman E. The LAM/MPI Checkpoint/Restart Framework: System-Initiated Checkpointing, Proceedings, LACSI Symposium, October 2003, Sante Fe, New Mexico, USA.
19. Chiba S. A Metaobject Protocol for C++ , In: Proceedings of the ACM Conference on Object-Oriented Programming Systems, Languages, and Applications (OOPSLA), page 285-299, October 1995.http://www.csg.is.titech.ac.jp/~chiba/openc++.html

NumGrid Middleware: MPI Support for Computational Grids[1]

D. Fougere[†], M. Gorodnichev[‡], N. Malyshkin[‡], V. Malyshkin[‡],
A. Merkulov[‡], and B. Roux[†]

[‡] Institute of Computational Mathematics and
Mathematical Geophysics (ICM&MG),
Russian Academy of Sciences,
pr.Lavrentieva 6, 630090, Novosibirsk, Russia
{maxim, nikmal, malysh, merkulov}@ssd.sscc.ru
[†] L3M / UMR 6181 CNRS-Universités d'Aix-Marseille,
38, Rue Frédéric Joliot-Curie,
13451 Marseille cedex 20
{broux, fougere}@l3m.univ-mrs.fr

Abstract. The paper presents the design and the first stage of implementation of the NumGRID middleware that is devoted to the development of the multicomputer grid software for the large scale numerical simulation. Global addressing of the NumGRID computational resources and MPI programs execution is provided. This stage is the basis for the development of supporting system that automatically provides the dynamic properties of MPI applications.

1 Introduction

With evolution of mathematical modeling and creation of high-performance computer systems, many scientific applications have appeared that demands increasing computational performance, higher than any of available supercomputers can provide. In particular, for the super large scale numerical modeling it is necessary to integrate several supercomputers, i.e., to create a grid. Not any application can be well solved on grids because of slow communications. However, such application problems as search for alien civilizations [1] and decoding the human genome are successfully running on grids.

Another problem is rapid progress in microprocessor development which forces us to use heterogeneous computer systems for solution of the large scale problems. In particular, in 2005 the ICM&MG plans to exploit the following multicomputers: the 32 processors MVS-1000, based on the alpha microprocessor (833 Mhz), the 128 processors MVS-1000, based on the alpha microprocessor (633 Mhz) and the 60 processors HP cluster, based on the Intel Itanium II microprocessor. Therefore, there is a necessity to create the software that will provide the large-scale simulation in het-

---

[1] This work is partially supported by the grants of NWO-RFBS contracts NWO-RFBS 047.016.007; NWO-RFBS 047.016.018; Russian Fund for basic research, contract RFBR 04-01-00272 and PhD grant from the French Ministere Education Nationale (MEN-DRIC).

V. Malyshkin (Ed.): PaCT 2005, LNCS 3606, pp. 313–320, 2005.
© Springer-Verlag Berlin Heidelberg 2005

erogeneous environments. For now, numerous GRID projects oriented to different applications are under development [1-5].

The speed of communication is permanently growing and now it is possible to organize numerical simulation on GRID of multicomputers. In 2004, the co-operative project NumGRID intended for the creation of the necessary grid system software started in Novosibirsk (ICM&MG) and in Marseille (L3M, CNRS) [6].

2 Objectives

The main objective of the NumGRID project is to provide the use of remote multicomputers for large-scale numerical simulation. In the coming years the proper computational resources for simulation of protoplanetary disc evolution and galaxy formation [7,8] should be provided. These models, developed in the frame of the project, devoted to the investigation of the germ of the life on the Earth, demand practically unlimited resources for simulation.

Another objective is to provide the exploitation of the heterogeneous net of multicomputers for numerical simulation.

3 Basic Requirements

NumGRID requirements provide the conditions for supporting high performance execution of application MPI programs of numerical modeling. These requirements are:

1. Homogeneous nodes multicomputers only are included into NumGRID.
2. Each node of a multicomputer can be an SMP system (2 processors or more)
3. MPI programs should be executed on NumGRID without corrections. Global addressing of all the NumGRID resources should be provided.
4. Automatic providing of the dynamic properties of application programs (tunability, dynamic load balancing, program execution monitoring, reliability)
5. Security and safety of calculations on the Grid

4 Stages of the Project

Design and implementation of the NumGRID project is done in several stages. The first one includes:

- implementation of all the basic means of resource and job management,
- providing communication layer for sending messages between computational nodes of different multicomputers (clusters),
- implementation of MPI over this layer.

Thus, the first stage of NumGRID project, NumGRID-I, allows running MPI-jobs on several clusters. If dynamic properties of application are programmed then these properties will be also provided by NumGRID-I software.

The second stage includes a number of "assembler" level tool that facilitate programming of dynamic properties of application program. This tool includes the library for programming dynamic resources allocation, manager of dynamic memory and means of processes synchronization and monitoring. Thus, the second stage provides automation of programming of dynamic resources allocation, monitoring of the execution of application parallel program, dynamic redistribution of workload, tunability of application programs to all the available resources.

On the third stage the high level asynchronous programming system intended for use in numerical modeling should be developed.

The rest of this paper describes the design and implementation of the NumGRID-I.

5 Related Work

Here, we describe and discuss some more or less known Grid-enabled MPI[9,10] libraries and other solutions that could be employed to run MPI programs on grids. Some of them are more suitable for running MPI programs on Grids than others, but any of them either contains hard restrictions or is only a test prototype.

MPICH-G2 [11] is a well-known grid-enabled MPI library from Globus Toolkit. The main restriction is that all worker nodes inside clusters should have public IP addresses (not from private networks) and have a possibility to be addressed from outside the cluster.

MPICH-MAD III [12]. This is french grid-enabled MPI library. The restrictions are:

- The source code is based on MPICH1.2.x. There is no support for other versions of MPICH
- MPICH (v 1.2.x) is only supported. There is no support for other MPI libraries, for example, LAM-MPI, SCALI MPI, MPICH2
- There are problems with compilation, the system functioning is not stable.

MP-MPICH [13]. The restrictions are:

- The source code is based on MPICH1.2.0. There is no support for other versions of MPICH
- The last version appeared three years ago.
- Myrinet and SCI cards are not supported
- MPICH (v 1.2.x) is only supported. There is no support for other MPI libraries, for example LAM-MPI, SCALI MPI, MPICH2

PACX-MPI [14]. The restrictions and problems are:

- The software is buggy (compiling, working with sockets, etc)
- There should be two special gateway nodes in every cluster that uses PACX MPI. These nodes are involved in MPI topology (+ 2 MPI_Size) and should have the same network interfaces as worker nodes. Thus, master node cannot be used as a gateway. This leads to several problems in cluster development and maintenance.

Virtual Private Networks, SSH tunneling, NAT etc. These solutions are very inefficient because tunneling mechanisms know nothing about the topology of MPI tasks.

6 NumGRID Approach

One of the problems of MPI use on global grids is that all the multicomputers restrict access to their internal nodes from outside. Thus, MPI packets cannot reach their addresses.

The initial idea of NumGRID-I is the following. A special program is loaded into master-nodes of all the multicomputers included into the NumGRID. This program is called MPI_gateway. This program is actually a gateway service for the MPI-packets routing. MPI_gateway provides receiving and sending packets to the internal (private) nodes of any NumGRID multicomputer. MPI_gateway transfers MPI packets from the internal nodes of a multicomputer (Cluster 1) to the MPI_gateway installed on the master of another multicomputer (Cluster 2). Later the second MPI_gateway transfers the received MPI messages to its internal nodes (inside cluster 2)

Another part of the NumGRID software is a special NumGRID_MPI library with an opportunity to send messages not only within a local network, but also through MPI_gateway server to global networks. We proceed from the assumption that there are some MPI libraries pre-installed on each cluster/SMP-system. Usually these MPI libraries are installed by the cluster's vendors and are well optimized (for example SCALI MPI). Therefore, it is desirable that application programs use these optimized MPI libraries. Implementing this idea, the NumGRID_MPI library should be actually a "wrapper" of the pre-installed MPI functions. That is, inside a component of a grid (clusters and/or the SMP), all messages are transferred using pre-installed MPI library, and all messages "outside" are transferred using the developed NumGRID_MPI library through MPI_gateway.

7 Implementation of NumGRID-I

NumGRID software is developed as a cross-platform environment that can be freely used on different hardware and with different operating systems. As the first NumGRID software implementation is done for the GRID of clusters both terms "multicomputer" and "cluster" are used here equally.

For now the NumGRID software was tested on:

Processors: Intel Celeron/P3, AMD Athlon, Alpha
OS: Windows 2000/XP, Red Hat Linux
Compilers: Visual C++ 6.0, VS.NET, GNU C++
MPI implementations: MPICH, LAM-MPI

The NumGRID software consists of 6 components: 1).NumGRID_MPI library, 2).NumGRID_gateway, 3).Cluster management module, 4).Client module (console tools & IDE), 5).Security subsystem

NumGRID_MPI library is a set of "wrappers" for the pre-installed MPI functions.

NumGRID_gateway is the service for transferring MPI packages inside and outside of the NumGRID clusters.

Cluster management module allows NumGRID software to use the static cluster facilities such as starting users' jobs, data transfer to/from clients, allocation of resources and so on. The module can work with commonly used system software that manages cluster's queue. The first queue management systems that are supported are PBS, SGE (Sun Grid Engine) and MVS1000. This module is very close to Globus job-managers modules [3].

Client module (console tools & IDE). It is a cross-platform environment that unifies the process of running computational jobs on NumGRID. Jobs of the NumGRID can be represented as a set of source files, executable modules, data files, lists of computational resources on which these jobs can be run.

The algorithm of jobs running on NumGRID looks as follows:

- Copy source files to all remote multicomputers
- Compilation of the user's application on each multicomputer (if they have the same architecture it is possible to compile only once)
- Copy data files that are required by user's program (input)
- Run all the processes on all the multicomputers
- Get the program's result to the user's local host

For controlling of this operations sequence, a scenario for every user's job should be written. Program scenario includes: user's program source files description, compiling process description, running jobs description, input/output data files description, resources specifications and a specification of results gathering process.

Every scenario file has a blocked structure. Every block describes the job behavior on a separate multicomputer. Inside a block a specific for these multicomputer settings are described. There are also global directives that affect the whole grid. The jobs scenario file is similar to Globus .RSL files but contains additional, specific to NumGRID tags. The client module supports Windows and Unix platforms, graphical IDE is based on QT.

Security subsystem. One of the key moments when carrying out numerical experiments on grid is security providing. Current version of NumGRID security subsystem is based on Kerberos. Kerberos allows to carry out identification of network services and users. Each multicomputer that is planned to be included into NumGRID, should have Kerberos control center and be controlled by the network service, which can be accessed only by the users, registered in Kerberos. It is important, that access to Kerberos center should be closed for all except the master nodes of NumGRID clusters.

8   Experiments

A number of experiments have been carried out with the current implementations of MPI-gateway and grid-enabled MPI library. The experiments were

1. to demonstrate the possibility to run MPI-programs with the MPI-processes spread over several clusters using NumGRID software;
2. to reveal the problems, which could appear on the way.

Three clusters were involved in testing of NumGRID software. Two of them, namely Scali and CHOEUR, are interconnected with the Gigabit Ethernet network of L3M laboratory of CNRS-d'Aix-Marseille university. The third one, P2chpd-cluster, is located at UFR de Mecanique of the University of Lyon.

Cluster name	Choeur	Scali	P2chpd-cluster
Intranetwork	Fast Ethernet	SCI Dolphin	SCI Dolphin
Hosts	2 processors AMD Athlon MP 2000+ (1.67 GHz), Mem. 2Gb	2 proc. AMD Athlon MP 1800+ (1.5 GHz), Mem. 1Gb	2 proc. AMD Athlon MP 2000+ (1.67 GHz), Mem. 2Gb
Computational nodes	2 proc. AMD Athlon MP 1.53 GHz, Mem. 1Gb	2 proc. AMD Athlon MP 1800+ (1.5 GHz), Mem. 1Gb	2 proc. AMD Athlon MP 2000+ (1.67 GHz), Mem. 1Gb
Number of computational nodes	20	5	40

Test 1. Shift of data along the virtual circle of MPI-processes

Description: Each process with the rank R passes some double precision numbers to a process with the rank (R+1) mod P, where P is the number of processes.

Purpose: This is a simple example of MPI-program, which should demonstrate the capability of NumGRID software to support basic MPI communications.

Algorithm: For the sake of simplicity, the P is assumed to be even. First, all the processes with even ranks send their data to their "right" neighbors, and then odd-ranked processes do the same.

Result: This was the first test to try. It has been passed successfully for P=2,4,6,8 with different distributions of processes between Choeur and Scali and between Choeur and P2chpd-cluster. There were no problems with the Choeur and Scali. The same for the Choeur and P2chpd-cluster took a lot of efforts and time to achieve an agreement on policies of firewalls between these two clusters.

Test 2. Each process receives data from each other process

Description: In turns, the processes receive messages from all the other processes. The messages are ordered by the increasing rank of sending processes.

Purpose: This test demonstrates that NumGRID implementation of MPI keeps the supposed order of incoming messages.

Algorithm:

```
for i from 0 to P-1
    {if R equals I
        {for j from 0 to P-1:
            if not j equals R,
                receive a message from the process with rank j}
        else,
            send a message to the process with rank i
    }
```

Result: The test has passed for 2, 4, 6 and 8 processes distributed (in different combinations) between Choeur and Scali and between Choeur and P2chpd-cluster. All the messages have been received in the expected order.

Test 4. Speed of communication (O. Bessonov's test)

Description: The test is composed of several series of data exchanges between MPI-processes. The difference between the series lies in the number of exchange operations and the size of the messages. The results are given as the average speed observed during a series, i.e. the ratio of transferred data volume (Mbytes) in the series to the time the series took. The time of a series comprises not only the time of data transfer but also latencies, the time while the processes are waiting for each other and other overheads. O.Bessonov published the results of his experiments on Scali and Choeur in [15].

Purpose: The time costs of a series of data exchanges are studied depending on the number of exchanges and the sizes of the messages.

Algorithm: Exchanges are carried out in series. Within a series, two processes send messages to and receive from each other in turns. The parameters of the series are presented in the table, see Results section.

Results: The results again demonstrate the great difference between intra-cluster and inter-cluster communication speeds and show the role of latencies. The communication scheme is typical for numerical iterative computations.

Series	Number of send-recv pairs	Message size, in 8 bytes numbers	Amount of transfer for the series, Mbytes	Speed of communications, Mbytes/sec		
				Nodes of Choeur	Choeur-Scali	Choeur-P2chpd
1	8192	64	8	5.66	0.010	0.010
2	4096	128	8	8.48	0.019	0.014
3	2048	256	8	13.71	0.032	0.029
4	1024	512	8	22.92	0.064	0.058
5	5120	1024	80	33.74	0.12	0.11
6	2560	2048	80	44.27	0.85	0.76
7	1280	4096	80	51.33	1.41	0.62
8	640	8192	80	54.54	0.93	0.71

Test 5. Parallel implementation of the explicit Poisson solver

Description: Solution of 2D Poisson equation with the finite differences explicit 5-point stencil scheme. It is one of the simplest examples of the somewhat real computational problem.

Purpose: This test demonstrates how NumGRID software copes with the execution of the computational MPI-program.

Algorithm: Data-partitioning parallelisation of the explicit scheme on a virtual line of processors.

Results: Test successfully passed for 2, 4, 6 and 8 processes. The correctness of data transfers has been demonstrated. When the size of the mesh (that is equal actually to the size of the problem) is large enough, good speed up can be observed when calculations begin to dominate over communications.

9 Conclusions and Future Work

A lot of firewalls between clusters make great administrative problems. This is because NumGRID uses TCP protocol for communications between host machines and most of the TCP ports are closed by the firewalls. The solution is to use some standard communication services that are always open. The most widely used is SSH protocol and it is desirable to use in NumGRID two transport subsystems.

The measurements of communications speed between differently located processes reveal the ultimate heterogeneity of the target computer system. It is important to note that the performance of different nodes is different as well. Moreover, in a general setting, nodes might be of different architectures. The later should be taken into account when NumGRID_MPI is designed and implemented. Also, the heterogeneity of the network and processor elements should be taken in to account when application programs to be run on such a computer system are developed.

This work was scheduled in such a way in order to start NumGRID software exploitation on ICM&MG + NSU, L3M Marseille + UFR Lyon clusters as soon as possible. Now our main efforts are concentrated on the implementation of the executive subsystem.

References

1. SETI program, http://setiathome.berkeley.edu
2. European CrossGrid TestBed, http://cgi.di.uoa.gr/~xgrid/archive.htm
3. European DataGrid , http://eu-datagrid.web.cern.ch/eu-datagrid/
4. LHC Grid, http://lcg.web.cern.ch/LCG/
5. Globus Toolkit, www.globus.org
6. D.Fougere, N.V.Malyshkin, V.E.Malyhskin, B.Roux. The NumGRID metacomputing system. Bulletin of the Novosibirsk Computing Center, p.57-69. NCC Publisher. Novosibirsk.2004.
7. Snytnikov V.N., Dudnikova G.I., Gleaves J.T., Nikitin S.A., Parmon V.N., Stoyanovsky V.O., Vshivkov V.A., Yablonsky G.S., Zakharenko V.S. Space chemical reactor of protoplanetary disk // Adv. Space Res., V. 30, No. 6, pp. 1461-1467, 2002.
8. V.N.Snytnikov, V.A.Vshivkov, E.A.Kuksheva, E.V.Neupokoev, S.A.Nikitin, A.V.Snytnikov. Three-Dimensional Numerical Simulation of a Nonstationary Gravitating N-Body System with Gas // Astronomy Letters, v. 30, no. 2, pp.124-138, 2004.
9. MPI standard, http://www-unix.mcs.anl.gov/mpi/
10. MPICH, http://www-unix.mcs.anl.gov/mpi/mpich/
11. MPICH-G2, http://www.hpclab.niu.edu/mpi/
12. MPICH-MAD III http://dept-info.labri.fr/~mercier/mpi.html
13. MP-MPICH http://www.lfbs.rwth-aachen.de/content/mp-mpich
14. PACX-MPI http://www.hlrs.de/organization/pds/projects/pacx-mpi/
15. O.Bessonov, D.Fougere, B.Roux. Using a Parallel CFD Code for Evaluation of Clusters and MPPs. / Proceedings of IPDPS, 2003, p.65-73, Nice, France. IEEE, PR01926, 2003.

A Practical Tool for Detecting Races in OpenMP Programs*

Young-Joo Kim,[1] Mi-Young Park,[1] So-Hee Park,[2] and Yong-Kee Jun[1,**]

[1] Gyeongsang National University, Jinju
jun@gsnu.ac.kr
[2] Kyungsung University, Busan,
Tel +82-55-751-5996, Fax +82-55-762-1944,
South Korea
heeya@star.ks.ac.kr

Abstract. Detecting data races or just *races* is important for debugging OpenMP programs, because races result in unintended nondeterministic executions of the program. The previous tool to detect the races in OpenMP programs monitors a serial execution of the program, but unfortunately cannot guarantee to verify the existence of races even in the programs only with the directives. This paper presents a practical tool which monitors a parallel execution of standard OpenMP program, and not only verifies the existence of races but also detects first races for each shared variable in the programs.

1 Introduction

It is still more difficult to debug the industry-standard OpenMP programs [2] than sequential programs because of unintended nondeterministic executions incurred by the notorious parallel program bugs, called *data races* or shortly *races* [11]. A race is a pair of instructions in a set of parallel threads accessing a shared variable with at least one write-access without appropriate inter-thread coordination.

Traditional cyclic debugging with breakpoints is not often effective in the presence of races, because the breakpoints can change the execution timing causing the erroneous behavior to disappear. The previous tool [4] to detect the races in OpenMP programs monitors a serial execution of the program, but unfortunately cannot guarantee to verify the existence [3,12] of races even in the programs only with the directives.

This paper presents a practical tool called *RaceStand* which monitors a parallel execution of standard OpenMP program, and not only verifies the existence of races but also detects first races [1,10] for each shared variable in the programs. RaceStand is based on scalably efficient techniques of on-the-fly race detection,

---

* This work was supported in part by IT Leading R&D Support Project funded by Ministry of Information and Communication, Republic of Korea.
** In Gyeongsang National University, he is also involved in the Research Institute for Computer and Information Communication (RICIC).

V. Malyshkin (Ed.): PaCT 2005, LNCS 3606, pp. 321–330, 2005.

```
        . . .
C$OMP PARALLEL DO
C$OMP+PRIVATE(I)
      DO I = 2, N
          . . .
          IF (X(I-M) .EQ. ···) ···
          IF (···) X(I) = ···
          X(I+M) = ···
          . . .
      ENDDO
C$OMP END PARALLEL DO
        . . .
```

Fig. 1. An OpenMP Parallel Program

and can be accessed remotely via the web interface of the Internet through the client-server relationship between programmers and RaceStand.

The following section first introduces the issues on debugging races in shared-memory parallel programs, and then Section 3 explains the practical techniques employed in RaceStand to detect the races occurred in an execution instance of OpenMP program. Section 4 presents the web-based structure of RaceStand to preprocess the debugged programs and monitor their execution instances remotely through client-server relationship. The final section concludes our work suggesting some future work.

2   Background

An industry-standard OpenMP program [2] may include a set of compiler directives and runtime routines for parallel loops and two kinds of inter-thread coordination: PARALLEL DO directive to fork a thread team, END PARALLEL DO directive for a team to join, BARRIER directive to synchronize all at once, and CRITICAL/ORDERED directive or locking routines to create critical sections. We consider that event synchronization may be defined as user-defined routines. The *nesting level* of an individual loop is equal to one plus the number of enclosing outer loops; a loop may enclose zero or more disjoint loops at the same level. The *nesting depth* of a loop is the maximum nesting level of the loop. In Figure 1, the forked threads share the work specified with the DO statement and the loop body, where the index variable I is private to each thread, and two variables {N, M} and one array X are shared among the threads.

The most serious problem of effective OpenMP programming is that it is more difficult to debug the parallel programs than sequential programs for uni-processor computers. Such the difficulty is mainly caused by unintended nonde-terministic executions of parallel programs which are incurred by uncoordinated parallel threads accessing a shared variable with at least one write-access. Such a kind of behaviors are called *data race* or shortly *race* [11] which is the most notorious kind of bugs in parallel programs including OpenMP programs. This program shown in Figure 1 have data races depending on the values of N and M. For example, consider the case in which the value of M is 1 and the two IF-conditions of each thread are satisfied in such the case that I is 2 and 3. The first thread with I = 2 may perform one read access to X(1) and then two write accesses to X(2) and X(3). The second thread with I = 3 may perform one read access to X(2) and then two write accesses to X(3) and X(4). In this case, the execution instance involves two data races between the two parallel threads, because these two uncoordinated parallel threads may access shared variables X(2) and X(3) with at least one write-access, respectively. Theses data races result in the nondeterministic values of X(2) and X(3).

It is ineffective to use traditional breakpoints for detecting data races, because the breakpoints can make the execution timing interfered and then may make erroneous behaviors disappear. Most parallel debuggers are not effective to detect data races either, but often resorts only on programmer's ability. To dynamically detect threading errors including data races in the *relaxed sequential programs* which is parallelized with only OpenMP directives, the *projection technology* [4] of Intel Thread Checker compiles the program with binary instrumentation to analyzes threading errors while every instruction in the program is executed, and then monitors a *serial execution* of the instrumented program to project the parallel memory traces of logical threads derived from the annotated sequential memory trace that is treated as the specification for the OpenMP program. However, Thread Checker cannot guarantee to verify the existence [3,12] of races even in such the programs only with the directives, because it cannot discriminate a logical thread with its parent or children in nested parallelism.

As in all kinds of debugging process, locating and eliminating the first races [1,7,11] is also important in debugging parallel programs, because the removal of such races may make other races disappear. Intuitively, the races that occurred first are the races between two accesses that are not causally preceded by any other accesses also involved in races. The functionality for detecting first races also has the property of race verification, because there does not exist a race in an execution if and only if there does not exists a first race in the execution. However, it is preferable to verify the races appropriately, since the indefinite iterations of detecting first races must incur still greater monitoring overhead than verifying races in parallel programs which are usually large in the scale of their execution time.

3   The Practical Techniques

This paper presents a practical race detection tool called RaceStand which is based on on-the-fly techniques and then requires still less storage space than post-mortem trace analysis. In order to detect races, we determine during the monitored execution if a thread's access to a shared variable is logically concurrent with any previous accesses to this variable and results in a race. This requires monitoring the parallel threads accessing shared variables, and maintaining an *access history* for each shared variable during an execution instance of program. We call this monitoring algorithm the *race detection protocol* [1,3,8,12,13]. For this protocol to operate whenever an access to a shared variable occurs, we need to determine the logical concurrency between the current thread and each previous thread in the access history of the variable. This logical concurrency between

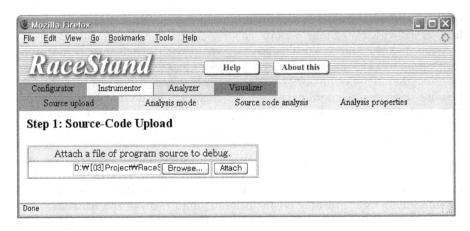

Fig. 2. The User Interface of RaceStand Step 1

two threads is determined from on-line information of each thread, called the *thread label*. A thread label is generated by the *labeling algorithm* [5,12,14] on each thread operation such as fork/join operation or each inter-thread coordination such as barrier operation, and may be stored in the access history of the corresponding shared variable.

Previous on-the-fly tools often show the serious on-line labeling bottleneck which is incurred from using a centralized data structure which is globally-shared among the threads. RaceStand is based on the scalable labeling schemes [5,14] which generate each label of the newly created threads using only the private labels of the parent threads. And, another drawback of existing on-the-fly race-debugging tools is the serious bottleneck of run-time protocol which is incurred from serializing all accesses to the same shared access history. RaceStand is based on access filtering schemes [6,8] which examine to filter the current access if it is possible to be involved in a first race.

RaceStand supports two kinds of effective techniques for debugging races: verifying [3,12] the existence of races, and locating the first races [1,7,8,9,10,13] appeared in an execution instance of program with nested parallelism and inter-thread coordination by barriers [7,8], critical sections [10], and event synchronization [1,9,13]. For the programs with explicit event synchronization, one technique [9] for RaceStand restructures the monitored program to generates the corresponding sequential program which preserves the semantics of the original program. Monitoring an execution instance of the restructured program uses either the two-pass [13] or multi-pass [1] detection protocol to detect the first races in the corresponding execution instance of the original program. Although the two-pass protocol works only for the programs with ordered synchronization, it can detect the first races in the restructured programs with the event synchronization, because any pair of the corresponding points of the event synchronization are executed in an ordered sequence in the corresponding execution of the sequential program.

The storage space consists of two components: the space to store access histories for all shared variables monitored, and the space to store thread labels of

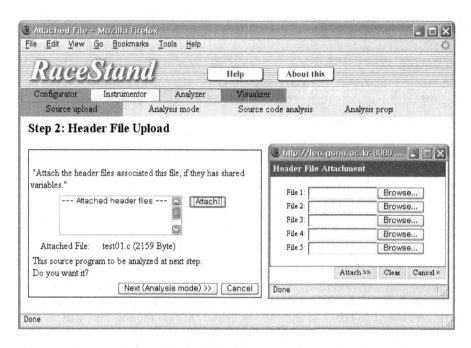

Fig. 3. The User Interface of RaceStand: Step 2

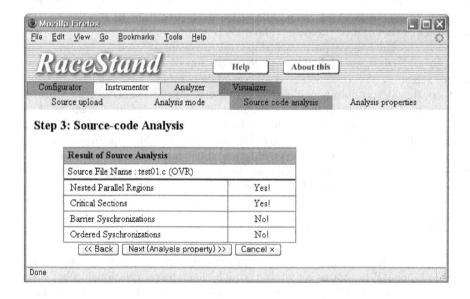

Fig. 4. The User Interface of RaceStand: Step 3

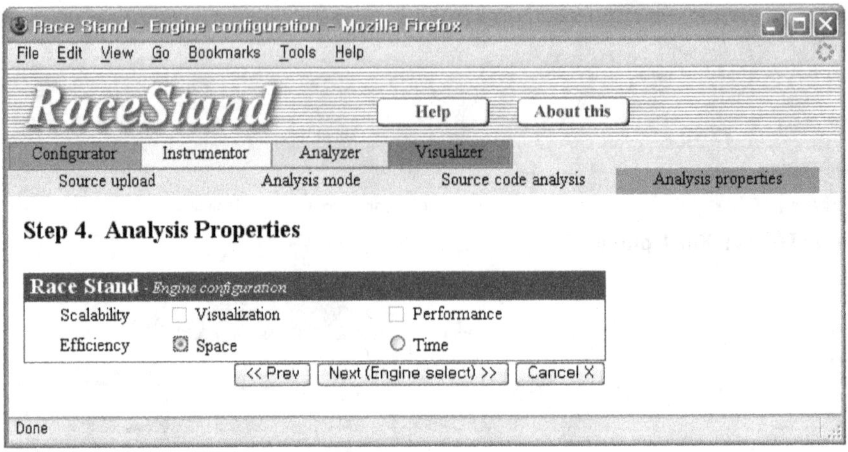

Fig. 5. The User Interface of RaceStand: Step 4

simultaneously active threads. RaceStand basically stores a constant-sized label generated by scalable labeling schemes [5,14] in each entry of access histories, and stores only two labels in each access history in case of programs with nested parallelism and no other inter-thread coordination. We may monitor programs in the canonical sequential order to store only one thread label for simultaneously active threads. For the programs even with explicit event synchronization, RaceStand supports a practical technique [9] which restructures the monitored program to generates the corresponding sequential program which preserves the semantics of the original program. The detection time consists of two main components: the time to perform race detection protocol at each access, and the time to perform thread labeling on every creation of threads in the execution. Since each entry of access history is a thread label and every access performs the protocol that determines logical concurrency with a previous access, the time to perform race detection protocol mainly depends on the labeling scheme used.

RaceStand is based on two efficient labeling schemes [5,14]: *T-BD Labeling* used for all cases of monitored programs, and *NR Labeling* optimized for the programs without inter-thread coordination. The time consumed by these two labeling schemes each depends only on the maximum nesting depth of the program that has no inter-thread coordination.

4   The Structure and Interface

We have been developing a web-based RaceStand to make it practical to debug races in OpenMP programs remotely through client-server relationship between programmers and RaceStand. Its web interface is implemented with Java Server Pages (JSP) to serve the user at the client site and execute the commands received from the client at the server site.

JSP technology enables rapid development of Web-based applications that are platform independent, and separates the user interface from content gener-

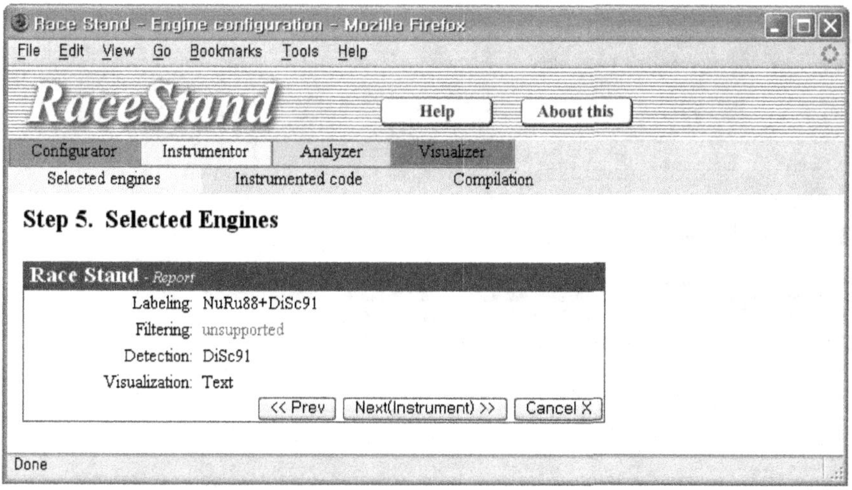

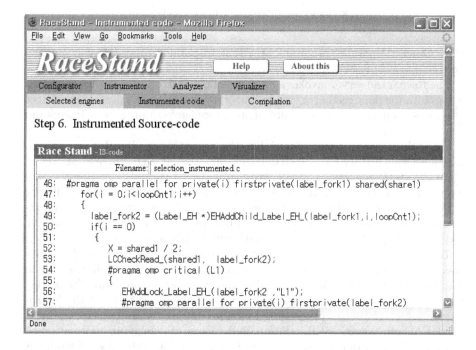

Fig. 6. The User Interface of RaceStand: Step 5

Fig. 7. The User Interface of RaceStand: Step 6

ation, enabling designers to change the overall page layout without altering the underlying dynamic content. Using JSP technology, the client programmers can

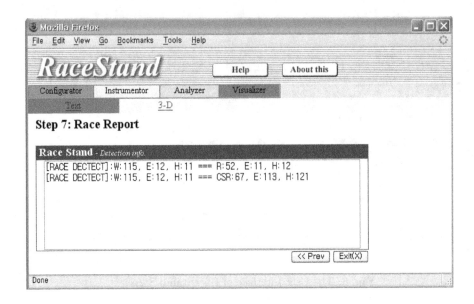

Fig. 8. The User Interface of RaceStand: Step 7

debug OpenMP parallel programs at a remote parallel computer without any additional tool but their web browser.

The RaceStand server invokes a preprocessor to instrument the race-detection engines into the debugged program, executes the instrumented program to detect data races, and notifies the results of monitored execution to the RaceStand client.

For each access to a shared variable, the preprocessor allocates an array to store one access history for each shared variable. And, at each source location just before the static reference to read/write to a shared variable, the preprocessor inserts one of two function calls which inspect and may update the access history for either race verification or first race detection. The preprocessor also inserts other function calls to generate thread labels at each location just before the static operations of fork/join and inter-thread coordination.

To support the intuitive visualization, the preprocessor inserts the corresponding function calls to compute graphic information for displaying thread structure and its abstraction captured in the execution of program. For source-level debugging, the preprocessor add a flag variable to hide all of the instrumented codes. The set of monitoring functions can be chosen by the user in its initial debugging session of RaceStand, and generates debugging information on the detected races during an execution instance of the debugged program. A report to detected races includes both of the shared variables associated with the race and the static locations of accesses involved in the race.

RaceStand provide the users with four main menus: the Configurator to configure detection engines at their own will, the Instrumentor to make object program instrumented with the selected engines, the Analyzer to execute the instrumented program, and the Visualizer to report the detected races with debugging information either in text or three-dimensional graphs. The six figures shown Figure 2-7 shows a session instance of six steps displayed at a client site of RaceStand. Figure 2 shows the first step in RaceStand Configurator, in which users can upload a source file to be debugged; Figure 3 shows the second step in Configurator for case that the source file requires a set of header files. Figure 4 shows the third step in Configurator for users to make sure the thread model of the debugged program which is analyzed by RaceStand to select the appropriate set of race detection engines. Figure 5 shows the fourth step in Configurator for users to suggest their priorities in selecting the detection engines in their scalability of visualization, scalability of performance, and efficiency in required space or time.

As the fifth step, Figure 6 shows the set of detection engines selected by RaceStand Instrumentor with reference to both the results of source-code analysis and user's selection of analysis properties. As the sixth step, Figure 7 shows the instrumented source code with the selected engines shown in Figure 6. In the figure, *label_fork*2 is the declared space to allocate the label space to be consumed by English-Hebrew (EH) Labeling [3]; *EH AddChild_Label_EH_()* (or *EH AddLock_Label_EH_())* is the engine call for each forked thread (or critical section) to generate an EH label; and *LCCheckRead_()* for the read access to execute the race detection protocol. Figure 8 shows a report of two races as the final step which is detected during an execution of the instrumented program shown in Figure 7. In the figure, RaceStand produces three pairs of race components each of which is delimited by semi-colons: the source line number of (locked) read/write access involved in the race, and the values of English and Hebrew labels stored in the corresponding threads.

5   Conclusions

RaceStand monitors a parallel execution of standard OpenMP program based on scalably efficient techniques of on-the-fly race detection, and can be accessed remotely via the web interface of the Internet through the client-server relationship between programmers and RaceStand. Since RaceStand determines during the monitored execution if a thread's access to a shared variable is logically concurrent with any previous accesses to this variable and results in a race, it can not only verify the existence of races but also detect first races for each shared variable in the programs. We now have a plan to work on extending RaceStand to include more elaborate facilities that may help users easy to understand the debugging information and to add to RaceStand more detection engines to be developed in the future.

References

1. Choi, J., and S. L. Min, "Race Frontier: Reproducing Data Races in Parallel-Program Debugging," *3rd Symposium on Principles and Practice of Parallel Programming* (PPoPP), pp. 145-154, ACM, April 1991.

2. Dagum, L., and R. Menon, "OpenMP: An Industry-Standard API for Shared-Memory Programming," *Computational Science and Engineering*, 5(1): 46-55, IEEE, January-March 1998.

3. Dinning, A., and E. Schonberg, "Detecting Access Anomalies in Programs with Critical Sections," *2nd Workshop on Parallel and Distributed Debugging* (WPDD), pp. 85-96, ACM, May 1991.

4. Intel Corp., *Getting Started with the Intel Thread Checker*, 2200 Mission College Blvd., Santa Clara, CA 95052-8119, USA, 2004.

5. Jun, Y., and K. Koh, "On-the-fly Detection of Access Anomalies in Nested Parallel Loops," *3rd Workshop on Parallel and Distributed Debugging* (WPDD), pp. 107-117, ACM, May 1993.

6. Jun, Y., and C. E. McDowell, "Scalable Monitoring Technique for Detecting Races in Parallel Programs," *5th Int'l Workshop on High-Level Parallel Prog. Models and Supportive Environments* (HIPS), pp. 340-347, IEEE, Cancun, Mexico, May 2000.

7. Jun, Y., and C. E. McDowell, "On-the-fly Detection of the First Races in Programs with Nested Parallelism," *2nd Int'l Conf. on Parallel and Distributed Processing Techniques and Applications* (PDPTA), pp. 1549-1560, CSREA, August 1996.

8. Kim, J., and Y. Jun, "Scalable On-the-fly Detection of the First Races in Parallel Programs," *12nd Intl. Conf. on Supercomputing* (ICS), pp. 345-352, ACM, Melbourne, Australia, July 1998.

9. Kim, Y., and Y. Jun, "Restructuring Parallel Programs for On-the-fly Race Detection," *5th Int'l Conf. on Parallel Computing Technologies* (PaCT), pp. 446-451, Russian Academy of Science (RAS), St. Petersburg, Russia, Sept. 1999.

10. Kim, J., D. Kim, and Y. Jun, "Scalable Visualization for Debugging Races in OpenMP Programs," *The 3rd Int'l Conf. on Communications in Computing* (CIC), pp. 259-265, Las Vegas, Nevada, June 2002.

11. Netzer, R. H. B., and B. P. Miller, "What Are Race Conditions? Some Issues and Formalizations," *Letters on Programming Lang. and Systems*, 1(1): 74-88, ACM, March 1992.

12. Mellor-Crummey, J., "On-the-fly Detection of Data Races for Programs with Nested Fork-Join Parallelism," *Supercomputing*, pp. 24-33, ACM/IEEE, Nov. 1991.

13. Park, H., and Y. Jun, "Detecting the First Races in Parallel Programs with Ordered Synchronization," *6th Int'l Conf. on Parallel and Distributed Systems* (ICPADS), pp. 201-208, IEEE, Tainan, Taiwan, Dec. 1998.

14. Park, S., M. Park, and Y. Jun, "A Comparison of Scalable Labeling Schemes for Detecting Races in OpenMP Programs," *Int'l Workshop on OpenMP Applications and Tools* (Wompat), pp. 68-80, West Lafayette, Indiana, July 2001.

Comprehensive Cache Inspection with Hardware Monitors

Jie Tao[1], Jürgen Jeitner[2], Carsten Trinitis[2], Wolfgang Karl[1],
and Josef Weidendorfer[2]

[1] Institut für Technische Informatik,
Universität Karlsruhe (TH), 76128 Karlsruhe, Germany
{tao, karl}@ira.uka.de
[2] Lehrstuhl für Rechnertechnik und Rechnerorganisation,
Technische Universität München, Boltzmannstr.3, 85748 Garching, Germany
{jeitner, trinitic, josef.weidendorfer}@in.tum.de

Abstract. Computer systems usually rely on hardware counters and
software instrumentation to acquire performance information about the
cache access behavior. These approaches either provide only limited data
or are restricted in their applicability. This paper introduces a novel approach based on a hardware cache monitoring facility that exhibits both
the details of traditional software mechanisms and the low–overhead of
hardware counters. More specially, the cache monitor can be combined
with any location of the memory hierarchy and present a detailed view
of the complete memory access behavior of applications. The monitoring concept has been verified using a multiprocessor simulator. Initial
experimental results show its feasibility in terms of hardware design and
functionality with respect to providing comprehensive performance data.

1 Introduction

Within the last decades, both processor and memory speed have been growing
at an exponential rate. Nevertheless, the growth rate of the memory speed is
rather lower, leading to a significant and continously growing gap. Caches, as
fast buffers for reused data, have been introduced to compensate for this. Due to
the complex structure of applications and the memory system, however, the data
stored in caches often can not be reused by the running programs. Cache locality
optimization becomes hence a critical issue for achieving high performance.

A prerequisite for such optimization is performance data that shows the
cache access behavior of applications. Currently, computer systems acquire this
information usually relying on either software profiling and simulation systems
[9] , or hardware counters embedded in modern processors like Intel Pentium
series [6] and Itanium Architecture [5], the IBM PowerPC Architecture [12], and
the DEC/Compaq/Intel Alpha series [3].

The software approaches usually sample a source code or the executables
and record the access information during the execution of a program. These

V. Malyshkin (Ed.): PaCT 2005, LNCS 3606, pp. 331–345, 2005.
© Springer-Verlag Berlin Heidelberg 2005

systems can provide very detailed performance data and also enable examination of the access behavior in individual code fragments. However, they are not generally applicable and lead to large output data sets. The second approach, the hardware counters, on the other hand, allow precise and low–intrusive on-line measurements and can provide valuable information about the performance of critical regions in programs. However, this information is restricted to very specific, mostly global events like the total number of cache misses or the number of memory accesses. Information about important performance metrics, like false sharing, cache line invalidation, cache line replacement, and access pattern, is missing. Therefore, it is not sufficient for a comprehensive analysis and optimization.

Hence, it is necessary to use a novel approach capable of achieving accurate, comprehensive performance data, and at the same time not introducing major overhead or hardware complexity. For this, we have designed a cache monitor and are currently working on the hardware implementation. This cache monitor is a flexible device capable of observing the memory traffic on all levels of the memory hierarchy and collecting detailed information about the cache access behavior. It can be configured to a variety of working modes at the runtime and provide different information needed for understanding the various access patterns of applications and for the selection of appropriate optimization techniques. In order to avoid delivering fine-grained, low-level performance data, a multilayer software infrastructure has been developed for transforming the original monitoring information into a high level abstraction with respect to data structures. This includes both APIs for address transformation and interfaces for convenient access of the performance information. In combination with the software interface, the cache monitor provides, for example:

- Access histograms on individual location or the whole memory hierarchy. They records the access distribution to the complete working set at granularity of cache lines [1]. This gives the user a global overview of the memory accesses allowing an easy detection of access hotspots.
- Statistics on single events, like cache misses and total references to a specific memory region or performed inside an individual iteration, loop, or function; number of cache line replacements within an array; and number of first references with respect to memory regions, arrays, or code regions. This allows to find the source causing cache miss and inefficiency.
- Profile of access addresses. Based on this information, accesses at close intervals can be grouped into the same cache line, thus reducing cache misses caused by first references and also increasing spatial reuse of the cached data.
- Histogram of cache events which records the runtime actions of individual cache sets in chronological orders. This allows to detect overmapping and interference misses, helping to prohibit frequent replacement and reloading.

---

[1] In order to reduce monitoring data, a coarse granularity can be specified for creating histograms showing hotspot regions. These regions can then be monitored at cache line granularity.

- Additional information for multiprocessor systems, e.g. information about false sharing and invalidation behavior. This helps to reduce the number of cache line invalidations and thereby improve the cache efficiency.

The monitor concept has been verified using a simulation platform that models both uniprocessor architecture and multiprocessor systems with shared memory. Experimental results have shown the feasibility and effectiveness of this hardware design.

The remainder of this paper is organized as follows. Section 2 introduces common used approaches for acquiring cache performance data. This is followed by a detailed description of this approach, the cache monitor, in Section 3. In Section 4 some initial simulation-based experimental results are illustrated. The paper concludes in Section 5 with a short summary and a few future directions.

2   Related Work

As locality tuning requires information about memory accesses, various approaches have been developed for collecting performance data with respect to the memory system. These approaches can be roughly divided into three categories: compiler-based, simulation-based, and hardware supported.

First, modern compilers trend to transparently optimize data locality during the compiling time. They usually rely on heuristic analysis and mathematical frameworks to understand the runtime access pattern. Ghosh et al. [4] present an example in this area. Within this research work, a framework was developed that automatically diagnoses the causes of cache misses in a compiler. This framework is based on the Cache Miss Equations (CMEs), an analytical representation of cache misses in a loop nest. Besides CMEs, a CME table is used to describe the loop-level cache behavior and enable an automated diagnosis of the source of cache misses. The diagnosis is then used to select program transformations that improve cache performance.

For simulation based schemes, well-known examples are SIP [1] and MemSpy [8]. SIP (Source Interdependence Profiler) is a profiling tool that uses SimICS [7], a full-system simulator, to run the applications for collecting cache behavior data. It then analyzes the acquired data and provides detailed information about cache usage, such as spatial and temporal use of floating point and integer loads and stores, cache miss ratios with respect to data structures, and a summary of the complete statement. MemSpy is a performance monitoring tool designed for helping programmers to discern memory bottlenecks. It uses cache simulation to gather detailed memory statistics and then shows frequency and reason of cache misses.

On the area of hardware, modern processors provide performance counters for recording important information about the runtime execution. The UltraSPARC IIi Architecture [10] provides two registers to count up to 20 events like cache misses, cache stall cycles, floating-point operations, branch mispredictions, and CPU cycles. The IBM POWER2 [12] has 5 performance counters enabling the concurrent monitoring of five events, such as the number of executed instructions, elapsed cycles, counts and delays associated with cache and TLB misses, and utilization of the various execution elements. Intel's Itanium Architecture [5] offers 8 and Pentium4 [6] even 18 performance counters to allow the collection of more information, like that about specific instructions and pipeline conflict.

Overall, the compiler-based approaches can analyze the cache access behavior, but can not observe the runtime dynamic access pattern. The simulation based approaches compensate for this, however, introduce significant overhead with respect to profiling and are also not generally available. For hardware counters, only limited performance data about the memory system can be achieved and details are missing; programmers often have to do hard work in analyzing the applications in order to understand the code and the data structure. We therefore design a cache monitor in order to provide the programmers with detailed, understandable, and easy-to-use performance data, and at the same time hold the hardware properties such as enabling on-line processing with only probe intrusion.

3   The Cache Monitor

The goal of this hardware monitor is to deliver comprehensive cache performance data that not only shows the various aspects of cache access behavior but also is easy to use, e.g. in the form of statistics and at high-level in terms of data structures. We achieve these features with both flexible hardware design and a multi-layer software infrastructure.

3.1   Hardware Design

The hardware monitor, as shown in Figure 1, consists of four modules: monitor control, bus interface, counter module, and the memory transfer buffer. The monitor control is the user interface of the monitor. The bus interface is the connection to a bus system and responsible for acquiring data about bus traffic. The data is then handed on to the counter module, which is responsible for keeping track of those events that relate to the parameters defined by the user. The data can then be transferred to a user-defined ring buffer in main memory (Data-Buffer) through the memory transfer buffer. The memory transfer buffer forms bundles of several event data and enables e.g. the utilization of memory burst write accesses to reduce monitoring influence on observed systems.

Monitor Control Component (MCC). Figure 2 shows the structure of the Monitor Control Component. For monitor configuration four registers are deployed. Two of them are used for communication with the monitor, while the others are related with the user-defined ring buffer in the main memory.

The first register defines a time stamp and some control and configuration parameters. Time Stamp is a simple counter incremented when a monitoring event is written to the memory transfer buffer. It can be used for event ordering. Control parameters are used to reset, start, flush, and suspend the monitoring.

The last parameter, the configuration bits, contains both specifications for enabling/disabling individual cache levels (up to 5) and for activating the dynamic working mode of the hardware monitor.

The second register defines a few bits reflecting the states of the MESI protocol. This is an extension for monitoring cache behavior with regard to cache line states and can be used to understand the cache coherence protocols.

The last two registers, RegionStartPtr & RegionEndPtr, specify two independent address regions of interest. Accesses out of these regions will be ignored by the event filter. By a null value, the whole address space is monitored.

As can be seen in Figure 2, these registers are organized in rows and columns. To achieve greater flexibility, an additional bit field, called level, is introduced. This allows to couple more than one counter module to a single monitor control component.

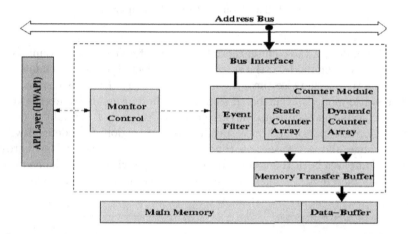

Fig. 1. The cache monitor on the top level

Main Memory Ring Buffer. In order to observe all memory accesses with limited registers, a ring buffer is maintained in the main memory for monitoring data delivered from the hardware. Two registers in the MCC, BufferStartPtr and BufferEndPtr, serve as pointers of the ring buffer. Each time a monitoring data is written to the ring buffer, the BufferStartPtr is incremented. If BufferStartPtr is equal to BufferEndPtr, an interrupt is created and delivered to the software layer for clearing the ring buffer for further use.

Counter Module and the Two Working Modes. The cache monitor can be configured to one of two working modes: static and dynamic. The former only triggers predefined events and can be used to monitor specific memory regions. The latter implements a histogram-driven monitoring, in which the counting is not controlled by events, but rather all events can be traced. This mode can hence be used for generating complete access histograms.

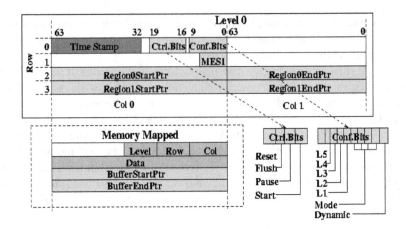

Fig. 2. The Monitor Control Component

Correspondingly, the counter module consists of two groups of counters, each for a single working mode. If the static mode is selected, the static counter array (SCA) is active. Otherwise the dynamic counter array (DCA) is chosen.

The static mode is event-based sampling, where users define events and the monitor counts the occurrence of these events. An event is actually a group of memory accesses performed on a specific memory region. It is defined with an address range and a transaction type. By each memory access the hardware monitor compares both the access address and type with the predefined events. In case of a matching, the memory access is stored as an event in SCA.

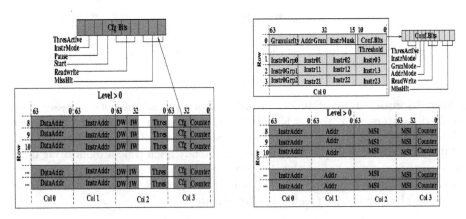

Fig. 3. Static (left) and dynamic (right) counter array

Figure 3 (left) illustrates the structure of the static counter array. It is comprised of several registers, again organized in the form of rows and columns. While rows 0-7 are reserved for user-defined settings, the others are used to store information about the monitored events. These registers can be configured using the following parameters:

- DataAddr: start address of the monitored event.
- InstrAddr: start address of an optional instruction region that issues the event.
- DataWidth (DW): width of the event-related data region.
- InstrWidth (IW): width of the instruction region.
- Threshold (Thres): optional threshold for restricting the maximal count of the corresponding event.
- Cfg: configuration flags, where InstrMode for activating instruction region observation, Start for activating the corresponding counter, ReadWrite for specifying access type, and MissHit for selecting miss/hit events.
- Counter: the event counter.

Figure 3 (right) also illustrates the organization of the dynamic counter array. As shown in the bottom of this figure, each counter (from Row 8) can be used to store information concerning a single event, including instruction address (InstrAddr), access address (Addr), and the counting to the event. In addition, an MSI (Mode Specific Information) field is combined with each counter for submodes to store additional information.

As mentioned, the dynamic mode supports submodes in order to enable various functions and allow the generation of different monitoring data. For example, submode0 observes all data accesses performed at runtime. In order to sort and categorize various events, it uses MSI to store the time stamp and transaction type for each event. Besides this submode, the dynamic monitoring supports another three submodes, where submode1 enables the observation of instructions and instruction groups in relation to their memory access behavior, submode2 traces the instruction addresses of applications, and submode3 counts cache hits on individual cache lines between two single invalidations and is specially designed for improving cache coherence protocols. Overall, each submode aims at creating different monitoring data for various need with respect to locality optimization.

In addition, the monitoring concept provides a dynamic granularity control, where the tracing unit can be configured. This allows to monitor single words for e.g. detecting false sharing and also enables the aggregation of neighboring events in case of access histograms where fine granularity is not required. For this granularity control the counter 0 in the dynamic counter array provides a field "Granularity" to store a user–definable parameter that specifies the maximal range of addresses which are allowed to be combined. In addition, counter 0 also defines granularity for optional address observation (AddrGran) and for masking single instructions or whole instruction groups (InstrMask).

3.2   Software Infrastructure

The monitoring data directly delivered by the cache monitor is low-level, fine-grained, and based on physical addresses. It can hence not be provided to users who need high-level abstractions to reason about cache misses and to understand the access pattern of applications. For this, a software infrastructure has been designed.

As illustrated in Figure 4, the software infrastructure contains several layers, each processing a step further of the monitoring information. As mentioned, the original monitoring data is stored in the ring buffer in main memory. From there, the data is first processed by the low level API of the hardware monitor. Within this step, data is sorted and then a histogram chain is generated that stores the monitoring data in the order of memory blocks in cache line size, so called memory lines. In addition, the low level monitor API also combines the monitoring data from different monitors and probably different processors, and translates physical addresses to virtual ones.

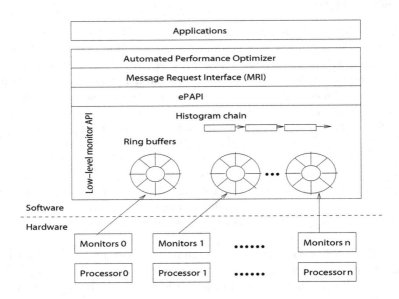

Fig. 4. Software framework for data processing

On top of the monitor API, the ePAPI library further processes the monitoring data into statistical forms such as total number of single events and access histograms. Finally, the Monitoring Request Interface (MRI) maps the virtual addresses into data structures using the context table provided by some compilers or using the debugging information. Also from this component, the final high-level data abstraction is delivered to performance tools and applications for performance analysis.

As the primary data processing component, ePAPI provides a set of functions not only for data processing but also for configuration of the monitoring hardware. Similar to the PAPI [2] library for hardware counters, ePAPI is capable of generating statistical numbers on individual events like cache hits and misses. Besides this, ePAPI generates access histograms recording the occurrence of single events over the complete working set. These histograms can be used to find critical regions where individual metrics, like cache locality, show a poor performance. In addition, ePAPI provides functions for analyzing the access addresses and invalidation operations. These functions can be used to provide address groups and to create invalidation sequences, which are needed in address grouping and false sharing detection.

As an information request interface, the main function of MRI is to allow tools and applications to specify runtime requests that hold definitions of the required information, like information type, source code region, and the concerned data structure. The runtime information type can be individual events and access histograms in combination with program regions. Typical program regions are program units, loops, parallel regions, and function call sites. According to the requests, MRI calls appropriate ePAPI functions and delivers information to the consumer in a push and pull fashion.

4   Verification of the Hardware Design and Functionality

In order to evaluate the hardware concept, the cache monitor has been simulated with a monitor simulator. This component closely models the hardware details and the working principles. The monitor simulator is then combined with an existing multiprocessor simulator SIMT [11], which simulates the execution of serial and parallel applications on SMP/NUMA architectures and generates events like cache hits/misses, replacements, and cache line invalidations.

The applications used for the following experiments are from the SPLASH-II Benchmarks suite [13]. This includes a Fast Fourier Transformation (FFT), an LU-decomposition for dense matrices (LU), an integer radix sort (RADIX), the OCEAN code for simulation of large scale ocean movements, and the WATER code for evaluating water molecule systems. We use these applications to determine hardware parameters like the number of registers in the counter arrays, and to verify the feasibility of the cache monitor in terms of providing performance data. All applications were simulated using their default working set size.

Events Interval. An important design issue with a cache monitor is to know how fast it has to process an event or how many registers have to be provided as store buffer, in order to guarantee that no event is missing, especially for the histogram-driven dynamic working mode. This parameter depends on the frequency of events issued at the runtime. Using the simulation platform we have measured the interval between two events. Figure 5 shows the results.

We divided the events into four groups: those with intervals less than 5 CPU cycles, intervals between 5 and 9 cycles, intervals between 10 and 14 cycles, and intervals greater than 14 cycles. We first measured the number of events within each group and then computed the percentage. As shown in Figure 5, for all applications 20–30% of the total events lie in the third group, i.e. with intervals between 10 and 14 CPU cycles. This indicates that the cache monitor can probably directly process these events without buffering. However, it can also be observed that for four applications more than 60% events occur one after another with an interval less than 5 CPU cycles. This means that a number of registers is necessary for storing the events, since the hardware monitor is not possible to handle the events at this speed. Overall, the experimental result renders a buffer as necessary.

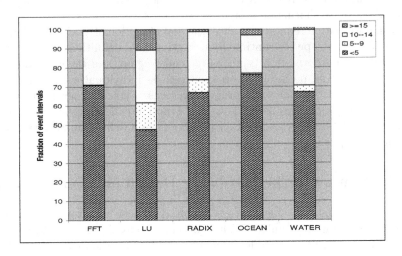

Fig. 5. Statistics on events with different intervals

Number of Registers. Another important parameter with hardware capacity is the number of registers in the counter arrays. This is actually a trade-off between hardware cost and efficiency. Few registers can potentially result in a significant amount of data transfers from the hardware counters to the ring buffer, and on the other hand, excessive counters lead to a waste of hardware resources. In order to find reasonable setup, we measured the frequency of flushes with all applications in case of different number of hardware counters in the dynamic counter array. Figure 6 shows the experimental results.

For each application a curve presents the concrete numbers of flushes, when the number of hardware counters vary from 4 to 128. Examining these curves, it can be seen that 4–16 counters still result in large number of flushes, while more than 16 counters could not introduce drastic reduction of flushes any more. Hence it can be concluded that the best configuration for the dynamic counter array is 16 registers.

Access Histogram. Besides the hardware concept, the functionality of the cache monitor is also important. Actually, the cache monitor is capable of supplying a variety of performance data, like statistics on single events, individual access histogram on a single cache level, combined histogram on the whole memory hierarchy, and operation histogram showing ordered events. We choose three examples to verify the function: complete access histogram, reason of cache misses, and statistics on false sharing.

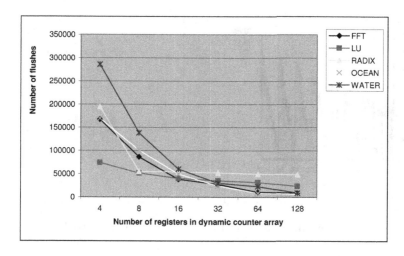

Fig. 6. Flushes of the dynamic counter array with different number of registers

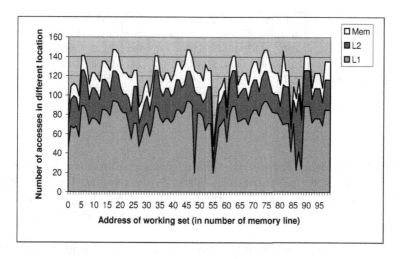

Fig. 7. Combined memory access histogram of WATER

Figure 7 illustrates a sample histogram with WATER, which shows the combined data for all monitors on a memory hierarchy with two level caches. The x-axis of this figure presents the first 100 memory lines of the complete working set and the y-axis presents the number of accesses performed on each memory line. These accesses can be either an L1 hit, an L2 hit, or have to be performed in the main memory. As can be seen, most memory references can be found in the caches, however, for this concrete example there also exists memory regions with a high access rate of the main memory.

In summary, the access histogram enables a direct observation of distinct memory access behaviors within a single code. This allows to find access hot spots, forming the first step towards cache optimization.

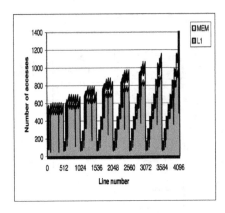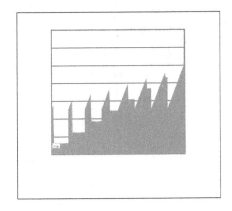

Fig. 8. Memory access distribution of LU before (left) and after (right) locality optimizations

Table 1. Number of false sharing with different cache coherence schemes

	MESI		FULL		OPT		SCOPE	
	inva.	false	inva.	false	inva.	false	inva.	false
FFT	2670	1057	18517	2626	992	496	2110	1647
LU	16185	487	304137	4728	3392	24	106380	3886
RADIX	7274	4716	63857	5488	654	160	15937	4774
OCEAN	17990	2875	253808	4405	8411	2538	133490	2748
WATER	9302	2704	70662	4486	2920	2557	20590	2378

Cache Miss Reason. For a comprehensive cache optimization, however, additional information, e.g. source of cache misses, is also required. For this the cache monitors again provide detailed information. We use the LU code as an easy-to-follow example to depict how the monitoring information helps to improve the cache behavior.

LU factors a dense matrix into the product of a lower triangular and an upper triangular matrix. The dense matrix is divided into blocks to exploit temporal locality on submatrix elements. We simulated this program using a 128×128 matrix with *double* type and with a block size of 8 bytes. The first simulation results show high cache misses.

According to the monitoring report, we found that these cache misses are mainly caused by accessing the matrix being decomposed. Besides this, the monitoring data shows that theses misses are caused by cache line replacement on the matrix itself. This detection led us to examine the memory distribution of this data structure. We then found that several matrix blocks of LU, which are needed for a single computation, are allocated in a way that they are mapped into the same cache sets at the runtime, leading to replacement. According to this detection, we optimized the LU code with a better data placement and an improvement with cache locality is achieved.

Figure 8 shows the memory access distribution of the complete matrix before (left diagram) and after (right diagram) optimizations. For a better observation of the different behavior with the cache and the memory, the second level cache is disabled within this experiment. Both diagrams in the figure show the absolute number of access hits on both L1 and the main memory, with the L1 hits on the bottom and the memory hits on the top. It can be clearly seen that less references are performed on the main memory for the optimized version. This again proves the feasibility of the cache monitor, since it directs the users to the correct point where optimizations are needed.

False Sharing. For shared memory multiprocessor systems, cache line invalidation is a critical issue causing cache misses. Such invalidations, however, could be unnecessary. A specific case is false sharing, where a cache line on a processor is invalidated because another processor has modified a word of the same data copy, but the processor needs a different word within the cache block. In this case, the cache line has not to be invalidated.

For supporting the optimization with respect to false sharing, the cache monitor provides event profile that records the histogram of memory operations in a serial order. This allows its API to compare the target of a shared write with all following shared reads thus to detect false sharing. Table 1 shows the statistics reported by the cache monitor API. This result was acquired by simulating all applications on a 32-node multiprocessor system.

We have measured the number of false sharing for four different cache coherence protocols. MESI is a common used scheme for hardware-based shared memory machines. This scheme performs cache line invalidation by each write operation to shared data. FULL is a kind of release consistency model usually deployed on systems with distributed shared memory. This scheme performs whole cache invalidation at each synchronization event like lock and barrier. OPT is an optimal scheme that invalidates a cache line by a read operation and only when the accessed cache line has been modified. SCOPE is an optimized version of FULL, where only the cache lines holding remote data are invalidated rather than the complete cache. In principle, OPT should performs better than MESI, MESI better than FULL, and SCOPE better than FULL.

Table 1 depicts the absolute number of total invalidations and false sharing of them. It can be observed that applications vary in this behavior. For FFT, 40% of the invalidations with MESI are false sharing, 50% with OPT, and even 78% with SCOPE. For the FULL scheme, it is senseless to compute this proportion because most validations are performed on invalid cache lines. However, more false sharing can be observed with this protocol. LU performs better than FFT with a slight percentage of false sharing, e.g. 3% with MESI. RADIX reports the highest false sharing (65% with MESI) and the other two applications perform better than RADIX and FFT.

Overall, the experimental results indicate that for most applications optimization with false sharing is necessary in order to alleviate cache misses. For this the cache monitor provides required data for analysis.

5   Conclusions

This paper introduces the design and working principles of a hardware monitor for observing the access behavior of caches. This monitor is comprised of control registers and counter arrays for hardware configurations and monitoring data. It can be configured into a static mode for event triggering and action processing on special memory regions of interest, and a dynamic mode for providing fine-grain monitoring statistics across the complete application's working set. In addition, the cache monitor is capable of supplying different performance data allowing the adaptation to various cache optimization techniques. The design of the hardware monitor has been evaluated using simulation and the results have shown the feasibility and effectiveness of the monitoring approach.

In the next step of this research work, the hardware will be implemented using FPGAs. In addition, performance tools will be developed for supporting the locality optimization. This includes a visualizer that shows the cache behavior in graphical views and an automatic optimizer that improves the cache performance transparently at runtime. The latter forms a base for building autonomous systems.

References

1. E. Berg and E. Hagersten. SIP: Performance Tuning through Source Code Interdependence. In *Proceedings of the 8th International Euro-Par Conference*, pages 177–186, August 2002.
2. S. Browne, J. Dongarra, N. Garner, G. Ho, and P. Mucci. A portable programming interface for performance evaluation on modern processors. *The International Journal of High Performance Computing Applications*, 14(3):189–204, Fall 2000.
3. Digital Equipment Cooperation. Alpha 21164 Microprocessor Hardware Reference Manual. Technical report, 1995.
4. S. Ghosh, M. Martonosi, and S. Malik. Automated Cache Optimizations using CME Driven Diagnosis. In *Proceedings of the 2000 International Conference on Supercomputing*, pages 316–326, 2000.
5. Intel Corporation. *Intel Itanium Architecture Software Developer's Manual*, volume 1–3. 2002. available at http://developer.intel.com/design/itanium/manuals/iiasdmanual.htm.
6. Intel Corporation. *IA-32 Intel Architecture Software Developer's Manual*, volume 1–3. 2004. available at Intel's developer website.
7. P. S. Magnusson and B. Werner. Efficient Memory Simulation in SimICS. In *Proceedings of the 8th Annual Simulation Symposium*, Phoenix, Arizona, USA, April 1995.
8. M. Martonosi, A. Gupta, and T. Anderson. Tuning Memory Performance of Sequential and Parallel Programs. *Computer*, 28(4):32–40, April 1995.
9. M. Martonosi, A. Gupta, and T. E. Anderson. Tuning Memory Performance in Sequential and Parallel Programs. *IEEE Computer*, pages 32–40, April 1995.
10. Sun Microsystems. *UltraSPARC IIi User's Manual*. October 1997. available at http://www.sun.com/processors/documentation.html.

11. J. Tao, M. Schulz, and W. Karl. A Simulation Tool for Evaluating Shared Memory Systems. In *Proceedings of the 36th Annual Simulation Symposium*, pages 335–342, Orlando, Florida, April 2003.

12. E. Welbon and et al. The POWER2 Performance Monitor. *IBM Journal of Research and Development*, 38(5), 1994.

13. S. C. Woo, M. Ohara, E. Torrie, J. P. Singh, and A. Gupta. The SPLASH-2 Programs: Characterization and Methodological Considerations. In *Proceedings of the 22nd Annual International Symposium on Computer Architecture*, pages 24–36, June 1995.

A Fast Technique for Constructing Evolutionary Tree with the Application of Compact Sets*

Kun-Ming Yu[1,**], Yu-Weir Chang[1], YaoHua Yang[2], Jiayi Zhou[1], Chun-Yuan Lin[3,†], and Chuan Yi Tang[4]

[1] Department of Computer Science and Information Engineering, Chung Hua University
[2] Department of Information Management, Chung Hua University
[3] Institute of Molecular and Cellular Biology, National Tsing Hua University
[4] Department of Computer Science, National Tsing Hua University
Hsinchu, Taiwan 300, R.O.C.
yu@chu.edu.tw

Abstract. Constructing an evolutionary tree has many techniques, and usually biologists use distance matrix on this activity. The evolutionary tree can assist in taxonomy for biologists to analyze the phylogeny. In this paper, we specifically employ the compact sets to convert the original matrix into several small matrices for constructing evolutionary tree in parallel. By the properties of compact sets, we do not spend much time and do keep the correct relations among species. Besides, we adopt both Human Mitochondrial DNAs and randomly generated matrix as input data in the experiments. In comparison with conventional technique, the experimental results show that utilizing compact sets can definitely construct the evolutionary tree in a reasonable time. Keywords: computational biology, evolutionary tree, compact sets, branch-and-bound.

1 Introduction[1]

An evolutionary tree is a model of evolutional histories for a set of species. It is an important and fundamental model in bioinformatical field to observe livening species. A meaning evolutionary tree enhances biologists to evaluate the relationship of a set of species in taxonomy. Hence, many methods have been proposed to construct the evolutionary tree.

The majority of these methods are all based on two models, i.e., the sequences and a distance matrix. In the sequences model, they do multiple sequence alignment (MSA) for a set of species with corresponding DNA sequence first. Then an evolutionary tree is constructed according to the MSA result. However, the MSA problem is NP-hard. In a distance matrix model, they determine the distance as the edit distance for any two of species first. Then these distances are formed as a distance matrix. Finally, an evolutionary tree is constructed according to a distance matrix. Unfor-

---

* This work was supported in part by the NSC of ROC, under grant NSC93-2213-E-216-037.
** Corresponding author.
† Post doctor fellowship is supported by NSC under contract NSC92-3112-B-007-002 and NSC93-3112-B-007-008.

V. Malyshkin (Ed.): PaCT 2005, LNCS 3606, pp. 346–354, 2005.
© Springer-Verlag Berlin Heidelberg 2005

tunately, it is also an NP-hard problem to construct a minimum cost evolutionary tree from a distance matrix.

A category of evolutionary tree called ultrametric tree (UT) assumes that the rate of evolution is constant. An UT is a rooted and edge weighted binary tree in which every internal node has the same path length to all the leaves in its sub tree. The minimum UT for a distance matrix is an UT that the distance between any pair of leaves on the tree is no less than the given distance and the total weight on the tree edges is minimized.

In the distance matrix, shown in figure 1, each value represents the distance between two species. The distance matrix D is symmetric, i.e. for all $0 \leq i \leq n$, $D[i,i] = 0$. Also, the matrix D follows the triangle inequality, i.e. for all $1 \leq i, j, k \leq n$, $D[i,j] + D[j,k] \geq D[i,k]$.

	V_1	V_2	V_3	V_4	V_5	V_6
V_1	0	3	1	12	6	13
V_2		0	7	9	5	16
V_3			0	11	4	15
V_4				0	14	2
V_5					0	8
V_6						0

Fig. 1. An example of distance matrix

Some studies on constructing optimal evolutionary tree have been proven to be an NP-hard problem [3, 4, 6, 8, 9, 15]. The scientists could use the branch-and-bound technique to construct optimal evolutionary tree in a reasonable time [12] when the number of species is small. Although the branch-and-bound algorithm would detect an optimal solution, such capacities cannot effectively support the optimal evolutionary tree construction when the number of species exceeds 26.

In this paper, we specifically utilize the compact sets to convert the distance matrix into several small matrices for constructing an UT in parallel. We can not only obtain nearly optimal evolutionary tree but also keep the precise relations among species through compact sets by the property - the least common ancestor [14]. Of such an advantage, our work might contribute to the findings on the phylogeny.

The rest of the paper is organized as follows: section 2 proposes some preliminaries. Section 3 describes the methods for constructing the ultrametric tree in detail. The experimental results are presented in section 4. Finally, the conclusion is placed in section 5.

2 Preliminaries

An ultrametric tree is a rooted, leaf labeled binary tree, and each edge associates with a distance cost. The length from root to any leaf is equal. We can construct an UT through a distance matrix D representing a complete, weighted and undirected graph G. The graph $G = (V, E)$ includes vertices V and edges E. We give some definitions below:

Definition 1. Assume that P is a given topology and $i, j \in L(P)$. $LCA(i,j)$ represents the lowest common ancestor of i and j. Assume a and b are two vertices in P, we denote $a \rightarrow b$ if and only if a is an ancestor of b.

Definition 2. Assume P is a tree topology. $R(P)$ is a relation - $\{(i,j,k)|a,b,c \in L(P), LCA(i,k)=LCA(j,k) \rightarrow LCA(i,j)\}$.

The compact set has been extensively studied [5] but have not been applied to the evolutionary tree construction problem. We will list some properties of compact sets below:

Lemma 1: Assume compact sets C exist in a tree T including elements i, j and k. The compact sets must satisfy a relation — least common ancestor. If and only if the relations $((i, j), k)$ and $LCA(i, j) < LCA(i, k) = LCA(j, k)$ exist, then there is an adjacency relation in T like figure 2.

Lemma 2: Let C be a subset of vertices V. If C is compact, then the maximum edge in C should be smaller than any edges between an element in C and that in V but not in C.

Lemma 3: Let A and B be two different compact sets of V_l. If A and B have intersection, then either $A \subset B$ or $B \subset A$[5].

Lemma 4: If sub graph g is compact set, then the sub tree in g also belongs to the minimum spanning tree $\overline{T}$.

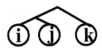

Fig. 2. An example of least common ancestor

3   Proposed Solutions

To construct nearly optimal UT for mass spices in reasonable time, we utilize the idea of compact set in our work. Firstly, we will find the compact sets from distance matrix D and explore them to create several small distance matrices D'. Then we input the smaller distance matrices D' to parallel branch-and-bound algorithm. Finally we can obtain sub trees T' and merge them into an ultrametric tree T. We describe the details in the subsection.

3.1   Compact Sets

As above, we explore compact sets to separate the distance matrix D into several small distance matrices D'. If the elements in a subset S of X are closer than those outside S but in X, then S is a compact set. Also we could continuously find compact sets in S until exploring all sub sets. In this work we can find all the compact sets to classify the organisms by collecting the more relative species on the graph[17]. The found

found groups will keep the correct relations and could conduce to analyze the phylogeny. Thus we utilize compact sets to construct a more precise ultrametric tree.

Initially we must find the minimum cost spanning tree to converge the closest groups and can probe the elements inside each group to discover all the compact sets. Take the figure 3 for example; if using the Kruskal's algorithm, we can locate a minimum spanning tree $\overline{T}$ like figure 4, and the compact sets are $\{(1,3),(4,6),(1,2,3,5)\}$. We will continue using the algorithm below to verify the subsets in $\overline{T}$ to discover all the compact sets.

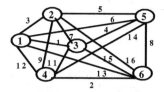

Fig. 3. The complete, weighted, undirected graph

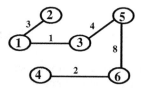

Fig. 4. The minimum spanning tree

```
Algorithm Compact Sets
Input: A graph G = (V, E) with the vertex set V ={V₁,
          V₂, …, Vₙ} and edge set E. Each edge has a weight.
Output: All of the compact sets on the graph G.
Step 1. Find the minimum spanning tree T̄ on the graph
          G. )        //here we use Kruskal's algorithm.
Step 2. Sort the edges in T̄ in ascending order, which is
          marked as (e₁, e₂, …, eₙ₋₁).
Step 3. P ← {{V₁}, {V₂,…, Vₙ}.
Step 4. for i := 1 to n-2
          {
            1. Let a and b to be the end vertices of edge
               eᵢ, i.e., eᵢ = (a, b).
            2. Find A, B in P such that a belongs to A and b
               belongs to B
            3. A ← merge A and B
            4. Delete B from P
            5. Find the maximum edge in A, denoted Max(A).
            6. Find the minimum edge between a vertex in A
               and a vertex not in A, denoted Min(A, !A).
            7. If Max(A) < Min(A, !A), then A is a compact
               set.
}
```

According to the algorithm, the order of edges is (1, 3), (4, 6), (1, 2), (3, 5) and (5, 6) after sorting by the weights. The population P includes all the vertices in $\overline{T}$, i.e. P = $\{(1), (2), (3), (4), (5), (6)\}$. We will firstly merge (1) and (3) together while coming to step 4. After the mergence, the P becomes $\{(1, 3), (2), (4), (5), (6)\}$. Continuously, we will find compact sets, (1, 3) and (4, 6). Worthy to be noticed is when we merge (1, 2) with (1, 3), we must examine if (1, 2, 3) satisfies the lemma 2. The maximum distance in (1, 2, 3) is less than the minimum distance between vertices in (1, 2, 3) and (4, 5, 6). Thus, (1, 2, 3) is a compact set. In the end, all the compact sets are (1, 3), (4, 6), (1, 2, 3) and (1, 2, 3, 5) like figure 5.

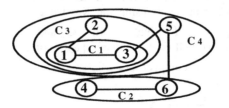

Fig. 5. Compact sets for the example

We then create several small distance matrices D' of three types which differ in the distance lengths stored in D'. These three matrices separately called *maximum, minimum,* and *average*. In this paper, we only study the ultrametric tree constructed from *maximum* matrix. The construction procedure is as follows. While creating the *maximum* matrix of C_4, we will examine the distances between elements in C_4, i.e. (C_1, C_3, 5). When considering C_3 and (5), we must select the maximum distance, which is 6, between (5) and any element in C_3, i.e. (1), (3) or (2). The resulted *maximum* matrix of C_4 shows in figure 7.

We shall discuss a situation that if there more than one $\overline{T}$ exists. In the previous step when finding $\overline{T}$, we need to examine and will obtain another $\overline{T}$ while replacing the edge of $\overline{T}$ with that holding the same weight on the graph. Indeed the new $\overline{T}$ should satisfy all conditions after the replacement. Figure 7(a) and (b) provides an example that two $\overline{T}$ s coexist in a graph.

Maximum	C_1	C_2	5
C_1	0	7	6
C_2		0	6
5			0

Fig. 6. Maximum matrix of C_4

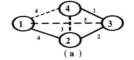 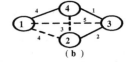

Fig. 7. Two minimum spanning trees in a graph

We can keep the precise relations among species by discovering all the compact sets on the graph. Thus we could ensure the relationship of every species in the ultrametric tree is precisely preserved by the characteristics of compact set. Then we can use the parallel branch-and-bound technique to construct an ultrametric tree from the small matrices D'. The following is an introduction to parallel branch-and-bound technique.

3.2 Parallel Branch-and-Bound Algorithm

We input several small distance matrices D' to the parallel branch-and-bound algorithm to find sub trees T'. Branch-and-bound algorithm is an efficient tree search algorithm for NP-hard problems. Some results about ultrametric trees have been proposed in [2]. In the previous researches, Wu et al., [19] had proposed a sequential branch-and-bound algorithm to construct minimum ultrametric trees from distance matrices.

For the parallel branch-and-bound algorithm, we utilize a heuristic algorithm UPGMM (Unweighted Pair Group Method with Maximum), which is altered from algorithm UPGMA [15], to find the cost values as bound values in our algorithm. If any computing nodes are notified that the branching unable to create any better solution, we then remove the branch. Compared with the single processor system, the solution space in the multi-processor system will decrease greatly. Thus, the parallel branch-and-bound algorithm could achieve super-leaner speedup.

The parallel branch-and-bound algorithm in the master and slave paradigm is listed as follows.

```
Parallel Branch-and-Bound Algorithm
Input: An n * n distance matrix D.
Output: The minimum ultrametric tree for D.
Step 1: Master control node re-label the species such
        that (1, 2, …, n) is a maxmin permutation.
Step 2: Master control node creates the root of the BBT
        (branch-and-bound Tree).
Step 3: Master control node run UPGMM and using the
        result as the initial UB (upper bound).
Step 4: Master control node branches the BBT until the
        branched BBT reach 2 times of total nodes in
        the computing environment.
Step 5: Master control node broadcasts the global UB
        and send the sorted matrix the nodes cycli-
cally.
Step 6: while number of UTs in LP (Local Pools) > 0 or
        number of UTs in GP (Global Pools) > 0 do
          if number of UTs in LP = 0 then
            if number of UTs in GP <> 0 then
              receive UTs from GP
            end if
          end if
          v = get the tree for branch using DFS
          if LB(v) > UB then
            continue
          end if
          insert next species to v and branch it
          if v branched completed then
            if LB (v) < UB then
              update the GUB (Global Upper Bound) to
              every nodes
              add the v to results set
            end if
          end if
          if number of UTs in GP = 0 then
            send the last UT in sorted LP to GP
          end if
        end while
Step 7: Gather all solutions from each node and output.
```

When obtaining the sub tree T' from the small matrix D', each node will return it to the master control node. Finally, the master control node will merge all the sub trees T' into the ultrametric tree T.

4   The Experimental Results

The experimental environment is built by a Linux-based cluster incorporating one master control node and 16 computational nodes. Computational nodes have the same hardware specification and connect with each other at 100Mbps and 1Gbs to server. Human Mitochondrial DNAs and randomly generated species matrix are the data instances stored in the distance matrix. The experiments will process in two conditions: To construct ultrametric tree (1) with application of compact sets and (2) without utilizing compact sets. We will compare the differences in computing time and total tree cost. We can find compact sets on a graph and determine the *maximum* distances of elements in each compact set as the total tree cost while considering the ultrametric tree based on *maximum* matrix. The following experimental results of compact sets are shown based on the data of *maximum* matrix.

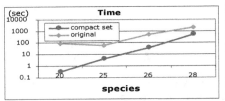
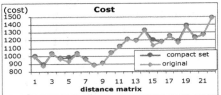

Fig. 8. The computing time for random data set

Fig. 9. The total tree cost for random data set

As the experiments on the randomly generated sequences, the averages computing time is shown in figure 8. Figure 8 illustrates the more species the more computing time we spend. In comparison with the method without applying compact set, the most time we save is about 99.7% and the least is 77.19% while using compact sets. Also we present the differences in cost between condition 1 and 2 in figure 9 and the results are based on randomly generated sequences. Figure 9 illustrates the total tree costs under two conditions are almost equal and the difference is less than 5%.

As the experiments on Human Mitochondrial DNAs, we use 15 data set containing 26 species for each and the total tree cost is presented in figure 10. The results show the maximum difference is 1.5%. In other words, the results demonstrate compact sets have the same effect not only on generated sequences but also on Human Mitochondrial DNAs. Figure 11 shows the computing time. Using compact sets can definitely save time but unexpectedly the experiments without compact sets also take little time except the last data.

We also experiment with 30 DNAs and figure 12 represents the costs of 10 data set each including 30 DNAs. As figure 12, using compact sets could keep the cost down when we experiment on 30 DNAs as well as generated data or 26 DNAs. According to figure 13, for computing time, the performances of the experiments on both 26 and 30 DNAs are alike.

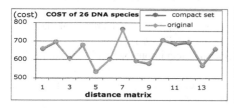

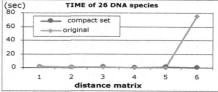

Fig. 10. The total tree cost for 26 DNAs   **Fig. 11.** The computing time for 26 DNAs

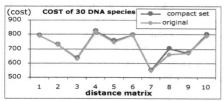

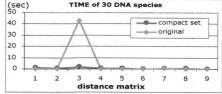

Fig. 12. The total tree cost of 30 DNAs   **Fig. 13.** The computing time of 30 DNAs

No matter how many species on which we experiment, the computing speed is still extremely rapid without using compact sets. Although the experiments using compact sets do not take much less time, we suppose the phenomenon is relevant to the population of the data. The computing time resulted from the experiment with randomly generated data can be a reference for any circumstance.

5   The Conclusions

In this paper, we employ the compact sets to convert the original matrix into several small matrices for constructing ultrametric tree in parallel. Of the compact sets, the precise phylogeny remains and facilitates biologists to analyze the species in taxonomy. Although we experiment with both Human Mitochondrial DNAs and randomly generated sequences, the results from generated data can represent any real instance. Therefore our technique could be applied in any condition.

References

1. H.J. Bandelt, "Recognition of tree metrics," *SIAM Journal on Discrete Mathematics*, vol. 3, no. 1, pp.1-6, 1990.
2. E. Dahlhaus, "Fast parallel recognition of ultrametrics and tree metrics," *SIAM Journal on Discrete Mathematics*, vol. 6, no. 4, pp. 523-532, 1993.
3. W.H.E. Day, "Computationally difficult parsimony problems in phylogenetic systematics," Journal of Theoretic Biology, vol. 103, pp. 429-438, 1983.
4. W.H.E. Day, "Computational complexity of inferring phylogenies from dissimilarity matrices," Bulletin of Mathematical Biology, vol. 49, no. 4, pp. 461-467, 1987.

5. E. Dekel, J. Hu, and W. Ouyang. An optimal algorithm for finding compact sets. Information Processing Letters, 44:285-289, 1992.
6. M. Farach, S. Kannan, and T. Warnow, "A robust model for finding optimal evolutionary trees," *Algorithmica*, vol. 13, pp. 155-179, 1995.
7. W.M. Fitch, "A non-sequential method for constructing trees and hierarchical classifications," *Journal of Molecular Evolution*, vol. 18, pp. 30-37, 1981.
8. L.R. Foulds, "Maximum savings in the Steiner problem in phylogency," *Journal of theoretic Biology*, vol. 107, pp.471-474, 1984.
9. L.R. Foulds and R.L. Graham, "The Steiner problem in phylogeny is NP-complete," *Advances in Applied Mathematics*, vol. 3, pp. 43-49, 1982.
10. M.R. Garey and D.S. Johnson, *Computers and Intractability: A Guide to the Theory of NP-Completeness*, Freeman: San Fransisco, 1979.
11. D. Gusfield, "Algorithms on Strings, Trees, and Sequences, computer science and computational biology," *Cambridge University Press, 1997.*
12. M.D. Henry and D. Penny, "Branch and bound algorithms to determine minimal evolutionary trees," *Mathematical Biosciences*, vol. 59, pp. 277-290, 1982.
13. R.M. Karp, "Reducibility among combinatorial problems," in *Complexity of Computer Computations*, R.E. Miller and J.W. Thatcher (Eds.), Plenum Press: New York, 1972, pp. 85-103.
14. SungKwon Kim, "A note on finding compact sets in graphs represented by an adjacency list" Information Processing Letters, vol. 57, pp. 335-238, 1996.
15. M. Krivanek, "The complexity of ultrametric partitions on graphs," *Information Processing Letter*, vol. 27, no. 5, pp. 265-270, 1988.
16. W.H. Li and D.Graur, Fundamentals of Molecular Evolution, Sinauer Associates, 1991.
17. Chiou-Kuo Liang, "An $O(n^2)$ Algorithm for Finding the Compact Sets of a Graph," BIT, vol. 33, pp 390-395, 1993.
18. N. Saitou and M. Nei. The neighbor-joining method: a new method for reconstructing phylogenetic trees. Molecular Biology and Evolution, 4:406-425, 1987.
19. B.Y. Wu, K.M. Chao, C.Y. Tang, "Approximation and Exact Algorithms for Constructing minimum Ultrametric Tree from Distance Matrices," Journal of Combinatorial Optimization, vol. 3, pp.199-211, 1999.

XenoCluster: A Grid Computing Approach to Finding Ancient Evolutionary Genetic Anomalies

Jesse D. Walters[2, 4], Thomas L. Casavant[1, 2, 3, 4], John P. Robinson[2, 4], Thomas B. Bair[2], Terry A. Braun[1, 2, 3, 5], and Todd E. Scheetz[1, 2, 3, 5]

[1] Center for Bioinformatics and Computational Biology, Iowa City, IA
http://genome.uiowa.edu
[2] Coordinated Laboratory for Computational Genomics, Iowa City, IA
{jwalters, tomc, tbair, tabraun, tscheetz}@eng.uiowa.edu
john-robinson@uiowa.edu
http://genome.uiowa.edu/clcg.html
[3] Department of Biomedical Engineering, Iowa City, IA
http://www.bme.engineering.uiowa.edu/
[4] Department of Electrical and Computer Engineering, Iowa City, IA
http://www.ece.engineering.uiowa.edu/
[5] Department of Ophthalmology and Visual Sciences, Iowa City, IA
http://webeye.ophth.uiowa.edu/

Abstract. This paper describes and evaluates a coarse-grained parallel computational approach to identifying rare evolutionary events often referred to as "horizontal gene transfers". Unlike classical genetic evolution, in which variations in genes accumulate gradually within and among species, horizontal transfer events result in a set of potentially important genes which "jump" directly from the genetic material of one species to another. Such genes, known as xenologs, appear as anomalies when phylogenetic trees are compared for normal and xenologous genes from the same sets of species. However, this has not been previously possible due to a lack of data and computational capacity. With the availability of large numbers of computer clusters, as well as genomic sequence from more than 2,000 species containing as many as 35,000 genes each, and trillions of sequence nucleotides in all, the possibility exists to examine "clusters" of genes using phylogenetic tree "similarity" as a distance metric. The full version of this problem requires years of CPU time, yet only makes modest IPC and memory demands; thus, it is an ideal candidate for a grid computing approach. This paper describes such a solution and preliminary benchmarking results that show a reduction in total execution time from approximately two years to less than two weeks. Finally, we report on several trade-off issues in various partitions of the problem across WAN nodes, and LAN/WAN networks of tightly coupled computing clusters.

1 Introduction

The mass availability of trillions of nucleotides of genomic sequence from more than 2,000 species containing as many as 35,000 genes each, makes it possible to pose biological and biomedical questions that just a few years ago would have been inconceivable. However, without large-scale parallel computational power, it would still be infeasible to practically address and answer these same questions. These two

V. Malyshkin (Ed.): PaCT 2005, LNCS 3606, pp. 355–366, 2005.

necessary elements have met in a number of fascinating settings within the genomics and bioinformatics communities; this paper describes a grid-parallelizable [1] algorithm and implementation called *XenoCluster* which addresses one such setting known as *horizontal gene transfer*. In addition, general issues facing the use of heterogeneous networks for such problems are addressed. The result of XenoCluster will be to identify genes in a species which are candidate xenologs -- or genes that were introduced into a species by horizontal gene transfer, rather than by random mutation and natural selection. The underlying methods employed to detect xenologs are proven methods, used by biologists on small sets of species and genes for decades. This paper is reporting on a scaled implementation for benchmark purposes. The ultimate goal of this work is to develop a robust, grid-deployed version to identify xenolog candidates to be verified with traditional biological means. Our benchmark results show that it is possible to efficiently harness more than 2,048 processors organized in a heterogeneous grid of modest sized compute clusters to reduce the overall computation time of a typical problem setting from more than 2 years to roughly 12 days. Our work is continuing in the development of new parallel methods to allow even more efficient implementation of XenoCluster on larger numbers of processors, as well as a generic grid implementation using emerging grid computing platforms such as BIRN [2], Globus [3], or other OGSA [4] platforms.

2   Background and Related Work

2.1   Biological Background

Typical genes are transferred through lineages, from one generation to the next within a species. However, an alternate form of "inheritance" is possible in which genetic material crosses species boundaries. This form of inheritance is termed horizontal gene transfer. This may occur from a single gene transferred via a viral vector, or through an endosymbiotic event resulting in the acquisition of an entire genome. Such events are generally accepted theories throughout evolution (e.g., eukaryotic acquisition of mitochondria via an endosymbiosis of blue-green algae). Thus the ability to identify patterns of horizontal gene transfer can increase our understanding of the evolution of species and the structure of the tree of life.

General features of horizontal gene transfer include higher inter-species sequence similarity between two taxa (species) that are in different clades (branches) of the consensus tree. To accomplish this, a broad set of species must be sampled. Ideally all species for which gene sequence is available would be utilized. The limiting factors are thus the availability of sequence for a large number of taxa, sampled across a broad set of phyla, and the capability to harness sufficient computational power to identify orthologous sequences, construct phylogenetic trees for each orthologous set of genes, and then compare the trees derived from each orthologous set to identify "non-consensus" inheritance patterns.

2.2   Computational Background

Several operations are necessary to identify horizontal gene transfers, or other anomalous gene inheritance events. First, orthologous sequences must be identified.

Orthologs are the same gene in different species (e.g., hemoglobin alpha in human and mouse). Next these sequences must be aligned, and phylogenetic trees created. Finally, the tree structures are compared to identify atypical patterns of inheritance.

There are several computational methods for determining orthology. The most commonly accepted method is based upon a strongly connected graph constructed of nodes representing genes across species in which each element is more similar to the others in the set than to genes from outside the set. In graph theoretical terms, this is analogous to a strongly connected component. In practice, this definition may be performed in an NxN comparison of all sequences to all other sequences or it may be performed using a "root" species upon which all other comparisons are based. The latter method is known as a Star multi-alignment, and is the only computationally feasible method for moderate to large numbers of sequences.

Additionally, there are several previously generated set of orthologs publicly available. These include COG (Clusters of Orthologous Groups), and KOG (Eukaryotic Orthologous Groups) from NCBI [5], as well as OrthoMCL [6] from the University of Pennsylvania and EGO Eukaryotic Gene Orthologs; [7] from TIGR. The primary limitation on each of these data sets is the scope of sequences utilized in the construction. OrthoMCL only includes the genes from 10 specific well-curated species. The method described in this paper presents a more dynamic version that incorporates sequences from all organisms available in the NCBI's non-redundant amino acid database (NR).

Phylogenetic analysis allows determination of the most likely pattern of inheritance of a gene. In other words, it estimates the evolutionary relationship between the species for which orthologous sequences of the same gene (or set of genes) are available. Such analyses may be done with either nucleotide or amino acid sequences, and yield a phylogenetic tree. Dendrograms are the most frequently used representation of a phylogenetic tree. After a phylogenetic tree has been created, its structure is evaluated through repeated construction of trees based upon randomly reconstructing replicate data sets based upon the original data set. Programs such as PHYLIP [8] and PAUP [9] are commonly used to construct phylogenetic trees, based upon an aligned set of orthologous sequences. Both programs support multiple construction methods, including distance-based construction as well as maximum likelihood-based construction methods.

3   Approach and Methods

In this section, we present an outline of the computational methods needed to solve this problem in general, and then discuss the way in which this solution may be parallelized for a *grid of clusters* solution in heterogeneous-latency networks. The algorithm is divided into 3 major phases:

1. Identification of a maximal set of orthologous genes.
2. Generation of phylogenetic trees resulting from orthologous groups.
3. Clustering of these trees into groups corresponding to genes which show consistent evolutionary behavior.

In phase 1, it is necessary to identify potential homologous genes for every gene in the union of a complex set of 1000s of species. This is accomplished by BLASTing

[10] each gene against the set of all known genes in all species, and then performing a reciprocal BLAST operation to verify that the best hit for each gene hits the original gene with the highest rank score. This becomes the base set of orthologous gene groups to be used in phase 2 among which xenologs may be identified. The second phase involves the sequence trimming and multiple alignment of all members of each of the orthologous gene groups, followed by the automated generation of a phylogenetic tree for each aligned group. The final phase performs an all-pairs distance analysis of phylogenetic trees for all gene groups, and then uses a clustering technique to identify maximal sets of trees, which represent sets of genes which share a common evolutionary history. This two-level clustering is illustrated by the tree of trees figure shown in Figure 1.

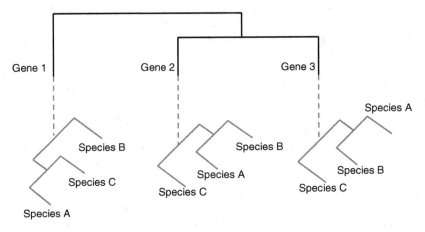

Fig. 1. An illustration of the clustering of phylogenetic trees. The overall tree is partitioning based on genes, and each tree at a leaf node represents a tree of species based on the genes in a single orthologous group. Leaves that are "close" together are similar based on common patterns of evolutionary descent

Relatively small clusters of genes (shown as trees grouped together as leaves of the main tree) are likely to implicate xenologs, and would eventually need to be verified by closer biological examination.

Important design details of the procedure outlined above are presented in the following sections, and are illustrated summarily in Figure 2.

3.1 Orthologous Set Identification

Ortholog identification was performed using the COE (Computational Orthology Engine) system, developed at the University of Iowa. COE identifies orthologous sequence groups using a reciprocal best-alignment strategy. Each mRNA RefSeq [11] sequence for a base species was BLASTed against NCBI's non-redundant amino acid database.

For each BLAST result, the top hit of each species was selected, if and only if it met a stringent quality threshold criterion. The threshold criteria included

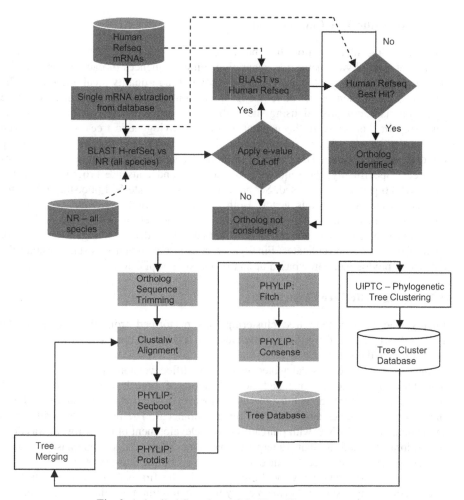

Fig. 2. A detailed flowchart of the XenoCluster approach

minimum length of matching region, alignment score and statistical significance (e-value). If these criteria were not met, then a reciprocal BLAST was not performed and ortholog investigation for the particular alignment was aborted.

If the threshold criterion was met, a reciprocal BLAST was performed with these top species hits against the RefSeq database [11] to further support the orthology inference. A reciprocal BLAST that did not yield the original RefSeq sequence as the best BLAST hit, was discarded and not considered an ortholog. If the reciprocal BLAST yielded the original RefSeq sequence as the best hit, then the reciprocal BLAST sequence and species information was added to the orthologous group for the current mRNA sequence.

Text parsing of the BLAST results was performed using custom Perl scripts with the BioPerl [12] package. Batch scheduling of all BLAST operations in phase 1 was performed using the Portable Batch System [13].

3.2 Phylogentic Tree Construction

Once ortholog identification has been performed, the next phase is trimming, alignment, and phylogenetic tree generation. First, sequences of each group must be trimmed to contain only the subsequences showing high-quality local alignment. The trimming of sequences is done using a custom Perl script. Multiple sequence alignment is accomplished using the well-established clustalw software [14]. The final step in this phase is the generation of the phylogenetic trees – one for each orthologous group of genes identified in phase 1. Each gene and its corresponding ortholog set form a tree. The PHYLIP [8] software suite was used to generate each of the trees. Specifically, the seqboot, protdist, fitch and consense programs from the PHYLIP 3.6 package were used. Seqboot was used to create 500 bootstrap replicates for each set of orthologous genes. Both protdist and fitch were run with default parameters, except that they analyzed the complete set of 500 replicates. These programs generated the sequence distance matrices and the phylogenetic trees for each of the bootstrap replicates. Finally, the consense program was run to obtain the consensus phylogenetic tree based upon the bootstrap replicates.

3.3 Phylogenetic Tree Clustering

Finally, the phylogenetic tree clustering was performed from the results of the PHYLIP software package. This involves two main sub-phases – distance matrix generation, and clustering.

Inter-tree distance was calculated using a modified version of the TreeRank [15] algorithm. Modifications included normalization of branch lengths and up-down distances to reflect tree branch lengths as phylogenetic distances. In the published form, this algorithm assumes unit length for all tree branches. The modified algorithm was implemented in POSIX C with pthread support. Development of this software was done on Fedora 9.0 and Redhat Enterprise machines. The second sub-phase involved clustering, given a complete distance matrix from every tree to every other tree.

The second sub-phase involved clustering via the first sub-phase's tree distance matrix containing distances between every tree. A minimum similarity parameter was used to specify the minimum tree to tree similarity allowed to add a tree to an existing cluster. If a given tree met or exceeded *any* tree in a cluster, it was added to that cluster and no further comparisons were performed for that tree. The tree clustering system was implemented in POSIX C with pthread support. Development of this software was done on Fedora 9.0 and Redhat Enterprise machines.

3.4 Grid/Cluster Implementation and Benchmarking Approach

Each of the phases described in detail above were implemented in a LINUX environment (2.2GHz dual Athlon with 2GB RAM running either Fedora or Redhat 9.0), and benchmark executions were performed using the largest set of human genes known at the time of publication. For this analysis, and all benchmarks, this consisted of the set of all 20,364 known human RefSeq mRNA sequences. Runtime estimates for the first phase of the computation, which involved the COE system, varied significantly with system threshold parameters. The initial iteration of the system yielded an average of 588 cpu seconds per RefSeq mRNA. Variations of the aforementioned match length, alignment score and e-value thresholds can change the number of reciprocal BLASTs performed and therefore the average runtime. Thus, the values reported in Table 1 are an average taken across the entire set of 20,364 genes. The average COE benchmark time per RefSeq gene also varied substantially with the size of the mRNA nucleotide sequence, and the novelty of the RefSeq gene. For example, a gene that was highly conserved across several species would have many more reciprocal alignments to perform than a gene that only appears in the human species. The COE results yielded an average of 12.6 orthologs per RefSeq mRNA. More relevant to performance, a mean of 39 reciprocal BLASTs were performed for each RefSeq mRNA. This meant that approximately 32% of the reciprocal alignments were considered orthologs while the remaining 68% were not considered to be the RefSeq mRNA's true ortholog because a better hit was found to a different RefSeq. An important trade-off for future investigation is the sensitivity and specificity of the ortholog search versus execution time. Lowering the match criteria in the initial BLAST phase will improve sensitivity, while requiring more work to be performed in the reciprocal BLAST phase to address specificity.

Currently, work is underway which will allow phase 1 and phase 2 to be deployed on a globus [3] administered grid. In addition to PBS, other cluster scheduling tools hope to be deployed, such as Condor [16] and SGE [17] to provide users with a robust job submission environment. With the ongoing development of the Open Grid Services Architecture [4] and projects such as caGrid [18], additional modification and portability development will be done to take advantage of future computer resource architectures.

In the next section, we will discuss the effect of deployment of XenoCluster on a large-scale grid of compute clusters. The average benchmark time of 588 seconds could potentially be extrapolated to reveal the runtime of the entire dataset through the COE system. To validate the accuracy of our predictive model, 20,364 mRNAs at an average of 588 seconds would yield 3,326 cpu hours. A benchmark was then performed on our 16-node Linux cluster (same nodes as reported above). The wall clock time was shortened to 207 cluster hours. This was very close to the expected time of approximately 12 days. Runtime of the PHYLIP software increased linearly with the number of bootstrap iterations performed. Preliminary averages show a runtime of 579 cpu seconds at 100 bootstrap iterations, while an average of 2,518 cpu seconds was achieved at 500 bootstrap iterations. The tree clustering phase (UIPTC) results were extrapolated to reveal the estimated runtime of the large 20,364 gene set.

Table 1 summarizes the detailed times (in wall-clock time units of seconds) of 5 computational and 2 communication elements of XenoCluster. The intra-cluster communication overhead was approximated as the average time to transfer the NR database between two Linux clusters via a 100 Mb connection. Similarly, the inter-cluster communication cost overhead was calculated as the average time to transfer the NR database between compute nodes in the same cluster over a 1 Gb connection.

Phase 1 as described in section 3.1 is represented by two benchmark elements – Initial BLAST and Reciprocal BLAST respectively– because these two phases are differently affected by parallelization. Similarly, the phylogenetic tree generation phase described in section 3.2 is divided into a Sequence Alignment (including trimming) and PHYLIP Tree Generation. Note that these four computational elements parallelize cleanly across all genes, and in the case of reciprocal BLASTing, the degree of parallelization is increased to an average of 39x due to the fact that the number of reciprocal BLASTs depends on the number of potential orthologs identified in the Initial BLAST sub-phase. However, in the final phase, tree clustering has not been parallelized effectively at the time of this manuscript preparation and strategies for this phase are outlined in the conclusion of the paper. The pie-chart illustrates the fact that the PHYLIP phase is the single most costly in terms of execution, and thus was the first target of our parallelization strategy.

4   Results and Discussion

Based on the extensive measurements made in the benchmarking of the component phases of XenoCluster reported above, and its parallelization on a 16-node cluster, we have been able to predict performance in a grid computing environment of 1000s of compute nodes. Key to understanding the potential impact of this parallelization is two key parameters describing the grid – **K**: the number of clusters, and **N**: the number of nodes in each cluster. Note, the number of total nodes in the grid is then simply the product **K*N**. While not simulating the effect of varying sizes of clusters,

Table 1. Benchmark timings on 20,364 genes for the component phases of XenoCluster run with 1 dual CPU node (cluster size 1). Timings taken on a 2.2GHz dual Athlon with 2GB RAM running Fedora Redhat 9.0

Phase/component	Time (Seconds)	# of Iterations	Total (Seconds)
Intra Cluster IPC	124	1	124
Inter Cluster IPC	311	1	311
Initial BLAST	301	20364	6129564
Reciprocal BLAST	12	794196	9530352
Sequence Alignment	33	20364	672012
PHYLIP tree generation	2518	20364	51276552
Tree Clustering	1036800	1	1036800
Total	**1,040,099**	**855,291**	**68,645,715**
CPU Efficiency			**100.00%**
Days to completion			**794.5106**

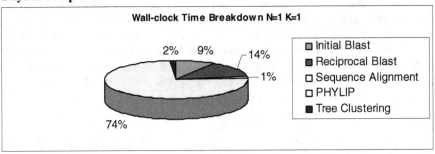

this analysis does shed meaningful light on the question of how heterogeneous communication times within a grid environment affect the overall performance and the ability of this application to effectively scale to large numbers of processors in a high-latency environment.

We first examined the effect of increasing overall system size while maintaining the number of clusters constant. Figure 3 shows a constant value of K=4, while N varies from 64 to 1024. In this graph, note the Inter-cluster IPC (Inter-Process Communication) times do not vary, as would be expected with a fixed number of clusters. However, the Intra-cluster IPC costs steadily increase. Also, as shown in Figure 3, note that all compute phases decrease overall execution up to the maximum system size of 4,096 processors. With a coarse-grained problem such as identifying xenologs, this is not surprising. The issue of trade-off with communication time is addressed later.

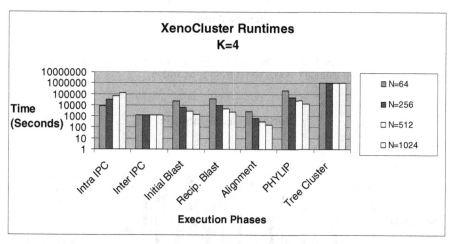

Fig. 3. XenoCluster component execution times with number of clusters (K) fixed, cluster size (N) varying. Total number of compute nodes varies from 256 to 4096

Figure 4 examines the case of holding the cluster size (N) fixed, while varying cluster size (K). Now, the Intra-cluster IPC costs are fixed as cluster size increases, but the Inter-IPC costs increase. However, the effect of increasing the volume of data between clusters has a more harmful overall affect due to higher latency, than increasing intra-cluster IPC as demonstrated in Figure 3. This is most striking when comparing the Intra-IPC costs with K=4, N=1,024 at 126,976 seconds, with the Inter-IPC costs with K=1,024, N=4 at 318,464 seconds.

Bringing the communication and computation costs together, and examining a range of combinations of K and N, Figure 5 illustrates the potential benefits of a grid solution to the xenolog problem. Performing an optimization search of this parameter space (not described here) produces the optimal configuration of K=16, and N=128. Such a 2,048 node grid solution would yield an execution time of 12.8 days. Also shown in Figure 5 are the execution times of the extreme cases of N=1, K=1, and N=1, K=16384, clearly demonstrating the tradeoff between communication and computation, and the need to construct a grid configuration of a significant number of clusters.

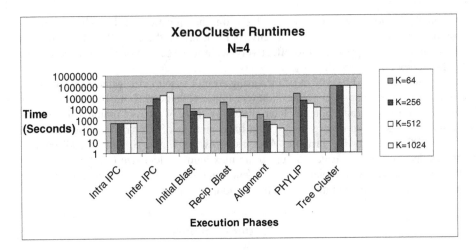

Fig. 4. XenoCluster component execution times with cluster size (N) fixed, number of clusters (K) varying. Number of compute nodes varies from 256 to 4096

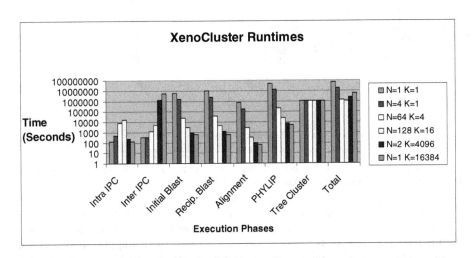

Fig. 5. XenoCluster execution times for varying number of clusters and cluster sizes. Total number of compute nodes varies from 1 to 16384

Each of the three phases of the system lent themselves to different forms of parallelization and optimization. Since each of the 20,364 mRNAs through the COE system are non-causally related and independent, a simple batch scheduling system was employed to gain close to linear speed up. However, the bandwidth needs of BLAST for database access hindered the ideal linear speed up. At 1.8 GB, the non-redundant nucleotide (NR) database presented a significant load even for modern gigabit networks to transfer. Therefore, cached copies of the databases were stored on the compute nodes. Future work in this area would involve modifying the database caching system to integrate into existing grid computing infrastructures. One solution would involve creating a hierarchy of cached NR databases across all clusters in a grid.

The tree generation phase of the computation benefits most from a grid computing approach – even with small cluster sizes. This stage requires relatively little data per node, while CPU demands are high – the ideal large-grained application characteristic. These properties lend themselves to a grid architecture where CPUs are inexpensive and network bandwidth is at a premium.

Finally, the third phase of the computation which involves the clustering of all 20,364 trees stands as the best candidate for further parallelization. The inter-tree distance matrix could be broken in to smaller sub-matrices and distributed via inter-process communication, a la MPI. An MPI solution of the problem is currently being implemented which would reduce the final overall computation time to a fraction of the current best performance. This solution partitions the distance matrix in a virtual 2-D mesh of processors which seeks to minimize interprocessor communication by careful assignment of trees to processors.

5 Conclusions

This paper has shown a large class of applications which just a few years ago would not have been possible due to both a lack of genomic data, but more importantly, the lack of an effective parallel computational strategy. XenoCluster has shown an effective speedup of a prototype scaled version of the xenolog-finding problem from roughly 2 years to less than one day in a grid environment of 1000s of processors in varying sizes of compute clusters.

However, it must be pointed out that the full solution of this biologically-driven problem will only be accomplished by an overall iterative refinement of the clustering by re-aligning concatenated cluster members, generation of trees and comparison of resulting tree clusters with predicted trees. This interpretation step must be done with close collaboration with evolutionary biologists. Thus, the need for an efficient grid deployment to this problem becomes even more paramount, and is the subject of our ongoing work.

Acknowledgments

TES was supported under a Career Development Award from Research to Prevent Blindness.

TBB was supported by an NRSA post-doctoral fellowship no 1F32HG002881.

References

[1] Computational Grids., I. Foster, C. Kesselman. Chapter 2 of "The Grid: Blueprint for a New Computing Infrastructure", Morgan-Kaufman, 1999.

[2] Ellisman, M. and Peltier, S. Medical data federation: The biomedical informatics research network. In *The Grid: Blueprint for a New Computing Infrastructure, 2nd Ed.,* I. Foster and C. Kesselman, Eds. Morgan Kaufmann, San Francisco, 2004.

[3] Globus: A Metacomputing Infrastructure Toolkit. I. Foster, C. Kesselman. *Intl J. Supercomputer Applications*, 11(2):115-128, 1997.

[4] Open Grid Services Architecture. http://www.globus.org/ogsa/

[5] Tatusov RL, Fedorova ND, Jackson JD, Jacobs AR, Kiryutin B, Koonin EV, Krylov DM, Mazumder R, Mekhedov SL, Nikolskaya AN, Rao BS, Smirnov S, Sverdlov AV, Vasudevan S, Wolf YI, Yin JJ, Natale DA. (2003) The COG database: an updated version includes eukaryotes. BMC Bioinformatics. 4(1):41.

[6] Li, L., Stoeckert, C. J. Jr., Roos, D. S. (2003). OrthoMCL: Identification of Ortholog Groups for Eukaryotic Genomes. Genome Res. 13: 2178-2189

[7] Lee Y, Sultana R, Pertea G, Cho J, Karamycheva S, Tsia J, Parvizi B, Cheung F, Antonescu V, White J, Holt I, Liang F, and Quackenbush J. (2002) Cross-referencing eukaryotic genomes: TIGR orthologous gene alignments (TOGA). Genome Research 12(3): 493-502.

[8] Felsenstein, J. 1989. PHYLIP - Phylogeny Inference Package (Version 3.2). Cladistics 5: 164-166.

[9] Swofford, D. L. 2003. PAUP*. Phylogenetic Analysis Using Parsimony (*and Other Methods). Version 4. Sinauer Associates, Sunderland, Massachusetts.

[10] Altschul SF, Gish W, Miller W, Myers EW, Lipman DJ. Basic local alignment search tool. J Mol Biol 1990;215:403-410

[11] Pruitt KD, Katz KS, Sicotte H, Maglott DR. (2000) Introducing RefSeq and LocusLink: curated human genome resources at the NCBI. Trends Genet. 16(1):44-47.

[12] Stajich JE, Block D, Boulez K, Brenner SE, Chervitz SA, Dagdigian C, Fuellen G, Gilbert JGR, Korf I, Lapp H, Lehvaslaiho H, Matsalla C, Mungall CJ, Osborne BI, Pocock MR, Schattner P, Senger M, Stein LD, Stupka ED, Wilkinson M, Birney E. The Bioperl Toolkit: Perl modules for the life sciences. Genome Research. 2002 Oct;12(10):1611-8.

[13] PBS Pro. http://www.pbspro.com/

[14] Thompson J D, Higgins D G and Gibson T J (1994). CLUSTAL W: improving the sensitivity of progressive multiple sequence alignment through sequence weighting, positions-specific gap penalties and weight matrix choice. *Nucleic Acids Res.*, **22**, 4673-4680.

[15] Wang JTL, Shan H, Shasha D and Piel WH. (2003) TreeRank: A Similarity Measure for Nearest Neighbor Searching in Phylogenetic Databases. Proceedings of the 15th International Conference on Scientific and Statistical Database Management (SSDBM 2003), Cambridge, Massachusetts, pp. 171-180.

[16] Michael Litzkow, Miron Livny, and Matt Mutka, "Condor - A Hunter of Idle Workstations", *Proceedings of the 8th International Conference of Distributed Computing Systems,* pages 104-111, June, 1988.

[17] Sun Grid Engine. http://gridengine.sunsource.net/

[18] caGrid. https://cabig.nci.nih.gov/guidelines_documentation/caGRIDWhitepaper.pdf

A Model for Designing and Implementing Parallel Applications Using Extensible Architectural Skeletons

Mohammad Mursalin Akon[1], Dhrubajyoti Goswami[2], and Hon Fung Li[2]

[1] Department of ECE, University of Waterloo, Canada
[2] Department of Computer Science, Concordia University, Montreal, Canada
{mm_akon, goswami, hfli}@cs.concordia.ca

Abstract. With the advent of hardware technologies, high-performance parallel computers and commodity clusters are becoming affordable. However, complexity of parallel application development remains one of the major obstacles towards the mainstream adoption of parallel computing. As one of the solution techniques, researchers are actively investigating the pattern-based approaches to parallel programming. As re-usable components, patterns are intended to ease the design and development phases of a parallel applications. While using patterns, a developer supplies the application specific code-components whereas the underlying environment generates most of the code for parallelization. PAS (Parallel Architectural Skeleton) is one such pattern-based parallel programming model and tool, which defines the architectural aspects of parallel computational patterns. Like many other pattern-based models and tools, the PAS model was hampered by its lack of extensibility, i.e., lacking of support for the systematic addition of new skeletons to an existing skeleton repository. Lack of extensibility significantly reduces the flexibility and hence the usability of a particular approach. SuperPAS is an extension of PAS that defines a model for systematically designing and implementing PAS skeletons by a skeleton designer. The newly implemented skeletons can subsequently be used by an application developer. SuperPAS model is realized through a Skeleton Description Language (SDL), which assists both a skeleton designer and an application developer. The paper discusses the SuperPAS model through examples that use the SDL. The paper also discusses some of the recent usability and performance studies, which demonstrate that SuperPAS is a practical and usable parallel programming model and tool.

1 Introduction

With time, computer hardware is getting inexpensive and faster. At the same time, scientists are investigating increasingly complex problems with finer level of detail, requiring larger computing power, sophisticated algorithms and cutting-edge software. Research in High Performance Computing (HPC) is exploring different aspects of available and foreseeable technology to realize those complex problems.

V. Malyshkin (Ed.): PaCT 2005, LNCS 3606, pp. 367–380, 2005.

Parallel application design and development is complex and hence is a major area of focus in the domain of HPC. Numerous research has been conducted and several approaches have been proposed for hiding some of these complexities. This research focuses on one such approach, which is based on the idea of (frequently occurring) design patterns in parallel computing. In the domain of parallel computing, (parallel) design patterns specify recurring parallel computational problems with similar structural and behavioral components, and their solution strategies. Several parallel programming systems have been built with the intent to facilitate rapid development of parallel applications through the use of design patterns as reusable components. Some of these systems are *Enterprise* [1], *Tracs* [2], *DPnDP* [3], *COPS* [4], *PAS* [5], and *ASSIST* [6].

Most of the previous research in this direction focused on the algorithmic or behavioral aspects of patterns, popularly known as *algorithmic skeletons* [7]. On the contrary, Parallel Architectural Skeletons (PAS) [8, 5] focus on the architectural or structural aspects of message-passing parallel patterns. Each architectural skeleton in PAS encapsulates the various structural attributes of a pattern in a generic (i.e., pattern- and application-independent) fashion. An architectural skeleton can be considered as a pattern-specific virtual machine with its own communication, synchronization and structural primitives. A developer, depending upon the specific needs of an application, chooses the appropriate skeletons, supplies the required parameters for the generic attributes, and finally fills in the application-specific code. Architectural skeletons supply most of the code that is necessary for the low-level and parallelism-related issues. Consequently, there exists a clear separation between application dependent and application independent issues (i.e., *separation of concerns*).

Each skeleton is a reusable component, which can be configured to the needs of an application and also can be composed with other skeletons to create a complete parallel application. Though re-usability is an obvious benefit, the lack of extensibility is one of the major concerns associated with many of the pattern-based parallel programming systems, including PAS. Most existing systems support a limited and fixed set of patterns that are hard-coded into those systems. Generally, there is no provision for adding a new pattern without understanding the entire system (including its implementation) and writing the pattern from scratch (i.e., lack of extensibility). Consequently, if a required parallel computing pattern demanded by an application is not supported, generally the designer has no alternative but to abandon the idea of using the particular approach altogether (lack of flexibility). Obviously, lack of flexibility hampers the usability of a particular approach.

SuperPAS is an extension of the PAS system and it addresses the drawbacks mentioned previously. An earlier discussion of SuperPAS based on the initial phase of this research appeared in [9]. In this paper, we discuss the complete SuperPAS model via examples that use the Skeleton Description Language (SDL), mainly targeted for a skeleton designer. Using the SDL, a skeleton designer can design and implement a new skeleton without understanding the low level details of the system and its implementation. We elaborate the SDL via examples.

Note that the SDL is mainly for assisting a skeleton designer. An application developer has to do most of the development work using pure C++.

We also describe some of the recent usability and performance studies. The studies show that the SuperPAS significantly reduces the development time without compromising the performance of the developed applications.

In the next section, we introduce the necessary preliminaries. In Section 3, the SDL constructs are discussed through examples. A step-by-step application development procedure is described in Section 4. Section 5 describes the usability and performance tests and results. Finally, Section 6 concludes our discussion emphasizing on current research trends and future directions.

2   Preliminaries

Parallel Architectural Skeletons (abbreviated as PAS) [5, 8] generically encapsulate the structural/architectural attributes of message-passing parallel computing patterns. Each PAS skeleton is parameterized where each parameter is associated with some attribute. The value of a parameter is determined during the application development phase. A PAS skeleton with unbound parameters is called an *abstract skeleton* or an *abstract module*. An abstract skeleton becomes a *concrete skeleton* or a *concrete module*, when the parameters of the skeleton are bounded to actual values. A concrete skeleton is yet to be filled in with application-specific code. Filling a concrete skeleton with application-specific code results in a *code-complete parallel module* or simply a *module*. Various phases of an application development using PAS are roughly illustrated in Figure 1(a). The figure shows that different parameter bindings to the same abstract skeleton can result in different concrete skeletons.

Each abstract skeleton (or abstract module) consists of the following set of attributes: (i) *Representative* of a skeleton represents the module in its action and interactions with other modules. The initial representative is empty and is subsequently filled with application-specific code during application development. (ii) The *back-end* of an abstract module A_m can be formally represented as $\{A_{m1}, A_{m2}, ..., A_{mn}\}$, where each A_{mi} is itself an abstract module. The type of each A_{mi} is determined after the abstract module A_m is concretized. Note that collection of concrete modules inside another concrete module results in a (tree-structured) hierarchy. Consequently, each A_{mi} is called a *child* of A_m, and A_m is called the *parent*. The children of a module are *peers* of one another. In this paper, the children of a module are also referred as *computational nodes* of the associated skeleton or patterns. (iii) *Topology* is the logical connectivity between the children inside the back-end as well as the connectivity between the children and the representative. (iv) *Internal primitives* are the pattern-specific communication, synchronization or structural primitives. Interactions among the various modules are performed using these primitives. The internal primitives, the inherent properties of the skeleton, capture the parallel computing model of the associated pattern as well as the topology. Figure 1(b) diagrammatically illustrates attributes of an abstract and a concrete 2-D Mesh skeleton.

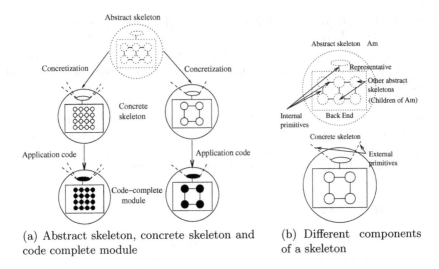

(a) Abstract skeleton, concrete skeleton and code complete module

(b) Different components of a skeleton

Fig. 1. PAS skeletons and their components

There are pattern-specific parameters associated with some of the previous attributes. For instance, if the topology is a Mesh, then the number of dimensions of the mesh is one parameter, and the nature of the connectivities among the nodes at the edges (i.e., toroidal or non-toroidal) is another parameter. Binding these parameters to actual values, based on the needs of an application, results in a concrete module. A concrete module C_m becomes a code-complete module when: (i) the representative of C_m is filled in with application-specific code, and (ii) each child of C_m is code-complete.

All of the attributes of an abstract skeleton are inherited by the corresponding concrete skeletons as well as the code-complete modules. In addition, we define the term *external primitives* of a concrete or a code complete module as the set of primitives using which the module (i.e., its representative) can interact with its parent (i.e., representative of the parent) and peers (i.e., representatives of the peers). Unlike internal primitives, which are inherent properties of a skeleton, external primitives are adaptable, i.e., a module adapts to the context of its parent by using the internal primitives of its parent as its external primitives. While filling in the representative of a concrete module with application-specific code, the application developer uses the internal and external primitives to interact with other modules in the hierarchy.

A parallel application developed using PAS is a hierarchical collection of (code-complete) modules. Conceptually, each concrete module can be considered as a pattern-specific virtual machine with its own communication, synchronization and structural primitives. A user fills in these virtual machines with application-specific code, starting bottoms-up in the hierarchy, to create the complete parallel application. The root of the hierarchy, i.e. a code-complete module with no parent, represents a complete parallel application. Each non-root node of the hierarchy represents a partial parallel application. Each leaf of the hierarchy is called a *singleton module* (and correspondingly, a *singleton skeleton* for the abstract counterpart).

3 SuperPAS Model and the Associated SDL

In this section, we discuss about the model of SuperPAS with the help of the associated Skeleton Description Language (SDL). First, we give a brief overview of SuperPAS. The subsequent discussion describes the SDL for designing and implementing abstract and concrete skeletons.

3.1 Basic Idea Behind the SuperPAS Model

SuperPAS model incorporates the PAS model, and provides extra features to facilitate design and implementation of new abstract skeletons. SuperPAS provides a set of multidimensional grids to embed the topologies of newly designed (abstract) skeletons. Each node of the grid is considered as a virtual processor. Each multidimensional *virtual processor grid* (*VPG*) is equipped with its own communication and synchronization primitives. These primitives include operations for synchronous and asynchronous peer-to-peer communication, collective communication, and synchronization-specific primitives. We chose to make the VPG primitives a super-set of the basic communication-synchronization primitives supported in some of the prominent parallel programming environments. Our choice is influenced by the MPI standard, PVM documentations, our experiences with PAS and other pattern-based systems, and various research articles (e.g., [10]). In the process of designing an abstract skeleton, the skeleton designer needs to embed the topology of the newly designed skeleton to the existing grid topology provided by SuperPAS, and consequently map each of its children (i.e., abstract modules of the back-end) into a VPG node. The embedding of a skeleton into a VPG is complete when the associated communication, synchronization and structural primitives of the skeleton are defined. These primitives are defined on top of the existing SuperPAS-provided primitives for the VPG. The following discussion elaborates and exemplifies these issues.

3.2 The SDL for Abstract Skeletons

As mentioned before, the SDL is mainly targeted towards a skeleton designer who designs and implements new abstract skeletons and integrates them into the existing skeleton repository. We demonstrate the different language features by describing the design procedure of an abstract *Wavefront* skeleton, which implements the *Wavefront* pattern. Figure 2(a) is the visualization of the Wavefront skeleton where its constituents and topology are shown. The visualization helps the designer to make several design decisions. At first, she decides about the *parameters* of the skeleton. For example, in this case, the structure of a Wavefront skeleton becomes generic if the the number of rows (or the number of columns)

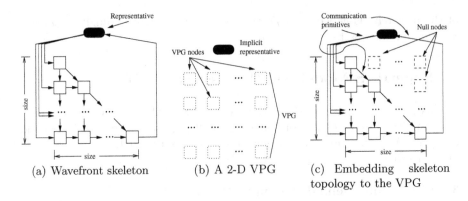

(a) Wavefront skeleton   (b) A 2-D VPG   (c) Embedding   skeleton
                                                        topology to the VPG

Fig. 2. Mapping wavefront skeleton components into a 2-D VPG

of the skeleton is considered to be a parameter rather than a constant. In this
example, we name this parameter as *size*.

In the case of a Wavefront skeleton, the choice of a two dimensional VPG (Figure 2(b)) for embedding the topology of the skeleton is an obvious choice because
it facilitates a one-to-one mapping of the children (of the skeleton) into the nodes
of the VPG. Figure 2(c) shows one such mapping. Note that each VPG has an implicit representative node, to which the representative of the skeleton is mapped
onto. From the figure, it can be found that even after limiting the height and
width of the VPG (to the parameter *size*), there are virtual processors to which
no child of the skeleton are mapped onto. Those virtual processors are called
null virtual processors or *null nodes*.

```
00 integer size; // The parameter for the skeleton
01 // Design of the the Wavefront skeleton follows:
02 skeleton Wavefront(2) { // Embedded into a  2 dimensional VPG
03    LOCAL  = {
04      void init(void) { // The initialization function
05        // Set the dimensions of the skeleton topology
06        for (int i = 0; i < GetDimension(); i++)
07          SetDimensionLimit(i, size);
08      }
09      bool non_null(const Location & loc) { // Define non-null nodes
10        // loc[0], loc[1], .. indicate position of a VPG node in a
11        // specific dimension, i.e. loc[0] is for the lowest
12        // dimension, loc[1] is for next dimension, etc.
13        if (loc[1] <= loc[0]) // column number <= row number
14          return true;
15        return false;
16      }
17    };
18    INITIALIZE = init; // Set the name of the initialization function
19    MAPPING    = non_null; // Set the name of the mapping function
20    PRIVATE    = { ... }; // Private primitives
21    PUBLIC     = { ... }; // Public primitives
22 }
```

As is shown in the previous SDL code, the skeleton description starts with
the declaration of the parameters, and subsequently the definitions of the con-

stituents of the skeleton and their embeddings to the 2-D VPG. The initialization
function *init* (line 18) limits the length of both of the dimensions of the VPG to
the parameter *size*. The function *non_null* (line 19) returns true for all non-null
VPG nodes, i.e., nodes located on or below the upper diagonal of the VPG.
Consequently it defines the embedding of the Wavefront skeleton into the VPG.
It should be noted that *GetDimension* and *SetDimensionLimit* are two of the
built-in structural primitives provided by SuperPAS.

The definition of the skeleton is not complete unless the topology (i.e., connectivity) of the skeleton components is defined. In practice, the (virtual) connectivity is established via defining the internal communication primitives of
the skeleton. SuperPAS divides the internal primitives into two categories: *private* primitives are to be used exclusively by the representative of the skeleton,
whereas *public* primitives are inherited by the children as external primitives. In
the case of the Wavefront skeleton, a *receive message from the child, located at
the last column* is a private primitive whereas a *send message to the left peer* is
a public primitive. The SDL code for defining the private and public primitives
is shown next:

```
...
skeleton Wavefront (2) { // Embedded into a  2 dimensional VPG
    LOCAL = { ... };
    INITIALIZE = ...;
    MAPPING = ...;
    // private primitives
    PRIVATE = {
        // Send a message to a child located at <nRow, 0>
        bool SendToNodeAt(int nRow, Msg & m) {
            Location loc;
            loc[1] = 0, loc[0] = nRow;
            return SendChild(loc, m); // VPG primitive provided by SuperPAS
        }
        // Receive a message from the child located at <size - 1, size - 1>
        bool RecvFromLastNode(Msg & m) {
            Location loc;
            loc[0] = loc[1] = size - 1;
            return RecvChild(loc, m); // VPG primitive provided by SuperPAS
        } ...
    };
    // Public primitives
    PUBLIC = {
        // COMMUNICATION PRIMITIVES
        // Send message from node <i, j> to <i, j+1>
        void SendRight(Msg &m) {
            Location loc = GetLocation();
            loc[1] = loc[1] + 1;
            SendPeer(loc, m); // VPG primitive provided by SuperPAS
        }
        // Node <i, j> receive message from node <i, j+1>
        void RecvRight(Msg &m) { ... }
        // Receive message from the representative
        void RecvRepresentative(Msg &m) {
            RecvParent(m); // VPG primitive provided by SuperPAS
        }
        // STRUCTURAL PRIMITIVES
        // Check if node is located at the first column
        bool IsAtFirstColumn() {
            Location loc = GetLocation();
```

```
      return loc[1] == 0; // is column number == 0?
   }
   // Check if node is located at the diagonal
   bool IsAtDiagonal() {
      Location loc = GetLocation();
      return loc[0] == loc[1]; // is column number == row number?
   }
       ...
   };
}
```

In the previous code, the skeleton-specific private primitives (e.g., *SendToN-odeAt, RecvFromLastNode*, etc.) and the public primitives (e.g., *SendRight, IsAt-Diagonal*, etc.) are defined inside the language constructs *PUBLIC* and *PRIVATE* respectively. These skeleton-specific primitives are built on top of the basic SuperPAS-provided primitives for the 2-D VPG, i.e. *SendChild, RecvPeer, GetLocation*, etc.

3.3 The SDL for Concrete Skeletons

The SDL also provides supports to an application developer during the concretization phase. However, it should be noted that the application developer has to do majority of the development work using pure C++. According to the PAS model, concretization of skeletons during application development is a top-down procedure, starting at the root of the hierarchy. While developing an application, a developer chooses the appropriate skeleton, from the repository of abstract skeletons, as the root of the hierarchy. Then she binds the parameters of the skeleton with appropriate values and decides about the types of its children (i.e., labeling each children with an abstract skeleton type). The labeled (abstract) children are subsequently concretized and consequently concretization proceeds in a top-down fashion.

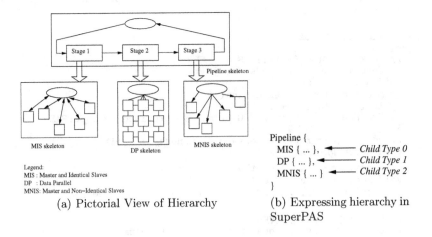

(a) Pictorial View of Hierarchy

(b) Expressing hierarchy in SuperPAS

Fig. 3. Two levels of skeleton hierarchy

For example, let us consider the skeleton hierarchy of Figure 3(a), decided by an application developer. The root of the hierarchy is constituted by a *Pipeline* skeleton. Subsequently, the first child (i.e., the first stage) of the *Pipeline* is labeled with the abstract MIS (*Master and Identical Slaves*) skeleton. The second and the third stages are labeled with DP and MNIS skeletons respectively, which stand for *Data Parallel* and *Master and Non-Identical Slaves* skeletons. The corresponding SDL code for expressing this hierarchy in SuperPAS is shown in Figure 3(b). The labelled children are subsequently concretized and thus concretization proceeds top down in the hierarchy. The example in the next section elaborates it further.

4   Example: An Image Convolution Application

Image convolution is an important application in the domain of image processing [11]. Here we describe a step by step procedure to develop a parallel image convolution application using SuperPAS.

4.1   Problem Description

Image convolution is performed by applying a mask to each of the image pixels. The simplest way to make the operations parallel is to divide the whole image into columns and/or rows. Different parts of the image are distributed to different processes and each process computes the convolution of its assigned part. Unfortunately, there are dependencies among these computing processes, i.e., each process needs to exchange data with its logically neighboring processes.

4.2   Concretizing Abstract Skeletons

As the problem description suggests, the application demands a 2-D *Mesh* skeleton with identical children (i.e., which actually represents data-parallel computation on a virtual mesh). The representative of the skeleton is mainly responsible for data partitioning (and all the file system I/O, depending on the underlying hardware constraints). The identical children of the mesh skeleton perform the actual convolution. In this case, each child of the mesh is a *Singleton* skeleton, i.e., a skeleton with an empty back-end which is analogous to a traditional sequential process. The two-level hierarchy for this application is shown in Figure 4. In the figure, *icmesh* is an instance of an abstract mesh skeleton, and *icsingleton* is an instance of an abstract singleton skeleton. It should be noted that *icsingleton* represents each identical child of the mesh skeleton.

The cluster on which this application runs consists of 10 dual-processors. Consequently, for better performance, we decided to have 20 sequential processes performing the convolution. For an input image of size 2048×1536, we chose to divide the image among 5×4 children, each of which is a singleton module and hence performs sequential computation. Based on this decision, we concretize the *icmesh* skeleton as follows:

```
// File name: image_conv.htree
icmesh { // icmesh is an isntance of Mesh skeleton
    icsingleton { // icsingleton is an instance of Singleton skeleton
    }
}
```
0−th Child Type for icmesh

Fig. 4. The two-level skeleton hierarchy for an image convolution application

```
// File name: icmesh.skel
// The icmesh skeleton: an instance of Mesh skeleton
integer k = 2; // A k-D VPG to which mesh is embedded into
// Bind the different parameters for the mesh as follows:
bool fWrapping = false; // A non-toroidal mesh
skeleton Mesh (k) {
    LIMITS = {4, 5}; // Binding: columns = 4 and row = 5
}  ...
```

We also need to specify a labeling function that labels each of the identical children of the *icmesh* skeleton as *icsingleton*, an instance of the abstract singleton skeleton. The corresponding SDL code is shown in the following :

```
// File name: icmesh.skel
skeleton Mesh (k) {
  ...
}
LOCAL = {
    void label(void) {
        Location loc;
        // for all children ....
        for (loc[1] = 0; loc[1] < GetDimensionLimit(1); loc[1]++) {
            for (loc[0] = 0; loc[0] < GetDimensionLimit(0); loc[0]++) {
                // Label each child as icsingleton (0-th child type)
                AddLabel(&Mesh, loc, 0);
            }
        }
    }
};
RULE = label;
}
```

At the second level of the hierarchy, the *icsingleton* skeleton has no parameter to bind. Moreover, a singleton skeleton has an empty back-end and hence it has no children to be labeled. Consequently, concretization of the *icsingleton* skeleton is a void procedure. The corresponding SDL code is omitted due to space constraints.

4.3   Code-Complete Modules

Filling in the representatives of each of the *icmesh* and *icsingleton* skeleton results in the respective code complete modules and hence the complete parallel application (refer to section 2). Before implementing the code complete modules, we need to first generate the C++ code for the skeleton hierarchy. The SuperPAS-provided tools generate one C++ object per skeleton. The developer subsequently needs to fill in the representative code for each skeleton object. The *Rep* method of each of the generated skeleton objects is interpreted as the representative of the corresponding skeleton. In the case of the image convolution application, the *icsingleton* and *icmesh* objects are generated, and subsequently they are filled in with application-specific code as follows:

```
class icmesh : ... {
public:
    icmesh(...) : ... { ... }
    void Rep(void) { // Representative of mesh module
        // Fill in application-specific code as follows:
        MsgImage imgMain, mask;
        // Read the image and the mask from file into imgMain
        // and mask objects

        // Now partition the image
        int nParts = GetDimensionLimits(0) * GetDimensionLimits(1);
        MsgImage * imgParts = new MsgImage[nParts];
        ... // Divide imgMain among imgParts
        // Now send the partitions to the children
        ScatterToChildren(imgParts); // An internal primitive (section 2)
        BroadcastToChildren(mask); // An internal primitive (section 2)

        // Now gather the convoluted image partitions from children
        GatherFromChildren(imgParts);

        // Combine the convoluted image partitions into the imgMain object

        // Write the result back to a file
        ...
    }
}

class icsingleton : ... {
public:
    icsingleton(...) : ... { ... }
    // NEWLY ADDED METHODS (BY DEVELOPER) BEGINS
    void RecvRight(Msg &m) {
        static int * p = {+1, 0}; // Right node in a 2-d mesh
        External.RecvNeighbor(p, m); // ''External'' stands for an external
                                     // primitive. Refer to section 2.
    }
    void SendLeft(Msg &m) {
        static int * p = {-1, 0}; // Left node in a 2-d mesh
        External.SendNeighbor(p, m);
    }
    bool IsAtFirstColumn(void) {
        return External.IsAtBeginning(0);
    }
    // ADDED METHODS ENDS
    void Rep(void) { // Representative of singleton module
        // Fill in with your code
        MsgImage imageIn, imgi, mask; // The image partition and the mask

        // receive the image partition from parent
        External.RecvRepresentative(imageIn);
        // Receive the mask
        External.RecvRepresentative(mask);
        // Exchange information with neighbors

        // Now convolute
        ...
```

```
    // imageOut contains only the part of the image to be sent back
    MsgImage imageOut(imageIn.dx(), imageIn.dy());
    // Send the result back to parent
    External.SendRepresentative(imageOut);
  }
};
...
```

The previous code uses the *MsgImage* class. This class is inherited from SuperPAS library-provided *Msg* class. The *Msg* class is a generic message container used by all SuperPAS-provided built-in communication primitives. It has two abstract methods: *Marshal()* and *Unmarshal()*, which specify how the corresponding message object should be packed into buffer and subsequently unpacked upon receipt. These two abstract methods need to be overwritten by an application developer, as is shown below for the *MsgImage* class:

```
class MsgImage : public Msg {
    int width, height;
    int * data;
public:
    MsgImage(void) : Msg(), width(0), height(0), data(NULL) { }
    MsgImage(int _height, int _width) : Msg(), height(_height),
        width(_width) {
        data = ...;
    }
    void SetImage(const gdImagePtr im) { ... }
    int GetWidth(void) { return width; }
    // other methods
    // FOLLOWING METHODS MUST BE OVER WRITTEN
    // How to marshal  this object
    void Marshal(void) {
        // marshal width
        MarshalData(width);
        // marshal height
        MarshalData(height);
        // marshal image data
        MarshalData(data, width * height);
    }
    // How to unmarshal this object
    void Unmarshal(void) {
        // unmarshalling must be in same order of marshalling
        // unmarshal width
        UnmarshalData(width);
        // and height
        UnmarshalData(height);
        if (data) delete []data;
        data = new int[width * height];
        // we have proper memory, now unmarshal image data
        UnmarshalData(data, height * width);
    }
};
```

5 Usability and Performance Studies

SuperPAS is currently implemented using C++ on top of MPI and is ported onto a Beowulf cluster. To conduct our usability tests, we chose a group of twelve students, enrolled in an introductory graduate-level course on parallel and distributed computing. Students were asked to compare their experiences with MPI and SuperPAS. The study pointed out four important points: (1) the learning curve for the SuperPAS model is more than the MPI model. On the average, the time to learn the SuperPAS model and the SDL is approximately 30% more than that of the MPI model and its API; (2) developing parallel applications is significantly easier and less time consuming, if the required abstract skeletons already exist in the repository. In the case of SuperPAS, it took approximately 50% less time and coding effort as compared to MPI; (3) the SuperPAS system becomes more beneficial with increased complexity of the given application problem, i.e., if the problem structure is simple, it is better to use MPI provided that the required abstract skeleton(s) do not already exist in the repository; (4) the object-oriented interface and skeleton-specific primitives for communication-synchronization are easier to use as compared to the primitives provided by MPI.

To test the performance of SuperPAS system, we developed two image processing applications. The first application convolutes a series of images and has already been discussed. The second application finds the contours of objects in images of maps of buildings and roads. The applications were developed using both MPI and SuperPAS. The run-times of the applications were measured as an average of at least 10 runs. The results showed that the performance degradation using SuperPAS as compared to MPI is rather negligible (less than 1%). Since the SuperPAS run-time system is a thin layer over MPI, this performance degradation is expected. It is also found that the initial environment initialization phase for a SuperPAS application is much more complex and hence more time consuming than that of a similar MPI application. However, it should be noted that this initialization takes place only once during the life time of the application. Though the initialization time grows proportional to the complexity of the skeleton hierarchy, it becomes rather insignificant if the application has a relatively long run-time. More performance results about the PAS system can be found in [5].

6   Conclusion and Future Work

SuperPAS is a step towards making PAS more flexible and usable by supporting both extensibility and skeleton composition. In this paper, we describe the SuperPAS model for designing abstract PAS skeletons. We also extend the model for supporting composition of abstract skeletons to design new abstract skeletons. Recent usability studies have demonstrated that SuperPAS might ease the development process for big and complex applications. We have also found that there is no significant performance degradation (less than 1%) while using SuperPAS.

Currently our research team is working on several other issues of the PAS system. We are investigating the issues of *performance modelling and profiling* for PAS skeletons. *Synchronous slicing*, a method to extract the communication synchronization behaviour of a given application, is of particular interest. We are also working on the issues of *static and dynamic optimizations* and *fault tolerance* aspects of applications developed using PAS. Many of these aspects of our current research will be reported in our future works.

References

1. Schaeffer, J., Szafron, D., Lobe, G., Parsons, I.: The enterprise model for developing distributed applications. IEEE Parallel and Distributed Technology: Systems and Applications **1** (1993) 85–96
2. Bartoli, A., Corsini, P., Dini, G., Prete, C.A.: Graphical design of distributed applications through reusable components. IEEE Parallel and Distributed Technology **3** (1995) 37–50
3. Siu, S., Singh, A.: Design patterns for parallel computing using a network of processors. In: 6th International Symposium on High Performance Distributed Computing (HPDC '97), Portland, OR (1997) 293–304
4. MacDonald, S., Szafron, D., Schaffer, J., Bromling, S.: From patterns to frameworks to parallel programs. Parallel Computing **28** (2002) 1663–1683
5. Goswami, D., Singh, A., Preiss, B.R.: From design patterns to parallel architectural skeletons. Journal of Parallel and Distributed Computing **62** (2002) 669–695
6. Vanneschi, M.: The programming model of assist, an environment for parallel and distributed portable applications. Parallel Computing **28** (2002) 1709–1732
7. Cole, M.: Algorithmic Skeletons: Structured Management of Parallel Computation. MIT Press, Cambridge, Massachusetts (1989)
8. Goswami, D.: Parallel Architectural Skeletons: Re-Usable Building Blocks for Parallel Applications. PhD thesis, University of Waterloo, Canada (2001)
9. Akon, M.M., Goswami, D., Li, H.F.: A parallel architectural skeleton model supporting extensibility and skeleton composition. In: Second International Symposium on Parallel and Distributed Processing and Applications, Hong Kong (2004) Lecture Notes in Computer Science, Vol. 3358, pp. 985-996.
10. Chan, F., Cao, J., Sun, Y.: High-level abstractions for message passing parallel programming. Parallel Computing **29** (2003) 1589–1621
11. Myler, H.R., Weeks, A.R.: The Pocket Handbook of Image Processing Algorithms In C. Prentice-Hall, Englewood Cliffs, N.J (1993)

A Parallel Computational Code for the Education of Coherent Structures of Turbulence in Fluid Dynamics

Giancarlo Alfonsi[1] and Leonardo Primavera[2]

[1] Dipartimento di Difesa del Suolo, Università della Calabria
Via P. Bucci 42b, 87036 Rende (Cosenza), Italy
Phone: + 39 0984 496571, Fax: + 39 0984 496578
alfonsi@dds.unical.it
[2] Dipartimento di Fisica, Università della Calabria
Via P. Bucci 33b, 87036 Rende (Cosenza), Italy
Phone: + 39 0984 496138, Fax: + 39 0984 494401
lprimavera@fis.unical.it

Abstract. A parallel computational code is developed for the execution of the Proper Orthogonal Decomposition (*POD*) of turbulent flow fields in fluid dynamics. The *POD* is an analytically-founded statistical technique that permits the eduction of appropriately-defined modes of the flow from the background flow, allowing the determination of the coherent structures of turbulence. The computational aspects of the different phases of the computing procedure are analyzed and the development of the related parallel computational code is described. Computational tests corresponding to different computing domains and number of processors are executed on a *HP-V2500* parallel computing system and the results are shown in terms of parallel performance of the different phases of the calculations separately considered and of the computational code in the whole.

1 Introduction

In fluid dynamics and turbulence research a wide class of methods of investigation involves numerical simulations.

Numerical simulation of turbulence via digital computers implies the execution of the numerical integration of the three-dimensional unsteady Navier-Stokes equations on an appropriate computing domain, for an adequate number of time steps. Different numerical techniques, ranging from finite differences, finite elements, spectral methods and appropriate combinations of the basic algorithms in mixed techniques (Alfonsi et al. [1], Passoni et al. [2]) can be used.

One of the problems involved in this activity at sufficiently high Reynolds numbers is the remarkable difference existing between a solution of the Navier-Stokes equations as an exercise of numerical analysis – however complex it may result – and a solution of the same equations with the aim of obtaining a precise correlation of the results with turbulence physics. In the latter case the accuracy of the calculations has to be deeply monitored and the equations have eventually to be further manipulated in following one of the existing approaches to the numerical simulation and/or modeling of turbulence.

V. Malyshkin (Ed.): PaCT 2005, LNCS 3606, pp. 381–392, 2005.

There are three main approaches to the numerical simulation and modeling of turbulent flows: *RANS* (Reynolds Averaged Navier-Stokes equations), *LES* (Large Eddy Simulation) and *DNS* (Direct Numerical Simulation of turbulence). One can refer to Speziale [3], Lesieur & Métais [4] and Moin & Mahesh [5] for review works of the three approaches, respectively.

Within the *RANS* approach Reynolds averaging is performed. Reynolds decomposition and averaging consists in: *i)* separating the dependent variables of the Navier-Stokes equations into mean and fluctuating parts, *ii)* substituting the decomposed variables into the equations, *iii)* taking the average of the equations themselves. Due to the nonlinear character of the system of the equations, the result is that a new term in the momentum equation arises, the Reynolds stress term, a non-zero correlation between fluctuating components of the velocity. One has:

$$\partial_t \bar{u}_i + \partial_j \left(\bar{u}_i \bar{u}_j \right) + \partial_j \left(\overline{u_i' u_j'} \right) = -\frac{1}{\rho} \partial_i \bar{p} + \nu \partial_j \partial_j \bar{u}_i \tag{1}$$

where u_i is the fluid velocity, p is the pressure, overbars denote time averaging and primes denote fluctuating components, being ν and ρ the fluid kinematic viscosity and density, respectively. Different models have been devised to face the problem of the closure of the system of the Navier-Stokes equations: *i)* zero-equation models, in which simple formulas are adopted for the Reynolds stress term, *ii)* one-equation models, in which an additional differential equation is involved in the system of the governing equations, in terms of turbulent kinetic energy κ, *iii)* two-equation models, in which two additional differential equations are involved in terms of turbulent kinetic energy κ and rate of dissipation of kinetic energy ε, *iv)* stress-equation models, involving a number of additional partial differential equations (and related models) for the description of the evolution of the terms representing the Reynolds stress tensor.

In following the *LES* approach one wants to actually simulate the larger scales of the flow and use a model for the smallest, based on the hypotesis of universal, isotropic and purely dissipative behavior of the latter. A filter is applied to the Navier-Stokes equations for scale separation (usually a convolution integral) and a model is sought (the subgrid-scale model) for the term of the momentum equation that do not result a function of the filtered variables, the subgrid-scale stress term. One has:

$$\partial_t \bar{u}_i + \partial_j \left(\overline{\bar{u}_i \bar{u}_j} + \overline{\bar{u}_i u_j'} + \overline{u_i' \bar{u}_j} + \overline{u_i' u_j'} \right) = -\frac{1}{\rho} \partial_i \bar{p} + \nu \partial_j \partial_j \bar{u}_i \tag{2}$$

where overbars now denote filtering and primes denote subgrid-scale components.

Several subgrid-scale models have been devised for *LES* calculations of turbulent flows, the Smagorinsky's model ([6]), the Scale Similarity model (Bardina *et al.* [7]), the Spectral Eddy Viscosity group of models (Kraichnan [8]), the Structure-Function model (Métais & Lesieur [9]), the *RNG* model (Yakhot *et al.* [10]), the Dynamic Model (Germano [11]).

In the *DNS* approach the attitude of directly simulating all turbulent scales is followed and the momentum equation (besides continuity) is considered without modifications of any kind. One has:

$$\partial_t u_i + \partial_j \left(u_i u_j \right) = -\frac{1}{\rho} \partial_i p + \nu \partial_j \partial_j u_i . \tag{3}$$

The critical aspect in following this method is the accuracy of the calculations that in theory should be as high as to resolve the Kolmogorov microscales in both space and time (or at most limited multiples of them, see, among others, Spalart [12]).

In all the three approaches outlined above, the major difficulty in performing calculations at Reynolds numbers of practical interest lies in the remarkable amount of computational resources required. The consequence for a long time has been that only simple flow cases have been investigated numerically. The advent of the supercomputing technologies has completely changed this scenario, opening new perspectives in the field of the *high-performance computational fluid dynamics* (see Passoni *et al.* [13],[14] and the list of references therein, for an account of recent progresses in turbulence research using supercomputers).

Modern techniques of investigation of numerical and supercomputational nature applied to turbulence research have the potential of greatly increasing the amount of information gathered during a research (see Fischer & Patera [15] for a review) and the continuous effort in studying turbulence in its full complexity (three-dimensionality and unsteadiness) has brought researchers to manage very large amounts of data.

A typical turbulent-flow database includes all three components of the velocity in all points of a three-dimensional domain, gathered for an adequate number of time steps of the turbulent statistically steady state. Such a database contains much information about the character of a given turbulent flow but in the formation of the value of each variable all turbulent scales have contributed and the effect of each scale is nonlinearly combined with that of all other scales. It is otherwise recognized that not all the scales of turbulence contribute to the same degree in determinig the physical properties of a turbulent flow.

Methods can be devised to extract from a turbulent-flow database only the *relevant information*, that has to be meant as to separate the effect of appropriately-defined modes of the flow from the background flow or, finally, to extract the coherent structures of the flow, whatever definition of coherent structure is adopted. There are several techniques of both qualitative and quantitative nature for the eduction of the coherent structures of turbulence (see Cantwell [16] and Robinson [17] for review works on this subject). Of all the existing methods, a powerful technique for the determination of the coherent structures of turbulence is that of the Proper Orthogonal Decomposition (*POD*).

2 Proper Orthogonal Decomposition

The *POD* is an analytically-founded statistical technique that can be applied for the extraction of the coherent structures of a turbulent flow field in fluid dynamics. The method has been first introduced in turbulent flow analysis by Lumley [18] and has been indipendently suggested by Kosambi [19], Loéve [20], Karhunen [21], Pougachev [22] and Obukhov [23]. Besides turbulence it has been applied to other fields of science such as oceanography, image processing and data compression. On its basis, starting from the Navier-Stokes equations, it is also possible to construct low-dimensional dinamical models for the analysis of the interaction of predetermined spatial and temporal, local, coherent structures. The method is extensively presented in Sirovich [24] and Berkooz *et al.* [25], and it is here summarized.

By considering an ensemble of temporal realizations of a non-homogeneous, square integrable, three-dimensional, real-valued velocity field $u_i(x_j,t)$ on a finite domain D $(i, j = 1,2,3)$, one wants to find the most similar function to the elements of the ensemble on average, i.e. to determine highest-mean-square correlated structure with all the elements of the ensemble. This corresponds to find a deterministic vector function $\phi_i(x_j)$, so that:

$$\max_{\psi} \frac{\left\langle \left| (u_i(x_j,t), \psi_i(x_j)) \right|^2 \right\rangle}{(\psi_i(x_j), \psi_i(x_j))} = \frac{\left\langle \left| (u_i(x_j,t), \phi_i(x_j)) \right|^2 \right\rangle}{(\phi_i(x_j), \phi_i(x_j))} \tag{4}$$

or, equivalently, find the member that maximizes the normalized inner product of the candidate structure with the field $u_i(x_j,t)$. A necessary condition for problem (4) is that $\phi_i(x_j)$ is an eigenfunction, solution of the eigenvalue problem and Fredholm integral equation of the first kind:

$$\int_D R_{ij}(x_l, x_k')\phi_j(x_k')dx_k' = \int_D \left\langle u_i(x_k,t)u_j(x_k',t)\right\rangle \phi_j(x_k')dx_k' = \lambda\phi_i(x_l) \tag{5}$$

where $R_{ij} = \left\langle u_i(x_l,t)u_j(x_k',t)\right\rangle$ is the two-point velocity correlation tensor. When D is bounded, there exists a denumerable infinity of solutions of (5) and these solutions are called the empirical eigenfunctions $\phi_i^{(n)}(x_j)$ (normalized, $\left\| \phi_i^{(n)}(x_j) \right\| = 1$). To each eigenfunction is associated a real positive eigenvalue $\lambda^{(n)}$ (R_{ij} is non-negative by construction) and the eigenfunctions form a complete set. Every member of the ensemble can be reconstructed by means of a modal decomposition in the eigenfunctions themselves:

$$u_i(x_j,t) = \sum_n a_n(t)\phi_i^{(n)}(x_j) \tag{6}$$

that can be seen as a decomposition of the originary random field into deterministic structures $\phi_i^{(n)}(x_j)$, with random coefficients. The modal amplitudes are uncorrelated and their mean square values are the eigenvalues themselves:

$$\left\langle a_n(t)a_m(t)\right\rangle = \delta_{nm}\lambda^{(n)}, \tag{7}$$

being δ_{nm} the Kroneker's delta. A diagonal decomposition of R_{ij} holds:

$$R_{ij}(x_l, x_k') = \sum_n \lambda^{(n)}\phi_i^{(n)}(x_l)\phi_j^{(n)}(x_k') \tag{8}$$

implying that the contribution of each different structure to the average content of turbulent kinetic energy of the flow can be separately calculated:

$$E = \int_D \left\langle u_i(x_j,t)u_i(x_j,t)\right\rangle dx_j = \sum_n \lambda^{(n)} \tag{9}$$

where E is the total turbulent kinetic energy in the domain D. Thus, each eigenvalue $\lambda^{(n)}$ represents the contribution of each correspondent structure $\phi^{(n)}$ to the total amount of kinetic energy.

Among other cases, the *POD* has been used in wall bounded turbulent-flow problems by Bakewell & Lumley [26], Aubry *et al.* [27], Moin & Moser [28],

Sirovich *et al.* [29], Ball *et al.* [30] and Webber *et al.* [31]. In most of the aforementioned works, mainly to limit the computational resources involved in the *POD* calculations, flow cases exhibiting specific symmetries have been considered. A typical example is that of the flow in a plane channel ([28],[31]), a problem characterized by two homogeneous directions in which the correlation tensor has to be evaluated – for all the three velocity components – only along the non-homogeneous direction. Fully non-homogeneous problems (the majority in the field of practical applications) require remarkably higher computational resources and thus supercomputing technologies.

In this work a parallel computational code for the Proper Orthogonal Decomposition of turbulent flow fields is developed. The code is general, it handles three-dimensional velocity fields in physical space onto three-dimensional spatial domains and can be used in all kind of problems since it does not require any particular symmetry.

The two-point velocity correlation tensor at the left hand-side of equation (5) is calculated in its complete form:

$$R_{ij}(x, x', y, y', z, z') = \langle u_i(x, y, z, t) v_j(x', y', z', t) \rangle \tag{10}$$

so that the optimal representation of the velocity field outlined above is calculated in all the three directions x, y, z.

3   The Computational Algorithm

The computational code for the implementation of the *POD* technique involves several mathematical operations of different kind and in particular includes the following main phases:

- evaluation of the two-point correlation tensor of the velocity components of equation (5), phase *CORR*;
- evaluation of the integral of equation (5) on the computational domain D with the use of the trapezoidal rule, phase *TRAPEZ*;
- execution of the tridiagonalization operations for the resulting matrix with the use of the Householder method, phase *TRED2* (see also [32]);
- solution of the eigenvalue problem (5) with determination of the eigenfunctions and corresponding eigenvalues, phase *TQLI* (Tridiagonal *QL* Implicit, see also [32]);
- execution of a test to ensure the correct representation of the energy content of the eigenvalues, phase *TESTENERG*;
- evaluation of the time dependent coefficients of equation (6) by means of a standard inversion procedure, phase *COEFF*.

In terms of computer memory, the velocity database to which the *POD* procedure has to be applied, requires a matrix of size $NCOMP \times NMAX \times ITMAX$ (*NCOMP* is the number of the velocity components considered, *NMAX* is the number of grid points in which the velocity field has been calculated and *ITMAX* is the number the time steps of the temporal sequence of the instantaneous velocity data). The two-point velocity correlation tensor requires a matrix of size $(NCOMP \times NMAX)^2$.

4 The Parallelization Technique

In devising a parallelization strategy for the *POD* code, each different phase of the calculations is analyzed and a parallelization technique is implemented, with the aim of minimizing the communications and balancing the computational load among the processors for the whole code.

4.1 Phase *CORR*

For the evaluation of the two-point correlation tensor R_{ij} of equation (5) this phase of the calculations utilizes the velocity components stored in a matrix (matrix *U*). Both matrices *U* and R_{ij} have to be distributed onto the *n* available processors. The procedures connected with the execution of *CORR* strongly depend on how matrix *U* is distributed among the processors, rather than R_{ij}. Matrix *U* is divided along the time axis, i.e. to each processor is attributed a subset of velocity components corresponding to the time interval *ITMAX/n* (*n* is the number of processors).

Communications are needed among the processors in this case, in the sense that each processor has to cyclically communicate to the others its own portion of matrix *U*.

4.2 Phase *TRAPEZ*

In this phase the evaluation of the integral in equation (5) with the trapezoidal rule is performed, together with the transformation of R_{ij} into the equivalent symmetric problem. The quadrature formula utilizes appropriate weight functions occupying a limited amount of memory that, when duplicated onto each processor, actually eliminate the need of communications among processors in this phase of the calculations.

4.3 Phase *TRED2*

The calculations incorporated in this phase can be logically divided in two parts, the tridiagonalization of the symmetric matrix R_{ij} (the most relevant part) and the build-up of a rotation matrix *Q* for the transformation of the symmetric matrix R_{ij} into the tridiagonal matrix $R'_{ij} = Q R_{ij} Q^T$ (^{T} is transpose). In order to avoid an unbalanced load distribution among the processors, a solution called *cyclic parallelization* of *TRED2* is adopted. This solution can be implemented through both the rows or columns of R_{ij} because of its symmetry. Working with the rows of R_{ij}, they are *distributed cyclically* among processors as follows:

- the first processor receives row *0*, row *n*, row *2n*, row *3n*, ...
- the second processor receives row *1*, row *(n+1)*, row *(2n+1)*, row *(3n+1)*, ...
- the third processor receives row *2*, row *(n+2)*, row *(2n+2)*, row *(3n+2)*, ...

Each processor receives in total a number of rows equal to the total number of the rows divided by the number of processors. In this way the load of each processor increases uniformly and the parallel performance remains constant.

4.4 Phase *TQLI*

In this phase of the calculations the eigenvalue problem associated to the matrix that has been tridiagonalized during *TRED2*, is solved. Two sub-phases are incorporated in this cycle, the calculation of the *i-th* eigenvalue and the updating of the correspondent eigenvector, being the process of evaluation of the eigenvalues characterized by a complexity of one order of magnitude less than that of the calculation of the eigenvectors.

The computation of the eigenvalues has been duplicated onto the n available processors and the updating of the eigenvectors has been parallelized. In this sub-phase, being the matrix of the velocity correlation tensor distributed among the processors by rows, no communications are required because of the fact that a dependency exists in this direction, in the sense that the element $(i, j+1)$ depends on the element (i, j).

4.5 Phase *TESTENERG*

This phase is not particularly complex. The calculations are executed by all the processors in parallel, being U distributed onto the processors along the temporal axis (subsection 4.1).

4.6 Phase *COEFF*

In this phase of the calculations the processors have to operate independently on their own portion of the tridiagonal matrix of the velocity correlation tensor. A cycle is implemented, in which three elements belonging to three consecutive rows are multiplied. Thus, in order to parallelize this phase efficiently – limiting the communications among the processors – a *cyclic partition* of the matrix of the correlation tensor among the processors is again needed, this time in groups formed by *three consecutive rows.*

On the basis of the analysis of each of the different phases of the calculations to be performed, the most relevant factors for the parallelization of the whole *POD* procedure appear to be related to the optimization of *TRED2, TQLI* and *COEFF*. For what *TRED2* is concerned, the so-called *cyclic distribution* of the matrix R_{ij} among the processors is mainly needed (subsection 4.3). For what *TQLI* is concerned, it is needed that an entire line is avaliable to each processor. In the case of *COEFF*, at least three entire rows are needed for each processor (subsection 4.6). Thus, the optimal solution for the parallelization of the code in the whole is the *cyclic distribution of the matrix of the correlation tensor in groups of three consecutive rows* onto each of the n avaliable processors.

Moreover, computational tests of preliminary nature have shown that only four of the six main phases of the computing procedure significantly influence the execution time, *TRED2, TQLI, CORR* and *COEFF*. *TRED2* uses around 70% of the total time with one processor in use, decreasing with the number of processors. *TQLI* uses around 15% of the total time with one processor, also decreasing with the number of processors. *CORR* on the contrary increases its execution time with the number of processors, while the time used by *COEFF* is practically constant with the number of processors. The remaining two phases weigh for less than the 1% of the total execution time.

5 Results

The computer that has been used for the performance tests is a *HP-V2500*. It includes 20 processors *PA-RISC 8500*, all arranged in a single hypernode and totaling 16 Gbyte of *RAM* and 180 Gbyte of mass memory (up to 16 processors have been used in the present calculations). The *PA-RISC 8500* is a 64 bit processor, 440 Mhz of frequency clock, 1 Mbyte of Data Cache on chip and 0.5 Mbyte of Instruction Cache on chip per processor. The memory architecture is a crossbar-based symmetric multiprocessor (*SMP*) of 8×8 non-blocking multiported crossbar type. The maximum bandwidth allowed is 15.36 Gbyte/s.

The parallel performance of the whole *POD* code and of its different phases separately considered has been investigated for two different datasets. Dataset *A* with *NMAX*=250 (*NX*=10, *NY*=5, *NZ*=5 are the grid points along *x*, *y* and *z*, respectively) and *ITMAX*=50. Dataset *B* with *NMAX* =500 (*NX*=10, *NY*=10, *NZ*=5) and *ITMAX*=50 (*NCOMP*=3 in both cases). Groups of 2, 4, 8 and 16 processors have been used in the calculations.

In Figures 1 and 2 the speed-up*s* of the four more relevant phases of the calculations separately considered with the number of processors, are shown for both datasets. The speed-up is defined as the run-time with one processor divided by the run-time with a given number of processors.

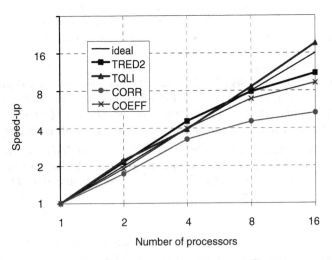

Fig. 1. Dataset A. Speed-up of the four most relevant phases of the *POD* procedure separately considered with the number of processors

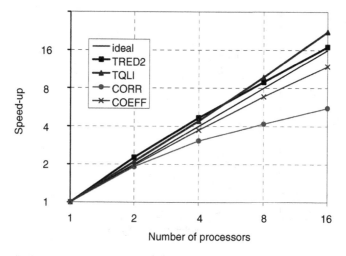

Fig. 2. Dataset B. Speed-up of the four most relevant phases of the *POD* procedure separately considered with the number of processors

Figure 1 shows the speed-up of the four relevant phases with the number of processors for daset *A*. *TQLI* exhibits a superlinear behavior, *TRED2* is superlinear up to 4 processors involved in the calculations, is linear with 8 processors and decays with 16 processors. *COEFF* and *CORR* remain under the linear limit up to 16 processors.

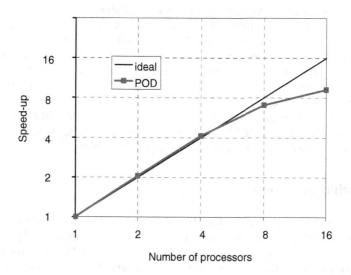

Fig. 3. Dataset A. Speed-up of the whole parallel *POD* computational code with the number of processors

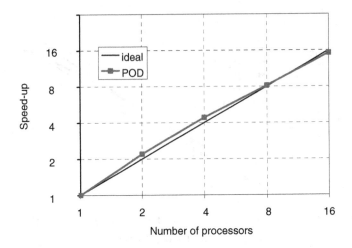

Fig. 4. Dataset B. Speed-up of the whole parallel *POD* computational code with the number of processors

Figure 2 shows the speed-up of the four relevant phases with the number of processors for dataset *B*. *TQLI* and *TRED2* exhibit a superlinear (or almost linear) behavior up to 16 processors. The superlinear results are related to the involvement of the cache. By increasing the amount of the processors, the memory required by each processor decreases and so do the cache-miss events. The linear behavior of *TQLI* is a permanent factor in the execution of the program, due to the absence of significant amounts of communications in the parallelized *TQLI* phase.

In Figure 3 and 4 the speed-up*s* of the whole *POD* code are reported for both datasets *A* and *B*. In the case of dataset *A* (Figure 3) the speed-up of the code is nearly linear up to 4 processors and then the efficiency reaches about the level of the 60% with 16 processors. In the case of dataset *B* (Figure 4) the speed-up is nearly linear up to 8 processors and then the efficiency reaches about the level of the 95% with 16 processors (almost ideal).

Overall, the superlinear character of subroutines *TRED2* and *TQLI* compensate the behavior of subroutines *COEFF* and *CORR*, giving at the end satisfactory levels of speed-up to the parallel *POD* computational code in the whole.

6   Concluding Remarks

A parallel computational code for the execution of the *POD* technique in fluid dynamics is developed. The most relevant phases of the computational procedure are analyzed and a parallelization strategy is devised. The parallel code for the Proper Orthogonal Decomposition exhibits satisfactory levels of speed-up with an increasing number of processors involved in the calculations, mainly because of the superlinear behavior of some of the phases of the calculations.

References

1. Alfonsi G., Passoni G., Pancaldo L. & Zampaglione D.: A spectral-finite difference solution of the Navier-Stokes equations in three dimensions. *Int. J. Num. Meth. Fluids.* **28** (1998) 129

2. Passoni G., Alfonsi G. & Galbiati M.: Analysis of hybrid algorithms for the Navier-Stokes equations with respect to hydrodynamic stability theory. *Int. J. Num. Meth. Fluids.* **38** (2002) 1069

3. Speziale C.G.: Analytical methods for the development of Reynolds-stress closures in turbulence. *Ann. Rev. Fluid Mech.* **23** (1991) 107

4. Lesieur M. & Métais O.: New trends in Large-Eddy simulation of turbulence. *Ann. Rev. Fluid Mech.* **28** (1996) 45

5. Moin P. & Mahesh K.: Direct Numerical Simulation: a tool in turbulence research. *Ann. Rev. Fluid Mech.* **30** (1998) 539

6. Smagorinsky J.: General circulation experiments with the primitive equations. *Mon. Weather Rev.* **91** (1963) 99

7. Bardina J., Ferziger J.H. & Reynolds W.C.: Improved subgrid models for large-eddy simulation. *AIAA Pap. 80-1357* (1980)

8. Kraichnan R.H.: Eddy viscosity in two and three dimensions. *J. Atmos. Sci.* **33** (1976) 1521

9. Métais O. & Lesieur M.: Statistical predictability of decaying turbulence. *J. Atmos. Sci.* **43** (1986) 857

10. Yakhot A., Orszag S.A., Yakhot V. & Israeli M.: Renormalization group formulation of large-eddy simulation. *J. Sci. Comput.* **4** (1989) 139

11. Germano M.: Turbulence, the filtering approach. *J. Fluid Mech.* **238** (1992) 325

12. Spalart P.R.: Direct simulation of a turbulent boundary layer up to $Re_\theta \approx 1410$. *J. Fluid Mech.* **187** (1988) 61

13. Passoni G., Alfonsi G., Tula G. & Cardu U.: A wavenumber parallel computational code for the numerical integration of the Navier-Stokes equations. *Parall. Comput.* **25** (1999) 593

14. Passoni G., Cremonesi P. & Alfonsi G.: Analysis and implementation of a parallelization strategy on a Navier-Stokes solver for shear flow simulations. *Parall. Comput.* **27** (2001) 1665

15. Fischer P.F. & Patera A.T.: Parallel simulation of viscous incompressible flows. *Ann. Rev. Fluid Mech.* **26** (1994) 483

16. Cantwell B.J.: Organized motion in turbulent flow. *Ann. Rev. Fluid Mech.* **13** (1981) 457

17. Robinson S.K.: Coherent motions in the turbulent boundary layer. *Ann. Rev. Fluid Mech.* **23** (1991) 601

18. Lumley J.L.: *Stochastic tools in turbulence.* Academic Press (1971)

19. Kosambi D.D.: Statistics in function space. *J. Indian Math. Soc.* **7** (1943) 76

20. Loéve M. : Functions aleatoire de second ordre. *C. R. Acad. Sci. Paris.* **220** (1945)

21. Karhunen K.: Zur spektral theorie stochastischer prozesse. *Ann. Acad. Sci. Fenicae.* **A1** (1946) 34

22. Pougachev V.S.: General theory of the correlations of random functions. *Izv. Akad. Nauk. SSSR, Ser. Math.* **17** (1953) 1401

23. Obukhov A.M.: Statistical description of continuous fields. *Trans. Geophys. Int. Akad. Nauk. SSSR.* **24** (1954) 3

24. Sirovich L.: Turbulence and the dynamics of coherent structures. Parts I-III. *Quart. Appl. Math.* **45** (1987) 561

25. Berkooz G., Holmes P. & Lumley J.L.: The Proper Orthogonal Decomposition in the analysis of turbulent flows. *Ann. Rev. Fluid Mech.* **25** (1993) 539

26. Bakewell P. & Lumley J.L.: Viscous sublayer and adjacent wall region in turbulent pipe flows. *Phys. Fluids.* **10** (1967) 1880

27. Aubry N., Holmes P., Lumley J.L. & Stone E.: The dynamics of coherent structures in the wall region of a turbulent boundary layer. *J. Fluid Mech.* **192** (1988) 115

28. Moin P. & Moser R.D. : Characteristic-eddy decomposition of turbulence in a channel. *J. Fluid Mech.* **200** (1989) 471

29. Sirovich L., Ball K.S. & Keefe L.R.: Plane waves and structures in turbulent channel flow. *Phys. Fluids.* **A2** (1990) 2217

30. Ball K.S., Sirovich L. & Keefe L.R.: Dynamical eigenfunction decomposition of turbulent channel flow. *Int. J. Num. Meth. Fluids.* **12** (1991) 585

31. Webber G.A., Handler R.A. & Sirovich L.: The Karhunen-Loéve decomposition of minimal channel flow. *Phys. Fluids.* **9** (1997) 1054

32. Press W.H., Teukolsky S.A., Vetterling W.T. & Flannery B.P.: *Numerical Recipes in Fortran 77.* Cambridge University Press (1992)

Experimenting with a Multi-agent E-Commerce Environment

Costin Bădică[1], Maria Ganzha[2], Marcin Paprzycki[3], and Amalia Pîrvănescu[4]

[1] University of Craiova, Software Engineering Department,
Bvd.Decebal 107, Craiova, 200440, Romania
badica_costin@software.ucv.ro
[2] Gizycko Private Higher Educational Institute,
Department of Informatics, Gizycko, Poland
ganzha@pwsz.net
[3] Oklahoma State University, Computer Science Department,
Tulsa, OK, 74106, USA and
Computer Science, SWPS, 03-815 Warsaw, Poland
marcin@cs.okstate.edu
[4] SoftExpert SRL,
Str.Vasile Conta, bl.U25, Craiova, Romania
amaliap@soft-expert.com

Abstract. Agent technology is often claimed to be the most natural approach for automating e-commerce business processes. Despite these claims, up till now, the most successful e-commerce systems are still based on humans to make the most important decisions in various stages of an e-commerce transaction. Consequently, it is difficult to find successful actually implemented and working large-scale agent-based e-commerce applications to confirm agents superiority. Here, we discuss an abstract e-commerce environment that allows agents of different types to interact with each other and operate with an overarching goal of supporting an e-commerce transaction. A prototype system that implements this vision using JADE agent platform is also described. Finally, we report on experiments with the implemented system skeleton.

1 Introduction

E-commerce involves complex processes with many facets, spanning areas that cover business modeling, information technology and social and legal aspects ([9]). A recent survey ([8]) pointed out to useful applications of intelligent and mobile agents in support of advanced e-commerce. The main message permeating his (and other) work is that agent technology is expected to bring efficiency to businesses and thus improve its profitability (e.g. by improving the rate of successful transactions from the total number of attempted transactions, or by decreasing the total time required to complete a transaction), but also to benefit individual users (e.g. by assuring "price-optimality" of purchases or by increasing customer satisfaction). However, taking into account the high diversity of e-commerce activities involving electronic payments, business document

V. Malyshkin (Ed.): PaCT 2005, LNCS 3606, pp. 393–402, 2005.

processing (orders, bills, requests for quotes, etc.), advertising, negotiation, user mobility, delivery of goods, security etc., it is clear that a lot more work needs to be done to achieve the vision of a global distributed e-commerce environment supported by intelligent software agents. This claim is further supported by the fact that it is almost impossible to point out to an existing (and used in day-to-day operation) large-scale implementation of an e-commerce agent system. While a number of possible reasons for this situation have been suggested (see, for instance, [10]), one of them has been recently dispelled. It was shown that modern agent environments (e.g. JADE, [7]) can easily scale to 1500 agents and 300000 messages ([3]). Since these results have been obtained on a set of 8 anti-quated Sun workstations, it is easy to extrapolate the true scalability of JADE on modern computers and thus *it is possible to build and experiment with large-scale agent systems*. This is the general direction of agent system development that will be addressed in this paper. If mobile and intelligent software agents are to become an important part of the e-commerce infrastructure, we have to start implementing such systems that involve large number of agents interacting in a way that is to model realistic scenarios arising in an e-marketplace. This process has to have at least two goals in mind: (1) to focus on the technical aspects of the system, such as agent functionalities, their interactions and communication, agent mobility etc., and (2) to focus on modeling the economical processes occurring in an e-marketplace, such as: effects of pricing strategies, of negotiation protocols and strategies, flow of commodities etc. The first goal attempts to address the problem of lack of large-scale agent systems implemented using agent environments (we are aware of large bio-inspired agent simulations written in C, but this is not what we are interested in). Without being able to show that it is actually possible to implement such systems, using tools that are apparently designed with this goal in mind, agent research will never be able to reach beyond academia. The second goal points to a possible application of the system. While we do not try to convince anyone that as system like ours will be immediately usable in real-life e-commerce, we can point to an interesting way to utilize our system. This possible application is e-commerce modeling. Due to the agent flexibility it will be relatively easy to experiment with the above described as well as other factors appearing in various e-commerce scenarios. While both of these developmental paths are very closely related to each other in this paper we are more concerned with the former.

In this broad context, our goal is to create a system with a multitude of agents that play variety of roles and interact with each-other in an abstract e-commerce environment. Currently, we follow our earlier work, where first, we have implemented a set of lightweight agents capable of adaptive behavior in context of price negotiations (by dynamically loading appropriate software modules; see [11] and work referenced there). Second, we have implemented a simplistic skeleton for an e-commerce simulation ([2]). Third, we have combined these two developmental threads into a unified e-commerce environment [12]. One of the important limitations of our work reported thus far was the fact that we have experimented only with a very limited number artifacts populating our system (products, negotiation mechanisms and strategies, agents of various types, computers). The aim of this paper is to report on the results of our experiments when the size of the system has been increased considerably. In the remaining parts of this paper we, first, present the top level description of the system. We follow by a summary of the implementation-specific information as well as an example illustrating its work in a larger-scale setting.

2   System Description

In our work we aim at implementing a multi-agent e-commerce system that in a long run will help carrying out experiments with real-world e-commerce scenarios. In this context, note the exploratory nature of our work: the system is based on an abstract e-commerce environment describing an artificial world in which e-commerce agents perform variety of functions typically involved in e-commerce, rather than on a solution to a specific business problem in terms of a limited number of application-specific agents.

Our e-commerce model extends and builds on the e-commerce structures presented in [2] and [11]. Basically, our environment acts as a distributed marketplace that hosts e-shops and allows e-clients to visit them and purchase products. Clients have the option to negotiate with the shops, to bid for products and to choose the shop from which to make a purchase. Conversely, shops may be approached "instantly" by multiple clients and consequently, through negotiation mechanisms (including auctions), have an option to choose the buyer. At this stage the system is under development and has a number of limitations. (1) Only four negotiation protocols have been implemented: FIPA English auction, FIPA Dutch auction, iterative bargaining and fixed price (also known as take-it-or-leave-it). Note that the first two are one-to-many negotiations while the last two are one-to-one negotiations (see [1] for a discussion on how various negotiation mechanisms can be parameterized). (2) The two strategy modules are trivial and are there only to show that such modules can be downloaded upon request. (3) We have only shops that are allowed to advertise commodities (clients cannot advertise products they are seeking). (4) While various strategies could be employed to decide where to buy from (e.g. the best price, the safest offer, the most trusted offer, etc.), we are using only the best negotiated price. (5) We have implemented only single-item negotiations. In the case of multi-item negotiations there exist a much large number of factors influencing purchase decision. (6) Our system can be (but is not) made adaptable through data mining (e.g. history of buyer-seller interactions can lead to negotiation strategy adjustment). We plan to address these serious restrictions in the near future.

Shops and clients can be created through a GUI interface that links users (buyers and sellers) with their *Personal Agents*. However, these agents are in many ways spurious for the operation of our system (especially in the context of e-commerce modeling - goal (2) above). Furthermore, a *Personal Agent* is considered to be an envoy of the user that resides on her machine and represents her interests in all aspects of e-life. Thus, in the context of our system its role is "only" to create *Client* / *Shop* agents that will be a part of the e-commerce system; and therefore the *Personal Agent* is not further discussed. Note that it is also possible to create *Client* and *Shop* agents via a command-line line interface. This facility extremely is useful for preparing experiments via scripting programs.

The top level conceptual architecture of the system illustrating proposed types of agents and their interactions in a particular configuration is shown in Figure 1. Let us now describe each agent appearing in that figure and their respective functionalities.

A *Client agent* (*CA*) is created by the *Personal agent* to act within the marketplace on behalf of a user that attempts to buy "something." Similarly, a *Shop agent* represents user who plans to sell "something" within the e-marketplace. After being created both *Shop* and *Client* agents register with the *CIC* agent to be able to operate within the marketplace. Returning agents will receive their existing IDs. In this way we provide support for the future goal of agent behavior adaptability. Here, agents in the system are able to recognize status of their counterparts and differentiate their behavior depending if this is a "returning" or a "new" agent that they interact with.

There is only one *Client Information Center* (*CIC*) agent in the system (in the future we may need to address this potential bottleneck [3]). It is responsible for storing, managing and providing information about all "participants" existing in the system. To be able to participate in the marketplace all *Shop* and *Client* agents must register with the *CIC* agent, which stores information in the *Client Information Database* (*CICDB*). The *CICDB* combines the function of *client registry*, by storing information about and unique IDs for all users and of *yellow pages*, by storing information about of all shops known in the marketplace. Thus *Client* agents (new and returning) communicate with the *CIC* agent to find out which stores are available in the system at any given time. In this way we are (i) following the general philosophy of agent system development, where each function is embodied in an agent and (ii) utilizing the publisher-subscriber mechanism based on distributed object oriented systems. Furthermore, this approach provides us with a simple mechanism of correctly handling the concurrent accesses to a shared repository without having to deal with typical problems of mutual exclusion etc. Actually, all these problems are automatically handled by JADE's agent communication service.

A *Client* agent is created for each customer that is using the system. Each *Client* agent creates an appropriate number of "slave" negotiation agents with the "buyer role" (*Buyer* agents hereafter). One *Buyer* agent is created for each store, within the marketplace, selling sought goods.

On the supply side, a single *Shop* agent is created for each merchant in the system and it is responsible for creating a slave negotiation agent with the "seller role" (*Seller* agent hereafter) for each product sold by the merchant within her e-store.

Finally, *Database* agents are responsible for performing all database operations (updates and queries). For each database in the system we create one database agent (in the future we may need to address this possible bottleneck

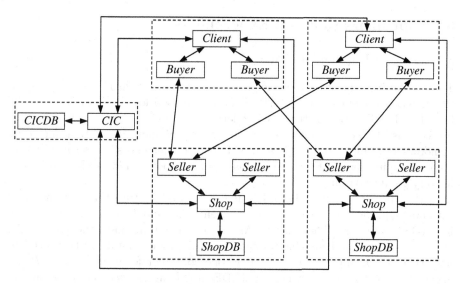

Fig. 1. The abstract e-commerce environment (two-client; two-shop version)

[3]. In this way we decouple the actual database management activities from the rest of the system (i.e. the database management system can be modified in any way without affecting the agent side of the system and vice-versa). Currently, there are two databases in the system: a single *CICDB* database (operated by the *CICDB* agent containing the information about clients, shops and product catalogues, and a single *Shop Database* (*ShopDB*) operated by the *ShopDB* agent storing information about sales and available supplies for each merchant registered within the system.

The central part of the system operation is comprised by price negotiations. *Buyer* agents negotiate price with *Seller agents*. For this purpose *Buyer agents* migrate to the e-stores known by the *CIC* agent to carry sought after commodity. In case of multiple *Buyer* agents attempting at purchasing the same item, they may compete in an auction. Results of price negotiations are send by the *Shop* agent to the *Client* agent that decides where to attempt at making a purchase. Note that the system is fully asynchronous and thus an attempt at making a purchase does not have to result in a success as by the time the offer is made other *Buyer* agents may have already purchased the last available item. In this way we proceed with an e-commerce model similar to the airline ticket reservation where until an actual purchase is made item is reserved, but may not be available at a later time. Note that once the complete system is created, changing this policy will require only a limited amount of work. Furthermore, it will be possible to add different scenarios of completing negotiations to the system and build a mega-system, where all of these strategies will exist together. Ability to achieve this goal by simply adding new agents with new behaviors illustrates the power of agent-based system design.

3   Implementation and Experiments

3.1   System Implementation

The current implementation of the proposed environment has been made within the JADE 3.3 agent platform ([7]). The main reason for this selection was the fact that JADE is one of the best modern agent environments. JADE is open-source, it is FIPA compliant and runs on a variety of operating systems including Windows and Linux (and, as illustrated below, it is also possible to run JADE in a mixed environment). Furthermore, as reported above, in [3] we have observed its very good scalability.

JADE provides a flexible and configurable architecture that matches well with our requirements. Negotiations between *Seller* and *Buyer* agents take place in JADE containers. There is one Main container that hosts the *CIC* agent. Users (customers and merchants) can create as many containers they need to hold their *Client* and *Shop* agents (e.g. one container for each e-store). *Buyer* agents created by *Client* agents use JADE mobile agent technology to migrate to the *Shop* agent containers to engage in negotiations. In this context, a container simulates a marketplace where various *Seller* and *Buyer* agents meet and negotiate. Moreover, all these containers linked via the agent platform simulate a bazaar filled with marketplaces filled with trading agents.

The current implementation is based on several Java classes organized into several categories. Each category is implemented as a separate Java package.

- *Agent classes.* Classes of this package are used for describing various agent types used in the system. Each agent class incorporates a subset of agent activity classes, also called behaviors. Behaviors are used as an abstraction that represents an atomic activity performed by an agent.
- *Database classes.* Classes of this package are used for describing agents that are responsible for management of database connections.
- *Negotiation classes.* Classes of this package implement a simple framework for describing various negotiation protocols. This framework uses the Initiator and Participant roles, as defined by the FIPA Contract Net Interaction protocol ([5]).
- *Reasoning classes.* These classes used for the implementation of the various reasoning models employed by the negotiation agents; see [11] for more details concerning model of negotiation agents. Our implementation supports agents that dynamically load their negotiation protocols and reasoning modules. The implementation combines the Factory design pattern ([4]) and dynamical loading of Java classes ([11]).
- *Ontology classes.* These classes are necessary for implementing agent communication semantics, using concepts and relations. Current implementation uses an extremely simple ontology that defines a single concept for describing *Client* and *Shop* preferences including prices, product names and negotiation protocols.
- *Other classes.* This package contains various helper classes.

In our system, agent communication is implemented using FIPA ACL messages [5]. We have used the following messages: SUBSCRIBE, REQUEST, INFORM, FAILURE, CFP, PROPOSE, ACCEPT-PROPOSAL, REJECT-PROPOSAL, REFUSE. SUBSCRIBE messages are used by the Shop and Client agents to register with the CIC agent and for the Buyer agents to register (to participate in auctions) with the Seller agent. REQUEST messages are used by Client agents to query the CIC agent about what shops are selling a specific product and for Client agents to ask the Shop agent for a final confirmation of a transaction. INFORM messages are used as responses to SUBSCRIBE or REQUEST messages. For example, after subscribing to the CIC agent, a Client agent will get an INFORM message that contains its ID, or after requesting the names of the shops that sell a specific product, a Client agent will receive a list of the Shop agent IDs in an INFORM message. Buyer agents are using FAILURE messages to inform the master Client agents about the unsuccessful result of an auction. Finally, CFP, PROPOSE, ACCEPT-PROPOSAL, REJECT-PROPOSAL and REFUSE messages are being used by negotiating agents.

3.2   Experiments

The system can be run in a simple setting for demonstration purposes by manually creating *Shop* and *Client* agents via the GUI, or directly from command-line when a large number of agents, containers, products etc. is to be created [6].

For the purpose of this paper we have utilized experiments involving multiple agents residing on multiple computers. First, *Client* agents resided on a single computer and *Buyers* migrated to *Shop* agents residing on the remaining 19 machines. Second, *Client* agents resided on 4 computers, while the remaining 16 machines contained *Shop* agents. Furthermore, to illustrate heterogeneity of the environment in which our system can run, in both experimental settings the Main container of the agent platform resided on a computer running Linux, while the remaining 20 computers run Windows. In addition JADEs *Sniffer* agent also was executed, on the Linux PC,. This agent is provided by JADE and its role is to report on communications between agents in the system. Figure 2 presents agent communication captured with help of this agent (note Linux environment).

In the experiment shown in Fig 2 every *Shop* had three different products. Thus, at the beginning of an experimental run every *Shop* registered with the *CIC agent*, then created 3 *Sellers* (one *Seller* for each product). *Seller* agents also registered with the *CIC agent* and then waited for the incoming *Buyer(s)*. Communication involved in these operations can be seen in Fig 2. There exist two events which are necessary for to start negotiations: appearance of at least one *Buyer* and an interrupt caused by the timer (see Figure 3).

After creation, *Client* registered with the *CIC agent*. Upon user request, it obtained list of *Shops*, where product(s) of interest were sold and created *Buyer* agents and sends them to the selected *Shops*. When *Buyer* arrived at the marketplace it asked about current negotiation protocol, communicated with its *Client* and obtained a corresponding strategy module and waited for start

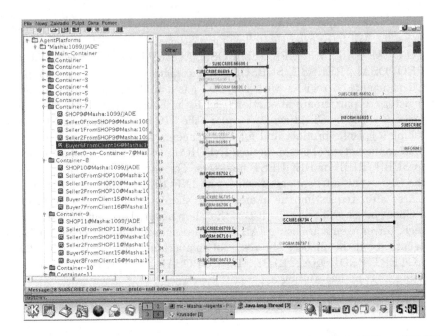

Fig. 2. The beginning of work of the system — registration with CIC and CICDB agents

Fig. 3. The beginning of work of the system — DOS window

of negotiations. After finishing negotiations, *Seller* informed *Shop* agent about their results and *Shop* agent notified appropriate *Client* about successful result of negotiations (see also Fig 2).

In the experiment represented in Fig 2 and Fig 3 we used three products, which *Client* could buy. Thus, we had a total of more than 200 agents populating the system. It should be pointed out that the most time-consuming operation is system initialization (creation of containers). However, since containers are created once, they have only minimal impact on the operations of the system.

We have run multiple experiments, changing the number of (a) containers, (b) computers, (c) *Clients*, (d) *Shops*, (e) negotiation protocols, (f) products (g) mixture of Linux and Windows environments, etc. In each case experiments run smoothly and supported our general claim that the proposed system, when further developed can: (1) can be scaled to a truly large size, and (2) be used for e-commerce modeling.

4   Concluding Remarks

In this paper we have introduced an agent-based e-commerce system that has actually been implemented and show to fulfill the basic promises of agent systems. The most important of them were: (1) system scalability, (2) flexibility, and (3) heterogeneity. Obviously, the proposed system has a number of shortcomings that we are aware off, and we will work vigorously to remove them and develop and implement a truly comprehensive system. We will report on our progress in subsequent reports.

References

1. Bartolini, C., Preist, C., Jennings, N.R.: A Software Framework for Automated Negotiation. In: *Proceedings of SELMAS'2004*, LNCS 3390, Springer Verlag (2005) 213–235.
2. Chmiel, K. et al.: Agent Technology in Modelling E-Commerce Processes; Sample Implementation. In: C. Danilowicz (ed.): *Multimedia and Network Information Systems*, Volume 2, Wroclaw University of Technology Press, (2004) 13–22.
3. Chmiel, K. et al.: Testing the Efficiency of JADE Agent Platform. In: *Proceedings of the 3rd International Symposium on Parallel and Distributed Computing, Cork, Ireland*, IEEE Computer Society Press, Los Alamitos, CA, (2004) 49–57.
4. Cooper, J.W.: *Java Design Patterns. A Tutorial*. Addison-Wesley, (2000).
5. FIPA: *The foundation for intelligent physical agents*. See http://www.fipa.org.
6. Ganzha, M., Paprzycki, M., Pîrvănescu, A., Bădică, C., Abraham, A.: JADE-based Multi-Agent E-Commerce Environment: Initial Implementation. In: *Analele Universităţii din Timişoara, Seria Matematică-Informatică* (to appear), (2005).
7. JADE: Java Agent Development Framework. See http://jade.cselt.it.
8. Kowalczyk, R. et al.: Integrating Mobile and Intelligent Agents. In: *Advanced E-commerce: A Survey. Agent Technologies, Infrastructures, Tools, and Applications for E-Services, Proceedings NODe'2002 Agent-Related Workshops, Erfurt, Germany, LNAI 2592*, Springer Verlag, (2002) 295–313.

9. Laudon, K.C., Traver, C.G.: *E-Commerce. Business, Technology, Society (2nd ed.)*. Pearson Addison-Wesley, (2004).

10. Paprzycki, M., Abraham, A.: Agent Systems Today; Methodological Considerations. In: *Proceedings of 2003 International Conference on Management of e-Commerce and e-Government*, Jangxi Science and Technology Press, Nanchang, China, (2003) 416–421.

11. Paprzycki, M., Abraham, A.. Pîrvănescu, A., Bădică, C.: Implementing Agents Capable of Dynamic Negotiations. In: Petcu, P. and Negru, V. (eds.): *Proceedings of SYNASC'04: Symbolic and Numeric Algorithms for Scientific Computing*, Timişoara, Romania, Mirton Press, Timişoara, Romania (2004) 369–380.

12. Pîrvănescu, A., Bădică, C., Paprzycki, M.: Developing a JADE-based Multi-Agent E-Commerce Environment. In: Guimarães, N. and Isaías, P. (eds.): *Proceedings IADIS AC'05: International Conference on Applied Computing*, Algarve, Portugal, IADIS Press, Lisbon, Portugal (2005) 425–432.

A Parallel Version
for the Propagation Algorithm[*]

Márcio Bastos Castro, Lucas Baldo, Luiz Gustavo Fernandes, Mateus Raeder,
and Pedro Velho

Programa de Pós-Graduação em Ciência da Computação, PUCRS,
Avenida Ipiranga, 6681 - CEP 90619-900, Porto Alegre, Brazil
{mcastro, lbaldo, gustavo, mraeder, pedro}@inf.pucrs.br

Abstract. This paper presents a parallel version for the Propagation
Algorithm which belongs to the region growing family of algorithms.
The main goal of our implementation is to decrease de Propagation Algorithm execution time in order to allow its use on image interpolation
applications. Our solution is oriented to low cost high performance platforms such as clusters of workstations. Four different input data sets
represented by pairs of images were chosen in order to carry out experimental tests. The results obtained show that our parallel version of the
Propagation Algorithm presents significant speedups.

1 Introduction

Creating virtual in-between views from two scenes of the same subject taken
from different points of view can be a very interesting tool to economize resources in some practical applications [1]. One main example is typically found
in teleconferencing with limited network bandwidth. Image-based interpolation
is a method to create smooth and realistic virtual views between two original
view points. Interpolation applications are usually based on a three-phase algorithm [2]: construction of a dense matching map between the original images,
separations of matched areas from unmatched ones and finally the generation of
all in-between images. The matching phase is by far the most time consuming
one of this procedure. The general technique for matching areas from different
images is called region growing. Its basic principle is the use of images characteristics to group neighbor pixels and thus creating regions. In [3], a new region
growing algorithm was proposed. It is based on the construction of a quasi-dense
matching map between the two original views and it is able to perform more accurate matches. Its originality consists on the adoption of a "best first" strategy
to select the next match from a set of seed matches which is updated through the
addition of each new found match from the precedent algorithm iteration. This
new algorithm was called the Propagation Algorithm, and the improvements on
the matching procedure brought together an additional computational cost. This
paper proposes a parallel version for the Propagation Algorithm. The target architecture is a cluster of workstations and the implementation was carried out
using the standard message passing library MPI [4].

---

[*] This work was developed in collaboration with HP Brazil R&D.

V. Malyshkin (Ed.): PaCT 2005, LNCS 3606, pp. 403–412, 2005.

The parallelization of the region growing technique has been the subject of several different studies [5]. One of the most spread techniques is based on the "Split and Merge" strategy [6]. On this approach, the merge phase is done through the construction of a non-oriented graph to represent the problem. The graph boundaries are the image regions and the connections between the extremities stand for the neighbors relation of the regions. The first parallel versions of the regions growing algorithm based on the "Split and Merge" approach were implemented over SIMD machines and dynamic structures were used to store image regions information [7,8]. Another experimental study of the parallel versions of the image segmentation algorithm based on the regions growing technique (also based on the "Split and Merge" approach) was presented by [9]. On this work, the authors propose a new version of the algorithm to determinate the connected components of an image and a new parallel approach is presented for the merge phase.

The paper is organized as follows. In Section 2, the image interpolation application is reviewed, with emphasis to the propagation (region growing) algorithm. After, the proposed parallel approach is described in Section 3. Section 4 presents some experimental results for four different case studies. Finally, some concluding remarks and future directions are given in Section 5.

2   Propagation Algorithm

Before starting the Propagation Algorithm, a preparation phase is necessary to select the seed matches. Points of interest [10] are naturally good seed point candidates because they represent the points of the image that have the highest texture. These points are detected in each separated image. Next, they are matched using the ZNCC (zero-mean normalized cross correlation) measure [3]. At the end of this phase, a set of seed pairs is ready to be used to bootstrap a region growing type algorithm which propagates the matches in the neighborhood of seed points from the most textured pixels to the less textured ones. The Propagation Algorithm itself is based on a classic region growing method for image segmentation [11] which uses pixel homogeneity.

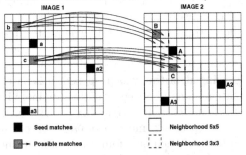

Fig. 1. Neighborhood propagation

However, instead of using pixel homogeneity property, a similar measure based on the matches correlation score is adopted. This propagation strategy could also be justified by the fact that seed pairs are composed by points of interest, which are the local maxima of the texture. Thus, these matches neighbors are also strongly textured what allows good propagation even though they are not local maxima. The neighborhood $N_5(a, A)$ is defined as being all pixels within the 5x5 window centered at these two points (one window per image).

For each neighboring pixel in the first image, a list of match candidates is constructed. This list consists of all pixels of a 3x3 window in the corresponding neighborhood of the second image (see Fig. 1). The complete definition of the neighborhood $\mathcal{N}(a, A)$ is given by:

$$\mathcal{N}(a, A) = \{(b, B), b \in \mathcal{N}_5(a), B \in \mathcal{N}_5(A), (B - A) - (b - a) \in \{-1, 0, 1\}^2\}.$$

The input of the algorithm is a set which contains the current seed pairs. This set is implemented by a heap data structure for a faster selection of the best pair. The output is an injective displacement mapping which contains all the good matches found by the Propagation Algorithm. Briefly, all initial seed pairs are starting points of concurrent propagations. At each step, a match (a, A) with the best ZNCC score is removed from the current set of seed pairs. Then, the algorithm looks for new matches in its match neighborhood and, when it finds one, it is added to the current seed pairs set and also to the set of accepted matches which is under construction.

3   Parallel Propagation

The parallel implementation for the Propagation Algorithm discussed on this section was developed in order to allow the use of this new algorithm on realistic situations. Thus, it was necessary to achieve better performances without using parallel programming models oriented to very expensive (but not frequently used) machines. Therefore, the natural choice was a cluster with a message passing programming model.

As seen before, the Propagation Algorithm advances by comparing neighbors pixels through out the source images surface. From some seed pairs, it can form large matching regions on both images surface. In fact, a single seed pair can start a propagation that grows through a large region over the images surface. This freedom of evolution guarantees the algorithm to achieve good results in terms of matched surfaces. Another characteristic is that the algorithm is based on global "best-first" strategy to choose the next seed pair that will start a new propagation, which also has a direct effect on the final match quality. These two characteristics are hard to deal with if one wants to propose a parallel distributed version of the algorithm without loosing quality at the final match. The "best-first" strategy implementation is based on a global knowledge of the seed pairs set, which is not appropriated to a non-shared

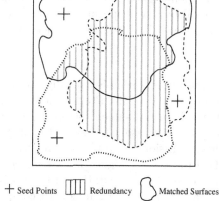

Fig. 2. Redundancy problem

memory context. In addition, the freedom of evolution through out the images surface assumes that the algorithm knows the entire surface of the images, and this can create a situation where several processors are propagating over the same regions at the same time creating a redundancy of computation (Fig. 2). Besides, it is not possible to know in advance how many new matches a seed pair will generate. Thus, from a parallel point of view, the Propagation Algorithm is an irregular and dynamic problem which exhibits unpredictable load fluctuations. Therefore, it requires the use of some load balancing scheme in order to achieve a more efficient parallel solution.

The parallel solution proposed in this paper is based on a master-slave scheme. One processor will be responsible for distributing the work and centralizing the final results. The others processors will be running the Propagation Algorithm, each one using a sub-set of the seed pairs and knowing a pair of corresponding slices over the images surface (coordinates of target slice). The master distributes the seed pairs over the nodes considering their location over the slices. This procedure replaces the global "best-first" strategy by several local "best-first" ones. Each local seed pairs sub-set is still implemented as a heap which is ordered by the pair ZNCC score. This strategy minimizes the problem of loosing quality at the final match.

Once the problem with the global "best-first" strategy is solved, it still remains the problem of the algorithm limitation of evolution over the images surface. As said before, each node can propagate just over the surface of its associated slice in order to avoid computation redundancy. However, forbidding the evolution out of the associated slice generates two kinds of losses. First, some matches are not done because they are just at the border of one slice and one of its points is placed outside it. Second, some regions in one slice may not be reached by any propagation started by a seed pair located inside of its surface, but instead they could be reached by a propagation started at a neighbor slice.

Such a limitation is partially solved by a technique called flexible slices. This technique allows the Propagation Algorithm to expand through the surface of its neighbor slices in a controlled way. As shown on Fig. 3, each processor works over its own associated slice, but it also knows its neighbor slices and it has the permission to propagate over them. But still, it is not interesting to leave the Propagation Algorithm free to compute its neighbors entire surface. This may cause the computation of too many repeated matches. To avoid that, each processor has the permission to compute just over a percentage of its neighbors surface. This percentage is related to the number of slices. A large number of slices implies in thinner slices. In this case, it is acceptable to allow a processor to advance over a large percentage of its neighbors surfaces. On the other hand, a small number of slices implies in larger slices. Here, the algorithm must not propagate too much over the neighbors surface. Finally, it is impor-

tant to mention that the master must
receive all matches generated by the
slaves and it must filter the unavoidable
duplicated ones. In order to send these
final matches to the master, each slave
has a communication buffer which is
filled progressively as the Propagation
Algorithm advances. When the buffer is
full, it is sent to the master. After that,
the slave immediately returns to its execution. All slaves do the same procedure, in a way that forces the master
to have a receiving queue. This queue
is dimensioned to avoid buffer losses by
the master. When a slave reaches the
end of its seed pairs sub-set, it sends

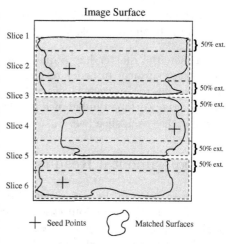

Fig. 3. Flexible slices approach

an incomplete buffer to the master. When the master receives an incomplete
buffer, it knows that the sender has finished its work and sends a new slice (seed
pairs sub-set) back to it (if there is still sub-sets available). Figure 4 shows the
complete flow-chart for the parallel Propagation Algorithm.

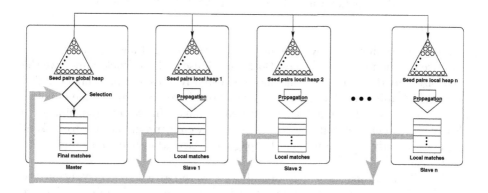

Fig. 4. Flow-chart of the parallel Propagation Algorithm

The last problem to deal with in the parallelization of the Propagation Algorithm is the workload distribution. If the source images are divided into more
slices than the number of nodes available, the following strategy is adopted:

1. the master divides the set of seed pairs into sub-sets based on their location
   over the slices;
2. each slave receives one slice with its associated sub-set;
3. each slave computes its own sub-set of seed pairs;
4. when there is no more seed pairs to compute, the slave sends a signal to the
   master;

5. if there is some available slices remaining, the master choose a new one and send it to the available slave.

In fact, the master has a queue of slices, organized by their position over the images surface. In order to choose which slice will be sent to an available slave, the master just gets the first slice of this queue. This procedure is sufficient to avoid the workload unbalance problem originated by the different amount of seed matches each slice has.

4   Experimental Results

In order to perform the experimental tests of the parallel implementation of the Propagation Algorithm, four case studies were selected. Table 1 presents the size of the images that compose those case studies with their respective sequential execution times obtained using a Pentium III 1 Ghz with 256 MB RAM.

Table 1. Execution times for the sequential Propagation Algorithm

Image	Flower	House	Rock	Trunk
Size (pxs)	368x384	768x512	512x768	360x240
Propagation time (s)	6.32	15.24	14.32	3.20

Each pair of images shows specific characteristics. The Flower pair is the only one based on non-realistic images. Both, the House and the Rock pairs have the same size, but the House pair has more textured regions and presents occluded elements. Finally, the Trunk pair is the only one based on a gray scale of colors and it has the smallest number of textured regions. This set of input images is clearly not exhaustive, but the pairs of images were carefully chosen to make it possible to verify the the parallel Propagation Algorithm behavior on different situations.

For all input images, experimental tests were carried out varying on the number of processors[1](N), number of slices per slave (fine grain and coarse grain) and the redundancy extension allowed over the slices. The number of slices per slaves is obtained by $2 \times N$ (coarse grain) and by $3 \times N$ (fine grain). Moreover, the slices redundancy extension used was 30% and 100% of the slices height. Figure 5 shows the speedup, execution time (T) and efficiency (E) of the parallel Propagation Algorithm for each case study. The experimental tests showed that, for all input images pairs, our parallel implementation achieved an execution time reduction about 81% ($\simeq$ 79.26% for the Rock, $\simeq$ 80.01% for the Trunk, $\simeq$ 81.49% for the House and $\simeq$ 83.86 for the Flower) using 9 processors. On the other hand, all executions carried out with more than 9 processors presented a significant lost of performance.

---

[1] The target architecture was a cluster with 8 nodes Pentium III 1 Ghz dual and 256 MB RAM connected by a 100 Mb Fast-Ethernet network.

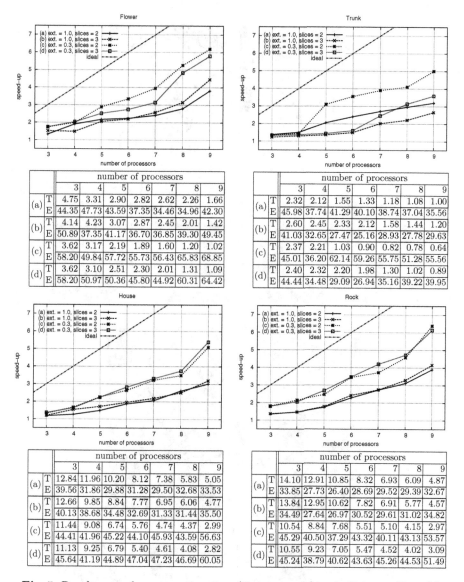

Fig. 5. Results: speedup, execution time (T, in seconds) and efficiency (E, in %)

The analysis of the curves on the graphs of Fig. 5, one can clearly identify that the 30% of redundancy extension always results in a better efficiency. This result was expected, since with a lower redundancy allowed there are less pairs to match. We could then expect even better results with less than 30% extension, however this is not possible due to the lost of matches at boundaries of each slice what compromises the final match quality.

Examples of the parallel Propagation Algorithm output for each case study ((a) Flower, (b) House, (c) Rock and (d) Trunk) can be visualized at Fig.6. The

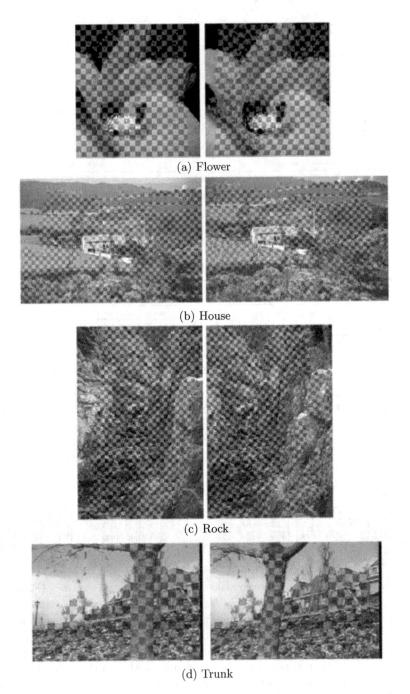

(a) Flower

(b) House

(c) Rock

(d) Trunk

Fig. 6. Output of the parallel Propagation Algorithm for each case study

squared regions in both images of each pair show the extension of the matched regions obtained from the seed matches. Readers can notice that the Propagation Algorithm advances better over the textured surfaces. Regions like the sky in the Trunk pair or the grass in the House pair were not matched due to absence of texture. Furthermore, some regions on the images boundaries cannot be matched because they do not appear in both views.

5   Conclusions

The implementation of a parallel version for the Propagation Algorithm was presented in this paper. The particularity of this algorithm consists on the adoption of a "best first" strategy to select the next match from a set of seed matches firing several propagations that can advance over the same images zones generating a large redundancy in the computation of the seed matches. Our parallel version is based on a master/slave scheme and we proposed a new technique called flexible slices to solve the redundancy problem. Several experiments were carried out in order to verify the usability of our approach and the results present a significant gain of performance. Finally, it is the authors opinion that the work developed so far was worthwhile. The results obtained are interesting and the implementation allowed a quite good understanding of the problem, leading to promising directions for further investigations.

References

1. Seitz, S., Dyer, C.: Physically-Valid View Synthesis by Image Interpolation. In: Proceedings of the International Workshop on Representations of Visual Scenes, Cambridge, Massachussets, USA (1995) 26–33
2. Lhuillier, M., Quan, L.: Image Interpolation by Joint View Triangulation. In: Proceedings of the International Conference on Computer Vision and Pattern Recognition, Fort Collins, Colorado, USA (1999) 139–145
3. Lhuillier, M., Quan, L.: Robust Dense Matching using Local and Global Geometric Constraints. In: Proceedings of the 15th International Conference on Pattern Recognition. (2000) 968–972
4. Snir, M., Otto, S., Huss-Lederman, S., Walker, D., Dongarra, J.: MPI: the complete reference. MIT Press (1996)
5. Alnuweiri, H., Prasanna, V.: Parallel architectures and algorithms for image component labeling. IEEE Trans. Patt. Anal. Machine Intell. **14** (1992) pp. 1014–1034
6. Horowitz, S., Pavlidis, T.: Picture segmentation by a directed split-and-merge procedure. In: Proceedings of the 2nd International Joint Conference on Pattern Recognition. (1974) pp. 424–433
7. Tilton, J.: Image segmentation by iterative parallel region growing with applications to data compression and image analysis. In: Proceedings of the 2nd Symposium on the Frontiers of Massively Parallel Computation. (1988) pp. 357–360
8. Willebeck-LeMair, M., Reeves, A.: Solving non-uniform problems on simd computers: case study on region growing. Journal of Paralle and Distributed Computing **8** (1990) pp. 135–149

9. Jájá, J., Bader, D., Harwood, D., Davis, L.: Parallel algorithms for image enhancement and segmentation by region growing with an experimental study. Technical report, Institute for Advanced Computer Studies, University of Maryland (1995)
10. Schimid, C., Mohr, R., Bauckhage, C.: Comparing and Evaluating Interest Points. In: Proceedings of the 6th International Conference on Computer Vision, Bombay, India (1998) 230–235
11. Monga, O.: An Optimal Region Growing Algorithm for Image Segmentation. International Journal of Pattern Recognition and Artificial Intelligence **1** (1987) 351–375

Parallelization Techniques for Multidimensional Hypercomplex Discrete Fourier Transform

Marina Chicheva[1], Marat Aliev[2], and Alexey Yershov[3]

[1] Image Processing Systems Institute of the RAS; 443001, Molodogvardeiskaya st. 151, Samara, Russia
+7 (8462) 320094, +7 (8462) 325620
[2] Adygeya State University; 352700, Universitetskaya st. 208, Maikop, Adygeya Republic, Russia
+7 (87722) 70273
[3] Samara State University; 443011, Academik Pavlov st. 1, Samara, Russia
+7 (8462) 345402
mchi@smr.ru, marat@adygnet.ru, yershov@ssu.samara.ru

Abstract. We consider techniques for parallelization of the multidimensional hypercomplex discrete Fourier transform. There are two potentials for parallel algorithm synthesis: specific structural properties of hypercomplex algebra and inner parallelism of multidimensional Cooley-Tukey scheme. Both approaches are developed; results of their experimental research are shown.

1 Introduction

The multidimensional hypercomplex discrete Fourier transform (HDFT) [1] of real signal, given by

$$F(m_1,...,m_d) = \sum_{n_1,...,n_d=0}^{N-1} f(n_1,...,n_d) W^{\langle \mathbf{m,n} \rangle} \ , \ W^{\langle \mathbf{m,n} \rangle} = \prod_{k=1}^{d} w_k^{m_k n_k} \ , \ w_k^N = 1 \qquad (1)$$

has increasingly been in the focus of attention of those working in image and multidimensional signal processing. A number of publications by the Russian and foreign researchers are devoted to the HDFT applications (see [3], [4], [5]).

The characteristic feature of the transform (1) is that the N-th roots w_k from unity are found in different sub-algebras isomorphic to complex algebra **C** of some 2^d algebra $\mathbf{B}_d$. Accordingly, the spectrum values $F(m_1,...,m_d)$ are found in algebra B_d. In the two-dimensional case ($d=2$), the transform (1) takes the form:

$$F(m_1,m_2) = \sum_{n_1=0}^{N-1} \sum_{n_2=0}^{N-1} f(n_1,n_2) \ w_1^{m_1 n_1} w_2^{m_2 n_2}, \ 0 \le m_1, m_2 \le N-1, \qquad (2)$$

where $w_1 = \exp\left\{ 2\pi\varepsilon_1 / N \right\}$, $w_2 = \exp\left\{ 2\pi\varepsilon_2 / N \right\}$, ε_1, ε_2 $\left(\varepsilon_1^2 = \varepsilon_2^2 = -1 \right)$ are the constituent elements of some four-dimensional hypercomplex algebra, with its arbitrary element defined as

V. Malyshkin (Ed.): PaCT 2005, LNCS 3606, pp. 413 – 419, 2005.
© Springer-Verlag Berlin Heidelberg 2005

$$z = \alpha + \beta\varepsilon_1 + \gamma\varepsilon_2 + \delta\varepsilon_1\varepsilon_2 . \tag{3}$$

Note that the classical discrete Fourier transform is a particular case of the transform (1) at $\varepsilon_1 = ... = \varepsilon_d = i \in \mathbf{C}$. Thus, we can state that besides a variety of special applications discussed in Refs. [3], [4], [5], the transform (1) provides an effective instrument for solving the entire scope of problems in digital signal processing, which rely upon the discrete Fourier transform (fast calculation of discrete convolutions, filtration, signal compression, etc.)

As noted in Ref. [1], the only principal property that determines the efficiency of the HDFT's applied use is not the specific structure of hypercomplex algebra $\mathbf{B}_d$, but the existence of a sufficient number of isomorphic copies of complex algebra in it. In Ref. [1] it was proved that the minimal number of real operations required for addition/multiplication of elements in $\mathbf{B}_d$ is achieved at

$$\mathbf{B}_d \cong \underbrace{\mathbf{C} \oplus \mathbf{C} \oplus ... \oplus \mathbf{C}}_{2^{d-1}} \tag{4}$$

Besides, in Refs. [1], [2] an automorphism system is constructed, an algorithm for fast multiplication of algebra $\mathbf{B}_d$ elements developed, and sequential HDFT algorithms are synthesized.

2 Parallel HDFT Algorithm Based on Hypercomplex Algebra

When implementing a multidimensional transform, a major problem is increasing computational effort with increasing dimensionality. A natural way of resolving the problem is parallel implementation of the transform (1). It stands to reason that a principal feasibility of such a parallelization is incorporated in the representation (4). Besides, additional opportunities for increasing the algorithm's parallelism and efficiency are offered by the inner parallelism of the Cooley-Tukey scheme, an analog of which is used for generating the hypercomplex spectrum.

Below, principles on which the algorithm is based are exemplified by the 2D transform. Let an arbitrary element z of four-dimensional algebra $\mathbf{B}_2$ be defined by the relation (3).

Introduce the change of variables:

$$u_0 = 1 + \varepsilon_1\varepsilon_2 , \quad u_1 = 1 - \varepsilon_1\varepsilon_2 , \quad u_2 = \varepsilon_1 - \varepsilon_2 , \quad u_3 = \varepsilon_1 + \varepsilon_2 .$$

Then, the hypercomplex number z is given by

$$z = \tfrac{1}{2}\big((\alpha+\delta)u_0 + (\alpha-\delta)u_1 + (\beta-\gamma)u_2 + (\beta+\gamma)u_3\big). \tag{5}$$

Obviously, for an arbitrary $z \in \mathbf{B}_2$ the change to (5) will call for four real additions. However, for the real (input signal) and complex (the roots w_k) numbers such a change does not require performing non-trivial arithmetic operations.

The inverse change to the original representation also calls for four real additions per hypercomplex spectrum pixel.

The multiplication rules for the new basis elements are given in Table 1.

Table 1. Multiplication rules for the basis elements

	u_0	u_1	u_2	u_3
u_0	$2u_0$	0	$2u_2$	0
u_1	0	$2u_1$	0	$2u_3$
u_2	$2u_2$	0	$-2u_0$	0
u_3	0	$2u_3$	0	$-2u_1$

It should be noted that in the above representation, the products of the elements u_0 and u_2 by the elements u_1 and u_3 are equal to zero. This implies that with such a representation the calculation of a product of two hypercomplex numbers consists in two entirely independent procedures. Instead of the product

$$\left(xu_0 + yu_1 + zu_2 + vu_3\right)\left(\alpha u_0 + \beta u_1 + \gamma u_2 + \delta u_3\right)$$

it will suffice to independently calculate two products:

$$\left(xu_0 + zu_2\right)\left(\alpha u_0 + \gamma u_2\right) = 2\left(\left(x\alpha - z\gamma\right)u_0 + \left(x\gamma + z\alpha\right)u_2\right),$$
$$\left(yu_1 + vu_3\right)\left(\beta u_1 + \delta u_3\right) = 2\left(\left(y\beta - v\delta\right)u_1 + \left(y\delta + v\beta\right)u_3\right).$$

Thus, the most cumbersome algorithm's operation - calculation of the product of hypercomplex numbers - can be parallelized into two independent branches which do not require data exchange. Thus, per-operation time will be reduced by nearly twice.

The structure of the sequential fast HDFT algorithm [1] is such that the representation (5) allows the calculation to be completely separated by the same principle. As a result, the parallel algorithm of the 2D HDFT is as follows:

- change from the original representation (3) to the representation (5);
- data distribution between two processors;
- taking the transform (2) using algorithms of Cooley-Tukey type [2];
- hypercomplex spectrum reconstruction.

The processing in two-dimensional case is illustrated by the Fig.1. During the talk the authors propose to discuss the case of an arbitrary dimension d.

The main advantage of the proposed algorithm is essential decrease of computational complexity of next operations:

- addition of hypercomplex numbers in 2^{d-1} times;
- multiplication of complex root by hypercomplex number in 2^{d-1} times;
- multiplication of two arbitrary hypercomplex numbers for $d=2$ in more than 3 times, for an arbitrary d – in $2^{d-1}(2d+1)/3$ times.

Besides, it is saved an important feature of sequential algorithm that is the use the symmetric properties of real signal hypercomplex spectrum (see, for example, [1], [2]). But to use the symmetry it is required to carry out additional data exchange, resulting in slight decrease of parallelization general efficiency.

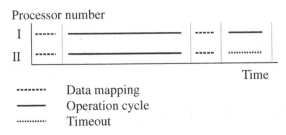

Fig. 1. Illustration of processor workloads for parallelization based on algebra properties (two-dimensional case)

3 Parallelization Using the Decomposition Structure

The above-described approach allows synthesis of a parallel algorithm for the d-dimensional HDFT paralleled between 2^{d-1} processors. Accordingly, the algorithm's speed up will not exceed the value of 2^{d-1}. With a greater number of processors available, it is expedient to implement an additional parallelization due to the multi-dimensional Cooley-Tukey decomposition structure. The data and computation distribution principle is exemplified below by a two-dimensional transform.

The basic relationship for "the radix 2" decomposition of the HDFT (2) [2] takes the form:

$$F\left(m_1, m_2\right) = \sum_{a,b=0}^{1} \tilde{F}_{ab}\left(m_1, m_2\right) w_1^{am_1} w_2^{bm_2} \tag{6}$$

where

$$\tilde{F}_{ab}\left(m_1, m_2\right) = \sum_{n_1,n_2=0}^{N/2-1} f\left(2n_1 + a, 2n_2 + b\right) \left(w_1^2\right)^{m_1 n_1} \left(w_2^2\right)^{m_2 n_2}.$$

The key operation of the algorithm is the reconstruction (6) of the complete spectrum $F\left(m_1, m_2\right)$ from the known (derived) values of partial spectra $\tilde{F}_{ab}\left(m_1, m_2\right)$. Assume that every partial spectrum has been calculated on a separate processor. Note that the processing time will be approximately the same for all the processors because the spectrum array sizes and the calculation algorithms are the same. Then, every processor performs multiplications of the partial spectra elements by the power of the roots w_1, w_2. Then, the values derived are transferred to a processor where the hypercomplex spectrum is finally formed.

It stands to reason that in this way the process can be parallelized between any number of processors divisible by four by using several decomposition steps of type (6). The expected time of the hypercomplex spectrum computation is in inverse proportion to the number of processors because the major computation effort is accounted for the computation of the smaller-size HDFTs. For the data dimensionality $d > 2$, a similar scheme involving stepwise parallelization between 2^d processors can be applied.

Fig.2 illustrates the described algorithm for two-dimensional case and one step of decomposition fulfilled.

Processor number

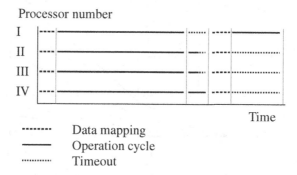

Data mapping
Operation cycle
Timeout

Fig. 2. Illustration of processor workloads for parallelization based on decomposition structure (two-dimensional case, one decomposition step)

The advantage of this approach is twofold reduction of transmitted data volume due to symmetry of hypercomplex spectrum of real signal.

4 Experimental Studies

To date, we have implemented and studied the parallel algorithms of two-dimensional hypercomplex discrete Fourier transform based on both algebra properties and decomposition structure, and also the combined algorithm. Below the parallelization results are given for next cases specified in table 2, where p is the required processor number.

The studies were conducted on the cluster of the Moscow State University R&D Computer Center (RDCC MSU), which consists of 16 two-processor nodes on the Pentium III platform, integrated into a high-speed network SCI. Fig. 3 shows the program execution time T_p (in seconds) as a function of N, where $N{\times}N$ is the two-dimensional HDFT size.

Tables 3 shows the experimentally derived values of the algorithm's speed up, $U = T_1/T_p$, and efficiency, $E = T_1/pT_p$.

Table 2. List of examined algorithms

p	Algorithm
1	Sequential algorithm
2	Algorithm based on algebra properties
4	Algorithm based on decomposition structure (1 step)
8	Combined algorithm
16	Algorithm based on decomposition structure (1 steps)

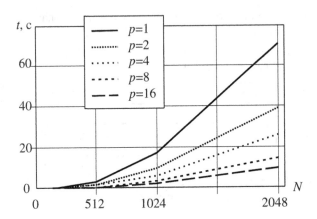

Fig. 3. Computation time for the $N{\times}N$ – HDFT

Table 3. Algorithm's speed up and efficiency

	Speed up				Efficiency			
N	$p=2$	$p=4$	$p=8$	$p=16$	$p=2$	$p=4$	$p=8$	$p=16$
128	1,805	2,261	4,082	6,545	0,903	0,565	0,510	0,409
256	1,802	2,795	5,035	6,444	0,901	0,699	0,629	0,403
512	1,790	2,372	4,246	6,382	0,895	0,593	0,531	0,399
1024	1,803	2,925	5,274	6,577	0,902	0,731	0,659	0,411
2048	1,791	2,725	4,881	7,243	0,896	0,681	0,610	0,453

5   Conclusions

Thus, in the presented paper the synthesis principles for parallel algorithms of hyper-complex DFT are developed. Two ways of DFT parallelization are implemented. The best efficiency was reached during parallelization based on structural properties of the algebra ($\approx$90%). The efficiency of parallelization based on Cooley-Tukey scheme and combined algorithm amounts to 40-73%. Efficiency decrease with increasing processors' number is connected with decreasing part of simultaneous calculation of partial spectra, which gives the main effect. Obtained results allow us to conclude that if number of dimensions will increase at limited number of processors the approach used structure of multidimensional hypercomplex algebra is the most preferable.

Acknowledgements

The work was financially supported by RF Ministry of Education, Samara Region Administration and U.S. Civilian Research & Development Foundation (CRDF Project SA-014-02) as part of the joint Russian-American program "Basic Research and Higher Education" (BRHE); and by Russian Foundation for Basic Research (RFBR), grants # 03-01-00736, #05-01-96501.

References

1. Aliev, M.V. Chernov V.M.: Two-dimensional FFT-like algorithms with overlapping. Optical Memory and Neural Networks (Information Optics), Vol. 11, No. 1 (2002) 29-38.
2. Aliev, M.V.: Synthesis of two-dimensional DFT algorithms in the hypercomplex algebra. Pattern recognition and image analysis, Vol. 13, No. 1 (2003) 61-63.
3. Furman, Ya.A., Krevetskii, A.V., Peredreev, A.K.: An introduction to contour analysis: applications to image and signal processing. FIZMATLIT, Moscow (2002) (in Russian)
4. Geometric Computing with Clifford Algebra (Sommer G. (Ed.)). Springer Series in Information Sciences. Springer-Verlag, Berlin (2001)
5. Labunets, E.V., Labunets, V.G., Egiazarian, K., Astola, J.: Hypercomplex moments application in invariant image recognition. Int. Conf. On Image Processing 98 (1998) 256–261

An Implementation of the Matrix Multiplication Algorithm SUMMA in mpF[*]

Alexey Kalinov, Ilya Ledovskikh, Mikhail Posypkin, Zakhar Levchenko, and Vladimir Chizhov

Institute for System Programming of the Russian Academy of Sciences,
109004, 25 B.Kommunisticheskaya str. Moscow, Russia
{ka, il, posypkin}@ispras.ru

Abstract. In this paper, we present a new parallel Fortran extension called mpF. The language based on both data and task parallelism allows explicit specification of data and computations distribution. We discuss some reasons for the language design and demonstrate the basic mpF features on an example of the parallel matrix multiplication algorithm SUMMA. The mpF implementation is compared with its MPI counterpart.

1 Introduction

There are two extremes of parallel programming. The first one is the use of a sequential language and a parallelizing compiler. It is the most comfortable approach for application developers but the least efficient. The second one is the use of a sequential language and the basic level libraries for synchronization and access to data. It is potentially the most efficient but the least comfortable approach.

The most common architecture for parallel computing now is distributed memory systems. The following approaches to the extremes: High Performance Fortran (HPF) [1] and Message Passing Interface (MPI) [2] are the most commonly used for parallel programming such systems now. HPF is easy in use but in general inefficient [3]. MPI is efficient but hard to use.

A parallel programming language called mpF [4] is an attempt to develop a parallel extension of Fortran 90 being a golden mean between easiness in use and efficiency. It was developed on base of experience of development and use of the mpC parallel programming language [5,6]. Both languages were developed in Institute for System Programming of the Russian Academy of Sciences. The important features of the mpF and the mpC are that they support efficiently portable parallel programming of heterogeneous platform and mixed data and task parallelism.

The language features are demonstrated on an example implementation of Scalable Universal Matrix Multiplication Algorithm (SUMMA) proposed in [7]. It was chosen for demonstration of mpF because this efficient and scalable algorithm is the base of the matrix multiplication algorithm in widely used parallel library ScaLAPACK [8]

[*] This research is supported by Computational and Information Aspects of Solving Large Problems program of the Division of Mathematical Sciences of the Russian Academy of Sciences.

V. Malyshkin (Ed.): PaCT 2005, LNCS 3606, pp. 420–432, 2005.

and its elegant MPI implementation is presented in [7] as an example, demonstrating the power of MPI for coding concurrent algorithms. Moreover the algorithm is intended to execution with heterogeneous distribution of data between processes.

The main contribution of the paper is presentation of the mpF implementation of the algorithm SUMMA and its comparison with the MPI counterpart. The mpF parallel programming language is introduced as well.

The rest of the paper is organized as follows. In section 2 we present our motivation of the language design. Section 3 introduces algorithm SUMMA. Its implementation in mpF is presented in section 4. In section 5 we compare mpF and MPI implementations. Section 6 concludes the paper.

2 Motivation of the Language Design

Fortran is still the main programming language for scientific and technical applications. Language dialects known as Fortran 90, Fortran 95, and defined by the new published standard ISO/IEC 1539-1:2004, are enough suitable for development of efficient and portable programs for sequential architectures, vector and superscalar computers, and for shared memory systems. These Fortran dialects support data parallel programming for SMP computers because provide whole array expressions, functions and assignment, and executable constructs like FORALL loop. Such language facilities allow both development of efficient programs and generation of efficient parallel target code. Automatic parallelization of source code is also possible for architectures listed above, and the existing parallelizing compilers can be successfully used for development of real-life applications. On the other hand, development of such parallelizing compiler is still the complicated and labor-consuming task.

The situation in area of applications for distributed memory systems (MPP computers) is different. Both automatic parallelization of sequential source code (we call it *compiler approach*) and array expressions and constructs do not allow yet producing an efficient parallel target code for wide class of applications. The existing parallelizing compilers still are prototypes, which stay far from the industrial level.

Presently two approaches are used for development of the real-life computational applications for MPPs: message passing libraries (*library approach*), or parallel extensions of Fortran (*language approach*) Library approach is very flexible and efficient, but looks to be tedious and error-prone for development of large and complex applications. Language approach based on data- or task parallelism is much more easy-to-use for development of computational applications.

The most widespread parallel extensions of Fortran are initially based on data parallelism and use the implicit approach to distribution of data and computations – parallelism is specified by the set of compiler directives. With exception of such compiler directives (designed usually as Fortran comments) the program is still the sequential Fortran program and can be developed and debugged on uniprocessors. Examples of such implicitly data parallel languages are HPF 1.1[9], Fortran D[10], Fortran DVM[11]. Data parallel languages allow the efficient implementation for big set of computational algorithms. But these languages do neither support heterogeneous computing and task parallelism.

On the other hand, the Fortran M language [12] is based on explicit task parallelism. The corresponding extensions of FORTRAN 77 are made in syntax of statements. The Fortran M program can be efficiently compiled for both distributed and shared memory systems. The language allows to specify the virtual computer (processor array), and its topology may differ from the size and shape of the physical multiprocessor. The mapping is performed using language constructs, which influence the programs performance but not correctness. It means, the programmer can develop his/her application on uniprocessor workstation and then tune performance on parallel system by changing mapping constructs. But the absence of data parallel constructs makes Fortran M almost similar (from the users point of view) to Fortran with MPI calls.

Thus, there is a need in Fortran language extension for MPP computers, suitable for efficient programming of wide class of applications. This language has to support both data- and task-parallel programming paradigms. Additionally, this language should be easy-to-use for the programmer, on the one hand, and not too complicated for the efficient implementation, on the other hand. The evolution of HPF (HPF 2.0) [1] and Fortran D (Fortran D95)[10] is directed to combination of data- and task-parallel facilities in one language. Thus, the set of parallel algorithms that can be efficiently implemented is extended, but additional extensions of such big language make it more and more complicated in use and in implementation.

The library approach to extension of data-parallel language also can be successfully applied to combine data- and task parallelism in one system. An example of such approach is HPF/MPI [13] – an HPF binding for Message Passing Interface, that allows making parallel applications consisting of different groups of processes. Processes of each group correspond to some data-parallel task that is coded in HPF; MPI calls are used for interaction between process groups. The portable implementation of HPF/MPI provides a significant speedup for many applications in comparison to pure HPF. It is necessary to say that such extension inherits not only benefits, but also drawbacks of low-level library approach – developers time consumption and debugging difficulties. Also, because the extended language is HPF, the problem of generation of efficient parallel code for data-parallel tasks is not eliminated.

In our opinion the implementation complexity of existing Fortran dialects and its relatively low flexibility are conditioned on implicit approach to data parallelism. The user has facilities to specify data distribution only, and compiler is responsible for extracting of efficient communication pattern. On the contrary, the library approach mentioned above is explicit but hard to use.

The proposed Fortran extension [4] is based on explicitly parallel approach and includes both data- and task parallelism. During design of the language called mpF we had used the principal concepts of the mpC language [5,6]. At that we worked for three goals: first, to provide high performance for wide class of applications; second, to make the extension not too big and easy in use; third, to raise the application reliability by means of language facilities. Like mpC mpF is aimed at efficient programming of irregular applications and allows obtaining good speedup on heterogeneous computing systems. Withal, the proposed Fortran extension is compact and introduces only some new entities and most new constructs are designed in traditional Fortran style and spirit. We choose for extension Fortran 90 as the simplest version of Fortran with whole array operations.

3 Scalable Universal Matrix Multiplication Algorithm SUMMA

Let us consider the formation of the matrix products $C = \alpha AB + \beta C$. We assume that each matrix X is of dimension $m^X \times n^X$, $X \in \{A, B, C\}$. Naturally, there are constraints on these dimensions: $m^A = m^C = m$, $n^A = m^B = k$, $n^B = n^C = n$. We consider processes of the parallel program as $r \times c$ grid. The $p = rc$ nodes are indexed by their row and column index and the (i, j) node will be denoted by P_{ij}.

We consider two dimensional data decompositions with the following assignment of data to nodes: Given $m^X \times n^X$ matrix X, $X \in \{A, B, C\}$, and an $r \times c$ logical process grid, we partition as follows:

$$X = \begin{pmatrix} X_{00} & \cdots & X_{0(p-1)} \\ \cdots & & \cdots \\ X_{(q-1)0} & \cdots & X_{(q-1)(p-1)} \end{pmatrix},$$

and assign X_{ij} to process P_{ij}. Submatrix X_{ij} has dimensions $m_i^X \times n_j^X$, with $\sum_i m_i^X = m^X$ and $\sum_i n_i^X = n^X$.

For simplicity, we will take $\alpha = 1$, $\beta = 0$ in our algorithm description. If a_{ij}, b_{ij} and c_{ij} denote the (i, j) element of the matrices, respectively, then the elements of C are given by

$$c_{ij} = \sum_{l=0}^{k-1} a_{il} b_{lj} .$$

Notice that rows of C are computed from rows of A, and columns of C are computed from columns of B. We hence restrict data decomposition so that rows of A and C are assigned to the same row of nodes and columns of B and C are assigned to the same column of nodes. Hence, $m_i^C = m_i^A$ and $n_j^C = n_j^B$.

Let us consider what computation is required to form C_{ij}

$$C_{ij} = \overbrace{\left(A_{i0} \mid A_{i1} \mid \ldots \mid A_{i(Q-1)} \right)}^{\tilde{A}_i} \overbrace{\begin{pmatrix} B_{0j} \\ B_{1j} \\ \cdots \\ B_{(P-1)j} \end{pmatrix}}^{\tilde{B}^j} .$$

Note that $\tilde{A}_i$ is entirely assigned to node row i, while $\tilde{B}^j$ is entirely assigned to node column j. Letting

$$\tilde{A}_i = \left(\tilde{a}_i^0 \mid \tilde{a}_i^1 \mid ... \mid \tilde{a}_i^{k-1}\right) \quad \tilde{B}^j = \begin{pmatrix} b_0^{j\,T} \\ b_1^{j\,T} \\ ... \\ b_{k-1}^{j\,T} \end{pmatrix}$$

we see that

$$C_{ij} = \sum_{l=0}^{k-1} \tilde{a}_i^l \tilde{b}_l^{j\,T} .$$

Hence the matrix-matrix multiply can be formulated as a sequence of rank-one updates.

It now suffices to parallelize each rank-one update. Pseudo-code for this, executed simultaneously on all nodes P_{ij} looks as follows:

```
Cᵢⱼ  = 0
for  l=0, k-1
        broadcast  ã_iˡ  within node row i
        broadcast  b̃_lʲ  within node column j
     Cᵢⱼ  =  Cᵢⱼ  +  ã_iˡ · b̃_lʲ^T
endfor
```

The process is illustrated in Fig. 1.

Further improvements can be obtained by observing that reformulating the method in terms of matrix-matrix multiplications instead of rank-one updates can greatly

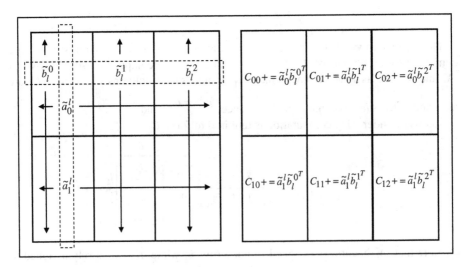

Fig. 1. Operations implementing the inner loop of matrix multiplication of a 2x3 grid of nodes

improve the performance of an individual node and reduce communication overhead. In our explanation, each column $\tilde{a}_i^l$ became a panel of columns and row $\tilde{b}_l^j$ a corresponding panel of rows.

Algorithm SUMMA is based on an implementation of the broadcast as passing of a message around the logical ring that forms the row or column. This allows pipelining computations and communications and making the algorithm scalable. The proof of the scalability as well as MPI code for the pipelined blocked algorithm is presented in [7].

4 Implementation of the SUMMA in mpF

In this section we present the mpF implementation of the algorithm SUMMA equivalent to the MPI implementation presented in [7].

```
module grid_nettype                                                     !1
! two dimensional grid                                                  !2
  nettype grid(p,q)                                                     !3
     integer p,q                                                        !4
     coord(p,q)                                                         !5
  end nettype                                                           !6
end module                                                              !7
                                                                        !8
subroutine pdgemm(                                                     &!9
       net,          &!network argument                                 !10
       p, q,         &!network dimensions                               !11
       m, n, k,      &!global matrix dimensions                         !12
       nbl,          &!panel width                                      !13
       alpha,        &!multiplication constant                          !14
       a,            &!array that holds local part of matrix A          !15
       lda,          &!leading dimension of a                           !16
       b,            &!array that holds local part of matrix B          !17
       ldb,          &!leading dimension of b                           !18
       beta,         &!multiplication constant                          !19
       c,            &!array that holds local part of matrix C          !20
       ldc,          &!leading dimension of c                           !21
       ma, na,       &!dimensions of blocks of A                        !22
       mb, nb,       &!dimensions of blocks of B                        !23
       mc, nc,       &!dimensions of blocks of C                        !24
       w1, w2)        !work arrays                                      !25
  use grid_nettype                                                      !26
  nettype(grid(p,q)) net                                               !27
  integer, replicated :: p,q,m,n,k,ma,na,mb,nb,mc,nc                    !28
  dimension ma(p), na(q), mb(p), nb(q), mc(p), nc(q)                    !29
  double precision a(lda,*),b(ldb,*),c(ldc,*),w1(*),w2(*)              !30
  replicated kk=1,iwrk,icr=1,icc=1,ii=1,jj=1,ic,ir,l,len               !31
  double precision d_one=1.0                                            !32
  subnet (net), allocatable :: s1(:,:)                                  !33
  distribution (s1) :: l,len                                           !34
                                                                        !35
  m1=1.coordof.net   !my row in network                                !36
  m2=2.coordof.net   !my column in network                             !37
! C=beta*C                                                              !38
```

```
      c[1:mc(m1),1:nc(m2)]=c[1:mc(m1),1:nc(m2)]*beta                !39
      main_loop: do while(kk.le.k)                                   !40
        iwrk=min(nbl,mb(icr)-ii,na(icc)-jj)                          !41
        A_panels_bcast: do ir=1,p                                    !42
          allocate (s1(ir:ir,q))                                     !43
          region(s1) block                                          !44
!    pack current iwrk columns of A into w1 on node (ir,icc)         !45
          len=ma(ir)*iwrk                                            !46
          region(s1(:,icc:icc))                                    &!47
            w1(1:len)=reshape(a(1:ma(ir),jj:jj+iwrk),(/len/))        !48
!          ring broadcast w1 within row ir                           !49
          do l=icc,icc+q-2                                           !50
            (net(ir,mod(l+1,q)))(w1(1:len))=                       &!51
                                (net(ir,mod(l,q)))(w1(1:len))        !52
          end do                                                    !53
          end region                                                !54
          deallocate (s1)                                           !55
        end do A_panels_bcast                                       !56
        B_panels_bcast: do ic=1,q                                   !57
          allocate (s1(p,ic:ic))                                    !58
          region(s1) block                                         !59
!    pack current iwrk rows of B into w2 on node (icr,ic)            !60
          len=nb(ic)*iwrk                                           !61
          region(s1(icr:icr,:))                                    &!62
            w2(1:len)=reshape(b(ii:ii+iwrk,1:nb(ic)),(/len/))       !63
!          ring broadcast w2 within column ic                       !64
          do l=icr,icr+p-2                                          !65
            (net(mod(l+1,p),ic))(w2(1:len))=                      &!66
                                (net(mod(l,p),ic))(w2(1:len))       !67
          end do                                                   !68
          end region                                               !69
          deallocate (s1)                                          !70
        end do B_panels_bcast                                      !71
!      update local block                                          !72
        call dgemm("N","N",mc(m1),nc(m2),iwrk,alpha,              &!73
                   w1,mb(m1),w2,iwrk,d_one,c,ldc)                   !74
!      update icr, icc, ii, jj, kk                                 !75
        ii=ii+iwrk                                                  !76
        jj=jj+iwrk                                                  !77
        if(jj.gt.na(icc)) then icc=icc+1; jj=1; endif               !78
        if(ii.gt.mb(icr)) then icr=icr+1; ii=1; endif               !79
        kk=kk+iwrk                                                  !80
      end do main_loop                                              !81
      return                                                        !82
      end                                                           !83
```

In mpF, the concept of the *computing space* is introduced. It is defined as a set of virtual processors (nodes), which may have different performance. Subsets of the computing space (called *regions of the computing space*) are used to distribute data, evaluate expressions, and execute statements. The computing space is managed via network objects or simply *networks*. Their network types characterize networks.

Lines 1-7 contain the definition of module `grid_nettype`, which holds the definition of network type `grid`. This network type (lines 3-6) describes two-dimensional networks consisting of p*q nodes with two-dimensional coordinate system. The nodes have the first coordinate ranging from 1 through p and the second coordinate ranging from 1 through q.

Data object distributed over a region of the computing space comprises a set of components of the same type so that any node of the region holds just one component.

In mpF, procedures (subroutines and functions) are divided into two classes: nodal and distributed procedures. Nodal procedures are executed by individual nodes of the computing space region. All subroutines and functions of Fortran 90 (including the intrinsic ones) are nodal procedures in mpF.

Nodes of a certain region of the computing space execute distributed subroutines and functions. The notion of distributed procedures is specific for task parallel languages. Syntactically, distributed procedures do not differ from nodal ones. The difference is in the list of formal parameters. In addition to the parameters with the names interpreted in the conventional Fortran way, any distributed subroutine or function must have exactly one *network parameter*. The name of this parameter is the name of a user-defined (in the scope of the procedure or outside it) network or an intrinsic network.

The subroutine `pdgemm` implementing algorithm SUMMA is an example of distributed procedure. Besides usual Fortran 90 formal parameters (lines 11-25) it has network parameter `net` (line 10). By default all formal parameters and data defined in the scope of the subroutine are distributed over the network `net`, which is defined in line 27 as a two-dimensional pxq grid of nodes.

Line 31 defines replicated variables. Distributed data object is called *replicated* if the values of all its components are identical.

An expression can be evaluated by a single node or by a region of the computing space. In the latter case, the expression is called distributed, and the region on which the expression is evaluated is called the expression distribution region.

There are three types of distributed expressions:

- An *asynchronous* expression does not require any communication between the nodes of the computing space for its evaluation; in fact, the evaluation of such an expression decomposes into independent computations performed at the nodes of the expression distribution region.
- A *synchronous* expression requires the communication between the nodes of the computing space for its evaluation.
- All components of *replicated* expressions value are equal. Replicated expressions can be both synchronous and asynchronous.

A network can be treat as an array of nodes. A *network section* (or simply *subnetwork*) is referenced in the way similar to an array section in Fortran. In distinction with array sections subnetworks can have names. A network or subnetwork can be declared as *allocatable*. Similar to allocatable arrays allocatable networks and subnetworks are expected to be allocated later in the program by respective ALLOCATE statement.

Line 33 defines the allocatable subnetwork `s1` of the network `net`.

Line 34 defines distribution of the variables `len` and `l` over the subnetwork `s1`. Note, that by default all other variables are distributed over the network `net`.

Lines 36 and 37 assign values of the first and second coordinates of the node in the network `net` to the distributed variables `m1` and `m2` respectively. The right parts of the assignments contain the binary operation `.COORDOF.`. The right-hand operand of `.COORDOF.` specifies the region of the computing space, and the left-hand operand specifies the dimension of the right-hand operand. The result of `.COORDOF.` is the distributed integer value with the components equal to the corresponding coordinate of the node that stores these components. `.COORDOF.` is an asynchronous operation and assignments in lines 36-37 are asynchronous statements.

The asynchronous statement in line 39 performs local update $C_{ij} = \beta C_{ij}$. All nodes of the network `net` perform this update in parallel.

Lines 40-81 express the main loop of the algorithm. It is finished when the index of the current row/column panel `kk` became greater then `k`.

Line 41 computes width of the current panels `iwrk`. It is computed so that the current panel of the matrix A belongs to the one node column and the current panel of the matrix B belongs to the one node row. Here `nbl` is default panel width, `mb(icr)` is the number of rows of matrix B distributed to the current node row, `icr`, `ii` is the number of the rows from this row nodes have been processed, `na(icc)` is the number of columns of matrix A distributed to the current node column `icc`, `jj` is the number of the columns from this column nodes have been processed.

The DO construct in lines 42-56 broadcasts current panel of matrix A over logical ring. The DO statement in line 42 iterates the node rows.

Line 43 allocates the subnetwork `s1` consisting of the nodes of the `ir`-th node row of the network `net`. To ensure correctness of the subnetwork allocation the coordinate expressions of the `allocate` statement must be replicated over the network `net`.

The REGION construct in lines 44-54 specifies that nodes of the `ir`-th node row execute code in lines 45-53. So, nodes of the different rows independently in parallel execute all computations inside the construct.

Line 45 compute the number of the elements in the part of current panel of matrix A distributed to the nodes of the `ir`-th node row.

The REGION statement in lines 47-48 specifies that the statement in line 48 is executed on the node with coordinates (`ir`,`icc`). The assignment in line 48 copies part of the current panel belonging to the node into one-dimensional buffer `w1`.

The DO construct in lines 50-53 performs passing of the buffer `w1` around node row `ir`. The assignment in line 51-52 copies first `len` elements of the buffer `w1` on the node with coordinates (`ir`,`mod(1,q)`) to the buffer `w1` on the node with coordinates (`ir`,`mod(1+1,q)`). Note that it is important that coordinate expressions specifying distribution of left and right parts of the assignment must be replicated over subnetwork `s1`.

The assignment in lines 51-52 is synchronous. Therefore enclosing constructs DO (lines 50-53), REGION (lines 44–54), DO (lines 42–56), and DO (lines 40–81) are synchronous as well. It is crucial that all nodes executing the DO constructs execute exactly the same number of iterations. This is ensured with requirements that logical expressions in loop control of the loop in lines 50-53 must be replicated over the subnetwork s1 and the ones of the loops in lines 42-56 and 40-81 must be replicated over the network net.

The line 55 deallocates the subnetwork s1.

Similar to the code in lines 42-56 the code in lines 57-71 broadcasts current panel of matrix B over logical ring.

Lines 73-74 call BLAS [14] subroutine dgemm for the sequential matrix multiplication to perform the local update $C_{ij} = C_{ij} + \alpha \cdot \tilde{a}_i^l \cdot \tilde{b}_l^{j^T}$ in parallel.

Lines 76-80 update the variables used for the main loop execution control.

5   Comparison with MPI

This section discusses benefits of parallel programming in mpF over parallel programming in MPI and compares efficiency of mpF and MPI implementations of SUMMA algorithm.

5.1   Writing in mpF Versus Using MPI

Mainly a program written in mpF differs from a program written in MPI in the way work splitting and interactions among parallel processes are specified. Communications part of the SUMMA performs broadcast of the current panel of the matrices A and B over logical ring. Let us compare implementation of the broadcast of the current panel of the matrix A using mpF (lines 42-56 in example above) and MPI below.

Suppose that separate communicator comm corresponds to each row of the node grid. MPI implementation looks as follows:

```
len=ma(m1)*iwrk                                               !mpi1
if(m2.eq.icc)                                               &!mpi2
    w1(1:len)=reshape(a(1:ma(m1),jj:jj+iwrk),(/len/))         !mpi3
if(mod(m2+1,q).ne.icc)                                      &!mpi6
    call mpi_send(w1,len, MPI_DOUBLE_PRECISION,             &!mpi4
                  mod(m2+1,q),tag,comm,ierr)                  !mpi5
if(m2.ne.icc)                                               &!mpi7
    call mpi_recv(w1,len,MPI_DOUBLE_PRECISION,              &!mpi8
                  mod(m2-1+q,q),tag,comm,status,ierr)         !mpi9
```

Note, that mpF implementation requires two DO constructs, ALLOCATE and DEALLOCATE statements, REGION construct and statement, and three assignments: for computing number of elements in buffer, for coping of the part of the current panel to the buffer w1, and for buffer exchange between nodes to express the broadcast. MPI implementations requires three IF statement, two assignments: for computing number of elements in buffer, and for coping of the part of the current panel to the buffer w1, and two call to MPI procedures to buffer exchange between processes to express the broadcast in Fortran 90 with call to MPI procedures. So the number of statements in the mpF implementation is even more then number of statements in the

MPI implementation. So it may seem that mpF language has no advantages over programming in MPI.

The main advantages we can point here correspond to the possibility to detect a wide class of errors in compile time.

- Communications in mpF are expressed with assignment statement. Therefore types and distributions of variable and expression (the left and the right parts of the assignment) can be checked. Expressions in distribution specifiers of the left and the right parts of the synchronous assignments must be replicated. This ensures the absence of deadlocks in mpF programs.
- One of the main source of hard to detect errors in MPI programs is violation of replication, that is equality of the values of the expression components in case that it is supposed. For example, in fragment of MPI code above it is supposed that the values of expressions m1, ma(m1) are the same for all processes of the same column of grid nodes, and the value of iwrk, icc, jj, and q are the same for all processes participating in computations. Violation of those conditions leads to incorrect MPI program behavior that can be detected on debugging stage only. In mpF, most if not all of replication violations will be detected in compile time.
- Semantics of the REGION statement in mpF fragment (lines 47-48) is the same as semantics of the IF statement (lines 2-3) in MPI fragment. Distribution specifier in REGION statement as well as logical expression in IF statement specifies which nodes/processes should execute the copying of the part of the current panel to the one-dimensional buffer. But Fortran 90 compiler does not know anything about this semantics and cannot check corresponding errors. Those errors can be detected on debugging stage only. On the contrary the information from the REGION construct or statement allows mpF compiler to check correctness of the distribution of the computations and communications. For example, if the statement in lines 51-52 of mpF implementation looks as

```
(net(ir,mod(1+1,q)))(w1(1:len))=          &!51
            (net(ir,mod(1,q+1)))(w1(1:len))  !52
```

the mpF compiler detect an error because nodes with coordinates (ir,mod(1,q+1)) do not belongs to the subnetwork s1.

5.2 Experimental Comparison of mpF and MPI Counterparts

Two implementations of SUMMA were compared on example of multiplication of two 2000x2000 dense matrices on square grid of processes of dimension varied from 1 (one process) to 10 (100 processes) on supercomputer cluster MVS-1000M: MPI implementation presented in [7] and mpF implementation presented in this paper. The cluster installed in Joint Supercomputer Center of the Russian Academy of Sciences consists of 384 dual Alpha21264A nodes interconnected via Myrinet (http://www.jscc.ru). For sequential matrix multiplication we use dgemm BLAS subroutine (implementation from http://www.netlib.org/blas/).

Fig. 2 presents speedup of mpF and MPI implementations. One can see that the both implementations demonstrate super linear speedup. The most likely reason of super linearity is specific of the used BLAS implementation.

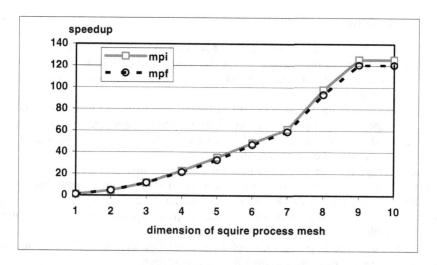

Fig. 2. Speedup obtained for MPI and mpF implementations on 2000x2000 matrix multiplication on square process grid as function of grid dimension on a cluster of dual Alpha21264A interconnected via Myrinet

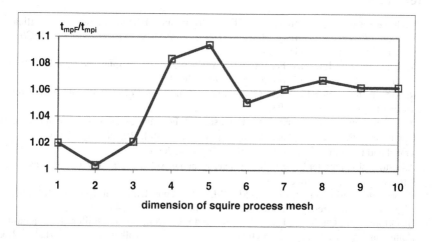

Fig. 3. A ratio of time of mpF implementation to time of MPI implementation for 2000x2000 matrix multiplication on square process grid as function of grid dimension on a cluster of dual Alpha21264A interconnected via Myrinet

Fig. 3 presents a ratio of time of mpF implementation to time of MPI implementation. The average ratio is 1.06.

Results presented on fig. 2 and fig. 3 allows us to say that subroutine of matrix multiplication implemented in high level parallel programming language mpF is insignificantly less efficient that its counterpart implemented in Fortran with call to low level message-passing library MPI.

6 Conclusions

We present implementation of matrix multiplication algorithm in the parallel programming language mpF. The algorithm has communication pattern, which rather cannot be extracted from data parallel Fortran extensions. So we demonstrate expressive power of the mpF.

We also stress attention to notion of replicated variables and expressions in the mpF language. Using replicated expressions in parallel assignments, distribution specifiers and control expressions of execution control constructs and statements avoids a lot of potential errors in parallel program.

The language combines task and data parallel programming paradigms. Notion of distributed procedures and possibility to specify distribution of computations with REGION construct explicitly is specific to task parallelism. Possibility to specify distribution of data and extract the information about distribution of computations from distribution of data is specific to data parallelism.

We show that mpF implementation of the nontrivial parallel algorithm demonstrate practically the same efficiency as the MPI implementation.

So we demonstrate that mpF is easy enough in use and efficient parallel programming language.

References

1. High Performance Fortran Forum. High Performance Fortran Language Specification, Version 2.0 (Rice University, Houston, 1997), http://dacnet.rice.edu/Depts/CRPC/HPFF/versions/hpf2/hpf-v20/index.html.
2. Message Passing Interface Forum. MPI: A Message Passing Interface Standard, Version 1.1, June, 1995, www.mpi-forum.org/docs/docs.html.
3. Report on the 1998 HPF Users Group's annual meeting. Porto, Portugal: IEEE Comput. Sci & Eng. 1998. V.5(3) 92-93.
4. A. Kalinov and I. Ledovskih: An Extension of Fortran for High Performance Parallel Computing, Programming and Computer Software, Vol. 30, No. 4 (2004) 209–217. Translated from Programmirovanie, Vol. 30, No. 4, 2004.
5. A.Lastovetsky: Parallel Computing on Heterogeneous Networks, John Wiley & Sons (2003)
6. http://www.ispras.ru/~mpc
7. R. van de Geijn and J. Watts. SUMMA: Scalable Universal Matrix Multiplication Algorithm. Concurrency: Practice and Experience, 9(4) 255-274 (1997)
8. Blackford, L.S., Choi, J., Cleary, A., d'Azevedo, E., Demmel, J., Dhillon, I., Dongarra, J., Hanmmarling, S., Henry, G., Petitet, A., Stanley, K., Walker, D., and Whaley, R.C., ScaLAPACK User's Guide, Philadelphia: SIAM, 1997.
9. High Performance Fortran Forum. High Performance Fortran Language Specification, Version 1.1 (Rice University, Houston, 1994)
10. The D System Home Page: http://www.cs.rice.edu/~dsystem/
11. DVM System: http://www.keldysh.ru/pages/dvm/
12. I.Foster, R.Olson, and S.Tuecke: Programming in Fortran M, Version 2.0 (Argonne National Lab., August 1994).
13. I.Foster, D.R.Kohr, R.Krishnaiyer, A.Choudhary: A Library-Based Approach to Task Parallelism in a Data-Parallel Language, Journal of Parallel and Distributed Computing, vol.45, 148-158, Sept. 1997.
14. J. J. Dongarra, J. Du Croz, I. S. Duff, and S. Hammarling: A set of Level 3 Basic Linear Algebra Subprograms, ACM Transactions on Mathematical Software vol. 16, 1-17 (1990)

The Parallel Implementation of the Algorithm Solution of Model for Two-Phase Cluster in Liquids*

V.D. Korneev[1], V.A. Vshivkov[1], G.G. Lazareva[1], and V.K. Kedrinskii[2]

[1] ICMMG SB RAS, Novosibirsk, Russia
{korneev, vsh, lazareva}@ssd.sscc.ru
[2] LIH SB RAS, Novosibirsk, Russia
kedr@hidro.nsc.ru

Abstract. The new parallel algorithm has been developed and implemented for solving the axial-symmetric problem of the interaction of a plane shock wave with a free bubble system (cluster) resulting in the formation of a stationary oscillating shock wave. The important characteristics of the problem in question, such as acceleration, effectiveness, and the influence of heterogeneity on the time of calculation have been experimentally obtained. They enable us to evaluate the quality of the algorithm and the scope for obtaining appreciable results. With the use of the parallel algorithm discussed, the dynamics of the pressure fields in a distant zone of a cluster is investigated, including the pressure field of the shock wave radiated by a bubble cluster. It is fairly difficult over a reasonable period of time to obtain results of such an investigation in one computer due to the large size of the problem under consideration.

1 Introduction

Generation of pressure pulses in liquid and gases has been the subject of ongoing research for many years. This work resulted in the development of various pressure generators and shock-wave comulation methods. Research efforts were focused on the exploration of media in which the energy transferred by relatively weak pulsed loading can be absorbed, consentrated in a local region, and reemitted in a pulse of substantially higher amplitude. In [1], the model developed by Iordanskii, Kogarko, and van Wijngaarden was used in numerical studies to show that interaction between a plane shock wave and a bubble cluster gives rise to a shock wave with a pressure gradient tangent to its curved front. By focusing such a wave, its amplitude can be increased by one or two orders of magnitude. As another example of waves focusing in an axially symmetric geometry, processes taking place in interaction between a plane shock wave and a toroidal bubble cluster. The results of numerical study of near-axis wave structure was presented for a focusing shock wave emitted by a bubble cluster in [2].

* Supported by the Siberian Division of the Russian Academy of Sciences, Integration project no. 22.

V. Malyshkin (Ed.): PaCT 2005, LNCS 3606, pp. 433–445, 2005.

This paper proposes the new parallel algorithm of the axially symmetric problem of the interaction of the plane shock wave with a free bubble system (the toroidal cluster) resulting in the formation in the liquid of a stationary oscillating shock wave. The new approach to parallelization of the algorithm of the given problem is considered; The basic characteristics of the parallel algorithm, obtained for different sizes of a computer system, different sizes of a bubble cluster and different sizes of a problem are presented; The corresponding graphs of the numerical experiments are plotted; The results of solution to a concrete problem, obtained on the supercomputer system MVS1000 are presented; The new results when solving the problem of the interaction of the plane shock wave with a toroidal cluster have been obtained; Analysis of the wave field structure in a distant zone of a cluster for three sets of geometrical parameters of the toroidal bubble cluster was made; The improved values of the pressure dynamics when the Mach disk is propagating along the axis for large time intervals have been obtained. This paper proposes the new parallel algorithm of the axially symmetric problem of the interaction of the plane shock wave with a free bubble system (the toroidal cluster) resulting in the formation in the liquid of a stationary oscillating shock wave.

The new approach to parallelization of the algorithm of the given problem is considered. The basic characteristics of the parallel algorithm, obtained for different sizes of a computer system, different sizes of a bubble cluster and different sizes of a problem are presented. The corresponding graphs of the numerical experiments are plotted. The results of solution to a concrete problem, obtained on the supercomputer system MVS1000 are presented. The new results when solving the problem of the interaction of the plane shock wave with a toroidal cluster have been obtained. Analysis of the wave field structure in a distant zone of a cluster for three sets of geometrical parameters of the toroidal bubble cluster was made. The improved values of the pressure dynamics when the Mach disk is propagating along the axis for large time intervals have been obtained.

2   Statement of the Problem and Governing Equations

We consider the shock wave generated by piston motion at the end of a shock tube of radius r_{st} filled with a liquid at the moment $t = 0$. The shock tube contains a toroidal bubble cluster whose center is located on the shock-tube axis (denoted by z) at distance l_{cl} from its left boundary. The plane of the base circle of the torus (hereinafter called the toric plane), which has a radius R_{tor} ($R_{tor} < r_{st}$), is perpendicular to the shock-tube axis. he cross-sectional radius of the torus is R_{circ} (see Fig. 1). The initial volume fractin of the gas phase in the cluster is denoted by k_0. All gas bubbles have equal radii R_b, and their distribution over a cluster is uniform. At $t > 0$, the shock wave propagates along the positive z axis, interacts with the toroidal bubble cloud, bypassed around it, and is refracted as it encounters the cluster.

The focusing of the refracted wave by the cluster was computed by using a modified Iordanskii-Kogarko-van Wijngaarden model [1], based on the continuity

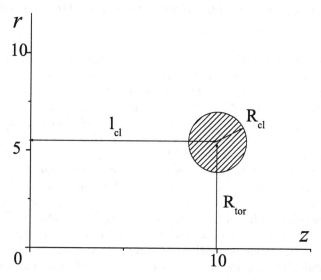

Fig. 1. Toroidal Bubble cluster: the hatched area is the toric section; z is the symmetry axis

and momentum equations written for the average pressure p, density ρ, and velocity $\boldsymbol{u}$:

$$\frac{\partial \rho}{\partial t} + div(\rho \boldsymbol{u}) = 0, \qquad \frac{\partial \boldsymbol{u}}{\partial t} + \boldsymbol{u}(\nabla \boldsymbol{u}) = -\frac{1}{\rho}\nabla p, \qquad (1)$$

$$p = p(\rho) = 1 + \frac{\rho_0 c_0^2}{n p_0}\left[\left(\frac{\rho}{1-k}\right)^n - 1\right], \qquad k = \frac{k_0}{1-k_0}\rho\beta^3,$$

where ρ_0 is unperturbed liquid density, c_0 is the speed of sound in liquid, and the ρ is the density of the bubble liquid normalized to the ρ_0. It is obvious that systen (1) is not closed: the Tait equation of state for the liquid phase contains the volume fraction k of gas in the cluster, which is expressed in terms of the dynamic variable $\beta = R/R_0$ (relative bubble radius).

In the Iordanskii-Kogarko-van Wijngaarden model, a physically heterogeneous medium is treated as homogeneous, and the Rayleigh equation for β:

$$\frac{\partial S}{\partial t} = -\frac{3}{2\beta}S^2 - \frac{C_1}{\beta^2} - C_2\frac{S}{\beta^2} - \frac{p}{\beta} + \beta^{-3\gamma}, \qquad (2)$$

where

$$S = \frac{\partial \beta}{\partial t}, \qquad C_1 = \frac{2\sigma}{R_0 p_0}, \qquad C_2 = \frac{4\mu}{R_0\sqrt{p_0\rho_0}},$$

is used as a closure for system (1). Here, σ is surface tension; μ is viscosity; $n = 7.15$; and p_0, ρ_0, R_0, $\sqrt{p_0/\rho_0}$, and $R_0\sqrt{\rho_0/p_0}$, are the reference parameters used to obtain a dimensionless system of equations.

3 Parallelization of the Solution Algorithm of the Problem

The computer system MVS1000 is a system with the distributed memory. Such systems are primarily intended for computing the MPMD- and the SPMD-programming models. As is known, the problems that are solved by finite difference methods can be effectively parallelized in the computer systems with the distributed memory using the SPMD- programming models or by the data decomposition method [3 - 9]. It is this method that is applied for the parallelization of the algorithm of the problem in question.

According to the definition given in Section 2, the computation model of the problem in question consists of the bulk of a homogeneous liquid medium and a bubble cluster included in it. Both the liquid medium and the bubble cluster "contribute" differently to the total time of calculation. Therefore, in order to reveal the features of a parallel algorithm it is necessary to determine the characteristics of the algorithm for computer systems of different size, for clusters of different size, and for the problems with different number of points.

3.1 The Computational Domain

The medium domain is set as a 2D rectangle of size $X_m * Y_m$ (in centimeters). The bubble cluster domain is a 2D domain of a design configuration. The bubble cluster domain is included into the medium domain.

In the domain of the medium a uniform rectangular grid is set that defines the computational domain of the medium (hereinafter: "medium domain" instead of "computational domain of the medium"). The grid has $N_m * K_m$ nodes along the coordinates r and Z, respectively. The same computational grid is used for the bubble cluster in the sub-domain of the medium domain where the cluster is located.

Three medium variables and one variable of the bubble cluster are calculated by the explicit five-point "cross" stencil. When all the other variables are calculated at the grid points during the k+1-th time step, the values of variables are only used that have already been obtained during the k-th time step.

3.2 Parallelization of the Algorithm

As stated above, the parallelization of the solution algorithm of the problem is carried out by the method of decomposition of computational domains when both the medium domain and the bubble cluster domain are divided into sub-domains, and these sub-domains are distributed among the processors of the computing system (multi-computer). The size and configuration of the sub-domains of the decomposed domains are automatically calculated at each processor according to the variables of these sub-domains and the value P that is equal to the number of the processors in the multi-computer. Both the decomposition of the medium domain and the decomposition of the bubble cluster domain have their own salient features.

Decomposition of the Computational Domain of the Medium. The computational domain of the medium is segmented into equal bands along the coordinate Z. The size of the bands is calculated by the following formula: $K_m/P * N_m$ where P is the number of processors in the multi-computer. That is, the domain is segmented along the direction of the plane wave propagation. Since the computational domain of the medium is represented by the values of 10 variables calculated at the grid points, all the arrays are cut into sub-arrays in accord with the segmentation of the domain. The arrays calculated by the five-point "cross" stencil are decomposed with the overlap of the values of the adjacent points of the boundary sub-domains. Decomposition of the other arrays is carried on without overlapping the boundary sub-domains. All parts of the arrays corresponding to these sub-domains are then distributed among the processors of the multi-computer.

Decomposition of the Computational Domain of the Bubble Cluster. The computational domain of the bubble cluster is segmented into bands along the coordinate Z as is the case with the medium domain (hereinafter: "cluster domain" instead of " computational domain of the bubble cluster"). The cutting lines of the cluster domain are specified by the cutting lines of the medium domain and coincide with them completely. The width of the bands in the medium domain depends on the number of processors P. As the cluster domain depends on the medium domain, the sizes of the sub-domains of the decomposed cluster domain and their configurations will be quite different for different values of P. The sub-domains of the decomposed cluster domain are distributed among the processors together with the corresponding sub-domains of the medium, to which the cluster is bound. Therefore, in the first place, the cluster sub-domains will not be distributed among all the processors, and, in the second place, the size and configuration of the cluster sub-domains allocated to the processors will be different. The processors to which the decomposed cluster sub-domains are allocated are to be able to simulate these parts of the cluster in their memory. In this case, the simulation is to be carried out automatically with different cuttings of this cluster. In the original sequential algorithm, the size of the bubble cluster, its configuration and location in the medium are set in a special way, by means of the variables. Every processor determines the cluster sub-domains by the cutting lines of the medium domain. The decomposition algorithm of the cluster domain is universal, and it is independent of the size and configuration of the cluster.

All the three arrays of the values of the variables determining the cluster domain are segmented into sub-arrays according to the segmentation of the medium domain. The array calculated by the "cross" stencil is decomposed with the overlap of the values at the adjacent points of the boundary sub-domains. The other arrays are decomposed without overlapping the boundary sub-domains.

3.3 Topology of the Computer System

It is known that the topology of a computer system is determined by the structure of the algorithm of a problem. In the case under consideration the topology is determined by the data structure, as the algorithm is parallelized by the data. The data in the algorithm are segmented into bands, and the data exchange in the course of calculation only happens between the adjacent bands. Therefore, the linear topology of the computer system is sufficient for the problem solution. The bands of the decomposed medium domain are sequentially distributed among the processors according to their numbers. The band with the smallest coordinates of the grid points locates at the 0-th processor, the one with the bigger coordinates - at the 1-st processor, etc. The band with the biggest grid coordinates locates at the last processor. The sub-domains of the bubble cluster are distributed among the processors according to the bands of the medium, in which they are found.

The specified boundary conditions of the computational domain of the medium along the coordinate Z are evaluated for the 0-th and the last processors, the boundary conditions along the coordinate r being evaluated for all the processors.

3.4   Acceleration and Efficiency of the Parallel Algorithm

When developing a parallel algorithm, it is important to be aware of the potentialities of the acceleration of calculations and of the amount of time needed to organize the interactions between the parallel branches of the algorithm. It is also important to know the efficiency indexes that allow us to compare the given algorithm with other parallel algorithms. These indexes also allow us to evaluate the quality of the algorithm in terms of the consumption of time needed for the data communication between the processors.

The acceleration index of a parallel algorithm in the computer system with $P > 1$ processors (hereinafter: $P > 1$) according to [3] will be assessed by the following value

$$U_p = \frac{T_1}{T_p},\qquad(3)$$

where T_1 is the computational time of a sequential algorithm in one processor, and T_p - the computational time of a parallel algorithm in the computer system with P processors.

The efficiency of parallelization in the computer system with P processors will be assessed by the following value:

$$F_p = \frac{T_{pc}}{T_{pc} + T_{pv} + T_{ps}},\qquad(4)$$

where T_{pc} is the computational time in the computer system with P processors; T_{pv} is the total time used for the data communication between the processors of the same system, T_{ps} - the total time needed for the synchronization of the branches of a parallel program.

The medium domain and the cluster domain differently affect the total time of calculations because these two domains are different in size and have a different number of the major parameters. Therefore, for a better verification of the main characteristics of a parallel algorithm two variants of testing procedures are considered: - in the first variant the size of the cluster domain remains constant, and the size of a computer system varies; - in the second variant the size of a computer system remains constant, and the size of the cluster domain varies.

In the first variant testing is carried out for two medium domains of different size.

Acceleration and Efficiency of the Parallel Algorithm When Calculating in the Systems of Different Size. This Section presents the results of the first variant of testing the parallel algorithm of the problem under study. In this variant, the characteristics of the algorithm are determined, in the first place, for two different sizes of the medium domain, and, in the second place, for two types of calculations in each of these domains. These two types of calculations are: 1) calculations for the medium with the cluster included in it, and 2) calculations for the homogeneous medium only. In practice, the cluster domain can differ in size. That is why, when calculating in the homogeneous medium without a cluster, the characteristics of the parallel algorithm are limiting for the problem as a whole. One more index is discussed here, the index of relative acceleration:

$$U_{p,2p} = \frac{T_p}{T_{2p}}$$

This index means the following: by what value the algorithm acceleration will change if the number of processors in the system is doubled.

Testing was carried out in the computer system MVS1000 with a different number of processors: one, two, four, eight, sixteen and thirty-two processors. The parallel programming system MPI [12, 13] was used. Two medium domains of different size were tested: O_1 and O_2. The size of the medium domain O_1 was equal to $N_m * K_m = 320 * 3200$ grid points along the coordinates r and Z, respectively. The medium domain O_2 was twice as large and was equal to $N_m * K_m = 640 * 3200$ grid points along the same coordinates. The cluster domain was the same for all the cases and represented a circle of $20 * 10^3$ points.

Here the indexes U_p, F_p, $U_{p,2p}$ and the total time of the problem solution T_p for calculations in the homogeneous medium O_1 will be denoted as U_p^{o1}, F_p^{o1}, $U_{p,2p}^{o1}$ and T_p^{o1}, and for calculations with a cluster in the same medium - as U_p^{k1}, F_p^{k1}, $U_{p,2p}^{k1}$ and T_p^{k1}. For calculations in the homogeneous medium O_2 we will use the following notations for the same indexes: U_p^{o2}, F_p^{o2}, $U_{p,2p}^{o2}$ and T_p^{o2}. While for calculations in the same medium with a cluster the indexes will be U_p^{k2}, F_p^{k2}, $U_{p,2p}^{k2}$ and T_p^{k2}.

Below we present the following plots of characteristics of a parallel algorithm when computing with the use of a different number of processors: 1) plots for the acceleration indexes U_p^{o1}, U_p^{k1} and U_p^{o2}, U_p^{k2}; 2) plots for the efficiency indexes F_p^{o1}, F_p^{k1} and F_p^{o2}, F_p^{k2}; 3) plots for the acceleration indexes $U_{p,2p}^{o1}$, $U_{p,2p}^{k1}$ and $U_{p,2p}^{o2}$, $U_{p,2p}^{k2}$; 4) plots for the time allotted for the problem solution T_p^{o1}, T_p^{k1} and T_p^{o2}, T_p^{k2}.

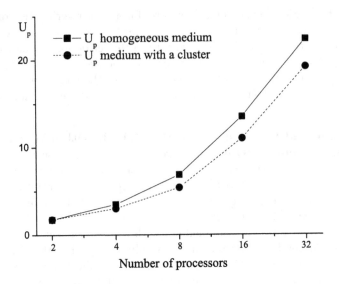

Fig. 2. Plots for the acceleration indexes of the algorithm for two types of calculations in medium O1 when computing with the use of a different number of processors

The acceleration indexes U_p^{o1} (see Fig. 2) appeared to be sufficiently good, for example, $U_2^{o1} = 1, 8$, $U_{32}^{o1} = 22$. That is, when using two processors the speed of the algorithm is almost twice as large as compared to one processor. And, when the multi-computer has thirty-two processors the speed of the algorithm becomes 32 times as large.

The indexes U_p^{o1} are limiting for U_p^{k1} , i.e., the smaller the cluster domain, the closer the plots U_p^{k1} to the plots U_p^{o1}. Acceleration indexes of both types of calculations in the medium O_2 are close to those in the medium O_1. We would remind you that O_2 is twice as large as O_1.

In the plot (see Fig. 3), the efficiency indexes show what extra time is taken in order to send data from one processor to another. As is evident from the plot, when the number of processors in the computer system increases, the efficiency of parallel calculations gradually decreases. For systems consisting of two or more processors, the communication channels between them essentially affect the speed of data exchange and, consequently, the total time of calculations. As follows from (2), the plot shows that time needed for parallel interactions relatively increases when the size of the computer system grows.

It should be noted that the plots for the efficiency indexes of the algorithm for calculations in the medium O_2 are similar to the plots presented in Figure 3.

The plots of the relative acceleration indexes $U_{p,2p}$ for different types of calculations (see Fig. 4) are also indicative. They help to answer the following question: how many times does the speed of calculations increase if the size of a computer system is doubled? As is clear from the plots if there are 32 processors in a system instead of 16, then the acceleration $U_{p,2p}^{o1}$ only increases by the factor of 1.65, and the acceleration $U_{p,2p}^{k1}$ - by the factor of 1.57. These plots

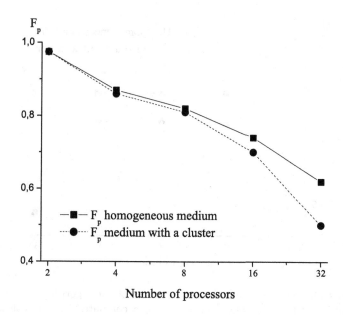

Fig. 3. Plots for the efficiency indexes of the algorithm for two types of calculations in medium O1 when computing in a computer system with a different number of processors

indicate that the speed of calculations decreases with an increase in the size of the computer system. This implies that with a certain size of a computer system, the speed of calculations will not grow at all or will even reduce. However, this is valid for the given size of the problem only.

The last two plots indicate that both the efficiency and the relative speed of calculations decrease with the growth in the size of the computer system. It should be so for the given problem. For a particular problem, with the growth of the computer system, the body of data assigned to each processor decreases proportionally with the size of the system (see Section 3.2). It means that the number of computational operations decreases when the size of the computer system grows while the number of exchange operations - between the parallel branches - remains the same. Here we mean the exchanges for the calculations of three variables of a medium and one cluster variable (see Section 3.1). It should be noted here that the plots of the relative acceleration indexes of the algorithm for calculations in the medium O_2 are similar to the plots in Figure 4.

And, finally, Figure 5 shows how the total time of calculations depends on the size of the computer system used for the media of different size.

Influence of the Size of a Bubble Cluster on the Total Time of Parallel Computations. In this Section, we present the results of the second variant of testing the parallel algorithm of the problem under study in the case where the size of the computer system remains constant and the size of the cluster domain varies.

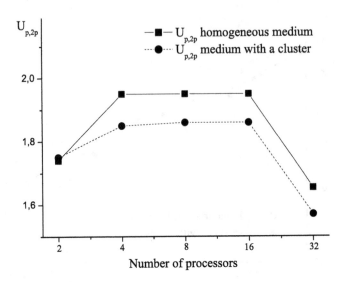

Fig. 4. Plots for the relative acceleration indexes of the algorithm for two types of calculations in medium O1 when computing in a computer system with a different number of processors

For the given problem it is also very important to know how the size of a bubble cluster influences the total time of parallel computations. The testing was carried out in the computer system MVS1000 with a constant number of processors, namely, four, but for clusters of different size. In all the cases, the medium domain was the same and equal to $N_m * K_m = 1280 * 1280$ grid points along both coordinates. Cluster domains of different size were used, and they were allocated to the processors differently.

Two sub-variants were considered that differed both in the size of clusters and in their location at the processors. In each sub-variant, the cluster domains differed in size only, their location at the processors being the same. The size of the cluster was determined by the number of points of the cluster domain, its configuration being unimportant. In the first variant four clusters were considered, their sizes being $K_1 = 50 * 10^3$, $K_2 = 100 * 10^3$, $K_3 = 150 * 10^3$, and $K_4 = 200 * 10^3$ points, respectively. In the second variant there also were four clusters with $KL_1 = 100 * 10^3$, $KL_2 = 200 * 10^3$, $KL_3 = 300 * 10^3$ and $KL_4 = 400 * 10^3$ points. In the first variant, the clusters were located at one processor, while in the second variant they were located at two processors with a uniform distribution of points between the processors. In both variants, the time of computations was compared both with the time of parallel computations in a homogeneous medium (without a cluster) and with the time of computations in a homogeneous medium for a sequential algorithm calculated at one processor.

Below there is a plot, which shows the time of parallel computations for both sub-variants of the tests obtained in the computer system consisting of four processors (see Fig. 6). Here nk denotes the time of calculations in a homogeneous

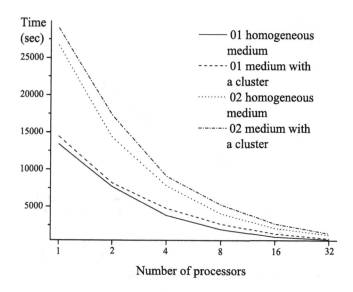

Fig. 5. Plots for the total computing time of the algorithm for two types of calculations in media O1 and O2 when computing in a computer system with a different number of processors

medium without a cluster. ki $(i = 1, 2, 3, 4)$ is the time of calculations in the medium with the corresponding cluster ki for both sub-variants 1 and 2 (the notation of clusters is presented above).

As is clear from the plot the size of a bubble cluster essentially affects the total time of calculating the problem. It should be noted that the lines representing the two sub-variants on the plot are not very different. It can be explained in the following way. When a cluster is only located at one processor, the time needed for calculations at this processor increases. As for the other processors, for further synchronization both in exchanges and on completion of cycles they have to wait until the processor with the cluster included finishes its part of the calculations. If at this very time another processor carries out the same task, the time delays will be almost the same.

4   Conclusion

This paper presents a new parallel algorithm of the axial-symmetric problem of the interaction of the plane shock wave with a free bubble system (the toroidal cluster). The result of the interaction is the formation of a stationary oscillating shock wave in the liquid. The tests have shown that:

1. the algorithm of the problem is parallelized fairly well in the computer systems with the distributed memory. When the size of the medium domain is $320 * 3200$ and the cluster domain has $20 * 10_3$ points, we attain the acceleration by 22 fold at the multi-computer with 32 processors;

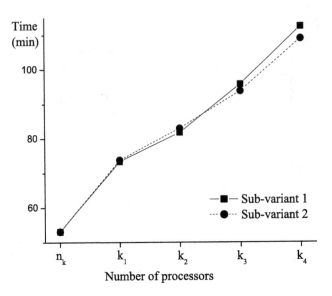

Fig. 6. Plots for the total computing time of the algorithm at four processors for two sub-variants

2. the characteristics of the parallel algorithm do not deteriorate when the size of the problem increases;

3. the new results have been obtained when solving a real problem: the structure of the wave field in a distant zone of the cluster has been analyzed for a wide range of geometrical variables of a toroidal bubble cluster. The improved values of the pressure dynamics have also been obtained for large time intervals when the Mach disk is propagating along the axis;

4. the calculations carried out at the supercomputer are more accurate and are characterized by a wider range of data to be obtained. A maximum value of the pressure amplitude in the Mach disk core, obtained at the supercomputer is approximately 1/3 times as large as the one obtained at a single computer.

It should be noted that each size of the problem in question corresponds to a certain size of a computer system that is optimal for solving the problem.

It should be noted that each dimension of the problem in question corresponds to a certain size of a computer system that is optimal for solving this problem.

References

1. V.K. Kedrinskii, Yu.I. Shokin, V.A. Vshivkov, et al.: Docl.Akad. Nauk **381**, 773 (2001) [Docl. Phys. **46**, 856 (2001)]
2. V.K. Kedrinskii, V.A. Vshivkov, G.I. Dudnikova, itet al.: Joarnal of Experimental and Theoretical Physics, Vol. 125, No. 6, (2004) 1302-1310
3. Evreinov E.V., Kosarev Yu.G.: High efficiency homogeneous universal computing systems. Nauka. Novosibirsk (1966)

4. Mirenkov N.N.: Parallel programming for multimodular computing systems. Radio i Svyaz. Moscow (1989)
5. Korneev V.D.: A system and methods of programming of multicomputers on an example of the computer complex PowrXplorer. Russ.Acad.Sci., Sib. Branch., Ins.Comp.Math.and Math.Geoph. Preprint, No. 1123. Novosibirsk (1998)
6. Korneev V.D.: Parallel algorithms deciding the task of linear algebra. Russ.Acad.Sci., Sib. Branch. Ins.Comp.Math. and Math.Geoph., Preprint, No. 1124. Novosibirsk (1998)
7. Korneev V.D.: Parallel programming in MPI. Russ.Acad.Sci. Sib. Branch. Novosibirsk (2002)
8. Malyshkin V.E.: Linearization of mass calculations. System Computer Science. Nauka, No. 1. Novosibirsk (1991) 229-259
9. V.E. Malyshkin, V.A.. Vshivkov, M.A. Kraeva.: About realization of the method of particles on multiprocessors. Russ.Acad.Sci. Sib. Branch. Ins.Comp.Math.and Math.Geoph. Preprint, No 1052. Novosibirsk (1995)
10. Snir M., Otto S. W., Huss-Lederman S., Walker D., and Dongarra J.: MPI. The Complete Reference. MIT Press. Boston (1996)
11. Dongarra J., Otto S. W., Snir M., and Walker D.: An Introduction to the MPI Standard. Technical report CS-95-274. University of Tennessee, January (1995)

Neural Network Approach for Parallel Construction of Adaptive Meshes[*]

Olga Nechaeva

Supercomputer Software Department,
ICMMG, Siberian Branch,
Russian Academy of Science,
Pr. Lavrentieva, 6, Novosibirsk, 630090, Russia
nechaeva@ssd.sscc.ru

Abstract. The neural network approach for parallel construction of adaptive mesh on two-dimensional area is proposed. The approach is based on unsupervised learning algorithm for Kohonen's Self Organizing Map and enables to obtain an adaptive mesh being isomorphic to a rectangular uniform one. A parallel algorithm for the construction of those meshes based on master-slave programming model is presented. The main feature of the obtained mesh is that their decomposition into subdomains required for parallel simulation on this mesh is reduced to partitioning of a rectangular array of nodes. The way of partitioning may be defined based on parallel simulations on the mesh. The efficiency of the parallel realization of the proposed algorithm is about 90%.

1 Introduction

Adaptive mesh methods have important applications in a variety of physical and engineering areas such as solid and fluid dynamics, combustion, heat transfer, material science etc. The use of those meshes enables to improve the accuracy of numerical solutions without essential increasing in number of nodes [1]. In addition, it is necessary for a mesh construction method to be well parallelized.

In this work, the neural network approach for curvilinear adaptive mesh construction on arbitrary two-dimensional simulation area is proposed. The approach is based on the iterative unsupervised learning algorithm for Kohonen's Self Organizing Map [2]. The idea is that an originally uniform rectangular mesh is being deformed and stretched all along the area during the iteration process. Density of the mesh is proportional to the values of a given nonnegative control function defined on the simulation area.

The inherent parallelism of the proposed algorithm is a natural base for its parallel implementation. Efficiency of the proposed parallel algorithm is about 90% that is the result of the low communication overhead.

The resulting adaptive mesh is isomorphic to the initial uniform one. Due to this property, mesh decomposition into subdomains required for parallel simulation on

---

[*] Supported by Presidium of Russian Academy of Sciences, Basic Research Program N17-6 (2004).

V. Malyshkin (Ed.): PaCT 2005, LNCS 3606, pp. 446–451, 2005.

this mesh is reduced to partitioning of a rectangular array of mesh nodes wherever the nodes are located in the simulation area.

It is important that the efficiency of parallelization is almost independent of the way of partitioning the array of mesh nodes. Therefore, the latter may be distributed among the processors in accordance with the requirements on parallel implementation of the problem under simulation, as well as with the properties of the parallel computer system used.

Existing methods of adaptive mesh construction not always provide the above properties. For example, equidistribution method [3] and Thompson method [4] are based on the solution of nonlinear partial differential equations, and parallelization of those methods is comparatively more complicated. Besides, they require an additional work on the construction of suitable initial mesh.

The paper is organized as follows. Section 2 contains a general idea and an algorithm for the proposed method of adaptive mesh construction. Section 3 presents parallel realization of the algorithm and time-efficiency diagrams of its implementation. Section 5 concludes the paper.

2   General Algorithm for Adaptive Mesh Construction

The Self-Organizing Map (SOM) is a neural network used for a topology-preserving mapping of arbitrary dimensional data onto a low dimensional space, usually a 2D space [5]. The adaptive mesh construction algorithm is similar to the iterative unsupervised learning process for SOM where neurons correspond to the mesh nodes [6].

Let G be an arbitrary two-dimensional simply connected area. An uniform rectangular mesh of $N_1 \times N_2$ nodes is placed inside G arbitrarily as Fig.1(a) shows. The mesh can be regarded as an initial one for the iterative process of adaptive mesh construction. Let G_N be an array of mesh nodes:

$$G_N = \begin{pmatrix} x_{11} & \cdots & x_{1N_2} \\ \cdots & \cdots & \cdots \\ x_{N_1 1} & \cdots & x_{N_1 N_2} \end{pmatrix}, \tag{1}$$

where each node x_{ij} is represented by a pair of real coordinates $x_{ij} = (x^1_{ij}, x^2_{ij})$, $i = 1, ..., N_1$, $j = 1, ..., N_2$ in G. The algorithm of mesh construction is as follows.

Algorithm

0. Set initial locations of mesh nodes $x_{ij}(0)$, $i = 1, ..., N_1, j = 1, ..., N_2$.
1. Perform the following operations at each iteration t.

a) *Point generation.* Generate a random point $y \in G$ in accordance with some probability distribution $P(G)$.

b) *Winner determination.* Calculate Euclid distances between y and all nodes $x_{ij}(t)$ and choose the node $x_{mn}(t)$ which is closest to y, i.e.

$$\left\| y - x_{mn}(t) \right\| \leq \left\| y - x_{ij}(t) \right\| \tag{2}$$

for all $i = 1, ..., N_1, j = 1, ..., N_2$. The node $x_{mn}(t)$ is called a *winner.*

c) *Node coordinates correction.* Adjust the locations of the nodes using the follow-ing rule:

$$x_{ij}(t+1) = x_{ij}(t) + \theta(t, i, j)(y - x_{ij}(t)) \tag{3}$$

for all $i = 1, ..., N_1, j = 1, ..., N_2$, where $\theta(t, i, j) \in (0, 1]$ is a *learning rate*.

2. Repeat step 1 until changes of the node locations become small enough.

At each iteration, mesh nodes move towards the generated point y. The shift length for each node is defined by the learning rate $\theta(t, i, j)$. Quality and speed of mesh construction depend on the selection of $\theta(t, i, j)$. Usually, the learning rate is given by the following formula [7].

$$\theta_{mn}(t, i, j) = \delta(t)\, e^{-\frac{(i-m)^2+(j-n)^2}{2\sigma^2(t)}} \tag{4}$$

The form of $\theta_{mn}(t, i, j)$ provides conditions according to which winner gets maximum shift, while other nodes change their locations the less the larger the differ-ence between indices (i, j) and (m, n). Based on experiments, the functions $\delta(t)$ and $\sigma(t)$ have been selected as

$$\delta(t) = \frac{1}{\sqrt[5]{t}}, \quad \sigma(t) = \frac{a}{\sqrt[5]{t}}. \tag{5}$$

Changing a point generation probability in particular regions of G, the required density of the mesh can be obtained on those regions. Fig.1 shows an example of the adaptive mesh obtained by the proposed method. Density of the resulting mesh is proportional to grey tones on the input area G (Fig.1 (b)).

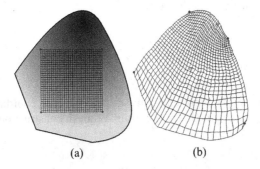

(a)   (b)

Fig. 1. (a) – input area G and mesh at $t = 1$; (b) – resulting adaptive mesh at $t = 100000$

In general, during the mesh construction, nodes change only their location in G ac-cording to the learning rate (4). Therefore, the structure of node connections remains the same as that in the initial rectangular uniform mesh wherever the mesh nodes are located.

3 Parallel Adaptive Mesh Construction

In the sequential version of the adaptive mesh construction algorithm (Sect. 2), the calculation of distances $\left\| y - w_{ij}(t) \right\|$ in (2) and of node locations $x_{ij}(t+1)$ in (3) are the most time-consuming operations, since they require looking over all mesh nodes. Fortunately, both operations may be computed independently for all pairs $(i, j) \in N_1 \times N_2$. So these steps can be parallelized using distribution of the array G_N among the processors.

The proposed parallel algorithm is based on a master-slave programming model, having one processor P (Master) that controls the other processors P_0 , ..., P_{p-1} (Slaves). Master stores information about the input area, each Slave P_k contains a part G_N^k of the array G_N, $k = 0, ..., p-1$. During the mesh construction, Master generates random points and controls the global winner calculations whereas Slaves determine local winners and perform the correction of the node locations.

Parallel Algorithm

0. Master gets information about the input area G, quantities N_1 and N_2 and parameters of the learning rate (4). Then it sets the initial location of mesh nodes $x_{ij}(0)$ and distributes the array G_N among Slaves.

1. The following operations are performed on each iteration t.

a) *Point generation.* Master generates a random point $y \in G$ in accordance with probability distribution $P(G)$ and broadcasts its coordinates to all Slaves.

b) *Winner determination.* According to (2) each Slave P_k searches for the node $x_{mn}^k(t)$ that is the closest to y in G_N^k (a local winner) and sends the indices $(m, n)_k$ and the value of $\left\| y - x_{mn}^k(t) \right\|$ to Master. Master calculates $k_{win} = \arg\min_k \left\| y - x_{mn}^k(t) \right\|$ – the rank of Slave in which a global winner is situated, broadcasts k_{win} and the indices $(m, n)_{k_{win}}$ to all Slaves and then turns to step 1a if a termination condition is false.

c) *Node coordinates correction.* Each Slave P_k converts the indices $(m, n)_{k_{win}}$ in the local array G_N^k into indices (m, n) in the global array G_N and then adjusts the locations of the nodes depending on k.

2. Repeat step 1 until changes of the node locations become small enough.

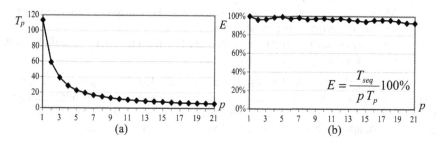

Fig. 2. Computation time (a) and efficiency (b) for 1000 iterations of the parallel algorithm

The parallel program has been implemented using MPI library. Fig.2 shows computation time and efficiency dependence on the number of Slaves. Time has been measured for 1000 iterations of the algorithm. The array G_N size has been 500 by 500. All measurements have been made in Siberian Supercomputer Center using MVS-1000 system that consists of 24 processors Alpha, 833MHz, connected to each other by Myrinet.

The efficiency of parallelization obtained (Fig.2(b)) is greater then 90%. The explanation of this is as follows. First, there are no communications between Slaves, data transmission occurs only among Master and Slaves. Second, total amount of data that is transmitted at each iteration is equal to eight numbers per Slave independently on sizes of adaptive mesh. Third, a random point generation (Master) and correction of the node locations (Slaves) are performed simultaneously.

Parallel algorithm for different partition of G_N (e.g. line or grid of processors) is the same except for the converting local indices to global. Because of the absence of communications between Slaves, the efficiency of parallelization is almost independent on the way of partition of the array G_N.

Therefore, the partition of G_N may be carried out in accordance with requirements on parallel implementation of the problem to be simulated on the mesh, as well as with properties of parallel computer system used. Existing methods of adaptive mesh construction not always provide this property. For example, parallelization of the most allied equidistribution method [3] is reduced to parallelization of the alternating directions method [8]. The latter can be performed with acceptable efficiency using a line of processors only.

The above feature is important also when using a moving mesh, because the mesh tuning is required at each iteration of a simulation process on the adaptive mesh. So, it is necessary to perform the tuning efficiently.

5 Conclusion

In this paper, the application of Kohonen's Self Organizing Map for parallel construction of adaptive mesh has been presented. Implemented algorithms show that the proposed approach allows to obtain adaptive meshes with the following properties:

- The resulting mesh is isomorphic to a rectangular uniform one.
- The efficiency of parallel mesh construction is about 90%.
- Mesh decomposition for parallel simulations is reduced to partitioning of the rectangular array of the mesh nodes.
- The way of partitioning may be defined based on parallel simulations on the mesh or a computer system used.

In the future, the proposed method is to be extended for generation of moving meshes with preservation of the above properties. Quality of the resulting adaptive meshes will be studied in details. In addition, comparative analysis of the proposed neural network approach and equidistribution method will be performed.

References

1. Lebedev, A.S., Liseikin, V.D., Khakimzyanov, G.S.: Development of methods for generating adaptive grids. Vychislitelnye tehnologii, Vol. 7, No. 3 (2002), 29
2. Kohonen, T.K.: Self-organization and associative memory. Springer Verlag, New York (1989)
3. Khakimzyanov, G.S., Shokin, Yu.I., Barakhnin, V.B., Shokina, N.Y.: Numerical Modelling of Fluid Flows with Surface Waves. SB RAS, Novosibirsk (2001)
4. Thompson, J.F., Warsi Z.U.A., Mastin C.W.: Numerical grid generation, foundations and applications. North-Holland, Amsterdam (1985)
5. Ritter, H., Martinetz, T., Schulten, K.: Neural Computation and Self-Organizing Maps: An Introduction. Addison-Wesley, New York (1992)
6. Nechaeva, O. I.: Adaptive curvilinear mesh construction on arbitrary two-dimensional convex area with applying of Kohonen's Self Organizing Map. Neuroinformatics and its applications: The XII National Workshop. ICM SB RAS, Krasnoyarsk (2004) 101-102
7. Ghahramani, Z.: Unsupervised Learning. In: Bousquet, O. et al. (eds.): Machine Learning 2003. Lecture Notes in Artificial Intelligence, Vol. 3176. Springer-Verlag, Berlin Heidelberg (2004) 72–112
8. Eisemann, P.R.: Alternating Direction Adaptive Grid Generation. AIAA Paper 83-1937, AIAA 6th Computational Fluid Dynamics Conference, (1983)

Clustering Multiple and Cooperative Instances of Computational Intensive Software Tools

Dana Petcu[1,2], Marcin Paprzycki[3,4], and Maria Ganzha[5]

[1] Computer Science Department, Western University of Timişoara, Romania
[2] Institute e-Austria, Timişoara, Romania
[3] Computer Science Department, Oklahoma State University, USA
[4] SWPS, Warsaw, Poland
[5] Computer Science Dep., Gizycko Private Higher Educational Institute, Poland
petcu@info.uvt.ro, marcin@cs.okstate.edu, ganzha@pwsz.net

Abstract. In this note a general approach to designing distributed systems based on coupling existing software tools is presented and illustrated by two examples. Utilization of this approach to the development of intelligent ODE solver is also described.

1 Introduction

Developing from the scratch parallel systems to solve computationally intensive problems, while efficient, is in most cases rather difficult. Moreover, in initial stages of development, only few parallel algorithms within such a system are usually fully implemented and tested, making the resulting system too limited for practical uses. An alternative approach is to gradually add parallelism to an existing system consisting of a large number of fully tested sequential algorithms. In this case parallelism becomes an added value to an existing environment. Several software tools, based on different requirements and targeted for different hardware architectures, have been developed in this way. Such development followed the same general path leading from single-processor computers, through tightly-coupled parallel systems, to loosely-coupled distributed environments.

In this note we consider requirements imposed on system architecture that allow connecting several instances of a given software tool (possibly combined with single or multiple instances of other tools) in a cluster environment. Architecture discussed here is designed so that the system can be easily ported to the grid or to a web-based environment. The proposed architecture was implemented to couple instances of software tools from symbolic computing and from expert systems. The efficiency of implementation on a cluster is also reported.

2 Overview of the Proposed Architecture

Coupling several instances of software is an example of transforming software components into a conglomerate system. One of possible ways of accomplishing this transformation, is by implementing a *wrapper* that becomes the desired

V. Malyshkin (Ed.): PaCT 2005, LNCS 3606, pp. 452–456, 2005.

interface between components, translates external *interactions across native interfaces* and deals with *global syntax* of the system. Automatic wrapper generators for legacy codes that would be able to wrap the entire code or selected subroutines / modules, are still not available outside of the academia [8]. Here, we try to identify the requirements that have to be imposed on such a wrapper for the particular case of coupling software components within cluster environments.

We make the following assumptions about the software module that is to be interfaced with the system. (1) It has a user interactive interface, (2) it can be installed on several machines of a cluster or is accessible by each cluster machine via an NFS, (3) it has TCP/IP communication facilities, or its source code is available in a language having TCP/IP communication library, or it has I/O facilities, and (4) user knows how to split the problem into subproblems. Specifically, user wants to use the interface of an existing software module to launch several copies on nodes of a cluster and, in the next step, to send to them separate subproblems to be solved. Separately, we assume that cooperation between instances is possible. Finally, other users of the same cluster may want to use (within the same scenario) the same software module(s) within their applications. For example, each node of an 8-processor cluster has a copy of Maple running and various users may utilize groups of 1 through 8 kernels.

Designing cluster wrappers for software tools satisfying our assumptions can be done by combining two pieces of software (Figure 1). The first one is a set of simple commands, functions, procedures or methods, written in a language of that software tool; designed as user interface for controlling remote instances, sending and receiving information to and from them (parallel API – PAPI). The second one is a set of commands, functions, procedures or methods written in a language of the cluster middleware, catching the user commands and executing them (communication middleware, CMW). The PAPI is the cluster wrapper

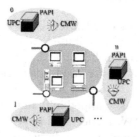

Fig. 1. Wrapping the user code (UPC) to clone it in a cluster environment: two main components, the PAPI depending on the UPC and the general CMW

component depending on the user provided software (denoted UPC), while the CMW is more general, it must be useable by several PAPIs. On a particular node of the cluster where an instance of the software tool is running, the PAPI set is loaded and any specific call to it leads to communication with the CMW

Table 1. The commands send by a PAPI to its twin CMW

Command	meaning
spawn n	CMW launches in the cluster environment n copies of the UPC
send d t "c"	CMW forwards to the dth copy of the UPC the text c to be interpreted by the UPC; the label t is used to match sends with receives;
receive s t	CMW and UPC wait until a message from the instance s is received; then forward it to the UPC which has requested the receive
probe s t	CMW tests if a message has arrived from s and responds 'true' or 'false'
kill s	Shutdown the UPC and the CMW from the node hosting the instance of s
exit	All remote UPCs and their twin CMWs are stopped
proc_no	CMW replace it with a no. representing the no. of current UPC copies
proc_id	CMW replace it with the identifier of the UPC copy

component activated on the same machine (by the classical TCP/IP or the I/O operations). A minimal language must be specified for such communication. For example, a minimal set of such messages can be as presented in Table 1. In this case, while user loads interactively the PAPI set within its UPC, the UPCs launched remotely also load the PAPI set, recognize their identifier in the system and constantly probe requests their twin CMW, i.e. if they do not work they expect to receive information from the other instances. Let us now illustrate most important details of implementation of the proposed architecture.

3   Implementation

We introduce two examples: (1) coupling several instances of Maple; (2) coupling several instances of Jess. Let us note that our main goal is to reduce the solution time when the two software tools are used to solve complex problems.

Coupling Several Instances of Maple. There exist a large number of efforts to extend Maple to parallel and distributed environments and a comprehensive review of the state-of-the-art can be found in [9]. Within last 5 years we have implemented two variants of cluster (and grid) oriented Maple: PVMaple and Maple2g.

In PVMaple [4], Maple was wrapped into an external software that manages execution of tasks. The CMW, a special binary, written in C and using PVM, is responsible for the message exchanges between Maple processes, coordinates interaction between Maple kernels via PVM daemons, and schedules tasks among nodes. The PAPI, a Maple library, consists of a set of parallel programming commands available within Maple itself and supports connections with the CMW (Table 2). Communication between Maple and CMW is achieved via text files.

The more recent wrapper – Maple2g [6] - also consists of two parts, the PAPI, the computer algebra dependent one – m2g, a Maple library of functions allowing Maple users to interact with the grid or cluster middleware – and the CMW, the grid-dependent one – MGProxy, a package of Java classes acting as

Table 2. PAPI to CMW communication in PVMaple, Maple2g, and Parallel Jess

PAPI	pvm lib for PVMaple	m2g library for Maple2g	ParJess lib
spawn n	spawn(IP,proc_no)	m2g_maple(n)	(kernels n)
send d t "c"	t:=send(d,c)	m2g_send(d,t,c)	(send d t s)
receive s t	receive(t,s)	m2g_recv(s,t)	(recv s t)
probe s t	-	m2g_prob(s,t)	(prob n t)
kill s	-	-	(kill s)
exit	exit	m2g_exit()	(exit)
proc_no	tasks	m2g_size	-
proc_id	TaskId	m2g_rank	?*p*
-	ProcId, MachId,	m2g_connect(), m2g_getservice(c,l)	(connection)
	setttime(), time(),	m2g_jobsubmit(t,c), m2g_jobstop(t)	
	version()	m2g_status(t), m2g_MGProxy_start(),	
		m2g_results(t), m2g_MGProxy_end()	

an interface between m2g and the grid or cluster environment. MpiJava was selected as the message-passing interface for the CMW, due to ist compatibility with the Globus Toolkit. Communication between Maple and the MGProxy is achieved using socket library available in Maple. The most important features of Maple2g are summarized in Table 2. Maple2g was tested on a cluster of 9 PCs connected with a fast Myrinet switch (2Gbs) on which Maple7 was installed. To indicate an order of the efficiency, for 2 integers of 10 millions multiplied with Karatsuba algorithm (the implicit procedure in Maple7): 88% for 3 processors, 71% for 9 processors. Subsequent examples in the grid case can be found in [6]. All experiments indicate reasonable scalability of both PVMMaple and Maple2g (scalability depends primarily on network throughput).

Coupling Several Instances of Jess. Standard benchmarks [2], show that current rule-based systems, running on modern hardware, may need hours to reach an answer when the number of rules is of order of thousand. Therefore, parallel approaches are needed for real applications and first parallel implementations were already available in early 1990s [1]. There are several approaches to parallelization [10]: (a) parallel matching leads to a limited speedup caused by the sequential execution of rules; (b) multiple rule firing approach parallelizes the match phase and the act phase by firing multiple rules in parallel, but involves extra cost due to synchronization; (c) special techniques like compatible rules or analysis of data dependency graphs, can improve efficiency of parallelization; (d) task-level parallelism, used here, based on the decomposition of the problem into a hierarchy of tasks is expected to lead to best results.

Jess, a rule-based programming environment written in Java was chosen because of its active development and support, and because there is no parallel version of Jess. The proposed architecture, recently reported in [7], also follows the wrapper-based design presented in Section 2.

The CMW in Parallel Jess consists of two parts: the Connector and the Messenger. The Connector is written in Java and uses standard ServerSockets methods of TCP/IP communication. Jess instance acts as a client and contacts (via socket) its Connector, the server. Each Messenger is associated with one local Connector and its purpose is (1) to execute commands received by the Connector, and (2) to communicate with Messengers associated with other instances of Jess. Messenger is written in Java and JPVM. Set of new commands added to Jess (the PAPI) is presented in Table 2.

In order to test Parallel Jess efficiency, we applied it to the Miss Manner problem [2] on the same cluster computer, obtaining an efficiency of 95% for 2 processors, and 45% for 8 processors. Several other examples can be found in [7] and all of then indicate reasonable efficiency of Parallel Jess.

Future Research Direction. The above described components will be used to develop a distributed cluster-based intelligent ODE solving environment. Here, the problem will be described in a user friendly environment of the latest version of the ODE numerical expert, EpODE [3]. The problem properties (stiffness, decomposability, etc) will be then analyzed using a Maple kernel residing in the cluster environment (e.g. eigenvalues of the linear part), or using EpODE facilities (e.g. Jacobian matrix). Decisions which analysis methods to apply will be made by a rule-based algorithm rewritten in Parallel Jess. Furthermore, if the problem is large, a Maple2g multiprocessor approach will be used (see also [5]).

References

1. Amaral J.N.: A Parallel architecture for serializable production systems, Ph.D. Thesis, University of Texas, Austin, 1994.
2. OPS5 Benchmark Suite, available at http://www.pst.com/benchcr2.htm, 2003.
3. Petcu D., Dragan M.: Designing an ODE solving environment, LNCSE 10, Procs. SciTools, eds. H.P. Langtangen et al(2000), 319-338.
4. Petcu D.: PVMaple – A distributed approach to cooperative work of Maple processes. LNCS 1908, eds. J.Dongarra et al., (2000), 216–224
5. Petcu D.: Numerical Solution of ODEs with Distributed Maple, LNCS 1988, Procs. NAA, eds. Lubin Vulkov et al, 666–674, 2001.
6. Petcu D., Dubu D., Paprzycki M.: Extending Maple to the Grid: Design and implementation, in Procs. ISPDC'04, J.Morrison et al. eds., IEEE CS Press, 209-216.
7. Petcu D., Parallel Jess, Proceedings for the ISPDC 2005 Conference, to appear.
8. Solomon A., Struble C.A.: JavaMath – an API for internet accessible mathematical services, Procs. 5th Asian Symposium on Computer Mathematics, (2001).
9. Schreiner W., Mittermaier C., Bosa K.: Distributed Maple – parallel computer algebra in networked environments, J. Symb. Comp. 35:3, (2003), 305–347.
10. S. Wu, D. Miranker, J. Browne: Towards semantic-based exploration of parallelism in production systems, TR-94-23, 1994.

A Multigrid Parallel Program for Protoplanetary Disc Simulation*

Alexey V. Snytnikov and Vitaly A. Vshivkov

Institute of Computational Mathematics and Mathematical Geophysics SB RAS,
Lavrientieva av. 6, Novosibirsk, 630090, Russia
{snytav, vsh}@ssd.sscc.ru

Abstract. In this paper we present a program for simulation of the two-component protoplanetary disc evolution. The model includes gas dynamics and collisionless solid body dynamics. Multigrid method for solution of Poisson equation in cylindrical coordinate system is described. An essentially parallel Poisson equation solver is constructed by means of applying Fast Fourier Transform along the angular direction. Processor workload rearrangement is performed in order to increase the speedup. The results of computational experiments are given to demonstrate the physical validity of the program.

1 Introduction

Protoplanetary discs are widely studied in recent time (e.g. [1], [5], [8]). The problem of organic matter genesis in the Solar System is a matter of special interest. In [12] the protoplanetary disc is considered as a catalytic chemical reactor for synthesis of primary organic compounds. The mean density and temperature in protoplanetary disc are very small. But the chemical synthesis requires high values of gas temperature, pressure and also density of both gas and dust particles. Due to this reason it is extremely important to find out how do these high values of temperature, pressure and density appear. The solitons that appeared in our computational experiments are one of the possible answers to this question.

The strong mutual influence of gas and dust components was found out in our computational experiments. Namely, the whole disc becomes unstable due to dynamic heating of the very small dust component. Thus the presented program is capable to achieve more accurate results than in one-component (purely gaseous) protoplanetary disc analysis (for example, [10]). The physical consideration of these phenomena is out of the present paper. Here we just want to say that our program produces results that are interesting from the physical point of view.

---

* The present work was supported by SB RAS integration project number 148, Subprogram 2 of RAS Presidium Program "Biosphere genesis and evolution", and RFBR (grant 05-01-00665), Dutch-Russian NWO-GRID project, contract NWO-RFBS 047.016.007 and Dutch-Russian NWO-Plasma project, contract NWO-RFBS 047.016.018.

V. Malyshkin (Ed.): PaCT 2005, LNCS 3606, pp. 457–467, 2005.

Protoplanetary disc simulation involves solution of the complex system of equations: Vlasov-Liouville kinetic equation, Poisson equation and gas dynamics equations. Vlasov-Liouville equation is solved by the Particle-in-Cell method. The parallelisation of the method is very simple and leads to almost linear speedup for kinetic equation solution [6]. Gas dynamics equatons are solved very rapidly (compared to Poisson and Vlasov-Liouville equations) by The Fluids-in-Cells (FlIC) method [2]. Due to this reason the FlIC method parallelisation is not discussed in the present paper. The implemented methods for solution of Vlasov equation and gas dynamics equations are described in more detail in [13]. Parallelisation scheme is presented in [9].

Poisson equation solution takes the most time in protoplanetary disc simulation. The survey of Poisson equation solvers could be found, for example, in [7]. The cylindrical geometry employed in our program together with the necessity to compute on very fine grids give special requirements for Poisson equation solver. The widely used 3D FFT method is limited to rectangular cartesian grids. The fastest techniques based on circular reduction (e.g. FACR, DCR) could not be used on fine grids due to intrinsic numerical instability. Poisson equation must be solved at every timestep of the computational experiment. Thus the iterational methods are worth using since they are able to take the potential from the previous timestep into account.

In [11] the Poisson equation solver is described that is a combination of FFT along the angular coordinate and Block Succesive Over-Relaxation (BSOR) method. The solver provides rapid potential evaluation. Unfortunately, the straightforward parallelisation of this solver results in rather a small speedup. The reason is that the number of BSOR iterations differ dramatically for different potential harmonics. In the present paper the solver is presented that employs multigrid method for the harmonics with greatest number of iterations and BSOR method for all the others. Thus a better speedup is achieved. All the computations were carried out on the MVS-1000M multicomputer in Siberian Supercomputer Centre, Novosibirsk and Joint Supercomputer Centre, Moscow.

2   Source Equations

The dynamics of the dust component of protoplanetary disc is described by the Vlasov-Liouville kinetic equation. In the following text dust particles will be called simply particles. To consider the motion of the gas component the equations of gas dynamics are employed. The gravitational field is determined by Poisson equation.

If we employ the collisionless approximation of the mean self-consistent field, then Vlasov-Liouville kinetic equation is written in the following form

$$\frac{\partial f}{\partial t} + v\nabla f + a\frac{\partial f}{\partial v} = 0,$$

where $f(t, r, v)$ is the time-dependent one-particle distribution function along coordinates and velocities, $a = -\nabla \Phi + F_{fr}$ is the acceleration of unit mass particle, F_{fr} is the friction force between gas and dust components of the medium. Gravitational potential Φ could be divided into two parts:

$$\Phi = \Phi_1 + \Phi_2,$$

where Φ_1 presents either the potential of immobile central mass (galactic black hole or protostar) or the potential of a rigid system which is out of disc plane (galactic halo or molecular cloud). The second part of potential Φ_2 is determined by the additive distribution of the moving particles and gas. Φ_2 satisfies Poisson equation:

$$\Delta\Phi_2 = 4\pi G \Sigma \rho.$$

In the case of infinitesimally thin disc the bulk density of the mobile media $\Sigma\rho = \rho_{part} + \rho_{gas}$ is equal to zero (ρ_{part} is the particle density, ρ_{gas} is the gas density). There is a shear of the normal derivative of potential at the disc surface. This shear gives a boundary condition for the normal derivative of potential Φ_2:

$$\frac{\partial \Phi_2}{\partial z} = 2\pi G \sigma.$$

here σ is the surface density.

Gas dynamics equations are used in the common form. The implementation of the Fluids-in-Cells method for the solution of gas dynamics equations is discussed in [13].

In the full description of the protoplanetary disc these equations are complemented with the equations for chemical reactions in gas component and the equations for simulation of dust particles coagulation.

Since the real physical quantities related to protoplanetary discs are very large, sizeless variables must be used to avoid the loss of precision in computations. The following quantities were chosen as basic characteristic parameters for transition to sizeless variables:

— distance from the Sun to the Earth $R_0 = 1.5 \cdot 10^{11}$ m;
— mass of the Sun $M_\odot = 2 \cdot 10^{30}$ kg;
— gravitational constant $G = 6.672 \cdot 10^{-11} \cdot$ m^2/kg^2.

Corresponding characteristic values of the particle velocity (V_0), time (t_0), potential (Φ_0) and surface density (σ_0) are written as

$$V_0 = \sqrt{\frac{GM_\odot}{R_0}} = 30 \text{ km/s},$$

$$t_0 = \frac{R_0}{V_0} = 5 \cdot 10^6 \text{ s} = 1/6 \text{ year},$$

$$\Phi_0 = V_0^2 = \frac{GM_\odot}{R_0},$$

$$\sigma_0 = \frac{M_\odot}{R_0^2}.$$

In the following text all the parameters are given in sizeless units.

Initial distribution of the particle and gas density is set according to the model of solid body rotation [13].

3   Multigrid Poisson Equation Solver

In this section the essentially parallel Poisson equation solver is constructed. The first step is the Fast Fourier Transform along angular coordinate. It results in a set of linear algebraic equation systems. Each system of linear algebraic equations describes one harmonic of the potential:

$$\frac{1}{h_r^2 r_{i-1/2}} \left[r_{i-1} H_{i-3/2,l-1/2}(m) + r_i H_{i+1/2,l-1/2}(m) \right] +$$

$$\frac{1}{h_z^2} \left[H_{i-1/2,l-3/2}(m) + H_{i-1/2,l+1/2}(m) \right]$$

$$-\frac{2}{h_\varphi^2 r_{i-1/2}^2} \left[1 + 2\sin^2 \frac{\pi m}{K_{max}} \right] H_{i-1/2,l-1/2}(m)$$

$$= 4\pi R_{i-1/2,l-1/2}(m) \cos \frac{2\pi}{K_{max}} km,$$

$$m = 1, ..., K_{max}.$$

where m is the number of harmonic or angular wavenumber, K_{max} is equal to the number of grid points along the angular coordinate. These systems are completely independent from each other, thus they could be solved concurrently with no interprocessor communications.

The 2D linear algebraic equation system is solved by Block Successive Over-Relaxation method (BSOR). Figure 1 shows that the most time is spent on solving the system for the first harmonic ($m = 0$). Diagonal domination in the linear system matrix is weak for $m = 0$ and the iterational process converges very slowly.

Multigrid method is employed to solve the system for the first harmonic. The general description of the multigrid method is given for example, in [4]. The method itself is well-known, but there is no multigrid scheme which is optimal in all the cases. Due to this reason the implementation of multigrid method was built that takes the cylindrical geometry into account.

The multigrid method is implemented in the form of the Full MultiGrid (FMG, [15]) loop. This scheme contains of the following parts: smoothing operator S, restriction operator R and prolongation operator P. Smoothing operator is used to suppress the high-frequency error. R restricts the fine-grid values onto the coarse grid. The operator P does the opposite: it interpolates the solution

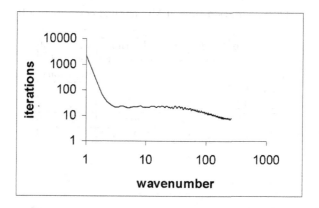

Fig. 1. Number of BSOR iterations depending on wavenumber

from coarse grid to fine grid. Finally, there is a procedure that solves the linear equation system on the coarsest grid level. The main difficulty is the following: common restriction, prolongation and smoothing operators result in slow convergence in the case of cylindrical geometry. In the present work the special form of these operators was designed. Also their combination was chosen that gives fast convergence of the multigrid method.

The number of grid nodes along each coordinate line is equal to $N_l = 2^l - 1$ for the number l grid. The size of the source (finest) grid is $N_0 = 2^L - 1$.

For smoothing operator BSOR method was chosen. Chan et al. [3] construct the interpolation operator by solving local PDE. In our case it means that Poisson equation should be satisfied in the neighbourhood of the fine-grid node with the given values in the nodes of the coarse grid. Thus the interpolation operator has the following form:

$$H^{l-1}_{i-1/2,k} = \frac{1}{4} \frac{1}{r_{i-1/2}} \left[r_i H^l_{i+1/2,k} + r_{i-1} H^l_{i-3/2,k} \right] +$$

$$+ \frac{1}{4} \left[H^l_{i-1/2,k-1} + H^l_{i-1/2,k+1} \right],$$

$$i = 1, ..., I_{max} \qquad k = 1, ..., K_{max} \qquad l = 1..., L.$$

here l is the number of the grid. The values in the coarse grid nodes that belong also to the fine grid are transmitted with no changes.

Both operators R and P are just matrices. In the present work R is a transpose of P: $R = P^T$.

Multigrid method (MG) works faster than BSOR as table 1 shows. The number of BSOR iterations the smoothing operator S performs depend on the grid size. They are usually called nested iterations. Small number of nested iterations makes the process unstable, large number makes it too slow.

Table 1. Computation time of MG method compared to BSOR

Grid size	BSOR time (in seconds)	MG time (in seconds)	Number of nested iterations
63×63	0.13	1.08	5
127×127	2.27	1.3	25
255×255	49.89	20.06	120
511×511	1119.8	204.33	500

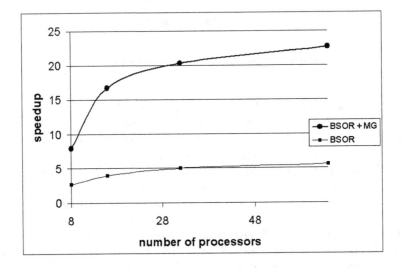

Fig. 2. Speedup. Linear equation system for the first harmonic is solved with the MG method on the detached processor, all the other harmonics with BSOR (*circles*). All the harmonics are evaluated with the BSOR method, uniform workload distribution (*squares*)

The computation time for the first harmonic of potential on the large grid is reduced by the factor 5.4. Thus the processor workload becomes more uniform.

Finally the first harmonic is assigned to a detached processor. During the potential evaluation stage the workload is the following for 512 harmonics and 8 processors. Processor number 0 has only the first harmonic, processor number 1 has the harmonics from the 2nd to 74 and so on, 73 harmonics for each processor. This enables to improve the speedup, as it is shown in figure 2. The computation is done for the grid size $511 \times 512 \times 511$, 100 million particles. The time of real computation on 8, 16, 32, 64 processors is compared to the virtual single processor computation. Actually the problem of such a large size does not fit into less than 8 processors.

4   Simulation Results

4.1   Disc Instability Due to Dust Component Heating

The goal of the first computational experiment was the demonstration of the mutual influence of gas and dust components of the protoplanetary disc. The dynamic temperature of the dust component varied from 0.01 to 0.1, the other parameters of the disc are shown in table 2.

Table 2. Disc parameters for computational experiment 1

Dust component mass	0.01
Gas component mass	1.0
Central body mass	1.0
Dust disc radius	2.0
Gas disc radius	2.0
Gas pressure in the disc centre	0.001
Timestep	0.002
Number of timesteps	4000
Grid size	$120 \times 128 \times 100$
Number of particles	10^7

Toomre [14] criterion states the the one-component disc (dust component only) becomes more stable with the increase of the dynamic temperature. Figure 3 shows gas density distribution in the disc. White colour means the maximal density, black means zero density, the scale is logarithmical. Three cases are given: stable disc ($Q = 0.01$), marginal disc ($Q = 0.05$) and unstable disc ($Q = 0.1$). For each case the value of dynamic temperature Q is given.

Thus with increase of the dynamic temperature of the dust component the whole disc looses axial symmetry and becomes unstable. The most interesting fact is that the dust component, having very small mass (about 1 % of the whole disc mass), has a strong influence on the stability of the disc. Let us remind once more that this situation is impossible for a one-component disc.

This effect means that dust and gas components of the protoplanetary disc could not be considered separately. As it is shown in this section, the presented program suits for studying mutual influence of gas and dust components.

4.2   Soliton Interaction

In the second computational experiment the interaction of solitons (lone density waves) occurred, fig. 4. The parameters of the disc are shown in table 3.

First the density wave arises (fig. 4, A), then it approaches the standing soliton (fig. 4, B). After absorption of the wave the soliton deviates from the initial position (fig. 4, C) but then returns back (fig. 4, D). It should be noticed that such a phenomenon is impossible for clumps of dust. Thus figure 4 proves wave nature of the structures observed in our computational experiments - the solitons.

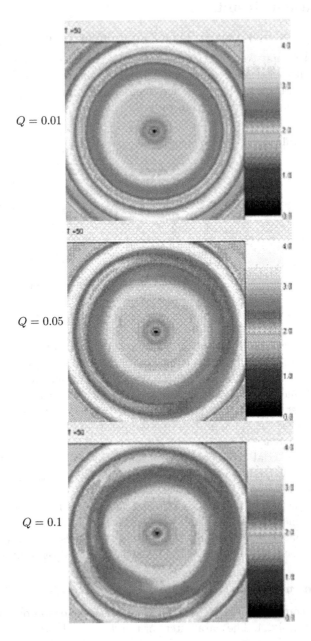

Fig. 3. Gas density distribution. The instability arises with the increase of the dynamic temperature of particles

Table 3. Disc parameters for computational experiment 2

Dust component mass	1.0
Gas component mass	1.0
Central body mass	2.0
Dust disc radius	1.0
Gas disc radius	1.0
Gas pressure in the disc centre	0.001
Timestep	0.0005
Number of timesteps	16000
Grid size	$300 \times 256 \times 128$
Number of particles	5×10^7

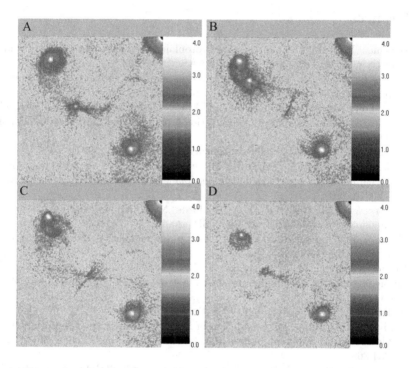

Fig. 4. Absorption of a density wave by the soliton. The size of the exposed domain is 1.0×1.0, the centre of it is in (-0.5, -0.5). Figure A shows particle density distribution for the moment of time 4.76, figure B for the moment of time 4.96, figure C for 5.04 and figure D for 5.2

Moreover, white colour of the soliton kernel means that the density of the dust particles in that place is much higher (by 6 orders of magnitude) then in surrounding disc. There are also high values of gas density and pressure. These conditions probably make the catalytic synthesis of primary organic compounds possible.

5   Conclusion

The use of multigrid method and processor workload rearrangement enable to increase the speedup twice compared to uniform processor workload. The results of computational experiments show, in the first place, strong mutual influence of the gas and dust components of the disc, and second, soliton formation and interaction. Both effects are important for simulation of primary organic compound synthesis in protoplanetary disc.

Acknowledgements. The authors want to thank Valery N.Snytnikov and Victor E.Malyshkin for their help and interest to our work.

References

1. Barranco J., Marcus P.: Vortices in Protoplanetary Disks and the Formation of Planetesimals. In DPS 2001 meeting BAAS. (2001). 33.
2. Belotserkovsky O.M., Davydov Yu.M.: Fluids-in-cells method in gas dynamics. Moscow, Nauka Publishers. (1982). - in Russian.
3. Chan T.F., Wan W.L.: Robust multigrid methods for nonsmooth coefficient elliptic linear systems. Journal of Computational and Applied Mathematics. Vol. 123. (2000). 323-352.
4. Demmel J.W.: Applied Numerical Linear Algebra. SIAM. (1997).
5. De la Fuente Marcos C., Barge P.: The effect of long-lived vortical circulation on the dynamics of dust particles in the mid-plane of a protoplanetary disc. MNRAS, 323. 2001b. 601
6. Grigoryev Yu.N., Vshivkov V.A., Fedoruk M.P.: Numerical "Particle-in-Cell" Methods. Theory and Applications. VSP. (2002).
7. Hockney, R.W. and Eastwood, J.W.: Computer Simulation Using Particles. IOP Publishing, Bristol. (1988).
8. Kornet K., Stepinski T., Rozyczka M.: Diversity of planetary systems from evolution of solids in protoplanetary disks. Astronomy and Astrophysics. Vol. 378. (2001). 180.
9. Kuksheva E.A., Malyshkin V.E., Nikitin S.A., Snytnikov A.V., Snytnikov V.N., Vshivkov V.A.: Numerical Simulation of Self-Organisation in Gravitationally Unstable Media on Supercomputers. PaCT-2003 proceedings. LNCS 2763. (2003). pp.354-368.
10. Pickett B.K., Durisen R.H., Davis G.A.: The Dynamic Stability of Rotating Protostars and Protostellar Disks. I. The Effects of Angular Momentum Distribution. Astrophysical Journal. 458. (1996). 714-738.
11. Snytnikov A.V.. A Parallel Program for Simulation of Disc-Shaped Self-Gravitating Systems. Bull.Nov.Comp.Center, Comp.Science. Vol. 19. (2003). 73-81.
12. Snytnikov V.N., Dudnikova G.I., Gleaves J.T., Nikitin S.A., Parmon V.N., Stoyanovsky V.O., Vshivkov V.A., Yablonsky G.S.,Zakharenko V.S.: Space chemical reactor of protoplanetary disk. Adv. Space Res. Vol. 30, No. 6. (2002). 1461-1467.

13. Snytnikov V.N., Vshivkov V.A., E.V.Neupokoev, Nikitin S.A., Parmon V.N., Snytnikov A.V.: Three-Dimensional Numerical Simulation of a Nonstationary Gravitating N-Body System with Gas. Astronomy Letters, vol. 30, no. 2. (2004). 124-138.
14. Toomre A.: On the gravitational stabilty of a disc of stars. Astrophys. J. Vol. 139. (1964). 1217.
15. Wesseling P.: An Introduction to Multigrid Methods. John Wiley & Sons. (1992).

Author Index

Lecture Notes in Computer Science

For information about Vols. 1–3516

please contact your bookseller or Springer

Vol. 3566: J.-P. Banâtre, P. Fradet, J.-L. Giavitto, O. Michel (Eds.), Unconventional Programming Paradigms. XI, 367 pages. 2005.

Vol. 3565: G.E. Christensen, M. Sonka (Eds.), Information Processing in Medical Imaging. XXI, 777 pages. 2005.

Vol. 3564: N. Eisinger, J. Małuszyński (Eds.), Reasoning Web. IX, 319 pages. 2005.

Vol. 3562: J. Mira, J.R. Álvarez (Eds.), Artificial Intelligence and Knowledge Engineering Applications: A Bioinspired Approach, Part II. XXIV, 636 pages. 2005.

Vol. 3561: J. Mira, J.R. Álvarez (Eds.), Mechanisms, Symbols, and Models Underlying Cognition, Part I. XXIV, 532 pages. 2005.

Vol. 3560: V.K. Prasanna, S. Iyengar, P.G. Spirakis, M. Welsh (Eds.), Distributed Computing in Sensor Systems. XV, 423 pages. 2005.

Vol. 3559: P. Auer, R. Meir (Eds.), Learning Theory. XI, 692 pages. 2005. (Subseries LNAI).

Vol. 3558: V. Torra, Y. Narukawa, S. Miyamoto (Eds.), Modeling Decisions for Artificial Intelligence. XII, 470 pages. 2005. (Subseries LNAI).

Vol. 3557: H. Gilbert, H. Handschuh (Eds.), Fast Software Encryption. XI, 443 pages. 2005.

Vol. 3556: H. Baumeister, M. Marchesi, M. Holcombe (Eds.), Extreme Programming and Agile Processes in Software Engineering. XIV, 332 pages. 2005.

Vol. 3555: T. Vardanega, A.J. Wellings (Eds.), Reliable Software Technology – Ada-Europe 2005. XV, 273 pages. 2005.

Vol. 3554: A. Dey, B. Kokinov, D. Leake, R. Turner (Eds.), Modeling and Using Context. XIV, 572 pages. 2005. (Subseries LNAI).

Vol. 3553: T.D. Hämäläinen, A.D. Pimentel, J. Takala, S. Vassiliadis (Eds.), Embedded Computer Systems: Architectures, Modeling, and Simulation. XV, 476 pages. 2005.

Vol. 3552: H. de Meer, N. Bhatti (Eds.), Quality of Service – IWQoS 2005. XVIII, 400 pages. 2005.

Vol. 3551: T. Härder, W. Lehner (Eds.), Data Management in a Connected World. XIX, 371 pages. 2005.

Vol. 3548: K. Julisch, C. Kruegel (Eds.), Intrusion and Malware Detection and Vulnerability Assessment. X, 241 pages. 2005.

Vol. 3547: F. Bomarius, S. Komi-Sirviö (Eds.), Product Focused Software Process Improvement. XIII, 588 pages. 2005.

Vol. 3546: T. Kanade, A. Jain, N.K. Ratha (Eds.), Audio- and Video-Based Biometric Person Authentication. XX, 1134 pages. 2005.

Vol. 3544: T. Higashino (Ed.), Principles of Distributed Systems. XII, 460 pages. 2005.

Vol. 3543: L. Kutvonen, N. Alonistioti (Eds.), Distributed Applications and Interoperable Systems. XI, 235 pages. 2005.

Vol. 3542: H.H. Hoos, D.G. Mitchell (Eds.), Theory and Applications of Satisfiability Testing. XIII, 393 pages. 2005.

Vol. 3541: N.C. Oza, R. Polikar, J. Kittler, F. Roli (Eds.), Multiple Classifier Systems. XII, 430 pages. 2005.

Vol. 3540: H. Kalviainen, J. Parkkinen, A. Kaarna (Eds.), Image Analysis. XXII, 1270 pages. 2005.

Vol. 3539: K. Morik, J.-F. Boulicaut, A. Siebes (Eds.), Local Pattern Detection. XI, 233 pages. 2005. (Subseries LNAI).

Vol. 3538: L. Ardissono, P. Brna, A. Mitrovic (Eds.), User Modeling 2005. XVI, 533 pages. 2005. (Subseries LNAI).

Vol. 3537: A. Apostolico, M. Crochemore, K. Park (Eds.), Combinatorial Pattern Matching. XI, 444 pages. 2005.

Vol. 3536: G. Ciardo, P. Darondeau (Eds.), Applications and Theory of Petri Nets 2005. XI, 470 pages. 2005.

Vol. 3535: M. Steffen, G. Zavattaro (Eds.), Formal Methods for Open Object-Based Distributed Systems. X, 323 pages. 2005.

Vol. 3534: S. Spaccapietra, E. Zimányi (Eds.), Journal on Data Semantics III. XI, 213 pages. 2005.

Vol. 3533: M. Ali, F. Esposito (Eds.), Innovations in Applied Artificial Intelligence. XX, 858 pages. 2005. (Subseries LNAI).

Vol. 3532: A. Gómez-Pérez, J. Euzenat (Eds.), The Semantic Web: Research and Applications. XV, 728 pages. 2005.

Vol. 3531: J. Ioannidis, A. Keromytis, M. Yung (Eds.), Applied Cryptography and Network Security. XI, 530 pages. 2005.

Vol. 3530: A. Prinz, R. Reed, J. Reed (Eds.), SDL 2005: Model Driven. XI, 361 pages. 2005.

Vol. 3528: P.S. Szczepaniak, J. Kacprzyk, A. Niewiadomski (Eds.), Advances in Web Intelligence. XVII, 513 pages. 2005. (Subseries LNAI).

Vol. 3527: R. Morrison, F. Oquendo (Eds.), Software Architecture. XII, 263 pages. 2005.

Vol. 3526: S. B. Cooper, B. Löwe, L. Torenvliet (Eds.), New Computational Paradigms. XVII, 574 pages. 2005.

Vol. 3525: A.E. Abdallah, C.B. Jones, J.W. Sanders (Eds.), Communicating Sequential Processes. XIV, 321 pages. 2005.

Vol. 3524: R. Barták, M. Milano (Eds.), Integration of AI and OR Techniques in Constraint Programming for Combinatorial Optimization Problems. XI, 320 pages. 2005.

Vol. 3523: J.S. Marques, N. Pérez de la Blanca, P. Pina (Eds.), Pattern Recognition and Image Analysis, Part II. XXVI, 733 pages. 2005.

Vol. 3522: J.S. Marques, N. Pérez de la Blanca, P. Pina (Eds.), Pattern Recognition and Image Analysis, Part I. XXVI, 703 pages. 2005.

Vol. 3521: N. Megiddo, Y. Xu, B. Zhu (Eds.), Algorithmic Applications in Management. XIII, 484 pages. 2005.

Vol. 3520: O. Pastor, J. Falcão e Cunha (Eds.), Advanced Information Systems Engineering. XVI, 584 pages. 2005.

Vol. 3519: H. Li, P. J. Olver, G. Sommer (Eds.), Computer Algebra and Geometric Algebra with Applications. IX, 449 pages. 2005.

Vol. 3518: T.B. Ho, D. Cheung, H. Liu (Eds.), Advances in Knowledge Discovery and Data Mining. XXI, 864 pages. 2005. (Subseries LNAI).

Vol. 3517: H.S. Baird, D.P. Lopresti (Eds.), Human Interactive Proofs. IX, 143 pages. 2005.